Wartime Washington

EBL at age 18, portrait by
Thomas Sully. Courtesy of
the P. Blair Lee family.

SPL, ca. 1844, portrait by
Thomas Sully. Courtesy of
the P. Blair Lee family.

Wartime Washington

The Civil War Letters of Elizabeth Blair Lee

EDITED BY

Virginia Jeans Laas

FOREWORD BY

Dudley T. Cornish

UNIVERSITY OF ILLINOIS PRESS

Urbana and Chicago

Publication of this work has been supported in part by grants from
the Lee Brooke Family Trust and the National Endowment for the
Humanities, an independent federal agency.

This book is printed on acid-free paper.

Library of Congress Cataloging-in-Publication Data

Lee, Elizabeth Blair.
    Wartime Washington : the Civil War letters of Elizabeth Blair Lee /
edited by Virginia Jeans Laas.
        p. cm.
    Includes bibliographical references and index.
    ISBN 0-252-01802-8 (alk. paper)
    1. Lee, Elizabeth Blair—Correspondence. 2. United States—
History—Civil War, 1861–1865—Personal narratives. 3. Washington
(D.C.)—History—Civil War, 1861–1865—Personal narratives.
4. Wives—United States—Correspondence. I. Laas, Virginia Jeans.
II. Title.
E601.L44 1991
973.7'81—dc20   90-25762
                                                              CIP

For my mother
Virginia Kring Jeans
and in memory of my friend
Dorothy Doty Duffy
(1934–90)

Contents

Illustrations follow pp. 12, 350.

Foreword

Over twenty years ago E. B. Smith of Maryland suggested the wisdom, even the historical necessity, of editing Elizabeth Blair Lee's Civil War letters. Indeed, there was some serious discussion of the practicality of giving her superb correspondence priority over a biography of her sailor-husband, Samuel Phillips Lee; the Admiral's male descendants quickly brought the ship back on course. *After* the biography, Virginia and I often said, we'll edit those incomparable letters. The ultimate result of our long collaboration in research and writing was the 1986 publication of our biography, *Lincoln's Lee.*

Although I perforce retired and removed to San Francisco, Virginia pushed ahead on and in those letters. She quickly went beyond my untutored editorial efforts and learned modern methodology, practice, and style—on her own motion. Beyond that, she put her increasingly sophisticated skills to practical purpose in essays and papers for historical conferences. Predictably, her work appeared in professional journals: "Elizabeth Blair Lee: Union Counterpart of Mary Boykin Chesnut" (*Journal of Southern History,* 1984); "The Courtship and Marriage of Elizabeth Blair and Samuel Phillips Lee: A Problem in Historical Detection" (*Midwest Quarterly,* 1985); and "The View from Blair House: The Civil War Letters of Elizabeth Blair Lee" (*Documentary Editing,* 1988). By the time I returned to Kansas after a long year in California, she had practically completed selecting and editing hundreds of Lizzie's wartime letters to her "Dearest Phil." By the summer of 1988 she had completed the monumental task.

Elizabeth Blair Lee has been incredibly fortunate in her editor. Put another way, if ever writer and editor were made for each other, these two were. From her first sampling of those letters during Christmas of 1979, Virginia has concentrated on the happy work of bringing them out of the archives and into public view. She brought to that work an inquiring mind, scholarly eagerness, indefatigable tenacity of purpose, thorough involvement without sentimental softness, indeed a sort of tough-minded tenderness.

Well grounded in the mystique of the nineteenth-century "cult of true womanhood," Virginia has sensitively introduced Elizabeth to our century as a representative individual, member of a privileged elite, and acute observer writing from the very center of a nation at war with itself. Fragile in health but blessed with an iron constitution, Lizzie never lost faith in her cause, her family, her husband, or herself. Thanks to Virginia Jeans Laas, Elizabeth Blair Lee takes on deserved immortality, and our understanding of Civil War America becomes the richer thereby.

Dudley T. Cornish

Pittsburg, Kansas, 1990

Acknowledgments

It is a happy task to acknowledge the debts one accumulates en route to the completion of a manuscript. In the beginning, there was Elbert B. Smith of the University of Maryland, who had first used these letters and recognized their value for historians of nineteenth-century America. In the honorable tradition of scholarly generosity, he has permitted the long-term loan of his ten microfilm reels of Elizabeth Blair Lee's letters to her husband. Sanford W. Higginbotham, former editor of the *Journal of Southern History*, gave early hope that these letters were indeed significant by the alacrity with which he accepted an article for his journal. Later, he agreed to read the entire, long manuscript. His careful reading and precise editorial comments were invaluable and gave me confidence: if the manuscript had passed a Higginbotham examination, then it was in good shape. Dudley T. Cornish, who admits to being in love with Lizzie Lee, gave continual encouragement through endless hours of discussion and analysis. He has read and reread the manuscript, in parts and in its entirety, more times than I can count. His enthusiasm, historical judgment, stylistic suggestions, and just plain sound advice are only some of the reasons he is a valued colleague and cherished friend. Throughout this long process, Elizabeth Wayne Lee and her husband, the late P. Blair Lee (E. B. Lee's grandson), were staunch supporters and gracious hosts. She generously provided the superb color photographs of the Sully portraits. Elizabeth Blair Lee would have rejoiced to know that her grandson had found a reflection of herself in Elizabeth Wayne Lee.

Numerous trips to Princeton University Library were not only productive but also a genuine pleasure. Jean Preston and Anne Van Arsdale were consistently helpful and accommodating; their hospitality gives returning scholars a feeling of homecoming. These letters are published with permission of Princeton University Library. The knowledgeable archivists and staff of the library of the State Historical Society of Wisconsin in Madison made work in that mecca for historical research an easy and rewarding experience. In Washington, D.C., the staffs of the Naval Historical Center, the Library of Congress, and the National Archives lightened the load and eased the way in tracking down all manner of obscure documentation. Jane C. Sween, librarian of the Montgomery County, Maryland, Historical Society, found answers for innumerable queries about denizens in the Silver Spring vicinity; her precision and knowledge are greatly appreciated. An important help was the photographic skill and artistry of Gary Shepard in Media Services at the University of Arkansas. At the same institution, Chris Syphus and the Computer Science Engineering department gave technical assistance. The libraries at two local institutions have done everything within their means to push this project forward: Missouri Southern State College in Joplin and Pittsburg State University in Kansas. Their librarians and staff are always unstinting in their assistance, providing friendship as well as professional services.

The National Historical Publications and Records Commission deserves special praise for its promotion of documentary editions. Their summer institute for training documentary editors was essential for this project, and I am grateful to institute director Richard Sheldon and resident advisors Elizabeth Hughes of the Eisenhower Papers and Kenneth Bowling of the First Federal Congress project. In addition to technical training, the 1986 editing institute fostered lasting friendship and camaraderie among the participants. Continued interest and encouragement from fellow interns John Muldowny, Elaine Pascu, Esther Katz, Brooks Simpson, and Jean Berlin have been especially valued. Mary Giunta, acting director of NHPRC, has been unstinting in her support, encouragement, and active involvement in helping this project to publication.

Finally, I give special appreciation to those at home: to my husband Fred, who has never doubted the importance of this work and always seemed to say the right thing at the appropriate time to keep me going; to our sons Andy, Matt, and Gil who have consistently appreciated what I was doing and helped make it possible by willingly shouldering additional family responsibilities, and at the same time making me laugh. To Andy, a fellow historian, I owe a professional debt; he responded with alacrity and enthusiasm to my requests to check facts and locate photographs in a variety of Washington, D.C., archives. This book is dedicated to two women who, if they had lived a century earlier, could easily have been Elizabeth Lee's best friends.

Wartime Washington

Introduction

Elizabeth Blair Lee

BORN JUNE 20, 1818, IN FRANKFORT, KENTUCKY, Elizabeth Blair was the only daughter of Francis Preston Blair, Franklin County circuit court clerk, land speculator, and newspaperman. Her mother, Eliza Gist, was the daughter of the Revolutionary War hero Nathaniel Gist and the stepdaughter of Gen. Charles Scott, governor of Kentucky. In addition to Elizabeth, the Blair family circle included three sons: Montgomery, born in 1813, James in 1819, and Francis Preston, Jr. (Frank), in 1821. The Blair household was lively and energetic, filled with the activity of four exuberant children. It was also a close-knit and loving family. The father, called Preston by his family and friends, may have been a fierce political competitor, but at home he was a doting, warmhearted, and generous parent. The mother, Eliza, whose strong personality earned her the nickname of "the Lioness," was an equal partner in her marriage, nearly matching Preston in intellect and tenaciousness. At her death, her son-in-law described her as "one of the noblest of women— of a great good & generous nature of wonderful mental powers—."

Politics permeated Elizabeth's childhood years as her father plunged headlong into the tumultuous Kentucky fray, arguing the issues of tariff, national bank, land policy, taxes, nationalism, and states' rights. By 1826 Preston Blair was a staunch supporter of the hero of New Orleans and played a substantial role in Andrew Jackson's election to the presidency in 1828. Called to Washington in 1830 by President Jackson, Blair became editor of the Democratic newspaper, the *Globe,* and a member of the Kitchen Cabinet.

The years of Jackson's presidency were exhilarating times for the Blair family. Preston Blair was not only a firm political ally; he and his family also developed a deep and abiding love for Jackson. Elizabeth spent many hours sitting at the feet of the tall, gaunt president, listening to the political discussions of her father and his close friend. Jackson, as well as her father, enlisted her help to transcribe documents, correspondence, and editorials. Her father claimed she was "brought up in caucus." In his final years Old Hickory gave

Elizabeth one of his most cherished possessions: the wedding ring of his beloved
wife Rachel.

In Washington, Elizabeth Blair blossomed into an attractive, slender, and
vivacious young woman. As an only daughter, she was the apple of her father's
eye, and her delicate constitution caused all the family to be overly protective.
Her own sparkling personality, ready wit, and refined good looks, coupled with
her father's political position, ensured Elizabeth's role in society as a belle of
Washington. With a love of dance and exceptional ability as a conversational-
ist, she thoroughly enjoyed the balls, theater outings, and social gatherings in
the nation's capital, often overtaxing her physical strength. In addition to the
political acumen acquired within the family circle, Elizabeth benefited from
several years' experience at Madame Adele Sigoigne's fashionable school in
Philadelphia. Meanwhile, in 1836 her father had purchased a two-story brick
home across the avenue from the White House. Blair House remained a family
home until 1942, when it was purchased by the United States government and
became the presidential guesthouse.

In August 1839 Elizabeth Blair vacationed at White Sulphur Springs in
western Virginia. It was there that she first met the handsome and quietly
resolute young naval officer, Lt. Samuel Phillips Lee. Although a member of
that noble family, the Lees of Virginia, Phillips was an impecunious relation,
visiting the Springs in an attempt to restore his broken health. More than
that, he was also recovering from his ignominious dismissal by Charles Wilkes
from the great United States exploring expedition to the Antarctic. It would
not have been surprising if Miss Blair had not noticed him, but she did. For
his part, the young lieutenant fell immediately and deeply in love. For four
years their courtship was a romantic tale of the trials and tribulations of young
love. Her father vehemently objected to her choice, as did her brother Montgomery, and she struggled with the demands of filial duty and heart's desire.
At last, on April 27, 1843, Elizabeth Blair married Samuel Phillips Lee. Unable to reconcile his feelings, Preston Blair traveled west to visit his eldest son
and did not witness the ceremony. The passage of time, however, healed the
breach; the father came to regard Phillips Lee as another son, and they enjoyed
a close and affectionate relationship for many years. Montgomery, however,
never overcame his dislike for Phillips Lee. Through the years the relationship
of the brothers-in-law was, at best, cool and on occasion, downright hostile.

Throughout the 1840s and 1850s Elizabeth's world revolved around her
husband's career. A conventional nineteenth-century woman, she confined
herself to her sphere and was content to be a dutiful wife. Only within the
privacy of their marriage did she stray from the ideals of the cult of true womanhood. Throughout their long partnership, Elizabeth Blair Lee gave her husband sound, frank, thoughtful, and straightforward advice, influencing him in
career decisions and professional relationships. Her letters to him demonstrate
the extent and importance of her role as confidante and counselor.

During the extended periods of her husband's active sea duty, she lived with her parents. In 1845 Preston Blair built a second home, Silver Spring. Located just east of the northernmost boundary of the District of Columbia, it was only six miles from the White House. Most of the time Blair rented his Washington home to governmental officials, and the family lived in the country. The mouse-brown house at Silver Spring was unpretentious; Blair concentrated his energies and enthusiasms on the land. The estate was a profusion of flower and vegetable gardens, orchards, and fields. It was from this idyllic setting that Elizabeth Lee wrote many letters to her absent husband. Politicians, men of affairs, military leaders, relatives, and friends congregated at Silver Spring to consult with Preston Blair. It was not unusual for her to report that "there were ten to dinner beside our own family" (Sept. 5, 1863).

In 1852 Montgomery Blair moved back to Washington from St. Louis and took up residence in the Blairs' Pennsylvania Avenue home and soon added a third story. Seven years later, when it seemed possible that Phillips Lee might be permanently stationed in the city, Blair decided to build a house for his beloved daughter and her husband. The three-story structure was adjacent to and a duplicate of Montgomery's home, sharing a common wall. It was a congenial arrangement for the elder Blairs, who were never on good terms with Montgomery's wife; they continued to live in the country but used their daughter's home as a convenient haven when in the city. During the war, Elizabeth experimented with renting the house but found it only added to her troubles. Thereafter, she usually spent her summers at Silver Spring and wintered in the city. Military and political notables called regularly at both homes, and she routinely reported the considerable news she heard to Phillips Lee.

Central to Mrs. Lee's life was their only child Francis Preston Blair Lee. Called Blair, he was born August 9, 1857, and was a great consolation to his mother during the war years. As she wrote on his birthday in 1863, "I sometimes wonder what would have become of me in these last three years of separation from you & bitter miseries of the War— I have been many times felt most gratefully that he was an endless source of occupation, comfort & joy to me."

Beyond her roles of wife and mother, Elizabeth participated in a traditional form of benevolent work. Inspired by her aunt Rebecca Gratz, a leading philanthropist in Philadelphia, she devoted herself to the Washington City Orphan Asylum and joined its board in 1849. She devoted endless hours to asylum work, raising money, establishing a Sunday school, and hiring and firing employees. She believed in the value of her work but also appreciated her personal benefits: "I love this work for all the good it has done others & to me— I took it to get rid of myself when pining into sickness for my husband— [It] gave me work for head, heart & hands— & a refuge ever ready for me when my life was too lonesome to be happy— & no matter how much faith one has we must do something for others to be happy so you see all my charity is after all selfishness—" (Feb. 7, 1865). In 1862 Elizabeth became first directress, a title she retained until 1906. She was also a founder of the first Washington chapter of the Daughters of the American Revolution.

When war came, Elizabeth and Blair only rarely strayed from her home environs. In the summer of 1861, after the disastrous rout of the Union army at Bull Run, there was general fear that Washington was in danger, and toward the end of July she left the capital, searching for safety. Mother and son visited Atlantic City, stayed with relatives in Philadelphia, rented a cottage for a few weeks in Bethlehem, Pennsylvania, and finally returned to Silver Spring in mid-October. A year later, when Phillips Lee gained command of the North Atlantic Blockading Squadron and was ordered to report to Norfolk, she again left her home. Because rumors swirled of an attack on the North by Robert E. Lee, Elizabeth and Blair visited their Philadelphia relatives until the bloodbath of Antietam was over and Robert Lee's threat had ended. Never again did she run from danger, although she was vacationing at Cape May during Jubal Early's 1864 raid on Washington, when Silver Spring was ransacked and her brother Montgomery's country home burned.

Vivacious and intelligent, Elizabeth Lee was an attractive woman. Thin but energetic, she combined the faint vestiges of tomboyishness that came from growing up with three brothers with the natural refinement of a pleasant, well-bred, and somewhat delicate woman. Talkative, optimistic, and blessed with a saving sense of fun, Elizabeth was an appealing personality. Regrettably, only one photograph of her in maturity has survived. Family legend asserts that she claimed the picture showed the ravages of war. It does. Looking older than her forty-four years, she appears somber and worn down by the anxieties of the time. Only careful examination uncovers her wide, well-formed mouth, her lovely oval face, and her large and gentle eyes. Despite the cares of war, Elizabeth retained her optimistic outlook, commenting that her usual attitude was "bouyant hopeful even when there's little save faith to make one so." She recognized that "tis my nature to believe the best until I know the worst—" (Mar. 20, 1862; Oct. 15, 1863).

Generosity of spirit was an essential element of Elizabeth Lee's character and endeared her to family and friends. When S. P. Lee's brother John thought he could not send his sons to college, Elizabeth wrote to her husband: "I really cannot resist suggesting that if possible without hurting your Brother you ought help him to educate his sons. tis the best way to help them in life— & I regard it as the best storage in life for our own child These are all fine children & they are the band of Brothers to which I hope our little one will belong & I hope with mutual benefit—" (Aug. 9, 1863). Her absolute devotion to the Union did not cloud her judgment of her country's foes: "I heard this morning that Stonewall Jackson is to [be] buried at Richmond today— He was an able Genl & an earnest man & I hope is taken away to be spared the sorrow which I think the cause he earnestly espoused is to come to— I have thought him a sort of

Cromwell only a far better man & in times to come I think we as Nation will take pride in his heroism even in spite of the miserable cause which won his heart—" (May 13, 1863). The only Southerner for whom she had no sympathy was Robert E. Lee. She could not forgive his refusal of the command of the Union armies which her father offered him in Lincoln's name: "In my opinion no vain woman was ever more easily lured from honor and duty by flattery than was this weak man by the overtures of wily politicians" (May 18, 1862).

Elizabeth Lee's attitude toward slavery is an excellent example of the workings of moderate minds and hearts in America during this turbulent period. Preservation of the Union was the ultimate goal of the war; slavery was only significant in its relationship to that end. She approved of her brother Frank's vow which she quoted to Phil, "to support the Constitution & Union— about which we care more than we do the niggers—" (Dec. 15, 1861). For the Blair family, slavery was a political problem, albeit a knotty one, that called for a practical national solution, and they clung to the chimerical idea of gradual emancipation and colonization. Sharing the attitudes of the vast majority of white Americans, Elizabeth Lee believed the black race to be inferior. At the same time, she loved individual blacks such as Blair's nurse Becky. When the possibility of emancipation in Maryland became reality, her solution was simple and pragmatic: "If I was a large owner of that property I would put them on wages now and be sure of my crops" (Oct. 3, 1863). When the new railroad in Washington, unlike the older lines, permitted black passengers, she explained, "this of course excludes the fastidious who are touchy on these points— I have always thought making them altogether useless— I so use what is convenient & agreeable— & say nothing about it—" (Jan. 14, 1865).

Although Robert E. Lee surrendered to Ulysses Grant at Appomattox Court House on April 9, 1865, the war did not end for Elizabeth Lee until the following August when Phillips Lee at last returned home after the deactivation of his last wartime command, the Mississippi Squadron. For the next five years the family was reunited, although a variety of his land-based duties required frequent separation of husband and wife. Shortly after his promotion to rear admiral in 1870, Lee again went to sea as commander of the Atlantic Fleet and served in that capacity until August 1872. After his retirement on his sixty-first birthday, February 13, 1873, Lee became a gentleman farmer at Silver Spring, and the couple enjoyed another twenty-four years of domesticity.

In the years after the war, Mrs. Lee followed her established pattern of living at Silver Spring during the summer and moving into the city for the winter months. The Lees continued to share living accommodations with her parents; Elizabeth always considered herself as first lieutenant of the home and Eliza as commander. After Francis Preston Blair's death in October 1876, "the Lioness" lived only another nine months.

Son Blair progressed steadily and easily to manhood, and graduated from

Princeton in 1880. In 1883 he began his career as a lawyer. Soon he was involved in politics, and he eventually became the first popularly elected United States senator from the state of Maryland. In 1891 he married Anne Clymer Brooke of Birdsboro, Pennsylvania, and they lived in the Lees' Washington home. After Phillips Lee's death in 1897 Elizabeth lived with her son and his family, and Blair provided a loving family circle for his mother, just as she had done for her parents.

In her final years, Elizabeth grew increasingly feeble, suffering from a variety of debilitating ailments, and failing eyesight progressively restricted her activities. In 1895 blindness in her right eye was diagnosed as glaucoma, and after 1898 she was forced to give up her work for the Washington City Orphan Asylum. Despite her inability to participate actively in this most-cherished philanthropic work, the board of directors continued to reelect her first directress for the rest of her life. Eventually she was totally blind and deaf. Until the end, however, she continued to visit with her friends occasionally to talk over old times. Blair cared for and nursed her tenderly in her declining years. Each Sunday he slowly walked her across Lafayette Square to St. John's Church. The frail, small woman leaning on the arm of her grown son as they passed Jackson's equestrian statue was a touching sight for any who witnessed it. After her death, John Maddox wrote to Blair describing the impression it made on him. Whether he knew Mrs. Lee and her son is problematical; at best, he was only an acquaintance. As a member of Epiphany Church, Maddox also crossed Lafayette Square on Sunday mornings. He wrote that he made it a practice to start early for church so that he could stand in the park and watch mother and son pass.

On September 13, 1906, Elizabeth Blair Lee quietly died at home on Pennsylvania Avenue. She had lived a long and full life, and to her family and friends had seemed the ideal incarnation of a nineteenth-century woman; she had fulfilled, in the words of one acquaintance, all that is contained in "that beautiful old word 'gentlewoman.'" A devoted daughter, sister, wife, and mother, she left the example of a life well lived.

The Letters

In 1942 while clearing out the farm at Silver Spring, Mrs. Lee's grandsons discovered trunks of family papers and letters stored in the hayloft of the stable. They gathered them up and deposited them in the library at Princeton University, where they comprise the Blair-Lee Papers. Included in this rich collection are the papers of Samuel Phillips and Elizabeth Blair Lee, Francis Preston Blair and his sons Frank and Montgomery, and Phillips's brother John Lee.

When Elizabeth Blair married Samuel Phillips Lee in 1843 she promised to write him every day they were apart. As a professional naval officer, Lee was away from home a good deal of the time, and in their fifty-four years of marriage Elizabeth fulfilled her vow, writing thousands of letters to her "Dear Phil." Fortunately, Phillips Lee cherished her letters and saved them; happily, their descendants preserved them.

Of the 930 existing Civil War letters from Elizabeth Lee to Phillips, 368 have been chosen for publication. Portions of the remaining letters have been incorporated in the annotations. The only major break in the run of the letters occurs in the first year of the war. There are no letters for the months of March, April, and May 1861. During that period, Mrs. Lee thought her husband was en route to the China Station and sent her letters to Batavia. Anticipating the outbreak of civil war, Lee disobeyed his orders and returned home from the Cape of Good Hope. Evidently, the letters written by Mrs. Lee during those months never returned from the Far East.

Letters, described by Goethe as "the most beautiful, the most immediate breath of life," give voice to ideas and feelings of the moment, evoking the emotional milieu of the time. Elizabeth Lee's Civil War letters are a direct and immediate account of life during the United States' greatest crisis. Writing for the one person she most trusted, with no thought of a wider audience, she wrote frankly and without pretense. Her letters express her spontaneous thoughts and feelings, untainted by hindsight. Indeed, she described her letters as "thinking aloud" and assured her husband that she never read over them or considered "how I am saying or writing my utterances" (Feb. 12, 1864).

Enlarging our vision of the war are Elizabeth's graphic eyewitness accounts of wartime events. Immediately after the stunning Union loss at First Bull Run, she wrote from her home on Pennsylvania Avenue: "I saw many of the soldiers straggling in late last night & early [in] the morning— One of them sat in the rain on the stone foundation of brother's front fence— I asked if he was hungry? No! thirsty? no, sick? no,— wounded no no only mad— we are beat & badly because we have no generals— no competent officers He was almost heart broken from his tone & manner— a very respectable looking man—" (July 23, 1861). From her moving description of the resignations by Southern senators on January 21, 1861, to the dramatic interruption of her letter-writing by a messenger bringing the shocking news of Lincoln's assassination, Elizabeth Lee re-creates the emotion and reality of the Union in crisis.

These letters document not only the domestic and social life of the nation's capital but its politics as well, for Mrs. Lee's vantage point was unique. Her editor-father Francis Preston Blair was a significant political power in Washington from the administration of Andrew Jackson through the presidency of Andrew Johnson. Her elder brother Montgomery served Lincoln as postmaster general. Her younger brother Frank, a Union general, congressman, and senator, helped save Missouri for the Union. Her husband, a Lee of Virginia, fought to preserve the Union and served his country with distinction. During the war Mrs. Lee lived either at Blair House, two hundred yards from the White House, or at her parents' country home, Silver Spring, six miles away. Both residences drew a constant stream of distinguished visitors. Elizabeth Lee kept the promise she had made to her husband in 1851: "I shall cultivate politics this winter to keep me alive & . . . give you a clear, prompt understanding account of what goes on" (Sept. 19, 1851). Especially during the war she found solace in her "talks" to Phillips Lee and poured out a steady stream of political news and her own analyses of events. In the early months of the war she wrote: "I cannot think England will take any part in this war— she knows that the power of this nation is north to help her in her time of need which may not be afar off— Our Blockade must be an effective one & when they have lost a good many ships— they will cease to run blockade as it is not sufficiently profitable—" (June 1, 1861).

The following year she commented upon political machinations within the cabinet, lashing out at "fussy tricky" Secretary of War Edwin M. Stanton, "who is pretty much divided between his intrigues and jobbing and devotions to the White House where he is ever so prostrate that one can scarce approach old Abe with [out] giving him a shove to get at him— He and Chase now hunt in couples and both have mounted the Extreme Abolition lacky" (May 26, 1862). Even when writing of her family members, she almost never lost her sense of balance or her adroitness with the pen. When her tempestuous brother Frank became embroiled in a congressional wrangle, she commented: "Frank will not let even a great man set his small dogs on him without kicking the dog & giving his master some share of his resentment" (Oct. 24, 1863).

Intelligent, perceptive, and thoroughly immersed in politics, Mrs. Lee wrote acute judgments of public figures, vivid descriptions of behind-the-scenes political activities, and sensible assessments of the tide of events. With two decades of experience in letter-writing, she gave her "inside view," producing the thoughtful and concise reports which her husband expected. Throughout her letters she cleverly drew quick vignettes of personalities: Preston King "rolls about the house like a huge body of feathers—" (Mar. 8, 1865); Joseph Hooker "has the gift of appreciating clever men & maybe to use them— if so he will get along & well— but I think he lacks everything but courage—" (Jan. 27, 1863); the feud between Benjamin Butler and David Porter after the failure of the first Union attack on Wilmington, North Carolina, she thought was "a hot fight between two gas bags who may puncture each other" (Dec. 31, 1864).

Devoted to the cause of the Union, Elizabeth Lee's attitude is typified by her cry, "This wicked Secession Conspiracy! How many hearts it has mourning and broken" (Mar. 3, 1862). She hated secession, yet felt great compassion for the Southern people, as she wrote on April 10, 1862, "I cannot for an instant divest myself of feeling that they are my people, my countrymen, mad men as they are, my heart aches for them." For her old friend Varina Davis, wife of Confederate president Jefferson Davis, she felt great sympathy: "She is one of the victims of this war— I shrink from looking her future in the face— & yet she may escape all the sorrow I fear for her how sincerely I wish her no ill— & yet how fervently I pray that our Government may go thro the trials which now beset it— & come out— greater & better than ever" (June 11, 1861). By war's end she could only think of her foes as "these poor sinful men" with "their bad and now hopeless cause" (Apr. 7, 1865).

Elizabeth Lee was at the center of an extended and affectionate nineteenth-century family. Through her correspondence, she bound that family together. She recognized her role, commenting in 1863, "my letters are a family institution" (Aug. 12, 1863). She wrote regularly to her absent brothers, to her husband's relatives, particularly brother John and his wife Nelly and to sister Fanny. She never neglected her treasured "Aunt Becky" in Philadelphia. The renowned Rebecca Gratz is a classic example of the Blair-Lee extended family. Rebecca's brother Benjamin Gratz had married Eliza Blair's sister. Although not technically her aunt, Rebecca, in fact, performed and was treated as if she had been. It was through the Gratz family that Elizabeth Lee found her lifelong friend, Sara Gratz Moses Joseph, who was a daughter of Rebecca's sister, Rachel. The Gratz connection brought a host of fond relatives from the Hays, Etting, and Mordecai families. On the Blair and Gist side, intermarriages brought Prestons, Breckinridges, and McDowells into the family circle. Lee relations are legion. Phillips Lee was third cousin to Robert E. Lee. John Lee had married into the extensive Hill family of Prince Georges County, and the ties with that family were intimate and widespread. Elizabeth's brother Montgomery explained the importance of her correspondence when he wrote: "I never feel indeed how much I owe to you & how much we all owe to you till I get away & think how true you are not only to me but to us all & how much you have been instrumental in keeping up & cherishing the love for each other which makes the happiness of our family more than all things else" (Apr. 29, 1854).

Beyond their abundant political insights, these letters make an important contribution to understanding nineteenth-century American life. They provide an intimate picture of a strong and stable marriage, even though the partners were separated a good deal of the time. They help explain how a woman who nearly embodies the nineteenth-century ideal of "true womanhood" could yet maintain her sense of self; indeed, they contribute a substantial picture of the inner workings of a marriage between two strong individuals. The letters offer an excellent running commentary on child-raising—the pitfalls of theory and the pratfalls of actuality. There is much to be learned from them about intergenerational relationships and extended family ties. They help explain the value of benevolent work to middle- and upper-class women: what they contributed to it and what they gained from it. They also give greater understanding of nineteenth-century women, whose value was measured by their husbands' success: how they helped to promote their men and how they influenced careers. Elizabeth Lee was her husband's wisest and closest confidante. She had seen "the ropes well pulled" and could effectively plead his case in the Navy Department, the halls of Congress, and even the White House. The significance to social historians of Mrs. Lee's letters is equally as great as their value to political historians. Full of life herself, Elizabeth Lee brings the past to life in vibrant letters, animating the drama of Civil War Washington with immediacy, intimacy, and spontaneity.

Individually, the letters of Elizabeth Blair Lee offer striking statements of political attitudes, personal judgments, and immediate reactions to events. Collectively, they re-create the atmosphere of the period, building daily life through the recitation of the mundane acts that comprise much of ordinary life. Her regular references to weather, health, and daily chores bring history to life, giving substance and texture to her world. That day-to-day routine, punctuated by shattering events of war, impresses us with what it was like to be there.

Editorial Method

The primary goal of the editor has been to preserve the style and spirit of Elizabeth Blair Lee's correspondence to her husband Samuel Phillips Lee. Because she considered her letters to her husband casual "talks," she frequently neglected orthodox sentence structure and rules of grammar, and she ignored paragraphing altogether. Guided by the principle of preserving the integrity of the documents, I have attempted to reproduce the original text as nearly as possible, given the limitations of typesetting. All editorial interventions are clearly indicated, either in this essay or in notes.

Notes following each letter identify and explain people, places, and events. People are identified at their first mention with sufficient biographical information for understanding the text; these identifications are not comprehensive biographical sketches. The index indicates where those identifications appear and include all other references to that person.

In every case, the dateline has been regularized and salutations have been run into the text. Because she had no uniform style for ending her letters, the closing has been run in with the last paragraph. Frequently, the last few sentences of a letter were written in the margins and across the top of the pages; these sentences have been included as part of the last page. Interlineal additions are placed within the text at the point indicated by Mrs. Lee. Superscriptions have been brought down to the line. Abbreviations and contractions have been retained; those that might cause confusion are explained in the notes.

Mrs. Lee adopted the practice of numbering her letters so that her husband could easily tell when one had gone astray. The theory was better than the practice, for she often forgot the number of her previous letter, and either repeated or skipped a number. Sometimes she neglected to use any number at all. Because these numbers can be more confusing than helpful, they are not reproduced.

Misspellings may be assumed to be those of Elizabeth Lee and not typographical errors. Misspelled proper names stand as written and are corrected in notes at their first appearance and in the index. A misspelled or misused word sometimes makes the meaning of a sentence particularly obscure. In those few instances, the correct word is immediately inserted in square brackets. An optimistic person, Mrs. Lee tended to omit negatives, a confusing practice for the casual reader. Only in those cases in which her meaning is exceptionally obscure is the negative added in square brackets. This device has been used sparingly; if there exists any possibility that the addition further confuses the meaning, the sentence stands as originally written. On a few occasions Mrs. Lee repeated the last word of the preceding page. Because this practice was not her usual style, the repetition has been eliminated. I have attempted to keep all editorial interventions within the text to a minimum; those that occur are always indicated by square brackets.

Mrs. Lee's free-form style is most obvious in her devotion to the common nineteenth-century use of the dash for commas, semicolons, and periods. The dash has been retained, and no attempt has been made to determine whether she intended a comma, semicolon, period, or simply a dash. Likewise, Mrs. Lee's placement of her dashes (and their length) was erratic and haphazard; they have been rendered in uniform length, consistently placed next to the preceding word, and followed by a space. Although Mrs. Lee's style of capitalization is more modern than that of many nineteenth-century writers, her handwriting is hurried, and the problem of deciphering upper and lowercase letters is difficult. I relied on my best judgment from the experience of reading hundreds of her letters.

The letters are almost innocent of paragraphing. To give some relief from solid print, I have introduced some paragraphing. Because Mrs. Lee often moved from one subject to another in successive sentences, there is no infallible rule for establishing paragraphs, other than to intrude into the letters as infrequently as possible. When a sentence or a thought was completed at the end of a line, Mrs. Lee rarely added any sort of punctuation. When a thought is obviously a complete sentence, a period has been added. If the meaning is unclear or there exists the possibility of more than one reading, the words are reproduced as they appear in the original.

Occasionally, the letters contain references to enclosures; most often they have not survived. If they were found, they are summarized in a note. Strike-outs are omitted unless they significantly alter the meaning. Most of Mrs. Lee's strike-outs are caused by hasty writing, for example, "Post Genl Master Genl." Frequently in her haste Mrs. Lee neglected to indicate opening or closing quotation marks. Where the beginning or end of the quotation is obvious, the quotation mark has been supplied; but often she has moved between direct and indirect quotation with no exact indication of which is which.

I am weak & nervous but keep a quiet exterior even amid all this excitement — I think of Joy over our Glorious victories — but none offer up more heartfelt thanks givings than your wife This experience has made come to this conclusion that I will await your return home if the Dr says I can safely do so + — [if it returns] I could not shake off the feeling that morning that I should die under that knife & chloroform & to leave the world without seeing you again seemed more than death — there was nothing reasonable or right in this feeling & I controlled it — still I suffered more than I will do again willingly.

11 OcK Friday night

Oh horror upon us again — I was sun [missed just now] by the ringing of the door bell — every one was sleeping but me — I went to the door — Mry Rochester said — It was he so I opened it — & he announced the assassination of our President & the attempt upon Mr Seward — My brother was out — Charles had gone to the Country — At the moment Luke took his stand at on front door — I told him

Letter of Apr. 14, 1865, when EBL learned of Lincoln's assassination.

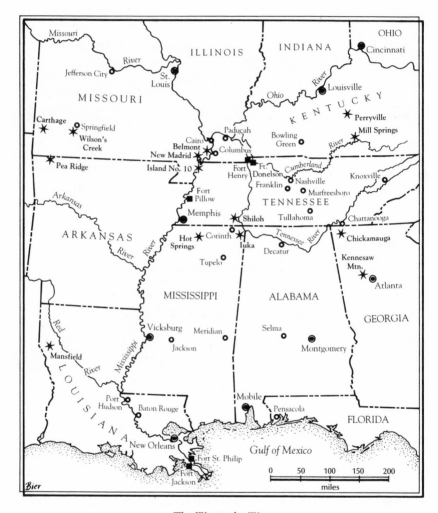

The War in the West

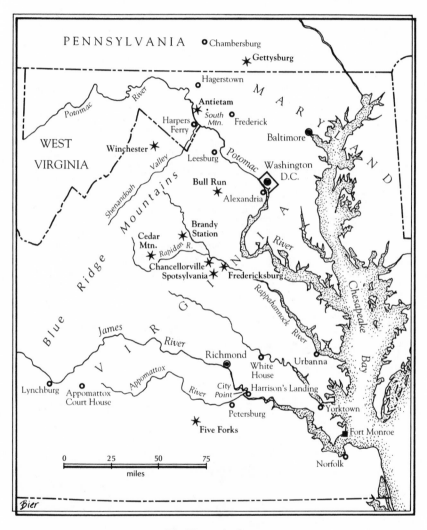

The War in the East

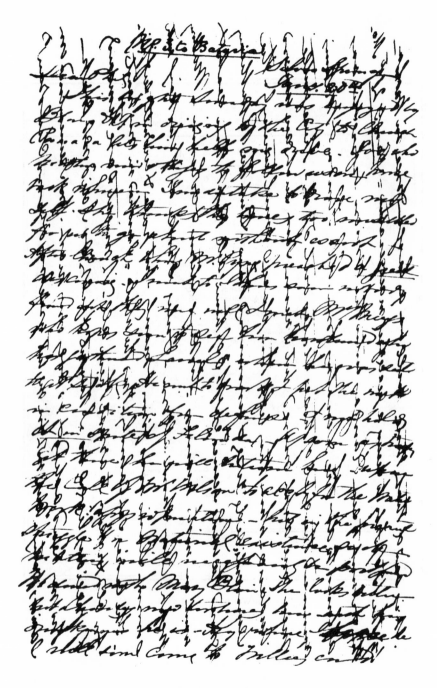

"No. 3 to Batavia," letter of Jan. 20, 1861.

1

"Civil War seems inevitable— even at friendly dinner parties"

January 12, 1861

IN THE FINAL MONTHS OF 1860, as the nation teetered on the brink of civil war, Secretary of the Navy Isaac Toucey ordered Comdr. S. P. Lee to join the East India Squadron in the China Sea. Departing New York on December 9, 1860, Lee's ship *Vandalia* made port at Cape Town, South Africa, on February 27, 1861. While refitting his ship he must have learned of the secession of South Carolina, and after a few weeks of hesitation, he decided upon his course of action: on March 25, 1861, disregarding his orders, he sailed for home and arrived in New York on May 15.

Upon his departure from home, Elizabeth Lee resumed her accustomed practice and wrote to her absent husband, directing her letters either to Cape Town or to Batavia. Because of the great distance her letters were to travel, she wrote in journal form, covering the events of several days in one letter. She also often wrote two letters of the same date or overlapping dates.

Her letters during these uncertain months were highlighted by descriptions of the continual efforts to find a means of compromise between North and South and of the resignations of Southern senators, and of her own speculations about the incoming administration of Abraham Lincoln.

There are no letters for the months of March, April, and May; it is probable that she continued to direct her mail to Batavia, and those letters never returned.

Silver Spring   December [5, 1860]
Dear Phil   Your letter of yesterday was handed to me by Father this evening— He is oppressed to night from fatigue & trouble. He is satisfied as to the cause determined upon by his friends— no white feather but no retaliating speeches no bitter words— a calm dignified patience— & leave all action to the other side as they have the power & responsibility—[1] Iversons speech let the cat out of the bag and it is very evident if the north holds off that the cotton states &

middle states will soon be at logger heads— Mr Iverson speech was applauded by the galleries— when he proposed a Brutus (ie) Wigfall) for Houston—[2] Mrs Davis[3] & other southern-people filled the gallery— but Mr. I's was amazing to his friends— "*in vino* veritas" so read it—

Mrs. D & our new family convert to Republicanism— are no longer friends— Mrs. D. having announced in *her presence* she would not associate with Republicans— Mrs. D. has shown me extra civility this fall— but my country home[4] helps me thro all such points— I intend to call her Queen Varina from this time forth & that will put me in high favor— Tho' she may be pretend to be mad—[5] Our defeated candidate who offered to make Mrs. D. Secy of State's wife— is all civility to Father urged him to take part in the *Senatorial* caucus— who replied— he *knew his own place* better than that— upon which there was some talk— of course all in good humor— *Our Sunday Company* is very excited— I suppose the more so because of his opposition to the proposition in the Eve Journal Albany—

Father saw John[6] today & tried to comfort him with his own conviction that slaves are safer in Md. than south & tobacco will keep high even war time Thursday morning   I am off to the City with Mary & my boy—[7] the ride is good for him & I want him to go see Mary Blair[8] who is the most unhappy looking person I know— her brother's unhappy end— said to be by suicide has affected even more than the loss of her Father— & Charly is here with his burdens in addition— She takes great notice of our boy   I go to her whenever in the city for her sorrows have endeared her to me very very much— I hear the Forts South are to be taken by States a civil process against each individual soldier— So far Father think the good nature of the north is imperturbable but I fear old Wade[9] wont hold out much longer

1. Francis Preston Blair had always followed a moderate course in his approach to the problem of slavery. Originally from Kentucky and owning a few slaves himself, he had viewed slavery as a political p oblem, albeit a knotty one. He clung to the notion of gradual emancipation and colonization. As a member of the Republican platform committee, he had favored a statement that would not provide the South with a cause to secede. Although he had supported the candidacy of Edward Bates, he was pleased with the nomination of Abraham Lincoln and became a devoted advocate. For Blair, finding a middle ground on the slavery issue was one thing; acquiescing in secession was quite another. Preservation of the Union was the cardinal principle that guided all his political activities.

2. Georgia senator Alfred Iverson minced no words in his speech of December 5, 1860: "We believe that the only security for the institution to which we attach so much importance is secession and a southern confederacy. . . . Our true policy is, to go out of this Union now while we have strength to resist any attempt on the part of the Federal Government to coerce us." He referred to Sam Houston as "a clog in the way of the lone-star State of Texas," and threatened, "if he does not yield to public sentiment, some Texan Brutus will arise to rid his country of the hoary-headed incubus that stands

between the people and their sovereign will." *Congressional Globe*, 36th Cong., 2d sess., 1860–61, 30, pt. 1:11. Texas senator Louis T. Wigfall was an adamant fire-eater while Texas governor Sam Houston opposed all efforts toward secession.

3. Varina Howell Davis, wife of Mississippi senator and Confederate president Jefferson Davis, was a good friend of EBL.

4. EBL's country home at Silver Spring, Maryland, belonged to her parents.

5. On January 10, 1861, EBL reported: "My sobriquet Queen Varina is universal now."

6. Maj. John Fitzgerald Lee, S. P. Lee's younger brother, owned a farm, The Lodge, in Prince Georges County, Maryland. A West Point graduate in 1834, he was a career army officer, appointed in 1849 as judge advocate of the army. He remained in that position until it was abolished by a congressional act of July 17, 1862, when he retired to his country home.

7. Mary Martin, eldest daughter of E. T. T. Martin of Auburn, New York. Her family had been close to the Blair family since the days of Andrew Jackson's presidency. The Lees' son Blair was three years old.

8. Mary Serena Jesup Blair was the widow of EBL's brother James. Mary Blair's father, Thomas S. Jesup, died June 10, 1860. Her brother William resigned from the U.S. Military Academy and died at the age of twenty-six, five months after the general. Her brother Charles Jesup (USMA 1858) resigned on August 20, 1860, because of ill health and died April 22, 1861.

9. Benjamin Wade, Republican senator from Ohio (1851–69), was a leader of the extremists in Congress.

Silver Spring   December 6, 1860

Dear Phil   Many thanks for your letter the "Directions for letters" is invaluable— to me— when I saw how much pains you had taken I reproached myself for having asked it[1] I might have studied it out by myself & saved your precious eyes that labor—

I failed in seeing Judge T.[2] I missed him between the Senate & his home for I was on my way to the Capitol when I saw the flag was down—[3] As I took Blair in with me— & I dont want to be out late— the roads bad I hurried home without following up the Judge— When I saw the flag was down something that Father said about Berta Young—[4] made me feel anxious to see her— I called & found her home Oh— what a sad visit— She says for the last 3 months half of her waking hours have been spent on her knees, she asked about Blair— & then exclaimed Oh our sons!! What a noble heritage we thought them born to, in our wide spread— fine, happy country— Now they have no future & with that her tears streamed— & her anguish was— but I must grieve you with her gloom I hope I left her happier than I found her— I rallied all the time & talked with the abiding faith that lives in me that— God will be merciful— to us sinful as we are As I told the Bishop (Catholic) of Richmond[5] at Johns there are too many praying people in this country to endure such a chastisement as civil war— He replied "Universal suffrage will not do—" But in all religion the people are ever more devout & earnest that the priests & it is in the people I hope & trust— as the instrument to save us, thro' God's great goodness to us— I am full of this trust & therefore not cast down— but I hope this Refuge is now so continually pressed upon my head & heart that I do hope it will make me ever a more earnest & devout woman— As yet I am well & calm— sleep generally 5 & 6 hours soundly— dont weep in my sleep— walk 3 miles & sometimes more a day— read & talk the evenings to my Parents— in my room write to you & read my bible &c— here is a full acct of myself that you may see I am trying to do my duty earnestly when undergoing a trial that would have utterly prostrated me formerly And if you & Blair have health & happiness— my life will be one of joy & thankfulness— Bertys husband[6] sent word by me to Father he was coming here before he went home— he is as gloomy as his wife

I left Mary at Capt Sands[7] with Betty—[8] that is the rendezvous now in the City— with Betty & Mary!!— I went to buy a Herald & met Mr. Colfax & Mr McPherson[9] both inquired after you— they spoke cheerfully of things— & it is evident to me they dont think the South in earnest— Some think that the middle states are to stay in to mediate dictate terms for the return of the Cotton States to the Union—[10] *this* is from an extreme southern source— Hale[11] has give great disgust to the Republicans their programme is— *imperturble silence* & a zealous following up of business— Good night. there is an irrepressible conflict in my heart— I yearn to look at even that beard— which I quarrel with sometimes—

Friday morning Decr 7 Blair wants to go on board the Vandalia this morning— I asked why he wanted to go on "board in it"— he replied— that yr ship had no "black smoke steam pipe in it" & that you must put one in "Bandalia & he was going to help you do it" This subject has not been mentioned by me to any one— so I asked him who told him you wanted a steam pipe ship— "I heard my Papa liking a steam pipe Ship" When talking about you & yr picture— he said Papa has his hair all over his face now You cant see his face like the picture   he lost his pencil & after looking about for it he told Becky—[12] "You look for my pencil my Papa pays you money to wait on me"— One of the little colored girls has been sent away & when I can manage to get the other off little Henry— who is a very good child will be a very good play mate for him— He has no thing like Blair's activity or hardihood— so wont lead He sets up a great cry when out in the cold now tho' more heavily clad with yarn socks &etc—

Vincent[13] waits to take this in & to get tidings from you Blair says [line of Blair's scribbles] that is his love & is pestering to write more love with that of   Your devoted Lizzie

1. On December 5, 1860, Lee sent his wife a long and elaborate letter of instructions for mailing letters to him. He included postage rates for letters and newspapers via

England in either British or American vessels; he meticulously described the number of days to allow for a letter to reach New York or Boston, how many days it would take to reach England and the connections for overland mail; he suggested careful scrutiny of the New York *Herald* and *Tribune* for steamship sailings; and he recommended Cunard steamers as the most reliable. Lizzie was to send her letters to the Cape of Good Hope until January 5, then to Batavia until February 25. These letters, he advised, should only be abstracts, and his regular letters should be sent to Hong Kong.

2. Judge Lyman Trumbull, Republican senator from Illinois and friend to SPL, had served on his state's Supreme Court.

3. The flag was flown only when Congress was in session.

4. Roberta Young Brown was the wife of A. G. Brown, senator from Mississippi. They had two sons, Robert Y. Brown and Joseph A. Brown.

5. The bishop of Richmond was John McGill.

6. Albert Gallatin Brown, Mississippi senator (1854–61) and Confederate senator (1862–65).

7. Benjamin Franklin Sands was SPL's old friend; they had served together on the brig *Washington* in the Mexican War in 1847.

8. Betty Blair was Montgomery's daughter by his first marriage to Elizabeth Buckner. After her mother died, Betty was adopted by her grandparents Eliza and Francis Preston Blair.

9. Schulyer Colfax was a Republican congressman from Indiana and Edward McPherson a Republican congressman from Pennsylvania.

10. After listening to congressional debates, EBL was confirmed in her opinion, writing on December 10: "Revolution alone is the theme of our public men & at same time feels like the stillness which presages a storm— which I do hope will be confined to the hurricane region— & the bitterness of the discussion— in the councils of the Cotton states— as to their subsequent steps— disposes the middle men to hold on to the evils they know rather fly— to those they know not— besides the fire eaters want them in to help them back when their exit obtains concessions they want— this *one* of them told me— But they will have rope enough & then Dictator & etc will soon make all things work well for those who are merciful & good."

11. John P. Hale was a strong antislavery senator from New Hampshire (1847–53, 1855–65).

12. Becky Smith was a black hired slave and Blair's devoted nurse. She began working for the Lees in March 1859.

13. Vincent was a black house servant of the Blairs.

Silver Spring   December 17, 1860

Dear Phil   When Joe took my letter to the PO. Saturday in the snow storm the Post Mr— told him that if I sent a letter as late as tomorrow any time before twelve olk it would be in time for the Asia[1]

Since hearing about Walters[2] going with you he [Blair] is quite eager to go too asserting that he is a big boy & dont any nurse to go with him— & for little time rebels out right against Beckys attendance

Yesterday was my Sunday to nurse— but the burden of it was assumed by

Birney[3] who still takes every opportunity of watching over her nursling— I went to the Country church[4] the service is very enjoyable & I've no doubt in the end I'll give up going to the [City] to Church altogether— the preacher is a well educated & earnest man— & I feel that I can probably do most good to myself & help to keep the service going on— & thereby do good to others— I shall study all my Church music & enter the choir in this humble flock next spring— & may most of this winter These are my present thoughts about this matter

Blair & I went to the city this morning with all the family who crowded in to hear Mr. Wade make a speech— A most manly conservative one it was too. He resists secession as a breach upon the constitution— Cannot see how Mr. Lincoln[5] can avoid carrying out the Revenue Laws— quoted Jackson— Webster Clay[6] & and all the great lights of 1851 & 2 & 3— Would never consent to any more compromises could not even think of any under the menace of the South but would live & die under the Constitution— made by the bravest & noblest men on Earth he would abide by that Compact in all it comprises— and in good faith carry out its letter & spirit— But he would hold on just as tenaciously to the Flag of the Revolution— the Capital founded by Washington— he had lived under that banner & with Gods permission die under— It was an unadulterated white man's speech & I think it will sober the South for they will have to look fearful consequences full in the face—[7]

Everybody well at Johns to day. John is getting over his cold & looks better Maj Wayne[8] & other army & navy talk about resigning They even talk of Old Buck[9] resign— Mrs. Anderson[10] the wife of the officer in command a Fort Moultrie[11] is making a great stir in town Her husband will not give it until every man is killed unless he has *orders* to do so— Mr. Taylor asked me if you had left yr resignation with me. I told you intended to hold onto your commission & yr Country & could not change your colors Mrs Jef asked me if I was going down south to fight her— I told her no. I would kiss & hug her too tight to let her break any *bonds* between us. The answer alluded to a figure in Mr. W. speech and was happy enough to get the approval of the immense crowd around us. I had a good deal of badinage with Mr. Taylor but all in perfect good nature he said there was a fireeater near me. I replied that my observation led me to think that Genus hurt themselves more than they ever did any one else.

I got a very affectionate note from *Cyntine*— Mrs. Holcomb[12] I will not forget her if I can help her in any way—

Tuesday Decr 18. I must hasten off to the City to secure this a passage in the Asia— We are all well— & it is a bright cold clear winters day I fancy you in the tropics & the talk of War makes me more reconciled to your far away station. Blair knelt of his own accord & asked God to make him good & bless his Papa. the feeling ever uppermost in your devoted wife's heart Lizzie

1. The Cunard steamer *Asia* carried mail from New York to Liverpool.

2. Walter Trumbull, Lyman Trumbull's teenage son, sailed with SPL on *Vandalia*.

3. Martha Byrne Cook had been Blair's nurse from babyhood. In the 1850s she had married Joseph Cook and was no longer a regular employee.

4. St. Paul's Episcopal Church at Rock Creek. The rector from 1852 to 1897 was James A. Buck.

5. In a December 28 letter, EBL gave her appraisal of Abraham Lincoln: "From all I hear— Lincoln so far gives great satisfaction not only to our *set* but to all sets— he is frank, cool— brave— but *very very* prudent—."

6. Andrew Jackson, Daniel Webster, and Henry Clay had all played significant roles in averting earlier breaks with the South, from the South Carolina nullification crisis in 1831 to the Compromise of 1850.

7. In a December 10, 1860, letter, EBL wrote of Southern motivation: "it is becoming evident that *local* necessities rather than northern aggressions have made protecting actions necessary." She also "feared a Civil & servile war."

8. Captain Henry C. Wayne resigned from the U.S. army December 31, 1860.

9. Democratic President James Buchanan was often called "Buck."

10. Elizabeth Clinch Anderson was the wife of Robert Anderson of Kentucky, commander of the Union garrison at Charleston.

11. As a defensive measure, Anderson moved his force from Fort Moultrie at Charleston to Fort Sumter in the harbor.

12. Anne Selden Watts married James P. Holcombe of Virginia. He was a secession member of the 1861 Virginia Convention, a Confederate congressman (1862–64), and Confederate commissioner to Canada in 1864.

Silver Spring   December 25, 1860

Dear Phil   It might happen that currents winds & waves might prevent you from stopping at the Cape of Good Hope & on getting to Batavia you would want to know how even these 15 days have passed with us Well your pilot letter alone made me feel you had gone when for a time not even the perpetual talk of civil war around me here reconciled me— however I rally quickly & now I can feel thankful for all the mercies of God on this day of rejoicing— Tho I so miss you aching to share with me the exhuberance of Blair in Xmas gifts & joys

No political event has occurred except that South Carolina ordained herself on the 20th out of the Union whereupon the stocks rise. Patriotism is now above par. The Union Flag streams from nearly every house top— Father returned home from the City last night singing & happier about politics than Ive seen him since the election— Still he & all thinking men are sure that peaceable secession is a fallacy

Our party are in the labors of Cabinet Making & from all I hear it will hardly get through safely for the party— Bates[1] has certainly got a place & L[incoln] feels obliged to ask Seward[2] & yet he dont want him to accept— but *he will.* so it hangs at present Our Maryland nominee[3] has also got a promise in writing— but *all* are yet held under advisement— Things pecuniary are not any brighter in St Louis Frank from necessity has gone to work at Law with Bay as a partner[4]

Jany 9th 1861 I concluded to make this letter cover the first month of your absence & it has been a long weary one This year commences with a warlike aspect Majr Anderson in command at Fort Moultrie denyed reinforcement tho his importunate wife insulted the President when her entreaties failed to move him to send them— But Providence over rules even the most determined— An immense theft to the amount of several Millions of State Bonds lodged in the Interior Dept was discovered or confessed by a Mr. Bailey book keeper—[5] Floyd was implicated in this fraud & he availed himself of Maj Andersons transfer of his forces to Fort Sumter to make a plea for resignation— These changes have produced a change of policy in the administration— Old Buck is now odius to the South because he has concluded not to act any longer in concert with Traitors and to execute the Laws & protect Govt property—[6] Andersons movement was masterly & has made him now the Hero of the day.[7] On yesterday there was nearly as many guns fired in his honor as that of Genl Jackson— whose spirit is now invoked daily for the protection of the Country. Mississippi is to secede to day & tomorrow King Jeff[8] is to make his adieux to the Senate. He will take his wrath out of old Buck— But on this change of policy in the President— Stocks begin to rise again & there is a tone of firmness & hope in the community—[9] that has given at least more fortitude to bear our troubles with—

Jany 10th Mr. Slidell[10] and Mr. Davis were intense in the bitterness of their denunciations of the President around whom now the Republicans rally as it is a great onus off the Republican party that he devotes to the South & Democracy should begin the War— which I fear was commenced yesterday— A Steamer[11] was sent to Maj Anderson by Scotts orders under Holt—[12] now acting Secy of War with more men & provisions. She was fired at by the South Carolinians from Fort Moultrie & a light house battery when she put back— Anderson sent an officer to Govr Pickens— they say with a threat to destroy Charleston if that attack on the Steamer was repeated to day. Her owners are telegraphed today that she safely unloading at Fort Sumter— it looks like a back down in S.C. & it will be no misfortune to the Country to prove she is unequal to any of her threats Anderson says he could hold his position in defiance of the whole South— I see to day that Hartstene has resigned—[13] he is the highest on the list who have done so & there are very few resignations— Comre Shubrick[14] went to Charleston & has returned saying they are all stark mad— *save men of large estates* & it is evident they are to be fleeced The Jews have already quit— The monied men north will not take the U State Loan— whilst the Treasury Department is in the hands of a Secessionist— Our Party are in great distress at the idea of having Cameron[15] in the Treasury it is said to day he declines but that tis thought a ruse— to quiet the protest now being made against this appointment— Even the Sun— the hotest Secession paper in Maryland gives up that Maryland will go out— there is no disunion or secession in the State—[16] Our neighbors are all civil & even when there was talk of attacking Washn we were to be protected. But the Presidents change of front has quieted all *that talk* for it never amounted to anything else— The North rallies unitedly to the Union & for the execution of the Laws & a maintenance of the Constitution— in letter & spirit— Thus your people are on the strongest & safest side of the Contest— Missouri is to go thro the ferment of her democratic Legislature— but she is considered safe & so is Kentucky— North Carolina & Tennesse— but Virginia is shaky— but it will go back to the people there & that will give time— & confidently hoped a happy result   Thompson[17] resigned when reinforcements were sent to Majr Anderson who is a kinsman of Mary Blair & a Kentuckian were at the Brevort with the Jesups this fall

Our home routine has been unaltered & so far this winter we have good health— Blair is rarely kept indoors all day— The winter is very wet so far & tho frequent snow— no ice yet to put up for summer— Mary & Betty in town   I do less reading than ever before. They have got used to doing without me & want to keep the habit— but so far my home here is comfortable— Our boy is sturdy & well & everybodys pet & particularly his Grand Pa's— who is of late struck with his abiding loyal love to my Papa— it was only yesterday he ordered Becky to Pack his clothing— "I am going to Sea to talk to Papa— he would not take either Becky or I with "Papa will take care of me" Yours ever Lizzie

1. A former Whig, Edward Bates of Missouri had been the Blair's choice for the Republican presidential nomination in 1860. A moderate man from a border state, he was chosen by Lincoln to be attorney general.

2. William Henry Seward, New York senator, became Lincoln's secretary of state.

3. Montgomery Blair became Lincoln's postmaster general.

4. EBL's brother Frank Blair has lost an election in Missouri to fill out an unexpired congressional term. He had, however, been elected to a full term, but it did not begin until December 1861. His law partner was St. Louis attorney William V. N. Bay.

5. John B. Floyd of Virginia was secretary of war. Floyd's administrative negligence and carelessness, bordering on malfeasance, caught up with him. He had fallen into the habit of issuing "acceptances" to the army supply contracting firm of Russell, Majors and Waddell. The company used these acceptances as collateral for funds borrowed from banks. As the financial situation of the company became worse, Russell struck a bargain with Floyd's relative Goddard Bailey who was a clerk in the Land Office of the Interior Department. Bailey loaned Russell bonds belonging to the Indian Trust

Fund. On December 22, the scandal became public. There was never any evidence that either Bailey or Floyd profited from these arrangements.

6. Howell Cobb of Georgia, Buchanan's secretary of treasury, resigned from the cabinet on December 8.

7. In her journal letter begun December 16, EBL reported on January 8, that "Mrs. Anderson had 6000 visits New Years & is showered with flowers & all sorts of civility." In her December 28 letter, EBL wrote that Mrs. Anderson "must have obtained permission in some shape— for her husband to secure himself. she was backed by Genl Scott— She did not spare old Buck— finding S.C got things by bullying— she got her objects by something like it draped in hoops & lace."

8. EBL referred to Jefferson Davis as "King Jeff," just as she called Varina Davis "Queen Varina."

9. Almost always optimistic, EBL made a shrewd, although erroneous, evaluation in her December 28 letter: "I think the cry for bread south will soon supercede the call for anything else The reign of Terror is nearly at an end—."

10. John Slidell, Democratic senator from Louisiana, became the Confederate minister to France.

11. The Union supply ship *Star of the West* withdrew from Charleston harbor without relieving the besieged Fort Sumter.

12. Joseph Holt, Kentucky War Democrat, served as Buchanan's postmaster general, then as secretary of war. On September 3, 1862, when he was appointed judge advocate general of the army.

13. Commander Henry J. Hartstene resigned from the U.S. navy on January 9, after thirty-three years of service.

14. Captain W. Branford Shubrick retired from the navy on December 21, 1861.

15. Republican senator from Pennsylvania Simon Cameron had given Lincoln support for the presidential nomination in exchange for appointment as secretary of war. In a letter of January 14, 1861, Francis Preston Blair advised Lincoln on the selection of his cabinet. Adamantly opposed to both Cameron and Seward, Blair suggested a long list of possible candidates, among them Charles Francis Adams, John Andrew, Edwin D. Morgan, Preston King, Salmon P. Chase, Sam Houston, and John Minor Botts. For Blair's letter, see Elbert B. Smith, *Francis Preston Blair,* 271.

16. Under the date December 29, EBL described Maryland's situation: "Every effort is being made to get up the Secession fever in this State— but Govr Hicks is firm & the State is peaceful & as yet safe & unexcited— So ends the year with a gloomy sunset over a deep snow—."

17. Jacob Thompson of Mississippi, the secretary of the interior, resigned because he had not been informed of the decision to reinforce Anderson at Fort Sumter.

Silver Spring   January 1861

I've sent a journal already to Batavia

Jany 12 Father returned this evening after a sojourn of 24 hours in the City— It seems Anderson backed out & not S.C. he has sent Lt Talbot[1] to get the instructions of the Govt & it is a wise delay as there are now so many of the southern Conventions going on at the moment— so as not to take the onus of aggression off S.C. in any way— Mr. Tombs & Genl Scott[2] had a *bout* at No. 4 (John R's)[3] The first called the Old Hero a liar— whereupon the Genl rushed into him— but they were promptly parted— it was at a dinner party— Civil War seems inevitable— even at friendly dinner parties

The Secessionist are making a great rush at Missouri but Mr. Corbin[4] *one of them* says in vain— Frank *has his ship fixed to ride out this storm & has at his command too many neighbors to make it practicable*— in that State. The Bell Everetts hold to their platform in Mo. *"enforcement* of Laws" These added to the Republicans make a majority—

It turns out that Douglass and Crittenden[5] are in Caucus with the Secessionists & are playing into their hands Mr. Cameron gives up— he says of his own free will *on dit* because he was forced— he & Mr. Seward are in cahoot— but they put in for their set too strong— & are in check now but for how long no man knoweth— Davis is likely to be the nominee— in this State & Graham[6] of N.C. in the Navy— which would suit you *better*

Jany 13 Mary M. & I went to the Country Church had a good Union sermon— Berney had Blair— by which simple name Becky called him yesterday— "Becky dont call me Blair—" What must I call you? Blair *Lee* quoth the youngster— "I think Blair is enough to call you—" "No Lee is my Papas name Mr. Hill[7] asked me if I was not Capt Lee of Navy—" I asked what he said to Mr. H. "I told him No— but I was Capt Lee's Boy Blair Lee—" Becky says this conversation with Oliver Hill occurred some weeks since

Father says I must tell you for him that you will find when you return the U. States with the same boundaries of Lakes north— Gulf South— Oceans East & West that you left— but in the meantime the country will go thro' very great trouble & trials The North is a unit for the Union[8] The Democrats taking the lead of Republicans for the enforcement of laws & the Constitution as it is— putting state volunteers at the Presidents disposal &c

The Aikens[9] are in Washington & give doleful accts S.C. The organization of minute men is a system of depredation upon the men of substance— Mr A refused to be elected to the convention of South Carolina

Jany 14 A snow storm prevents me from going to the City & sending you the latest papers but I try to get them off to you by the Servant at the Trumbulls— We are all well and every thing looks as you left it in this home circle except Blair grows taller & more knowing daily— he's fatter than when we parted— I think the worst part of getting his big teeth is past— they are nearly thro' the gums are very large & he slobbers just like a little baby— his cheeks ruddy— & *every* sign of good health— but I have to be very careful about his diet— Becky & I watch everything he eats I'll write again to Capetown but from this time constantly to *Batavia* Devotedly yr wife Lizzie

1. Lt. Theodore Talbot served at Fort Sumter. After the *Star of the West* turned back, Anderson sent messages north.

2. Robert A. Toombs, Democratic senator from Georgia, resigned his seat and became Confederate secretary of state. "Old Fuss and Feathers," Winfield Scott, was general-in-chief of the Union Army.

3. John R. is John R. Thomson, Democratic senator from New Jersey. Scott at this time was seventy-five years old and in such poor health that he could not mount a horse or even enter his carriage by himself.

4. Abel R. Corbin of St. Louis was editor of the *Missouri Argus* in the 1840s.

5. Stephen Douglas, Democratic senator of Illinois, leading exponent of popular sovereignty and defeated presidential candidate, was a member of the Committee of Thirteen in the Senate. John J. Crittenden, also a committee member, offered several resolutions in an attempt to placate the South. He resurrected the Missouri Compromise line of 36°30′ and offered a variety of conciliatory policies as concessions to the Southern states.

6. Henry Winter Davis, Maryland congressman (1855–61). He was defeated in the 1860 election then elected on the Unconditional Union party ticket and served from 1863 to 1865. William A. Graham was governor of North Carolina (1845–49); secretary of the navy (1850–52); Whig vice presidential candidate (1852); and senator in the Second Confederate Congress.

7. Oliver Hill, a relative of John Lee's wife Ellen Hill Lee.

8. On December 23, EBL reported "12 hats on the rack," including those of John Albion, Benjamin Wade, Lyman Trumbull, Preston King, and James Doolittle. After serving them all dinner, she concluded: "Tis settled that all the Northern governors are to recommend— arming & mustering the registered Militia of their States— & are to recommend the enforcement of the Laws— & loyalty to the Constitution in word spirit & deed."

9. William Aikens had been a member of Congress from South Carolina from 1851 to 1857. He was again elected in 1866, but he was not allowed to take his seat.

Silver Spring   January 17, 1861

Dear Phil   I see that a Steamer leaves New York day after tomorrow for Liverpool— So if the West winds will blow hard these last papers & letter to Cape Town may reach England by the 5th— & carry you some home tidings— Tho' so far this week has given no utterance of any great import—

The Va convention's doings are to be voted upon by the people to which the Secessionist are opposed— I see the vote given for secessionists in these Conventions— both in Ala— Geo— & Louisiana are very little ones a forth of the vote given at the Presidential election[1] The whole secession business has been brought about by secret Leagers & societies[2] & this State would have now been in the hands of the few voters & unprincipled politicians but for the firm stand of Govr. Hicks[3] & some other steady brave men— These Leaguers have roamed over the State threatening the men in their way— from all they have got one answer "we are as ready to risk our lives in self defense as you to

risk yours in attacking us—" The Union men here are up— doing— & not at
all fearful of the result & now that the people are to vote in Virginia— even
secessionist cease to boast— All their deeds are done in secret which at once
stamps their wickedness & doom—

Another thing is bringing the South to its senses it was willing to suffice if
they could bring ruin on the north— but a mild winter & an abundant har-
vest has prevented any unusual amount of suffering none out of the Cities—
Where I suppose some envoy has made the rich more than ever ready to relieve
the poor— In the South the drought of last summer— & the total cessation
of business, makes the scene there very different— they wont allow the papers
to speak of it— but letters teem with nothing else— & this seems to account
for the rabid action of the poor whites who in ignorance & poverty attribute
all their troubles to the election of Lincoln— But the actions of Virginia-
N Carolina— & the delays in Geo— & the strong opposition in Louisiana to
secession— the change in Mr. Buchanans Cabinet—[4] the rise in stocks & the
taking so promptly of the U.S. debt on the advent of Govr Dix[5] to the Treas
Dept— all look propitious— & as if the darkest hour was past— in this night
of trial to the Country

Very few Army & Navy men resign Hartstene is the only one that I
know— & he cant get any more fancy trips so quits No body as yet above you
& southern patriotism cant get that high.

The Father of *Young Lady*[6] who accompanied us to Mt Vernon writes to
Father that he has been offered the Treasury Dept. he is indisposed to take
it— but will do so— if Leaders here think he ought his tone is affectionate
as a son He will be urged by all to accept— He writes that Democrats of Ohio
are more bitter towards the South than the Republicans— Douglas holds to a
few men in Illinois but McClernand[7] & endless others have quit him—

The young ladies are in the City trying to be gay— but as yet politics has
entire sway & there is nothing else thought or talked of— Nelly[8] says she must
do something to get them out of heart & hand I recommend a good novel—
I've indulged in two— but must stop for they keep me awake too long— so it
is only a variety of dissipation I was telling Blair a story— when I said I must
go & write to you— Yes Mama go write to Papa— what must I say for you—
"Tell him come back to us now"—

Father went to the City & brought us the papers— The Republicans have
rebuked Sewards proffer "to meet violence with the right hand of peace"—
& has passed a resolution refusing all amendments to the Constitution thus
putting to an end to Mr. Crittendens plans This will help to get Seward to
England Europe where all the Senators want to send him— Col Hayne[9] was
sent back to Charleston to day with a flea in his ear from Mr. Buchanan—
who they say is enraged at Comre Armstrong for giving up Pensacola Yard to
Florida— Jim Watson protested[10]

John & family are all well

Jany 18. We are all well this morning & I have so little hope of you getting this that I'll only add   Your affectionate Lizzie   Blair told me to go to New York to see you again

1. Candidates for election to the state conventions to decide the question of secession were labeled either secessionists or cooperationists. There were, however, no clear-cut delineations, for the term "cooperationist" had many meanings, and therefore the campaign results are difficult to evaluate; but it appears Lizzie was correct: the results were generally close. In Mississippi, votes cast for known secessionists and cooperationists were 16,800 to 12,218. In Florida, cooperationists garnered between 36 and 43 percent of the vote. Secessionist-cooperationist votes in other states were as follows: Alabama, 35,600 to 28,100; Georgia, 44,152 to 41,632; Louisiana, 20,214 to 18,415.

2. After John Brown's raid on Harpers Ferry in the fall of 1859, volunteer vigilance committees sprang up thoughout the South. Under a variety of names, such as the League of United Southerners and Minute Men for the Defence of Southern Rights, these organizations, in the winter of 1860–61, turned from their original motivation of controlling the Negro to promoting secessionist sentiment.

3. An opponent of secession, Thomas Hicks was governor of Maryland from 1857 to 1862. He was then elected to the Senate and served until his death in 1865.

4. In January 1861, Philip Thomas of Maryland resigned as secretary of the treasury and was replaced by New Yorker John A. Dix. This change, along with the resignation of Jacob Thompson, gave the cabinet a majority of antisecession Democrats.

5. John A. Dix had been an unsuccessful candidate for governor of New York in 1848, running on the Free-Soil ticket. He was eventually elected to that office in 1872. Dix served briefly as Buchanan's secretary of the treasury from January to March 1861 and was a major general in the U.S. army from 1861 to 1865.

6. Kate Chase was the daughter of Salmon P. Chase. He had been governor of Ohio from 1855 to 1859. Elected to the U.S. Senate in 1861, Chase took his seat on March 4 and two days later resigned to become secretary of the treasury.

7. John A. McClernand, Democratic congressman from Illinois, resigned in October 1861 to become brigadier general of volunteers.

8. Eleanor Anne Hill Lee (called Ellen or Nelly in the letters), from a prominent Prince Georges County, Maryland, family, was the wife of SPL's brother John.

9. Isaac W. Hayne, attorney general of South Carolina

10. On January 12, 1861, without any attempt to resist the Florida militia, Capt. James Armstrong surrendered the Warrington Navy Yard at Pensacola. Josiah Watson was captain of the marines on duty at the Navy Yard.

Silver Spring   January 20, 1861

Dear Phil   This bright Sunday was enjoyed by Blair & I in driving to the City to Church   Canada[1] lets him help me drive— Joe who Mother now obliges to follow us on horse back whenever I undertake to drive myself. She thinks the times too unstable for me to go about without escort— After Church where

Mr. Pyne[2] preached a great discourse— I went to Johns saw nobody found out they were well & met Mrs. Meigs[3] who hopes soon to see her husband who has gathered Laurels when he was sent to get sick— He went to work & put the works in condition for defense— & now holds it in spite of Florida—[4] As soon as Navy gets there he will return here— upon the call of Mr. Wilson[5] to acct for the Water Work appropriations— but in the present struggle for National existence such matters will necessarily be postponed

We dined with Mary Blair— She looks better but Charley now tortures her with his drunkenness he is Ky where I fear he will soon come to Willie's end

It is said that there will be a large force in Washn by the 15 of Feby to secure a peaceful inauguration—

Jany 21st Mother & I went to see Kanzas enter the Union—[6] before she was allowed to do [so] the Senators from Ala Florida & Mr. Davis announced the exit of these States out of it—[7] These gentlemen were deeply moved but I never saw such an aroused audience when they left their places simultaneously— the Democratic side rose & surrounded them— But the Republicans ignored the whole scene & except 3 of them, all kept their seats & went on with business— looking stern & solemn— Mallory wept. Clay shook all over— Yulee spoke as if choking with sorrow— Davis was firm & manly— but pale & evidently suffering— The ladies sat calmly— thro the whole— I wished in my heart for Old Hickory to arrest them all— it might save thousands of precious lives, so I thought & felt & so I did not weep tho' my head ached & so does my heart— for I remembered our Savior's parting— "Weep not for me but yrselves & your children"

Jany 22nd. Father returned frome the city without news tonight. He evidently begins to dispair of avoiding Civil War— I cannot give up hope for it is so evident a death knell for slavery in all those States who throw away the shield of our National Government— I cannot conceive the owners so mad as to put themselves between the fire rear & front—

Jany 23. As it is best for me to keep quiet Ive busied myself with letter writing— to you Aunt Becky & Fanny—[8] The papers to night are full of Genl Scotts gathering troops at Washn The two arsenals & Genl Lawson[9] riding school are all filled & I hear Mr. Cobbs late residence is to be officers quarters I grieve over Capt Tom Brents[10] resignation I talked it over to Father & he thought I ought to try & get his friends here to stop it & write to him— but I found thro Mr. Sands that it was accepted so I did & said nothing about it— Capt Faren[11] has resigned & gets from Florida the Pensacola [yard] he thinks perhaps a life estate— poor short sighted man Troops are already en route reinforcing Fort Pickens— which commands the whole entrance & Bay & yard Genl Gibson[12] says he has a new lease on life— to keep those deserters from the Army & Navy from ever re entering the service— that shall [be] his sole vocation hereafter.

Jany 24 There are endless rumors about the commencement of hostility at Charleston & Pensacola How long this lull will last none of us know but Father thinks most likely until March. He says Corwins [13] proposition will pass— The middle states will accept this or any overture & my hope is that they will to use Mr. Browns phrase to *mediate* the return of the Cotton States— when once their own position is settled & now they all refer the action of their Conventions back to the people & even the extremest Secessionists give up that when this is done the game is up with them— Arkansas is considered safe on this account—[14] Govr Hicks has so far kept down the rioters & is supported by 3 fourths of the state in union meetings & thus we keep in peace & quiet whilst every other Slave State is full of contention & trouble—

Blair is house bound & rebellious to day by an easterly rain storm— Dogs Toys & little Henry all fail to reconcile him to the house— He informed me betimes today he was going to China to see you No day passes without many queries about you & yr present whereabouts

Jany 25 Blair & Grandma had a fine ride on horse back— & our boy is glowing with fresh air & exercise which seems as essential to his happiness as to his health.

The contest waxes warm in Missouri Green [15] writes with more anxiety as to the result than Frank They have begun the game of minute men & terrorisms but I think that will not do where they have as much of freedom of press & speech left as in Missouri— The same thing is going on in Virginia What strikes me in this contest— is the extreme supineness & noninterference of the north in every way— except when War comes they are *keen for it*— Nine tenths of the northern men evidently only want to hear the trumpets blast This temper amazes me— There are a thousand ways in which they might assist the Union men South but not one iota do they give or inch do they move but immense war preparations are going on in every northern state drilling every grown man— factories in full blast & every thing seems tending to the that dreadful end— & if war comes they will emancipate the Negroes & send them out of the country—

Now this is gloomy talk but in the end it may sober the South and let them see what is really before them— & in that way bring peace at present through Floyd they have all the Cannon & arms which belong to the United States *All South*— & this makes them bold now— but the makers are in the north & are not idle— This is why precipitation is the watchword with the Revolutionist—

Congress is idle tho the Republicans are now in power there— Etheridge [16] comes up to the Patriots standard & so do many Tennessee & North Carolina men— but they are all without organization & spirit & the other side have had their secret Leagues working for several years past— It is all a struggle for power & naught else— My faith is still strong in the law abiding tenor of the people— & a higher trust in the God of Mercy— The United States will have to muster volunteers into service & that measure is the next one to be moved in Congress. Old Buck's Cowardice is still the great misfortune to the Country— He does nothing in time *to prevent* mischief—[17] Upon the surface things look more cheeful in the city— & they are beginning their dances & frolics The place is full of officers & the jails bad boys troubles I have not been to the city for many days— So give second hand ideas—

January 26 The most violent snowstorm I ever saw Blairs smile is the only sunshine in the house— Now I am not troubled at all for our personal safety that is a thing that is not taken into our troubles at all— for women children & old men are very safe but it is the martial mien of the Country & its unhappy condition— Even all of our family yours & mine are now free of any war like exposure except Frank who has now to meet this Contest in St Louis rather Mo— but he is brave & more safe from that & tis now agreed that the Contest there— settles it for all west of the Alleghanies— *Frank's tone is perfectly confident*— & some of the Members Democrats elect to Congress have joined him from the South East corner of the State John Bell[18] is out at last— *Boldly* for the Union— so I think— he is very sure of the State— & best of all they are all working like men for dear life & dearer Country—

Saturday eve— We are all quite elated tonight with the news from Kentucky the Legislature has refused even to call a convention to *talk* about secession— This result in Ky. in spite of Coz John[19] will have an immense effect on Virginia & above all Missouri— This is a great comfort to us just now for it sustains Govr Hicks & now if Missouri votes down Secession *all of our family concerns* are out of the ditch of disunion *&* confines that disease to the yellow fever region— for there is a border warfare between N. Carolina & S. Carolina already— They ran up a palmetto flag in a fort near Washington in N.C. The people let it stay there all Sunday— but on Monday— they went [to] work & soon ran off the intruders— treated the Palmetto flag with every possible indignity & they ran up the Stars & Stripes— How much more feeling I now have for that flag— In Frankfort they flung that banner to the breeze & saluted it [with] the cannons roar— I am more than ever proud of my Native State. The newspapers talk of Franks call to Springfield—[20] & the long secret sessions— It is the Chicago battle over again

Sunday Jany 27 This is a low spirited letter but I write as I feel— & you know my health has something always to do with my spirits— I have been out today walked in the snow up to the Country Church & I cannot tell you how much cheerfulness this release from the house has given me— Then the Cause of Kentucky is reviving— will have an excellent effect upon all the Middle States These safe— *Secession practically will not touch us*— I've read the St Louis Democrat carefully it is full of spirit— & Union meetings all over the State— Old Houston talks bravely in Texas wont let them take any short cut to disunion there & the M.C. here is against it—[21] I see in the Tribune that there was a move in this county against Father— that was weeks ago & more   some drunken fellows about Rockville & from Prince Georges— & was rebuked by Mr. Valdenar & some of Roger Brooke fraternity—[22] & was never anything to give us any trouble at all— Old Roger died a few weeks ago— We really have no enemies— the poor are under too many obligations & hoping for more— The better classes are generally our friends. I repeat this for your own comfort & it is one to be thankful for when the homes of so many are now so unhappy What would add most to my happiness now within reasonable expectations is a letter from you. I hunger & thirst to hear from— Blair was as frisky as a snow bird today— Truly & fondly yr own Lizzie

1. Canada, a horse owned by the Blairs.

2. Smith Pyne, rector of St. John's Episcopal Church in Washington, D.C. (1845–64).

3. Louisa Rodgers married Montgomery Meigs on May 2, 1841. She was the daughter of Commodore John Rodgers.

4. In 1857, Montgomery Meigs was on detached duty as the supervising engineer for the construction of the Capitol and the Washington Aqueduct; his immediate superior was John Floyd, newly appointed secretary of war. Floyd's careless administrative practices and propensity to award contracts to partisan political friends led to numerous confrontations between the two. Floyd finally rid himself of the scrupulously honest Meigs by banishing him to the Dry Tortugas in September 1860. From mid-November 1860 until February 13, 1861, when he was ordered to resume supervision of the Aqueduct project, Meigs worked diligently to make Fort Jefferson defensible. Commenting on Meigs's exile, Francis Preston Blair concluded, "They sent Meigs to gather a thistle, but Thank God, he has plucked a laurel." Meigs was appointed quartermaster general May 15, 1861.

5. Henry Wilson, Republican Massachusetts senator from 1855 to 1873. He resigned to become U. S. Grant's vice president.

6. The vote on Kansas's admission did not come until January 29, 1861.

7. Senators Jefferson Davis of Mississippi, Stephen Mallory of Florida, Clement C. Clay of Alabama, and David L. Yulee of Florida gave farewell speeches on January 21.

8. Rebecca Gratz was EBL's aunt by marriage. A moving force in numerous Philadelphia philanthropic endeavors, Aunt Becky provided a role model for EBL, who devoted much of her energies to the Washington Orphan Asylum. Reportedly, Rebecca Gratz was Sir Walter Scott's model for Rebecca in *Ivanhoe*. Frances Ann Lee Pettit, born in 1816, was SPL's younger sister.

9. Probably Surgeon General Thomas Lawson who died May 15, 1861, after forty-eight years in the army.

10. Thomas W. Brent resigned January 19, 1861.

11. Ebenezer Farrand resigned January 21, 1861, after thirty-eight years in the navy.

12. Gen. George Gibson, commissary general of the U.S., died September 30, 1861.

13. Thomas Corwin, Republican congressman from Ohio. As chairman of the House Committee of Thirty-three, he vainly looked for a compromise with the South in January 1861.

14. On January 17, EBL wrote, "Arkansas goes about secession like a snail—."

15. Colton Greene, a captain in the Missouri state guard, was a South Carolinian of considerable wealth. A strong advocate of secession, he supported Claiborne Jackson and attempted to garner Confederate support for the fight in Missouri.

16. Emerson Etheridge, Whig Unionist congressman from Tennessee.

17. The following summer, on July 2, 1861, EBL claimed: "The people in Pa treat [Buck] with great contempt." EBL's obituary states that Major Abraham Van Buren said, "Buchanan sat for four years in Washington like a large, white milk and bread poultice drawing rebellion to a head." Draft of her obituary, Blair-Lee Papers, Princeton University Library.

18. John Bell, Whig senator from Tennessee and Constitutional Union candidate for president (1860).

19. John C. Breckinridge of Kentucky was Buchanan's vice president. In 1860, he was a defeated presidential candidate but was elected to the Senate. After he entered the Confederate army as a brigadier general, the Kentucky legislature asked him to resign his Senate seat, and on November 6, 1861, the federal district court at Frankfort, Kentucky, indicted him for treason. The U.S. Senate finally expelled him on December 4, 1861. EBL considered Breckinridge a distant cousin and frequently referred to him as "coz." The Blair family was thoroughly intermarried with many of the leading families of Kentucky and Virginia.

20. Frank called on Lincoln in Springfield, Illinois, on January 23, 1861, to urge his brother Montgomery for a cabinet post.

21. But the state convention passed an ordinance of secession on February 1, 1861, by 166 to 8.

22. Francis Valdenar was a Montgomery County, Maryland, commissioner from 1842 to 1845. He was also a delegate to the Montgomery County slaveholders meeting in 1859. Roger Brooke, a descendant of one of Maryland's first colonists, had a large and successful farm, Brooke Grove, near Sandy Springs.

Silver Spring   February 3, 1861

Dear Phil   Sunday— After going to Church & communion I stop to see Nelly & John   he looks better— The state of affairs has worried him sadly. We left Father in the City in Caucus   he goes to see John & tho he has said nothing to him is dreadfully anxious that he should keep out of these disunionist intrigues— Rust[1] blows hot & cold so that he is evidently no longer an oracle with J. If he had been steady there is no doubt that he would have come again in Arkansas— which up to this time has called no Convention & from all accts is averse to this whole movement at the South— Evarts Sewards man is defeated for the Senate— Greely beat him Caucus but Judge Harris—[2] a man of high character was elected—

Feby 4th The Mo Democrat sticks to it that no avowed secessionist will get

into the convention— tho some are trying to get in as Constitutional Unionist &etc— In spite of the awful roads I must go hear the result in Virginia
tomorrow— as well as go to the Asylum[3] Father came out weary from a run
away on the Sluggard—[4] he has been a peace making & hopeful Blair told him
he must not stay in the City again that he & Grandma didnt like it. in spite
of his love for GrandPa no bribery can induce him to say he is any bodys but
Papas Boy Got a letter from Sara Joseph[5] telling of wet snows & inviting us to
go there & escape the tumults she fears here— Ill stick to my home where it is
an effort to keep content & elsewhere I would be utterly miserable— I am no
runaway— yet while—

Feby [5] Your old native State Stands up gloriously to the good work of our
forefathers— & is for the Union— by unanimous vote— & requires all done
by the Convention to be submitted to the people *almost* unanimously— thats
her verdict on politicians—[6] Consequently we are all to stay in bonds of Union
& Safety— Oh be joyful— Sent some of our children[7] to the far west today—
I felt reluctant about it— but the hard times makes me cautious about keeping
them when we can make any other sure provision for them— The Democrat
which I read for you says all business is prostrate in St Louis The Crisis has
been dreadful on the business of the whole country except New York— but far
more to the Slave States than elswhere

Feby 6 I shouted for joy over your letter from Cape Verde Islands which
came to me this evening by Savannah It was the short letter dated the 4th
of Jany. It brought me as much relief as the Virginia elections— Surely this
has been a week of good things to me— Blair exulted in my joy & it would
have touched you to see him when in my lap *reading* over yr letter with pat it
with his fat hand as he does living things he likes— I am on the qui vive for
the long letter which I expect went to Quebec & is delayed by the unknown
depths of snow in those parts— A letter from Mr. J Sherman[8] says Frémont[9]
wants to go to Frank to be Secy of War— He is likely to get the post— The
papers tonight brought the St Louis nominees for the State Convention—
One is a combination between the Democrats & Bellmen as *Constitutional
Union* ticket— The other is the Union Ticket "unreservedly" which is the
Republican ticket— it will be a hard fought battle but our people are out in
earnest— The troops are withdrawn from Pensacola by Ala— Florida & L—
so the paper says Fort Pickens has been reinforced There's talk of a court martial on Comre Armstrong—[10] & impeachment of Secy Toucy—[11] who has kept
the home Squadron by special orders at Vera Cruz until entirely out of provision & now they have to go to Havana or to a northern port for provisions—
before they can go to Pensacola where the supplies have been seized— If the
squadron had been there according to routine would have prevented all this
row at Pensacola & great loss to the Government—

Feby 7— Went to the City with Mary Martin who met her Father—[12] they return home tomorrow— I went to see Mrs. Trumbull[13] to share my tidings & accompanied her to the Capitol to hear Winter Davis' speech— which fully qualified him for a cabinet place   he spoke well & to the rather *hot* point[14] Roads desperate full 2 hours getting home

Feby 8th. Mr. Martin & Mary came out dined   she packed & departed for their home   her health is vastly improved— The Va news has acted like a perfect sedative to the political fuss makers— It ensures peace home & comfort— & that a great deal to you as well as all & keep John out of all trouble. In the strongest negro districts where they've tried to vote by an unauthorized election— to put down Govr Hicks— these revolutionists have all been put down as you by the enclosed slip—[15] The arrival of a 1000 of U.S. Troops & the departure of the Secessionists has rendered the City very gay— a party every night

Feby 9 Spent the day in walking with Mother & Blair on my return copied for Father all evening tho I took a peep in the papers— to get the news The Democrat has a letter in the Ed column saying 19 twentieths of the people in St Louis were for the Union— plain & simple— Telegraphs show them up doing all over the State— Ill send you the Post with my days work in it— I was grieved to the heart to learn by the city papers that Capt Tilton[16] had committed suicide yesterday   I have not met him this winter & think I saw him across the Senate one day— The paper says it was owing to the Countrys troubles— forgetting that there is a "better country" for which we ought to work on bravely & honestly in this one. Oh the bitter pang to his wife to feel that there was no love of God or any of his creatures not of himself even to protect them from such wretchedness The amount of unhappiness to result in such a deed is fearful to think of May God be more merciful to him than he has been to himself— He looked ill when I saw him here in the summer & pehaps his mind was clouded with illness— His State was still in the Union & all prospect of Md. seceding is given up by the frantic fire eaters

Feby 10. This Sunday two months ago you sailed & I feel almost impatient about my Quebec letter tho the Savannah one was such a relief that I ought to have promised myself to be patient about the other   Brother & 3 MC were here today— Jeff Davis is elected President & Stephens[17] Vice P. in the Conclave at Montgomery— These men are *"moderates"*— & both *in private* antisecession— There are signs of revolt to secession in some of the cotton states & we hear more of it sub rosa among the Republicans— who get letters from them, by indirection so Mr. Trumbull tells me— War has appeared so inevitable & that we are so long preserved from it is by Gods Mercy— & it makes me hope that it will be averted— there are many things to make me hope it—[18] Mrs. Davis is a warm personal friend— of Anderson— Mrs. A went to him for counsel & *got it* when she came here about having her husband reinforced— There are other things just of this type which make me hopeful—

Frank writes triumphant about his State— & so on— *a reaction has certainly commenced*—

Poor Capt Tiltons fate arose from his health— he had every symtom of a softening of the brain & it affected his mind— & for days he had kept at home— & was violent threatened to kill one of his daughters— The day he turned on himself was Claras birthday— Miss Buchanan & others were driving there for that reason & when dining (he saying he was too sick to eat) shot himself in his room I shall go there as soon as I think it will be acceptable We all feel deep commiseration for the helpless family

The band of *minute men* who congregated at Grave's—[19] (thro whom we were secretly posted) have had fights & quarrels nightly since the Virginia elections & last night— so many with drew from the "*company*" that it is regarded as a *break up* of the whole thing— Tho' they professed great friendship *to us* I rejoice over their dispersion— tho they never cost me *but one* night of disquietude— even then I slept half of it— so you may know I was not very anxious As I am nurse tomorrow morning— I have to close this— full of love & kisses from your boy and your devoted wife Lizzie

Aunt Becky in her letters desires me to say she worries in yr absence— & send love to you from all at her house

1. Albert Rust, Democratic congressman from Arkansas (1855–57, 1859–61).

2. William M. Evarts, respected New York lawyer, had been a delegate to the 1860 Republican convention. He later served as U.S. attorney general, defending Andrew Johnson in impeachment proceedings, and from 1877 to 1881, he was secretary of state. Evarts finally became a senator, serving New York from 1885 until 1891. Republican Judge Ira Harris had defeated Evarts and New York *Tribune* editor Horace Greeley in the New York Senate race of 1861. Harris had previously served on the state supreme court (1847–59).

3. EBL was first directress of the Washington City Orphan Asylum.

4. The Sluggard was Blair's horse, a mean and unruly animal. For years the Blairs risked their lives by riding him.

5. Sara Gratz Moses Joseph was Lizzie's cousin and closest friend from childhood. Lizzie's aunt Maria Gist (her mother's sister) married Benjamin Gratz, who was the brother of Sara's mother, Rachel Moses. After Rachel died in 1823, another sister, Rebecca Gratz, cared for all of the Moses children. For generations the Blairs and then the Lees maintained extremely close ties not only with the immediate Gratz family (which was quite large) but also with many of its numerous extensions.

6. On February 4, 1861, Virginians elected delegates for a convention to decide the issue of secession. Forty-six secessionists and 106 moderates were elected.

7. Children from the Orphan Asylum.

8. John Sherman, Republican congressman from Ohio (1855–61); U.S. senator (1861–77).

9. John C. Frémont, Republican candidate for president in 1856, was the son-in-law of Blair's old friend Thomas Hart Benton.

10. James Armstrong requested a court of inquiry, which found him guilty of neglect of duty, "disobedience of orders and conduct unbecoming an officer." After fifty-two years of service in the navy, he was suspended from duty for five years with loss of pay for half that time.

11. Secretary of the Navy Isaac Toucey, a Connecticut lawyer and former governor, was a Northerner with Southern sympathies. His policy of running his department on a business-as-usual basis brought criticism from ardent Unionists.

12. E. T. T. Martin, a lawyer, was the nephew of Enos T. Throop, Jacksonian ally of Francis Preston Blair. When Throop became governor of New York upon the resignation of Martin Van Buren in 1829, Martin went to Albany as his uncle's private secretary. He and his family remained close to the Blair family. Throop gave his nephew his home, Willowbrook, on Lake Owasco near Auburn, New York.

13. Julia Jayne had married Lyman Trumbull in June 1843. Her father, Dr. Gershom Jayne, was a prominent Springfield, Illinois, physician.

14. Only a week earlier, on January 31, EBL witnessed a scene of congressional speechmaking: "I went to the Capitol & heard an animated debate between Seward Mason Douglas— Hale & wigfall— & was sorry when— Father came after me ere the last had finished his wild vagaries— some of my friends smiled at me when he said— He did not see how Harry Lee & Lightfoot Lees Washingtons & such proud blood could submit to the domination of the North— I said they only supported the Constitution made by their Fathers & would not submit to a Conspiracy of Cotton Aristocrats."

15. Enclosed with the letter was a newspaper account headlined "CONSERVATIVE SENTIMENT IN MARYLAND."

16. Capt. Edward G. Tilton shot himself in the head while his family was one floor below him at their home. He and his wife Josephine had five children, ranging in ages from nine to twenty-three.

17. Alexander H. Stephens, vice president of the Confederacy, had served as congressman from Georgia from 1843 to 1859. A moderate, he opposed secession until it was a fact.

18. On February 1, EBL explained: "From some of the talk I heard yesterday it is evidently a sore disappointment to the Secessionist that their course has not affect the north more permanently— & that there was no anarchy & no more than usual suffering among the poor— The middle states are steady— The whole country will soon rally from this winters doings."

19. A. L. Graves lived north and west of the Blairs' Silver Spring farm, near the Sligo Post Office.

Silver Spring   February 12, 1861

My dear Phil   Yours of Jany 8th came yesterday as Nos. 1 & 3 are still due— it was the first talk I had for so long that it was delightful— All the black ink was as plain as print— after experiments I find it best to use black ink altogether As I know my writing is not good[1] I've tried all helps to it— & find *real* black ink best—

I have cogitated a great deal about your orders— If there is Civil War— there no doubt but you with all the rest of the Navy may be called home—

& with that fear before me & to carry out our plans if it we are so happy
as to escape war of which Father is *now* for the first time for weeks past *very*
hopeful I shall get you ordered according to pro[cedure] to the Pacific— & at
San Francisco if there is war we had best take counsel then what to do— The
Seceding States threaten privateering in which case there would have to be
a strong force on our Western coast & there you would probably be kept—
which is far better than any duty on this [side] of the continent— You will
write to me from Hong Kong— your views about matters— & I can get them
(or try to) carried out 'ere you reach San Francisco I went to see Mrs. Trumbull
& duly impressed on her the sickliness of the Chinese port— thats enough for
present purposes & the reasons for making you stay so long in them

Tennessee has refused to call even a convention by 20 thousand majority
& for the Union by 50— thousand   Missouri comes off next & Frank has the
question put there right— without any *if*— I see he has *Gantt* & Gamble[2] on
the City ticket which is about 1 third Douglas men— 1 third Bell men 1 of
Republicans & he writes that there will not be an avowed secessionist elected
to the State Convention— Jeff Davis— & Stephens are elected President and
Vice at Montgomery by delegates elected by the delegates to their several state
conventions Since this change of Leaders is hopeful for a peaceful solution of
our troubles— I take more heart from a speech of Yancey[3] in which he urges
the Convention not to refer *anything* back to the people for fear that this "*whole
noble movement may be overthrown*"— South Carolina is trying to *precipitate*
War— as she did secession— but to that Jeff Davis is opposed & will do his
utmost to avert an attack upon Anderson— his *intimate* friend to whom his
wife came & got counsel about what she should do to obtain reinforcements
for her husband— I wrote you what she did & said & *by advice*—

Feby 13th Your birthday of which I was duly reminded 'ere half awake before
7 olk by a conversation between Blair & Grandma She inquired of me if I
was going to the City for Church & asked Blair to stay home & ride with her
"Oh, no Grandma this is my Papa birthday & I am going to get fire crackers
& a gun to fire off"— all of which I had promised some days ago— There is
great talk about celebrating the 22nd & Blair want to know what for?— being
informed on the subject— he approves the idea hence & is keen to celebrate
your natal day— which he & I did each in our own way   he bought his fire
crackers spent his money that Grandma had given him will [shoot] them & a
new gun I bought him— & then went to Mary Blairs where they were making
some ado for Jesups[4] fete— so with the fixing & the dinner party— Blair had
a fine frolick— They all smiled at Blairs hearty zeal in it all   he is so honestly
loving & joyous that Mary says his visits are invaluable to them there— I went
to church & my thoughts followed you lovingly & prayerfully— Mr. Pynes
sermon was especially to humankind— whose bitterness of speech was to be
repented of this Lent. I went again to see Mrs. Trumbull to take a confab about

the orders to San Francisco which she is quite as eager as I am— I feel that that point is one of very easy management.

Feby 14 I paid a visit to old Mrs. Speakman— her husband makes such a pet of Blair that the courtesy was due in her illness she is getting well I hope— On my return I took to gardening I've quite a little conservatory in the little south room up stairs— my geraniums are growing finely. I sometimes think of recommencing my hen house it is expensive & I find my money goes very fast so am reluctant to open any new outlets I [am] reading [of] the devastations in the Chinese Emperors palace— it seemed a sin to let those soldiers use crimson damask for saddle clothing—[5]

Father has returned home full of hope that these troubles will pass away without bloodshed— but the Leaders of secession are with but few exceptions bad men— Floyd's stealings are growing fast to 7 millions— & likely to be discovered to greatly exceed that—[6] Slidell & Benjamins[7] Human hunt. Mrs. Merrick[8] classed them on that act as no better than Mr. Floyd— Wigfall & Yancey are desperate men both killing their men & not according to *the* code so tis said— & our friend Jeff loveth power over much to relax the grasp he has over some & resign it without *an* effort— Still I hope much from his many good qualities— But the money gathered for this conspiracy by Floyd can [not] last long— & the drought & want of sale for cotton deprives the South of much to contribute & they have no credit— so it must come to an end before very long— I see denunciations of the *selfish rich* already in the leading papers in Ala— S Carolina & threats of confiscation— they've spent one forced loan already in the last state— & still cannot take by themselves Fort Sumpter or I believe they would have done so ere this— Father thinks they wont bring their raw levies to the cannon's mouth—

The Peace Congress stay at Willards & he has put his Concert Hall as their place of meeting—[9] Genl Butler[10] is here & had too many invitations to accept Brothers yet awhile— met Father with his olden affection— & professed joy that they are together again— *Union Party* is to be the party name after this any how south of the Potomac Frank will be here this time next week— he says no avowed secessionist will elected to the Missouri Convention. I forgot to mention I've begun to cultivate Mrs. Latham[11] of Cal. she is an intimate of Jessie's[12] & I take to her vastly

Feby 15 Blair & I took a run between showers it has turned so warm that I am afraid our fruits will bud Joe went for the papers— the Democrat looks like it did in August before the election— & says all business is at a stand still—

Mr. Lincoln is en route to Washn & in triumph all the way— his talk is *firm* & undismayed tho fully impressed with the trials before him. he has taken issue already with Seward by saying— "We must execute the laws— & are oath bound to support the Constitution— & to protect the property of the U S—"

Feby 16— I must start early tomorrow to the city so as to do an erand for Father before Church So close this now— Blair was rolling on the floor today & seemed very quiet— when he said "I wants to see My Papa so bad I'll cry—" Now he has not heard me utter anything but joy over your late letters— Last night he gave his Grandma a handful of scrawled papers— for Joe to put in the Post Office for you & on Monday— when taking a letter in to the P.O. for you— he took & put it to his mouth   his Grandpa promptly protested against his spoiling my letter— "I wont spoil it for it is to my Papa I am only sending him kisses is on it—" & "I'll give him the one Aunt Becky sent tother day too"— Father was very much touched— the dear little fellow was so earnest about it—

There is no news of import today   I'll try to get you the result of the Mo. election in this mail to Batavia as tis my last one to that port— I send you an Eve Post which you will see has a long piece in it from Father— it is his peace offering— & yet I fear more will be required to get it— the accusation agt Wigfall on stealing— is not Father's & I take a note in to the Eds of the Post to retract it— Father did not know he was a lawyer & cant vouch for the facts so wont stand sponsor— of course— this has not been desired by Mr. Wigfall   Father says tis due to himself & tis a great liberty with Father & he is very much annoyed— I will write again on Monday— to go by the Steamer—

South Carolina growls at Jeff's election— & the whole provisional Govt & talks of seceding again— Mr. Janney[13] of Loudon is elected President of the Va convention so you will feel she is in very safe hands   I think it is feared now— therell be an attack on Fort Sumpter to precipitate War & stop the reaction evidently now set in South— North Ala has raised the old flag & is in open rebellion to the seceders— So it goes & God help them— & take care of you   devotedly yr Lizzie

1. In a December 10, 1860, letter, EBL apologized for her penmanship: "I've tried to make this legible but it is not very easily accomplished by my mothers daughters heavy hand."

2. Thomas Tasker Gantt, former law partner of Montgomery Blair, was also an ardent Unionist. He served on McClellan's staff from 1861 until 1862, then was appointed provost marshal general of Missouri in 1862. Hamilton R. Gamble of Missouri, a staunch Unionist, had served on the Missouri Supreme Court from 1850 until 1854 and wrote the dissenting opinion in the Dred Scott case. He was the Unionist acting governor of Missouri from June 1861 until he died in January 1864.

3. William L. Yancey of Alabama was an early secessionist. He was the Confederate commissioner to England in 1861.

4. Jesup Blair, EBL's nephew, was the son of Mary and James Blair. He was born February 13, 1852.

5. In retribution for the Chinese seizure of British envoys Harry Parkes and Henry

Loch, British and French troops destroyed the emperor's Summer Palace in Peking on October 8, 1860.

6. In her December 28 letter, EBL claimed: "Robing is the leading trait of this administration— next to cowardice in the President—."

7. Judah P. Benjamin of Louisiana served his state in the U.S. Senate from 1853 to 1861. An ardent secessionist, he served as Confederate attorney general, then secretary of war, and finally secretary of state.

8. Mary Wickliffe Merrick, wife of U.S. Circuit Court judge William M. Merrick, served on the Washington City Orphan Asylum board with EBL.

9. Labeled the "Old Gentleman's Convention" by Horace Greeley, the Washington Peace Conference was called at the request of the Virginia legislature to make yet another attempt at compromise. Twenty-one states sent delegates to the meeting which convened on February 4 at Willard's Hall in Washington and was chaired by former president John Tyler.

10. Benjamin F. Butler, Massachusetts Democratic politican, began his Civil War career as a brigadier general of militia.

11. In 1853, Sophia Birsall married Milton S. Latham, Democratic senator from California.

12. Jessie Benton Frémont, wife of John C. Frémont and daughter of Thomas Hart Benton.

13. John Janney of Virginia was elected president of the Virginia convention. A conservative and Unionist, he tried to find a solution short of secession. Into the month of April, the Virginia convention continued to reject secession.

2

"There is now 75 thousand men in front of— &
in the City of Washington— & one universal grumble
at Genl Scotts do nothing policy with
such immense means—"

June 25, 1861

IN MID-MAY S. P. LEE RETURNED to the United States to find his country
at war. Although he had disobeyed his orders, the Navy Department desperately needed his ship to assist in enforcing the blockade of Southern ports
proclaimed by President Lincoln on April 19. After a brief visit with his family
in New York, S. P. Lee departed to begin blockading duty off Charleston,
South Carolina. Elizabeth and Blair stopped for a short visit in Philadelphia,
reaching Silver Spring on June 7. The early summer months were filled with
uncertainty: saving the border states of Maryland, Kentucky, and Missouri
for the Union was essential; the resignations of army and navy officers caused
anguish; building and equipping a fighting force took time; the possibility of
foreign intervention threatened an already tenuous situation. The first battle
of Bull Run, within hearing of Silver Spring, sobered Americans to the reality
of a long and desperate struggle.

Philadelphia   June 1, 1861
Dear Phil   Yours of yesterday has just been read. I had but little hope of seeing
you tonight— but that little dies hard— If you remain until Monday I shall
feel sorry Blair & I did not go to Sands Street— Still I feel it was right to escape
instantly from the house— & it is a matter of congratulation that I did not go
to Mrs. Upshurs[1] rooms & that as far as we know our little one was never in
contact with those children— for Becky made up Blair bed always & had the
sole handling of his bedding which was in a trunk during the day. I tell you all
this as it is a comfort to me that all human precautions have been taken & for
the rest we must trust cheerfully to Gods mercy.

I cannot think England will take any part in this war— she knows that the

power of this nation is north to help her in her time of need which may not
be afar off— Our Blockade must be an effective one & when they have lost
a good many ships— they will cease to run blockade as it is not sufficiently
profitable— You will see that congress will have to take up the Negro *Deportation immediately* & then that disposed of & such an up *rising of poor white folks*
as will astonish our aristocrats as much as the *up* rising at the north I cannot
distrust that the result will be for our ultimate benefit to our noble Government & all the world— tho the grand result will come thro great tribulation &
endless individual suffering & sorrow— But you can always hold a protecting
hand over our two heads by taking *good care* of my precious husband— & if we
try to do right, God will surely be good to us— & this is my abiding faith &
comfort

I saw Midge[2] yesterday She says her husband writes that Genl Harney[3] is
doing them endless harm— & if not soon removed would soon put the State
out of the Union as he once before nearly accomplished So you may imagine
my joy today in seeing that he had been recalled for having disbanded the
secessionists with arms in their hands. to go about the State & prey upon all
those who disagreed with them— Dick[4] writes her— that they will soon get
the whole state under the control of the Union men if they can get rid of Genl
Harney— She says that Apo[5] was troubled at the idea of the order to Fortress
Monroe & they will all rejoice to hear that it is recalled

I see by the papers the U.S. has now 80 thousand men— actively— on the
scene of War— 40 days ago we had but eleven hundred men— I went yesterday to see Mrs. Mordicai[6] who looks ill— tho her face did beam with real joy
when she told me that her son had resolved to stand by the Government &
that was but the poor return he could make the education he had received at
it hands but such was his devotion to it that if not a regular soldier he would be
a volunteer one this her & Aunt Becky's great comfort— poor Maj Mordicai[7]
looks miserable tho every body is kind & considerate of him— He has offers
from the Confederates— but will not accept—

I will go home next Thursday— without something happens in the meantime to make it right to delay going— Blair is restless here— wants to go back
to you or go on home & when I tell you are to sail tomorrow he will be almost
uncontrollable about going home— He must look after your goat & endless
other good reasons which has to express his impatience of this delay— but it is
due to Aunt Becky & my feelings for her— I will write to you until I know the
positive time of your sailing— & then will commence to direct daily letters to
Old Point Comfort, where you will certainly be for a while— & I hope until
the crisis of matters in Virginia are settled— which will I think soon come to
pass now—

I met Mrs. Stockton & Miss Mary[8] they are boarding next door to this
house— & Clem & Laura Pleasonton[9] on the other side I could get but little

news out either party— Mrs Stockton told me that Mrs. Roger Jones[10] is in great affliction about a son in Texas who has deserted his flag— & that Lucien & Tom also talk of going to Virginia when— she says Roger will her only joy & pride left in life— this was my only item of Washington talk— Blair is out walking— or would make his marks of love for you on this letter— Your devoted Lizzie

1. Kate Williams married John Henry Upshur in 1851; they had four children. An 1848 graduate of the Naval Academy, Upshur was selected by SPL in 1863 to be his chief of staff of the North Atlantic Blockading Squadron.

2. Mira (Midge) Dick was Apo Blair's sister and the wife of Franklin Dick.

3. Brig. Gen. William S. Harney, commander of the Department of the West, had pursued a conciliatory policy with Missouri state officials. The pro-Unionist faction had succeeded in having him recalled to Washington in April, but Harney had returned to his post in May. Ultimately, through the influence of Frank Blair, Franklin Dick, and others, Harney was removed from the command.

4. Franklin A. Dick, a prominent St. Louis lawyer and lieutenant colonel in the Missouri state militia, was provost marshal general, Department of Missouri. He was Frank Blair's brother-in-law.

5. Appoline Alexander married Frank Blair on September 8, 1847.

6. Sara Hays had married Alfred Mordecai in 1836. Their son, Alfred, Jr., fought for the Union, rising to the rank of brigadier general.

7. Maj. Alfred Mordecai (USMA 1823) had commanded the Washington Arsenal during the Mexican War. When the Civil War began, he resigned his commission and refused to fight for either side.

8. Harriet Maria Potter Stockton, wife of naval officer Robert F. Stockton who had resigned in 1850. He was a U.S. senator from New Jersey (1851–53) and a delegate to the Washington Peace Conference in 1861. Mary Stockton McKnight, born 1830, was the Stocktons' daughter.

9. Clementine and Laura Pleasonton were sisters of Gen. Alfred Pleasonton and all were children of Stephen Pleasonton. From 1817 until his death in 1855, Stephen was fifth auditor in the Treasury Department and an old friend of James Buchanan.

10. Mary Anne Page Jones, wife of Maj. Gen. Roger Jones, adjutant general of the United States. Four of their sons went south: Catesby ap Roger and Charles Lucian to the Confederate navy and Thomas Skelton and Walter to the army. Another son, Roger, became inspector general of the United States Army.

Philadelphia June 4, 1861

My Dear Phil   Your letter enclosing the list reached me this moment— I will follow your directions closely   I would have made arrangements to remain here longer but for the reluctance to keep Blair in cities at this season so long a time— all Doctors say June is the hardest month on children in the Cities

Our home generally is as secure as John's—[1] We are never at night with less than 4 or eight Soldiers sleeping in the house— of which Joe Cook & Capt Morrison[2] are in command— & in the day I will keep in our lawn— my own garden & Hen house will be my chief out door resorts— with Becky & Blair trotting after me Father has followed the precaution you suggest for months past. he & our Coachman too *have* been armed— our horses are fast— & our neighbors reliable— Scouts about us on the Harpers Ferry road day & night so I can retreat to Johns when ever theres a necessity. & I therefore will *now* go to Silver Spring for Blair's sake especially— but shall be often with John— as I have been during this whole winter & spring— But as all this keeps you uneasy Ill come back to this part of the world if the Confederates have any success.

Our people are not prompt & are not conducting the Campaign upon the brilliant plan— but raw troops are not to rushed on— & so it may be the safest tho' much can be said on the other side of the case— I think today things look well in the mountains— here there is an intense distrust of Patterson—[3] But after all said, I feel happiest & safest under my home shelter than any where else when from under your wings— & as I can not nestle there with my little one I'll go where we are both most cared for, loved, — & happiest—

I had a letter from Mrs Upshur asking me to make inquiries about board here & Bethlehem for her— I'll do all I can to help her— Miss Mary McKnight told me a long story by which she makes it appear that Comre Shubrick is to blame for the Resignation of Comre Tatnall[4] & others in the commencement— Commre Shubrick was brought to Anchor by Dr Clymer[5] who announced to him that he had to war upon his own offspring if he warred for Carolina When he backed out & left others in the lurch. His account of the Roger Jones concern is sad   none but Edmonia[6] stand by Young Roger really,   Mrs. Smith Lee[7] holds to her resolve— has sent Fitzhugh back to West Point. & she stick to the north end of Long Bridge— with her little boy who she told me was now her *only* protector— & he looked so proud— pleased & handsome that I felt she was not so poorly off after all for her Robert is a splendid boy of 12 yrs— he, added to grey hair & wrinkles will at least give safety.

"Papa Blair wants to see you" was the meaning of those marks[8] uttered as they were made— He is now writing more to you with the pencil you gave him— You would pack me off home today if you could hear him beg to go out of this "Old City"— It is his first thought & just now he was threatening "to leave dis minute & go home." Beck pack up"— is a reiterated order & your powers of resistance I think would soon vanish under his pleadings & his evident weariness. He did go to the square & played with the little Dicks but that & the squirrels are now no longer a resource to him— I will write until I know you've pulled up anchor & off— I do hope you will get detained in the Chespeake tis now upper most wish— Your devoted Lizzie

1. John Lee's plantation near Upper Marlboro in Prince Georges County, Maryland, was more remote from danger than the Blairs' Silver Spring home.

2. Joseph H. Cook of Company L of the First Maryland Cavalry. Capt. Washington Morrison of the Potomac Home Brigade cavalry.

3. Gen. Robert Patterson of Pennsylvania. "Granny Patterson" was a sixty-nine-year-old veteran of both the War of 1812 and the Mexican War.

4. After forty-nine years of service, Josiah Tatnall had resigned from the U.S. navy on February 21 to become a captain in the Confederate navy. Eight months later, on February 18, 1862, EBL gave this report of Tatnall: "Dr. Russell of the London Times told me he was a broken hearted man & that the old man's face only brightened when speaking of the gunnery of American sailors—."

5. Dr. George Clymer, surgeon in the U.S. navy, was married to Schubrick's only daughter.

6. Edmonia Jones was the daughter of Maj. Gen. Roger Jones and sister of the inspector general of the United States.

7. Anna Maria Lee was the wife of Sydney Smith Lee. Their son Lt. Fitzhugh Lee (USMA 1856) had already left West Point where he had been a cavalry instructor.

8. A line of Blair's scribbles

Philadelphia June 5, 1861

Dear Phil   I feel lonesome & as badly as I did the day I left New York Ive seen your ship all day going out of the New York Bay   I will not send a letter to New York as you said your's which came today— that you sail today "*certainly*—" so my occupation of a daily letter is gone & the getting of one too which is of more import to me—

Silver Spring—June 7. I got home last night tired & with a head ache— found my Parents invalidish & with nobody staying with them— so rejoiced doubly in my heart that I was [not] lingering away from them— when I had nothing to compensate me in it

This morning young Emory[1] was out here to breakfast They made a pull altogether today to get Emory[2] back into the Army— I knew from Mr Cameron's talk with me it was a hopeless effort but I said nothing— to deter any efforts to save him— but Mr C. is anti-Coburg—[3] most bitterly & he let out to me as he suspected me of being sympathetic— I plead guilty— yet I said I believed Col Emory was loyal— for he could have got a good place from the Davis' but the plea was not admitted— "No *really good places to give*" or something to that effect— Father's absence all day— & my occupations in the gardens has given me no *news* opportunity—

Mr. Holt was here today & said that Kentucky is in for it he is very zealous— I was busy tying up asparagus to save Mother from her rhumatism & she saw him but she was delighted with his visit— & Both of my Parents are pleased with my visit to the Mann's[4] in Brooklyn— Saw John for a moment only am going there tomorrow—

June 8 No news of import to day. except a Silence to be observed about the movement of the Troops— Mr Kelly[5] says there are to day 20 thousand at Chambersburg— He has just come here with the Miss Cameron[6] as an escort—

Monday June 10 Two days of bad head ache has prevented me from going to the city to see about getting letters to you— Sands is ordered to California— Miegs is to be Quarter Master Genl— Emory is not to get back— & *Genl apathy* is again in full command & likely to keep it until Congress meets I've full faith the mercy of Providence so am not troubled tho' many around me are— I can see no harm to come out of delay to us— & great evils to the other side— Hunger is a very troublesome one & that is imminent— Blair keeps well— enjoy every thing with his peculiar exuberance— kissed me over & over this morning to send to Papa— who goes away very often— too much[7]

Monday afternoon I received your letters from Sandy Hook & am hot after a steamer for you today—[8] I told them that Nelson was never more eager for frigates than you for a steamer— that you are off in old ship willing to do for the Country in any & every way— but Steamers are alone effective & that I must have a steamer— All this I said to Father & will keep on But I've not much hope of any thing until Frank comes

There is a grand move of troops to Harpers Ferry today about three thousand on the road between the City & Silver Spring All with the bearing of gentlemen Father was cheered by the New Hampshire Regiment— I had a talk with Mr. Dick's nephew in the Phila Regiment. Dick is expected here tonight I dined at Johns he is very cheerful— & talks *well*— He thinks there will be a fight in a week or ten days there is now some 35 or 40 thousand between us and the Confederates I shall retreat farther than they can if they are whipped by Joe Johnston's[9] troops

I have just made an arrangement with Mr. Fox[10] that he is to send a letter once a week for me & oftener when he knows of a chance that is direct to you— Davenport[11] is home— & sick has two diseases but the worst is a sympathetic affection of secession type— We had a guest from the New Jersey Camp at John's to day. All well & in haste but ever your own Lizzie

1. Campbell Emory, a twenty-year-old USMA cadet, was the son of William H. Emory.

2. William Hemsley Emory resigned from the U.S. army on May 9, 1861, and was reappointed May 14.

3. A "coburger" was an army or navy man who received promotion or easy assignments through political influence.

4. Abijah Mann, Jr., Jacksonian Democrat, had served in the House of Representatives from 1833 to 1837. Like Francis Preston Blair, he had turned to the Republican party in 1856.

5. William Darrah Kelley, outspoken critic of McClellan, had been elected Republican congressman from Pennsylvania in 1860.

6. Simon Cameron had two unmarried daughters in 1861: Virginia Rolette Cameron and Margaretta Cameron.

7. In her June 2 letter, EBL explained: "I try to conceal all I can of expressions of grief about your absence for the dear little fellow feels it too much for one of his age & I try to build castles already about our doings & sayings when we three get together again Our little trio is not bad company is it?"

8. On June 3, EBL had written: "I shall go right to work & beg of the Govt the Iroquois for you." In June 1861, the blockade off Charleston was a paltry affair, consisting of only three vessels: the steamers *Union* and *Wabash* and Lee's sailing sloop *Vandalia*, built in 1828.

9. Confederate Gen. Joseph E. Johnston, in command at Harpers Ferry, was an old family friend of the Blairs and Lees.

10. Gustavus Vasa Fox, assistant secretary of the navy, was related by marriage to the Lees; his wife, Virginia Woodbury, was the sister of Montgomery Blair's wife.

11. Lt. Henry K. Davenport apparently recovered from his maladies and any sympathy for secession. In November 1861, he was given command of USS *Hetzel* at Newport News, Virginia.

Silver Spring   June 11, 1861

Dear Phil   Becky is sick & I am nurse so I am busy all day & when Blair sleeps I am nearly as tired as he if not as sleepy. My thoughts have been most of this day in Leesburg— strange as it may appear but I learned late last night that the 12,000 troops which left Washn yesterday for Harper's Ferry are to be concentrated by different routes today at Leesburg— So it is well John's family did not accept Mr. Harrisons[1] invitation!! Poor Kate's[2] fear has often disturbed me today

They have sent there the best displined troops— the Rhode Island— New Hampshire & Phila troops— I know some of them & they are chiefly comprised of gentlemen & this is now a comfort to me. I can scarce conceive that sequestered place— a scene of tumult— & war— but it is to cut off one of the railroad retreats from Harpers Ferry.

June 12 My spirits rose high today upon hearing that the English will allow no privateers to be sold in their ports & *the tone* of Lord John Russell[3] is altogether friendly to the United States— The *Times* too is on a lower key— Our people have had a fight at Bethel & captured a thousand men— but I grieve to say that a rumor says 700 were killed— it is awful to think of—[4] It has been our first real summer's day— Blair is chirping Becky is well again— Our people here are in a fever about the election— All are keen to elect Calvert[5] It will be a great Union triumph I hope— The fight down the Bay will insure a quiet election in Baltimore No news from Harpers Ferry or Leesburg— I must say I prefer Henry May's election to that of Winter Davis—[6] tho perhaps I ought to remember his vote for Frank more gratefully— The news papers are just filled with speculations on the movements of the troops & the probabilities of a battle— & comments on *Russel*[7] letters from the London Times— about Royalty in the South I enclose it— Queen Varina will feel snubbed— I also send you a letter from Andrew Blair[8] George Alexander[9] is here & say Blairs donkey is en route

June 13. This day has been a *country* day— No tidings from the City as Geo Alexander was to bring them & he did come & consequently the mail was not sent for— for the first time these many long days. I have been busy with garden & went visit the Clagetts—[10] with Father who returned from the polls in great glee— a large vote & all our side— save a dozen or so of *the gentry* which will soon become an opprobrious epithet in this country I expect Henry May will be elected from what the Doctor said & I'll not be sorry— I've had much sympathy for you today in being cut off from tidings at this fearful time— I wish you knew that we are well & under our own vine— in quietness & safety— so far tis a very long two weeks today since we parted

June 14th Harpers Ferry is evacuated! & Western Virginia— delivered of secession thraldom—[11] Our news from St Louis is uncomfortable Claibe Jackson[12] has made a final effort to take out Missouri— calls out 50000 troops— burnt the bridges & in going give fight Blair is by me & sends you this kiss ( ) & he gave a hearty one too Nicholas Hill[13] is just from Dixie— bearer of a gift from the Lady who cut off Blair's curls— to Minna's little boy Gist—[14] a dress— She burst into tears on getting it!! Nich says she Mrs D.[15] talks all the time of Washn & of her friends with unaltered feelings She is one of the victims of this war— I shrink from looking her future in the face— & yet she may escape all the sorrow I fear for her how sincerely I wish her no ill— & yet how fervently I pray that our Government may go thro the trials which now beset it & come out— greater & better than ever This prayer is so earnest that it is seems a part of those constantly in my heart— on my lips for you & our dear Boy whose best inheritance is this noble free Govt of our goodly country— Prince Georges went for Mr. Calvert— & Maryland for the Union almost without disent— Mr Calvert's vote is a great tribute to his character He was Father's & Bonifant's[16] nominee & so managed that our Prince Georges friends feel as if he was theirs— but dont *ever* tell this

June 15— Blair is well again Worms *again* that fever he had when in Brooklyn was from that cause— it returned on him I sent for Dr. May— who was out of the City— & John sent Dr. Miller[17] to see him— he gave big doses but I reduced them to the *May* quantity— Genl Jones[18] is staying with Dr. Miller They live together the Dr. says good naturedly— The Miller girls are in Leesburg— & the Dr. looks very unhappy & most heartily wishes them at home— he tries to be secessionist— but admitted that his trip to Chicago almost vanquished him— they were so kind

The St Louis Republican denounces Govr Jackson who has already Jeffn City so you see *our* side is the strongest— Joe Johnston has quit Harpers Ferry he was very nearly surrounded our forces had reached Martinsburg— & were rapturously welcomed— & that was not far from the Winchester railroad— Ive not heard who got to Leesburg first— but is was a race— Robt Lee is concentrating at Manassas Gap— where theyve 60 thousand troops— we have 80— to confront them—[19] Father saw Meigs in the Quarter Master's place— he had on a busy look— I think this a great *moral* appointment— It is of course the Presidents own doings—

June 16 Sunday. I did not feel like leaving Blair this morning— so did not go to Church until evening— when I felt easy about my boy who is really over his feverishness— I left word with John— that he was well— as they had heard of his sickness— & now write to you 'lest by some accident you might do so too— it was just such a fever as he had in Brooklyn only it came 3 nights in succession— It was from indigestion & worms of [which] he is now clear— I'll alter his diet in some respects hereafter— No news— Mr. Holt dined here he talks well & patriotically

June 17. Blair rode on horse back today with GrandMa seven miles— is very bright & well— Your letter of last Tuesday by the Privateer was recieved tonight— I have talked steam— & got Father to do it twice at the Dept. already. but I shall keep it up at high pressure all the time— but have small hopes of accomplishing much until Frank comes They promise Father— but Frank will make them do it He took of possession yesterday of Jefferson city— & they are in hot pursuit of Jackson who has fled— they will organize things at Jefferson— Mr. Blow[20] is here tonight he referred to your Springfield trip with the greatest pleasure He is anxious about things but says Frank is in fine spirits— that Jackson has thrown up the game & that now they will soon organize at least 40, thousand men all over Missouri & keep thing all right which would have been done long ago but for Harneys reappearance in St Louis— Their fear now is an invasion in the South West *after lead* which the Confederates need from Arkansas & Texas— Cortinas [?] is playing the last— & I think Mo. & Kanzas will take care of the last— Wigfall was in the City yesterday & has gone north to see his wife— he is in disguise but no body seems to care a fig about him— He will see nothing to comfort him except his wife in the north

They say Scott has moved up towards— the Confederate lines— But— there are all sorts of rumors— & nothing true but the evacuation of Harper's Ferry— & Leesburg in which place they have bur[n]t all that belong to the Railroad cars— Depot & etc— Imagine Harrison's sensation which witnessing these Vandal proceedings!! They are now calling the Secessionists— "Bridge Burners—" Union Army the "Bridge & Railroad Bulders" & it is really very

characteristic of the destructive & conservative missions of the two Armies—
The Convention of Western Virginia are going to have a provisional Govt. &
send Senators & etc to Congress in July— This is the way the Union will be
rebuilt & is therefore an important movement—[21]

I got a polite note from Mrs. Eberfield [?][22] sending the enclosed— I have
been busy all day in my garden & playing & nursing Blair who follows me
everywhere when out doors— The weather is fine— cool nights & warm
days   we have had but 2 hot days as yet—

The Armies stand now very much— as when you left save the Harpers
Ferry movement— & the Regiment stationed above us at Rockville— which
is treated there by the Ladies with every sort of kindness The officers are
"Smothered in Strawberries & Cream— so writes *Smedb*urg[23] to Betty &
Young Pyne[24] to his Mama— So *our* situation even in defeat is safe for we have
a retreat to Rockville & thence to Penny— if in the worst sort disasters occur
in Virginia— Maryland has sent an entire Union delegation to Congress by
50,000 majority

I heard that Fox said that they intended to finish the work commenced by
the Charleston people— sink old ship filled with stones in the channel & stop
it tight

June 18. Blair is bright & well today & as it is cool— he will go to the City
with Grandma & Becky— to get his hair cut when his head was hot his thick
hair was a trouble to me *No* news from Fanny since we parted. They are all well
at Johns & here— & as Grandma waits I must stop with yours ever devotedly
Lizzie

1. Henry Harrison, who lived in Leesburg, was the husband of S. P. Lee's eldest
sister, Jane Elizabeth, who died in 1837. In 1841, he married Elizabeth Mary Jones,
daughter of Gen. Walter and Anne Lucinda Lee Jones.

2. Kate Harrison, the emotionally unstable and wayward daughter of Henry Harrison and SPL's late sister Jane Elizabeth.

3. Lord John Russell, British foreign secretary.

4. The Battle of Big Bethel, Virginia, a Union defeat, occurred on June 10. The
actual statistics were: Union casualties—18 killed, 53 wounded, 5 missing; Confederate
casualties—1 killed, 7 wounded.

5. Charles Benedict Calvert, a Union Whig, won election to Congress from Maryland and served from 1861 to 1863.

6. Henry Winter Davis had been an American Party congressman in the Thirty-
fourth Congress, then had been elected to the Thirty-fifth and Thirty-sixth as a Republican from 1855 to 1861. In 1860, he lost his seat to Henry May but was reelected
on the Unconditional Union party ticket in 1863. Henry May had been a Democratic
congressman from 1853 to 1855 when he lost his seat. He ran again in 1860 against
Davis and served from 1861 to 1863.

7. William H. Russell's article in the *Times* of London, May 30, 1861, included the

mocking comment: "Why not Presidents of State of Georgia or of Alabama? Why not King of South Carolina, or Emperor of Florida? Soldiers of fortune! make your game!"

8. Andrew Blair was Frank Blair's oldest son, born September 20, 1848.

9. George Alexander was Apo's brother.

10. John Brice Clagett, Washington merchant and son of Darius Clagett. His home was Pomona, located in the northernmost part of the District of Columbia, not far from the Blairs' Silver Spring home.

11. On June 14, the Confederates under Joe Johnston abandoned Harpers Ferry. On June 13, Union Col. Lew Wallace had led a raid into western Virginia to protect pro-Northern citizens.

12. Claiborne F. Jackson, proslavery governor of Missouri, tried to take the state out of the Union. On June 11, Jackson and Sterling Price met in St. Louis with Frank Blair and Nathaniel Lyon. The attempt to work out a compromise between the state and federal officials was unsuccessful, and Jackson returned to Jefferson City. En route, he burned bridges over the Gasconade and Osage rivers. Back in his capital, he issued a call for 50,000 volunteers for the state guard.

13. Nicholas Hill, a first cousin of S. P. Lee's sister-in-law Ellen Hill Lee.

14. Gist Blair, son of Montgomery Blair, was born September 10, 1860. Minna, Mary Elizabeth Woodbury Blair, was Montgomery's wife.

15. Varina Davis.

16. U.S. marshal Washington Bonifant was a founder of the *Maryland Republican* and friend of Montgomery Blair.

17. Dr. George May, an eminent Washington physician, was married to Catherine Hite Lee. Dr. Thomas Miller, another leading physician of the city, married Virginia Collins Jones, a daughter of Gen. Walter Jones.

18. Gen. Walter Jones, outstanding Washington lawyer, was Maj. Gen. Roger Jones's first cousin and father-in-law to Dr. Miller.

19. Robert E. Lee was S. P. Lee's third cousin. Francis Preston Blair, at Lincoln's request, had offered Lee command of the Union army. Joseph E. Johnston fell back into the Shenandoah Valley and fulfilled his twofold purpose: to hold the Union troops in the Valley and to allow his own troops to slip away and reinforce P. G. T. Beauregard at Manassas.

20. Henry T. Blow was a strong Union supporter in Missouri. He had been an early Free-Soiler, a delegate to the Republican convention in Chicago in 1860, and was appointed by Lincoln to be minister to Venezuela from 1861 to 1862. He served Missouri as a Republican congressman from 1863 to 1867.

21. Pro-Union advocates representing thirty-four counties met in convention in Wheeling, western Virginia. On June 17, the members adopted unanimously a Declaration of the People calling for reorganization of the Virginia government.

22. Possibly Mary Clagett Eversfield, wife of John Eversfield.

23. William R. Smedburg, from New York, joined the Fourteenth Infantry in May 1861, and was promoted to captain in October.

24. Lt. Charles M. Pyne, son of Smith Pyne, rector of St. John's Episcopal Church in Washington.

Silver Spring   June 25, 1861

Dear Phil   This has been house cleaning day here consequently every body was turned out of this house but it is all clean & sweet tonight   I have sat out doors, played with Blair & sewed worked & watered my flowers— for it has not rained here now for 15 days— Vincent is now off to the City— we hear all day the rub be dud of the drums & cannot for a moment forget the nearness to Camps There is now 75 thousand men in front of— & in the City of Washington—[1] & one universal grumble at Genl Scotts do nothing policy with such immense means—

The mail has come & brings me two letters from you Dont be afraid of my acting with lack of pride where you are concerned—[2] You are biggest pride of my heart. & you know from the fullness of that part of me I am prone to speak— No I have spoken to Father twice about a steamer for you & he has been to the Dept. & asked for one you— I said one day to Mr. Fox that I saw that the Baltre Atlantic & Iroquois were to go on blockade & that you thought none but a steamer could do good service— He remarked that he "did not agree with you about that— & he thought Palmer[3] would swap with you "the Steamers rolled so" There the talk stopped for I thought it *indicative* enough— I then thought of going around to see Comre Paulding— but to avoid observation from No 6[4] postponed it until too late   I have concluded to await Franks return— as I've been up to this time unsuccessful in all my attempts to see Comre P.[5] I will not go to the Dept— & living out here & never go alone to the city These draw backs added to Blair's sickness has kept me active besides Father has told me he would secure one for you & that I need not move in the matter at all— He says Fox tells him to advise you not to be in a hurry & then you will get a good steamer— at present there none but poor concerns & that a bad steamer is the worst box a man can be in—"

Blair is now entirely well & I shall feel easy about going all day away from him but I fear to take him to the City so full of small pox & etc— I have never taken him there since I heard that disease was there— The Claret has not come— I'll be glad to get it to build our boy up again— He was biting ice, I said I was afraid it would break his teeth— & then I would have to pull it out— "Did you ever see a tooth pulled out? was his inquiry— I showed him the place in my mouth from which one was pulled out & remarked it was done long before he was born— "Well I think God must have a long time making me" was his comment   Mother says he looks better than he has done since April so you see he must have got back all he had when you saw him— when I did not think him looking well at all— He had lost his bloom so entirely— tho I tried to think it was the warm weather—

Now dont be angry or say anything about Fox— but I will explain the Case fully to Frank & he has managed one Fox so well that I think he will help me— & it ought to be *managed No Body* in that Concern can beat me in good temper & it is a great point in all matters— save in war & that I am not making on any body

I am glad to know about the Lyceum   Ill send there twice a week & to the Dept once— & send you papers by the Lyceum the Intelligencer as it gives local items— Your prize money I'll turn over to John[6] I never want Blair to own a cent in his own right until he makes it— I think boys get too soon out of the guidance of Parents— I want Blair taught the use of money but dont spoil him with it— that is my great fear for our child— in our great tenderness we may not develop his really fine nature so far— he has shown a good heart & head & I shall feel like a faithless Steward if he does not make a clever & a good man— But it is a great point to keep him until manhood *entirely dependant upon you* & I am glad of a chance to put this wish of mine down in writing He is the only treasure I have to dispose of & I sometimes feel even now when I enjoy him most that I could part with him for your pleasure & comfort— And he dont hesitate to say now he wants to be with you— tho he softens it by saying "he will soon be back again to me— Then tells me has been so long with me— but his cheerful prattle has been all the Sunlight in this house until tonight when we heard of Franks return to St Louis— it was a great relief

June 26 We hope Frank will be here by Saturday night   his election as Speaker is conceded—[7] but I shall tell him to be as active as if it was not thought so probable for Seward is the craftiest of old fellows & as Mr. Mann says wants watching— No news of import today Nothing we know of is done or doing save more troops are going over to the Virginia side The Tribune & other papers are pitching into the administration for its torpor— & all hold Frank & Genl Lyon[8] up as models— Times Press Tribune Herald & etc even the Post— I got five applications yesterday to get offices for people— it may be selfish but I cannot undertake it as I have been too unsuccessful in my previous efforts—

Blair is just eating a hearty meal— dinner & is merry & well & Franks coming has cheered the whole house— Your letters telling me lightened my heart   these frequent letters as compared with the winter past gives me brighter hues to my nights & days— & when I heard you were in the Chespeake I was elated but twas not true   Ever your devoted   Lizzie

1. On June 27, EBL described the scene: "Everything looks as it did a year ago until you get to the College Hill & then you will seen one vast encampment—."

2. In her June 21 letter, EBL reiterates SPL's instructions "not *to beg*," concluding, "I wait until I cant get it without that process—."

3. Comdr. James S. Palmer of *Iroquois* had received orders on May 13, 1861, to return from the Mediterranean to New York. On July 6, he was ordered to the Atlantic Blockading Squadron.

4. EBL referred to her brother's home on Pennsylvania Avenue, attached to hers by

a common wall, as No. 6. Not on the best of terms with Minna Blair, she often referred to her as Mrs. No. 6. The Lee house was No. 4.

5. In April, Commodore Hiram Paulding had been given the special duty of destroying the Norfolk Navy Yard before its abandonment to the Confederates. On August 8, he was appointed to the Iron Clad Board; in November he became commandant of the New York Navy Yard.

6. On June 18, only two days after joining the blockade off Charleston, Lee's ship *Vandalia* was within sight when *Union* captured a prize. According to law, *Vandalia* would share in any resulting prize money. For the duration of the war, Lee relied on his brother John to invest all prize money awarded to him.

7. On June 23, EBL reported: "Mr. Cameron— Forney— Haskins & Brother dined here today They say nothing can prevent Franks election as Speaker except his absence—."

8. On May 31, Brig. Gen. Nathaniel Lyon superseded William Harney in command of the Department of the West. After the Confederate defeat at Booneville, Governor Jackson retreated to southwest Missouri with Lyon and Union troops following. Frank Blair and his regiment of Missouri Volunteers had been part of Lyon's force, but after the battle at Booneville, Blair had returned to Washington.

Silver Spring   June 28, 1861

Dear Phil   Spent most of yesterday at John's— the arrest of Marshal Kane[1] made him a little bitter but when he sees by to days papers— the Cannon Caps— guns & all sorts of warlike provisions found secreted in his cellers &etc I think he will feel that Genl Banks[2] was right As you supposed— it is evident that there was arrangements made by the Secessionists in Baltimore to rise & act if there was a reverse met by the federal troops— they are now disarmed & the City police will soon be reorganized & then it will be a safe city— The people by 2 thirds are unconditionally for the Union as the late vote shows— & the whole state is of the same way of thinking except St Mary Charles & Prince Georges This last County only gave 28 majority for Calvert The Secessionists expected to beat him by hundred but they dont know the people— same way in Kentucky— they are amazed with [results] there—[3]

The arrival of Frank in Phila is announced   he is now with his wife & will be here tomorrow— They to want seranade him— If I could get out home to my boy at night I would go & see the affair— but cant stay away from Baby boy for it would not pay me for leaving him all night— So Mother & I'll stay home— Blair enjoyed the Claret today— It has been at John's sometime— but they forgot to tell me until they were relating to Eliza Graham[4] how Phil protested against any body drinking his except Cousin George— & Annie—[5] All [word indistinct] pronounce it excellent John's Clerk Wright[6] is denounced by Calvert as a Secessionist & demands his removal— John says is perfectly trustworthy

June 29. We were joined by Col Frémont at breakfast this morning— to our great Surprise as we heard only last night of his arrival in Boston He expects Jessie & to be a Majr Genl very soon   he will command I suppose a western division— The death of Capt Ward[7] has hurt us all here— it made me shudder— I remember his cordiality on the North Carolina last fall— poor fellow— poor wife! poor children— I feel for them all— Brother says that Motley[8] the Historian told him that Mr. Dallas[9] has been all winter & spring the hottest Secessionist in London— & Falkner[10] has been less loud— but quite as earnest a one in Paris no wonder the Secessionist were sanguine of recognition when so ably represented abroad— Col. F says the change of tone in England among the Government people is wonderful— *the people* were always all the time with us—

I got another letter from Fanny today   they are all well—[11] Blair drinks the claret & calls it "*clabber*" much to our amusement He & GrandMa enjoy it vastly— They are great cronies— the absence of all the other children this past winter— & this summer makes the little essential to her comfort— He rides— walks & talks with her almost daily— Frank did not arrive tonight much to the family disappointment

June 30 It rained & I could not go to Church— but was Compensated by the arrival of Frank— looking thin but healthy— full of spirit & said "he was no sooner out of one scramble than he got into another"   the speaker-ship is contested— by Grow[12] Colfax, Crittenden & etc— but our people talk confidently

Whilst we in family circle were talking— Mr. Cameron arrived— said he had no family— no dinner— & knew where he wanted to come & enjoy both— The table was consequently enlarged— it was hardly fixed when Fré-mont drove up— & ere fixing was quite done— Govr Sprague[13] & a Rhode Island reinforcement came— now the the whole table was cleared off & en-larged & additional dinner— It was all done by *4 olck*— to my amazement & with Becky's & my help Frank & Frémont were known to be in the city & were hunted up— The dinner was just over when others came too in the same hunt—

July 1st M.Cs are all treated our best now a days— but it is hard to get up desserts fruit all gone— Every body went to the City but Blair & I— Mother wanted a seat for Apo to return with her so he & I gave up gave up turn which I am glad resign for him— Going by these green Volunteers I am afraid of a stray shot for him & yet I go without a tremor for myself   indeed I forget it except when reminded of it in some way—

Mother says Frank got a letter from you & it seems she pitched into Fox Whereupon Frank burst out on all the tribe and said he meant to demand a Steamer as *Your right & not as* a favor from anybody & that right away too— So you see Frank goes in the right way about the matter & he can do it better than your wife— Although I have sorely tempted

July 2nd All well but in great haste

1. George P. Kane, chief of police of Baltimore and a Southern sympathizer, was arrested on June 27.

2. Nathaniel P. Banks, major general of volunteers, ordered Kane's arrest.

3. On June 20, Kentucky, in a special congressional election, voted overwhelmingly for the Union. Nine of the ten congressional districts elected Unionist candidates.

4. Eliza was Elizabeth Gaston, daughter of William Gaston, congressman from North Carolina, and Eliza Ann Worthington of Georgetown. She married George Graham of Prince Georges County on November 14, 1842. George Graham was related to the Hills on his mother's side; he was the son of John Graham (of Washington) and Susan Hill.

5. Anne Lee, daughter of John Lee, was born April 24, 1851.

6. James M. Wright of Maryland, clerk in the judge advocate's office.

7. James H. Ward, commander of the Potomac Flotilla, was killed off Mathias Point, June 27.

8. John L. Motley, historian and diplomat, was appointed by Lincoln to be minister to Austria. He served at that post from November 1861 until July 1867.

9. George M. Dallas had been a Democratic senator from Pennsylvania (1831–33), minister to Russia (1837–39), and vice president to James K. Polk (1845–49). President Franklin Pierce appointed him minister to Great Britain, where he served from 1856 to May 1861.

10. Charles J. Faulkner, U.S. minister to France when the war began, was recalled. On August 12, 1861, he was arrested for procuring arms for the rebels in Europe.

11. Correspondence with SPL's sister called for diplomacy; occasionally EBL was not up to the task, as she related on June 19: "I got a real Secession letter from Fanny to day about ten pages long & feel the greatest temptation to respond to it but have made up my mind not to save on the personal points." Only a few pages later, she admitted that the next day "I wrote to Fanny a long letter I did not keep my good resolution & gave her a dose."

12. Galusha A. Grow of Pennsylvania was a Free-Soil Democratic and then Republican congressman from 1851 to 1863. He had unsuccessfully sought the speakership in 1857 but was elected to that post in 1861.

13. William Sprague was elected governor of Rhode Island on the Unionist ticket and served from 1860 to 1863. He then served as a Republican senator from 1863 to 1875.

Silver Spring   July 3, 1861

Dear Phil   Sent papers & letters to you this morning & one to Fanny She said in a late letter that her boy had a great many secession papers sent to them & had no Union papers except Prentice's[1] which they would not read— So I send a different paper almost daily to them We get a great number in Franks & Brother's mail—

Fanny has seceded— in heart— since she has got a letter from Mary Lee[2] saying— that Robt took his resignation into prayerful consideration for two days— I wish he had read over his commission as well as his prayers— his fall-

ing off from grace is a puzzle to Fanny so she thinks he must be doing right—
I am sure— he wishes to do right— but Ill tell her you are far more infallible
than Robt— when a practical duty belonging to this world presents itself.
Upon a Church doctrine & practice he may be the best guide but even here he
has not gone by Our Church— which usually sticks very close to the powers
that be "So says the Bishop of Maryland[3] & I'll go by him as long as he does
right!! the *Bible* being my rule of right doing—

July 5 I had a dismal day yesterday— Went to the City dressed my best—
stopped at Brothers [Montgomery's] & found them all blue enough went to
the capitol & saw Frank take his defeat with the best grace in the world[4] to see
him play his part— it was infecting— such an easy good nature— He was surrounded & to the eye from the gallery you would have thought him the winner
in the scene— The Republican party voted against him— Potter— Curtis[5]
& etc all having promised their votes 2 years ago to Grow— Such being the
case Frank made a mistake in being a candidate save it showed his strength
outside of the party— Congress looked any thing but broken up— Carolinas
& etc were in calling over the States— passed like California & Oregon as not
having "yet elected— Virginia— Maryland Mo & Ky were there— & Tennessee will soon be here— Grow did his part tolerably & it was a good deed
to get rid of Forney[6] whose fulsome speech added to Hickmans[7] in a seranade
gotten up by them & Haskin[8] hurt Frank with many as well as disgusted him
& us at the time— It was got up before Franks arrival & declined it for Sunday
& hoped it was altogether put aside as this is not time exultations— but they
persevered to his loss

I reached the city too late to see the President review 21 thousand New
York Troops & was too sick with headache & disappointment to stay see the
fireworks— so came home & went supperless to bed— with one of my worst
attacks of headache which is all past now— & I wonder I felt so badly about
things as I then did— Genl Scott has put in a clause in the Military [Pay Bill]
for himself to *retire on full* pay— This is now confidential— Mr. Fox remarked
that they would go *wall up* Charleston harbor— he remarked Genl Butler took
too much of the fleet— to take care of him—

Minna goes off to day & leaves Apo in command of No 6— Mr. Calvert
demands the dismissal of John's clerk as the most incendiary secessionist in all
his part of the country his son is a good Republican so I am going to ask Mr
Cameron to let him have the place— John feels very badly about it— but I
hope will be patient Mr Cameron I hear is very reluctant to do it

Friday night— Recd yr letter of the 27. I wrote to you about Franks move to
get you a Steamer he says you shall have Up to this moment the Speakership
& Committees have absorbed his whole thoughts— but 'ere this time next
week I hope he will secure you some steamer or the promise of one at any rate

be assured my dear Phil that I am saying all I can to get it done & since your rebuking letter about begging I am afraid of being too pertinatious— but I feel I have in Frank an able zealous ally & am more hopeful & really should have gone to the President & Secy long since myself but for the prospect of Frank's coming—

I have heard nothing about prize money & dont know who to inquire after it— but suppose it will take some time to dispose of the ship & etc *&* divide— I'll furnish our home with your earnings— with extra arm chair & resting places for you to take some comfort & rest out of your present discomfort— I am no advocate for "laying by" for Blair— he will be all the smarter fellow if like his Father he has to take care of himself & deny himself for others— he has no sisters & brothers to do that for as you had— but I'll try & make him charitable & the poor he "will always have" with him

I feel so sorry that you have no news from us as I know you are so anxious about your little household *company*— The Army is still in front of Washington within hearing & seeing of the Confederate— why no battle has occurred is inexplicable Genl Scott— cavalry & artillery & at first declined both— such is the growlings— but *he is in sole command of everything* & some think him too old & others that his heart is averse to an attack upon Virginia— but all this is speculation I only know he says he is not ready yet & that horses & cannon & men & wagons are now pouring in to the city

Johnston & Calwalder[9] had a fight & a Penny regt went up & *over* a battery near Martinsburg— losing 10 men Virginians fled— as they do in the Mnts before McClellan[10] for they are Union men forced to the C Army & when the Secessionists are beat go home— & throw up their hats for the Union— John says tis the regulars— In every skirmish so far when face to face— the Confederates fly— Frank says the rank & file are against them even in the Army All well here Yrs ever Lizzie

I've sent letters by the Lyceum & Dept & papers—

1. George D. Prentice, Unionist editor of the Louisville *Journal.*

2. Mary Custis Lee, wife of Robert E. Lee.

3. The bishop of Maryland was William Rollinson Whittingham.

4. Although Frank was defeated in the speakership race by Galusha Grow, he was appointed chairman of the House Committee on Military Affairs.

5. John F. Potter, Republican congressman from Wisconsin (1857–63). Samuel R. Curtis, Republican congressman from Iowa (1857–61). A graduate of the United States Military Academy in 1831, he became a major general of volunteers.

6. John W. Forney, editor of the *Philadelphia Press* and the *Washington Chronicle,* was Republican clerk of the House (1860–61) and secretary of the Senate (1861–68).

7. John Hickman, congressman from Pennsylvania, served from 1855 to 1863, first as a Democrat, then a Republican.

8. John B. Haskin, Democratic congressman from New York (1857–61).

9. On July 2, there was a skirmish at Falling Waters on Hoke's Run, a Union success. On July 3 Patterson advanced toward Martinsburg, and Joe Johnston fell back toward Winchester. Brig. Gen. George Cadwalader commanded the First Division of the Department of Pennsylvania.

10. Maj. Gen. George Brinton McClellan commanded Union operations in western Virginia.

Silver Spring   July 6, 1861

Dear Phil   Father went with Frank to see Mr Welles[1] about a steamer for you today.[2]— & it is promised & you are to be transfered right away— Yet there was a hitch in Fox's saying— as he was called & ordered by the Secy to give you the steamer   I believe the one Capt Thomson[3] has— But I am not certain & will go try to get at the Specialties from Comre Paulding who I am going *to ask* to carry out yr program for me— Frank says he is going again a few days to see if the order has gone— for you & will jog jog until it does—

I must say my heart is lighter than for a long time & yet I am afraid they will order you to New Orleans or somewhere I will live in terror about you— the fever will surely rage there this year   The truth is you Mercer[4] & *all active* southern officers to be relied on are to be kept on this blockade— for foreign effect & I am hopeless about getting you home & panic stricken when you tell me about boats taking you in light winds   I would be in dispair if the Secessionists ever get hold of you— & shall never be at rest— now until you are in a ship which can *move* at all times in some way & have a long gun & when you have the means of self preservation I have no earthly fear as to the result barring— hurricanes & etc & it never struck me about your exposure— until yr letter— I *say* nothing on *that* point— but I assure you no digging or reading or anything gets it out of my mind & tho I've tried not to fret about this matter they all see here that I feel intensely about it & I am sure your wishes will be promptly carried out—

Frank & Apo are here tonight— he is worn out & down   I never saw him so thin & they all say *we* look now exactly alike— he is as thin as I am & assure you I dont fatten tho' I do take great care of your little woman so she may be able to wait on you some— in return for all the watchings you gave her in years gone by— & happy tho they were sick years to me

July 9. Sunday. it became suddenly hot— & I had Blair to run after & indoors he would not be amused so I was fagged out by night between him & the usual company here— on Sunday. Yesterday we went to the City to keep our engagement with Mr. Bigelow[5] to go over to see the embankments & encampments over in Virginia— The day proved hot so I left Blair home

At dinner at Brother's we were joined by Mr. Russell of the London Times— he is a chuncky sample of John Bull evidently relishing our quarrels vastly   He remarked that the Southern women had more zeal than we Union women that they were making lint & bandages— &etc. I replied they were preparing to be whipped[6] & for defeat— We did not anticipate that We went to Arlington. the first time since my childhood. he questioned me as to our relationship. I made your reply on that point— He laughed at the House— but said he was amazed that they (the Confederates ever retreat from that Hill He said he walked over the long bridge one night when five hundred Cavalry could taken the city & that they had— but did not use their advantages & if Genl Scott had advanced his *Vanguard* there in Virginia— there would never have been any Secession in the Mother of States— He talked with ease & pleasantries— Evidently wearied of our close carriage was not comfortable to him— Frank intends to bring in a bill repealing the retrocession of Alexandria Co— Whilst we were at head quarters a flag of truce was brought in by Mr. Taylor a Frankfort Man born near our Benson home the flag was a mere pretense his real object espionage like those sent out to you—

I received a letter for you yesterday from Mr. Simmons[7] enclosing a check for $80 dollars which I gave (letter & all) over to John— Commerce is in St Louis as every where else defunct— people get no rents allowing tenets to hold their houses for nothing almost Frank is at the head of the Military Committee & Mr. Grow put nobody at the head of Navy Matters— that suited the *Dept.* All say the session will be short

July 10 Washington Came in this morning on business for Mother found no news— except that Genl Scott has put a stop on all telegraphs save for military use & troops are marching over into Va every hour of the day— All the three months troops whose time is up— next week are now in Fairfax— So they must expect to go after the Confederates

I enclose you a note from John to me— Father has just gone to Johns office & will he says fix matters for him & is resolved that Calvert shall not *go it* over him Blair is bright & well tho he expresses great discontent at the hot weather he says it makes him wet all the time— he perspires as much as you do— save in this respect tis delicious to me— Ever your affectionate Lizzie

1. In her August 10, 1861, letter EBL explained: "I tried in every way to get hold of the Secy of the Navy without going to the Dept but he was not in lodgings which was a formidable place— crowded with men Willards— not a woman there— I sent him invitations to dine at Silver Spring & the old man was 'too worn out' for so long a drive— I got Father to ask him to come stay out there but he did not come— I sent Father & Frank twice to the Dept. & Frank was most importunate & they always assured him you should have the 'first steamer they could get hold of— You see Capt Foote has got none yet & he has been trying all he *can*— Fox will not stand in your way to get anything— but he will not facilitate— You made him an enemy long since & I have done all I can but go around a la Mrs Emory— & that I would have done—

but I know it would offend you— but now as a want of success in yr wishes offends— I might just as well take that in another shape & have my self the satisfaction of getting things done that you wish for so I am going home early next week— & go to work I know the ropes for Ive seen them well pulled—."

2. Gideon Welles, old Jacksonian friend of Francis Preston Blair, was Lincoln's secretary of the navy and Montgomery Blair's closest friend in the cabinet.

3. Comdr. Edward R. Thomson, in *Seminole* (commissioned in 1860), joined the Atlantic Blockading Squadron in July.

4. Capt. Samuel Mercer was squadron commander in the attempt to provision Fort Sumter on April 5. In August, he was commanding USS *Wabash* off Charleston.

5. John Bigelow, editor of the New York *Evening Post.*

6. Line drawn through "whipped."

7. Samuel Simmons, S. P. Lee's St. Louis financial agent.

Silver Spring   July 11, 1861

Dear Phil   We have had no communication with the outer world today & the only item of News which has affected to our knowledge this incircle of yours is that the officers in command in New Mexico have deserted en mass U.S.— & took off with their men, munitions of war[1] & George Alexander fears his wife's servants her clothes and *Blair's donkey*!! however this would have been an encumbrance & thus tis hoped they may have let it drift along to him

Blair Becky, & I spent the morning blackberry hunting around the circle walk (which I never venture along now adays) Blair was in great glee— & as usual waited to divide with you & me his berries Your prize money has cost me some thought I did not like to prevent his feeling that you meant to do so much for him— So I've talked about your working very hard for his future— & yet dont mention money for I fear to cultivate a love of it in him— Your return is the great event of our future— I must say however— the Donkey has had a precedence lately so much so I've refrained from mentioning even its probable loss to him yet—

George Alexander & his wife are in the city— Father could not get Wright retained or his sons put in— but got a young man out Richard Bowies[2] office put in Wright's place thus disappointing Calverts ill will & thats some comfort to John— You have no idea how bitter the war is making people— in political feeling John let out his ire on Calvert by Wright alias Carlisle suing him for defamation & if he gets the suit Father is pledged to get him a place as well as his damages of $10,000—

As we returned home we met troops en route for Va no battle as yet of import The Congress & the people are dissatisfied with this delay— but I feel it is all for the best— I see by the papers Georgia has refused the Constitution of the Confederacy & when these divisions increase & are followed by a defeat after so many retreats— it may end the war expeditiously after all— There is great jealousy in giving Frémont an extensive command Frank will visit upon the *Mississippi Column* both sides   McClellan will take the Mountains— Genl Scott & his Lieutenants— east slope of the Mts & thus march South each Column over a 100,000 men

July 12 Friday— Father went to the City & got back too tired to tell us the News   the Papers report a fight in Mo. between Col Sigel[3] at Carthage & Jackson— in which Sigel got the best of it over an immensely superior force— his reinforcement were rapidly going to him— There is a fight in the Mts between Wise & Morris—[4] the last was holding his position & McClelland maneuvering to surround Wise— Our Army in Fairfax— have got the Court House & advance steadily & the Confederates are retreating

July 13 Apo & Frank are out here tonight & tomorrow there is to be a big dinner out here   I'll make the dessert & help set table & then go to Church for is a month tomorrow since I have been & it is a privilege I cannot relinquish—

The fight in the mountains is confirmed— but the Seceders ran before many were hurt & thus loss is in their waggons & guns[5] They evidently are counting on some grand rally at Richmond there are really but few troops at Manasses or Fairfax & they retreat everywhere   I asked Frank if Fox had sent you the order about the Steamer— he replied that your Steamer was a certain thing— but there was not one now ready but that they are working day & night— the one intended for you— I will continue to jog— but it is evident Frank says that at this moment you cannot be spared   I suppose they intend to keep you out the three months then recall you for refreshments— half that time now has expired— They dont say this to me about you— but of others— Frank is overwhelmed with business— but he will not neglect you—

July 14*th* made a dessert— fixed table & dressed and off to Church having a little chat with Mr. Grimes & Mr. Fessenden[6] before going & they brought tidings of McClellans victory & capture of Col Pelgram[7] & all his soldiers who did not *run* The Confederates impress the Western & *poor* Virginians & at the first fire— they generally take to the woods & get to their homes as fast as they can serving the Confederates *just right*

July 14 [15] A broken tooth ought to take me to the city today but I'll postpone it as was a lovely cool day to get my flowers well worked— Frank & Apo went off early & Father   they want me to go to the Levee tomorrow 'eve but I dont go to such places even you are home often & now I cant get up to the point tho' they urge very good reasons— the women kind are giving Mrs Lincoln[8] the cold shoulder in the City & consequently we Republicans ought to Rally— but it would be a turn out on my part & I have not the spirit in—

McClellan has captured Genl Garnetts[9] camp & a thousand men— Garnett was killed in his effort to rally his men Betty knew young Garnett well— he was a love of Ellen Hill & Betty says like him better than she did Saunders who she has now discarded after *ordering* him to go to "*secesh*—" Garnet was a Lieutenant in our Service— but there are so many *Bob* Garnetts that it is hard to say who it is— but Genl Garnett is killed— thats certain & his body sent to his home— Western Virginia is certainly delivered now— Wise is reported wounded some say killed Our forces are at a *Standstill* yet— in Fairfax— & been *just* on the move for ten days—

Henry May has just returned from Richmond in effort to coax "Secesh" to be reasonable & has returned home sick & says they will take nothing less than a recognition of their Independence— & of course he as a Union man is disappointed[10] the Maryland secessionist since they cant get out— are very eager now to get *"the south"* all back again but— its present master are to whipped 'ere that end attained—

Mr. Seward dined here yesterday— & he mentioned that Every European Power had written to this Government letters of sympathy & *encouragement* England alone excepted— Individuals in large numbers had written with the greatest interest & affection our old Stepdame— was missed Russell remarked that England would feel more sure of the Solution this question when our armies were in Richmond—

July 16th No more news today Nelly & Betty are going with me to hear John Breckinridge make a speech Nell waits in the carriage All well at Johns Will & Arthur[11] down the Country with Eliza Graham Blair begged to come in today but I think country is best until Washn is less of a camp Ever yr own Lizzie

1. On July 3 Union forces abandoned Fort McLane in New Mexico; on July 27 Fort Fillmore surrendered without a fight; on August 1, Confederates claimed the New Mexico Territory.

2. Richard Bowie, chief judge of the Maryland Court of Appeals (1861–67).

3. Col. Franz Sigel engaged the secessionist forces of Claiborne Jackson at Carthage, Missouri, on July 5. Sigel got the worst of it and was forced to retreat toward Springfield.

4. Jacob Cox rather than U.S. Brig. Gen. Thomas A. Morris engaged Henry Wise; Morris fought and pursued the forces of R. S. Garnett on July 11 and 12. Wise, former governor of Virginia (1856–60), was a brigadier general in the Confederate army.

5. The Union efforts at Rich Mountain, Laurel Hill, and in the Kanawha Valley, begun on July 11, resulted in defeat for the rebels. McClellan discontinued pursuit of the Confederate forces on July 13.

6. James W. Grimes, Republican senator from Iowa (1859–69), had been governor of Iowa from 1854 to 1858. William P. Fessenden, Republican senator from Maine from 1854 to 1864. He resigned his seat to become secretary of the treasury, in which office he served until March 1865.

7. On July 11, C.S.A. Lt. Col. John Pelgram was attacked at Rich Mountain, western Virginia, by McClellan's forces led by William S. Rosecrans. On July 13, Pelgram surrendered 555 men.

8. Mary Todd Lincoln, wife of the president.

9. C.S.A. Brig. Gen. Robert S. Garnett was killed July 13 while retreating from Laurel Hill.

10. Staunch Unionist Henry May went to Richmond, with Lincoln's approval, to attempt negotiations with Southern leaders. While he was on this mission, efforts were made to expel him from Congress, and on his return, he spent several weeks in prison.

11. William Hill Lee, born March 7, 1846, and Arthur Lee, born June 1, 1847, were sons of John and Ellen Lee.

Silver Spring   July 17, 1861

Dear Phil   Yesterday after I dispatched my letter to you Nelly Betty & I went to the Capitol to hear John Breckinridge's speech— He said nothing new attacked the President for violating the Constitution— & talk constitution so hypocritically that I almost lost my patience & would have left 'ere he finished but I knew Nel wished to hear the speech— All he said was easily answered— but I held my tongue & endured his specious pleading— & a very bad head ache until he was through— took Nel home— & was just leaving Betty at No 6— she is staying with Apo there— when we were greeted by Mr. Riggs[1] just back from Europe & Jane from "Jany" who was in great distress about her husband Gus Nicholson[2] being ordered over into Va with 300 Marines

After our inquiries about Mary[3] & the children were ended we went off to F Street[4] & found Jany in tears— I was sympathetic first & then tried to stir her up to go see about her husbands confirmation who Col Harris[5] wishes to defeat I left her in active mood & ready to brain the Col with more than her fan if she had a chance After these long delays I got home & went dinnerless to bed— but tho' I could not eat I could talk & went thro the speech— Genl Scott review of the 50,000 over the River & the Commencement of the "March upon Richmond" Genl Johnstons retreat to Winchester with temples thumping like a drum corp— These headaches are for the time overpowering— but my general health is regular & excellent— & I see no bad consequences from them except a loss of sight— Your specs are now really necessary to me

The news of the day is that H. A. Wise & his son O. Jennings[6] are routed at Ripley Western Va— These easy Victories in that Country of McClellans Army must create great consterna[tion] in "Secesh"— & all the greater when the learn that pins & lead are found in the touch holes of soldiers muskets— showing a fixed purpose not to fight for "the Gentry" This fact is not published here & for very obvious reasons contradicted tho an ascertained fact— in a vast number of cases—

July 18th. It seems that Palmer has determined to hold on to the Iroquois— & now Frank has put in for some other Steamer He thinks none of these chartered vessels worth having— & so they promise to give you the first new Steamer they buy. & they will purchase as soon as the appropriations are

passed— this makes the prospect near— I've made Currant Jelly & Straw-
berry & blackberry jelly (the best thing for weak bowels) I say all for the new
Steamer— & yet sometimes there is a hope in my heart we may enjoy our
sweetmeats together

The row made by the Jeff Davis & Sumter[7] (last said to have slipped out
Charleston on the 28th of June) is making a great stir on the ocean— & in
Commercial places They have sent six steamers (among them the Iroquois)
in search of these privateers This evening we had a visit from Mrs. Temple—
wants a commission for a nephew Temple— Fairfax Country House was evacuated in haste— South Carolina Regts left all their tents— sick. Hospital
stores & etc— Johnston is too quick for old Patterson— he will join Beauregard—[8] & at Manassas there will be a big fight— Our people will surround
them— & not attack their entrenchments & cut off the Retreat to Richmond
if possible— The Campaign *is just now* where you thought it was when you
left with this difference— Harpers Ferry & all Western Va is now delivered of
Secession & Balt is quite well purged of Treason So *our rear* is in a far more safe
condition than you thought it when we parted— & subsequent events have
proved that your fears would have been realized if Genl Scott had then pushed
things & met a rebuff Balt would have risen under Kanes lead— He is now
indicted for Treason by the Grand Jury of that City. where the *"good society"*
are all traitors & *the people* nearly all loyal

The vote in Maryland & its consequent Union position has made Thompson Mason & a great many other leading Secessionists now the most zealous
Unionist— they are running to Richmond— (said Henry May) to coax the
Confederacy back that failing *they'll go for whipping them back*— anything but
making Maryland northern frontier— to the South— the devastations on the
Ohio & Baltr Railroad— *has cured* a great many people in this State of Secession— Our Army marched to Manassas Junction today— Jane Jesup followed
her husband to Fairfax Court House— was sent back last night. She evidently
felt like a heroine!! Troop & Evy Martin[9] expected here tomorrow— they
come to get Troop at the Naval School

July 19. We have been on tiptoe of expectation all day Father returned late
saying that our advanced brigade had been repulsed and the *Bull Run* Battery
of the Enemy— Genl Scott ordered the army to stop— rest reconnoitre— &
he says nothing *can* happen until this evening— that at ten olk tonight he will
have dispatches from Genl McDowell—[10] This he said to the President— who
replied— Genl it is your duty to report to me every movement & action—"
The General look up to find he had a superior officer & promptly replied—
"Yes sir & in that & as in all else I'll do my duty" This the P. told Father—
who repeated it confidentially to Govr Gibbs[11] who has known Genl Scott
intimately for years— & who after a long silence— Well Mr L knows him &
knows how to manage him—"

There is a good deal of skirmishing in Missouri Frank— Apo— Betty— the Martins— Evy & Troop— go tomorrow down to Fort Monroe— & return Monday I suppose Frank goes on business Congress adjourned until Monday & the Members are off to the battlefield tomorrow— Mother & I have as usual been quiet at home— from which She wont go— & I really feel loth to leave her so much alone so I staid home today— I have not taken Blair to the City for a month or more

July 20 Got your letters by Capt G—[12] It was as water to a thirsty land to my heart— I wrote some of my joy & thanks today & sent it by Frank who I asked to give it to Comre Stringham [13] & tell him I meant to send almost daily letters— for I had been unfortunate in getting my letters to you— They are expected back Monday— Martin, Apo, Betty, Evy Martin— Marion Sands [14] all went with Frank to see Fortress Monroe— & Mother to get a change of air at my entreaty as she was not well

A house full came back home with us I invited Geo Alexander & his wife to come in Franks carriage— then went after Maria Mechlin [15] & when we called for Father we found he had invited Mr Riggs— So on getting home I was pushed for a dinner— Riggs gives bad accounts of the prospects for the Confederates in Europe Says even Bev Tucker [16] had not brass enough to endure the Coventry in which the Americans put all these Confederate Representatives abroad Bev bet him in March in Paris that Washington would be taken by the South— *in April* said he knew all about it— so you see how long & well this program was understood—

July 21st Sunday A day long long to be remembered in the annals of the world This morning at dailight the morning guns seem very loud to me— & when the[y] continued to rumble rumble I grew too restless— & got up about nine After breakfast I begged Maria to go walk hoping the woods would stop the *roar* in my ears— but down at the Grotto— I heard it plainer & then spoke of it to Maria told her it was the Battle at Bull Run— 30 miles off She soon distinguished the sounds & on our return to the house— All the house soon became listeners Brother & Mr Dennison [17] came out early & said that Genl Scott had sent word to Mr. Lincoln that the attack would commence with dailight— It was some time 'ere Mr. Dennison could distinguish in the Vally by Violets spring— the belchings of the Cannon & strange it was not heard in the city— but just as plain— oh so torturingly plain to me— all all this long day— When last news at 5 olk came in our side were victorious 3 batteries taken— the Confederate lines broken— & they retreating to their entrenchment at the Junction— but at 8 olk— as I was rocking our boy to sleep I heard that dreadful roar still— & it ceased— or I to hear it from about 15 minutes after eight Oh what a sad long weary day has this sabbath been to me—

Becky went to church & I had to look after Blair as well as the house— &

as so often in his precious life— he was such a stay & comfort to me— My duty in looking after an[d] amusing him just kept me wailing & weeping over the terrific scene of carnage of my own kindred & countrymen— within my hearing—

Washington *July 22nd* I enclose you a note from John— Father when we first heard the fearful rout of our army said Betty Blair Appo & I must go north at 2 olk   I sent for John— as in yr absence I never feel willing to ought of moment without your Brother's counsel He said go at first & then with me the enclosed[18] when I sent word Father said I might stay to consult John over again So here I am— going to stay Our army was overcome by numbers they have ascertained that one hundred & ten thousand troops in battle— John says this defeat *cements* Maryland in the Union

1. Elisha Riggs had replaced his half brother George W. Riggs in the banking firm of Corcoran and Riggs in 1848. When Corcoran retired in 1854, George bought his interest and the firm name became Riggs and Company.

2. Jane Jesup, daughter of Thomas Jesup and sister of Mary Blair, was married to Lt. Augustus S. Nicholson of the Marines.

3. Mary Boswell Riggs, wife of Elisha Riggs, had been the ward of Benjamin Gratz who had married EBL's aunt.

4. The Jesups' address was the south side of F Street north between Twelfth and Thirteenth.

5. Col. John Harris, commandant of the Marine Corps.

6. Capt. O. Jennings Wise, of the Richmond Blues, was Henry Wise's son. The Confederates under Henry Wise temporarily held up the Union advance, led by Jacob Cox, toward Charleston, western Virginia. Ripley is just north of Charleston.

7. CSS *Sumter*, commanded by Raphael Semmes, ran the blockade at New Orleans on June 30. The New York *Commercial Advertiser* of July 13 described the *Jeff Davis* as a pirate brig. She had been off Nantucket South shoals and had made several captures during the week. The article states that *Jeff Davis* was "commanded by Captain Postell formerly of the United States navy"; however, the official naval reports list Louis M. Coxetter as captain and William R. Postell as first lieutenant.

8. Confederate Brig. Gen. Pierre Gustave Toutant de Beauregard commanded rebel troops in northern Virginia.

9. Throop and Evy Martin were the children of E. T. T. Martin. Throop attended the Naval Academy at Newport but did not graduate. Evelina married Andrew J. Alexander, brother of Apo Blair.

10. Brig. Gen. Irvin McDowell was appointed commander of Army of the Potomac, May 29, 1861.

11. William Channing Gibbs had been elected governor of Rhode Island on the Democratic-Republican ticket in 1820; he served until 1824.

12. Captain John R. Goldsborough, commanding USS *Union*, was on blockade off Charleston with *Vandalia* and *Wabash*. On July 15, he was ordered to Hampton Roads.

13. Captain Silas H. Stringham, flag officer of the Atlantic Blockading Squadron.

14. Marion Sands, daughter of Benjamin F. Sands.

15. Maria Mechlin, an old friend of EBL's, had married Fred A. Smith in 1840.

16. Nathaniel Beverly Tucker resigned his post as U.S. consul at Liverpool and later joined the rebel army.

17. Ohio governor William Dennison replaced Montgomery Blair as postmaster general in 1864.

18. The letter from John Lee states his belief that Washington was safe but encouraged EBL to stay at his home in town, not at Silver Spring.

3

"A poet and a General are things rare to find"

October 7, 1861

THE SHOCKING UNION LOSS AT BULL RUN caused Elizabeth Lee to seek safety far from the sound of battle. She visited in Philadelphia, Atlantic City, and Bethlehem, Pennsylvania, before returning to Silver Spring on October 19. Elizabeth enlisted the aid of her father and brothers to fulfill S. P. Lee's wish to replace his sailing vessel with a steamer. In October he was ordered to command the *Oneida*, which was still under construction. While waiting for his ship, Lee traveled to St. Louis to look after his business interests there.

The final six months of the first year of war were dominated by the appointment of George B. McClellan to command the Army of the Potomac and his reorganization of federal forces. Events in Kentucky placed her firmly in the Union, but Missouri took longer and directly involved the Blair family. Growing disaffection with the performance of John C. Frémont led brother Frank to opposition which caused a permanent rift between the Blair and Frémont-Benton families. The tragedy of war came home with the death of cousin Cary Gratz, killed in battle at Wilson's Creek, Missouri. Although no other major battles occurred as both sides concentrated on preparation for war, the *Trent* affair sent tremors through the north that England might intervene to support the Southern cause.

Philadelphia   July 23, 1861

Dear Phil   The most comfortable sensation I have about this move from my home is that it will be a relief to you & that after this you will never have an anxious thought about us— feeling we have the most cautious care taken of us—

News from Washington indicates a revival of energy in Washn[1] They are sad & the secessionist too are equally busy over their dead & wounded   Mr. Pryor[2] a brother of the M.C. says their loss was awful even before he was taken prisoner early in the day— It must have been or they would have followed up their Victory more vigorously which they had not done at 2 olk today Patterson's men are ready to mob him so one of them told me today They say he is as more of an ally to the South than even Genl Jo Johnston The rumors about our loss is all uncertain for the rolls were not called at midday to day & I saw many of the soldiers straggling in late last night & early the morning— One of them sat in the rain on the stone foundation of brother's front fence— I asked if he was hungry? No! Thirsty? no, sick? no,— wounded no no only mad— we are beat & badly because we have no generals— no competent officers He was almost heart broken from his tone & manner— a very respectable looking man— The Citizens treated them well— fed & sheltered them from the storm— Maryland seems *steady*— All was quiet in Balt— as we came thro it— & I saw 50 flags where I saw ten in June—

I shall still stay here a few days & then go to Bethlehem for Mary Blairs party without Dr Hodge[3] advises me to go to the Sea shore for these headaches which I think comes from the same cause that makes specs comfortable— & if he advises me to go to the sea— Ill go with Mira & Mr. Dick to the Atlantic City— across New Jersey & just 2 hours from here & until this is settled I'll home here under Aunt Becky's care— Blair & Becky are my best protection in my wanderings— & our dear child is certainly a great comfort— He was joyous today in the Cars with hope of going to see Papa   I do hope you will soon come into port— tho this Rhode Island provision[4] looks like keeping you all out but the rest have had their turn & you ought to have yours-Ever yr devoted Lizzie

Betty & Apo go to New York tomorrow— Betty to Martins & Apo to Connecticut

1. In her July 25 letter, EBL reported on morale in Philadelphia: "There is no external evidence of depression here abouts now— only a renewed war spirit of twofold zeal-The recruiting places are thronged—."
2. Mr. Pryor was possibly Lt. John W. Pryor of the Eighty-first Pennsylvania Infantry Volunteers.
3. Dr. Hugh Hodge, professor of obstetrics at the University of Pennsylvania, was EBL's personal physician.
4. *Rhode Island* served as a supply ship for the North Atlantic Blockading Squadron.

Philadelphia   July 28, 1861
Dear Phil   As the time draws near for my plunging into the sea— & among strangers you cant concieve how I shrink from it— But the Doctor says I ought to go— & health is too precious to forgo for mere nervousness for my child & nurse are ample protection— Becky is very efficient as a traveller when she has to look out for things— she sleeps always in my room & locks & bars up every night no matter where we are The Doctor thinks two weeks at the sea

shore will do & if at the end of that time I cannot return home— I'll go to Bethlehem— where I'll be with Mary— in the country & in cheap lodgings & *good ones* & there I'll stay until you come back to the north— The weather here has been cool until today— midday was hot— but it now rains & wind easterly— I think in this we are fortunate for the Dr did not wish me to go until he had seen the effect of his medicine— Today he says we may be off on Wednesday, so I'll write for a room tomorrow— At the Surf House Atlantic City N Jersey— it is only a two hours ride from here— in the cars

Blair said to me today "Mama My Papa stays away so long I am afraid the Secessioners has caught him." I asked what made him say so— "A little Secession told me so—" & no cross examination could get out of him any thing else on the subject— trifling as it is— the prattle has depressed me more than I can tell you— There is no news since I last wrote from Washn

July 29 Monday— There is no news of import this morning Our loss in Bull Run in every way is now estimated to be about 1,000 men— 300 killed the rest wounded & prisoners. & yet since this estimate has been promulgated I hear that many stragglers have come in—[1] I have no letters from home today. It is evident that Fairfax is to be the battle ground & therefore it was well for Father to send us away at least until our home is no longer within the reach of the sounds of the battle field— I confess now I am better for being away— Yet I do wish my Parents were with me— both are now contentious

You see by the Herald I send you that they are pitching into Father & yet the P[resident] is taking advice *now* which was proffered 2 months ago— hence the Cabinet jealousy— which is leaking out—[2] But there is *now* no jealousy in *head* quarters & I do hope things will be more energetically done— Troops are going thro here daily to Washington— The three months men— which Brother opposed calling for that time are being disbanded at this moment. I remember well the day of great satisfaction— felt by Father when they got the 3 years men called— where would we be now without out them— they have been in camps drilling for near 2 months & tis said make a fine appearance as they pass through here Making laws for the military service— & to get money— drilling & reorganizing the army is now the work going on at Washington— Wade Hampton was killed & he and Genl Albert Johnson[3] are the only noted Rebels killed— the Confederate papers say their loss is over two thousand & that behind brest works!!

I saw by the yesterdays paper that the Rhode Island had not sailed yet so will enclose this to go by her to Capt Foot[4] care— As the Lyceum letters are slow getting to you— I shall be off to the sea tomorrow or certainly next day. it is very warm here to day. Blair prattles lovingly about seeing you when we get at the sea side I can never feel grateful enough for the comfort & company of this dear child in the past year— He has just be splashing in the big bath up stairs his joyous frolick enlivens this house as well as my heart— I have not

called on any body here out of the famly circle— Went to church with the
Dicks who say they will join us at Atlantic City where a sister of Mr. Dick's
is now there with a sick child— Waiter will take this in a moment so good
by   Yr devoted Lizzie

1. The figures on losses at Bull Run are: Federals: 460 killed, 1124 wounded, 1312
missing, for a total of 2896; Confederates: 387 killed, 1582 wounded, 13 missing,
totaling 1982.

2. A July 27, 1861, editorial in the New York *Herald* placed major blame for the
Bull Run disaster on "a weak, inharmonious and inefficient Cabinet." The article also
castigates the Blair family: "At the same time we would recommend a vigilant eye and a
tight rein upon that mysterious branch of government known as the Kitchen Cabinet.
In the declining days of President Jackson this institution, under the able, talented,
energetic and dictatorial head of the central democratic organ, the venerable Francis P.
Blair, Senior, played the part of Richelieu to the King. It is alleged that this terrible
thunderer of the old *Globe*, whose edicts under Jackson were as those of the Prime
Minister of the Czar, has at this late day assumed to control 'Honest Abe Lincoln;'
that F. P. Blair, Jr., of Congress, and his brother, the Postmaster General, all radical
members of the church militant, are largely responsible for our late army disaster, in
hurrying the President into forward movement" (p. 4).

3. Albert Sidney Johnston (USMA 1826) resigned from the U.S. army when Texas
seceded and was promoted to Confederate general August 31. Wade Hampton III of
South Carolina led Hampton's Legion at Bull Run. The rumors were false; neither
Johnston nor Hampton was killed.

4. Captain Andrew Hull Foote, commandant of the New York Navy Yard, was
appointed to command naval operations on the western waters on August 30.

Philadelphia   August 14, 1861

Dear Phil   I was startled this morning by a telegraph from Father saying "Stay
till you hear from me—" I of course stopped all my preparations for departure
& sat down to grieve over poor Genl Lyon & my anxieties about Cary Gratz[1]
walked about til worn out with fatigue— left for bed early but not sleep

Thursday Augst 15— All my forbodings of last night are fulfilled this morning— Cary Gratz is killed— His beautiful infancy was a great pleasure to my
childhood & his fine manly character has made him a very dear kinsman to
me— I mourn over his loss in sincere grief— & have a shuddering at the
thoughts of my Brother Frank rushing on to share in the perillous struggle
now going on in Missouri— I see that Frémont has declared Martial Law in St
Louis & is surrounding the City with batteries— & everything looks in battle
array there—[2]

I had a few moments since a letter from Father in Washington say— defences were being thrown up all around the City to the north— even "around
Silver Spring vicinicty—" & adds "until things are settled you had better stay

at Bethlehem or somewhere in a healthy Pa region or go to Mrs. Martin—"[3] Lyon's fate may propel the Beauregards in this direction— They are making great preparations—" "If I ascertain that there is no danger here I will advise you immediately to come home"

Blair takes this disappointment sorely to heart— I shall go tomorrow or next day to Bethlehem— & there stay until Father writes again "come home—" You will be satisfied to have us out of the cannons sound— & thats some comfort to me— tho' its din will never be forgotten by me in life again Bethlehem is near here or New York if you should come home & is near home— is cheap & healthy & Mary Blair & her little flock of dear children to me are my attractions there— Blair is well I ventured peaches two days without harm to him

Aunt Becky is very much overcome by Cary's death she says it will be a crushing blow to Uncle Ben[4] to whom he was the dearest of all his children— It would be a sad picture of this fratracidal war— to find that Joe Shelby & Henry Hart[5] & his son were with the Confederates on that day I send you the papers with all the tidings I have from these scenes of sorrow to us all—

The Confederates are now pushing matters as every day we are getting our three year's army better drilled— increased— & organized & will never again be as weak as now as all the three months are returned home— the last of them quit yesterday[6] so now is the propitious hour for them to strike— they'll never have the same opportunities again— for altho the Army around Washington is large— it is without drill— none have been in the field over six weeks except the reenlisted three months men— & they are as yet a small propotion the rest are still at home reorganizing into regiments & only in a state of preparation for departure to the field again Blair sent his love to you this morning saying "I wish Papa would come home & never go away any more" and utterance from his Mother's heart[7] Your affectionate Lizzie

1. Cary Gist Gratz, son of Benjamin and Maria Cecil Gist Gratz, was killed at Wilson's Creek, Missouri, on August 10, 1861. His mother was Eliza Blair's younger sister. Nathaniel Lyon, leading the Union forces, also died in the battle. The Blairs blamed Gratz's death on Frémont's negligence in failing to reinforce Lyon.

2. In her August 19 letter, EBL reported: "The point which Father has been laboring for is at last attained— McClellan has the eastern division & Frémont the West— & with that act instantly companies & parts of Regts are ordered to Washington & this City shows today in every face that *new* activity & energy is now at work in behalf of our Country— For nearly two months this has been labored for by our *se̲t*— to get the work out of *luke warm hands heads & hearts.*"

3. About 1834 Cornelia S. Williams of Utica, New York, married E. T. T. Martin. They lived at Willowbrook, Auburn, New York.

4. Benjamin Gratz of Lexington, Kentucky, was EBL's uncle by marriage; his first

wife had been Eliza Blair's sister. Gratz was a brother of Rebecca Gratz of Philadelphia, EBL's Aunt Becky.

5. Joseph Shelby was the son of Anna Boswell by her first marriage. He was indeed in the Confederate ranks at the Battle of Wilson's Creek. Anna was Benjamin Gratz's second wife. Henry Clay Hart was the son of Eliza Blair's older sister, Anna Maria Gist, and Nathaniel Gray Hart.

6. On August 5, 1861, EBL commented: "I met some the 3 months volunteers whose camp I saw en route to Harpers Ferry They talk like *Veterans*— I laughed a little at them."

7. On Blair's birthday, August 9, EBL mused: "It has been a long eventful year since we took our birthday dinner on chops & mushrooms tomatoes & potatoes— amid the bustle of packing up our little chattels— of housekeeping Well we will know how to appreciate a home together in peaceful times even more than ever did & I flatter myself we never underated that joy— no matter how or where I have been always happiest in our home together—."

Philadelphia   August 20, 1861

My Dear Phil   After a delay of a week here in which I have vibrated in my plans nearly each day— I've settled down to going to Bethlehem— for which place I'll start now in an hour or so— I have just received 7 letters from Atlantic City PO. all which I ought to have received when there— Mr. Dick went to the Post Office & I daily reminded to enquire for me— & he did for Mr. Phillips Lee— but not for Mrs S P. or E. B. Lee— here they are today—

In response to my letters about you Father says that Fox said that Paulding wanted you with him in the fall at New York Navy Yard— & that was probably your choice & that "he & Frank need not worry about a steamer for you."[1] The prospect of our home is delicious to me & therefore all I'll do now is to "worry" to get you relieved— which I have done nearly every day for the last two weeks   I'll go to Bethlehem because the prospects *are certain* of battle at no distant day near Washington   I confess to shrinking from the *hearing* of another battle— it is an agony that I'll not endure again without it is from a duty to you my child or Parents— Father has ordered me to stay away! for "*a while*"

I saw a letter this morning to Mr Dick from Ben Farrar[2]   he says the Confederates are on the borders of Mo. with an Army of 50,000 there—[3]   Frémont & Frank are busy organizing an Army to meet these invaders He describes Frank's distress as very great over Cary & Lyon— the first is a blow at our hearthstone— Aunt Maria's boys are our dearest of kin— she was a most devoted Aunt to us in our years of want & her boys were playmates & Bernard[4] & Cary have seem to be worthy sons to such a Mother— He has been so entirely with Frank during the past year of trouble All winter he has feared assasination for Frank & the instances of his watching over & sticking closer than a brother have been many in these our dark days— Frémont has stirred up things in St Louis & given new life there— spending money there in employing the people there to minister to the wants of the Army— the local effect has been "*fine*—" Frémont has plenary powers in the West— & plenty of money[5] & if he & Frank cant take care of Missouri I am mistaken in the men*[6] I only wish I felt as secure that my man Frank was safe

Blair is well & gay— he said you must come quick or he will take his foot away from you— He never fails to wish you back again in our talks about you I'll write again tomorrow by the Connecticut Your devoted Lizzie

1. On August 23, EBL told her husband that her father had assured her: " 'I'll look most jealously after Phils affairs & that he has hopes of getting Welles to turn out of his office some of the drones who have impeded its activity— & when you return you can have a shore or an active station to suit you— nothing will be fixed until you return & it was impossible from the necessities of the Govt & the foreign pressures to call in a single vessel which could stay out."

2. Maj. Bernard G. Farrar, aide de camp in the Missouri state troops.

3. A Missouri state convention had voted to remain in the Union and had declared state offices vacant. On July 31, a Union state government was formed with Hamilton Gamble as governor. At the same time, Gov. Claiborne Jackson and his pro-Confederate administration claimed to represent the state.

4. Bernard Gratz, born in 1822, was the son of Maria and Ben Gratz.

5. In her August 19 letter, EBL asserted: "Certainly never did a nation put *means* in its Government's hands more munificently than this does—."

6. SPL marginal note to *: "Sepr 9. You are mistaken & they are too late & slow. The last Administration did not suit the South better in the then state of affairs than this does in the present. Treason & venality then; greeness & venality now. S. P. Lee."

Bethlehem   August 31, 1861
Dear Phil   I was regaled to day with yours of the 9th & 19th— it was a feast after a long fast   I read them over & over to Blair   he was quite well please with his share of them "said he did say a word to make that boy set the dog on him did we Beck?— who replied that neither of them had spoken at all— Jesup has a little dugout boat— given him by his teacher with a sail on it when Jesup plays with it in the little rill of water near us it is evidently a source of envy on Blairs part— he lends his own play things freely to get a play with it & Jesup is generous about it however Saturday Blair sighed— then after a while said— Tell Papa to make me a little ship— just no bigger than Jesups (the size of this paper) & if he cant do it— I know old Uncle Dick[1] will—" Your promise of toys was very refreshing after such a wish had been uttered— I wrote to Fanny to share with her the comfort of your letters— & I'll write to John Monday for the same reason in part—

Sunday September 1st I went to Church & enjoyed the service even more than Sunday last—[2] after dinner I went to the *Love Feast*— where for the first time I realized how solemn eating & drinking can be made— Men & went around with baskets of *bunns* & mugs of coffee on trays— whilst the choir (one of the finest Ive ever heard) sang chants & hymns some of the last composed for the occasion— it lasted over an hour— to me a very short one— I brought the *bun* home for Blair & drank a part of the coffee (tolerably good). The Germans are without doubt the best musicians in the world— here nine tenths of the houses are two stories (brick) with 4 or six rooms— every house has its piano— & in the afternoon when the days work is done (Nobody has servants) some work the flower garden & others of the family play or practice the piano— There is something vastly attractive to me in the simple enjoyments & thrift of this *village* of *white* people—

Monday I had a letter today from Father saying they were all well "& that until I know what those fellows over in Dixie mean to do, I do not think it advisable for you to come home— I really & firmly believe that the enemy will not dare to cross the River, but if they do, we shall be in the midst of the battlefield & that is where I would not have my young brood— Every thing looks full of war, & *earnestly* & I doubt not that our folks will win wherever they fight for McClellan is a good General & we have the best troops that have ever been seen at the Capitol— Yet the race is not always to the swift nor the battle for the strong So I am clear that it is best for my younglings who can neither run nor fight to keep away from a place where it is possible that both may be necessary"

"I have not had a line from Frank though I got a letter today under his frank from St Louis— He is busy there recruiting his Regt which is to be of Artillery 2000 strong— I supose that Frémont & Frank will not, as force is pouring into them, venture another battle until they are strong enough to win it— & I suspect that then they will only have to chase the enemy not to fight McCulloch[3] who found when he was four to one that he could not hold his ground, nor follow— will not stay to meet a much superior force"

I have counted up the troops as they arrived at St Louis & they have Sixty thousand— Blair is regaining his flesh & complexion— & such spirits!! That are uplifting to me— Every body says he looks like you. Dick. Mary Blair Julia—[4] Jane Aunt Becky— & I see as I've always done your loving looks in his eyes his face dont change to me in the least but he grows tall & more active & boyish— I have got his whole boy outfit in Phil— for winter & to be donned for the first time when you come home to be "Papa's big boy" & he says mamas baby like Uncle Frank is Grand Ma's baby—" Your affectionate Lizzie

1. Uncle Dick was a slave.

2. The prior week, on August 23, EBL had commented: "I went to the Moravian Church— the service was so like that of the Episcopal Church in its Litany & singing

that I was quite at home there— & it proved to me that all Sects what take the Bible as their standard of faith do not disagree— I could be a Moravian without a change scarcely even of Church discipline—."

3. Gen. Ben McCulloch led Confederate troops at Wilson's Creek.

4. Julia Jesup, born 1840, was the daughter of Gen. Thomas Jesup; she was Jane's and Mary's sister.

Bethlehem   September 3, 1861

Dear Phil   I believe your catching the schooner of 250 tons[1] gave me greater satisfaction than the Hatteras conquest— but that is the most delightful victory— nobody hurt on our side & but few on the other— & if we had plenty of big guns— the whole war might be carried through in this style— Mrs. Janey— Nicholson has been searching this village all over for house— & cannot get one for all are occupied— So far as *my* observation goes— out of the shopping streets in Phil— I see no lack of business & prosperity every where I have been   Atlantic City was thronged this place— equally so the manufacturers all busy here & in Phila & see by the many articles that St Louis is doing some business. Frémont is doing all he can to give the people there occupation— & it seems that the Republican supports Frémonts course with zeal

Sept 4th I send as heretofore the papers tho' much discouraged for you have never acknowledged the receipt of any I have sent & they have not been less than a hundred   one a day since you sailed— for no letters can keep one posted like the papers— I have no news from home to day or yesterday & Nicholson nothing of military matters to his wife if he does she keeps it to herself— which I doubt the possibility— Blair came in sucking a great pear just now looking so hearty & happy that I wish I could transmit to you the vision— he is a universal favorite here as everywhere so jolly & good natured that he win his way along so far in life

Sept 5 I see your prize reached New York. I'll get some toys as well as Blair & what is better to me I'll get a letter tomorrow or next day. I thought a great deal about Mrs. Davis last night— of the day she ran out in the street to tell us "Jeff had a congestive chill & she had telegraphed Dr. Miller—" As a wife I pity her with all my heart— Blair in the park playing marbles with some german boys, & if I had spent the summer here he would talk german— I make Becky cultivate them to play with them & but for his cousins here he would do so altogether— but he enjoys his romps with them vastly. he full of play & fun— No news from home or St Louis to day— things seem to getting on better there as our people get stronger   I expect there is a muss between Gamble & Frémont   I am going to write to Jessie   I must hear from Frank— Your affecate Lizzie

1. On August 21, 1861, Lee's ship *Vandalia* captured the schooner *Henry Middleton*, out of Charleston, carrying a cargo of turpentine and rosin.

                                          Bethlehem   September 10, 1861
Dear Phil   No letters from home— & the Armies on the Potomac are still looking each other in the face— each trying to circumvent the other[1] last night I dream the Rebels had taken one of our Forts. & that I was on the Avenue in a scene of great anguish & trouble—   I tell you this to let you see how these terrible times haunt me   I never realized my own feebleness so entirely as now & never struggled more steadily to keep up a cheerful trusting spirit in the mercy of God for I see that when I droop it affects our dear sensitive child & I never chill his tender years with the frosts of my troubles— So I was never as tender to & or more watchful over him in his life— & he is so loving & comforting to me— I am sure much as you love him— his loving ways to me now are sweet indeed   today a gentleman met him on the street & gave him the finest fruit (plum) a perfect stranger— & so it is all the time So many notice him as he goes along in the park & streets

I had a long letter from Aunt Becky today— saying Uncle Ben is better— Frank Etting[2] has an army paymasters place Father got because Aunt asked for it— & she evidently is highly gratified

Sept 11th. I received the longest sort of a *secesh* letter from Fanny She is getting rampant   I shall decline discussion saying I cannot bear to the idea of associating her in my mind with the enemies of my country husband brothers & everything that gives life value to me— & therefore I must try to banish that subject from my mind when talking & thinking of her— She does not give me an item of news of any sort— but from the tone of her letter I infer they are all well— It is a rainy day & Blair has written a brown piece of paper all over as large as half the Herald for a letter to you— he is tired of the rainy day. I must amuse him some

Sept 12— Good news from Ky— she is out for the Union & hope will give Mr. Breckinridge[,] Magoffin[3] their quietess for they are both traitors of the most hypocritical stamp   I see Jessie is at Washington but I have not had a line from there for near a week & I expect Frémont is [in] a peck of trouble about his proclamation—[4] I *do not know* it only *infer* from *signs*— Just returned from a long walk with Mary & our children— The Pleasontons are here— Clem & I talk over Oakland experiences & the contrasts between now & then are certainly striking— we hear Mrs. Jeff. has another Baby[5] & old Jeff is still alive— I see the Richmond papers are beginning to kick at him— I cant pump an item out of the Pleasontons tho' I catch them pumping me all the time I see that Mrs. Pearson's out houses have all been burnt   they say by the soldiers— Majr Nicholson writes that every open space in Washington is now filled with soldiers & I calculate from his & Fathers letter, that we have between 150 to 200 thousand soldiers in & about Washington— There are now 50,000 on the Va side & Nicholson writes that the improved discipline is perfectly wonderful— & that we will have *no* Bull *running* of this Army   God Grant it— The P[leastonton]s asked of our circle & inquire for & send kind words to you Ever your own Lizzie   Clem P says Blair is handsome boy

1. In her September 6 letter, EBL states: "An immense army is being gathered mid way between Harper's Ferry & Washington to be ready for the Confederates anywhere on the Potomac line— Father seems perfectly satisfied so far with McClellan & writes constantly of his great improvement in discipline & every thing else since his installment   I believe they are going to concentrate all their forces— & fight it out at Washington—." She also relayed Maj. Gus Nicholson's opinion that the army was " 'all the time on the eve of battle'— & consequently that Washington is the most excited & yet saddest place in the world—."

2. Frank Marx Etting (1833–90) was the nephew of Edward J. Etting who, in turn, was the nephew of Benjamin and Rebecca Gratz.

3. Kentucky governor Beriah Magoffin (1859–62), an advocate of the Crittenden Compromise, refused calls for troops from both the Union and the Confederacy. In September 1861, he would not cooperate with the state legislature in ordering rebel troops out of the state. In 1862, he resigned his office.

4. Frémont's proclamation of August 30, 1861, freed the slaves and confiscated all property of those in rebellion. The Congressional Confiscation Act of August 6, 1861, affected only that property actually used in rebellion. Lincoln promptly revoked the proclamation.

5. The Davises' new baby, William Howell Davis, was not born until December 16, 1861.

Bethlehem   Sept 17, 1861   *Confidential*
My dear Phil   I return from our jaunt to the mountains this evening   I am grieved & cut to the heart by Frémont's treatment of Frank—[1] Who I see intends to fight it out with him. Were there ever people who were so false to themselves & to others   I can now say with old scotch man "you may shoot noo"— I felt bitterly angry all day— but have held my tongue & it is most seemly never to speak intemperately among strangers—

Sept 18th— I got last night a long letter from Father he says— "he & mother are getting over the feeling provoked by Jessie Frémonts ingratitude   She has proved to be to us what Old Benton[2] proved to be at the close of his life when his inveterate ambition mastered all his faculties— as he was to us & his own children, so Jessie & her man have shown themselves to all who have contributed to put them in a position to make their jealousy oppressive—"

He says he wrote to Jessie before Frank went west that Frank ought to have Frost[3] that he had declined to take a generals place from the administration because he would have to resign his seat in Congress which our friends the party desired him to return for the general military success of the cause— This he thinks alarmed them— Frémont instantly telegraph to the President that he objected to Gambles calling out the state troops— & he treated Gamble with the greatest indignity— who came straight to Washington The President authorized Gamble to raise the state troops & wrote to Frémont to cooperate with the Governor & with these letters Gamble returned—

Meanwhile— Jessie so Frank writes had set up a Court in St Louis in Louis Napoleon fashion— was producing universal discontent— his Italian attaches taking precedence & excluding our leading men from the presence & counsels of Frémont— the soldiers wandering about the streets drunk discipline neglected— while the maladministration of the army concerns seemed as apparent as it had been even in his private affairs. The President sent Meigs and Brother out to see after & try to reconcile matters & put some rein upon Frémonts *"absolutism"* Jessie is here putting all the blame on the Cabinet for the delinquincy in the Western department— She told me that it was the aspirants here for the presidency which prevented the Genl from reinforcing Lyon— which withheld the Tennessee Kny Regiment & this saved Memphis from being taken— & again it was saved by withholding from Frémont the 10 Indiana Regiments In a word they hate & fear Frank & are also hostile to everybody in the administration who is supposed to stand between them & imperial power which is they think to be clutched as easily as martial law by proclamation— I talked 3 hours & sounded her to the bottom her natural secretiveness Benton cunning giving way under the passion I provoked—

Toward the close of our talk Sherman[4] of New York came in I then repeated all the charges she had made against Frank that he might know how she abused him— closing with the last, that Frank had stopped his Frémonts march down the River & had so saved Memphis I then stated what Frank had done to give him his command— what I & Montgomery had done to elevate him in the public eye— what we had done to advance his private fortune— I boring for his claims in Congress— Montgomery securing his property in the Courts & with what special zeal we had pressed his requisitions through the Departments & as She bridled up at this & put on a very *high* look— I told him she saw she was to play the part of Empress Catherine "Not Catherine but Josephine she said— I said you are too imperious for her & too ungrateful for me— You have never made any return for services & you never shall— so I quit her—"

He bids me not to talk about this to any body so I mark it confidential— The matter is ventilated in the papers which I send you

Apo is very near Phila I have concluded to accept Aunt Beckys invitation day after tomorrow instead of next week— & go out to see & comfort Apo with all the attention & kindness I can proffer— the sympathy of all my heart she has I have written to Frank today & will write to her too— Brother has returned I see to Washington & I shall have further accounts from home which I will duly send you— but I somehow feel that you must be on your way home I ding dong about it in ever letter home & also to Comre Paulding. I am exasperated by this ill treatment of you I expect will be as wrinkled as a withered with just vexation of spirit & when I fret I feel I am wicked for when so many are having their dear ones slaughtered in this awful war— I must be thankful for the mercy of life to mine—

The weather here is wet and cold— and Blair & I will be more comfortable in warmer quarters— these are for summer only Mary Blair & Jane have the room with open fireplaces a stove is my abomination The cold is bitter— Blair enjoyed our mountain trip especially the carload of soldiers who came down with us—

Mary hot on the Frémonts tells me how she warned me— I thought many times last night of your saying about *our* tremors if they had been elected in 1856.[5] may be this will be a deliverance as then Frank is certainly clear of all the late bad management in Missouri for he tried his best to get Lyons re-inforced— & did all he could to save him & his gallant men Poor Frank has had a year of great struggles sorrow & suffering— but still he is spared to us & we must labor on to do a faithful part in this dreadful era Mine of doing nothing— when I sigh to be useful to you is one my burdens

Little Janey[6] came to me just now & reproached me for not sending her love to you— She & Blair are great cronies I am sorry to leave them but feel it is best for many reasons For you must come home soon— Blair sends his love & takes your papers letters to the Post Office nearly every day devotedly your Lizzie

1. In her September 19 letter, EBL explained: "Frémont is warring on Lincoln who ordered him to square his proclamation with the law— F refused & bade him do it himself Frank was requested by Lincoln to 'inform him of everything— that went on in the West for Frank it is your home & mine & I can rely on you—' Frémont heard of this & immediately issued an order forbidding any officer to write any criticisms of his Department to Newspapers or to any body— Frank says this order was a cap to fit his case The letters were intercepted & he arrested— 'which is to me a personal benefit.' for nothing can be more easy than to take care of myself in this matter' this whole letter to his wife is only sad about matters in Missouri— but his own affairs seem only to trouble him as it will make her unhappy & vexed— This whole letter is so firm & moderate— cool— about himself— sad about his state— anxious mostly about his wife— that it made me take courage & breathe freer—."

2. Missouri senator Thomas Hart Benton, father of Jessie Frémont and old Jacksonian ally of Francis Preston Blair.

3. Gen. Daniel Marsh Frost was commander of the First Military District of state militia with headquarters in St. Louis. Cooperating with the prorebel Claiborne Jack-

son, Frost commanded at Camp Jackson until May 10 when he was forced to surrender by the Federals. He then joined the Confederate army.

4. Isaac Sherman, wealthy New York businessman, was a close political associate of Nathaniel Banks and had been active in Frémont's 1856 presidential campaign.

5. On the first national Republican ticket in 1856, John Frémont was the presidential candidate.

6. Janey Nicholson was the daughter of Jane Jesup and Augustus Nicholson.

Philadelphia   October 1, 1861
Dear Phil   I have just torn up a letter to you so full of anxieties about your delay in returning home that it was silly— but I do so yearn to have you come that I am no longer reasonable— Yesterday I would not write my usual note of the day because I felt depressed & tho' this entire silence on the Coast ought satisfy me that there is a cause for delay— I still ruminate by night & by day on the why's & wherefores

Majr Schofield[1] spent Sunday at Silver Spring with Father & Mother & tells me they are all well & says Frémont has to act very vigorously to save himself   it is certainly risking matters some & yet it may be right to be patient—[2] Majr S. says he is surrounded with a set of sharpers & all busy plundering the Govt & *doing nothing* else— of course Frank was detrop among such a set & was not slow to see it— Majr S— has gone to West Chester after Apo— just now— & may take her west with him & cannot account for her delay about coming to the city— I fear they are sick— I have taken rooms for her & she was to have been here yesterday at ten oclk

I have been thinking of poor Fanny Hunt a great deal— Genl Gibson died yesterday— her sister is in N Carolina & Brother in our Army— Helen Smith's death makes her essential to the Smiths who are very anxious about their Father—[3] Mrs Steadman[4] was here just now to go spend the day with her Mrs Emory Mrs Gillespie—[5] I could not go— but thought it was a good chance to get news— but feared being pumped myself—

Affairs look gloomy in the West—[6] Kentucky is being invaded with 50,000 so says Mrs White (Mag Woolley)[7]— her 2 brothers are gone with Wm Preston[8] & John Breckinridge to the Con Army & our people *are as usual slow*   Anderson[9] is brave but not efficient I fear & Missouri is equally distressed   Mrs. White made me promise to send her "affectionate remembrances to you that you always called to see her & seemed more her cousin than I— Your kin are ever my best friends so I did not object & told her so   she is very pretty

Blair is out as usual but he looked so handsome rosy & merry this morning I felt more than ever the craving to show him to you— beauty bloom & life itself seems so fleeting in these sad days Majr. Schofield says things will soon take a very decisive shape opposite to Washington— & now is about the time

I ought to have left there— but women are born to obey & therefore tis no use to grumble— Nelly & John go on the even tenor of their ways I dont know *any* people whose routine has been so untouched by the times—

Every thing looks cheerful here   Horace [10] said Chestnut Street looked last eve as gay as ever he saw it— & I can not discover any where in the north one single sign of hard times— All the manufactures are going   I see no more poor in the streets than usual & wherever I have been I seen nothing but a busy— prosperous people   plenty to eat, to wear, & to do Even the cotton factories are spinning wool— the Iron mongers growl but that they always do & yet their steam pipes puff all day & night— & at Bethlehem kept me awake many an hour— There is less extravagance in dress so they say but I think I never saw women look *so fine*— Every body is knitting for the soldiers tis the *fashion*— I am a great teacher in the art   Aunt Becky even is a pupil— she is so good kind to your boy & your devoted Lizzie

1. John M. Schofield, major in the First Missouri Volunteers and first lieutenant of the First Artillery, served as General Lyon's acting adjutant general at Wilson's Creek.

2. On October 3, EBL reported that Charles Steedman had written his wife, "Frémont was 'odiously incompetent'— from all he hears & is condemned by every body."

3. Richard Smith was a Washington banker. Helen Smith was his daughter, and Fanny Hunt was a relative living with the Smith family.

4. Sarah Bishop married Charles Steedman in 1843. Her husband was a commander in the navy on blockade duty. Their home, Tarresdale, was twelve miles from Philadelphia.

5. Elizabeth Gillespie, wife of Archibald Gillespie, formerly of the Marine Corps. Mrs. Emory was Matilda Bache Emory, wife of William H. Emory. She was called Tilly.

6. The navy as well as the army had their problems in the West, as EBL wrote on September 27 that Charles Steedman "says there is [not] an officer connected with that Western flotilla worth his salt but Foote— the rest are *retired* 'resuscitated gentry— who will disgrace the Service in the West—.'"

7. Margaret Howard Woolley, daughter of Sarah Howard Wickliffe and Aaron Kitchell Woolley, married Peter A. White in 1856. Her brother Robert Wickliffe Woolley served on the staff of Gen. William Preston. Her brother Frank W. Woolley was a student at the Maryland Military Institute.

8. William Preston, Kentucky congressman (1852–56) served as Buchanan's minister to Spain from 1858 to 1860. In September 1861, he joined the Confederate army, serving under Albert Sidney Johnston.

9. Brig. Gen. Robert Anderson, who had commanded the federal army at Fort Sumter and now commanded the Department of Cumberland, was ordered to establish headquarters at Lousiville and organize the Union effort in Kentucky.

10. Horace Moses was Sara Moses Joseph's brother; their aunt was Rebecca Gratz. They were EBL's first cousins by marriage.

Philadelphia   October 7, 1861

Dear Phil   I was surprised to find how much I was ahead of time in my dates in my last letter   I was 6th of Oct. Well I wish the time was all gone that had to elapse 'ere you return home   I got a letter from Father saying that the order had been sent to the Comre in charge of the squadron[1] six weeks ago to send you in port & yet you are not here— & I have not heard a word since 19th of Augt

I have just read Frémonts charges against Frank— they are puerile & would never have got in to the Frémonts power but for the want of a right reserve on on the part of Brother & Father—[2] Frank may well say save me from my friends. he has written I hear a furious letter to Brother in which he evidently feels as I think he has a right to do   Father was most incautious in his talk with Jessie— & Brother more than followed his example— his telegram to Frémont made me mad. I dont what it did to Frank—

Oct 8th Late last— I received this telegraph "Have seen yr Father there is no cause of anxiety— the last vessel up spoke the Vandalia" G. V. Fox Washn Oct 7   So You are still on watch at Charleston & hard as it is tis a relief to know even that about you after so many long long days & nights of anxiety about you— Father says they expect you at the Dept daily to arrive So I must hope & pray & possess my soul with patience enough to be a comfortable inmate to these kind friends where I shall remain until you come, tho I have been here over a week indeed two of them— Aunt wont listen to my taking lodgings as I did last summer when she had the Mordecais[3] with her   says I am a comfort and Blair an enjoyment to her— Every body praises him for his gentle cheerful ways & he is a universal pet—

No letter about Frank today   It is rumored that Banks will be superseded by McCall[4] & that Frémont will be given a little more rope— Butler & Stringham only did half their duty at Hatteras so both are laid up in their homes[5] Indeed they will soon have an Army Navy in young & I hope efficient hands— No letter yet from Apo. I will keep this open in hopes Cousin Mira will have some tidings— I think G. Alexander the Dicks & Mama Alexander[6] will winter here— Mary Blair too thinks of taking a house here to share it with Mrs. Sitgreaves & Julia—[7] Jany is now in Washn to see if her husband has to go off on a secret expedition— Dick Wainwright[8] has got the Command of 500 marines— whilst Nicholson & Russel[9] are taking it easy in Washington— I suppose Dick W. is wanted on ship & Nicholson has to go to the field— I hear that John & Nelly are well   that Mrs. Bayard Smith[10] is threatened with Fort Lafayette— & is quite repentent—

Blair says let me send my myself   Becky says Mrs. Alexander has received no letter from Apo today & the latest tidings from there about Frank was that he was making himself comfortable at the Barracks— His Regt is stationed not far from there— he will not get much comfort out of Mr Dick   I never saw the little man so blue as he was yesterday But I dont agree with him I think our affairs on the mend on a great scale & Lincoln tho slow is a good true man & is doing a good work for his country & earning great renown for himself His cool way of doing things will I hope teach the Blairs a lesson not to rush on at things or people so violently I feel as if we were possessed about the Frémonts— & can only console myself by thinking— that a poet & a General are things rare to find & a parting over leaders is common enough Ever yr devoted Lizzie B. Lee

1. Louis M. Goldsborough was appointed to the command of the North Atlantic Blockading Squadron in September 1861.

2. On September 20, after Frémont had arrested Frank Blair for insubordination, Montgomery Blair wrote Frémont a conciliatory letter and enclosed a copy of a September 1 letter from Frank to his brother. Frank's letter expressed regret at Frémont's apparent lack of ability in military matters but did not condemn the general. Frémont ordered Frank's release, but Frank was furious. On September 26, wanting to bring Frémont to court martial, Frank preferred formal charges against Frémont, and Frémont arrested Blair for a second time. The controversy finally ended when Lincoln removed Frémont from the western command.

3. The Mordecai family was related to the Gratz family by an intricate web of marriages.

4. Brig. Gen. George Archibald McCall commanded a division under General Patterson, but he did not supersede Banks.

5. The army-navy attack on Fort Hatteras, August 26–27, was the first Civil War combined operation. Benjamin Butler and Silas Stringham commanded the successful attack.

6. Mama Alexander was Mrs. Mira Madison Alexander, widow of Andrew Jonathan Alexander and mother of both Franklin Dick's wife, Mira, and Apo Blair.

7. Lucy Ann Jesup married Lorenzo Sitgreaves in 1854. He graduated from West Point in 1827.

8. Richard Wainwright, career naval officer, was commanding at Fort Ellsworth and was ordered to take five hundred seamen to A. H. Foote at Cairo, Illinois.

9. Maj. William Russell, paymaster of the U.S. Marine Corps.

10. Henrietta Henley, daughter of Commodore John D. Henley, married Jonathan Bayard H. Smith in 1842.

Philadelphia   October 14, 1861
Dear Phil I have sent so many letters not heard of since[1] that I will not send the enclosed to Old Point— but by Lt Barnes[2] whose good offices I can obtain thro Miss Susan Hays[3] his betrothed whose acquaintance I made at Bethlehem & as he will return the letter to me thro her if he does not meet you I'll send one of the photographs I had taken for you to go by Comre Dupont—[4] Who I afterwards found had left this city 'ere I reached it I found Mrs Hays & her sisters[5] (all daughters of Comre Banbridges most charming acquaintances— at Bethlehem & Atlantic city—

I shall return home day after tomorrow if nothing happens to prevent Father having sent his permission last week but Blair was not well— having another attack of *worms* & Dr Hays[6] thinking it best for me to remain to let him watch the affects of the medicine he gave which has acted very effectively & the child tho pale & thin is now entirely well & I hope will soon regain his roses in the pines of his native place— I also hoped Mr. Dick would go with me but he has postponed his movements so Becky Blair & I will take up our march alone— Horace put us on the Cars here— & Henry meets us at them in Washington— Aunt Becky is very loth to have us go but I would gladly have returned ten weeks ago— if I could have obtained Father's permission & at last it is a reluctant consent but I feel so wretchedly homesick heartsick I must go & may take some joy in Blair's happy antics & my Parents kindnesses to him & their own forlorn child who may find something to do— which is ever my remedy for misery Here I find knitting socks for soldiers only makes thought as busy as my fingers— but not about the knitting— Apo writes today that it is certain now that Price[7] has escaped Frémont out generalled him & that he will be superseded— Mr. Cameron is now out there— Jessies part in this matter has disappointed me sorely— Things which I had learnt to believe about her husband made me think him unreliable— but only added to my pity & affection for her— I am now convinced that in countenancing & covering his sins she has shared & been degraded by them— & yet I can see in her efforts to elevate him & excite his ambition a struggle to win him from his grovelling nature—

Our news from Kentucky is cheering— the people are rising there en masse to defend their State In front of Washington— Our troops are undergoing the drill & awaiting attack & making a slow advance— They are some times ordered in battle array several times a week— but *tis all* for practice— every thing is done of that sort to enure our troops to battle or the idea of it— Some here have been certain of a battle today— but it has not come off— & I expect I shall yet be in the sound of those guns so long avoided & dreaded by me but I will endure that to be home now for I am a weary sad wanderer

Blair wants me to send his picture in pants but I'll keep that as I must surprise you when you come back with *that display* I have only got two left— one for you & one for myself— out of the dozen— but of the enclosed I have plenty of my dozen to risk the loss of the enclosed— Ever yr devoted Lizzie

Oct 15. All well & I hope to go home tomorrow—

1. EBL began her October 11 letter: "I have crossed my knees & wished & wished all this day long for a letter from you & none came & I nearly lost my faith in Old Hickory's way of wishing to get a thing—."

2. Lt. John S. Barnes served aboard USS *Wabash* and later became SPL's chief of staff for the North Atlantic Blockading Squadron.

3. Susan Hayes was the daughter of Susan Bainbridge Hayes and Thomas Hayes.

4. Capt. Samuel F. Du Pont, commandant of the Philadelphia Navy Yard, was appointed commander of the South Atlantic Blockading Squadron on September 18.

5. Commodore William Bainbridge's daughters were: Susan Parker Bainbridge, who married Thomas Hayes in 1825; Lucy Ann Bainbridge, who married Ashbel G. Jaudon in 1833; Louisa Alexina Bainbridge, who married Henry K. Hoff in 1838; and Mary Taylor Bainbridge, who married Charles B. Jaudon in 1849.

6. Isaac Hays, Philadelphia physician related to the Gratz family, was a leading ophthalmologist and a founder of the American Medical Association in 1847. His mother was Benjamin Gratz's sister.

7. Sterling Price had been governor of Missouri (1853–57) and was a major general of the Confederate militia in Missouri. On September 20, federal forces surrendered Lexington, in the northwest part of Missouri, to rebel Missourians led by Price. Frémont was castigated for not sending reinforcements. Price and his army could not hold the town and were soon retreating to the south, with Frémont in slow pursuit.

Philadelphia October 16, 1861

Dear Phil When at dinner yesterday I received the following from Father "I have your letter fixing your return for Wednesday— About that time I think the greatest battle ever fought on this continent will be brought to issue— All our side of the River is for most part stript of Troops & the white tents which yesterday covered the hills around Arlington with their snow, have during the night melted away in darkness— Several days since McClellan had driven a wedge of his force into the enemys column opening the way out to the Leesburg turnpike with the design evidently of cutting off the Communication between Beauregard & Johnston—"

["]Frank, Tilly tells me, stands better today than ever before in Missouri I think he will ultimately triumph over Frémont— The latter has set up for himself & Frank says it is very doubtful whether he would ever obey an order of recall from the President— He addresses himself to the foreign force in his Army & to the abolition horde in the north & on this anti patriotic party which he is building up he relies for support in a candidacy for the next Presidency or to resist an order of supercession—" This was written in Washington— Monday Oct 14th—

I received a letter this morning from Apo who says "people here are in better spirits Cameron & Thomas[1] will be here this morning— We are all hoping they are coming to call a Court Martial on Frémont— What rich developments it would bring out His expedition is now the laughing stock of the whole Country— Price has made good his escape to the South West. The expense & fuss of Frémonts grand move are for nothing— However it has been a grand affair— He travels with a grand cuisine & his fine travelling carriage— Jessie went to Jefferson in a special train & saw the Army off Frank is in better spirits & well— tho every day brings its trials— for all the homeless houseless refugees come to him to pour out their Sorrows— & he seems to take it to himself. Yesterday a soldier came in from Springfield, one of poor dear Carys men He was shot at the same moment with Cary & was with him until he died They were shot at eight oclk & dear Cary lived until two in the afternoon the man was only wounded in the leg so was able to give him water put a shade over him— It touched me to hear the man speak of Cary He was so beloved by his company. Frank say no man ever did his part more nobly"— This letter was dated Oct 11th

Cousin Mira got one at the same time dated Oct 12th saying— "Genl Cameron told Frank today every thing would be straight— Thomas & he went to Sedalia to day to remove the Genl I suppose— Frémont is sticking in the mud somewhere there— & Price in Arkansas" She mentions people calling on her who were *"too secesh"* last spring to speak when she met them— The telegraph tells of Camerons return— from Sedalia— he has stopped all of Frémonts works around St Louis & Jefferson— & the payt of all contracts until carefully examined into—

I telegraphed yesterday to Father that I would await the grand Battle until Friday day after tomorrow When I'll go home nothing happening to prevent Blair is wofully disappointed but is good natured about it as he is about every thing— He looks bright & well to day with some color back again— I hear the Wabash is to sail on Friday & I'll send papers & letter— today & tomorrow by her— I have sent them daily (papers to Old Pt. & letters three times a week— but not a line have I received for two months from you— I cogitate all sorts of reasons for this— but it all ends in making me very unhappy

Aunt Becky wishes me to give up going home until this impending battle is fought out but I think that with each movement in the advance of McClellan a battle has been anticipated & he fortifies as he goes & is not likely to fall back again upon Washington as he takes Railroads along with the Army— as well as waggons for its supplies— I think the Rebels are retreating to Richmond for winter— they are without clothing & must soon be in better quarters than tents— consequently they just keep up a show as at Munson Hill[2] to cover their Retreat but this will be ascertained by Friday & by that discovery I'll shape my movements for you see by Fathers letter he dont want me there during a fight. This movement of troops mentioned in his letter is not in the morning papers at all at last accts by them. Munson's Hill was the last one occupied by the Union Army— Mr. Dick is here still busy with George Alexanders invention[3] of which Father is not hopeful as to its adoption—

You will see by the papers that Genl Jones (Walter is dead the papers notice him with marked respect— he was 85 yrs old— I hear that Mrs. Roger Jones had to take the oath to get her pension but that she talks the bitterest *secesh* All of her sons are South except Roger who is with John in the Adgt Generals Office— He is perfectly loyal— tho sad by the course of his brothers— how blessed we are in having all of our brothers with us   it is a source of daily thankfulness to me—

In nothing would southern people feel the fatality of their cause than in its consequences to the North   I sometimes wish they could be uplifted & see with their own eyes how it goes on rejoicing in plenty & prosperity   I think they would lay down their arms & give up their darkies & do likewise. Chesnut Street never was more brilliant in beauty & apparel than yesterday— & I see far less than ever before of beggars & such like evidences of suffering & poverty— & As to the Country— there is no indication of war save in the passage of troops & the partings with friends & now all that is over it is only in eagerness for news & *in talk* you hear or realize that there is a war— You see now but few uniforms in the streets here   Blair is out or would send his love & kiss to Papa with that of your devoted Lizzie

1. Lincoln had sent Secretary of War Simon Cameron and Brig. Gen. Lorenzo Thomas, adjutant general, to Missouri to investigate Frémont's activities.
2. Munson's Hill, Virginia, was evacuated by rebels September 28.
3. George Alexander, Apo Blair's brother, had become involved in an ill-fated cartridge business. He claimed the cartridges could be soaked by water and still function.

                                        Silver Spring   October 19, 1861
My dear Phil   We reached here last night after a very comfortable ride from Philadelphia. I saw there the Secesh Army was on the retreat— in the morning & so I started for my house telegraphed to have the carriage at the Depot— I was met there by Fathers carriage & brother's too— brother did not know that Father was in town— so sent for me & one of his clerks to go home with me as he was too busy to go with me— I found all well— but my Parents are looking thin & wizened by anxiety and distress— they were overjoyed in getting us back gain

Father tells me that Cameron went out to relieve Frémont but was begged out of it by F.[1] Frank writes in great trouble as to the result— it seems that Ft— is an opium eater & is really imbecile—[2]

Blair slept well & is the most joyous little darling you ever saw— I had great relief in reaching the Depot last evening our dear little Phil[3] has been ill with dyptheria— & was for a long time very ill— but is now convolescing & out of all danger—

I find *no feeling of security here*— there is immense hosts gathered to settle this dreadful conflict & I fear ours is not yet strong enough to cope boldly with the enemy. I shall take flight upon the first reverse— in the meantime I have vast deal to do in my own little orbit— In sober truth I am so glad to get back home that— I felt no shudder when I heard the big guns this morning— only said tis but practice & went to sleep again— I am the most forlorn of mortals away from you & my Parents— I sometimes think I am ungrateful when I have such a comfort in Blair that I should repine so much for you & home— Wherever I have been too so much of kindness, loving hospitality has been extended to us— Every thing here is beautiful— the luxuriant growth of summer & fall united to the freshness of spring— My flower garden is just a vast bouquet nothing ever equalled it here before— I find the servants all well— poor Mary very sad— from the death of Sarah & her baby— she died of *her freedom*

Father says you had received permission by Ringgold[4] to come north & report to the Dept I cant understand this & getting no letters from you by the Flag or Wabash Father says he forwarded a letter from you to me not ten days ago— I never received it. but wrote on hearing this last evening to Horace to hunt it up at the Post Office for me— Never in my honeymoon days did I sigh to hear from you as much— I imagine you have been sick & all sorts of fears about your health from such long confinement to your ship— tho I dont say so to anybody

Saturday night— Father brought news from the city— no decision yet about Frémont Seigel Sturgis & Hunter[5] will all strive with their divisions to ship Price out of Missouri so as to get F's place so I am in hopes that the state will be cared for well after all No news as to where the 40 ships sailed from New York— I sent you letters by the Wabash & I have a suspicion that it goes to Beaufort & thence to Charleston and that you know it & that is why you wont come away— I am pressing a great many questions fruitlessly as yet—

Father has done well in farming, he has sold his grass— both growing & cut. has sold his wheat & made 1,500 dollars which is a great turn out for Silver Spring— he has grazed army beeves— altogether is in great farming feather— Father says Genl Scott is very Sick— he is getting dropsical & very old— when I compare Aunt Becky with any other old person I marvel the more at her great preservation both she & Horace urged me to return if there was any discomfort in remaining here but as yet I am too happy in getting back home to be troubled by any dangers sixteen miles off— & over the River—

Tomorrow I shall go to the Camp service opposite to Colclazers[6] where the 10th Mass Regt is encamped on Carberrys[7] place who built a fine stone house which blew down a little while since— The Fort just around the new brick church at little Emory is quite formidable and the aspect of the country around there is altered by cutting away the woods— I cannot go in to the city it smells so bad I will not take Blair there & Becky must go to see her friends— but Ill send Nelly some of my flowers & learn how Phil is who continued to improve when I heard last— Ever your affectionate Lizzie

1. On October 22, EBL reported: "Cameron reports for the removal of Frémont as he finds things worse than disclosed by Frank—."

2. In another reference to Frémont on October 22, EBL explained: "I never could account for this utter failure— but I hear now that Frémont's seclusion & torpor is accounted for by the fact of his being an opium eater— I cannot vouch for this rumor tho assured by one of his Staff & confidants."

3. Francis Phillips Lee, born May 8, 1856, was the son of John and Ellen Hill Lee.

4. Capt. Cadwalader Ringgold, commanding frigate *Sabine*.

5. Maj. Samuel D. Sturgis withdrew federal troops from battle at Wilson's Creek. Some thought the Union might have won the battle if they had continued the fight. On September 9, Maj. Gen. David Hunter was sent to advise Frémont and finally superseded him on November 2.

6. Either Daniel or Jacob Colclazer, who owned land not far from the Blairs' Silver Spring farm, near the Seventh Street Pike.

7. Thomas Carberry, former mayor of Washington and president of Bank Metropolis, lived north of the city on Seventh Street Pike. M. C. Emery owned property not far from Rock Creek Church.

Silver Spring   October 23, 1861

Dear Phil   I went today after Father & Mother had started off to the City with one of the Officers wives to the Camp of the Mass 10th on an errand of kindness & was fully repaid by getting a look at a morning paper and there seeing your arrival announced made it a jubilee to me—[1] Oh how thankful I am that you are at last come— & that joys may come together   I got yours of the 3rd of October which followed me back from Phila   Your coming brings me ten fold relief   I believe the huge expedition just fitted out is meant to attack Charleston—[2] 40 ships have sailed from New York— & I thought you were delayed to be there   All this was suspicion— I dont *know* anything about it— I have written & sent letters to Old Point Comfort regularly & there must be some five or six awaiting your arrival   One went yesterday.

We are all well & I would go to New York to meet you but I want you to come here— I want you to get the command of the Yard here— You have more rank & right to it than Dalghren[3] & I think you can get it— Any rate no harm to try   I got & opened a letter to you from Mr Quackenbush[4] wishing to help him to a gun boat— I'll keep until you come— I would go to the city to be there to greet you but our little Phil has had dyptheria— & it is undoubtedly contagious & I can[not] risk my child & Father says he cant risk his so I've not been there since my return— he was better today when Mother went to enquire for him— So you must come to us here— until our plans are settled for the winter—

I feel such comfort in your return that it is beyond all expression for the dire cloud of battle which hung over us for so many long months is about to burst upon & I feel as if I had somebody to take care of me— I staid away from home as long as I could but grew unhappy about my Parents & you too & came here feeling that I could easily retreat in case adversity to our Army which I pray God forbid I am happier here even under these circumstances than at the north— tho every body was as kind as my heart could wish— Blair is now well but had another worm attack which has made him pale— & thin— but as I will say no more as this may pass you on the way here All well & crave the sight of your face   Your devoted   Lizzie

1. Lee left *Vandalia* at Hampton Roads on October 22.
2. Actually, the fleet was en route to Port Royal.
3. Comdr. John A. Dahlgren had been appointed commandant of Washington Navy Yard upon the resignation of Franklin Buchanan, April 22, 1861.
4. Lt. Stephen P. Quackenbush had joined the navy in 1840. In July 1862, he was promoted to lieutenant commander, and he made rear admiral in 1884.

Silver Spring   December 15, 1861
Dear Phil   Yesterday was spent in visitings with Mary Martin the bride,[1] & other receptions & among others I intended seeing Mrs. Lincoln but staid too long at Carrolls[2] from all I can see & hear McClellan does not tell his secrets now to any body & that is a real comfort to me—

Our neighbor regiments are all building huts for winter & I am glad we are to have such respectable neighbors as the 10th Mass[3] Last night three Captains seranaded Miss Martin & took hot coffee afterwards & enjoyed it quite as much I hope as the musicians did something stronger— Blair was wide awake & was a very important body on the occasion & as he was to be roused I was glad it came before his bedtime   he is a great wood sawyer & I have many times thanked you for the saw it will be an invaluable rainy day resource—

Mr Doolittle[4] & Frank are to sleep here tonight— and discussed the Contraband question at length— they agree in their purpose— but not in the way of attaining it— Mr Thad Stevens[5] stumped it up to Frank (who now sits on the Democratic side)— said bitterly— you have deserted the Republican party—" "Well says Frank if so— I go with a majority of its members— who vowed with me to support the Constitution Union about which we care more than we do the niggers—" He is deep in a report on their deportation—

I went this morning over to the Camp to attend service— the sermon was good & the singing very enjoyable   Blair went with Mary Jim & I— & behaved very well   I think his health is now steadily improving— & this continued bright weather is a blessing to him— When putting him to sleep just now he told me to "*write my love to Papa*— & tomorrow morning Ill put in a kiss for him—" he talks about you constantly you & the saw are at this moment his themes of talk—

The shooting of the deserter yesterday has been the only army event— since you left— it makes us all shudder— Mr. Doolittle said to night we are in a great *crisis* at this moment not only on the field— but even a greater one

in the Capitol— which means— that about 30 abolitionists are rampant—
& they will fall as dead— in their present schemes as did old John Brown[6]
their prototype Mr. D. went to see you at No 4 Presidents Square— regrets
not meeting you & is most kind in his talk about you— Monday   all well   yrs
affecate Lizzie

1. Emma Twiggs Mason married Francis Wheaton of the U.S. army. She was the
daughter of George Mason and Margaret Hunter. After Mason died, his widow married
Don Carlos Buell in 1859.

2. Probably William Thomas Carroll, clerk of the U.S. Supreme Court.

3. The Tenth Massachusetts Regiment, under the command of Col. Henry I.
Briggs, had been stationed in Washington since July and continued there until March
1862.

4. James R. Doolittle, Republican senator from Wisconsin (1857–69), agreed with
the Blairs and Lincoln on a moderate approach to the slavery issue.

5. Thaddeus Stevens, radical Pennsylvania congressman, had introduced a resolution calling for freeing all slaves "who shall leave their masters, or who shall aid in
quelling the rebellion." The Democrats responded by offering a resolution to reaffirm
the Crittenden Resolution which had promised noninterference with slavery. Stevens
successfully led the fight to block its passage, but twenty-six conservative Republicans
had voted with the Democrats.

6. Abolitionist John Brown had been hanged for his ill-fated attempt to free slaves
at Harpers Ferry in 1859.

Silver Spring   December 17, 1861
Dear Phil   I never felt more gloomy than I did last night so I did not inflict
the mood upon you— as I know you were undergoing the same depression
when you read the last dispatches from England[1] so Ill not give you a double
portion of *the sensation* & have tried to get rid of it myself by hard work   I wish
you could see our hard working boy & his wheelbarrow of wood which he has
all sawed up finely—

Gen & Mrs. Lander[2] have just paid us a visit   She told me it was ascertained that the Confederates in Fairfax outnumbered us still— that they were
certainly & steadily approaching our lines— between Mt. Vernon & Alexandria— she is sprightly & plain & was formerly an actress Miss Davenport—
He has a fine face & is very impatient of the restraints inflicted by his wound   I
am busy gardening. the weather is perfection   Mary Martin is now at Franks
preliminary to a start for Nassau— I feel great sympathy for her but it is a great
relief to me to have her go on my own account first & then for herself as I am
quite convinced it is her only chance of life—

Wednesday Decr 18— Ellen Hill is out here today— so Ill seize the chance
of getting this mailed this morning whilst I was washing up the cups to give
Vincent time to ride Blair a private walked in & asked me if he might play on

the piano I consented— & never enjoyed a performance more— he played exquisitely

There is a good deal temper among the John *Brownites* in Congress. Frank is going act moderately & in keeping with the message which Mr. Crittenden says suits Ky Blair is by me & sends Papa (X) a kiss just where he put it— I must go to the city to morrow for Christmas gifts— for Blair & the other children— I do hope you will get back here to spend Christmas with your boy & your affectionate Lizzie

1. The United States became embroiled in international controversy when Charles Wilkes, commanding USS *San Jacinto,* stopped the British mail packet *Trent* on November 8, 1861, and took off James Mason and John Slidell, Confederate agents to London and Paris, respectively.

2. Gen. Frederick W. Lander had been appointed brigadier general of volunteers. In July he took over a brigade of Gen. C. P. Stone's division on the upper Potomac. Mrs. Lander, the former Jean Margaret Davenport, an actress, married Lander in October 1860.

Silver Spring   December 23, 1861

Dear Phil I sent you a letter without a signature for the first time since our engagement days— but I intended to add a line but Frank was off early & in the rain so to get it off I had just to enclose it hurriedly— I hear that the Donkey is forwarded by Mrs. Alexander as she could do so for thirteen dollars & that is scarcely more than it would cost to take care of it for six months— I would rejoice to have it by Xmas— but Blair is content without it— but is asking me all the time to take to the city— he has not been there since you left & I think he connects it with the loss of your visits here & seeing in the city at any rate I feel as if it were so—

Decr 24— I went to finish my Christmas gifts up & to my amaze found invitations for Father Mother You & I— to dine at the White House I do wish you would come as I have to go— Mother has some rhumatism & will & indeed cannot go so Father insists that I must particularly since you are a post Captain— That will force you to return here— as two post Captains will be too much in one expedition wont it?

Our people are for arbitration & will appeal to France— but England takes offense upon a technacality— because Wilkes[1] did [not] take the Trent in port— & prove the characters of Mason & Slidell whoever— contrabands or political refugees— is the point they make & on that insist upon their re-linquishment— S.[2] *will back down flat*— but what the P. will do is not yet known our set urge arbitration on this & other international points— *France is with us*— & when I remember yr accounts of their navy & ships I take hope & comfort— but I'll confess myself a lonesome sad woman this even when fixing out my boys Christmas pleasure— so many of my joys in him are lone-some— but he is getting stronger & better daily & you were well when I last heard— so I must & ought to be thankful—

Nelly is very joyous over her little tribe & her preparations for them— Julia Turner[3] is to spend Christmas with her— & they hope for a merry time— & as our darling will rouse me early I must say good night & God bless you   Ever your devoted Lizzie

1. EBL felt no great admiration for Wilkes and wrote on December 19, "to judge the tree by its fruit no agent of Dixie could have done so well to embroil us as Wilkes."

2. EBL expressed a stronger opinion of Secretary of State William Seward in her December 21 letter: "S. is an arrant coward & will back down when bullied if he is allowed to do so by the country—."

3. Julia Turner was the daughter of Henry and Julia M. Hunt Turner of St. Louis. In 1869, she married William Hill Lee.

Silver Spring   December 30, 1861

Dear Phil   Father had a most doleful letter from Mr. Dick   the Govt has ordered Seven full Regts of Cavalry into Missouri from Ill & Inda— So with what is there now Genl Halleck[1] will have the hundred thousand to hold the state— & take Arkansas if he is smart— As to Kentucky I have no fears— Uncle Ben & all the sources I hear from are satisfied with the Ps message— & the Secesh have gone off (the men except about Louisville & they are trades people who miss their southern customers— but are not over willing to help them— Poor Missouri has been most wofully maltreated— First Harney— then Frémont— but Halleck may deliver her from her tormentors— It is strange but a week ago Frank said that the war had developed Price's military genius & that he had more than any other secesh— Genl Johnston Beaure-gard not excepted but he said also that the Loyalty of the Republic was a sure sign that the tide had turned—

The English affair exercised us all so last week that we are now in a state of Collapse & reaction— but things will only be quickened up by it— our Navy & Forts *will now be put on a big* war footing & that too without loss of time— It is felt here that England wants *"the plantations of the South"* as a dependancy & will fight for it— After this week in which *plans & bills* are maturing you will see much stir & if the Cabinet dont come up to it— Congress will be after them   the members are in an explosive condition & must let off in some way— There is a sense of *injury* that is fierse & Wilkes will get his due share of it & that's not a small one in spite of his vote of thanks which he did well to hurry up   he couldnt get it now—

We are all well & the Smallpox panic is dying out— Our neighbor Regt dont receive or pay visits— Sent one case to the hospital & are in quarantine on that account— Genl Couch[2] is very careful to have this whole division vacinated & takes every precaution to avoid spreading it— Blair was riding today & walking— he is out even in this late cold weather from ten until dark save when eating— but still coughs   I never saw him look brighter or more gay— R Dale Owen[3] dined here today & George Alexander to dry cartridges— & I saw what you said on the explosive point but I said "*nauthing*"— Mr. Owen talked well— but nothing new—

Blair creeps in my bed now every night about 2 olk to *pat Mama*— I am going to the city tomorrow & shall report there   I hear that Mr. F[ox] says you will be here soon— I am entirely ignorant of yr movements or purpose He told me to expect to hear from you in 15 days after you left (as you promised to write) which he said had then passed— but which I told wanted 3 days more of the time— I enjoyed yr last letter *its points* were to the point Blair said this morning "Good morning Papa— I love you next to Mama"— Ever your affectionate Lizzie

1. Gen. Henry W. Halleck succeeded Frémont in command of the Department of Missouri, which included Illinois, Iowa, Minnesota, Wisconsin, Missouri, Arkansas, and western Kentucky.

2. Gen. Darius Nash Couch, a graduate of the U.S. Military Academy, had resigned from the service in the 1850s. He joined the volunteers in July 1861 as colonel of the Seventh Massachusetts Infantry and within weeks was promoted to brigadier general of volunteers.

3. Robert Dale Owen, social reformer, emancipationist, and son of the founder of the utopian experiment at New Harmony, Indiana. From May 1861 to February 1863, he was under commission from the governor of Indiana to purchase arms in Europe for state troops.

4

"This wicked Secession Conspiracy!
how many hearts it has mourning & broken—"

March 3, 1862

WAR IS A TERRIBLE INTERRUPTION in the lives of participants, but it does not stop the progression of the young through childhood. In the first months of 1862, Blair and most of his cousins suffered through a siege of measles, and Elizabeth gave regular health bulletins on the progress of each. Upon completion of his new steamer in New York, Phillips Lee left immediately for duty in the Gulf of Mexico under the command of David G. Farragut.

Much to the relief of Unionists, federal armies won important victories in the West. Forts Henry and Donelson fell in February, opening the state of Tennessee to invasion; in early March the *Monitor* and CSS *Virginia* battled to a draw in Hampton Roads, relieving the naval threat on the Potomac; at the same time the Northern victory at Pea Ridge, Arkansas, ended rebel chances in Missouri and the Union forces began to advance down the Mississippi to Island Number 10. McClellan, commanding the Army of the Potomac, moved south to begin the Peninsular Campaign. Stonewall Jackson's activities in the Shenandoah Valley lent a disquieting note to an otherwise optimistic outlook.

Silver Spring   January 29, 1862

My Dear Phil   Blair & I returned here late last evening— The young ladies got in so late that John was loth to have us return over our bad roads but we got here safe Blair quite happy to get back for he said to me when I was fixing to come— "Make haste Mama— Now that Papa is gone I am hungry to see Grandpa & Grandma"— & today he brought me a book of Bible stories & told me to tell him about Daniel— as Florida read it to him Sunday   I did so & was dilating on the necessity of prayer to God— if we wished to be happy in this world & the next too— & said you see how earnest Daniel was for he prayed three times a day.—" "Well I will pray a dozen times a day to get God to bring my Papa back to me, "well & happy—" the words I have taught him to use in prayer for you— The application of this Bible history gave evidence

of a good heart & head too— Vincent took him a long ride & he is very well
& bright tonight— The mud makes walking impossible in the Country— I
found Mother sick & worn out　Mrs. Andrew[1] & Father went to this [the city]
today— brought me good tidings from Nelly & Arthur first has no measels &
the last getting well

There is a rumor that we are to have Govr Banks for our Secy. he & his
wife[2] are in the city & he in *Citizens attire*— Hales report[3] may oust our grey-
beard[4] & our condition cannot I think be injured by any change The Mortars
for Foote are there ere this— so a movement there must soon come off The
Sewards & Mrs. Lincoln have invitations out for Soirees— no dancing. I
enclose Mr. Walshs letter[5] which I found in my drawer today when I got it
opened—

Jany 30th was a rainy day　nobody put their noses out but Blair who for
variety when running on the porch got an umbrella & went down to the
spring— Mrs. Andrew I fear will get very weary of her country visit— The girls
all take flight tomorrow— but her movements are dubious— I try to entertain
her but find it laborious　the fault may be more my own than hers— She is a
genuine Yankee in inquisitiveness— but is evidently a well bred woman— &
one accustomed to indulgence from all at her home— I saw in the Eve Post a
notice on "Physical Culture— by a Dr. Taylor—[6] who— has your idea about
not over exerting children muscles— being hardened & growth stopped by
it— Ill get the book— I would have sent a letter to day but had no chance

Friday Jany 31 Blair came to me just now & begged me to teach him to
read— I repeated your wishes about it & that quieted him for a while— but
he now says you will like to see him "so smart" when you get back He talks
about you & I try to do so cheerfully— he has fine plans for tying you in bed
next time we get you home to keep you from going away— "Ill bring him every
thing good to eat & wont starve him—" & so he prattles & comforts me with
his sympathy　I've done all I can to make him happy— but I am afraid without
much success the day you left. he fretted about every thing & fought Phil &
was not himself　I told him stories & played with him & he would be content
with no one else— he seems to fear that Ill go away too— but that is all past
now & all his happy moods were on him yesterday & today. We have no news
& are all well but my mother who looks & is sick　Blair sends kisses with his
Mamas love— Your affecate Lizzie

1. Eliza Jones Hersey married John Albion Andrew in 1848. He was governor of
Massachusetts from 1861 to 1866. They had four children between 1850 and 1858:
John, Elizabeth, Edith, and Henry.

2. Nathaniel Banks had been governor of Massachusetts from 1858 to 1861. His
wife was Mary I. Palmer Banks.

3. John Hale, Republican senator from New Hampshire, was chairman of the naval

affairs committee. On January 8, 1862, his committee recommended a change of authority in the overseeing of construction of twenty new ironclads. Wishing to substitute the president for the secretary of the navy, Hale questioned Welles's propriety in allowing his brother-in-law to act as agent for the department, stating flatly that he "did intend to convey a censure upon the Secretary for the manner in which he has disbursed the public funds that have been entrusted to him." *Congressional Globe*, 37th Cong., 2d sess., 1861–62, 32, pt. 1:219.

4. Secretary of the Navy Gideon Welles had a full, flowing grey beard.

5. Joseph C. Walsh to SPL, December 23, 1861. Walsh had retired from the navy in 1854 as a lieutenant, and he wanted to rejoin for the duration of the war. He explained to Lee that he desired appointment to something close to his former grade and that after the war, he did not want to retain his position. Walsh returned to the navy on February 11, 1862, with the rank of acting lieutenant; he then resigned the following May.

6. The New York *Evening Post* of January 29, 1862, ran an article on the theories of Dr. Charles Fayette Taylor (1827–99), orthopedic surgeon, and his recent publication in *United States Journal of Homeopathy*. Dr. Taylor advocated plenty of exercise for children and a lessening of the intensity of their scholastic training. He urged moderation in forcing children to their books "to ensure the healthful and harmonious performance of all bodily functions."

Silver Spring   February 5, 1862

Dear Phil   We were rejoicing over a small success last night but today see no mention of it   Capt Barton[1] was sent down with dispatches from Genl Lander— & told us he had returned to Romney[2] after a skirmish at Springfield which is half way between Romney & Cumberland   Capt Barton says that Genl Lander has now 18 thousand men & men used to fighting— & hard fare but that Genl Kellys[3] long illness had so relaxed all discipline that were harrassing the Country with their drunkeness but Genl Lander has gradually got them all under a very different regime—[4] but that he is out of all spirits to be tied down to Banks slow ways—wants direct communings with McClellan & then there be some go ahead— on the Railroad again I give you purport of the talk as I heard— I feel an interest in Genl L. as he says he is Fathers appointment & calls himself Mr. Blair's General so says his wife to me

The great Ball at the White House is [in] process now   I wrote an appology for us all— Mother received a beautiful knit shawl & hood from Mrs. Merrick today. Mr. Briggs[5] & other officers have brought their wives back here— I'll go see them as soon as I can but now the deep sluch of snow & mud confines our promenades to the Back porch— all of us except Blair— Who puts on his boots & roves as usual ever where. the extra effort of the movement giving him additional pleasure & roses   he helps all the farming process going on— to hear his talk   I told him I had written to his Aunt Fanny & thanked her for all the toys she had sent him & how well he kept them & what an endless quantity he had— Well said he "Is she such a hot secesh?? he seemed to think it would displease you sadly if she was—

Feby 6th A day of steady rain & sleet. No tidings from the city— & passed the day mostly with Blair— who is not happy when he cannot go out some part of the day— & has some cold today— so I dont dream of letting him go with umbrella besides I am very careful about any symtoms of cold just now as it might be measles in spite of my faith in Dr. May's saying the attack of sickness & eruption when he was 3 months old was measles— Birnie said it was not— & she might be right Father & I discussed our quandom friends the Bentons & Woodburys Concluded they were about equally valuable as friends & connections

Feby 7th Blair is writing his letter to you making big Os & putting kisses in them for you— that he caught a mouse in his trap— that Donkey is getting well he got the distemper from Old Charley— Our talk & love is all that we have to send you from this out of the world place Father goes in & may be will bring us some news to write— Your affectionate Lizzie

1. Capt. Fred Barton of the Tenth Massachusetts Infantry.

2. Romney, western Virginia.

3. Brig. Gen. Benjamin F. Kelley had been severely wounded during the Battle of Philippi on June 3. His principle duty was in western Virginia and Maryland, guarding the line of the B & O Railroad.

4. Lander led his troops in a skirmish at Bloomery Gap, western Virginia, on February 14, 1862.

5. Col. Henry Shaw Briggs of the Tenth Massachusetts Infantry.

Silver Spring   February 13, 1862

My dear Phil Blair enjoyed his dinner— all & when you letter came he was eating his supper— but he put down his bread & butter left his chair & little table to sit in my lap to hear your letter read— over twice— then got down & ate his supper— he seemed to think *we knew* this was your birthday first—

I got a letter from Horace about the Donkey Cart which is to have red wheels & 4 of them at that & springs— & a cover like an army waggon to keep off rain or sunshine as needed it will be here ten days hence— & by that time our little one will be well enough to go in it & its coming may be opportune— for it will be long 'ere I venture him on the damp cold earth after this sickness— he is very bright & cheerful— but you can imagine how he hates this confinement— Today I laughed at a remark of his to Becky she said the erruption was less red & added it is going in now & you will have no more fever— "Oh dont say going in Becky but going off. I dont want it in me any more its going off Becky—" said with the greatest positiveness—

His Grandpa went to the City today & he missed him very much. he played marbles with him yesterday & read to him for a while— He seemed pleased with your desire to nurse him— Mother wanted to take him down stairs as the day was mild— but after a struggle in my heart & head I concluded still to confine him to our room as the erruption is still thick upon him— I'll run no risks that I know are such Little George[1] is better but I got no tidings from John's Lewis brought us the papers.

Father remained in the City tonight— Stone's arrest[2] was from all I can learn entirely the act of McClellan & Stanton—[3] the Committee— on the progress of the War Claim to have developed the facts— I heard of the Fort last week from Capt Barton— who said the army up there were urging on a mutiny against their superior officers— Jim Byrne[4] told Becky the day you saw him here that the Rebels were building a fort "where we might hit them any time we pleased when they were at work—" This second dose of Sumpter is rather much— & I think implicates Banks & all around As Willie Lee said— "the Union Army men are not zealous—" & it will lose West Point much of its prestige if it goes on & it gives these abolitionist bill holds— Their last scheme is to turn all the States in Territories It is Chase hobby—[5] but the P[resident]. is down on it but wants it defeated in Congress & that may keep Father in to night— This is my second letter to day but it is your birthday & I ought *note* it doubly over other days. Ill add a few in the morning to tell you how Blair gets thro the night— God bless you & give you many & happy birthdays fondly prays yr devoted Lizzie

Feby 14 Friday Morning Blair had his first good night— he slept well & coughed but twice during the night & that not badly. So I feel as if he was almost well   Henry waits he goes in for the girls   Evy returns home on Monday   Yr affectionate Lizzie

1. George Madison Blair, born April 18, 1860, was Frank and Apo's son.

2. Gen. Charles Pomeroy Stone became the scapegoat for the death of Col. Edward Baker at Ball's Bluff. Arrested at midnight on February 8, 1862, he was placed in solitary confinement at Fort Lafayette for fifty days; he was finally released on August 16, 1862, and was ultimately exonerated. His first wife was Mary Louisa Clary, daughter of Gen. Robert Clary, who died during the investigation, leaving Stone with a small daughter to raise. EBL's initial reaction to his arrest came in her February 10 letter: "I feel as if we had lived over a magazine   I never saw the man in my life— but had learned to pity him for his misfortunes in his wife & do so more for his own sin— But now his treason gives me a double pang first because he professed to be a Christian Man— secondly that my country has produced another Arnold & worse—."

3. Edwin M. Stanton was appointed to succeed Simon Cameron as secretary of war on January 15, 1862. On March 2, 1862, EBL commented on his appointment: "Our fear was that he would take Frémont up behind him, but he has no idea of that— his poney cant carry double." Until his appointment, Stanton had been closely associated with McClellan. Within a week, their friendship had ended, and they became bitter opponents.

4. Jim Byrne, son of Blair's former nurse Martha Cook.

5. Chase and Charles Sumner promoted the idea that because of the act of secession, the Southern states should revert to the status of territories, and Congress then
had the authority to set the conditions for their readmission to the Union. One-fourth
of the House Republicans, along with Democrats and border-state men, defeated the
measure in 1862.

Silver Spring   February 14, 1862
Dear Phil   Blair has enjoyed full day light today— & has played with his toys
without stopping except when I made him sit in my lap & read to him just to
rest him— I'll let him go to the parlor tomorrow & enjoy the new Book which
Father brought him— Springtime will soon be here & then there is an end to
story telling— for he plays out doors all day— & when rainy days come then
toys are the resource— then there are no long evenings— one of Aunt Becky
reasons for teaching children to read early is— that they read slowly & simple
childish things & read them over & over again with relish— & that the mind
is really less worked & taxed than by this oral tale telling of old people. Blair
is eager to be taught— & I am sometimes sorely tempted to do so— but shall
resist until you say so— but if Blair was kept in the house like most children
he would teach himself in a few months to know a great deal. he now knows
his letters by some of his blocks— he will ask everybody he meets or sees what
is it— & when once told rarely forgets— his eyes bore the light well today—
has no inflammation or weakness about them— except they itch & I have to
remind him not to rub them—

Father was show the dispatches (private) to the Dept by Capt Goldsborough— which Father describes as beautifully written not only in style
which is very graphic but the handwriting is fine— Capt G. says their fortifications did them great credit but he evidently dont think much of the fighting
tho he dont say so in terms— Our men waded a swamp— & then drove them
from their batteries— at the point of the bayonet—[1] He says Govr Wise was
returning with reinforcements when taken ill & if he had not turned back he
would have reached there only in time to see his son die—[2] who was uncon-
cious of his situation & was urging Goldsborough to let him go upon parole—
a very little while before he expired— he could not make his men fight— The
poor whites have no heart in the cause & it is a battle of the gentry— & they
will do all the fighting—[3]

Father says the flag sent to the Dept is simply *a french flag*— with Stars
sewed on the blue stripe— Capt. G give a drawing of the fortifications & says
the Engineer of the Expedition says he would be proud enough to claim them
for they show great talent— as well as acquirements— Capt G. speaks of a
midshipman Porter[4] as having shown great courage & as deserving his epau-
lettes— but all of our sailors & officers were cool under fire— there were 10
or 12 killed on our ships— & the ship were under their fire two days— Golds-

borough says was there ever such *gunnery*!!— I hope they will hurry up the War & not give them any more time to learn how to shoot any better—

The appointment of Hitchcock[5] is bad for *us*— he is a second edition of Harney & it was done thro' Halleck— old California associations Frank has no end to his bad luck— but the girls say he is in the finest spirits— this routing out of Secesh in Missouri is really a comfort if we had nothing else to rejoice us— but Price's men are practiced runners and are very hard to catch—

Evy goes to New York on Tuesday & I think I'll send your boat cloak by Mr. Rochester[6] to be left at the Astor House for you— I hope you have recieved your luggage sent by Express— You asked John to attend to it for you most luckily for I have been a fixture at home ever since the day we parted I have not been but once out of the porch & that was to measure the Donkey for his harness— which I sent Horace & Old Dick brought him to the Carriage step— Brothers children have the mumps— so I'll be cautious for Blair in that quarter where he rarely goes at any rate— it is best for boys to have it in childhood— but Blair has had enough for this winter— Betty says he does not look much pulled down by his sickness—

I asked Father your question about Genl. Stone— his reply was "I have not heard his name mentioned since I have been in the City & cant say from what I know but all I have heard induces me to think it is Stanton & McClellan own doings Brother did not know it was done when here Sunday— Nor did Seward— have anything to do with it These two points I hear & believe— It was done so unexpectedly that it looks *military*—

Minna complains that the City is very dull— Nel had no beaux last night & Apo said to Father that the girls had made her house very gay— The girls are certainly very jolly over their *good times*— These are Fathers items & so is all my city news— Baby talk is all my own— Good night ever yr affecate Lizzie

Genl Stone was at the White House Wednesday night & at Lafayette Sunday next

1. On February 8, 1862, federal forces, led by Brig. Gen. Ambrose Burnside and Flag Officer Louis M. Goldsborough, captured Roanoke Island, North Carolina, in a joint expedition. Confederate Gen. Henry A. Wise was ill, and rebel forces were led by Col. H. M. Shaw.

2. Capt. O. Jennings Wise was wounded during the battle on Roanoke Island and died the next day.

3. In her February 15 letter, EBL commented: "I think when Secesh see that *the people* are not going to fight their battles they will conclude to all settle in South Caroline or give up— and if our cause is not *betrayed*— it will soon be gloriously victorious—."

4. Midshipman Benjamin H. Porter, in cooperation with the army, commanded a howitzer battery during the capture of Roanoke Island.

5. As commandant of cadets at the Military Academy, Ethan Allen Hitchcock

tangled with Andrew Jackson in 1833 when the president attacked the elitism of West Point. In addition, Hitchcock always blamed Jackson for the Seminole War. In March 1862, Hitchcock refused Lincoln's offer of McClellan's command of the Army of the Potomac because of age and poor health, but he became a military advisor. The Blairs, as staunch Jacksonians and advocates of McClellan, would not have been favorites of Hitchcock.

6. William Beatty Rochester, paymaster general of the army.

Silver Spring   February 16, 1862

Dear Phil   We have had a day of thankfulness that Ky is so near delivered from her enemies—[1] But the sucess in our war movements does not give me any greater joy there than the cry of joy for deliverance of the oppressed people of Tennessee—[2] & so it will be as our troops advance It is I admit— a rebellion of a whole caste— the gentry & a would be gentry— but the people are like our people hereabouts in our district where no effort was made to rally them— no breakfasts & waggons prepared for the election day— gave a larger vote than ever before & they were as sixty secesh to 200 loyal men— the first all our busy money making genteel acquaintance— the last the *Mortens* Collins— Bands Gaines & etc & so it is everywhere south— & Oh how my heart leaps with joy that foot of pride is to taken off of their necks— Frank brought us the good news about the evacuation of Bowling Green &etc— We are on the qui vive about Fort Donelson which must soon fall— this deliverance of Mo & Kentucky will I know give you great joy

This is Becky's Sunday rather she has had none for three & I sent her in today Which at once assures you how well Blair is today for she would not leave him in the least sick— he has played all day long without stopping until about Sundown he got in my lap & was still for a while   I frequently during the day had to coax him to a talk— for a rest— Frank says he is a deal pulled down, but was delighted with his brightness & evident improvement during the week— He has scarce coughed at all during the last 24 hours   I am quite at rest in my feelings about & sleep sound & long be his side— as before his sickness during which a half hours nap at time was about as long as my eyes could rest

I'll close this in the morning as the girls are going Ill have a chance for a mornings bulletin of health— Blair & I had a good night   Yr Lizzie   Monday

1. On February 11, the Confederates evacuated Bowling Green, Kentucky, and within a few days of the surrender of Fort Donelson, Tennessee, on February 16, there were virtually no rebel troops left in Kentucky.

2. The captures of Fort Henry on February 6, 1862, and Fort Donelson on February 16 opened the Tennessee and Cumberland rivers—and all of Tennessee—to Union forces. In her February 12 letter, EBL remarked of these developments: "Father saw

Andy Johnson who is exultingly happy in hopes of the deliverance of his home & people."

Washington   March 1, 1862

Dear Phil   As you rarely sail any day but Sunday I will send this in hopes it will reach you & let you know that Blair & I are both well— I have no letter to day from you but suppose Mothers stupid gardener has taken my letters to Silver Spring instead of bringing them to me first. Betty is so much better that I hope to go home tomorrow[1] & get a refreshing sleep She has had pneumonia with Measles— so you may know how very much the poor thing has suffered— I have just taken a walk & called at the Trumbull to tell them why I have not been to see them— for I did not wish to carry measles in my clothes to her two babies—

Yesterday as I went by the White House in my walk I concluded to walk up & enquire for the sick child & the Mother—[2] did so when Mrs. L sent me a kind message of thanks & sent her sister Mrs. Edwards[3] down to see me— when we had a very friendly chat she is ten times better looking than Mrs. Lincoln— Mrs. Edwards enquired for all the family— quite posted as to all of us I met Mr. Seward in the Vestibule going into the White House & in his gruffest tones he asked me "What are *you* doing here? I replied civilly which his Manner scarce deserved—

Frank said this morning that everything was really kept dark now— & it was he hoped all for our better success— It is believed here that Columbus is to be evacuated—[4] & that Winchester is surrounded by Banks & Lander.

Apos baby still lies in her arms with closed eyes & I think a steady fever   Dr. says however he is better   All well at Johns— Mrs. M Blair send man with white gloves to see how Miss Blair is every day   her children are recovering— Still in bed— the Baby[5] has mumps & measles & think it quite ill   George Alexander waits this so I must stop   Ever your affecate Lizzie

1. On February 26, EBL informed her husband that she was staying in the city to nurse Betty, who had the measles. Numerous Blair children were ill, as she wrote, "Apo has George ill with his eyes & I think typhoid fever Minna has Maria Gist & Woody all sick with measles & the Baby quite ill because he has mumps too & teething—."

2. William Wallace "Willie" Lincoln, the president's eleven year-old son, died of typhoid fever on February 20. Young Tad Lincoln was also ill but recovered.

3. Mrs. Ninian Edwards was Mary Lincoln's sister. On March 27, 1862, EBL reported another visit to Mrs. Lincoln: "Yesterday I went to see Mrs Lincoln she saw me— & was tearful but very kind— seemed to feel I had been attentive to her in her sorrow."

4. Confederates evacuated Columbus, Kentucky, on February 28.

5. Gist Blair, born September 10, 1860.

Silver Spring   March 3, 1862
Dear Phil   Received two letters today from you one of Friday & the other on
yesterday as you were starting on the trial trip— I wish you had a less stormy
day for it. that rolling tossing ship has been an ever present idea— with me
for I thought you were off to the Gulf I fear it will be a trial as well as a trip in
this furious storm of rain & sleet here— due South & East— & yet so cold
    I see the papers call the Oneida Sloop of War not gun boat— I'll call her
U.S. Steamer— Genl Landers death[1] was a blow to Father who knew & liked
him very much— & he has induced me to call on his wife who I now pity
very much for she appears to me to be an earnest frank warm hearted woman
& proudly devoted to her husband but as ambitious as he is— She & Mother
tanted me very cleverly for my want of spirit one day for saying I was very
patriotic in the abstract— & often wished to do something myself— but when
it came to risking my husband and Brother within reach of cannon shot I
shuddered, ached, & would not risk either for all the glories this world could
bestow if it was left to me— and now poor thing I expect she aches & cowers
as much as any other woman— This wicked Secession Conspiracy! how many
hearts it has mourning & broken—
Tuesday March 4th No photographs[2] which is a disappointment to Blair &
me— came either yesterday or today by mail but shall go to the City tomorrow
to see after Betty who has improved every hour since the irruption came out
Apo's George is still a sufferer & our accounts from him today were not good
    Washington   Wednesday   Glad I left Blair home   the roads are horrid,
horrid, I find all better but little Maria[3] who is dangerously ill— I am very
busy but well & hoped to hear of your return out of the stormy trial trip   In
haste   Your affectionate Lizzie

    1. Frederick W. Lander died March 2, 1862, of a "congestive chill."
    2. Before SPL left New York to join the Gulf Squadron, he had his photograph
taken.
    3. Maria Blair, born May 12, 1854, was Montgomery's daughter.

Silver Spring   March 6, 1862
Dear Phil   I see by the Times of Tuesday that you did not get out until Tuesday consequently I may get another bulletin to you You may see by the Tribune
that Frémont has published brothers letter[1] to him Are they not hard up—
but it turns out that the missive wrong as it is did the Fs more harm than
anybody else—
    Brother just took the letter up to the P. & asked him to read it— which
he declined— saying he did not intend to read it as it was never written for
that purpose— then Brother talked & told it fully to him & then said it was a
foolish letter & I regret it most sincerely— but it is due to you to make some

amends by resigning my place & explain fully what I meant— & omitted in a hasty private letter— I leave the whole thing to you & will do exactly as you wish about— Well replied the President Forget it, & never mention or think of it again I know what you meant for you very frank about your feelings & views at the time" Genl Scott was the Old Whiggism you meant— talked plainly enough— But the Old Hero has done his country noble service— & it was natural to trust him— but his vigor is past— &etc—

Then Brother went to Chase who was just reading it— Why says Chase "here is your dog days wrath— Yes replied brother & I owe you an apology for ever expressing it in that way I am heartily ashamed of it— Dont trouble yourself one moment on my account— it is not half as bad as you talked & I have got over that long ago— You middle state men have had more than enough to run you mad— & then he went on to talk in the best temper possible & so things stood when we left the City yesterday Did ever a man get out of so bad scrape so easily— Father is off to the City to see Mr. Lincoln & thank him for his kindness— it is evident they knew about the letter long long ago when you & I talk it over—

I find Apos Baby still very ill I am seriously alarmed about the Child Maria Blair has inflammatory Rheumatism & is a sad sufferer I never saw so much sickness & am thankful that Blair & Betty are both so well— I went to John's & there found your photographs It is an admirable likeness— I am delighted with it So is Blair who took it in his hand & looked at it & exclaimed— Oh Papa & kept looking at it & whilst I was talking to Mother he stole off in the corner of the room & sat down & then kissed the picture several times— Nobody said a word & there he sat for ten minutes & then came to me & asked me to put it where we can see it all the time. "I know it a heap better than that one—" pointing to the painting that dear young face that will ever live in my heart Mother thinks the photograph excellent & said I am going to keep this one— Yes says Blair you may have one but I wants two— & Mama all the rest is for you All well at Johns Blair is out doors playing with his wheel barrow merry & hearty. I'll send Fanny a photograph & your direction at Ship Island today— God bless you ever prays your devoted Lizzie

1. For weeks, the congressional Joint Committee on the Conduct of the War heard testimony on Frémont's activities in Missouri. Montgomery Blair's letter to Frémont was published March 4, 1862, in the New York *Tribune*. Part of that August 24 letter read: "The trouble is elsewhere. Chase has more horror of seeing Treasury notes below par than of seeing soldiers killed, and therefore has held back too much, I think. I don't believe at all in that style of managing the Treasury. It depends on the war, and it is better to get ready and beat the enemy by selling stocks at 50 percent discount than to wait to negotiate and lose a battle. . . . you must not expect too much of me in the Cabinet. I have as you know very little influence, and even now, when the policy I have advocated from the first is being inaugurated, it does not seem to bring me any great power over the administration. This, I can see, is partly my own fault.

I have been too obstreperous, perhaps, in my opposition, and men do not like those who have exposed their mistakes beforehand, and taunt them with them afterwards. The main difficulty is, however, with Lincoln himself. He is of the Whig school, and that brings him naturally not only to incline to the feeble policy of Whigs, but to give his confidence to such advisers. It costs me a great deal of labor to get anything done because of the inclination of mind on the part of the President or leading members of the Cabinet, including Chase, who never voted a Democratic ticket in his life."

Silver Spring   March 7, 1862

Dear Phil   I was very glad to get your letter of yesterday (6th inst)— the one of the day before is yet to come   I had not had a line since your trial trip until today tho the papers told me of your safe return out of the storm of Monday & part of Tuesday—

Frank is making his Frémont speech today   Father has counselled him to be moderate in tone & let facts *proved* facts, do the work— Julian[1] the abolitionist told Brother that Frémont's publication of brother's private letter had used Frémont up in his estimation with all honest men— for it showed two things 1st he was no gentleman to publish a letter of the kind— Secondly it disproved all Frémonts assertions that the Blairs had threatened him & were jealous of him— for nothing could prove more eager desire to forward all his plans— So the publication injured his own case & was simply done in malice

Father returned home tonight tired but in good spirits Mitchell[2] has a crony who is a Frémont follower— who remarked to Frémont that he thought he made a mistake in quarrelling with the Blairs— Oh replied Frémont I never intended to do it— but we thought it necessary rein Frank a little & felt quite sure the Old Man would make things all right again when it turned out that he was even more restive & violent than Frank ever was." I give you the talk as Mitchell repeated it— I was on the eve of sending Blair to see Jessie when I hear of her sickness & was only stopped by hearing that Mr. Gray said a Mrs Wright[3] of Cal a woman of very equivocal character was staying there with her this stopped me—

This has been a bitter cold windy day— so I have kept Blair in doors as I observed cold & wind make his eyes weep— showing they are still delicate & need care— this happened but once & the same exposure made him complain of a strangling affliction for nearly 24 hours he was never satisfied & had no relief in the slow languid discharge— Since then all this has gone well & his eyes never looked better— but it was a warning that for awhile he could not rough it out doors as of yore— it was a clear very cold windy day— & he was out about an hour & came in chilled From this time until summer I'll house him in all raw weather— & exercise in a carriage to keep him well   the roads after this will make that more practicable—

Our Mass 10th made a foray on Secesh above us— which has rather tarnished their good name— Over a hundred stole after day (eve) parade &

visited & frightened all our secesh neighbors up as far as Valdenar afrightened
the women & insisted on suppers & all sorts of cheer— shot all the fowls
they could find & was in a high frolick generally when Genl Couch who went
himself caught them by getting a Regt of Cavalry after them— They expect
to be off in Dixie next day as they are under marching orders & have been for
several days. Col Briggs had a whole company here all night. we did not know
it until afterwards to guard our premises fearing they would stop here drunk in
returning from their frolick— they had to drop about 20 of the fowls— which
has more than replaced those they took from the servants & Harvy found &
ate them all by the way I got an apology from them for taking my chickens
they thought they were Harvy[4] chickens who tho a Union man is unpopular
with some of the Soldiers— They say Secesh have got off too easy here after
shooting at the Pickets night after night in Augt. & Sept & so they intended
to pay off old scores 'ere they parted— It was evidently long premeditated for
3 or 4 men went out of every mess— of the 10th & 7th Mass Regts— Some
new Regts are stationed near the forts— & every time any of us go in we miss
some of those which have been here all winter— All the Cavalry on 7 Street
& on old Burns place are gone— & a new Regt is put on Corcoran's lawn—[5]
so he didnt escape after all—

Father says Betty George & Maria all better today— I feel for Capt Mercer
he has been badly treated[6] & I'll say so the next time I get a chance— it may
help to provide for some boy if he has one— I am off early to see about Betty &
the rest will add a note if I hear any news— Goodnight   Your devoted Lizzie

1. Abolitionist George Washington Julian of Indiana was first a Free-Soil then a
Republican congressman (1849–51 and 1861–71).

2. Probably Maj. Gen. Robert B. Mitchell who became chief of cavalry of the Army
of the Cumberland in 1863.

3. Mrs. George Washington Wright's husband had been congressman from California (1850–51); he was a longtime business associate and a staunch backer of Frémont
for president.

4. Harvey was FPB's farm manager. His wife Lavinia was sometimes employed as a
seamstress by EBL.

5. W. W. Corcoran, Washington banker and philanthropist, had a country home,
Glenwood, two miles north of Washington in the District.

6. Capt. Samuel Mercer died March 6, 1862.

Silver Spring   March 11, [1862]
Dear Phil   Went to the city for letter exercise & something to do   eyes too
bad to read or write & only make this note to thank you for your letters   told
Mrs. Alexander your message to George

March 12 Eyes still bad. but out door life is mending me up fast— eyes
much better   look little red & pain to use them   but nothing to what they
have been— The weather is good & Blair & I revel in out doors again—

March 13th. I went to the City— to hear the news & to get rid of my own thoughts— your departure from New York & talk of "*hand* grenades" [1]— other bitter words have made me writhe & "as weak eyed" as Leah of old but that is not the way to get the means of writing agreeable letters to you & that now is my first duty & pleasure I met Nelly & went home with her. she told me she had had a mass said at church for your safe return home to us all— I have asked Mr Pyne to pray on Sunday last the day which I anticipated you would sail on to pray for your safety— but alas I was not there to join in these prayer— either today or Sunday. first because I was not informed of her *purpose* & last because I was too sick to leave the house but you are ever in my prayers & thoughts— & those of your boy & now your dear Sisters too join me in these loving importunities and dear Aunt Kitty [2] too said & if I ever did pray earnestly for any I did your husband this day—" This is all comforting to me beyond utterance & I hope it may be so to you, not only as the assurance of love for you of those dear to you but of Him who moves our hearts to love and pray—

The running away of the Rebels from their stronghold [3] & the appointment of Frémont to the Mountain division of the army—[4] a narrow slip of the Country where there are no negroes or Secesh or many troops have been the themes of talk since Tuesday McClellan will have to achieve his Victories rapidly to hush up the sneering laugh of his enemies in the rear— but I hear he said— when he heard of the combination of Stanton Genl Turner—[5] Genl McDowell— & the Tribune Clique were combined against him Well said if I succeed they cannot hurt me— if I fail— nobody can help me— so it does not matter He evidently put his trust in doing his duty with all his might— & in God's mercy— The fact that painted Columbiads & stove pipes are found at Manassas makes people think that there has been a Sham force— & condition of things there all winter— but these were put up to cover their retreat— I heard that an Engineer had written back that the works were not even defencible— & if surrounded must have been vanquished—

Holt has returned from St Louis in extasies of the progress of these he says Halleck is a glorious General— & that Kentucky & the whole west is already on the rebound to prosperity & happiness— That he feels like an old man— who has been suddenly rejuvenated— that he is happy & will never murmur again since he has seen the dawn of the new day of national prosperity and grandeur—

Frémonts appointment I expect was the Presidents act urged by Chase— & Stanton who has his revenges too— Frank feels this accutely— but Brother takes it blandly— & says the President is the Wisest Man in the world. that he has now annihilated the abolition junto— & that we now present the South a United front I took up Brother's aspect of the case to Soften it to Father when I told it to him as he was sick— He says very little but is cheerful & now quite well again

Betty is home— has however a fearful cough— but is on the mend daily—

Blair is a gay bird since this bright weather he got some wings of a fowl & tied them to his arms & came running in the Library saying "Mama I am going to fly away to Ship Island." he looked all earnestness— & his rosy face made him as Father said the most beautiful Cupid he ever saw— I never heard more hearty peals of laughter than that excited his antics—

The movements of the Army are not published— but I heard that there were a hundred transports below Alexandria yesterday— & McC— evidently expects to be soon in Richmond— I met Mrs Taylor— she told me she had a letter from Varina— who had who wrote very affectionately— she said "Memory overleapt the horrid Gulf now between us & took her back to that happiest part of her life that spent at Washington & then went on to say that to *three* women out of the family circle she clung with an unaltered affection "Tilly Emory Lizzie Lee Minna Blair all so unlike— yet clever & to me dear unto life's end—" Minna mention this letter some weeks ago to me with great exultation mentioned Mrs Emory & herself but not me— as the unforgotten friends & yet Mrs. Taylor expressed great surprise I had not heard of her message to me—

Capt Barton was here just now says Genl Landon went to sleep & never again opened his eyes or spoke to any— lay 48 hours— 'ere he expired—

Friday. Another damp day but we are all well & I believe Blair & I will enjoy a day in our house plays— our resource so much since you left us— Vincent goes to get the mail without which it is hard to do these stirring times— Capt Barton says the Rebels have fortified Strausburg— he says the *let up* expression of people at Martinsburg & the wish for sugar— coffee— tea & comforts of all sorts— makes every body laugh— the Union men however are very bitter & revengeful— Goodbye devotedly yr Lizzie

1. On March 8, Lee had written his wife of his request for "some hand grenades which have been tried, & are much approved of, & which might be very useful if I am successful in carrying out a design I have formed." Blair-Lee Papers.

2. Catherine Smith, sister of Ellen Hill Lee's mother.

3. On March 9, the Confederates under Joe Johnston evacuated Manassas.

4. On March 11, Lincoln appointed Frémont commander of the new Mountain Department which included the mountainous areas of Virginia and western Virginia. At the same time, he relieved McClellan as general in chief but left him in command of the Army of the Potomac.

5. Gen. L. C. Turner of New York was appointed associate judge advocate for the army around Washington in August 1862. He worked with Stanton on arrests of draft evaders and questions of disloyalty.

Silver Spring   March 15, 1862

Dear Phil It has not rained but it has poured all day & my thoughts have been not a little exercised by our Soldier's exposure to it What the plans over the River are is not promulgated— but there is a huge Army being put on transports at Alexandria— Burnside[1] has the papers say been reinforced—

I am disgusted that the Officers & crew of the Monitor should be so noticed when those of the Cumberland are unmentioned[2] these were more exposed to danger— did their part nobly— & would have done it successfully had the Govt done their part at all   Father is down on me for digging in the Govt— but on this score I have a good right to growl— my ox was not gored but it was no fault of theirs— Father says it his particular request that his children shall quit fault finding & has commenced on his first *love about* it— The Herald and other papers are out on the Dept The fight in Arkansas has been a hard one   Curtis victorious over Van Dorn, Price, & McCulloch, who is reported killed again— losses great on both sides[3]

Monday March 17. New Madrid evacuated[4] & a million worth of stores left— I would have dispatched this to you yesterday but I waked with my left eye all swollen & had to keep in a dark room all day— but care has cured it up— & some redness in the corner is all left of the malady but reading & writing is forbidden so you must for a week put up with a few loving words for in my darkness my thoughts follow you all the time even Blair's visits are short for he says dark rooms are ugly. He is looking so fat & gay I think the measles really has improved rather than injured his constitution

The Keyes[5] division or Corps d'Armee are back here— awaiting transports   10th Mass are in their old encampments but one of the Aids said here that they expected to move any hour— Our people are following them up in middle Virginia   the enemy are on the Retreat everywhere Those who rested so lately at Winchester are now en route to Staunton   Jo Johnston at Gordonsville—[6] Our people are rushing down the River & will doubtless soon turn their right flank on Norfolk & Richmond— & it is thought Secesh will make no stand until they get in the Cotton States— where they will have to Stop— in their "last ditch" sure enough

It was all *fudge* about the removal of McClellan— Father the President today— *Nothing* could be more cordial[7] *affectionate* than their talk   Dick is here & says "All is right now in Missouri we have reached the granite & got solid foundations at last—" Frank feels well about his Bills *measures* now before Congress. I send you one of Franks speeches All our Invalids are getting strong again— & when I get the use of my eyes again I hope to have no sick reports to make— but I am *blindly* devotedly yr Lizzie

1. On March 14, Union troops under Gen. Ambrose E. Burnside captured New Berne, North Carolina.

2. On March 9, the battle of the ironclads *Monitor* and *Virginia* (formerly the USS *Merrimack*) ended in a draw. The wooden vessel *Cumberland* had sunk after being struck by the *Virginia.*

3. On March 7 and 8, Gen. Samuel R. Curtis and Union forces defeated Gen. Earl Van Dorn's Confederates at Pea Ridge, Arkansas. McCulloch was, indeed, killed during the action. The battle cleared Missouri of the rebel army and gave the Union control of northern Arkansas.

4. On March 14, federal troops occupied New Madrid, Missouri, which had been evacuated by the rebels on the previous day.

5. Brig. Gen. Erasmus Darwin Keyes commanded the Fourth Army Corps in the Peninsular Campaign.

6. In Virginia.

7. Line drawn through "cordial."

Silver Spring   March 18, 1862

Dear Phil   I too should dread old age if I lose my eyes when it comes I have really felt in bondage for ten days— And had I taken to a dark room & self denial at once would not have been a sufferer so long but tis past & next time I'll know better—

The Army below us had orders last night to move & it is now dragging it slow length along the streets & roads leading to Washington— the 10th being the farthest out moves tomorrow at day light & breaks up to return no more after all the Army which has been here all winter goes we will have a new army here— of thirty thousand troops about Washington & its surrounding Forts— The Round up in the country here has caused a great deal of fuss. Some anonymous writer has made complaint at Headquarters. After the officers of the 10th had been to every house & paid damages— the same day in Cash— for all injury done by the soldiers— This writer describes himself as if he was Father— The officers immediately pronounced it a forgery for Father would sign his name if he had complaints to make—[1] He has now gone to the Couch's Headquarters to set this matter— Father got Gallespie a Lt. place in New Mexico under Canby—[2] So he has a chance to fight himself up in life again— he has two brevets now— Russell is off now I suppose to do something to make him Chef of his Corp.

After all the Secesh ran off from Manassas in haste our Cavalry have Reconnoitred nearly up to Orange Court House & found the Country strewed with Guns hats coats— waggons— & full ones. Cars loaded with army stores— million of money will not replace these things Such retreats— must be nearly as disastrous to them as lost battles— it must demoralize the men & as well as diminish their means of war— & for us as nation it is the happiest of all things if the people wont fight for the conspirators how perfect again will be the Union & our future as Nation grander than ever— Every retreat & every Evacuation are the best of remedies for our political ailments—

Frank got a letter from Ariss Buckner[3]   he writes as if he was drunk   begs Frank to catch his negroes & employ them at Silver Spring. he is quite sure that they are thereabouts as George Massey's brother is among the Contrabands— 30 have run off speaks of the "infernal war" & hopes the North will put down the pewter & take the darkies off he does not care where— has heard poor Betty Blair was dead— says he feels like making his will & doing like wise ever since the war which has made every body penniless begs to have a paper sent to him or anything else that would look— taste, smell or speak of the civilized world again—[4]

My heart & head is today full of Capt Foote who is now or was yesterday battling away at No. 10 Island in the Missi—[5] & just as he was preparing for this battle he heard of the death of his son of 13 yrs old— I feel for his poor wife— her son gone & her husband in battle— could a woman have more anguish to bear—

Tuesday evening It is rumored to night that the Merrimac ran the blockade in the storm on Saturday night it made me shudder until I learned she could only carry 12 days of coal— I expect she will over haul some steamer & get replenished— but they can get off as she *is very very* slow So I am comforted as you can alway get out of her way— and shoot at her at long (and with your big guns but you be sure to run out of her way for no matter how gallantly you *sacrifice* yourself that goes for nothing success— & not sacrifice wins the guerdon— from our nation—

Wednesday March 19th I am going to the City for the ride— for eyes & nothing gets well with me in the house so with a thick veil I will go— Blair is well & the merriest little chap I ever saw as he was dressing I lay listening to his chirping no music much as I enjoy ever was more sweet to my ears

I got a letter from Mary Blair Little Jimmie[6] indeed all of those children wrote to me & always send love to Uncle Phil your visit there was very grati-fying to all of them— I will write to night any news I may get to day & keep a *stock* of letters on hand at New York to go by every chance— I know it is wearing to you to get so many *old* letters at once but you can glean from the latest & their no. and bulk will evince the constant thought & affection of yr own Lizzie

1. On March 24, 1862, EBL had commented: "There is a great of ferment about the visitation of the Soldiers up the Country— We take no part in it— but I must say privately that the Secesh deserved their *scare* & as they had inflicted quite that much on me this time last year I cant say I share any part of their indignation especially as all *damages* have been paid—."

2. Edward Richard Sprigg Canby commanded the Department of New Mexico until September 1862. Archibald H. Gillespie joined the marines in 1832 and resigned in 1854. He appears again in March 1862 as an assistant aide de camp. He was dismissed from the service June 4, 1863.

3. Ariss Buckner of Loudoun County, Virginia, was the father of Montgomery Blair's first wife Caroline Buckner.

4. On March 27, 1862, EBL reported: "Accounts private from Va say people suf-

fer for all the necessaries of life— Reverdy Johnson sent even bread to his Sister near Harpers Ferry—."

5. After the loss of New Madrid, Island Number 10 became the rebels' next line of defense on the Mississippi River.

6. Lucy James Blair, born December 26, 1855, was the daughter of James and Mary Blair. She was called Jimmie.

Silver Spring   March 20, 1862

Dear Phil   Yesterday saw Mr Dick at Frank's. his account of the *rabidness* of secesh is marvelous that is of *gentle* men & women officers— but the troops of prisoners are just the other way— they moved to tears by the unexpected un-dreamt of kindnesses extended to them— the Sick & wounded particularly— & those taken at Donelson of which he saw hundreds & talked to them they are emphatically *poor whites not one* of all the hundreds he spoke seemed to have any heart in the war & were generally ignorant of its causes or deceived and all nearly were men who could neither read nor write— Officers talked "Aristocracy & secesh" as we hear them all talk it— Hydra is under foot or Foote in the west— We are intensely anxious about the Battle going on at No. 10— No news from there when we left the City last night—

John Rogers[1] is in the City to beg for an Iron Steamer the Mystic will done in May— so tis said but Mrs. Fox[2] smiled incredulously when I said so— She rejoiced with me over the destruction of the Congress & Cumberland— on their ashes or ruin we will build an Iron Navy she says Fox has been begging for Iron Ship since the first day he went into office but that DuPonts success in wooden gun boats had defeated the Measure in Congress— & it was hope-less until the Merrimac emerged from Norfolk Then it may turn out that all our hopes in this war are eventually National gains— The Senate Commit-tee which rejected Iron Steamers 3 weeks ago— has now moved & got thro' the Senate 15 millions to build them The Dept are going to make a great ado over all our Officers & men on the Cumberland & Congress for they were all heroic— George Morris— quite dims Worden's[3] laurels in the City the last is at Wise's[4] with his eyes in a desparate condition— His wife is with him

I called at Johns— Nelly & Mrs. Graham are making a retreat so did not see them all well— Went to Franks where Father was to meet us & in walked Smith Van Buren[5] to go out home with us— We talked over old times— He is here simply to see the Army of the Potomac— Hentzelman's[6] division of 40 thousand men have all be stopped down the River. Transports are awaiting Keyes Corps d'armee— but have *no coal* hence a delay of 5 days where they are going no body knows rather tells me— Smith V.B gives bad accounts of his Fathers[7] health suffers from croup & has a bad time of it— John[8] is getting better. Smith is sprightly & pleasant as ever— thinner & smaller than ever— Said his Father wanted my photograph so I gave him one of mine with Blair at

my side— the only one I could ever get my own consent to sit for & Blair re-
deems it so much that I am less ashamed of my own face Smith says Blair looks
like me when he first knew me— I was about 12 years old we boarded at Willards present hotel together— Blair has a more regular face than mine ever
was & his blue eyes gives him beauty which I never had but we are alike in
temperament— bouyant hopeful even when there's little save faith to make
one so & I hope his *faith* will be as much stronger & fruitful than mine as his
man's nature is over my feeble woman hood—

Jim came out with me & is making this rainy day joyous to Blair in his
company & their romps & plays— Sawing & soldiering Capt Barton has
given Blair a huge Newfoundland dog a noble animal— he seems sorry to
part with him but he cannot carry him into Dixie with him We have nothing
definite from No 10 today Foote seems to move up slowly & it is more of a
seige than any thing that has occured— The Enemy will have surrender—
as they cannot run from their present position— We got a letter today from
Aunt Susan[9] at Nashville Money money is all the burden of her letter except
a reiterated desire to know how every body is & where we all are— No talk as
the past at all

March 21st— Father is off on horse to the City for the News whilst our Gun
Boats are battling away at Island No 10 There's no rest at heart for any us. You
will hear it all at once— our roads are as bad as in Feby from the late endless
rain & the clouds promise more of it— but it has stopped & Blair is off too
on a horse with Jim— who says the Country is "hateful" rainy weather— but
the spring birds begin to shirp & we cant have much bad weather— We are all
well both here & in the city & after so much sickness that is enough to rejoice
over Betty is looking better than for a long time past— & seems to fatten
daily— Father is helping John to get the Upshurs back to their house— No
news from the Knapps[10] Blair is not by me or would send kisses to Papa ever yr
devoted Lizzie

1. John Rodgers, career naval officer, was the son of Commodore John Rodgers. He
commanded the gunboat *Galena* and in May led a squadron up the James River during
the Peninsular Campaign.

2. Virginia Woodbury Fox was Gus Fox's wife and Minna Blair's sister.

3. John L. Worden commanded the *Monitor* in its fight with the *Virginia*. Lt. George
Morris served as executive officer on the USS *Cumberland*. In the absence of the
captain, Morris was in charge when *Virginia* struck and sank *Cumberland*.

4. Naval officer Henry Augustus Wise was assigned to the Bureau of Ordnance and
Hydrography.

5. Smith Thompson Van Buren was Martin Van Buren's son.

6. Gen. Samuel P. Heintzelman commanded the Third Corps during the Peninsular
Campaign. On March 27, 1862, EBL wrote of Heintzelman, "I know McC has more
confidence in him than any other man—."

7. Martin Van Buren, former president of the U.S., was a close personal friend and political ally of Francis Preston Blair. He died on July 24, 1862.

8. John Van Buren, older brother of Smith and son of Martin Van Buren.

9. Aunt Susan was FPB's sister Susanna Trigg Blair Ward Hunnicutt Stevenson.

10. The Knapps were related by marriage to the Lees. Ellen McMacken Lee, daughter of SPL's Uncle Ludwell, married the Reverend Nathaniel P. Knapp of Mobile, Alabama, in 1844.

Silver Spring   March 25, 1862

Dear Phil   I catch myself counting up the possibilities about yr arrival at Ship Island over & over again since the rumor of the New Orleans being taken has been floating around—[1] whence it comes no body knows— but this has occurred several times & always true save once— that was about Savannah. of course it comes thro' Secesh— & underground telegraph— but I am quite sure you were not there so try to be easy— for it took you a week at best to get there— & the news could scarce get here in less than ten days—

Secesh is making great efforts for the rescue of the South West Jeff to take the field On Sunday the Rebels turned on Shields[2] with 15 thousand but he whipped them with his 8000— All the troops are off again from those parts— Save those under Wadsworth—[3] about 30,000 They have gone to Richmond— & I have no doubt the attack on Shields is a feint to keep McC. from sending all his troops down the River— but he has Army enough to go both ways— he has quite three hundred thousand men   McDowels division has 40. thousand. ditto. Keyes— ditto Sumner—[4] & that does not include any artillery or Cavalry— or any of the Staff Corps sapper marines—[5] pontoon & any of that part of the business— just simple Infantry— Banks has about thirty thousand & ditto Wadsworth— You thus see here is *some army*— & it is my opinion that the whole Rebellion will be put down entirely by the 4th of July— next

Genl Wadsworth has taken the Markoe's[6] house & I am going to call them tomorrow & pay 14 other calls which Father has named tonight— I got two notices today telling me we had small pox at the Orphan Asylum— which was lucky as I was going there tomorrow Blair wrote you a long letter this morning & I was astonished to see P & H. as the beginning of your name— he says you have a long name & he forgot the other letters he dont know half of the Alphabet yet. I suppose Jim taught him this on the rainy days last week. I saw them spelling names with the blocks with letters on them   Fanny sent him the Mts. He rode out with Mother today & is the picture of health & happiness   Grandpa got him some chickens to put in the hen house now the soldiers have gone away. GrandPa constantly hopes as you do that I will not spoil him— & I never saw him love & pet anybody in the world as much as he & Mother do. his good conduct about Betty & when sick perfectly charmed them & they saw & heard him

Becky says the Secesh people are in good spirits in town yet— because they've got Leesburg again— of course that is not so— John has sent Henry & Sarah down to his farm but I fear he will have to send them off farther for Frank Thomas[7] told Father he meant to spend the rest of his life in speaking for emancipation in Md & H. May is inclined to do likewise so it is said but for this I have no authority— & dont believe it—

Wednesday. We are all well. Becky burnt Blairs letter I meant to have enclosed accidently— Genl Meigs rode out with Father to survey for a Railway up 7 Street— Brown's meadow & out at Grammers Place[8] going thro Whites & following up piney branch— All waiting for Your affectionate Lizzie

1. New Orleans was not taken until April 25.

2. Brig. Gen. James Shields, a division comander in the Shenandoah, was defeated by Stonewall Jackson on March 22.

3. When the Army of the Potomac moved to the Peninsula, James S. Wadsworth was left in command of the defenses of Washington. He was appointed military governor of the District of Columbia March 17.

4. Brig. Gen. Edwin Vose Sumner commanded the Second Corps in the Peninsular Campaign.

5. Sapper marines were combat engineers.

6. Francis Markoe was a chief clerk in the State Department. He lived at Nineteenth & I Streets.

7. Frank Thomas, Jacksonian Maryland congressman (1831–42), was returned to Congress in 1861 as a strong Unionist. He served until 1869 and was an enthusiastic supporter of the extreme Radicals.

8. G. C. Grammer's farm was to the east of the Blair property; it lay partly in Montgomery County and partly in the District.

Silver Spring   March 31, 1862

Dear Phil   In spite of the rain & snow as the carriage had to go for Father & Mother I at last had the priviledge of *my* Sunday at Church— & as we sat there the last Brigade march to a magnificent Band out of the City in *Va* upon whose sacred Soil there cannot be now less than three hundred thousand North Men— how any body could have been sneered at as "raving" if such an event had been fortold this time last year—

Fox told Father that he had been growling all winter at the blockade of the Potomac but since he had visited their Batteries & seen their huge guns spiked & burst— & many without any injury— that he rejoices that McClellan "sat them out" & it saves on battle & many many valuable lives on both sides. Now the Contest will be over Richmond & Norfolk & these they would have fought no matter what had happened at Richmond— There is a horrid story going the rounds told by officers & other who have been at Manassas A Ky Regt— refused en masse to re enlist Stacked their arms & moved off— homeward bound they were surrounded— & slaughtered by some Cotton

State Regiments— Fox is not easy about a second Visit from the Merrimack
or "Virginia"— Worden has been with irricipulous & really (says to me Mrs
Wise[1] who nursed him) not injured by the battle— They have been preparing ever since the Combat but the best preparation putting redoubled force at
work on the Mystic at Phila which will now be ready in few days

Hollins[2] has his Turtle at Island No 10— & I expect all the Iron Clad boats
on the Miss. will be used against Foote's progress down the River The delays
at No. 10 are to await moving south & west in Tennessee[3] Reinforcement
to Genl Pope at New Madrid— McClellan left Alexandria Saturday night
2 olk— The Railroads are all repaired now beyond Warrenton Junction &
our Running gear has come on in some transports from New York— Sumner[4]
said a railroad man had visited him Saturday night & said they the North had
made the Railways run again in Virginia— & had paid the money for their
first making— so it could never be doubted now to whom they belonged

Mrs. Kemble's[5] reading was a failure— Henry fifth is a play written to brag
of Englishmen over French & it was bullying to read such a play here now— &
it was received from end to end in sullen silence— Those who went enjoyed
her reading without giving her or her English bragging the faintest murmur of
applause— & she waited & waited for it & was evidently greatly chagrined as
she read well in the beginning did her best— She has sold out in this country
& return to live in England & I suppose this John Bullism at our Capitol was
to give her return some eclat— but it was treated with proper spirit— there
was but a slim audience— Congress generally was absent— I suppose they
were posted as the play & its purpose— Sumner seemed to understand it—
Mother met Mrs Schurtz[6] & says she is lovely. Father is full of the RailRoad
out this way   Meigs has reported in its favor & the Govt have made up their
mind to have some other Communication with the north than that thro Balt
as well as to be independent of Big & little Gunpower bridges which a foreign
gun boat could destroy without much notice if a march was stolen up us as
was threatened in the Trent affair— So the Old Gentleman finding it was to
come out into Mont. Co. has showed his Engineering up the water courses &
it proves a marvellous easy assent only 40 feet to the mile to the plain which
then runs level for many miles I forget how many— It will come in the rear
of the Morrings— & the nearest point here will be at Old Grammermans bars
on our way to Rock Creek Church— about one mile from here— A Shady
walk in old times— but now bleak enough as both Father & Shoemaker[7] had
to sell their wood to the Army after the Roads got impassable they had to cut
& take the wood nearest to the camps   Father sold his for 1000 dollars—

Tuesday Apl 1st Our almost first Spring morning— Got all my flowers put
out in a cold bed under glass & am ready for gardening but as tis too wet
yet for work I'll go to my orphan asylum business at Mrs Coxes[8] call which
I got yesterday   Mrs. Merrick keep the board in a stew most of the time— I

have not been there since you left having many excuses for not going　& no inclination to go Theres a regular fight betwee her & Mrs C and Mrs Rice[9]

The Cart is at Johns but the roads are too deep to bring it out yet　I wrote to Fanny to let her know of your arrival & departure from Key West　Blair is enjoying the half of a big red apple at this moment & says he is very busy but sends love to Papa He is full of fixing up his Donkey house & a place to keep his Cart & harness— since Pink Cook was caught riding off the donkey— the Bridles & saddle &ct are kept under key— I got a good letter from Joe Cook telling me of the battle of Winchester— he was in it The waggon waits Ever yr devoted Lizzie

1. Charlotte Brooks Everett, daughter of Congressman Edward Everett of Massachusetts, married Henry A. Wise.

2. Commodore George N. Hollins commanded Confederate naval forces on the Mississippi.

3. On March 1, Halleck had ordered Ulysses Grant to begin moving south from Fort Donelson, Tennessee. His march culminated in the battle at Shiloh.

4. Charles Sumner, Massachusetts Republican senator (1851–74), was chairman of the Senate Committee on Foreign Relations.

5. Fanny Kemble, popular English actress and one-time wife of South Carolina planter Pierce Butler.

6. Margarete Meyer Schurz was the wife of German immigrant Carl Schurz, who later became a Missouri senator (1869–75).

7. The Shoemakers owned land south and east of FPB in the District.

8. Susan R. Coxe, husband of Washington attorney Richard S. Coxe, was first directress of the Washington City Orphan Asylum Board.

9. Possibly Augusta E. McKim Rice, wife of Massachusetts congressman Alexander H. Rice.

5

"these dark days of anxiety"
April 15, 1862

IN THE SPRING OF 1862, ELIZABETH'S concern focused on the impending battle to capture New Orleans and open the Mississippi. Haunting thoughts of her husband under fire filled her with dread that pervaded her letters. Union successes at Shiloh and Island Number 10 encouraged optimism in the North; at the same time, the nation looked anxiously to the James and York rivers in Virginia where McClellan had begun his Peninsular Campaign. A fundamental problem for the North was to strike a balance between supplying troops for offensive action against Richmond and reserving forces sufficient for the defense of Washington. Events of the war forced the Union to confront the issue of slavery resulting first in emancipation in the District of Columbia.

                                                  Silver Spring   April 2, 1862
Dear Phil   Yesterday was entirely an orphan Asylum day but there was something of a scene between Mrs C[oxe] & Mrs Merrick & if you were here I fancy I could make you laugh with me— Mrs. M has all her powers at work for the place now held by Mrs C. I of course shall not aid & abet her as Mrs Cs much the most fit person & has been now 20 yrs devoted to the work—

    After the meeting was over I went to Johns & dined there— They were very anxious about Catherine[1] who has a bad attack of irricipulous now very prevelent in the city— Dr Miller said she was dangerously ill— & had a consultation— & today I was rejoice to find her very much better very suffering but quite in her mind & I think out of danger— John has had a letter from Mrs. Knapp asking him to take charge of her property— he informed Mrs. May[2] of this— & at the same time that he had an offer of a hundred dollars a month for it— She replied that it must a fictitious offer & the person could have not just appreciation of the house & adds that she has deposited every month $25— & she will now put $35— a month— John says that he will demand at least 60, or a hundred & threaten to enforce his rights— did you ever hear of such nefarious assurance?— I have not mentioned the names of any of the concern to any body but John since you left—

John says Mr Lincoln has sent him work entirely out of his office— & one case outside his line— was referred to him by the special request of the Govr[3] & all the members from the state of Illinois— not one of whom he had ever seen It is evident that he helps the President— who has found him able, & honest, & with a heart as good as his head— which is saying a great deal for it

I went with Betty to pay Visits to day— Called at the Wadsworth who are in the Markoe house. Welles & Sewards— & on the Marcys[4] who are at Mayor Berrets— I seized the opportunity to call on the Mayors wife[5]— I went to see Mrs. Trumbull & she is better— pitched into Mary of the White House— I had a good opportunity upon her assertion that "She had no un-kind feelings—" but &et— today I had been sounded as one of her friends by a person who I thought mean of to repeat my answers— as to what her feelings were when I repeat only such things that showed she had no unkind feelings— indeed I thought her too good a woman— to return ill will long towards anybody— She looked delighted— but added— that she wished all her friends had been as "*prudent*" in her behalf   I never saw a more lovely baby than this last one she has—

Mrs. Sands[6] came out with us brought with her little one who has lost the use of her limbs since she had the measles— Mrs S exclaimed when she saw Blair— Well he looks as if he had never been sick a day in his life. Mrs Trumbull was down on McClellan— asked me what I thought   I replied you said I only thought of people what I wished— & that I had so much staked on his success that I would be miserable if I doubted it a moment— She said "the War" Committee doubted him & she thought with reasons most ample— I thought of McClellans reply— when told of this combination in the War Dept— & Congress— Well if I succeed they cannot hurt me—if I fail— they cannot help me"— John told me this   John thought there was fighting on the whole line of the Rappahannock today   the Secesh confess to immense loss in the Winchester fight   our people say it amounts to two thousand— but this must be an exaggeration— I saw a party of Prisoners from that part of the world today— they look very jolly & had some of our Soldiers coats on to keep them warm— The Donkey Cart is at Johns but the Road is so bad I am afraid to bring it home   Phil is delighted with it & sent Blair word he would like to help him drive it— Fanny Hunt is said to be engaged to Genl Gibsons[7] nephew— I believe if she had accepted him in the Old Man's life time that he would have made them his heirs—

Apl 3rd A bright spring day— went with Mrs Sands to see Cousin Nancy[8] who looked badly— was alone with no one in the house but her darkies— her old age is sad— She asked with real interest about you— her mind is clear— No war news to night— & the movement of the troops are unknown to even the wives— Mrs Sands says her brothers wife has no tidings from Genl— French[9]   I see no one who knows but all suppose that Richmond is getting encircled by fire— Blair is bright & hearty as we could wish Indeed we are all well at Silver Spring Ever your devoted Lizzie In a letter from Mary Blair she says that Jesup prayed for his Uncle Phil's happy return to Aunt Lizzie that we both might always well & happy he is a warm hearted boy to his Aunty Always *Mary* sends her regards to you—

    1. Catherine was John Lee's servant.

    2. Catherine Hite Lee May was the wife of Dr. George May.

    3. Gov. Richard Yates of Illinois (1861–65).

    4. Randolph Barnes Marcy, father-in-law of George McClellan, served as McClellan's chief of staff. His wife was Mary A. Mann, daughter of Gen. Jonas Mann of Syracuse, New York.

    5. Julia M. Berret was the wife of Washington mayor James E. Berret.

    6. Henrietta Maria French Sands, wife of Benjamin Franklin Sands.

    7. Gen. George Gibson served in the War of 1812 and the Mexican War. He died on September 29, 1861.

    8. Cousin Nancy Ann ("Miss Nancy") Carroll, granddaughter of Daniel Carroll II, lived at The Cottage.

    9. Gen. William French commanded a brigade in the Peninsular Campaign. Henrietta Sands was his sister.

Silver Spring   April 4, [1862]

Dear Phil   I was glad to find Catherine out of danger today The poor creature in all her delirium never for one moment was disobedient to Nelly— & all her ideas were about Nelly & John & anxiety to help them— which she was doing with her strength when she was taken ill— John has sent Sarah & Old Henry down to the Country preparatory to this emancipation act in the District which will undoubtedly soon become a law— has already passed the Senate— this reduced Nelly's household considerably— They have now a dowdy looking Irish cook & Luke takes care of the Stable— as they keep but one horse— I expect the planters in Prince George will emmigrate their slaves to the Cotton states & get good prices for them as so many there will be freed by Confiscation—Henry & Becky say that nearly all the owners of slaves have sent them into Virginia & Maryland from the District I spent this day mostly in Orphan Asylum business, trying to make & keep the peace in vain I fear Mrs Coxe will resign

April 5th Jim's[1] first exclamation this morning was Well I must be a bad boy— it rains every time I come out here for fun— Still he did have a good time & enjoyed himself & the Donkey very much today— Blair thinks he would like to live in the City where he could have plenty of boys to play with— he gets quite lonesome for Jim after he leaves some times— they are devoted friends— Andrew was here & Woody—[2] so it was a noisy house all of day— Grandpa went off to the City he is on *tenters* to hear from *Island No.* 10— it is privately hinted in town (Frank told us that Foote is digging a sluice which

will circumvent the confederates & surround them so completely that they
will be *captivated*— without any more ado— The papers are full of the taking
of Forts St Philips & Jackson— but no body says whence comes the rumours
or who did it or when?— Fort Pulaski [3] is in the last ditch but wants to give up
with the honors of War— which is refused—

I see by the War Dept orders that McClellan has given up two more *slipes* of
his army— to Banks & McDowell— & it is believed in town that Virginia will
be evacuated without a fight The Rebels are certainly shrinking from the Rappahannock line already— Then of course North Carolina never was a willing
secesh victim so that will put the War in the right place at last in the seven
seceders I think Virginians (our Lee friends will feel bad when that happens
They ought to lay down their Arms & take the oath at once when Virginia is
evacuated— & I believe all but the ringleaders will escape the punishment of
their treason— From all I hear the seceded officers of the Army & Navy— will
have a hard time— & I sincerely wish some of them were safely & comfortably
fixed abroad— for they were some! victimized against their own principles—
& yet for that people are most sure to suffer in this & the next world—

I am very anxious about the attack on New Orleans because I know you
have had time to get there— & you cannot imagine how anxious these rumors
make me— I expect they are mere supposition, for nothing else is stated—
in the Richmond Dispatch The vote in Western Virginia is largely (by the
people) in favor of gradual emancipation so say this evenings papers Such
being the case I think Eastern Virginia will part with her gladly—

Mrs Sands little child is recovering marvellously fast— today she sat up
alone— & kicked her feet gaily— William Hills [4] daughter Anna— has become bedridden— her limbs as useless to her & as limber as rags & has been
so now ever since the 1st of January— Nelly seemed fear a serious end of the
case indeed is hopeless about it She had diptheria when Phil had it in the ears
& not the throat— this is a most singular disease Blair is the best pleased boy
with his cart & it is a very pretty diminutive Jersy waggon— well got up &
strong looking for its size— & Horace has your Squirril painted on the pan-
nel— He evidently took great interest in this big toy for Blair— his big dog
follows them everywhere— & Becky says she feels as if he was able to take
good care of the whole party he follows Blair & wont allow any body to jerk
or hurt him— he evidently is the Nurse No 2— & it forms quite a cortege the
donkey. dog— Henry Becky & Blair & Cart is the last addition

Birney got back from Poolesville— says she is going to the city to live—
I am going there next week & the one after to go to church on church days
& get my share of flowers from Franks gift— pay some visits & then I'll stay
home save to go to church days which Ill do until Easter— After that I'll gad
very little except on my Sunday to Church which is my best attraction & sole
pleasure in going there The Asylum worries me— but I'll hold on

I met Janet Powell to day— Just out from an attack of measles— expects soon to get some teeth— & any other juvenile performance that is due in childhood— says Powell[5] is luxuriating in the attentions & devotions of the Allies at Vera Cruz— appreciates better than ever the charm of belle ship— since he has had so many attentions *devotion* to his flag & himself Blair sleeps in his little bed at this sweetly— & looks ruddy & stout— I would be very proud to show him to you & happy too— So I'll go pray that that joy may be ours   Yr devoted Lizzie

1. Jim Blair, born 1854, was Frank and Apo Blair's son.
2. Woodbury Blair, born 1852, was Montgomery and Minna's son.
3. Fort Pulaski, Tennessee, well south of Nashville.
4. William B. Hill, born 1813, was Ellen Lee's eldest brother. Anna Smith Hill was his daughter.
5. Capt. Levin M. Powell, commanding U.S. frigate *Potomac*, was sent to Vera Cruz in February and dispatched regular reports to the Navy Department on events in Mexico. He returned to Key West May 29, 1862.

Silver Spring   April 6, 1862

Dear Phil   There were four or five gentlemen out here to dinner & before I came down to dinner some conversation about getting office was on the Topis— after I got to the table Mother said "Well I am glad to hear some grumbling on that score— for I too have my wrongs— I have asked employment but for one person the daughter of an old patriot Commodore who did battle for us in our last war with England— he was for years my neighbor & once saved my house from burning down— for his child a widow with house full of little children I begged bread— & have not got it yet even from my own son— He vowed twas the first he had heard of it— she appealed to Father & the rest of us— to testify how often it had been her earnest entreaty to Father & she thought to all & everybody she knew— we all had to testify she had been in season & out it too   I went off in a pleasant way but I think Brother will not invite such another attack by neglecting her wishes—

I had a long letter from Fanny today   she says her husband has started a one horse carriage as she is not so well as she had been & needed exercise of this sort— Mr Pettit[1] is certainly a most kind husband to her— & at this time she need care & kindness   She writes about the War the Hospitals where Mr P— will not consent to her going but her benevolence always abounding now overflows for our poor suffering soldiers

No news of import today— I was nurse & did not go to the City as I was loth to take Blair there whilst there's sickness in all the houses he frequents— Apo is still in Phila for Georges[2] eyes— Dr. Hays thinks them in a bad way— & their disorder wholly mistaken by Dr. Johnston[3]   Christine[4] is not well & I have been expecting a summons from Mrs. Alexander to go in to nurse her— which I offered to do if she was sick enough to go bed— She is better today   Blair & Preston[5] basked raced & rompted in the sunshine of this Spring day— Mrs Sands baby improves almost hourly— as she has nothing but debility the mat[t]er   eating & sleeping soon renovates such Cases—

I had not a chance to pump a single item of the *under* current out Frank Father or Mr Doolittle today   The last is vastly pleased with his emancipation feature in the Emancipation Bill presented by the Senate to the House a few days ago— Army & Navy were discussed Regulars nothing is more certain than that the Navy has won back all its old prestige over the Army somewhat dimmed by the Mexican War but that theres no depravity in the Navy is admitted by all   Mrs Morris[6] says she is very proud that her boy has at least shown his fathers courage

Monday April 6th We have a relapse with winter this morning— I had a person employed to come for my flower garden— but it is now indefinitely postponed   I never saw a more backward spring— all the better for our fruit— McDowell & Banks are left to protect Washington & McClellan has gone down the Bay to operate on Richmond & Norfolk   Vincent waits so Ive only time to say we are all well   Ever your devoted Lizzie

1. William Frederick Pettit, SPL's sister's second husband.
2. George Blair, born 1860, was the son of Frank and Apo Blair.
3. Washington physician W. P. Johnston.
4. Christine Biddle Blair, born 1852, was Frank and Apo Blair's daughter.
5. Francis Preston Blair, born 1856, was Frank and Apo Blair's son.
6. Eleanora Morris was the widow of Commodore Charles Morris. Her son was Lt. George U. Morris, executive officer on the *Cumberland.* When the *Virginia* attacked Union ships at Hampton Roads on March 8, Morris was in command in the absence of the captain. Morris fought bravely, but his ship was sunk.

Silver Spring   April 10, 1862

My dear Phil   We supped last night full of victory & horrors— the Papers report that Buell & Beauregard had met & that 30,000 men were killed in the conflict,[1] & our men were in hot pursuit to kill more— The only offset to this scene of blood is the complete surrounding & surrender of Island No. 10 without a loss of a man on our side—[2]   Genl Pope overtook & captured 50,000— of the those who retreated— Capt Foote says the place would have been impregnable if defended by men in a good cause

McClellan invested Yorktown on Saturday— where they have breastworks extending from the York— to the James River seven miles— The battle there I think will be the last one of huge propotions to be fought & it is a comfort to see the end of this sad war or even to hope we see it— I hope the defeat at Pittsburg Landing or as it is styled "The battle of Corinth[3] will make New Orleans fall easily in the hands of your gunboats— for the Delta & other papers are attacked by the Richmond Dispatch as "talking vile treason—" so I take comfort & hope & hope you may have no strife to go thro!

Fanny writes that she now only prays that the south will lay down their arms without another struggle— & make the best of their hopeless case— It is time for all of them to see their folly & wickedness— I cant for an instant divest myself of feeling that they are my people my countrymen— mad men as they are my heart aches for them— tho' I must confess I think of them with less patience at New Orleans than any where else There they are my enemies & I feel it but always think of them as frenchmen & quadroons This war news is only theme of talk— & of thought—

Thursday night— We had a visit from Mr. Briggs the brother of Mrs Merrick—[4] he brought us out more details of the battles of Corinth & the awful slaughter there— He says Mrs Merrick is still an invalid but she is well enough to make & send me a pretty gear to wear out doors— He says all this excitement about the battle just fought & being fought for I suppose that delayed at Yorktown by the three days storm has now commenced in earnest again to day in the soft sunshine which comes out strangely upon a deep snow here—

Blair was out today with his donkey & is Mr. Briggs says now quite stout enough to pass for a Yankee boy Mr. B saw a great change in him— both in his complexion & fullness of his figure & face— it would seem that the measles has wrought a change his constitution all for his good— so I am thankful— for the measles— and if we will keep our hearts true to our Creator all our troubles will ever work out for our good— for it is so promised You seem to think that you were over zealous in getting off so soon & might have been ordered Now that the Merrimac is at Craney Island hourly expected to make an onslaught on the vessels in Hampton Roads I am glad you are not there particularly as Foote is now in pursuit of the Turtle & all such craft on the Missippi—

April 11. 1862 You see who has been send you love & kisses to you[5] he says I would not let him tell you all about his cart & Donkey— We are all well & off in a few moments to the City I am going to Church & to do some shopping for Mother Blair & myself— tho it looks so much like winter it is hardly encouraging to buy spring clothing Ever your devoted Lizzie
Blair wants to tell you about the squirrel on the cart

1. Gen. Don Carlos Buell led the Army of Ohio in the capture of Nashville, then proceeded south and on April 7, joined Grant's army at Shiloh. The Union suffered 1,754 killed and the Confederates lost 1,723 killed.

2. On April 7, Gen. John Pope, commanding the Union Army of the Mississippi, took Island Number 10.

3. On April 6, Grant's forces were pushed back at Pittsburg Landing; on the seventh, they regained the ground.

4. Anne L. Merrick was the sister of Henry S. Briggs of the Tenth Massachusetts.
5. Lines of Blair's scribbles

Silver Spring   April 11, 1862
Dear Phil   On our way to the city we met Mrs. Hoban—[1] laden with the dreadful news of the death of Willie Sands—[2] he was drowned on the 2nd inst— & that is all the telegraph divulged— I did not return— but Betty went to Marion & Mrs. Sands came to the City immediately & I went to see her She grieves for herself— but says her son was a member of the Church & has been the best child any Mother ever had— her face is gentle, tearful, submissive— You know deeply I feel for them

I went to Church & there Mrs Harris[3] who told me I was unanimously elected to fill Mrs Coxes place she having resigned against my advice— This troubled me—[4] I went to My Brother's there learned Fox just returned from before Yorktown— McClellan has 80,000 troops— Rebels have over 100,000— behind entrenchments— He wants more Troops Stanton refuses them— has detached McDowell from his McClellans command— I ache all over in anxiety & sorrow this night & shall know no rest or comfort save in prayer for my husband my country & my friends

April 12th 1862— My Fathers *seventy first birthday*— Blair took him a pair of gloves & kissed him in bed— he then returned to my room ate his breakfast then off again to Grandpa— when they had "fun shaving—" Blair imitating Father with a piece of whalebone as a razor— I heard great laughing so the proceeding must have been comical— He is now off with the donkey cart Becky & the small darkies—

Altho Father said yesterday he would stay home & let the news come to him— but he took to his horse full of a letter to McClellan if he writes it I tell you its purport— Father came back just now— says no news— he wrote to Mc. not to let the Carpet Knights in Congress hurry or worry him into doing anything ignore them Reinforcements were sent to him last night & today 40,000 more troops— but McDowell stays opposite Washington— I think the Yorktown seige will be slow & long—

Sunday *Apl 13*. My day to go to Church so I am off in a few moments stop to say we are all well Blair & Ned Byrne[5] are playing by the window— Blair has on an old coat blue one in which you have seen him often— & it is much above his knees now & shows how rapidly he grows & now he is stout also I am thin as usual but quite well All well at Johns Ever your devoted Lizzie

1. Marion Hoban, widow of James Hoban, Jr., lived next door to the Sandses.
2. Willie Sands was the son of Henrietta and B. F. Sands.
3. Mary G. Harris was the wife of Marine Commandant John Harris. She served on the asylum board with EBL.
4. On April 14, EBL wrote that "I went to see our late Presidentess of the Asylum

board— we had a pleasant talk I told her I could not act without her permission & she was pleased evidently with her successor because she had not sought anything but to keep her in place— this has been a funny fight— & Mrs. Coxe told me the War would begin on me next— I told her I would make no fight first because I was a noncombatant— secondly because the post was a burden— & destroyed all my fun of which she knew I had a great deal when I was only looking on & then she I talked over some scenes past— enjoyed them all afresh— & parted in good spirits & good will she said she pitied me & I accepted her compassion with becoming humility and gratitude—."

5. Edward (Ned) Byrne was the deaf son of Blair's first nurse, Martha Byrne Cook. EBL often spelled the last name as it sounded, Birney.

Silver Spring   April 15, [1862]

Dear Phil   I sent Vincent off early & did his work in the pantry to get my letters by the Connecticut as promised on Sunday by Mr. Fox— none came & I even more on the anxious seat than ever for the "New Orleans battle" is again floating about in rumors— Fort Pulaski is taken at last[1] our guns broke the Walls off it so says the Telegraph I'll be off early myself in the morning— for letter for I am famished to hear from you— I never was as restless & nervous before in my life— & tho I try to take cheerful hopeful views of things yet no amount of fatigue & occupation drive away from me an aching misery that is both mental & physical—[2]

This spring is late like that during which we were married & the events of that time come back to me it seems to me as vividly as if they occurred yesterday & I know the vows I made then live as freshly in my heart as the hour I made them and how thankful I am to God that he did put it in my heart to love you so devotedly (even tho it makes me ache now) yet it in looking back over the past I can see how happily guided me thro the most troubles of my life— & of all my joys the best & dearest It will be nineteen years since were wedded— by the time this reaches you Last year up to the 27. I was in great distress about my home John & this dreadful Civil War— but I went to breakfast that day & Nelly said why you look so bright today. I said twas my wedding day. I added I always feel as if I would have some cause of special joy today— Soon after saying this I got your letters so long sighed for— but it has always been my bright day of the year & you see even now it gives light to these dark days of anxiety—

April 17. Went to Church this morning Thence to see Maria poor little child is still confined to the bed— did some shopping for Mother— the Sands & then awaited Bettys movements at Johns— talked over servants & spring [word illegible] with Nelly & came home tired out & with a headache

April 17— Thursday— Father had a very manly letter from McClellan[3] says he knows all the difficulties of his situation— but adds "that knowledge is an element of success." he is grateful for Fathers good advice— but I'll copy it for you. Jeff Davis has sent in to his Congress a message of thanksgiving for the

Victory of the 6th inst— he dont mention what occurred on the 7th[4] There is an elaborate account of the defences of New Orleans in the papers of today They are very formidable— but theres news from the south tonight which says that several steamers & the Mortars have gone by the Forts Jackson & Philip—[5] without opposition this comes by Pensacola & Key West— I had a letter from Horace saying Aunt Becky had a bad cough & was confined to the "second story" by it—

I believe I mentioned the advice alluded— it was to work deliberately— & emulate that virtue which Washington's enemies called rascally— his letter was short kind & I thought excellent. This response shows it was & well timed— Never mention this copy to any body. I believe you are posted as to the *Cabal* & their industry is wonderful[6] Mrs. Hatch[7] was here to day & mentioned how rife abuse about delays & everything else were today in the city— but the President is his staunch ally— & has proved himself so on this occasion tho at first misled— But we are all in the most anxious condition— New Orleans— & Yorktown are on the lips of all— & I can truly say you are ever in my thoughts for when sleeping I see you more plainly than ever in the garish light of day— Blair had a frolick with the boys today who are released from school by the holidays   Your ever devoted Lizzie

1. Fort Pulaski, Georgia, near Savannah, fell to federal troops on April 11, 1862.

2. In her May 1 letter, EBL described her attempts to keep occupied: "My flowers need attention & I must go to work it may help me thro this 'crisis' but my heart is far far away— my bread is as chips & no labor attracts or interest me & I hang about my child for quietness— & I can watch his plays with pleasure— & little does he know how much he really does take care of his Mama for his Papa—."

3. Name of McClellan marked out. The enclosed letter from McClellan to FPB was marked *Confidential:* "I beg to thank you for yr kind letter & the counsel it contains, at a moment when I have but partially shaken off the difficulties placed in my path by some who ought to be my friends. & when I am still face to face with the obstacles presented by the enemy, it is indeed a consolation & a source of new strength that one so honored & so venerated as yrself should take the trouble to adress such kind words to me— I have not been for a moment discouraged although I confess I have for a time felt sadly enough I fully appreciate the military difficulties of my position— but in that appreciation are the elements of success— I possess the means of ensuring victory— I think nothing human sure— but I do not for a moment doubt the result of this operation. I will take Y.— take it too without an undue loss of life— Again thanking you for yr kindness I am respectfully & truly yr friend—."

4. On April 6, the first day of the Battle of Shiloh, the Confederates pushed the federal forces back toward the Tennessee River. On April 7, reinforced by Buell, Grant regained the ground lost the previous day, and the rebels withdrew to Corinth, Mississippi.

5. Federal bombardment of Forts Jackson and St. Philip began on April 17; Farragut's fleet did not run past these forts until April 24.

6. On April 14 EBL had written: "I hope *somebody* will get tired of Presidential Candidates— Miss Kates father [Salmon Chase] has now got Genl McBowels as Frank calls him mounted behind him & they are trying the abolition nag together—full tilt versus the other Mc & his Commander in Chief—."
7. Probably Elizabeth Hatch, wife of Washington lawyer Nathaniel Hatch.

                                        Silver Spring   April 18, 1862
Dear Phil   A hot day in winter clothes not comfortably spent in going about the dirty City. No news from New Orleans & it was really a friday of penance to me— so I'll go to bed without grumbling over it to you— Mr. Fox's announcement of the Connecticut has made this a whole week of disappointment— for I've been in almost daily— & returned without letters & I fear I have grieved for them more than I ought to do but Ill stay home a day then maybe they will come—

April 19. 1862 Anniversary of the Baltimore Row[1] & it is whispered the emancipation Bill in the District[2] has renewed the rebellious spirit there & almost everywhere in the Secesh parts of Maryland Joe Cook was here this morning he is stationed near Balt & says things look very squally there— Vincent has announced his wish "to go *in the world* to better his condition" Father at first was puzzled what to do— but I begged him to let him go & to take Alick in the house & I am quite certain at the end of six weeks to make him a better house servant than Vincent & not doing great things either— The rest of the servants are going to remain on their old terms— Henry says he is content where he is— & is not used to knocking about among common folks. been used to quality all his days & wants to spend the rest of them with them—

The Lovejoys[3] were here today evidently to see the effect of the emancipation Act on us— They put direct questions on the subject when Father said his servants always knew they could go when they wished— & they were of course now at liberty to do so— but all but one declined "the priviledge They looked amazed— said they had heard of such things but never saw them before— I have enquiring in the City & can get other servants if we need them I have an idea that Mary "*wants to see the* world too" & as I can get a better Cook for Mother I am inclined to suggest Marys departure as an experiment for awhile for the above purpose— Mother of course cant bear any change but Marys pickings for her husband at Wilsons would pay a cook— She is a good cook & a kind creature but never honest— Mary has said nothing to me I hear however thro' Becky who advises her to stay where she is—

I expected all of them would put out for the City & was rather surprised when Nannie Olivia & Henry told their purpose Nanny says she knows when she is well off but is evidently delighted that her children are free This Bill has liberated about one thousand blacks & has made about two thousand very miserable— by having them sent away in Maryland Kentucky & Virginia— All of Beckys sisters neices nephews have been liberated by the Miss Bell— who have always been emancipationists— The Lovejoys say the Presidents messages have given the Republican party "*a policy*—" Emancipation compensation & colonization— satisfies all shades of Republicans— Frank says his bills are getting in favor daily—[4] I see that the Common Council of St Louis "*unanimously*" compliment & thank Frank about his Ship Canal & his zeal in behalf of Western interests—

Our papers are now filled with the melancholy lists of killed & wounded at Pittsburg Landing which battle in all its details and phases are discussed & the Generals on our side somewhat roughly handled and Sherman is in spite of Grant's[5] bolstering disgraced. The Navy comes out well in this as in every conflict essayed so far— Fox went down to Old Point & remained there until Goldsborough came & took command— I thought it a funny notion but said nauthing— Uncle Ben has not been to Phila   Joe Shelby[6] is with Beauregard & his Mother is too miserable about him to be left by her husband   Gratz Cohen[7] is among the prisoners taken at Fort Pulaski— William Preston is not killed but a John Preston either a cousin or Uncle of *Tom*—

Blair & I are to dine tomorrow with John & the boys who are now out of College When the children went home to day Blair was lonesome & asked what is tomorrow— I told him Easter Sunday "Oh then we are to dine with the boys & Uncle John—" he was immediately in a glee again told Becky about— & I saw he has his *town clothes* put out ready for the mornings Toilet He shares his toys very kindly with other children— Mother took them all fishing in Sligo yesterday had no luck but "lots of fun" She is never so happy as when surrounded by a troop of boys— Andrew took all the premiums & of course was duly recompensed here for it— I'll send you some of John's news tomorrow night They were all well there yesterday   Ever your affectionate Lizzie

1. On April 19, 1861, there was rioting in Baltimore when federal troops passed through the city.

2. On April 16, 1862, Lincoln signed the bill emancipating slaves in the District of Columbia.

3. Owen Lovejoy, abolitionist and brother of martyred Elijah Lovejoy, had been elected congressman from Illinois in 1856. His wife was Eunice Storrs Dunham.

4. On April 21, EBL reported that Frank planned to return to St. Louis shortly: "this move puzzles my Father— for he has been able to hold him here until he is intensely interested in the passage of his Bills to escheat Rebel estates for non payt of taxes & his ship canal— & Pacific Railroad Bills— All of which are just coming up now— he has reported on all long since & now he is off at the pinch of the game—." EBL offered her reason for "this new turn West— I fear tis the *finance* question— he has lately refunded all his Col's pay Father thinks tis to join the Army— but I speculate only to give you the family talk au courant."

5. U. S. Grant, Union commander at Shiloh. Brig. Gen. William T. Sherman, commanding the Fifth Division at Shiloh, was accused of being surprised by rebel attack—which he had been.

6. Joseph Shelby was the son of Anna Maria Boswell Shelby Gratz, Benjamin Gratz's second wife.

7. Gratz Cohen was related by marriage to the Blairs.

Silver Spring   April 23, 1862

My Dear Phil   I met Mrs Ro[d]gers yesterday who was enchanted that Capt John had got the "*Galena*" alias Mystic— Capt Alfred Taylor returning from his ship to the Charleston Navy Yard[1] I have heard that Taylor was loth to fight in this war as he was *sympathetic*" & I suppose gladly takes the Yard—

I had a business day with Mrs Franklin & Mrs Hodge[2] on Orphan Asylum matters & have to go again on Friday theres one comfort in this business— I am at home in it— for I feel nearly as homeless as you do— for tho' I love Silver Spring & all its dear inmates— I have been once uprooted & have never again put out my tendrils to take hold of it as a home again & tho I occupy myself in the garden— & flowers I never feel as if I were doing it for myself— I love those for whom I do it enough to do it gladly— Still it is not with the sensations of yore— but I have a home field of occupation in my child & how endless is the comfort this little one gives me— His sympathies are so warm & so in accord with my feelings in all things

Beckys former owners have freed Harriet & her children— & another sister of Beckys— but have taken away a niece which has grieved Becky very much indeed— Becky says the colored people all want "to *colonize* to Central America which is only half way to California—" John goes in for white labor *entirely* now in his household   I am rejoiced— the effect will be good upon his children   I heard that the abolitionists sent & said so many painful things to Mrs. McClelland[3] that her Mother has taken her off to New York among her friends— fearing the effects of her distress here upon her health— This I had from a next door neighbor

Blair Becky & I have put the dahlias out to sprout today— I gave this job to Neddy some days ago but he *shirked* it— So I had to do it today   this— & reading— have consumed the day— Good night—

April 24th Went to the City & first to the Post Office— but got no news or letters— The Secesh papers say there are 40 or 50 U.S. Gunboats below New Orleans & I never hear that now that I dont realize the tension under which I live   nothing can be more restless than this little woman of yours   I can still talk about you to Blair & consequently I know I am not so bad off as I might be for when I get too wretched about you I cant say your name even—[4] but I must talk of somebody else than myself in this letter   Blair's letter is full the donkey's feats— & his own kisses for Papa— he is full joyousness & health   Ever yr own Lizzie

April 25th Another rainy day but I am going to send Neddy Byrne for the mail this evening on horseback— Ned prefers staying here with Blair & me to going about the world with his mother & Joe— they board him & clothe him— I as have always done send him to school & he is here when he is not at school— he is devoted to the donkey & works about the place a little— but plays with Blair & gives him boyish plays with marbles & adds to the fellow's enjoyments I have had to keep Blair in the house from measles & the rain more this spring than ever before— We are all well but Mother who is very rheumatic— Betty is 21 today & groans over it as Mother does over her aches—

I went to see Mrs Winn[5] today who has the Dangerfield children staying with her a few days— the children are sturdy but the eldest *plain* & gauche Mary[6] is handsome— Madame La belle Mere is going to increase the tribe of Dangerfields— Mrs W. is sorry enough for it as she has been so far very kind to these children— who are evidently healthy & clean but riotous & rough enough—with considerable look of vigor which I think the first requisite— in rearing children— Blair told me to night that Luke tried to make him hurrah for Jeff Davis on Sunday & said he would shoot marbles at his head if he did not— & that was the reason he did not want to stay there on Sunday. John has this boy in the War Dept. & I feel sorely tempted to tell him about this but fear to do so for I get along there so well that I never like to utter a word about anything likely to ruffle my intercourse— but this boy has picked up this nonsense & thinks it a virtue to stick to his opinions— which I dont care about except that they might leak out & compromise John in the Dept— I think Ill suggest to John to change Lukes politics & give the hint in a joke— fearing the world might misjudge the Master by the Man The Emancipation act in the District has made Secesh very very bitter in these parts tho it stifled very much

I went to see Mrs Washington about Asylum business— & Mrs Davidge[7] for herself— they intimated too plainly they meant to return it here— so I put the whole of the visit on the Asylum— & kinship saying I could afford to waive formalities & etc— Mrs Washington was grieving for Mrs Talbot[8] in the loss of her son Theodore who was buried today— from there I did Mothers errands— then home again— one of the errands was to go to the Capitol gardener & claim Franks gift to me of some flowers for my borders but today is as cold as winter & grey & dreary but we have had rainbows just as during *our* spring 1843 & so it may be like that a harbinger of happier times

1. Capt. Alfred Taylor, born in Fairfax County, Virginia, in 1810, was a career naval officer. From 1862 to 1865 he was assigned to the Charleston Navy Yard at Boston.

2. Annie L. Clark married William B. Franklin in 1852. She was secretary-treasurer of the Washington City Orphan Asylum Board. Mrs. W. L. Hodge, wife of a Whig politician in the Fillmore administration, was the mother of Mrs. John Rodgers.

3. In 1860 Ellen Marcy married George B. McClellan. She was the daughter of Randolph B. Marcy.

4. On May 1, EBL wrote: "I am on the rack with anxiety about you— I have held on to all my home & town occupations until now but today when mother ordered me to make out her list for purchases for her— she looked at me & volunteered to say I was not fit to go & went herself— for she knows me well enough to be sure that I will muster a cheerful face as long as possible & when I cannot do it I like to be alone— aluxury I now enjoy—."

5. Mary L. Winn, an old friend of EBL's, was the sister of William Dulaney of the Marine Corps. She referred to EBL as "cousin." Mrs. Winn was also probably related to Timothy Winn who had served in the navy and became wealthy as one of the owners of the Anacostia River bridge.

6. Mary Dunlap married William Henry Daingerfield in 1848.

7. Mrs. D. Washington served with EBL on the asylum board. Anna Louisa Washington married Walter Dorsey Davidge, a distinguished lawyer. She was the daughter of Ann Matilda Lee and Dr. Bailey Washington.

8. Adelaide Talbot was the wife of Isham Talbot. He was U.S. senator from Kentucky (1815–19 and 1820–25).

Silver Spring   April 27, 1862

Dear Phil   I have spent this our wedding day mostly at Church & if I had dared murmur that it was not as happy as I had spent others it was hushed by the sight of Mrs Sands— whose face tells the whole misery of the giving up of ones first born— Ours is still here to gladden our future weddings I hope & I can pray that all those to come may be spent together Everybody was talking about the news to come from New Orleans— it was expected any hour— whence? or how? I could not fathom & yet I believe it was a longing hoping that kept me so late in town this evening. my wedding day brings me good tidings & good gifts & I confess I turn away home now feeling I had left my letters behind— but you'll think me foolish especially when I went to the Office the last thing & could hear of no news in any quarter— Still I believe it will come tonight & so believing will go to bed—

April 28 As I felt in my bones news did reach the City last evening that New Orleans had surrendered to our gunboats[1] so says the Secesh telegraph but Fox announces it as done by Porter's Mortar boats— God grant that you have escaped unharmed thro the perils of the ascent of the Mississippi River It will bore you but I can think of nothing but this matter & shall go to the City in the morning to see if I cannot get tidings from you—

Yesterday my Brother & Mr. Doolittle dined here I was glad to see him going out as our Old Crony P. King[2] is *cooled* off to all our concern except Father & me & even to us is not as of yore— His coming election makes him tender footed as to abolitionist— & they are evidently organizing in oppo-

sition to the Administration— taking issue on the habeus Corpus & all the
points in which it is assailable— The Germans are fortunately taking the lead
in this matter—

The President & Cabinet are very sweet on the french Steamer now at Our
Yard & they paid him Imperial honors when they received him on Board—
They say chickens cost $6 a pair in Norfolk— The Capt told Mrs Seward[3] that
he sent Jeff Davis some coffee who returned the compliment in Va hams—
They say they were astonished there so much at the warmth of friendship expressed by individuals separated by this War— When in Richmond he had to
make memoranda of the endless people who sent loving messages to friends
in Washington & some were uttered in a flood of tears They say the women
are crazy in Richmond— that is just my opinion all this secession is a suicidal
madness

I told Nelly Blair's speech "I will fight Luke & that speckled face boy
(Eugene Hill)[4] when I get to be a big boy—" She laughed & said Phil did.
not escape on that memorable Sunday as well as Blair did for the boys rolled
him down stairs— hurt his head then took him in the rain & he caught a bad
cold— wheras Blair only got a fit of ill temper— She laughed heartily & took
it in good part— I was glad thus to let her know Lukes talk—

Lizzie Pearson[5] & her Mother were here today terribly worked up by the
emancipation Bill— they got about 9,000 dollars!! for thirty servants[6] Lizzie
says Kate Gaston[7] writes frantically— When they were going away Blair as
usual refused to kiss the children I whispered to him "these little girls are your
Papa's Cousins" he instantly kissed one of them but the other refused after he
had been uncivil to her— They rode in the Donkey Cart— & took lunch
& were evidently well pleased with their visit— The little Jay boy was with
them— he is well grown & well mannered—

I have been working in the garden & now I hope am weary enough to sleep
a good thing not much enjoyed by me of late— Blair greeted you so joyously
this morning that he made feel better— how superstitions & nervous anxieties
makes one Everything plays upon one— but nothing comforts for the earnest
prayers for your welfare devotedly your Lizzie

1. The city of New Orleans was taken on April 25, 1862.

2. Preston King, Republican senator from New York (1857–63).

3. Frances Adeline Miller married William H. Seward in 1824.

4. Probably Eugene F. Hill, born 1845. His father, Charles Hill, Sr., and Ellen
Lee's father were brothers.

5. EBL's old friend Lizzie Pearson & her mother lived at Brentwood. They were
related to the Lees through the Brent family.

6. Lincoln signed the congressional emancipation bill for the District of Columbia

on April 16, 1862. It provided for average compensation to the owner of $300 per slave.
   7. Kate Gaston, the sister of Eliza Gaston Graham, lived with the Grahams in Prince Georges County.

                                              Silver Spring   April 29, [1862]
Dear Phil   Was off early in hopes of letters & two got a hearty welcome— Yr "long" from yr departure from Key West— your arrival at SW Pass— Your 9 days of fog & etc there and the letter from the Head of the Passes— to the 8th inst— 20 days ago— I have read them over & over & enjoyed your cheerful spirit until I felt almost light hearted myself but the knowledge that you had run the gauntlett of Rebel defences which appear frightfully formidable to me since these letters were written soon chocked all joy out of my heart & my fears haunt me waking & sleeping   I felt very thankful to Mr. Seward for reading prayers— I hope he continues it
   After reading my letters I went to the meeting of the Orphan board & was there from twelve to 3½ olk— Blair & Becky waited long at the door in the Carriage for to go comply with a promise to Maria Smith to take Blair to see her— as she had never seen him in *pants*— She was in an extasy over his beauty   I had to show her I did [not] like him to hear that sort of praise but she says he is a picture of "robust boyish beauty" he has grown much stouter than at any time since he has walked— All of his clothing has been or is to be en-large immediately— Of course I enjoy his good looks & that others should do so too but his warm heart is the best of him— & then his sweet joyous temper is his next best gift & that they may grow with his growth is my most frequent prayer for him— After this visit we called for Miss Mary Wright—[1] (Genl Ws daughter) & father & then trotted out home as fast as the bad roads would let us.
   Father laughed heartily over your notice of Brother's letter Father did not write a line of it— When Brother got in the carriage— he said to me The Dept— has receiving glowing accounts of yr husbands intelligent & unwearied activity—" I said Well he says there were some good points in that letter of your's— &etc he tried to look dignified then broke down in a radiant smile of satisfaction— So ended the talk— the first time he has mentioned you to me for nearly 4 yrs[2]
   When waiting for Mrs Hodge to go with to the Board— I called for her as she is not well)— Kate Riggs[3] stopped me to say that Sally Brent[4] died last night of typhoid fever   Anne told me Saturday she was getting better— but on Sunday she became ill & when better she said did not intend to murmur— but she had hoped her pilgrimmage here was at end— & when dying expressed great joy in the near prospect of Heaven   how plainly I can now see her gentle sad face   That pretty Miss Merkle died also of this disease— I shall go to the funeral at the Cottage Chapel & take some flowers with me to put on her grave

The Sea Service of our Church is beautiful & parts of it have of late been use at St Johns & all this State by order of the Bishop

April 30th I have read column after column in the Herald of the letters from your fleet & was enjoyable even tho' I read of facts I knew before— but I knew also the inside current of facts & that gave it zest. but the letters are two & three days later than yrs to me— for one is on the 11th & then I have read the Rebel account of your bombardment— & of the sharp shooters hitting an officer via epauletts I rejoice you never wear yr toggery— it me a comfortable assurance *that* time— The Rebels say on the 22nd two of our gun boats got by the Forts & chains & they were not joined by others of the fleet until next day that they met the Louisiana Iron Clad battery— & then all the fleet *thirty* men of war are in front of New Orleans on the 24th Nobody knows what to believe from Rebel sources— their report of the battle of Pittsburg Landing I know has given you many useless pangs— so I am warned not to believe them now— but tis all speculation & boring to you still— I am just now scarce able to think of anything else

I went this morning to Sally Brents grave joining the short cortege as it passed our gates— I took the flowers & was helped by Jim (Dr. H's man) to plant them— Cousin Mira & Apos children spent the day here—

Frank Father Brother Mr. Blow of St Louis Mr. Fox— Andrew & Wood— & sundry others whose name I dont know are to go to Old Point day after tomorrow— I wish they were all safe back— but you will call me coward if I write out so many *fears* But there is a great military gathering down there now & it is a sight to see & the siege is not likely to close at Yorktown for ten days yet— & they say the Merrimac knows now that she cannot cope with two mailed Steamers   John Rogers writes his wife that the Galena dont compare in efficiency or comfort to the Monitor The House censured Cameron & Frémont today by endorsing the Reports of the Committee of Inquiry into their doings   Frank took no part in the debate which was in good taste— No news from Yorktown of import All eyes & hearts are now turned to New Orleans I hear scarce anything else discussed— & I am not sorry to have all the world in sympathy with my ever besetting thoughts— Blair had a jolly day with the children & all are well & merry— Ever your devoted Lizzie

1. Mary Wright was the daughter of Gen. Horatio G. Wright.

2. The animosity between S. P. Lee and Montgomery Blair had begun when the latter opposed the marriage of his sister to Lee. Additional disagreements, slights, and grievances intensified the ill feeling, and in 1858 the two men had stopped speaking to each other. Montgomery had even refused to talk to his sister about her husband.

3. Catherine Shedden Riggs, born 1842, was the daughter of George Riggs.

4. Sally Brent, daughter of Robert Y. and Harriet Brent, died April 28, 1862.

Silver Spring   May 6, 1862

Dear Phil   When I tell you I sat still today for five hours listening to & talking *orphan asylum*, you may know I am a weary woman this night— This was my first day as 1st Directress & I was determined they should not call me "*arbitrary*" & depose me for such an unwomanly trait or excuse) as Mrs Coxe was for doing her duty— So I proposed certain rules & regulations & got them all adopted unanimously— & shall govern myself & the Ladies govern themselves by rules of their own making none of which I'll give them any chance to forget for I have got Mr. Gideon [1] to print them & each will have a copy & I'll have one nicely bound to remain on the table before us whenever the Board meets— So you see I had a job of some size & it took a long time to get each one to understand— & then to amend & vote &etc— but they all seemed delighted with the idea & their own way of carrying it out—

I could not get Father to go see about Cousin Cornelia [2] today he was fagged out by his Yorktown trip but goes tomorrow morning— Our Army is in hot pursuit of Joe Johnston—[3] who is so says the under current— broken in heart & health— but was not Captured as I wrote last night

You will enjoy all the glorification over the capture of New Orleans— but my heart has not yet felt one throb of exaltation— & will not until set in motion by the sight of your handwriting— I work body & mind to avoid depression & sickness— but it seems to me the days & nights never were so long & leaden before & you never so dear to me because it never occurred to me that you were in danger before— that sort of faith & reliance which is a wifes habit that you have the power to take care of me, of yrself & of all who depend on you was never suspended [?] in my feelings until now but now it is the big guns, barricades & forts which may shake the little wooden vessel which holds my sailor man that troubles me—

Mrs Washington asked very lovingly after you today & said many kind things about you— Our next meeting is at her house as there is some sickness— at the Asylum A committee of Ladies who have no children attend to it now   Father has me under bonds not to go near there— My hearts pledge is to you & my boy— who you well know I never risk knowingly— Mrs. Washington says Mary Jones has the Varioloid which now pervades the city but in a very mild form— Birny has come to take care of her boy Neddy which is a great relief to me— he suffers but is doing well according to the doctor—

I got a letter from Aunt Becky full of congratulations about New Orleans which is "*the* triumph of the war—" Uncle Ben & Horace join in joy & kind greetings to you   Aunt says Uncle Ben looks thin— "but his countenance is unaltered" by his loss. he is resigned to giving up his noble boy to his Country cause— tho he says it yet with quivering lips— Henry Etting [4] is in the city   I want to see him as he has seen you so lately

I met Mrs. Chandler [5] in Apo's parlor— she was very spiteful at McClellan

& the bottle of wrath are being cook up fast by a bitter opposition— & there will a new war of party start up on the return of peace & it will be strange to see the [word indistinct] Democrats— Embrace the blackest Abolitionist— The Trumbuls are too bitter to visit with pleasure altho I go— but bad roads & etc are excuse for not going oftener—

May 7. Every body went to the City but Blair & me   Mother wished me at breakfast to go pay some visits— I told her I could not visit— So she went— & they brought me an account of the Dispatches from New York from your Squadron Telling of the awful conflict you passed thro at the forts—[6] Mentioning the number of the killed & wounded but not the names— I shall feel no rest until I hear all about it but will not bore you with my anxieties any more— Our people are in a frenzy of exultation over New Orleans & it keeps all of McC's doings on the Yorktown line— under eclipse—

The Sands have the details of William loss— he lost his footing in jumping from the boat— to the ship on a dark stormy night— & was sunk by a heavy overcoat— All efforts of his Father & Brother to save him were in vain— & yet he was so close— that they heard him say— Father it is all no use   Mrs. Sands is now ill from anguish & has been for some days. Betty has been with them & look wan & worn from being there— I go often— but only for a short time—

The President has gone to Yorktown— Father went to see John to help right Cousin Cornelia he said he hoped to get it done without going to the President if he fail— he would then make the appeal to the President thro' Father— I think it is best for John not to make this appeal— against *his chief*— to the P— if to be avoided You will sympathise with this news even tho' *I cannot* now go into the minutia The Prince George people are amazingly sobered in their views on blacks— I expect to hear Emancipation talked soon as I hear white labor *exalted* now— I get raps all the time about Becky— which I take with a quiet satisfaction— so great that I give no raps back at all— plead old habits of old people— which my use of spectacles now numbers me— but in my old age as in my youth I am yr devoted Lizzie

1. Mr. George Gideon, a Washington printer and bookbinder.

2. Cornelia Lee Stuart was the wife of Charles Calvert Stuart who built Chantilly in Fairfax County near SPL's boyhood home, Sully.

3. On May 3, Joe Johnston and his army withdrew from Yorktown. In her May 4, 1862, letter EBL commented: "Poor Jo— in spite of the wickedness of this past year— I pity him—."

4. Henry Etting was related to the Blairs by marriage; his mother was a sister of Benjamin and Rebecca Gratz.

5. Letitia Grace Douglas of New York married Zachariah Chandler in 1844. Chandler, a strong antislavery senator from Michigan from 1857 to 1875, was an opponent of McClellan.

6. During the naval campaign to capture New Orleans, on four consecutive days beginning April 19, Farragut's force bombarded Forts Jackson and St. Philip. Lee's ship *Oneida* came under heavy fire as part of the advance guard. On April 24, the fleet withstood intense shelling and engaged in a furious battle with rebel gunboats as it successfully passed under the guns of the forts.

Silver Spring   May 8, 1862

Dear Phil   Yours of 12th ult. when on "Picket duty" came tonight but for once your letter did not comfort me the most— but Capt Porters[1] report— that "no officer was killed or wounded" did put my heart at rest— My letter was read afterwards as I glanced at its date— & then with ravenous eyes turned to Porters report— it was very thoughtful of him to send that dispatch & I like him for it—

Mother says Blair sat listening to my rapid reading out by snatches— & when I said "no officer was killed or wounded—" he said "then my Papa is safe—" with such an extraordinary expression on his face of relief & joy— that she & father spoke of it with emotion & asked me if I had talked to him about my anxiety— which I had never done— & it turned out that my Father had told him that you had been in a battle & won a great victory   Blair told Becky of this— & it was his own intelligence that made him appreciate it—

I try to share with him all my joys & he best comforts me in my troubles by his unclouded spirit— & I can oftener forget trouble listening to his joyous prattle than by any other means— He has been busy making a canteloupe patch today & he says his "Papa shall eat more of them than any body else—" His Grandpa called me twice to look at his energy in this work— adding he will be as industrious as Phil" who I suggested never showed much in the digging line— Goodnight for I am going to sleep & I hope one without dreams for I worked hard today & do not "fear ill tidings from a far country" as much as I have done— it may be ungrateful but it take "*the seeing*" of you again to make me happy after all this—

May 9th Capt Baily[2] telegraphed Brother to let me know that you were safe & well— goes on to say how "Brave Lee came to his rescue "in the nick of *time*—" The Times has a letter saying how many balls struck your ship & how many men injured— that ball which passed along your deck— cuting your cabin— makes me shudder & shiver Well all those days were earnestly prayerful with me as these are devoutly thankful— Nelly & Fanny I know they prayed daily for your safety— & are dearer than ever to me for this affectionate devotion— Capt Bailey is in the City this evening— I'll go in tomorrow— take Blair to ask him how you look & are— & above all to get yr letters— The Cayuga is to come up to Washington—

The President went down to Old Point & is doing what I exclaimed at Fox for delaying on Monday— send gun boats up the James River— Our Army are fighting gallantly their way up to Richmond— I do not give you details because they are so elaborately told in the papers— The Rebels retreat to Williamsburg (I think) was a success— but there they were whipped & their Retreat will I think be a disastrous every step they take—[3] it is evident that they intend crossing James River— & go to Petersburg (avoiding Richmond) & thence— fall back on the Cotton States— which is I hope "the last ditch where Session— will die in its birthplace Charleston— Genl McC. is so rapid in his pursuit— that I hope they will never cross James River[4] The President ordered the gunboats up James River & the attack— on their batteries— he is clean for taking Norfolk—[5] at once McC. says it will incur useless loss of life as the fall of Richmond insures that of Norfolk as did that of New Orleans that of the Forts— The attack of the Batteries checkmates the Merrimac & keeps all their forces at Norfolk— & so things stood this morning.

Govr Dennison is here tonight— full of hearty kindness for & about you—[6] When he learned you had gone to New Orleans he telegraphed the Dept to send him *all* your news as you were a dear friend— Blair heard him greet me about you on his arrival & then when he spoke to him to my surprise— instead of hanging his head & hiding behind me— he stepped forward gave his hand— & took the Govr's kiss— with a look of great satisfaction— he praised you & that went to your boy's heart & he forgot his habitual shyness— He showed some self denial of which I am proud the Martin's have sent Mother a huge quantity of maple sugar & molasses— It disagrees with Blair— I let him have some until I found it was making him sick then told him not to eat any more in any form— & tho often tempted in my absence— he has steadily resisted the temptation

May 10th I came in early for my letters[7] & some kind soul in mistaken kindness has taken my letters to Silver Spring I have just seen Capt Boggs[8] & given him my Fathers invitation to dine with us he spoke with great warmth friendship of you— & assured me of good health & spirits. The City is full of rumors & I believe that Franklin was repulsed by Robt. Lee until reinforced by Sedgewick—[9] Lee is said to be killed— nobody believes it Our people are to have a long hard fight on the Penninsula it is the dying struggle of the rebels[10] All well at our house & at Johns Ever your devoted Lizzie

1. At New Orleans, Capt. David Dixon Porter commanded a flotilla of vessels, each carrying a thirteen-inch mortar. In a second letter of May 8, EBL reported John and Ellen Lee's reaction: "both full of joy *for you*— but Nelly's heart is sadly on the other side of the question— I rarely broach it but today it was unavoidable— but nothing of hardness escaped me & now I am all thankfulness but I have felt very bitter sometimes of late— They joyed in my joy over your safety & as that is the biggest feeling in my heart— I was satisfied—."

2. Capt. Theodorus Bailey, commanding *Cayuga*. After Lee passed the forts guard-

ing New Orleans, he and Charles Boggs commanding *Varuna* found three rebel gunboats attempting to board Bailey's *Cayuga*. Bailey described the incident: "The Brave
Lee . . . came to my relief in the nick of time. I had more rebel steamers engaging me
than I could attend to without support when Lee & Boggs came dashing up delivering
a refreshing fire. The Enemy were so thick that it was like duck shooting. What missed
one Rebel hit another. With their aid we cleaned the kitchen. Please inform his wife."
Telegram, Bailey to Montgomery Blair, May 8, 1862, Blair-Lee Papers.

    3. EBL's father and brother Frank returned from a visit to Yorktown on May 5.
They reported that "the scene was that of a precipitate flight— blankets all sorts of
clothing—tents— fired ammunition & powder— all their cannon save those of the
flying artillery left standing & thousands of small arms. Store houses of John Brown
Spikes— the wharf was *muddy* inches deep with wet powder— Countless spades—
digging tools— everything indicating panic & flight."

    4. In her extra May 8 letter, EBL enlarged upon her opinion of McClellan: "Now he
has a fine opportunity of making his name famous and all sides are growing clamorous
in his praise Our Army expects to reach Richmond tomorrow evening."

    5. Under the date of May 11 in her extra May 8 letter, EBL announced, "Norfolk is
ours." She also commented, "The President ordered the attack on Norfolk & is taking
a pretty active part down there— & play chief of the Army & Navy with some eclat I
am glad of it as it endears him to the Country."

    6. In her extra May 8 letter, EBL proudly announced: "Mr Dennison suggested as
his own (yr idea about the *naming* of the Captains of yr squadron in a vote of thanks)—
. . . I did not go to my own people except Father about this— he like the idea & said
he would *see about* it tomorrow— I wanted it sooner— so talked & read it in to Govr.
D— & it is I think now— a fixed fact— He is a very sincere friend—."

    7. In her extra letter of May 8, EBL emphasized the importance of her husband's
letters: "they are precious to me I can follow you each day & nothing so satisfies in your
absence as to know each days doings & ideas Indeed it may be valuable hereafter—."

    8. Both Charles Boggs and Theodorus Bailey had recently arrived in Washington.
EBL was naturally anxious to invite them to dinner and hear their reports of the fights
at New Orleans.

    9. Gen. William B. Franklin, commanding a division of McDowell's corps, joined
McClellan on April 22. He was attacked at West Point, Virginia, by rebels under
G. W. Smith on May 7. John Sedgwick commanded the Second Division of the Second
Army Corps.

    10. With Norfolk lost, the rebels were forced to scuttle the *Virginia* on May 11. In her
extra letter of May 8, under the date of May 11, EBL wrote: "the Merrimac committed
suicide— off Sewalls point last night two ock— blown up— & Secesh surrenders the
Sea— & flies to the Mountains to pray & there cover its diminished head—."

6

"This carnage has made me heart sick body sick this day—"

July 3, 1862

DURING THE SUMMER OF 1862, NORTHERN attention focused on McClellan's slow advance up the Peninsula to threaten Richmond. Stonewall Jackson continued to confuse federal armies in the Shenandoah, and political infighting among Union generals became endemic. In the West, Farragut's naval force, including S. P. Lee, moved far up the Mississippi to the rebel stronghold of Vicksburg.

Elizabeth worked assiduously to get her husband out of the malarial Mississippi and to secure his advancement. To be promoted, it was necessary for an officer to win a congressional vote of thanks, and the Blairs did all they could to encourage Congress to name the officers involved in the capture of New Orleans.

Silver Spring   May 12, 1862

Dear Phil   There is a lull before the storm to come No reports from McClellan or Halleck Since Saturday & it is evident and will turn out that Chase & Stanton— have driven Huger[1] out of Norfolk. finished in that town & left the Navy yard without protection & of course it was burnt   Huger is off to aid Robt Lee to fight McC.— I think Chase & Wools[2] faux pas is at last worse than that of Wells— Smith Lee will make himself infamous by the destruction of old Virginia's only public work— of importance in the World's eye—[3] He never had much sense & Seceshism has destroyed that little   Blair & I have been the busiest bodies— cutting & tying up asparagus for Grandma this evening you ever saw—

May 13 Blair Becky & I took our first ride in the Rockaway since you went away so wretched have the roads been that I did not dare attempt to drive anywhere We found the City dusty & dull— all gaping after news— all filled with a breathless anxiety about the tremendous strife impending or actually in progress between Lee & McClellan— I think a great deal depends on the issue of the battle & if Mc. & Halleck are successfull the war is at end on a large scale[4] then comes the tug of war with politicians & the guerillas who will be very quickly hung up I hope for of all the shapes war takes that is the vilest & most dastardly—

I went to another orphan asylum meeting had a dull time this 1st Directress makes it all work & no fun at any time & you know that there was in times past some little undercurrent— Mrs. Harris bade me tell you that she has often thought of & prayed for your safety of late— Sue & I are getting to be very *cronyish* She got in to a disagreeable place in this last orphan asylum fuss— I saw it & came to her rescue— & she is very appreciative— of the kindness which I evinced— I told her of course I could fail to like anybody you thought so much— & etc Went to see Mrs. Bridge[5] & only met 2 Congressional (Rep) Ladies there— she does her part well to pass her winters in Washington— She looks wan & wasted— there are few people for whom I have so much pity— She does strive so hard to be active— & cheerful— but her face always reminds me of the Childless Racheal who could not be comforted—

I enclose you Horace's & Aunt Becky's letter about you I like them both so much that their congratulations are better than those of others— I met Mrs Alexander[6] (Soldiers home) at Johns today She says the Lincolns go out there the 10th of next month— I told her Mrs. L. was almost afraid to go among such *Secesh* but I had assured her that they were the best & most *loyal hearted* people in the world— Well she replied Mrs. L— is as much of a Kentuckian as I am & if we were Secesh I would be vastly afraid of her— but as I am not I anticipate her residence there with great pleasure— She begged me to come spend the day with her which I do before very long—

May 14th They are all off to the City as it is a rainy day I am going to put out of some of my plants— We are all well & send love to you Blair is singing away at this moment— & I wish I could seal up some of his merriment for you. ever your devoted Lizzie

1. Benjamin Huger resigned from the U.S. army April 22, 1861. He became a major general in the Confederate army, commanding the Department of Norfolk.

2. Seventy-eight-year-old Gen. John E. Wool was the oldest officer in either Union or Confederate army. He commanded the Department of Virginia from Fort Monroe until his retirement in August 1863.

3. Sydney Smith Lee, older brother of Robert E. Lee, was the Confederate commander of the navy yard at Norfolk. On May 9, the rebels had to abandon Norfolk, and they destroyed as much of it as they could.

4. On May 14, EBL wrote: "the very idea of more war takes all life out of me I am like Fanny panting for peace— Now that there is any prospect of it up to this time— it was an endless vista to me— but I do see daylight a far off. now— thro this dark night of our Countrys bitterest trial—."

5. George Washington Bridges was a Unionist from Tennessee, elected to the

Thirty-seventh Congress, but en route to Washington he was arrested by the rebels, returned to Tennessee, and held prisoner for over a year. He finally escaped, returned to Washington, and took his seat.

6. S. R. Alexander, from Kentucky, was the wife of Thomas L. Alexander, deputy governor of the Old Soldier's Home.

Silver Spring   May 17, 1862

Dear Phil No news is good news & this has been our good news for this week past it is evident our Generals are keeping their own Secrets & it is lucky for us if they can keep them & so manage their movements as to surround & capture the Army of Richmond—

Father says England in his opinion is trying to get France to intervene in our affairs & their whole scheme is spoiled by the Capture of New Orleans & that alone may have saved us this time— England is at war in heart with us & in this war as 1812 hates our prosperity— & Republican government Consequently naught can help to keep us out of trouble *but our* Navy is now our only safety & it is no small pleasure to me to hear the constant ovation to the Navy especially your Squadron— from the hearts of our people of all sides & shades—

I had a call from a M.C. from Penn[s]y[l]vania]. his wife & daughter (on whom none of us have called) because I was the wife of one of the New Orleans heroes— I was down in my garden hard at work— Father told them I was out & where & they came after— I wore your honors as meekly as I could Betty laughs at me & says I have a standing reply to all congratulations in my thanksgiving for your safety which is ever on my tongue from the heart's fullness— but the truth is I am not a whit more proud of you than I have been these twenty odd years— tho it is delicious to have others to appreciate you as I have ever done—

The Conkling[1] Mrs John R. Thomson were also among our visitors today— Mrs. JR. asked Betty to come pay her a visit— I suppose she wants to rebuke No 6 for not having Betty there— Betty is keen to go. has Fathers & my consent— but Mother who will talk by the year demurs if theres aught *done* is not agreeable to Mrs. No. 6—[2] but in all that concerns that part of the family— I am a noninterventione*r* in talk at any rate— save a little *bit* to you— in chronicling family affairs—

Apo & her youngster come here this next week greatly to Blairs amusement— Preston is so rough that it is lucky for Blair he has a body guard always in attendance they all spent the day here & the place was jubilant with their noises Mary writes that she goes to the Country near Phila on 1st June— Apo has a cottage for the Summer at Newport which Mother pronounces Bentonian— John & Nelly talk of the Mountains for the benefit of their household it will stretch their young limbs and do them all good I hope— but Phil is wonderfully strong & well & do not percieve any constitutional injury from his illness—

I am making changes in Blair clothes— he suffers from the heat— & looks paler already from it but I have his summer clothing & will relieve him of some his burden tomorrow He & GrandMa talk patriotism & drink yr health & are exhurant of your warlike deeds— Blair has a place in my garden he calls Fort Jackson "my fort—" & prattles all the time of his Papa— Mother wishes him to call you Father— but he says you never told him to do it so he wont because you say he is "papa's big boy" & bully boy," and "darling boy" You see like his Mama he does not forget your petting names or actions—

I read Fannys letter over & I've concluded to send it as it may interest you in many of its details & better told than by me Joe Cook & others (Capt Bartons Col Grafflin[3] for example)— give dreadful accounts of the Secesh enormities at Winchester & in that region— The women behaved so unseemly to the Union Soldiers in the hospitals when allowed to come there to administer to their own sick— brought from the battlefield by our men that they had to be excluded & if women behave badly in such a place as that what will they do out of it— As our troop passed thro Winchester to attack Jackson the insults heaped on them by women were indecent & were not resented save by the Maryland men who told them they would take their revenge out of *their* men— & they did with a vengance— This state of things may account for things told by Fanny— if true! but I doubt everything from Secesh sources— no matter whence they come—

Mother has read out as I write Comre Farraguts[4] order for prayer & thanksgiving in the fleet   if I ever see him I shall not fail to let him know how deeply I feel that act of his & may all of us ever remember the magnitude of the mercy then shown to us each one of us— I hope to impress its memory on our childs heart little as he is by sometimes putting it even in his short prayers— Frank Rives was out here yesterday says Wright[5] is now [with] McClernand as an aid camp near Corinth— All well in that concern Mr. Smith[6] (Capitol Gardener was with him gave me some good notions for my flowers— which is just now my occupation & Blairs, how the little one does enjoy it— helps (or tries everybody— & is a great delight & company for his Mama   Your devoted Lizzie

1. F. A. Conkling, New York congressman, was Roscoe Conkling's brother. He was elected to Congress in 1860 and defeated in 1862, after which he served as colonel of the Eighty-fourth New York volunteers.

2. Montgomery's daughter Betty, as well as most of the rest of the tribe, did not get along well with Minna Blair. On May 4, EBL reported an unpleasant incident: "Betty came from Church & her Fathers where she had a row with her amiable Step dame— & Mother took part against & the poor child came home sick with head ache & heart

ache—." On June 19, she again referred to family dissension: "All of No. 6 are here—
It is sad to see their & Betty manners to each other— mother is getting restive under—
tho she like all women will endure any thing from 'My son—' I get along on oiled
grooves with every body—."

3. Probably Maj. Charles Grafflin of the Third Regiment Potomac Home Brigade
of Maryland Volunteers.

4. Flag Officer David G. Farragut of the Gulf Blockading Squadron commanded the
attack on New Orleans.

5. Franklin and Wright Rives were sons of FPB's former partner John Rives. Capt.
Wright Rives was decorated for gallant and meritorious service during the advance on
Corinth.

6. Joseph Smith was not the official capitol gardener but was a gardener employed
by the Department of the Interior.

Silver Spring   May 18, 1862

Dear Phil   Blair & I went to Church today he staid until prayers were over—
then Woody took him out to Henry but when he got out the idea of going to
see Maria got hold of him & he walked back into church to ask my permission
which I gave   Mrs Minna was vastly amused as were others at his manner—
perfectly easy & quiet— She always makes a fuss over Blair & really he is now
the only person who gets always a hearty welcome & greeting whenever they
meet. In Maria's long illness— from which is still is quite helpless— Blair is
the only person out the whole family she asked to go to help amuse Maria &
they say this little girl is devoted to him— he sends her & Annie bouquets
& cuts them with some taste already— but I am training him about flowers—
& hope in his future life the love of them may give him a healthy & innocent
resource—   Mr Fox told him to come see a flag you had taken from the Rebels
& the next time I go in I'll send him to the Dept— for that purpose

Our fleet— on the James River has had to retreat— They encountered a
Battery— two hundred feet high— & the river chained— spiked & filled with
sunken vessels among them those steamers Jamestown & Yorktown— the Dispatch came whilst I was waiting for Blair to get ready to go home from Brothers
This will [word marked out] will give Rogers a great mortification his ship was
struck— & perforated more than a dozen times[1]

May 19 '62 Blair & I have been driving the donkey without Becky's aid
as this was her day in town & she was late getting out— We have made him
haul a great many loads in & out of the garden— just as we "turned *out for*
dinner— Minna Mrs Fox & Maria Smith drove out in what is called here the
Cabinet carriage— Mrs No 6. is getting the Castle on the Hill in order for
occupation—[2] there some fear of sickness in the City this summer— but they
are cleaning it up & will I hope make it healthy in spite of the bad odors of the
suburbs

Father talks of going to New York this week to see Mr. Van Buren— who is very ill & Mrs Gilpin[3] writes to Father that Mr. V.B. expressed a great desire to see him & yet she begs him to go without letting him know that he thinks the Ex P. very ill as that might alarm & injure him The letter for as a preparatory move for an invitation to come went off today— I received letters today— from Fanny Mrs Ives,[4] Mrs. Nathan[5] and Mary Blair full of congratulations & kindness about you—

Our news today is contained a shouting notice that the Rebels were passing the Chiccohominy & that our army was "pressing them—"[6] We had 14 hundred wounded brought to Washington last week & in all over three thousand have been sent north from the Penninsula— of our & the Rebel wounded for they leave both their wounded & dead to our care— as are certain of good care— perhaps better than it is in their power to give them they have hospitals here devoted to the Rebel wounded— & they make no difference in their treatment save they are not allowed to receive visits— which I have my private reasons for rejoicing over—

I got a letter to day from Fanny— about two thirds of it is devoted to her heartfelt joy over your safety & "*success.*" & then the rest is full of lamentation over the taking of the "White House— Mrs Robt Lees last refuge & home since leaving Arlington which is also the home of George Wickhams child now Fitzhugh Lee's wife—[7] dear Fanny's warm heart for her unhappy & mislead friends in Virginia is sorely touched by their misfortunes— But as much as I do pity them— I feel no exalted respect for a man who takes part in a movement in which he can see nothing but "anarchy & ruin as in secession" & yet that very utterance scarce passed Robt Lees lips to my Father[8] when he starts off with delegates from the Richmond Convention— to treat with Traitors— No vain woman in my opinion was ever more easily lured from honor & duty by flattering than was this weak man by the overtures of wily politicians but I'll not wound any who like him by saying so—

Frank thinks Mercier's[9] visit to Richmond was to induce the Southern leaders to take their Army & join the French in Mexico— if routed out of the South— They are evidently deserting Virginia as fast as they decently can— Mr Doolittle dined here yesterday & told me to tell you with his best regards & congratulations that since battle of New Orleans he has joined the Navy for life— he was very kind in his talk about you I took Nelly some asparagus yesterday. the boys all home enjoying a Sunday holiday all looking bright & well— John never was as stout & looks cheerful & is as tenderly kind to your boy for whom he has a feeling very akin to that for his own He insists that a man must love his brothers child better a sisters as it bears his name &etc— Frank says a sister child must be dearer than any other womans except one's own wife— & I say it depends how much one loves brother & sister—

Oh that I knew where & how you are tonight— Fox told me they had sent two steamers with dispatches to order you all up the Miss. "Davis is overmatched" & *things* are not well managed" I quote!!— If Farragut goes up he commands the whole— Foote is dangerously ill— It is evident Goldsborough thinks he has laurels enough & dont act cordially with the Army of the Potomac— he belongs to Chase!! Yr affectionate Lizzie

1. In the battle at Drewry's Bluff on May 15, *Galena* commanded by John Rodgers took eighteen hits and was seriously damaged. In her May 20 letter, EBL gave a more detailed report: "I heard thro John Rogers letter to his wife— that a shell cut his coat sleeve— & part bruised his cheek—."

2. Montgomery Blair had built a house near his parents' Silver Spring home; it was called Falkland.

3. Eliza Sibley Johnston Gilpin, wife of Henry D. Gilpin, Jacksonian supporter and Martin Van Buren's attorney general.

4. Mrs. Ives was the wife of Capt. Ralph O. Ives of the Tenth Massachusetts Infantry.

5. Rebecca Nathan was the sister of Sarah G. Moses Joseph and the wife of Jonathan Nathan.

6. On May 15, Joe Johnston's force had retreated across the Chickahominy, but McClellan did not vigorously press him.

7. George Wickham's daughter Charlotte married William Henry Fitzhugh Lee, R. E. Lee's second son. They lived at White House, the home of Martha Custis at the time of her marriage to George Washington. On May 20, EBL added this news: "I heard that Mrs. Robt. Lee left a letter at the White House for Genl. McClellan asking him to preserve the premises for their associations with Washington— McC had put a strict guard there & kept them inviolate."

8. At Lincoln's request, Francis Preston Blair had offered command of the Union army to Robert E. Lee, who declined the offer and joined the Confederate cause.

9. Henri Mercier, French minister at Washington.

Silver Spring   May 25, [1862]
My dear Phil   This was a delicious day   Betty & I went to church & as we drove off I did covet for you the sight of our Boy & Franks romping with freshly mowed grass— so full of glee & health— the lawn & children were all so beautiful to my partial eyes

On our return home we found that there were only 15 persons to dine exclusive of Apo (who would not keep so much company on Sunday) & the children— Apo was evidently in state of horror at the quantity of visitors— but Mother said that there were so few days in the year when so pleasant to drive to the Country & when our friends did come we ought always receive them gladly— & that we had many many days of the year which we could give our undivided attentions to our religious duties & that on every Sunday She required all who could to go to Church & that she hoped Apo would have many more than she had enjoyed— Upon the whole I dont think Apo was the most pious person in the house altho she certainly thought we were an ungodly set.

The moment I got to the door Father came in a sort of trepidation for me to go to the parlor where Mrs & Miss Gurly[1] of Cinnti were not as entertained as he wished them to be— but Betty & I brought up the rear— & remained in the company with Miss Chase[2] the Gerolts & the Buell Masons[3] & gentleman innumerable— until sunset— when they all went & we had a condoling quiet evening over Genl Banks & Genl. Frémonts defeats & retreats[4] which I concluded we all bore better than we could such disasters in any other places— or person & yet we were sobered by it— for it is horrid to have those good Union people again at the mercy of merciless Secessionist

John was not well— I did not see him— a swelled face from a bad cold & I sent him word that it more vanity than pain that prevented his seeing me— Nel— was more gay than usual— her seceshism was jubilant over the shameless rout of Banks[5] all produced by a scheme of Stantons to get McDowell at Richmond before McClellan

May 26— I am writing an extra to you tonight to go to Capt Davis—[6] for you at Memphis for if you all go up there you will be glad to get a greeting from yr little woman— *May 27* I sent off this morning an extra to Capt Davis at Cairo— it may greet you at Memphis & if it does not I have desired him to send it back to Father I have conned over this for a week nearly— & concluded it was no harm to trouble Capt Davis— that being my only way of getting this mail to you

I went to the City & made some calls for which Father has been talking at Mother Betty & me & at last said he wished me to go— so off we posted he & I. found all the formalities out— I *did up* the business then called on Mrs Chubb & Mrs Purser Warrington[7] As yet I have got nothing for the first— but promises— but I'll hold on to them & continue begging for her— The City all dullness & dust & as little like panic as ever you saw any place Mr Stantons *"scare"*[8] is a street joke The Senate did not vote thanks to any but Capt Farragut— Frank says the House Committee will report the Presidents recommendation & then he & others will debate it— & he feels sure of carrying it in the House when the Senate will have to come up to the mark— McDowell in town to confer about his & Stantons faux pas this makes a pretty fight among the Abolitionists— & if the Maryland troops were out of it I would not feel so bad about it but the people *here* are trying to put the blame on Frémonts slow doings— There is an ominous silence about the Richmond Army & Hallecks too My eyes strained in vain for news about yr movements but we hear of you at Vicksburg only All my thoughts are as turbid as the Mississippi water & my spirit as restless as its hurrying current— Blair is well & joyous Yr devoted Lizzie

1. John A. Gurley, Republican congressman (1859–63), was an opponent of McClellan.

2. In her May 20 letter, EBL mentioned, "We saw Miss Chase— bitter as gall on McLelland— I made no defense for him as I believe he will fight his countrys battles too well to need any but I was not so nonresistant on the darkey question, where I simply said if Congress did not deliver us of the freed ones we would dispose of them as the Yankees had the Pequods She is on the Wendall Phillips tack—." EBL referred to the 1637 Pequot War in which Massachusetts Bay colonists and Indian allies massacred at least four hundred Pequots, including women and children. The remainder of the tribe was captured and enslaved.

3. Baron Gerolt was the Prussian minister at Washington. Buell-Mason refers to the wife of Don Carlos Buell who was the widow of George Mason. She had two daughters, Emma Twiggs Mason and Elizabeth Ann Sally Mason.

4. For most of the month of May 1862, Gen. Thomas Jonathan (Stonewall) Jackson played havoc with the forces of Banks and Frémont in the Shenandoah Valley

5. On May 25, Jackson forced Banks to withdraw from Winchester.

6. Capt. Charles Henry Davis commanded the Union gunboat flotilla on the Mississippi River.

7. Eliza Warrington Chubb was the widow of Charles Chubb. Lewis Warrington, Jr., was a purser in the navy; he was dismissed in June 1863.

8. Stonewall Jackson's raid on Front Royal, Virginia, caused Lincoln and Stanton to withhold McDowell's troops from McClellan for the protection of Washington. Stanton also requested state governors to send their militia to Washington, and many felt that he had overreacted.

Silver Spring   May 26, 1862

Dear Phil   I tried to see Capt Fox yesterday to ascertain how get this to Capt Davis but as I failed to see him Minna brought me word today to send it Cairo— so here goes a few lines to meet & welcome you to Memphis whither yr last letter say will be yr destination & many is the anxious hour has it cost me for I had hoped the Iron Navy would *do up* all that part of the work—

We are all very well I am entirely over my attack (Mother says on New Orleans) & have got hearty & sunburnt in my garden over my rejoicings & thanksgivings at your wonderful deliverance from "all of yr enemies— I will never cease to be thankful for so great a mercy miraculous it appears to me the more I think of what you encountered   I lived in terror for weeks about the Forts— but it never occurred to me that they had any naval force of import above them— & I thought the Mortars would demolish them— but alas they were comparatively useless Maigre Fox & *Comre* Porter   I was proud of your good temper & patriotic desire to have all things done well & peaceably in the Squadron but it cost me some jealous pangs Ill confess—

I wish I could send you some glad tidings & just at this moment— but by a Cabal (a most pertinacious one) against McClellan Banks was deprived of all his troops but 6,000 & they were sent to McDowell to get him into Richmond via Fredericksburg before McClellan but as Genl fatty did not manage it & McClellan is now in sight of the Steeples of Richmond McDowell is ordered to rescue Banks after he is disgraced by a most disgraceful rout[1] Frémont to was whipped at Franklin by Jackson & then Banks which fact is suppressed by Stanton who is utterly abolitionized & was no doubt the promptor of Hunter's proclamation[2] so say Army people in the City— & Now he is telegraphing all creation & evidently trying to affright the world by his own scare which is described as dreadful— He wanted sink stone ships & block up the Potomac from the Merrimac— but Old Welles put his foot & commission on the proceeding & stopped & the other day when Rogers was repulsed at Fort Darling they say Stanton was all affright but Old Grey beard[3] assured them he was not discouraged & would not be if he lost all of our ships in the James River— I must say I like this calmness— it contrasts handsomely with this fuzzy tricky lawyer's jerks— Who is pretty much divided between his intrigues & jobbing & devotions to the White house where he is ever so prostrate that one can scarce approach old Abe" with giving him a shove to get at him— He and Chase now hunt in couples & both have mounted the Extreme Abolition lacky

I am sorry our friend P King too in his tremors about reelection has joined Wendall Phillips—[4] but our friend Doolittle is still a Republican & so is 9 tenths of the party still loyal to that platform & the Constitution of their Country & to white men rather than the black one— Our fat friend[5] has not been to see us this spring nor to see Frank— but we have been steady in our attentions & will continue them— in spite of his Frémont proclivities for which I say we all ought to be the last to make points upon as to the feelings of other people—

Frank & his family are now staying here with us— & Blair revels in so many juvenile companions & it is refreshing to see them playing with new mown hay on the lawn which never looked as beautiful before & I must add I think the children too were a fine looking set— so sturdy & rosy & joyous the Donkey Cart hauls off the hay & they rake & put it in & it is a lovely hay making to my partial eyes I went to Johns yesterday after church— I did not see who was too vain to let me see his swollen face which gives the poor fellow some pain he took cold when down in the Country a few days since Nelly was jubilant over Banks & Frémonts defeat tho she is very prudent in her talk to everybody but John & me— I have prayed her not to talk to her boys & she has quit it—

I had a long letter from Fanny She is in better health & spirits I sent you a long letter from her to Ship Island— They are all prospering again with the return of trade from Nashville where they are sending bread & meat for cotton & tobacco— in large quantities but secesh does all it can to conceal this revival of trade— they want the money but refuse to see the sources of their prosperity— May God enlighten them is my constant prayer when I think of southern people & the delirious frenzy now upon so many of them—

All of our kindred and friends are well & the papers will post you better than I can as to the progress of events Our whole well doing now seems to hang on the results at Corinth & Richmond— Some think here that the Battle of

New Orleans has stopped the Intervention project England hates our progress especially that of the Navy & will hurt whenever she can without ruin to herself & Louis Napoleon[6] only holds off because he hopes the growing enmity between us & England will move to his benefit or that of his Dynasty The people over the waters suffer more from this war than our northern people do who bear its whole expense in every sense & this *strength* is alarming— to all the crowned Heads Goodbye Ill write another Extra soon I send my regular bulletins to Ship Island still Blair sleeps or would join me in love & kisses Yr devoted Lizzie

1. On the next day, May 27, EBL commented, "Banks was Shamefully scared & fled from an equal force some say from *nobody*— He has had no discipline— consequently is a failure altogether & a disgrace—."

2. On August 30, 1861, Frémont, as commander of the Western Department, had issued an emancipation proclamation. On May 9, 1862, David Hunter, commander of the Department of the South, had freed the slaves in Florida, Georgia, and South Carolina. Lincoln disavowed both proclamations. On May 20, EBL wrote: "The Frémont mess has crazed Hunter too but the President has given all his Generals orders on that point today—."

3. Old Grey beard is Secretary of the Navy Gideon Welles.

4. Wendell Phillips, uncompromising abolitionist, was critical of Lincoln's policies.

5. Preston King.

6. Louis Napoleon, emperor of France, 1852–70.

Silver Spring   June 5, 1862

My dear Phil   I have not written to you since Saturday when I told you I was sea sick from Locust blossoms— I thought. I had been under the weather for some time then & since that day have had to go to bed & *be sick*— but today I am up— regaled with beef tea & brandy. champagne & ice— &etc & my first act after dressing is to write to you & thank you for yr letters of the 8th 11th & 14th of May with the log & official reports— all of which have been in bed with me read & reread— for five days past— if I were go in to details about my sickness you would think me more seriously sick than I am— but it is only a sick stomach from a liver affliction.[1] I have had no fever & Dr. May says I will be heartier than ever after I get over it which he said just now would be in a day or two I would have been troubled about not writing but I have a hope in my heart that you will be homeward bound 'ere this or even my late letters can get to you— I have counted up— the chances of yr return even to a day my birth day the 20th inst by which time I hope to have on my *best* (because happy & hearty) looks with which to greet you—

Beauregards breakdown of Corinth[2] reached here with your last letters great to my relief for I did not like the aspect of things from yr lookout point at all— but now the Halleck army will soon open the river— & cooperate with you

all on Mobile & I hope the whole business will be *settled up* quickly down on
the Gulf Coast   I read your cotton letter to Frank & Father— They reported
its purport to Brother thro whom it went to the Cabinet— Seward wanted the
exact words so I gave them to him— for European use— so Father told me—
There is a loud call for the Official reports of the New Orleans battle in the
papers— Father says I quoted him wrongly. I said that they had recd no report
from you— official— whereas the Secy said yr letter was the *best* report & *the*
only one written with spirit of the scene— I was struck with words *only* one.
& so related it but in subsequent talks found out my error— the Secy also said
it was his first *inside* view of the scene   John has the letter now— I have been
too *sick* to go after it—

The telegraphs are all broken down between here & Richmond by the
storms of this week but thing there are hurrying on to the end & it is believed they are evacuating it as fast as they can get out of it but they are
nearly surrounded— & will be so entirely if Dix moves promptly— Old Wool
& Goldsborough hampered McClellan all they could or it would have been
done ere this Neither will profit by it for McC. seems conquer his enemies
in the rear by using up those in front— Our Regt. 10th Mass was sadly cut
up—[3]   Casey's[4] troops were notorious here this whole past winter for bad
discipline & bad conduct in every way— they have all fixed on Sunday next
for the taking of Richmond— when I think the Rebellion will be "*used* up" or
as Mrs. Davis says "played out—" Oh how I sigh for peace— Blair is well &
enjoys the strawberries which are very fine   Your devoted Lizzie
If you keep your promise about returning when yr health *begins* to give way—
youll not get this

1. In her June 28 letter, EBL reported her recovery of health: "They laughed at me
for having what is called in town an attack of panic— It seems that other officers wives
have been sick— with the same disease of the liver with which I've suffered only some
had it more fatally— Dr. May told Nelly that it would have gone hard with me if I had
had fever— but I had none & was getting over it better than his other patients— it
seems that trouble stops the action of the liver— & hence the vulgar idea of the White
Liver being associated with Cowardice— I am now quite well."

2. The evacuation of rebel troops from Corinth brought this conclusion from EBL
in her May 27 letter: "The dear considerate Chivalry want to remove the War from
their own homes— Spare their own Cities— & carry on the War twenty years as Jeff
says in Virginia— & desolate her for that length what dear friends!."

3. In her June 10 letter, EBL gave details of the part played by the Tenth Massachusetts, who, she wrote, "has borne its part in a battle heroically When Casys men broke
& fled Couch's brigade came to their rescue & had nerve enough to bear up under this
panic & fight on with out flinching They had seven Captains shot down— Barton &
Ives are two of the three which escaped Capts Smart & Day were killed after being
wounded— by pistol & bayonet Col Briggs has three wounds— & my friends Capt

Parsons & miller both very religious men are wounded How ones acquaintance with the poor fellows guides interest to them & their men."

4. Silas Casey was appointed brigadier general of volunteers in August 1861, to organize volunteers in the area of the capital. He was assigned a division in Keyes's corps of the Army of the Potomac and received the first attack at Fair Oaks, May 31, 1862. Promoted to major general of volunteers, he commanded a division of the Washington defense troops from August 1862 to the end of the war.

Silver Spring   June 9, 1862

Dear Phil   As there is such a near prospect of your ship meeting that of Capt Davis I'll venture another extra that way to let you know that Blair & I are well & are on the tiptoe of expectation with the hope of your speedy return home   I recd your letters of the 8 11th & 14 of May in which the accounts of your health makes me crave yr return— do not I entreat you remain away any longer— a continuous affection of the bowels is the malady which of all others I dread most for you— do come home (without going to Mobile) up the river now that you have helped to open that great Avenue of commerce   thats glory enough for me plenty plenty—

I wrote you rather a sick letter this week via Ship Island as I was not well & low spirited— but since the Rebels have dispersed from Corinth I feel like a much stronger & healthier woman— & let Becky go to the City today feeling well enough to do her duties but Birnie came & took possession of Blair— & I had a most luxurious Sunday

No news today— from Richmond & I doubt if the fight will soon be renewed— the fight of the Oaks[1] this day a week ago was very like the Pittsburg Landing Affair   Casey a fussy political general got posted in advance— with troops which he had never drilled & got routed— Couches brigade saved us until Heintzelman & Sumner came to the rescue   Johnston is wounded with a Minie ball— added to his other wounds it will probably end his life If I were in his place & saw into the future with my optics tis the least of evils so to end such a career— The official report is today that our loss is 800— dead— 5000— wounded— but nine tenths slightly (with round ball & buckshot)— 500 hundred missing— we have about as many prisoners— they took Caseys men eating their breakfast & without even their guns in their hands. as he is a democratic politician all this will be hid in the War Dept— Frémont disobeyed orders— & let Jackson escape   Sigel is now sent in pursuit as Frémont is now *a failure* even to Colfax— Everybody laughs now at his fast riding in California

The bon bouche of this week is the defeat of the french in Mexico—[2] the chuckle all about the country is most hearty tho suppressed for policy sake in the papers— the news comes in two ways— via telegraph California & Vera Cruz— If the frenchmen begin to run from the Mexicans they will be

devoured for running is their strength— no racers like them on the Earth—
on two legs—

Our family circle here are all well— Franks family are here & go in about
two weeks to Newport for the summer— where they got a furnished house—
for six months for 225 dollars— with a large lawn with 12 rooms & in good
order   Johns family are preparing to leave too no place decided on— at which
I rejoice for change is very essential to Nelly after so much sickness— she needs
the rest— tho looking quite as well as usual— Fannys last letter were very
cheerful as to her health & all their family concerns— Louisville is already
benefitted by the partial return of trade & prosperity—

Frank wants to get off to St Louis Old Gamble— is playing a *bad* part not
only to Frank but to the Country—[3] & it is important for Frank to go see to
matters there He is receiving Price's men into the *Home* Guards— & really
turning traitor *fast*— under the negro pressure— about which I am rejoiced
to say our President is like a rock— Sumner & he had a regular bout on the
Stanly[4] affair of the negro school— the President said he had nothing to do
with schools in the States— white or black & would not recall Stanly or rebuke him— tho he regreted some things he had done— & the way it was
done— but he had no time even to discuss "nigger schools—" nor was the
present the time for anything of the sort— so Mr. Sumner was answered

Mr. Grow was out here today— came for "a little visit & spent the day.
things went off well— Mr. Doolittle was here too— he talks most kindly of
you & always sends you kind messages— he is full of glorification over the
Navy— Says Mr. King is lame in one knee from a fall— & in the other from
rheumatism— & is more than ever overwhelmed with fat— & patient as he
is— sighs for Heaven— since he is of earth so earthy— physically I mean—

My garden is a beauty— Blair & I dig there a great deal until this rainy weeks
since which I fear the weed will get the better of us— if it continues too damp
for us to work there much longer Today Blair got a letter from Mr. Stabler[5]
about a kite he promised him — He like endless others send you compliments
& kinesses. I got a very civil note from Capt Davis today inviting to send
letters thro him— thank him for me We have had but little hot weather still
Blair is thin from it— but in very good health eats & sleeps heartily & now
revels in strawberries So do all here— Ever yr own Lizzie

1. During the battle of Fair Oaks, May 31-June 1, Joe Johnston's rebels attacked a
federal army divided by the Chickahominy River. Initially successful, they were finally
pushed back by Union reinforcements. Johnston was seriously wounded, and Robert E.
Lee became the commander of the Army of Northern Virginia.

2. On May 5, 1862, six thousand French troops under General Lorencez were defeated by Benito Juarez outside Puebla. At the time, it appeared a major defeat for
Napoleon III's Mexican intervention, but in 1864, Archduke Maximilian of Austria
became emperor of Mexico.

3. On June 10, EBL explained, "Gamble is counting the negro secessionist parties[,] has enlisted some of Price returned men in the home Guard— & in his message treats the US Army which rescued the state from Anarchy as the source of much of their ruin— which Providence & '*the Noble* Convention alone prevented from being utterly overwhelming—.' "

4. Edward Stanly served as military governor of North Carolina, May 1862-January 1863. As a native son, he was looked upon as a traitor by the inhabitants; he was also unpopular with abolitionists. Stanly had opposed H. H. Helper's plan to establish a school for black children. The House of Representatives then passed a resolution inquiring, among other things, "whether the said Edward Stanley [sic] has interfered to prevent the education, white or black, in said State; and if so, by what authority, if any?" Stanly replied that he thought he "had been sent to restore the old order of things" and to return North Carolina to the Union. He defended his actions to Stanton by stating, "Unless I can give them some assurance that this is a war of restoration and not of abolition and destruction, no peace can be restored here for many years to come." *The War of the Rebellion: A Compilation of the Official Records of the Union and Confederate Armies,* series 1, vol. 9, 395, 400.

5. Edward Stabler, Quaker friend and hunting companion of Francis Preston Blair, was postmaster of Sandy Spring and a strong Maryland unionist.

Silver Spring   June 15, 1862

Dear Phil   I have been busy in my garden again today the first time for nearly 3 weeks— the weather is very comfortable to us but too cool to make flowers grow much— Still they are a great resource to Blair & I   we dig together & talk about flowers & fun & every thing— & my garden is consequently more than ever my hobby & promises great beauty this year

Tuesday June 16th   Apo & her troop of little took up their line of march for Newport today   Father is sorrowing that she does not go to St Louis & he fears it will injure her husband— but I try to console him by telling these revolutionary times makes it best to have an actor in them unencumbered with a wife in the scene of action & it is best for them all to have the helpless tucked away in safe places— but hereafter she ought to be anything but a non resident

Betty returned from the Headquarters of McClellan today where she & 15 others paid a flying visit on Sunday. within 2½ miles of Richmond— She says he looks thin but well— our army are sickening in the slashings of Hanover— Stewart[1] with cavalry made a dashing diversion out of Richmond on Sunday. but without damage to any one *save* some teamsters & some of his own men who were shot— Mrs. Ricketts[2] was one of their party & they found Wm Palmer[3] very ill & brought him back home with them today— I hope good nursing & home will soon set him up   McClellans Army has passed the Chicahominy— Betty says our army is in fine spirits[4] unhindered with the presence of the wounded or sick who are immediately dispatched— to the cities & hospitals— Our City is being filled with Hospitals 5 churches are now being fitted into Hospitals   I wanted to go to the City today but there was no room—

Old Judy from Auburn is here today— intends to return to Master Ariss— her accounts of that part of the Country are doleful

Wednesday June 17. As we are all anxiety as to the Army movements before Richmond Mother sends an express in today so I'll send this off hoping to hear from you that you are relieved from your Vicksburg duties—[5] which must end with the knowledge of the fall of Memphis I would be very miserable if I did believe so Blair & all are very well— Ever yr devoted Lizze

1. On Sunday June 15, James Ewell Brown "JEB" Stuart returned to Richmond from his sensational cavalry ride around McClellan's army on the Peninsula.

2. Frances Anne Pyne Lawrence married James B. Ricketts in 1856.

3. William Palmer, career army officer, died June 18, 1862. He was cited for gallant and meritorious service at Williamsburg, Virginia.

4. In her June 12 letter, EBL stated: "Father went to the City today saw Genl. Burnsides who has been to see McC. so they are pulling together   Burnside says weather permitting McC will be in Richmond now in a few days—."

5. On June 23, EBL reported rumors of "a land force— to aid in taking Vicksburg— it is nearly a month since your letters were written."

Silver Spring   June 25, 1862

Dear Phil   I dined with John & Nelly & they both pronounced me "an improved woman" looking better "than for many a long day"   I told them I was putting on my best looks to greet you with as I hope daily to hear of yr return— for I knew you were not well enough to remain on duty or in that sickly region— Frank returned home with us— & took Betty's room— So you see we are now pretty crowded— John says McKinstry[1] asks for a court martial

I forgot to tell you that Walter Trumbul[2] got a midshipmans warrant & is now at Newport & his parents say stands well No 18 in a class of 70— & he entered in April— he will do well if all their report is true & Mrs. T. speaks of you with *real* kindness asked me if I had a photograph of you that that of few persons would be so much valued by her— She is a devotee to the Hospitals to which places the Govt exhorts the ladies to attend & keep the menials there from neglecting the Soldiers   Mother is violent against my going to them & that I owe to you, Blair & to her not expose myself to sickness & I see I'll have to submit— & confine my charities to the Orphans & my home—[3] Still I can do a little— & that will keep conscience quiet which I assure you is restless when so many need help

June 26— We are again talking of intervention nobody seems to think anything of it— but it gives me a tremor— There is fighting going on today at Richmond— I can see by the looks of Brother— they seem confident of McClellans success— The Presidents visit to West Point if understood *here* is not expressed Mon face is sour—

June 27. A hot day & my thoughts live in the Miss River. It was a month since I have heard from you & it seemed to me many but your letter of 10th gave me a double relief first that the River below you was not commanded by the Rebels & next tho weak & weary you are not ill as my fears had made you— You had not heard of the Memphis evacuation & consequently I feel as if you were nearer getting out of the River than you then knew about

The papers all say Beauregard is at Richmond to which place they have called all their best troops— Mobile is reinforced— so is Charleston They seem to have given up the Misspi Valley much to the joy of the people who Wright Rives says "receive like Gods— & I am swearing in Rebel troops by Companies all the Southern paper doing much of this— & yet particularly those in South Carolina say Beauregard's army is scattered & demoralized & they have shorn him of all laurels— Jacksons Raid— was the result of the intrigue against McClellan— all of which I have written as fully as I could— McDowell was to get into Richmond first— so Shields[4] was sent to him— Blenker[5] was taken from McDowell & sent to Frémont— Shields took his place— & left Banks helpless & but for Jackson's slow movements he would have had the whole command at one mouthful at Winchester

Frémont you see by todays papers is deposed not a member of this family knew ought of the President's purpose until announced— today & we will be accredited with all the malice of it— but he— Banks, & McDowell & Shields all did so badly that I suppose the President felt it was a duty to put a man who could do better— Jackson has gone to Richmond so the President thinks— & says—

Mother talks of going to Newport— I'll stay here until you come unless Blair gets sick here I do what is best for him— Ever yr devoted Lizzie

Genl Rousseau[6] was here today— he says his Brigade fought John Breckinridge's at Shilo— Mrs Crittenden[7] has been paralyzed— but is getting over it— The Merciers were here too this evening— Count Mercier told Father that he got a letter from Thouvenal[8] today— who bade him assure the President that the Emperor[9] was unalterably the friend of the Union— This gave me *no* small comfort I do assure you— Blair looks pale from the heat— but is noisy & gay as ever he picked up rough ways from Preston & Jim— George Alexanders cartridge business is a failure

1. Maj. Justus McKinstry had been a member of Frémont's staff in St Louis in 1861. He had asked for a court martial, got it, and was dismissed in 1863.

2. Walter Trumbull, son of Lyman Trumbull, joined the navy as a midshipman in April 1862.

3. EBL added in her July 2 letter: "I never coveted robust health more than I might help to serve them for here theres a great want of good nurses— *head* nurses but I am useless save to you & my child— & you do enough for us for both for our Country."

4. On May 17, McDowell was ordered to move toward the Fredericksburg-Richmond railroad as soon as Brig. Gen. James Shields's division joined him. Shields

had been appointed brigadier general of volunteers August 19, 1861; he resigned March 28, 1863.

5. Ludwig Blenker, commissioned a brigadier general of volunteers, August 1861, had raised the Eighth Regiment of New York volunteers. He served with the Army of the Potomac until the beginning of the Peninsular Campaign, then he was sent to western Virginia. Blenker played an active role in the Battle of Cedar Keys, June 8, 1862; after the arrival of Frémont, he was succeeded by General Sigel and ordered to Washington. He was mustered out March 31, 1863.

6. Maj. Gen. Lovel Harrison Rousseau had raised a brigade for the Union early in the war; at Shiloh he led the Fourth Brigade, Second Division.

7. Elizabeth Ashley Crittenden was John J. Crittenden's third wife. They married in 1853.

8. Edouard Thouvenal, French foreign minister.

9. Emperor Napoleon III had wished to recognize the Confederacy but needed British cooperation. Thouvenal told John Slidell on May 14, 1862, that the losses of Donelson and New Orleans had been decisive in keeping the French from supporting the Confederacy.

Silver Spring   July 3, 1862

Dear Phil   The terrors with which I was possessed some days past— are stirring the world at large who know today for the first time of the terrific battle before Richmond—[1] Our loss is not known— even today I dread to hear it— McC is being reinforced rapidly. 20 thousand men were embarked to him today— Oh if they had been sent a month ago!! we might have been spared much sorrow on both sides of the lines— Majr Nicholson was here— his brother[2] is with Goldsborough— his officers are bitter about him— & Our Army disgusted with the conduct of the Govt—

4th July Long to be remembered in our Country as a day of mourning for many have learned their losses— & others dread to hear— & we all have to grieve that at least 30,000 of fellow country have been laid low— in that five days battle—[3] Our entire loss in killed, wounded & missing is twenty thousand— the Enemy acknowledge 25,000 of lost ones— & we have but very few prisoners— took a vast many but had not power to guard them & go on with the battle the men were allowed to go Our Army repulsed the enemy (who say they had 180,000 men to our 90 thousand) in every assault & retreated— with perfect order without loss of guns or anything else— save invaluable lives— This carnage has made me heart sick body sick this day— so Ill stop writing & try to do something that will relieve me of this oppressive thinking

July 5th We are all well here— Spending much of our time in pouring over the accts of the late long battle— they are so confused that theres but one thing certain— That we attained our object in gaining the James River— which has preserved our Army from utter destruction—[4] it has maintained it morale— & whipped the Rebels with help of the Gun boats grandly in the last encounter

& the defeat & route was so signal that even the Richmond papers admit their defeat—[5] The Army is safe & is being daily— reinforced—[6] Frank is ordered West to recruit a division or brigade & will command whatever he gets—[7]

Every body cries What is Halleck doing & done Beauregard's Army is at Richmond— his captured officers say so— Jackson is killed— & the feeling towards Halleck is akin to that— towards— Frémont Banks & Co—[8] When MC. wrote that Beauregards army was arriving in Richmond Halleck avers that it was in front of him & this is the Govt excuse— for not reinforcing MC.[9] who has begged for his Army from the hour he has faced the enemy who force he now is acknowledged to have reported accurately from that time to this— But these affairs are all absorbing and our city is hourly receiving the wounded & their number is appalling so I hear I would not be surprised if they made requisition of the private Houses in a few days— Hotels certainly— the last would have been taken before but for their being all so badly ventilated—

I went with Blair to the wheat field where they are cutting the finest crop ever made here He began to carry bundles & made up two little stacks himself— much to the amusement of the men— he is ever joyous & joy giving to his Mama more noisy than he was— since his acquaintance among boys has extended he is now entirely well— but has not the robust look he had in the spring— but I am thankful to have him so well— I am again quite as strong as it is my habit to be— Ever yr devoted Lizzie I hear Rogers is wonderfully happy at being in the fight Monday [10]

1. The Seven Days' Campaign ended on July 1 with the Battle of Malvern Hill, just north of the James River. McClellan retreated from Richmond, and the attempt to capture the Confederate capital was over.

2. Lt. Somerville Nicholson commanded the USS *Marblehead.* He was about to end his duty with the North Atlantic Blockading Squadron; on July 19, he was ordered to the South Atlantic Blockading Squadron under Admiral Du Pont.

3. The Battle of Malvern Hill (July 1), the last battle of the Seven Days' Campaign. Although rebel losses were greater than those of the Union, McClellan decided to retreat to Harrison's Landing.

4. On July 11, EBL made a more realistic assessment: "our whole loss killed— wounded & missing— is ten thousand instead of thirty as was reported by the Newspapers & I think from all I hear— ought to have marched into Richmond instead of going back to James River—."

5. On July 2, EBL had stated that McClellan's "Retreat from in front of Richmond is a virtual defeat on our part— brought about by taking his army from him to trot about after McDowell When McClellan found out that the enemy outnumbered him— so immensely by Beauregards & Jackson's Armies he altered his base of operations to save his army— he has done it— but with terrific fighting—." Actually, McClellan's force vastly outnumbered the Confederates.

6. EBL wrote on July 8: "Reinforcements are arriving & going to the Army— the

papers say litle about it & it is thought best I should not even here— Indeed there is a
sort of an estopal upon ones talk that is not comfortable— yet there is a want of spirit
or cheerfulness bout our affairs tho there is a deep resentment every where towards
those who are thought be the cause of our late troubles— All of our generals have a
grievance— & when I heard Genl & Mrs McDowell discourse yesterday— I felt that
there must be a victim somewhere to appease these Gods of War I must say that as the
war waxes on— I more & more put my trust in the God of Mercy."

7. EBL reported on July 2: "Stanton sent word to Frank today to know if he would
serve in the New Army called out— Frank replied yes— in any position from corpo-
ral up."

8. On July 2, EBL referred to "Halleck the Slowest of all General except Old Patterson."

9. Danger to Washington was the excuse for not reinforcing McClellan. Lincoln
wanted first to destroy Stonewall Jackson in the Valley, then reinforce McClellan.

10. After the Battle of Malvern Hill, naval forces under the command of Commodore John Rodgers successfully covered McClellan's retreat to Harrison's Landing.

Silver Spring   July 7, 1862
Dear Phil   The News papers can tell you all the details of the battles— I will
turn from them as my heart has been tortured by them for ten days past & I
can now be hopeful tho' I can never forget— the sorrow which fill my heart
for the carnage of my Country men— for I can not yet feel alien to the Rebels
Yesterday the papers were filled with the News that Vicksburg was taken—
but Mr Fox came out to dinner bringing Mr Gantt— & they said there was
nothing authentic in the Report G. is "broken down" but gives good account
of the spirit & courage of our Army I confess *this* was a reverse to me— for I
groan to think of your being up the Miss River this hot weather but hot as it
is Father was in the City all today— & has inspired others with his cheerful
energetic spirit—
Mr Crittenden Genl James Jackson & Mr Mallory[1] (who I found is an old
acquaintance of my dancing days) dined here yesterday & I never saw a more
animated cheerful set men— Govr Dennison & Lizzie[2] are staying with us—
& consequently it was a lucky hit— for not a soul was invited & yet including Blair 14 were at the table & had enough to eat Mr. Wise (Emmett)—
Mr. Sedgwick[3] among them— the first— told me across the table that "*people*"
would call him Commodore— I told I enjoyed it— for when he reached that
dignity I expected that "*people*" would make you Admiral— Mr Sedgewick
said that the House had passed a vote of thanks to you— I told him afterwards
quietly I heard the Senate meant to veto it— he replied that he would take
good care *it did not* I was I hope gracefully grateful to Mr Sedgewick & took
him to my garden where I found he was au fait & enjoyed it vastly There
seems no doubt entertained about its passage as even Hale & Grimes will cave
in now— since the late Naval feats on James River— they talk of the Cap-

ture of Vicksburg being a greater matter than that of New Orleans I cannot think that—

I would write fully as I have done about the personel of the Govt & its plans & etc— but Father thinks at this moment least said the better for our family concern— & probably for that of the Country & it is sufficient that all are up & doing— with great spirit as ever & I do hope the energies so willingly proffered of our people will be more intelligently used— I can only *hope*— & pray with all my heart

Lizzy D. is having a very dull time as even the last of Bettys young acquaintance who returned here some weeks ago wounded are now picked up for Pope's Staff— George Alexander came out with Frank— his cartridge business has proved a failure & I believe he will join the Army He looks even worse than ever— I feel sorry for the poor fellow & like him better than any of the family— He seemed refreshed by Mr Crittendens wit— I was struck with his & Fathers *superior tone* of mind & heart— over any body else yesterday— He said Stevens had taunted with being like David & Absolum— There was something so exquisitely feeling & touching in voice manner— when he added but David had no son Thomas—[4] The entente Cordiale between *our* people & these Kentuckians *is perfect*—

I intended yesterday to go to Church but could not take my boy to the City The weather is so hot— & I have lost another communion Sunday which I felt for all the means of strength vouchsafed to us are needed by me— for since my sickness I have lost something of my sanguine temper & that too when I gain daily physically about which I feel most thankful as nearly all those similarly attacked have since suffered with an unconquerable prostration— & even this hot day I enjoy work in the garden & walk— Blair rides daily and was out this morning bright & early with Grandma far away over the hills I can truly say— there is nobody's company she enjoys more his prattle & gayety she said today does me good"

I have not seen Johns family for a week & shall go in tomorrow to see what they have decided upon for the balance of the summer They are all all well Ever yr devoted Lizzie Father says the long journey this letter has to take & the excitement of the times make caution essential— *in us all*

1. Gen. James S. Jackson, former congressman from Kentucky, raised a Union regiment in the summer of 1861. On July 19, 1862, he was appointed brigadier general of volunteers. He was killed at Perryville, October 8, 1862. Robert Mallory, congressman from Louisville, Kentucky (1859–65).

2. Lizzie Dennison was the daughter of Governor William Dennison of Ohio.

3. Charles B. Sedgwick, Republican congressman from New York 1859–63, was chairman of the House Committee on Naval Affairs.

4. John J. Crittenden had sons in opposing armies: George B. was a major general in the Confederate army and Thomas L. was a major general in the U.S. army.

Silver Spring   July 12, 1862

My dear Phil   I was busy fixing currant jelly for us & on our household thoughts intent— when Becky brought me your letter about the Navy promotions— When I had read that— I turned to the papers— & the first thing to greet me was the appointments reorganizing— the Navy Dept   I confess to a bitter cry— I had set my heart on one of the bureaux for you— but it seems— I am not to be gratified in this— but on the promotion point— Father says he will resent as an outrage— upon justice & upon you & him if any body is put over you—[1] I would go to others about this matter but I have heard women so scandalized who have done this that I am deterred from any thing of the sort. But if any body should be put over your head it will cut me to the heart I have had some passes with Fox & Porter about this already—

Lizzie Pearson was here one day & twitted me "with *Comre Porter*" asked me how I endured such a slight upon you— I replied— I supposed it was earned by Porter when he was safely esconced behind the trees & woods when you were sent out to attract away from him all the fire of the Forts lest by accident one ball might intrude itself upon Comre Porters honors & enjoyments— You did the fighting— & he by favor would get the honors— Lizzie hates Gingy—[2] so of course regales her with my ill tempered resentment— for I never did have anything to make me more angry than the affair of Apl 19th—[3] The most useless exposure of you & your ship— for Porters protection— Mrs Porter[4] duly reported my talk to her husband— who in return sends me a most graceful eulogy of you— thro Mr. Fox & said what I believe is only what is due to you[5] In reply— I say— that he is but just to you— but to me he was generous to speak to me of you so handsomely in return for my envious talk— Mr Fox told me yesterday that he had a letter from Porter— is "hard on Boggs" If you mention this matter to Porter dont mention Lizzie Pearson's part or name in it— I would never fan family feuds— I suffer so much from one that I feel that none deserve Heaven like peace Makers—

I had a long letter from Fanny. she writes cheerfully— her boys are in the Tobacco business— both getting pay & learning a business into which they may embark when old enough— Harry Joseph[6] has made large fortune out of the Weed— Frank has gone West. Govr. Dennison wished him in McC's staff but F said No!

I wrote you twice yesterday having sent No 48 to Ship Island before I got your letter— so I sent another to Cairo— Mr. Fox came & asked my news saying that the Reports sent to the Dept— were not full— I replied that you sent me every detail about the Onieda— so I gave him the log— & the Genl. Order which he had not seen (so I understood him)— & he promised to return them— The Canal is a matter of much talk—[7] but I am distress as to the good it will do us— for you can not get by thro it I fear which was its only use profitable to us— however I am not sanguine now adays— & feel as if nothing but the sight your face & the sound of your voice will uplift my spirit again— Fellow feeling makes one a kin now that Frank has resumed his Army harness it is wonderful how much more of sympathy my Parents give me— You constantly like Frank in the War now— but his going even in spite of these sympathese but adds to my burden— Father has been writing to McC. if I dared I would send you Franks impressions of his late visit to him—[8]

Sunday— I am again disappointed about going to Church but have a chance to send this— freighted with love from Blair (who is standing by me) and your affectionate Lizzie

1. On July 15, EBL wrote: "Father went to the Department about the matter— to learn their purpose & to let them know his wishes— When he was informed there would be *no overslaughing* & that you would be made a Commre by the carrying out of the Bill."

2. Gingy refers to G. V. Fox's wife, Virginia Woodbury Fox.

3. In the New Orleans campaign, gunboats such as Lee's *Oneida* were sent ahead of Porter's mortar boats to provide protective fire and to draw the forts' bombardment. After his experience in the Mississippi, Lee had only praise for the commander of the mortar fleet and anticipated Porter's promotion: "He is entitled to, and worthy of it. I know no other junior to whom I would willingly defer my claims from rank and services." SPL to EBL, July 4, 1862.

4. Georgie Ann Patterson, daughter of Commodore Daniel T. Patterson, married David D. Porter in 1839.

5. Judging the action of "the brave Lee," Porter wrote: "I never saw a ship more beautifully fought and managed. He was under fire more than anyone else, excepting perhaps DeCamp and Guest. His ship was a good deal cut up. He had much more than his share of killed and wounded and said less about it than those who did not take the bull so closely by the horns. I admire Lee very much for his cool calm bravery, the highest quality an officer can possess, and he is properly estimated by the young officers, who after all are the best judges—. . . . When the toxsin sounded every may did his duty, though some may have been more fortunate than others, and some were doubtful before hand—Boggs, for instance, is a hero, but for Lee's assistance he would be at the bottom of the Mississippi River, —food for Catfish." D. D. Porter to G. V. Fox, June 2, 1862, Fox, *Confidential Correspondence*, 2:114–15.

6. Jacob Henry Joseph, husband of EBL's closest friend and cousin, Sara Gratz Moses Joseph.

7. The army attempted to dig a canal across Swampy Toe, an isthmus formed by a hairpin turn in the Mississippi at Vicksburg. They began digging on June 25 and finished on July 22, but the water was too low to fill the canal.

8. In her July 8 letter, EBL mentioned that Frank had accompanied the president on a visit to McClellan's headquarters. On July 18, she noted: "Frank was as heart sick as man could be when he went off to the Army but he & the President came back greatly cheered—."

Silver Spring   July 21, 1862
My Parents Golden Wedding day

Dear Phil   I have just returned from Court where I did my best— & if John is not appointed Col— in his Dept it will not be the fault his sister Lizzie— it is needless to tell it all— but Father & I go to the City to follow the matter up diligently— & this much I can assure he has shown an interest for John that has given me great satisfaction   I will write you the result as soon as I know it—[1]

The President told Father that the appointment of Halleck[2] was McClellands suggestion— As for himself he was willing to serve anywhere but that a military chief was an essential at Washington— I suppose to have this talk was one of the objects of the Ps visit to the Army

Mr. Fox spent last evening— He & Brother croaked until I felt almost in dispair— it was worthy of a Bull Run anniversary— But the P. is evidently relieved & cheerful & things must work better in the War Dept— now *where the disease* is seated— I will not characterize it— but have a mighty leaning to Dr Fs[3] notions of the matter— Fox says the promotions will soon be made & will be made by the recommendation of the board of officers— which is composed of Lavalette Shubrick— Gregory McKean & Gardner—[4] I think is the fifth— but I am not sure they will say if a man is morally— mentally— physically— fit for promotion— & then those pronounced upon are promoted according as they now stand on the list— No political favor is to be used— in the business & these old officers are retired Admirals—[5] The vote of thanks did not pass it got dropt in the Senate yet it was in the published list of bills passed   Fox told my Father there was no doubt of your promotion whatever—

F. said that Craven[6] has been summoned back to Washington for returning slaves back to some plantation owned & governed by "a Lady rather woman" who had them stript & lashed in sight of his ship— when they had been in service of the Govt— he is recalled here to make explanations— F went on to say that when he was put in Ward's[7] place where he wanted to put you but my Father & Brother said they would not have your life risked there— where it would be such a hopeless contest as the Govt refused troops to Ward— & continued to refuse troops to cooperate & raise the blockade of the Potomac— "Well replied Father I was right— Lee *would never have gone to sleep as you said Craven did*"— & I did not covet Wards fate for him who tried to do his duty & lost his *life* in a most hopeless struggle— & thus a noble fellow was cut off—" I give you the talk as near as I can remember it—

Your duties for this summer I tried to get at in vain— as to where you all were to be sent— my direct inquiry was answered by saying that it would be all left to Farragut & then I touched on big titles & big ships— to which he replied that the Dept would hereafter have to classify ships by tonnage instead of guns as the most effective Iron ships would only have two guns & in old style that might a Lts Command— I will go see Mrs Maury—[8] I did not know they were here & when the Footes come I will do my best to be civil—

1. John Lee was the first judge advocate of the army, appointed in 1849. On July 17, 1862, Congress enacted legislation which superseded John's office and created a new one, judge advocate general, to which John was not appointed because he opposed the use of military courts to try civilians accused of disloyalty. In September, he resigned from the army and retired to his farm in Prince Georges County.

2. Halleck assumed command as general in chief on July 23, 1862.

3. Surgeon Jonathan M. Foltz, serving on USS *Hartford*, had been at New Orleans and up the river with Farragut's force. Although there are no extant letters from Foltz to Lee during the summer of 1862, some notion of his opinions are evident in his letter of October 30, 1862: "The war has done some good in the Navy at least, and will probably do so in the Govt., and trust it will be restored stronger and better than it has ever been. I would not have it as it was. It must be reconstructed, and the stronger it is made the better I shall be pleased with it. let us have no more slavery, no more universal sufferage, & a stronger central power. . . . That the Rebellion will all end right, I have no fears, but it has been at a fearful cost of lives and treasures. The South must be punished for filling the land with widows and with orphans, and an export duty on cotton & sugar should aid to pay the national debt." Foltz to Lee, October 30, 1862, Blair-Lee Papers.

4. The Board of Promotions was composed of Elie A. F. La Valette, W. Branford Shubrick, and Francis Gregory, all promoted to rear admiral and placed on the retired list on July 16, 1862. Other members were William W. McKean and William H. Gardner, both promoted to commodore and put on the retired list.

5. The board, she informed Lee on July 16, was "to pass upon the merits of some 6 or 8 officers who are notoriously incompetent— & it suppose they will be overslaughed— for the rest they will be promoted as heretofore and there will be no chance of our Yankee friend being an admiral— He has made so much money by the war that ought to content him—." The Yankee admiral was Charles Wilkes, orginially from New York and an old adversary of SPL, dating back to the exploring expedition of 1839.

6. Capt. Thomas T. Craven, commanding USS *Brooklyn*, whose troubles stemmed from Lt. Selim Woodworth's complaint to D. D. Porter that without proper authority Craven had taken custody of some forty contrabands who had been given refuge by Woodworth.

7. James H. Ward, killed in attack on Mathias Point, June 26 or 27, 1861.

8. Possibly Ann Hull Herndon of Fredricksburg, Virginia, who was married to Matthew F. Maury in 1834. A career naval officer and scientist, Maury had resigned and gone with the Confederacy. His wife and children were at Fredericksburg and might have been able to get into Washington.

Silver Spring   July 22, 1862

Dear Phil   The Richmond panic is nothing to that I am under now— I have not had a sight of the papers yesterday they were all put out of sight & only those left about that [had] nothing about the Ram[1] in [them] & Fox told

them about it on Sunday when I went to put Blair to sleep— but your condition is not mention— & the accounts on our [their] side differ from those
on our side I got no letter from you is the point that makes it a serious matter to me— but Ill not add my troubles to yrs & as I can think of nothing
but my apprehensions— which I pray may never be realized— Ill say good
Good night—

Father had a long talk about Johns affairs with the President & Father says
he made no promise— save that it was an appointment which he would make
himself as it one he had *personal* interest in— Father came home satisfied—
the P. said you all seem deeply attached to Majr Lee— the Judge[2] has written
me a long letter on the point— Father saw John who seems easy about it

July 23rd I have just been over to the Navy Dept Mr Fox came down to the
carriage says they have no details of your doings at Vicksburg. He says Farragut
had gone below Vicksburg before the Ram passed down—[3] but the papers tell
a different story— He said Davis was caught napping— Secesh say you all
were dreadfully cut up in passing down— I ache with anxiety to hear from you
& even then I'll never know what peace is until I see you face to face after all
these perils & hardships[4]

Mother & Betty talk of going to the Sea Shore & Sara Moses is to be with
them— They all want me to go but Father who agrees with me that I am best
at home quiet where I can hear from you promptly— & should become hys-
terical if I went about the world anywhere— So I shall stay home as our darling
is well & enjoys life in the large range of Silver Spring where I can in routine
occupation "possess my soul with more patience than anywhere else— The
rest ought to go for they are all complain Mother particularly is depressed &
out her usual wholesome condition Ill ask Mrs. Sands or Miss Smith to stay
with me—

Mr. Holt was out here yesterday he is full of the emancipation project—[5]
Genl Speed[6] was there from Ky— he described this inroad of Morgan[7] as only
a large robbing horse thieving business it was meant as a recruiting foray but
the people are dead to his call— & he parts from fatigue & other causes much
smaller than when he first entered the State. He said the Govt had millions
of property at Louisville & only one hundred men— out of hospital— but
it was funny to see how many got well suddenly in one hour one thousand
invalids were under Arms— Morgan has gone about at the rate of 40 miles a
day— & took horses just as he needed them Robt Alexander lost his entire
stable The Humphries[8] too some of whom are Secesh all feared alike if they
had good horses— Thus it was literally a horse thieving foray— & has had a
good effect for the Union cause as the State Govt had requested particularly
that no troops should be encamped in the State if it was possible to avoid—
So Mr. Crittenden & all of them now see that they must either have northern
troops or have a military state organization & have it under the U.S. Control

as their own Govt. is not to be trusted a moment— this is Genl Speeds mission who was evidently well pleased that the disasters were not greater & the results for our cause— happy

Alfred Pleasonton[9] spent last evening at Silver Spring   he is just from the Army says they are all well & urges immediate reinforcements & prompt movements— I see Father's brow is vastly relieved by the advent of Halleck— The Army men are in great glee— over it say he is great at organizing & office work but not active enough for the field—[10] I suppose Buell[11] will have command in the West as Grant is not always to be relied on— Frank is getting on well. had some regiments proffered & he will have a division instead of a Brigade— So says rumor— We have cool weather & our invalids in hospital are getting well rapidly some already gone back to the Army. All well at Johns   Ever yr devoted Lizzie

1. On July 15, the new Confederate ram *Arkansas* came out of the Yazoo River into the Mississippi. The Union ships were unprepared: they lay at anchor with banked fires. The *Arkansas*, with barely steam enough to steer, slowly moved through the helpless Union fleet and took refuge at Vicksburg.

2. Montgomery Blair had been judge of the court of common pleas in St. Louis from 1845 to 1849.

3. On July 24, Farragut took most of his fleet down river, leaving five gunboats to patrol from Baton Rouge to Vicksburg.

4. In her July 23 letter under the date of July 25, EBL reported, "Fox sends me word that no officers were hurt when you all passed the Batteries—."

5. The Second Confiscation Act, July 17, 1862, provided freedom for slaves of those who participated in rebellion. The law also included a provision for colonization. On July 22, Lincoln presented to his cabinet his plan for an emancipation proclamation.

6. Louisville unionist James F. Speed had helped keep Kentucky in the Union. He was appointed attorney general by Lincoln on December 1, 1864.

7. John Hunt Morgan's cavalry raid in Kentucky, July 4–28, created general havoc by cutting telegraph lines, wrecking bridges, and destroying railroad track.

8. Morgan's raid threatened Lexington and Frankfort. Robert Alexander and David C. Humphries were both related to the Blairs through a tangle of marriages.

9. Alfred Pleasonton (USMA 1844) had commanded the Second Cavalry at the outbreak of war. He marched it from Utah to Washington, where he was assigned to capital defenses. He then served in the Peninsular Campaign and was promoted to brigadier general of volunteers in July 1862.

10. On July 23 EBL commented: "Halleck has gone to Head Quarters on the James River. He must endorse McC.'s Slowness as he is just as slow—."

11. In June 1862 Maj. Gen. Don Carlos Buell (USMA 1841) was to attempt to take Chattanooga. Morgan's cavalry cut his supply line in July, and in September Buell was ordered to Kentucky to stop a Confederate invasion led by Braxton Bragg and Edmund Kirby Smith.

Silver Spring   July 26, 1862
Dear Phil   On the receipt of your letter about detaching you from the Oneida
& the River Iron Clad Ships— &etc— I sat down & in the words of your own
letter made known your & my wishes on the matter to Mr. Fox in my most
civil way & had it next day backed up by Father So if it is not given to you it
is not for lack of asking—

On Sunday night when talking here I said— I hoped for promotion in the
way of ship as well as rank but I then thought get one at a time— would be
the best plan particularly as all this business of Rank & promotion— "is to
be settled in the next ten or 12 days" & *merit* is the sole recommendation—
On that test I have no fears— But when it comes to favoritism & political
influence I give up— but Fox said distinct *the whole* responsibility of selection
would rest upon the board— ie Shubrick McKean Gregory— Lavalette & I
think Gardener is the fifth—

Our household were put in alarm by the Minute Guns in mourning & horror of Mr. Van Burens death—[1] for they began at dawn of day & lasted until
sunset— & the whole country out here were put in a state of alarm— Our
gardner dropped his potatoes with a huckster & rushed back home as hard as
horse could bring him— saying there was such a firing over the Potomac that
the enemy must be at the bridge— he did [not] inquire— was too affrighted so
we all shared the panic until the Sewards came out & then Mr. S. had a good
laugh— at me— & as they say a *scare* is now my normal condition— I had it
all put on me— Altho I confess to having met considerable sympathy during
the day—

I went over to the Cottage— to see Cousin Nancy Carroll as I heard she
was ill— I think she is failing fast & cannot last much longer   she seemed to
have every comfort about her & to be well attended to— things looked cleaner
& more comfortable than I had ever seen them before—

Mr. King is out tonight to spend tomorrow his first holiday with us— We
are as cordial kindly as of yore— Tomorrow is my church day & as the weather
is cool I shall go— Minna thinks S[tanton] will have his way about Johns
matter— but Father who had the conversation with the President thinks differently— She says he will be ill treated— because he is "*our* friend—"[2]
As Dr. Wood—[3] who was overslaughed & now broken up out of his home
here simply because of his frienship for— her & Brother We are sorry for
"Mortimer" the *stylish* coachman of Chestnut— Hill a horse kicked & broke
his leg tonight & they have sent for Dr. May to set it— Good night   Ever your
devoted Lizzie

1. Martin Van Buren died at his home, Lindenwald, on July 24, 1862.
2. On August 5, EBL made this curious comment on the political implications of
John Lee's situation: "he has tried to help McC. out of a tight place— but the Genl
dont know his best friends and— but it is best not to say any more about it—."

3. Robert Crooke Wood was promoted to major surgeon July 1836. He served as colonel assistant surgeon general from June 1862 to October 1865.

Silver Spring   July 31, 1862

Dear Phil   Your situation on the 16th *inst* is my perpetual thought— I have been to see about your orders nothing *will* be done (not *can*) until you are promoted— what that promotion will be depends (they say) upon the Board now sitting in judgement upon all the Captains & Commanders— Fox remarked that there were not— 5 captains below Wilkes— (who now heads the active list) who were fit for promotion— & as he said to my Father that you were among the first men in all the Service— & as Brother said to Mother that all acknowledged you were the ablest man in F's Squadron. I cannot doubt that you will be made a Commodore— but I try not set my heart on it & will confess that its consequence to me *is now* greater as a means of deliverance from your present uncomfortable command— & such is my aching anxiety about you that I would take any thing or give any thing to get you home— I went to the City yesterday to shop for Mother & to the Asylum— The heat & the news together gave me a sick heart & head— Today Father & I went to Miss Nancy Carroll's funeral   I was with Mr. Geo Digges—[1] chief mourner (next to her servants) as nearest of kin present— I was sorry I had not taken Blair it was an uncommon funeral— A lovely day— Equisite Music— An Excellent sermon— a church full of friends

The arrest of secessionist in this region is because of their enticement to desertion of federal Soldiers— I saw Dr. John Fairfax—[2] he was very mad at the treatment of his Mother & family all for a parcel of horses & mules who got out by the soldiers pulling down the Bars themselves— & it has made a good laugh at such a charge of cavalry!! the old horse killed was blind & lame— but such is the movement of guerrillas in the Border States that I am glad our side are on the alert about Maryland— Where the emancipation in the District has made a great increase of *secession*— among slave owners   Miss Nancys kin will be furious at her She has left her slaves free— & her estate to be managed for that end & for their sole benefit—

I met Cullom at Botelers buying an ice Pitcher!! & sat on a pile of Rugs to ruminate on such a Chief of Staff at such a time!!![3] and fear I was bitter & scornful in my thoughts altho he did pay you huge compliments & me none— & an old woman a little while after told me I was "breaking very fast" I felt like telling her— if God in his mercy would give my heart one throb of joy— I would soon mend up again— but I said nothing— Blair is well & joyous & I can *see* his bright face— I see by Cullums talk that theres an entente Cordiale between Halleck & McC— Our whole cause depends— I think on this falls Campaign in Virginia— Frank has five Regiments nearly filled— Texas is I think to be his scene of action *but* is only talked of as yet— There is a great deal of talk about drafting & it will have to be done & that soon—[4]

You see by the enclosed that *Admirals* are made— & that there are five vacant places— I suppose Davis hopes for one— & Wilkes too as they have votes of thanks to get it with— Grimes stopped *our* thanks— in the Senate Boggs was the excuse— & others— in the fleet were considered unfit for promotion & who would get it— with such a passport for it— All well at Johns yesterday Ever yr devoted Lizzie I scarce know where to send this

1. George A. Digges was the son of William Dudley Digges and Catherine Brent. His home was Green Hill.

2. On July 28, EBL reported that Dr. John Fairfax had been arrested because of heightened fear of secessionist activity in Maryland, which activity prompted her to comment acidly: "I hope the Secessionists will be drafted here— (in this State) & then we will get rid of them."

3. Brig. Gen. George W. Cullum (USMA 1833), Halleck's chief of staff (1861–64), career officer, aide to Scott (1861), and superintendent of West Point (1864–66). In her July 28 letter, EBL worried: "Halleck has returned but I have misgivings about him— because he has the most incompetent Staff Cullum at the head of it, has no head & Halleck has need of many heads & hands to help him now."

4. To meet militia quotas in July and August 1862, the states were threatened with the possibility of conscription. On July 17, the president signed a federal militia draft for nine months' service, but it was never effectively used. Not until March 3, 1863, was there a national draft.

                                        Silver Spring   August 6, 1862
Dear Phil No letters, no news from you today none since that wrote in "Tribulation" on the 16th ult. I shall go gladly to the City in the morning with the hope of hearing of some way of getting you out of the Oneida I am pulling all my wires & have been to the City every day this week— & shall go tomorrow— with Mr Macawbers[1] hope— that something I hope for— (promotion) to get at this end— I want to go see Mrs Lincoln but have been able to get the carriage for only my own ends— & so take my chances—

Blair is well bears the heat better than he did— I dress him in one thin linen covering— pants & shirt— & one thin flannel over the stomach & bowels— he helped me work early this morning in my garden & tho his help is very troublesome— yet very enjoyable to me— Mrs Beale has lost her Uncle Wm Brown really a father to her— She calls her Baby Violet for Mother

Augt 7. When I received the commission— directed to you— from the Dept. I broke it open feeling assured you were made a Comre & consequently homeward bound— & that was the reason it was sent to you here A bitter burst of tears told Father my disappointment in find you only Captain & nothing said about relief Father seemed to think it was an injustice to you— & we posted to the Dept where learned that you were not reached— & I got the following list of Commodores for active list—

1	Wilkes head of the list	6	Blake
2	Eagle	7	Harwood
3	Long	8	Bailey
4	Van Brunt	9	Purviance
5	Glendy	10	Morris
		11.	Lardner

Craven suspended by a Court of inquiry as to the Negro matter

H K Hoff

Davis

Bell

Smith

Livingston

Missroon— present foot of list—[2]

Robt. Hitchcock[3] is at the head of the list of Captains— on which you are No. 12— & Mr Sands is at the foot of the list— there are eight Commodores who are retired at the end of this year by virtue of their ages— Schenck, Carter & Prentiss[4] are overslaughed— The first because of conduct lately in East Indies— I heard that now they were busy rating & arranging Commands & the point about which I wished to know was if the Oneida would be a Capts Command— & it was thought it would *not* be— The Iron ships will take rank by tonnage & not guns— & I got a promise from Father that he would ask for an Iron Ship for you I will leave no stone unturned to get you some relief—

I am sweet to everybody even went after *Tisha* McKean[5] & brought her out to the Hill when I knew there was such a thirst for gossip— that she would be as a "fresh spring in this hot weather— J & Nelly are off with their children to the Mountains— & they made their escape in the hotest weather we have had thus far— I went to see Mrs. Washington & took flowers— to Anna who is ill— Called on Mrs Jones[6] as I had to go to the house to see the bride Mrs. Rochester[7] Betty's friend Miss Martin— of Albany— did some business for Mother— got a new Cook— Went to see Maria Smith who I knew was very sick Met Genl. Wright in her parlor— he gave me an animated account of the Appearance— firing of the Vandalia at Hilton he went on board after it was over to see you & congratulate you on the spirited behavior of your ship— & was disappointed in not meeting you—[8] but told me to say *your crew* & ship did you great credit

I sent to know if I was expected to send your commission to you— Mr. Fox advised to send only a copy— which I enclose I got a letter from Appo & Betty all well with them but I got none from you so am a disappointed weary woman Ever your devoted wife Lizzie

1. Wilkens Micawber, character in Dickens's *David Copperfield* who always hoped that "something would turn up."

2. The following were promoted to commodore on July 16, 1862: Charles Wilkes, Henry Eagle, John C. Long (retired list), Gershom J. Van Brunt, William M. Glendy, George S. Blake, Andrew A. Harwood, Theodorus Bailey, Hugh Y. Purviance (retired list), Henry W. Morris, James L. Lardner, Thomas T. Craven, Henry K. Hoff, Charles H. Davis, Charles H. Bell (retired list), William Smith, John W. Livingston, and John S. Missroon.

3. Robert Hitchcock was promoted to captain on July 16. His promotion to commodore also dates from July 16.

4. James F. Schenk, John C. Carter, and George A. Prentiss did not receive their promotions until later: Schenck on January 1, 1863; Carter on April 4, 1867 (retired list); and Prentiss on October 24, 1864 (retired list).

5. Latisha McKean was one of the seven daughters of W. W. McKean, commanding the Gulf Blockading Squadron.

6. Fredericka B. Jones married Roger Jones in 1862.

7. Anna L. Martin married William Beatty Rochester in 1862. She was a second cousin of Evelina Martin, and he was a brother of Evelina's first husband James Hervey Rochester.

8. Lee had left *Vandalia* on October 22, 1861. *Vandalia* was part of Du Pont's naval force which captured Port Royal, South Carolina, on November 7, 1861.

Silver Spring   August 8, 1862
Dear Phil   The Papers say "all quiet along the lines—" & so things look— but there is much doing & it seems to me with more earnestness & method than ever evinced before in our affairs—

The theme of today is the weather There is an intense heat the more felt from the cool weather heretofore this is the first moonlight we have seen this year & as I can read by moonlight or do anything but dream over the past & pray for the future— Blair is full of talk of tomorrow his birthday which lives so vividly with me yet I can hardly believe it is five years ago

Today has been without events at Silver Spring— save that Father went to the City to have little Sara— (Charitys adopted) appraised & her papers given to her— When Vincent asked to have the same done for him—[1] Father agreed but the Court refused— Our new cook began today Our old one— Mary— gets 24 dollars a month for wages— it seems she & her husband are not satisfied with each he having sought a younger woman— for "a companion makes Mary more than content to quit him & her old home— Our new cook is an improvement on anything we have had for nearly a year past— Alick also does better than Vincent ever did— So we too are satisfied with the change

I sent one of your cartes to Dr. Palmer[2] through Apo who wrote that she promised to get one for him— he saw the one I gave Andrew in her book— Andrew never rested until I gave him one— when Apo took care of it for him in her book where you & Father shall hover around Jessie who was you know there last winter— She has written me twice— but I answered only today

She says Frank writes in excellent spirits & expects *now* to run for Congress without any opposition—

August 9th 1862 Blair's fifth birthday which has enjoyed hugely he had a grand cake— made by Becky which he invited the children from the Hill to help him eat and of which he ate less than any of them— We both sighed for Papa many times this day and I know he has thought of his boy with yearning heart today— It is two years today since we ate our last dinner in our own household and it has added a sadness to this day because I cannot forsee the time when we shall— a home feast together again

I went up to the Hill top to ask them to come eat Blair's cake & sat awhile for a chat with *Tish* McKean & Mrs. No 6— from the first— I heard— that Mary Scott (Scotia) was married to Harrington—[3] Chase's assistant Secy— some months ago that Smith Lee— had lost his mind— & so had Hartstene & Comre Tatnall loved the Yankees to much to fight them well— & all said his heart was broken— Huger was very much in the same condition— & were both *failures* south— Her accounts of the women of Washington attention to the Hospitals— does them great honor— they have given the Sanitary people— some good lessons in nursing & the number cured in our church Hospitals would be called miraculous if they were Roman Catholic & had *nuns* for nurses & the marvel would travel the world round— Gen Griffin[4] & his wife Sally Carroll were here tonight— He is a No 1 Soldier & has an abiding faith in Genl. McC— Yr affectionate wife Lizzie

1. On April 16, 1862, Lincoln signed the bill freeing slaves in the District of Columbia, with compensation up to $300. In her July 8 letter EBL had taken the news calmly, reporting: "Vincent & Mary have both got their leave to go—the first is a real deliverance but we miss Marys good cooking."

2. James C. Palmer, naval surgeon, had been a friend of SPL's since their earliest days in the navy.

3. George Harrington was assistant secretary of the treasury.

4. Gen. Charles P. Griffin (USMA 1847) married Sallie Carroll in 1861. During the Peninsular Campaign, he was promoted to brigadier general of volunteers.

7

"The Presidents proclamation took the breath out of me this morning"

September 23, 1862

PHILLIPS LEE RETURNED FROM DUTY on the Mississippi River to assume a new rank and position: acting rear admiral commanding the North Atlantic Blockading Squadron. After a three-week respite with his family, Lee again went to sea, and Elizabeth resumed her daily correspondence. Rumors of a Southern invasion of Maryland caused her to leave her home and visit her Philadelphia relatives. The Lees' anxieties were great enough to make them consider moving their possessions from Washington.

The frustration of a second Union defeat at Bull Run in August was partially alleviated by the repulse of Robert E. Lee's offensive at Antietam in mid-September. Lincoln's preliminary emancipation proclamation, issued shortly after that bloody battle, made the abolition of slavery a central Northern war aim.

Philadelphia   September 8, [1862]
Dear Phil   Yours written in pencil is just received— I think all the removals from the city ought now to be made by water— The Rebels are in Maryland & they may stop any train en route here[1] There is great activity here in war matters— Pope is here today— but Oh how differently would have been his advent here if he had been competent for his late position—[2]

Your orders about the money has been fully carried out—
$585 gold
115 in money paid*
$700
very nearly 19 per cent
*I kept 150— in paper for current uses if I needed it   I might do so— if I have to leave here with my child & board— as he is not well as when we parted but the soup here is too rich for him— but as he craved it Becky indulged him against my orders— her first indiscretion of the kind—

I had a letter from Father— he still writes in his old sanguine courageous tone—[3] Brother says to his wife— "we have ample means to annihilate the Rebels this side of the Potomac but if we cannot do it it would be best to close the war today—" He says the reception of McClellan by his Army is comforting[4] All agree he has its affection and confidence & nearly half of it refused to fight under any other General So if they have no excuse now for *not* fighting maybe they will do it little better than they did lately

Horace has entered today upon his duties as aid to Genl Pleasonton— there is to be every preparation made to meet the enemy here Horace says he will send Aunt & I to Canada where I would not last long— I shall remain here *this crisis* if Blair continues well & if he does wilt I run up to Bethlehem for a week or so—

When I came out of Church yesterday I was spoken to very kindly by Captain Rowan & Capt Poor[5] & each his wife— they are at Mrs. Sheezs[6] & Ill call on them tomorrow & Mrs Stockton— Our poor little Maria has absorbed my feelings for some days— & I am convinced she would have always been a sufferer— *her very bones* were distorted out of shape by the rhumatic fever of last winter— Her death is a release to her[7] I hear the telegraph has been cut by the Rebels in Balt— that the Railroad has been taken in charge by the military. Balt held down by Forts & gun boats— certain it is we are in awful times— Still I say— I do not dispair— & Oh how fervently I pray for Gods blessing upon you my precious husband—

I have written to Ellen— & strange I said— "The increase of titles & awful responsibilities & work upon husband does not guild this bitter pill for John is my very brother—[8] I felt nervous about Johnnie[9] & yearn to hear from them Blair has written you nearly as many letters as I have— he does love his dear Papa & so does your own affectionate Lizzie

1. On September 4, R. E. Lee's army began crossing the Potomac River into Maryland. On September 6 Stonewall Jackson had occupied Frederick, Maryland.

2. John Pope's Union Army of Virginia had been soundly defeated at Second Bull Run on August 29–30. On September 3, he was assigned to the Department of the Northwest and removed from the main actions of the war.

3. In her September 6 letter, EBL reported: "Mother & Father are at Silver Spring refused to go the the City but he says they are as safe there now as in the City—."

4. On September 2, McClellan was reappointed to command the Army of the Potomac in Virginia. On September 9, EBL stated that Montgomery "says that McC. is behaving well very laborious & active & hopeful—."

5. Career naval officers captains Stephen C. Rowan and C. H. Poor both served in the North Atlantic Blockading Squadron. Rowan's wife was Mary Stark Rowan.

6. Mrs. David Schietz ran a boarding house in Philadelphia at 812 Wallace.

7. On September 5, EBL had written about Maria: "I spent most of the day there & twice thought Maria dying toward night she became easier— & we thought her better she spoke gaily & laughed just ten minutes before the last dying convulsion

came upon her— All day yesterday her talk was so affectionate & intelligent— She put her arms around my neck— saying precious Aunt Lizzie will I die?" The next day EBL commented on Montgomery's reaction: "He is calm & very sad— he was wholly unprepared for the childs death."

8. Joseph Holt, who had been Buchanan's secretary of war, was appointed by Lincoln on September 8 to be judge advocate general, replacing John Lee. Holt, a Kentuckian, was a strong advocate of allowing military trials of civilians suspected of disloyalty. EBL anticipated the appointment on September 5: "it will grieve me to have John resign *now* & it does not seem to me to be any degradation in him to serve under his old chief— & a man who I believe he will find congenial & delightful as a colaborter."

9. John F. Lee, Jr., was born June 29, 1848.

Philadelphia   September 10, [1862]

My Dear Phil   I read with great distress John's resignation And I should have been better prepared for it by Ellens letter which I recd yesterday in which the only reply she makes to my inquiries about John is— that she is always assured of my loving sympathy— but I must now see how "beautifully & kindly are the ways of God to us—" She speaks in unmeasured terms of joy at having re-turned home on "*that Monday*" My Father had been to see her— & said all was well at Silver Spring— Johnny recovers slowly the fever had left him & he was gradually but slowly getting well— had no fever since Thursday   Ellen seems perfectly assured of the Success of the Rebels & her whole letter is evidently written in a joyous state of mind. I was so glad to hear that Johnny was better I was glad too— Your Brother is independent & it may be all for the best for their welfare & happiness—

Still I do not dispair of our good cause & believe this late chastening has been well merited & will eventually work out a quicker settlement of this frightful warfare As to News You know more than we do here Yesterday the city was filled with rumors— & I am most comfortable by disbelieving them all— As to moving our things— this place is really more in danger than Wash-ington— & after thinking it over for a long time I have concluded to let them take their chances just where they are— those under Johns roof are safe from pillage as his— & those at the Navy Yard are under gun boat protection— & all would be a heavy expense here & run now just the same chance of pillage with the increase of populace[1]

Minna left here yesterday at 2 olk for Portsmouth with her children all well— but she poor woman seemed only each day to realize more keenly her loss— I hope the change will procure her sleep & more composure—

Miss Mary McKnight was in here last night & was full of McDowells trea-son for which he is under arrest[2] Said among our military all was in good heart now that the traitors were found out— that the reception of McClel-lan by the Army was beyond description— All was working harmoniously

& heartily— hopefully in the Army now—" I give this as I know it comes straight from McClellans friends— Do make all the preparations possible to prepare for Merrimac No. 2 [3] but it does seem to me one of the best means is to find as her *reality*— if it is possible get information as our foes means & purposes— Your position I believe authorizes this as one of your duties— & in it all our other Chiefs have utterly failed— Horace says if South is victorious there the north will submit to their dominion— there *will be* but one Govt on the Continent—

Yours of the 8th recd yesterday— There is no panic here not even any excitement visible— but the people look anxious & unhappy [4] I send you Blairs letter tis all his own fixing up & is full of love if not of sense   Aunt & Horace send love   Ever yr devoted Lizzie

1. On September 11, EBL quoted her father's letter: "he says '*a hundred thousand men* man marched by Silver Spring— Jackson was stolen out of the pasture. Cupid was taken out of the Stable but Mother stopped the armed thief who dismounted & ran as *she* held the reins of the bridle   she is a Roman dame! All the apples, & the corn on the road is gone by Mothers leave who gladly gave anything she had to cheer our soldier on, in their duty."

2. Irvin McDowell, discredited commander at First Bull Run a year earlier, had now played a role in the second defeat, and the public found it easy to heap abuse on him.

3. There were numerous reports that the Confederates were building another ironclad at Richmond. The CSS *Virginia II* was not completed until 1864.

4. On September 12, EBL had noted: "up to this time there was repose in the faith they had in McClellan but since the enemy has reached Greencastle Pennsylvania— they have ceased to cry to Hercules & are now bestirring themselves to organize for resistance—."

Philadelphia   September 12, [1862]
Dear Phil   Yours enclosing Ad[mira]l G[oldsborough]'s note is recieved— I have never spoken to Capt Poor & Capt Rowan except at the Church door on Sunday when they sought me & then I could barely acknowledge their civility— for at the same moment Mrs Decharde & Mrs Chapman & Mrs Rockill [1] all old ladies & acquaintances of my girlhood came up & I walk away with Mrs. Chapman whose pew I always go to here & who is ever so very kind to me—

Capt Harrison [2] called today and asked me if you had heard anything about the New Merrimac   I said that the Norfolk people said they built her wooden work & represented of course the work of their own hands as formidable— & then he talked about his own health & wishes which I wrote to you today. [3] as he left I remarked that you had inquired of me if I had seen him his return from the south & had expressed solicitude about him & said I had no doubt you would be delighted to have him with you— he said— will you mention

my wish to be with him when you write— then I made enquiries about his wife
& etc as to Henry Etting I never talk to him— he always gets things wrong
end foremost— so I am extremely cautious in my talk & always say I dont·
know anything about Navy matters to *him* I called on these people next door
because— their wives were formerly intimate with Sara Moses— & they were
boarding & I was considered as a sort of home & at any rate with a resident
who desired me to visit them on her acct as well as my own— this Ill mention
when I see, They were out when I called Aunt Becky does not now visit out
of her family circle— I thought *it best* to call— as I see I'll be considered *stuck
up* if I alter my ways— & I never felt less so— for I never endured more anxious
feelings & yet I try to be calm & hopeful for I have no right to oppress those
about me— I ought to cheer them— Capt Harrison is the only naval man I
talk to at all & that was today in a visit of 15 minutes— when he did most
of the talk— he said there was a naval Battery here— which he & somebody
else— had been training— I mentioned this to Horace a few minutes after
& at a meeting of the Home Guards today they passed Resolution to apply to
the Govt for the immediate use of it & to get these Gentlemen to go act with
them— I'll keep your affairs to myself I have ever done so because I know it is
your own habit— & nature & it is instinctive with me to try to please you—
at least it one my hearts first wishes & from its fullness I generally speak—

I am not frightened about you—[4] it is a point of a woman love to have
faith in her husband & mine has ever had mine & when you can look out for
yourself— I am even more easy about you I have but one anxiety— that is
the many responsibility upon you health— but I take comfort in constantly
praying that God will aid & strengthen to do your duty & well

1. Mrs. Henry M. Dechert was the wife of a Philadelphia attorney; Mrs. George
Chapman was the former Emily Markoe; and Mrs. Rockhill was the wife of either
Daniel II or Edward Rockhill, clothing merchants in the city.

2. Comdr. Napoleon B. Harrison, commanding USS *Minnesota*, flagship of the
North Atlantic Blockading Squadron.

3. In her other letter of the same date, EBL wrote of Harrison's visit: "he says he
reported fit for duty day before yesterday & would like to serve wth you— wither on
your ship or in the Fleet— He seems very much yr friend."

4. In her September 13 letter, EBL corrects herself: "I did not say quite truly last
night when I said was not frightened about you I meant I gave my fears no utterance by
the help of God alone I endure quietly that burden in my heart with which it almost
breaks & would do so entirely but for faith that our Cause is righteous & God will
bless us."

Philadelphia   September 15, [1862]

Dear Phil   Your letter of Saturday telling me to write to you at Norfolk came
today also one from Father whose few lines are as follows

"We are in Statu quo here— all well— I am in the midst of an Army

& unless the Rebels destroy double their number they will not disturb Silver Spring— I will go to the City if they approach our Forts for this will be
necessary to escape our own Bullets

John very foolishly resigned without consulting me— He repented it— & I
went to the President to recall his resignation Lincoln went to the Dept to do
it— but it is possible that Stanton may have foreclosed his action I have not
heard— We have not suffered much from the intrusion of the troops except
'the loss of Jackson—' Yr affectionate fa[ther]

Nelly did [not] say any thing of Johns views— it was only indicative of her
own feelings which are *excessive* against the government—

McClellans reception by the people of Maryland is perfectly delightful to
me & when the Rebels retire from Maryland which they seem to be doing in
hot haste Johns only sympathy or principle with them is gone— States Rights
& this makes me intensely eager to get his Commission back again— I am as
sorry I did not go to Washington with you as Nelly is glad she did for then
as once before— I would have known of John's prospect & I believe again
prevented the acceptance of his resignation I am amazed at Ellen— who has
such a horror of her husband going into Battle *he* will not be let alone by the
Secessionists & in six months they will drag him into their horrid vortex &
ruin him now I will divide all I have in this world with them— & Ill even seek
their welfare as one of the dearest in life to me, but Johns heart will be broken
if he is improverished & cannot minister to his family's needs and it is this
that gives me the greatest solicitude— Not that they will ever suffer want—
but that he will anguish— When I read Fathers letter I felt like putting on my
wrappings & going to Washn but will now take up my pen & urge Father to
save this commission— if it is possible

Horace goes with Genl Pleasonton on Wednesday I think they mount a
campaign thro Maryland— I had a letter from Wright Rives in an agony about
his Father—[1] & says that men wept for joy when McClellan was restored
to his command— Nobody in the West would have trusted Pope He is with
McClernand at Springfield Ill. I will write to him there— & let him know
what was done about his promotion—

Dont repeat what I think about Nelly I write it because I think you will
be freer to express yr views to John— but be cautious as this is the time above
all others for me to cultivate the entente cordiale with Nelly & my heart feels
it— I heard today that Capt Turner[2] expected to sail on Saturday— his wife[3]
said he would I made no inquiries

Aunt & Horace who got back from Harrisburg this morning send love Blair
is very well is off in the square with Becky and the squirrels his great resource
here I showed him the garret room I had in my school days[4] he exclaimed
Why Becky you would not like being up there away from your Mother & Papa
& a little girl too— poor Mama! & he kissed me with exquisite tenderness

Horace says the wild enthusiasm at Harrisburg is beyond description & the numbers of men must already be fifty thousand They have already ten thousand today at Chambersburg 7 seven there yesterday— Ever yr devoted Lizzie

Our side begins to leap up again dont it?

1. John Rives, F. P. Blair's dearest friend and partner in the *Globe*. Rives's business talents and management provided Blair with financial stability. He died April 10, 1864.

2. Thomas Turner, captain of the *New Ironsides*, had served with Lee when they both were midshipmen. He was presently serving under Lee in the North Atlantic Blockading Squadron.

3. Flavia Prather, daughter of Henry A. Prather of the District, married Thomas Turner in 1834.

4. EBL had attended Madame Adele Sigoigne's School in Philadelphia in the 1830s and she had spent her weekends at her Aunt Becky's.

Philadelphia   September 16, 1862

Dear Phil   This is an outside grey day but Oh what a *let up* this last struggle has brought to us— & when I read your letter yesterday. saying you had no faith in McC, I must confess I exulted for once in my life *quietly* that you are mistaken— I have seen the inside view of the horrid treatment he has recieved at the hands of Mr Stanton[1] the endless hypocrasy & there is but one good old slang word— *bedeviling* to express it— He has born it well & as to his treatment of Pope in the first place— you must not believe one word uttered by Pope unless you know it to be true from other sources & as to serving under him, I would not do it first because morally Sickles[2] is a more moral man & I always justified the Mutiny of the Hylanders against him & then secondly tho brave & dashing— he has no sense & nobody ever thought he had. & how two such fat heads & his & McDowells ever got lifted up so high is only solved by the old saying about luck

Now McClellan is slow oh so slow & even now & I have a tremor of anxiety about his movements lest he will lose the fruits of this hard won fight— by following it up too *slowly*— You ought to remember he is our best man & consequently most hated by Secesh— then Abolitionist hate him because he is a lion in the way of their bad schemes for the uplifting of the African over white men   I have faith in him— & do fondly hope that he will be our successful General— because he is a good man— & will not use the power given by success to injure our Republic A point that has made me often feel that the characters of men who have been made Generals has not been sufficiently considered—

Capt Harrison was here last night with his wife to see me He has been ordered to go to Dupont— but has written to have his orders changed to go to you— he talked of going to Washn for the purpose today— he seems bent upon being with you— I told him exactly what you had said about it He remarked those are few words but you & I know it means more from him than flourishing sentences from others   I assented most cordially to this   I like him very much—

His wife has a little Baby & looks white from confinement but very pretty   I have no news to send— Blair is well— & is just now writing on a little slate which I got for a rainy day resource— Mrs. Hays[3] (Doctors wife) sent me the enclosed letter for her old mother   I told her that you could not send it as it was not permitted to send letters by Flags of truce Still she said— please send it he may know better about it & if it cannot go he can throw it in the sea— So here it is & I hope you will do as she says— The Rogers are next door to me— & all well—

Poor Genl Reno death[4] is a great alloy to this victory— he married Mary Cross—[5] Mary Blairs dearest friend & they look alike & now both widows & both widows indeed— I met Mrs Steedman she was very civil— but I would agree to go to the Country to see her— as she could not come to Silver Spring to see me   Aunt sends her love to you   Ever your devoted Lizzie

1. On July 2, 1862, EBL minced no words in her assessment of Stanton: "Stanton is a misfortune to his Country— & there is no good to come out of him— our present troubles are wholly due to his maladministration— & we should have been— utterly ruined if the President had not withstood his importunate counsels about half the time— One of his wickenesses is to keep the Country ignorant of the real state of the Army— & nothing can exceed the misery inflicted— the reality is not half as bad as the Rumors & terrors make the Condition of things— the papers talk strategy— but nobody believes it— & he like most bad men— delight in every rise of power without any other motive it seems to me in this case—."

2. Daniel E. Sickles, soon to be promoted to major general (November 1862), had gained notoriety in 1859, when he shot and killed his wife's unarmed lover Phillip Barton Key. He was acquitted on the grounds of temporary insanity, the first use of that defense.

3. In 1834 Sara Ann Minis married Isaac Hays in Savannah, Georgia.

4. Maj. Gen. Jesse Lee Reno was killed at South Mountain, Virginia, September 14, 1862.

5. In 1853 Mary Blanes Cross had married Jesse Reno.

Philadelphia   September 20, [1862]

Dear Phil   Yours of the 18 was recd yesterday evening— Sometimes I get letters the day after they are written— but most frequently it is two & three days.

We are vastly relieved here by the Exit of the Rebels out of Maryland—[1] where there has been no rising & where I have ever maintained there would be none because even those who were considered *Secesh* have ever evinced the greatest reluctance to anything of the sort & pronounced it ruinous—[2] They as you often said would if there is to be a division would prefer the north—

but Secession as a principle is as vile in their eyes as yours— & consequently there was *no spirit* or principle upon which they could or would rise— & then the Union men have ever outnumbered the sympathizers even in Secesh Counties the vote tell this— & never was an election held with so little interference— nowhere but in Prince Georges & Balt where violence was threatened was there any guard ever set at the poles— in our Neighborhood Secesh was insolent & violent— but were so few that they were laughed at only— This result in Maryland is delightful to me for too many reasons to enumerate— Horace is very much annoyed at the failure of his generals to go— he has gone to much expense to get equipped— uniform Crimean shirts Saddle & etc it is however very comfortable to Aunt Becky since she feels that our success renders his services unnecessary. So I shall probably go home the last of the Coming week or the first the next one when I will have been away four weeks eventful ones!! from home I will remain until the 1st of Oct I have written for Betty to turn her face homeward & shall take her with me— Letitia McKean dined here with me yesterday— she said Mr. Pyne's soldier son was desperately low from a wound—[3] & his life dispaired of— I could not extract another item tho I was very civil for that purpose

All thankful for our victories— but sad over our dead I still fear McC having lost so many generals will be too slow— & the slow set are the ones unhurt— Poor Will French— I mourn [?] him. I enclose you Blairs letter. I wish you could have heard his loving prattle over it— he kissed me & then cover certain places with his own kisses— Aunt Becky said last night he was a "delightful child—" which is kind of her for he is very noisy— Your coat will be done today & I send to know Paymaster Pettits[4] movements— I hear the Ironsides goes on Monday— I wish we had troops to go attack Richmond now— it would fall I think an easy conquest— I have no news save that in the papers Aunt is off to Synagogue Good day to you ever yr own Lizzie

1. In early September R. E. Lee began his invasion of the North which led to the battle at Antietam. By September 20 the rebels were retreating back across the Potomac.

2. On September 17, EBL had written: "Nothing can exceed the Military ardor of the people here— I know instances of a gentleman head of an establishment of enormous wealth is a private— under one of his apprentice boys who happen to devote his evenings to drilling— which has been the fashionable evening's occupation of the young men from 17 to 20 & these Boys consequently are in great demand—."

3. Charles M. Pyne had been wounded at Second Bull Run on August 30, 1862, but he did not die.

4. Paymaster Robert Pettit had joined the navy in 1837.

Philadelphia   September 22, [1862]

Dear Phil   Your's of the 19th came yesterday I did not write yesterday a dull headache in the evening made me too stupid for anything but sleep of which

I now get more than for some weeks past— It is astonishing how much quiet the exit of Rebels out of Md. gives me night & day.

I shall write to Father to day & see if I cannot return home next week Indeed I shall go surely If McClellan follows up the Rebels rightly This is my fear *now* he gives them time— to breathe & rally— too slow— thats his besetting Sin— & one that seems he cannot get over for none but his slow coaches— like Franklin & Sumner are left to him Noble, brave men, I feel hurt when I utter or write a word that reflects upon them—

I hear this morning from Jerusha Rogers[1] that Hooker is in danger of lockjaw & that Kingsbury—[2] Evy Taylors husband is mortally wounded There are a great many of the wounded here from the field of Antietam— but they are generally wounded with round balls & therefore with the good care they will get here— will all soon recover

I agree with Goldsborough now is the time to strike at Richmond— but I expect Stanton will order a discontinuance of recruiting & draft & every other preparation necessary to prosecute the war—[3] *there is our loose screw*— & every body knows— says it— nothing has been so fortunate for me as my having no acquaintances with that family for I am questioned daily as to my opinion— & I can reply truly— I do not know Mr Stanton "never saw him in my life—"[4] Situated as I am tis very fortunate I can wave off expressing any opinion— I always say I have liked McClellan all the time & believe he is an able good man & all of our generals have to get experience— & so wave off committing myself in any expression of opinion or feeling which is not publicly known as that of my people at home— but this endless inquiry shows the feeling & opinions of the Country & it may yet deliver us of this evil out of the Citadel Then we may hope to end this war with success—

Yours of the 19th with Adl G's letters & of his kinsman & Dr. Foltz to the life & etc Came just now— I heard from Becky last night that there were people here from Prince Georges by the shoals & they say, "*they was not going stay there for their masters to pack them* off to Georgia—" which they would be sure to do if the Rebels got in Maryland to stay even one Month"— She says— that the colored people at the Church last night went from one to another to get money to help these newcomers— How Strangely things turn out— A Yankee Army is stationed in Prince George's for nearly a year & but few slaves are lost— John not one— a Rebel one crosses the Potomac— for deliverance it seems of the black race & not their masters & they take flight—[5]

John's resignation— was a false step— for his own as well as his friend's sake— but we could not make him feel this until too late— If he had held his commission he would not have lost a slave— He is no longer in Bible phrase— "a man of authority" among his people

I went with the Harrisons to the Christening of their new Baby 7 weeks old yesterday— Blair was very much interested— They have twins— two boys nearly two years older than Blair a half head shorter— The Rowans have one boy just two years & 2 months older than ours— A fine boy & one that gives Blair great pleasure— they send here constantly for Blair & seem fond of him I have no letters from home today— Ever your affectionate Lizzie Of course Ill never say what I have written to Nelly or J— it would only *hurt* now.

    1. Jerusha Carolina Rodgers was the sister of John Rodgers and Louisa Rodgers Meigs.
    2. Col. Henry W. Kingsbury, Fifth U.S. Artillery, died September 18, 1862, of wounds inflicted at Antietam, where Joseph Hooker had been wounded in the foot.
    3. Stanton had closed recruiting depots on April 3, General War Order #33, and reestablished recruiting on June 6.
    4. On September 19, EBL gave her opinion of Stanton: "I would feel scarce a doubt of our success but for that *one* man— but a person without loyalty in such a place— is like one who holds the gate key— I hope I am unjust to him— & I never doubt the result of this great cause of good government—."
    5. From Philadelphia EBL had reported on September 14 that she had seen "some negroes who increase here so enormously that the people will soon take to driving them off & I must say their bearing must be aggravating to poor white men— I saw a negro woman dressed today more elegantly in silk & lace than I ever was in my whole life—."

Philadelphia   September 23, [1862]
Dear Phil   I went out with Aunt this morning & then went on after parting with her to return some visits from some acquaintances— Stopped a while at the Mordicai's— if ever there was a premature *old old* man it is the Major—[1] Even his daughters have lowered their tone of respect— they are unconscious of it— but he hangs about doing nothing not even reading & they are working in their school for bread— It is the most melancholy abode— in spite of the cheerful faces of these poor girls— who are trying so nobly do their duty— the Majr comes here Sunday evenings & sits for hours without saying scarce a word save the formula of greeting & parting— Horace seems to dread these visitations as much any of us womankind— Gladly would I do anything I could to help this poor family along.

    We are all intensely anxious about Louisville   Bragg[2] is advancing upon that city— & "Bull Nelson[3] is the Genl on the defensive— I have no great faith in his skill— McClellan went over into Virginia Yesterday & we are expecting Lee to attack him— I saw letters today from 2 of the troops under Casey & Heintzleman— which would at once show the difference between them & McClellan— who had order & discipline where ever he commands—

    The Presidents proclamation took the breath out of me this morning[4] He is in the hands of the Phillistines— but God will help us— & I do not dispair— it seems to me all that could be done to hurt our cause has been done there— Still we are not yet ruined   I still hope for successful end of the war & our Governments preservation— in spite of *all* its enemies—[5]

Blair is well— but weary of being here   I hope to go home next week some time— I have just recd yours of yesterday. I will wait McCs progress in Va— I will write to Father about Judge Goldsboroughs affairs   Ever your devoted Lizzie

1. A week later, on September 29, EBL commented: "Maj. Mordicai is falling into Melancholy— & is really important that something should be done to raise him— ere it is too late—."

2. Braxton Bragg (USMA 1837) was marching toward Louisville, but Buell got there first.

3. William "Bull" Nelson, promoted to major general in July 1862, was sent to Kentucky to oppose the invading force of Bragg and Kirby Smith. Nelson was badly defeated at Richmond, Kentucky, on August 30, 1862.

4. On September 22 Lincoln announced his preliminary emancipation proclamation that would, on January 1, 1863, free all slaves in those areas still in rebellion.

5. On the next day, September 24, EBL wrote more calmly about the Emanicipation Proclamation: "There is no excitement about the Presidents proclamation but the papers which speak here indicate that it is a mistake— it is really felt to be a paper pronunciamento & of no practical result the Southern people are not going to free the Blacks & the Govt cant enforce such a proceeding It may be to get Abolitionists to enlist but that is not their style & it will only organize a strong party against the Administration & that may be eventually be all for the real good of the Country   I write what I hear talked about me—." On September 29, she reported: "There is a rally being made against the emancipation policy of the President It is thought here that this state will vote largely against it—."

Silver Spring   October 1, 1862
Dear Phil   We reached here safely and comfortably in due course of Railway time   found Father & Betty in town waiting to take us out home— where I found as happy a greeting as heart could wish & my boy wild with joy & Grandpa— as much pleased as our little fellow the forest trees between our gate & Fort Massachusetts levelled to the ground[1]

I am tired— & only send this in haste   I asked Fox if Capt Rogers had come & I found I had put him in the wrong ship—[2] & misled his wife I'll write to her tomorrow   Fox says the Monitor will be repaired at Norfolk—

Fox looks sick My Parents looks bright hearty & oh so happy— Ever your own   Lizzie

1. On the next day, EBL reported: "What a scene of desolation presents itself at our gate every tree between here & the Forts felled to the ground— lie robed in their brown leaves— it is a sad sight—." In her October 6 letter, EBL reported: "they could have made a thousand dollars out of the orchards if the soldiers had not taken them— for days our people cooked all day long— the cows were milked & it streamed right into the soldiers can— & so with every thing— except the potatoes— which Mother

had dug in one day & this saved Sixty bushels— out of several hundred for she had an enormous crop— but Mother just bid them help themselves when they plead starvation of all good fruit & vegetables— & they all *asked* for things in troops— & do still— but I had the orchard cleared out yesterday—."

2. In another letter of October 1, EBL had written: "I let the Rogers know that the Galena was to go Washington to be repaired as I heard Mrs. Rogers say she would not go home until the 10th of Oct— so I sent word to her that I heard that her husband was to be home & to get ready for his summoning—." Ann Elizabeth Hodge of Washington married John Rodgers in 1857.

Silver Spring   October 3, 1862

Dear Phil   Who has my keys? This query was written this morning, since then I have found them at Johns in dear Nelly's care— I was at their house this morning when they arrived from the Country— we were very sad— They have rented their house to Mr. Arnold[1] for six months & may be for six years the boys to be put at the College & Annie at the Convent— where I told her she should never stay when ever I get or have a city home— they go to a small house on their place & build in the Spring   Nelly *did not* advise her husband to resign & I can see regrets it exceedingly— I shall remove my affairs next week early   George Beale[2] says theres room plenty

Fox ordered Govr Dennisons man to you Squadron to day Paymaster Benedict[3] John has rented the House to Mr. Arnold the new Senator from Rhode Island— they went down to G Grahams to see about it with Genl Stone[4] who says— Stanton says— McC imprisoned him & misused [?] his orders— McC says he has the reiterated order of the Secy— to do it When I get a cypher[5] Ill you another story about these people[6] We are certainly fallen into strange hands & times & there but little to rest upon but a firm faith in the Mercy of God— & be thankful to Him that he has placed my earthly happiness in the hands of my dear true hearted husband I am thankful for as much good & some real joy amid so much to grieve   Blair has written you a blotted page but it is too miserably to send   Ever yr devoted Lizzie I got your letters with Mr Allens letters & etc   His partner was here last night but A did not come

1. Isaac N. Arnold, Republican Illinois congressman (1861–65).

2. George N. Beale, naval storekeeper at the Washington Yard.

3. On October 2, EBL had told her husband that Governor Dennison had requested Benedict's assignment to Lee. George S. Benedict, son of the editor of the Cleveland *Herald,* was a newly appointed acting assistant paymaster.

4. Brig. Gen. Charles Stone was blamed for the Union disaster at Ball's Bluff. On February 8, 1862, he was arrested and imprisoned without being charged with any crime. He was finally released on August 6. Never was there any official acknowledgment of error or expression of regret.

5. In her October 3 letter, EBL had warned: "Of one thing we must be cautious in

our leter for I find that my letters to Father— have not reached him— & some of his to me— have failed to get to me— so please number yr letters & write in cyphur if need be—." Over the years, the couple had employed several different simple codes to mask the meaning of their letters.

    6. Also on October 3, EBL might have been referring to that "story." "McC— lost the fruits of his hard fight from his enemies in the rear— the whole Army was exhausted of Ammunition We can only hope that such frightful facts will convince the world— where the loose screw is—."

Silver Spring   October 7, 1862

Dear Phil   I believe this is the first letter I have ever commenced before break-fast but as Father goes in soon after it— I must make my report early & as Blair had me up by times to dress him here I am at your service He said to me this morning Mama— is it not happy to home again— dont you love home best

    Govr Andrew dined out here yesterday with one of his Wendall Phillipites whose talk was hateful but Father seem to think that the emancipation policy was inevitable sooner or later— & that his plan was rather different (& I may be excused for thinking it vastly wiser) than the Presidents— Still that fanat-ics on both sides— I think the Army is conservative but the result is the same if the War goes on— & I believe as I told John a year ago that the only slaves after this war will be found in Maryland & Ky & Missouri The Ada E. Douglas tied with white ribbon turns out to be a Chicago acquaintance of Father & not our fair widow

    I was to see Nelly yesterday after church   they are all well there— John went back into the Country for which I am thankful— He has been persecuted by S— who from all I hear has maligned him to the President   it all tends to embitter John— who talks too much from the fullness of his heart— there are now Spies everywhere— & I do hope he will not by *mere talk* incur fresh per-secution— I dont him to talk imprudently down in Prince Georges— because his friends there do it— I know it is very hard to be thus trammelled— but Father says John brought this whole trouble on himself— by neglecting a mere courtesy to S. who was his neighbor— & took it as indicative of contempt— & has been implacable ever since— Nobody mourns more than I that his proud Spirit should be thus tormented— but it seems a folly to bring misfor-tunes upon ones household just a lack of a small self denial— & this horrid civil war imposes that— & heart breaking sorrows on many noble natures—[1]

    There is evidently to be a move— in our army this week— nearly all of McC's Army is in Virginia— Andrew Alexander[2] slept here last night on his way to join his old chief Stoneman—[3] whose headquarters are at Pooles-ville   he says Heitzleman is repairing railways down towards Warrenton— & his whole account of the extent— & character of our army is very encourag-ing— Oh if McC would only pursue this war vigorously how much better it would be— *it is* suspected that Halleck— Buell— & Mc— have made delays for ends political indicated by the talk of Majr Key dismissed—[4] I have no doubt this discovery was the cause of the unexpected *proclamation*— tho it is almost imprudent to insinuate it— I must stop & will conclude my talk to night— Ever your affectionate Lizzie

    1. On October 20, EBL expressed her feelings for John and Nelly Lee: "in these years of yr absence— to me sometimes of intense loneliness they have been so kind & loving to me— I have gone there many days when Ive felt I must talk & be talked to you about— & to have every face beam with pleasure at your name & all respond to my yearning for sympathy   I cannot relate the endless kindnesses they the children & all the household have shown Blair & me— oh I shall miss them daily—."

    2. Andrew J. Alexander was Apo Blair's brother. He had joined the army in the summer of 1861, served in the Peninsular Campaign, and was a captain in the Third Cavalry.

    3. Gen. George Stoneman commanded the cavalry of the Army of the Potomac during the Peninsular Campaign. He then commanded the First Division of the Third Corps.

    4. Maj. John J. Key, who allegedly said after Antietam: "that neither army shall get much advantage of the other; that both shall be kept in the field till they are exhausted, when we will make a compromise and save slavery." Lincoln dismissed him from service on September 27, 1862.

                                         Silver Spring   October 10, [1862]
Dear Phil   I got no letter from you today & it reminded me that I was soon to do without that beverage— for a while during your trip on the coast   I hope you will not go in this easterly storm— The first good rain had here since we went our way to the Mountains— long ride it was—

    I went to the City today to keep an appointment with Mrs Merrick on Asylum   she is very smart & pretty put at me about the proclamation   I was reserved about it & at last said but I was a Quaker— she pushed Sumner at me   I then said— I never thought him a statesman— & went on about the asylum Sunday School— Which I started & have put her at work at it & she is so clever & energetic that it is a pleasure— to see the amount of work she does & how happy she is in it— She now wants to [hire] a gentleman Sunday School director   I refuse to have a man in the house & the Ladies seconded me So I want to get a lady to act but failed so far—

    I then did some shopping & was on my way to Johns when I overtook Nelly on the Avenue— & gave her a bouquet I had gathered for Annie from Uncle Phil who so often took them to her when he had the opportunity As the clouds looked threatening I was thinly dressed in the little open carriage— I hastened home— & got home ere the rain commenced— A soldier picked up Father's gold specs & brought them to him They were lost some weeks since among the rose bushes—

Saturday morning. Betty & Father go to the City immediately after I would go too but have some little matters to attend to at home about my flowers &etc I shall go to Church I hope tomorrow & dine with John & Nelly. I saw John in the City yesterday looking cheerful & well— There is the breakfast bell so good morning to you— Blair is merry as a cricket this rainy he has Wood to play with Ever your affectionate Lizzie

Silver Spring   October 15, [1862]
Dear Phil   I recd your letter with enclosure of Mr Fox's yr reply & etc— I sent you a letter & package by Mr. Fox of yr gloves towel &etc— I have worked very hard today & am very weary Becky was too sick to help me

Mr. Stabler & Col Graflin here tonight— the latter was taken prisoner at Harper Ferry— he was on the Md Heights & says there was just as much reason for surrendering Washington then as that place— he is convinced that we were sold— It makes me sorry that you are going to trust— I never believed in any of them at the same time I must remind you that it may be the result of ill temper on my part— besides Ill confess that in my young days when they were very civil to me I never liked any of the three brothers— but of the three I think the one you have to deal with— the best— he married a poor girl & has made her happy & Julia Hoffman[1] who knew them well always laughed at his peculiarities— but still thought he was true hearted where he owed allegiance— she spoke from an intimacy with his wife— I from the merest prejudice—

I am so glad you were kindly— I would always have some body with you in yr conversations Since he was so full of temper— forgetting that while he enjoyed the luxuries of his home— you were blockading & under the guns of Forts Jackson & St Philip Henry Turner[2] from my reading of his letters is for the saving of his property & is on the fence generally getting down occasionally first on one side & then the other His children are rebels— & he has lost a son lately— Capt Turner's children are Union soldiers— & he too lost a son lately from Camp fever— I think this indicates where the heart of the Parents is—

I am rejoiced that Nelly has concluded to take Annie to the Country with her to part with all her children & give up so much at once would accumulating self denials besides— I have an unmitigated horror of Boarding schools— for health & heart too— I tried to keep Betty out of one— & I never have ceased to regret my failure to do so— or sufficiently to thank Aunt Becky for her guardian care over me when I was incarcerated in one for the deliverance of two whole days out each week the two idle pernicious days

Oct 16 We had no mail— or tidings from the city today under which both Mother & are restive This evening Father recollected that Mrs John R. [Thomson] had sent word that she wished to see me— had I known this in the morning I would have been in the City— Blair when in Phila bit a bone & broke one of his under front teeth— last night he waked up & said "Mama— here is my tooth it was out of its place & I spit it out—" I am only sorry for it as his jaw may contract— & make the new teeth irregular— Still his new teeth will come soon— little Henry is changing his now & so is little Phil

I had a letter from Apo   Aunt Susan is to spend the winter with them— She writes cheerfully about Franks affairs— Father likes Franks speech I meant to have sent it to you, but he gave it to Col Graflin— he regrets some coarseness in it— I am glad you sent me F's letters— I enjoy the correspondences you send me— I never mention having them to any body—

I shall be off early in the morning to see about my affairs there, Asylum & House— servants clothes & etc   Blair is a busy boy, raking leaves— & wood in his wheelbarrow He talks a great deal about you Ever yr devoted Lizzie

1. Julia Hoffman, daughter of Judge Josiah Ogden Hoffman and Maria Fenno of New York. She was a half sister to Matilda, Washington Irving's beloved. Julia had died April 28, 1861.

2. Henry S. Turner had retired from an army career after the Mexican War. He had been a Constitutional Union nominee for the Missouri convention on secession. Originally from Virginia but also an old friend of William T. Sherman, Turner tried to remain neutral during the war. His son, Wilson Price Turner, was a first sergeant in Stuart's Horse Artillery and was killed at Second Bull Run on August 29, 1862. He was eighteen years old.

Silver Spring   October 17, 1862

Dear Phil   As I might have known ere I went to Mrs Thomson's[1] call she coaxed me into doing what I really did not want to do— that is in taking her gass fixtures— for which I can pay out of the rent due— on the 9th of next month— all of which I can spare save enough to pay washing— Becky— & some dues for making my winter dress the materials for which I paid out of your advance when I was in Phil— She is to send me Cornelius's[2] bills & I dont know what they are so I am afraid Ill have to pay more money than she sayes me or I can spare— so to night I am troubled about my bargains—

She wanted me to take wardrobes & etc   I refused all of them & the carpets then she gave me one huge wardrobe— & some glass shades which I declined to buy offered to buy my house which I declined & then came the gas fixtures— which I really like better than any I ever saw simply because they are simple— & cannot be hurt by dust & flies but I declined the one in the library as we have one suitable to it— & if I can manage to pay for them out my rent which otherwise *would all go loose* I shall be delighted with my investment—but if I have to call for help from you Ill be mortified about it—

I went after Mr Elliott[3] could not find out where his mother lived & met Frank Rives after having been to the Globe office in search of him— He says Elliot *drinks hard*— & supposes that is why he has not answered your letter— I told him to tell him I wished to know his inclinations about going to you but since I learned his habits— I would refer the matter to you again

Mrs. Thomson tried over & over again to get me to take charge of the house— but I told her that— I would aid her to rent it for one year but could do nothing more— that I should hold her responsible for the rent— she looked so full of tears & sorrowfull that I had to keep saying to myself *ten thousand a year* to do what was right even in this— I felt as if was so hard unfeeling— creature dealing with a sad widow— all the time we were talking business but I was greatly let up when she spoke of all her kind friends here & how eager they all were to serve her mentioning among others Capt Dalghren & that she hoped yet to live in dear Washington— if she ever again care much where she lived— but at present all places were alike to her" & etc She never looked prettier & her softened manner made her more than ever attractive to me— She inquired so very kindly for you & Blair Father & more than intimated I was the most fortunate of persons to have such friends, but above all such a house!!

Now you will laugh at me about the pretty widow— but I do believe if you had there we would have had now carpets wardrobes beds & etcetras— she did not want to carry off— with this consoling conclusion Ill thank you for yrs of the 14th & a large package of MSs every line of which is read with interest by me— I meant in all your letters as Mrs T. said she wrote to me & I never recd her letter— Blair is well— Ever yr own Lizzie

1. The Thomsons had been renting EBL's home, and when John R. Thomson died on September 13, 1862, his widow wished to end her lease.

2. James Cornelius, carpenter and finisher.

3. John M. Elliot was a clerk in the *Globe* office.

Silver Spring   October 20, 1862

Dear Phil   No news this morning of any kind— yesterday I heard the Rebels had made an attempt on No 10 Isd & were defeated— Grant has a division given him of West Tennessee & Ky— Great disgust is growing about the slowness of Buell—[1] & when you see the way he fought his Army by piecemeals there in Ky it is sickening

To tell you the truth West Point is not making much reputation by this war— Napolean never has been heard of there judging by the slowness of the movements & celerity is a thing never dreamt of— There is a conviction that there *is a system* & for a purpose May be, when the Democratic Generals get a Democratic Congress they may move with more accord— indeed there is something to my mind far from discouraging in this late infusion of an opposition element— I hope out good for the country in divers shape too numerous to mention!! I cannot see quite so much in the election of such a rotten set as Seymour,[2] for it is Hobson choice— bt him & Genl Wadsworth, still there is something in the foreign aspect of the election of Seymour that is to be dreaded[3] the North is a unit on the war— but not in the way it is conducted or as as to the results to be got out of it—

There's a blot which you must pardon as Aleck is waiting to go for Becky— & I have only a moment left to thank you for your sweet kind letter to Andrew Mother joins me in these feelings for she says it will save Andrew to get him out of the limits of the apron strings— Blair is well & happy as the day is long— & has this moment kissed these blots I hope that will make them less ugly— Ever your affecate Lizzie Tuesday All well today at home & no news I have heard in the city— I am going to see Mrs Welles—[4] have a beautiful bouquet for her— I shall probably dine with Nelly who is so busy that I refrain from long visits for she is busy with her Mothers house In haste Ever yrs Lizzie

1. On October 23, EBL commented: "Buell is a slow coach & it does seem to me that our Democratic Genls & Democratic Secy are making this the slowest war that world ever saw— One never believe such a man as Bouneparte had been heard of at West Point—."
2. Horatio Seymour, governor of New York (1853–55 and 1863–65).
3. Wadsworth ran for governor of New York on the Republican ticket but lost.
4. Mary Jane Hale of Lewistown, Pennsylvania, married Gideon Welles in 1835.

Silver Spring   October 21, [1862]

Dear Phil   When Father got thro his visits with me to Mrs Welles & Mrs Banks he said he was weary & seemed not very well so I returned home— Found Mother wrathy because we went off by Fathers order— without Betty who kept us waiting sitting in the carriage—

I found Luke had not put up cards in the window so I had it done I had paid him for it too— persons have called to rent it— but all want me to furnish it— It will be cheaper to me empty— Mrs. Hunter (Genl)[1] begged me just to put *some* furniture which she heard I had— I declined— Mrs Hills[2] house has rented for 1,500 empty— so I ought at least get 1,200 with gas fixtures— that some tell me— it is too high for these times— there are plenty of Contractors floating around— who will be glad to be next to a Secy that's my only profit out of that Office— Betty thinks the wardrobe left by Mrs T. is a small house & ought to rent for something—

I heard to day that there was a fuss between Pleasonton & Stoneman about

Stewarts escape— & theres to be a Court Martial— S. has been once before
rebuked for slowness— His wife[3] is hot Balt— secesh Mrs. Welles was very
civil I ought to say kind— Mrs Banks inquired also for you & was cordial
seemed really glad to see me— I met Mrs Almy—[4] & shall go see her my next
visit to the City—

I am disposed to get Blair's money— in US Stock Gold has got too high I
shall get whatever I conclude on in yr name for you know my opinion about
setting children up in possessions of any sort it would ruin my child John is
breaking his heart over the idea that his children will not be as well off as he
had hoped & is ready to deny himself any & every thing under that mistaken
unselfish tenderness If we have enough to give our boy a good constitution
& education & profession that is enough I'll not fret myself about his lack
of fortune— he will be better off in the end he will not be married for his
money for one thing & then his youth will be spent in some manly pursuit
& not wasted in dancing about Watering places— home & abroad in pursuit
of pleasure— which is the universal fate of our young men— & I do assure
you— no fellow is more known for that than our boy Willie— who was early
impressed to his Mother's sorrow that "Pa had nothing to do but make money
for his children"— poor fellow this is sadly checked now & I hear he is full of
feeling for his Parents— which shows that even John's overweening fondness
has not spoiled him—

Now what I mean is this not waste— but use your means for these boys
or Fannys as your heart prompts but I do not covet an estate for our child—
John seems to think me insincere when I say this but my experience in my own
family teaches me a bitter lesson— the poorest of my brothers now— is the
one who has wasted a fortune given to him by our father— the richest— is the
one who had the least— my brother M— Look at the Riggs— the two eldest
who had small beginnings are respectable men— the three younger ones are
foreign fops, gamblers & I know not what else contemptible— I heard it said
this war was a blessing to the rich young men of the north as it opened a career
of ambition— to allure them from that of vice & folly—

But you will think me prosy when I am only suggesting reasons for not
spoiling our youngling— & for you to cheer up John— whose overweening tenderness for his children makes him dread any of the mortifications or
struggles of poverty which he endured in his own youth— Nelly says this
apprehension burdens his heart & depresses him *Now dont repeat this*— but re-
assure him about their education— for that I am willing to deny myself of our
comforts— but not to give them or my own *"an estate"*— to be ridden down
or off in landaus— John has not written to Fanny or any body— but we ought
to *follow him* now— I will follow Nelly with my scrawls faithfully— You see I
have no news tonight so I have talked & from the fullness of my heart Nelly
is looking well John was up yesterday but I did not see him

Blair is bright & happy as the day is long & he complains that Silver Spring days are "too short for his play"— I took a note which Brother at the P.O.D. had on his table for Fox— which he wished Henry to leave as we pass the Navy Dept sent to know how you were as I got no letter to day— he replied— Admiral Lee never looked better in his life Ive just looked at *Lt Lees* picture— & we had some talks confidential nobody by but Blair asleep on this subject the Lt. seems to think himself the best looking— may be—[5] but the Admiral is just as dear to yr affecate Lizzie

    1. Maria Kinzie married David Hunter in 1832.
    2. Ann Smith Hill was Ellen Lee's mother.
    3. Mary O. Hardesty married George Stoneman in 1862.
    4. Sarah A. Gardner married John J. Almy in 1854.
    5. On October 25, EBL commented on her own appearance: "I am afraid you will be shocked with my head— it is getting grey very fast— & what I like less I am losing my hair more than ever before in my life—."

Silver Spring   October 24, 1862
My dear Phil   Yours of the 22nd came today— No news except that Rosencranz[1] is to have Buell's place who is superseded— & who is only fit for a camp of instruction I wish he was over the boors now in Washington— but his want of energy in pursuit of the enemy is exhausting all patience & good feeling towards him The talk about McClellan is that he says his Cavalry is not worth a sou (what you said a yr ago) & he is reorganizing it— but he is losing golden days— litterally for I never saw such weather except a year ago— when he *was organizing* but— I still have faith in him & dont blame him because *I know what is in his rear*—

Frank writes in sanguine tones about his election[2] who would have dreamed two years ago that the Republican would be more his friend at the next election than the Democrat & yet so it is— Gratz Brown[3] sends you his pronunciamento it has some ability— I forward it

I recd today yr gift of $30 for which I thank you— I am not in need of it— yet but lived in fear of it, as I *do* not know how much my bad bargains would come to— One Mrs *Nutt* has been to look at the house wishes to take it if I'll turn the Pantry into a kitchen!!— of course Ill decline the proffer— I am tired out to night shopping for mother & am in living hope of getting thro with it in one more such day as this—

I had a little talk with Nelly They are all well— I did *not* tell your veto on Prince George's I am glad she will take Catherine there with her she will be a help in every way to her— I met Mrs. Clem—[4] who asked me where Ellen was— & had Minna stood it?!—[5] She dreaded to see them. She was preparing to emerge from Country life— Nelly said to me for the first time "Oh how sorry I am that Fanny lives so far from us all She is so devoted to her Brothers & their families— dear Fanny is so truly loving & sympathetic & in all the trials of life one learns her value

You seem to get my letters irregularly. I write every evening to be ready for every chance in town next day Blair is well but is in diposed to night I would not put him to bed as he disobeyed me I am the most punished Ever your affecate Lizzie

1. Maj. Gen. William S. Rosecrans (USMA 1842) replaced Buell in Kentucky as commander of the Army of the Cumberland.

2. Frank Blair was running for a congressional seat in Missouri against Radical Samuel Knox. On October 28, EBL reported: "Father is intensely anxious about Frank— election [to] his position— opens him to assault from all sides. & the Secesh have at this eleventh hour brought out a man so Frank is the conservative between the two ultra parties & his election is almost a type of our government & we are sanguine as to political life of both— *but most anxious—*."

3. Gratz Brown, a cousin of the Blairs, was a St. Louis lawyer and newspaper editor. He eventually took the Radical position on emancipation. On October 28, EBL wrote: "Gratz Brown helped to get up a reception for him— [Frémont] She [Apo] is full of disgust about Gratz— who I think could be conciliated with a little tact— I think so because he sends all his papers here to you & Father showing an evident desire to keep in with us— & if the Union speaks truly it says that Gratz intends voting for Frank so if not driven by tongue lashing he might still be useful altho constantly betrayed into going off in a tangent by his jealousy & ambition—."

4. Sarah Ann Parker of Philadelphia married Ellen Hill's brother Clement in 1836.

5. Minna Blair and Ellen Lee were old and very close friends.

Silver Spring   October 31, 1862

My Dear Phil I did not write you last night I was hors de combat from a head ache— today I went early to the City & am glad to say finished up Mothers shopping for the servants about which she seemed impatient & as the weather is perfect I am glad now that she jogged me up—

I went up the City to see Mrs. Banks about a Col Freeman—[1] who has applied for the house found she had gone north with her husband so I wrote a few lines to Horace altho it is very much like the needle & hay stack to be enquiring the Character of a man in such a big town and is rather as troublesome business— I shall say so when I send Aunt Becky a long letter from uncle Ben in which he gives me an account of his loses— & he seems to think he was "less pillaged than most people" altho— they took his cattle, horses & provisions but Uncle Ben is down on our slow Generals— as is everybody. he adds "My best regard to your Husband who has always treated me as a relative for him I feel great interest—" He says Bernard was with Jackson in the fight at Perrysville & is now with McCook but he has written to him to come home—

or get some command— for which he thinks he is fitted, by his courage & energy—

I was shocked today to hear of the suicide of Majr Russell[2] the result from all I hear of hard drinking— No men thought more of or loved this world better or were as near being my idea of *worldly men* as he & poor Tilton & yet both have left it as it were in disgust— They were the last two men— I would have ever thought capable of such a deed But my ideas of Capt Tilton does not drag him to Russells standard— There was a great deal of the high toned gentleman in the first— & the last was devoted a devoted Brother— & I hear has watched tenderly over his children since left to his charge only— I feel sorry for them & him too— I recd a letter from Apo last night she is very sanguine about Frank— & I think Father feels less trepidation since Taylor[3] & all the Democratic nominees have declined one after the other the nomination of *the secesh*— But we will feel intensely relieved when the election is over— it is vastly important to Frank's future— A letter recd today from Preston King speaks hopefully of things in New York— Seymours imprudent friend John V.B.[4] may defeat him— but thats our best hope—

I recd today your reply to & the letter to Adl. DuPont— the first was read with anxious interest— & I was gratified by the last— for nothing so pleases me as such appreciation of your kindness— I am quite well tonight— but head pounds so to bed Ever yr own Lizzie

1. Probably Col. William Freeman of the adjutant general's department.

2. On October 30, 1862, Maj. William W. Russell, paymaster in the Marine Corps, committed suicide by stabbing himself with a sword, followed by a shot to the head. He was forty-two years old, a widower with six children.

3. Daniel G. Taylor, Democratic mayor of St. Louis (1861).

4. John Van Buren was the second son of Martin Van Buren.

8

"I am an abolitionist for the sake of my own race—"

December 31, 1862

THE CLOSING MONTHS OF 1862 BROUGHT Union victory no closer. Lincoln's repeated prodding of McClellan was fruitless, and presidential patience finally gave out: Lincoln replaced McClellan with Ambrose Burnside as commander of the Army of the Potomac. Although Burnside did not suffer from the "slows," he had his own faults. His headlong assaults at Fredericksburg ended in frightful slaughter and another retreat.

The Emancipation Proclamation had polarized political attitudes, and the Lincoln administration had feared its effect on the off-year elections. Republican losses were significant, and Lincoln welcomed Frank Blair's election in Missouri. Dissatisfaction, despondency, and pessimism spread across the land and into cabinet meetings. The rift between radical and moderate elements of the Republican party became more apparent and led to a cabinet crisis. While moderates like the Blairs pushed for gradual, compensated emancipation, Radicals became more insistent on immediate abolition. Lincoln restored the delicate balance among his advisors when he refused to accept the resignations of Secretary of the Treasury Salmon P. Chase and Secretary of State William Henry Seward.

Silver Spring   [November 1, 1862]
Dear Phil   Yours with business matters (St Louis) & the one of the 30th containing copy to G. V. F— all came today— I left the one about St Louis affairs with Nelly who expected John this evening— I shall go there to morrow if possible— to see John about this & another idea which Father has for him He thinks this war will bring an immense legal business to Washington & he thinks if John will turn the evenings & waste hours in the country to some *good* law reading as to process in civil suits & etc that with his great attainments in military law— he can at once establish himself here in a great business certainly at the end of the War— if not sooner— Father thinks neither J nor

Nelly will be happy in the Country besides he fears that John will overwork & expose himself   John will be up early & out constantly & that after his office life may go hard with him— besides he dont think much of the health of P. George Co

Dick Hill has another daughter[1] Nell says— "I used to joke him about it— but now it is no joke"— Annie said— "thats because they used to be so cross to your boys—" I am unused to thinking girls a misfortune— & therefore will not consider Dick an unlucky father— The News you got by Rogers was not without foundation but it was before any of the elections— & the proffer positively declined— & father who disproved the act was appealed to & the matter settled as you see— Subsequent events have rather justified the proceeding— & so it goes along well— I forgot to mention that Mrs Stanton[2] was out here a few days ago she is very handsome & is a Ky woman— Today Father went to the War Dept to introduce some Ky friends on business— The Secy was full of Mrs. S's enjoyment of her visit. & etc & *the* Ky friends were handsomely treated—

I paid a bridal visit to Mrs. Clephane[3] today— I am attentive to my social duties— & try to be cautious in my talk— There is a race going on now in Massachusetts— between Sumner & Chas. Adms—[4] for the Senate & it is thought that the last will carry the day— Neither of them have courage & force enough for our foreign affairs now a days where I hope & pray we may before too late have an able man— It would be however a great improvement to have Sumner at Paris or Everett—[5] & the other at Petersburg— consequently I believe I would vote for Adams in Mass if I was a strong minded woman of that latitude—

I heard today thro Secesh that the enemy were strongly fortified & entrenched at Gordonsville & that the Railroad between there & Richmond is in perfect order— under strong military guard— that they will use their cavalry to mislead our own people & to harm bridges & etc   they can fight us at Gordonsville & retreat on their Railroad & leave our people stuck in the Red Clay of the Mountains   Father says we ought to take Richmond right away— & attack the Railroad & destroy it between there & Gordonsville— then Lees Army would be in a very bad box— I enclose you a scrap of personal history Mrs. Turner had a pass from Brother— which her daughter abused so dis[6]

Birney was up at Fairfax when they were brought in she says the exposure & distress of the poor girl was pitiable & seems to think she was influenced in the whole procedure by the handsome young Revd Buck Bailey[7]   Joe Cook is a Captain— but is just now over at the Moorings quite sick with a bilious attack— Birney went to him— hearing of his illness— his Regt is ordered to Washn for reorganization— they have a poor set of officers if Majr Thistleton[8] is a specimen

Good night— Blair & all of us very well— his chesnuts are in a small paper candle box already to travel I will only sign my name side ways as that is now forbidden— I cant write & think so Ill have to copy if this is not plain enough Ever yr affecate Lizzie

1. Richard Hill and his wife Elizabeth Snowden Hall Hill had five daughters (Mary, Ann, Elizabeth, Clara, and Agnes) before their first son was born in 1864.

2. Ellen Hutchison Stanton, daughter of Lewis Hutchison of Pittsburgh, Pennsylvania married Edwin M. Stanton in 1856.

3. Annie M. Collins of Connecticut married Lewis Clephane in 1862.

4. Republican moderates in Massachusetts searched for a candidate to oppose Charles Sumner's reelection to the Senate. Some promoted Charles Francis Adams, U.S. minister to Great Britain, but he declined.

5. Massachusetts politician Edward Everett had been governor (1836–40), minister to Great Britain (1844–45), secretary of state (1852–53), and U.S. senator (1853–54). He was a moderate on the slave question.

6. The rest of the sentence is missing.

7. Louisa P. Buckner, Montgomery's niece by his first marriage to Carolyn Buckner of Virginia, was arrested along with a minister, Buck Bailey. She had tried to smuggle large amounts of quinine into the South.

8. George Thistleton had begun the war as captain of Thistleton's Company of the D.C. militia. He then became part of Company A, Fifth Battalion, D.C. militia infantry.

Silver Spring   November 5, 1862

Dear Phil   Frank is elected by five hundred majority!! & I am very sorry I was not well enough to to go to the City to send you the glad tidings this morning— but from an accidental bath I am not well— & will have to take great care, for Mother is very nervous & says at my time of life no sort of neglect is tolerable— I am *not suffering* in the least only a little debilitated— & feel sure that after this week I will be myself again— only a little more cautious about the use of cold water which is something you will not regret— I have long ceased (from your injunctions) to bathe Blair so much in it— & he is I think more sturdy from it— his skin is so much like yours, that I concluded your feelings in that respect would be a better guide for him— Now my dry hot skin is refreshed by its use— but you & he never enjoy it—

Father recieved yesterday a note from Mr. Fendall desiring an interview Father went to his office & he wants his son Philip[1] promoted to Russells place— Father applied for it immediately— Fox replied that loyalty of that corps was of the most sickly sort & that Mr. Fendall was from the South & came in the equivocal list— I wrote to Mr. Fendall— today *what was said of the Corps*— & that none but one of the *decided* loyal stamp would get the appointment & that I wrote to let him know this to give him the opportunity of seeing this— as my niece who knew his son well told me it was a matter of easy proof— Betty says— Phil is a witty & a *very* pleasant good fellow— & was a year ago zealous in the cause of the Union— Bet says his chance will be blue— for he was attentive to her & not to Miss *Ellen* in spite of all her hints to him to be so— but that a Bully Nelson acted on her hints but Phil was most amusingly obtuse & now he may feel it through Fox— or the influences around him—

The results in the north make Franks success a great thing for *us*. Abolitionists have *warred* on *the family* "& it is a comfort to be sustained when *niggerdom* of both sorts tried to defeat him— I am overjoyed The President said today that it was the *only good* news he had heard for many days— I think it settles the Frémonts & some more of that sort—[2] & well somebody realized that there has be a great deal of good advice wasted on him— Still I am sorry about the result in New York[3] Simply because of its effects south & abroad it deceives both

Capt Sands got home yesterday & his wife met him all joy & smiles tho he came back with one less of her boys than he took away— Blair[4] is here tonight & said his Father absolutely dreaded the meeting & to his amazement naught could be more calm or cheerful Two weeks ago Marion was here & her mother said she must come home & then told Betty she needed her child to help her to cheerfulness— My Will is not to return with his Father—" She is a good woman I think— Sands has applied for active duty—Blair is going to study law I did once think of suggesting him to you *not* to anybody else as yr clerk as he writes rapidly & well— but I think it best for the boy to go to some permanent pursuit & he has settled on the Law—

I have copied your letter to Capt Renshaw[5] I only recd it a few hours ago— & have enclosed it with a note to Mr. Fox saying— I meant to read him extracts but that I was too sick to have that pleasure so beg him to read & forward at his earliest convenience & greatly oblige &etc— I must now to bed— the best pleased woman I know— I forgot to say that the vote from the Army will greatly increase Franks majority— I can *sit still*— & write all day without hurt— so if you have any more copying send it to me— as tis good to have something to keep *me still* which is hard to do— these lovely autumn days & with an ache or pain to make it *feel* obligatory—

Blair wrote you a letter which I failed to send & lost you must forgive it as it was full of his kisses & love for you from him & your devoted Lizzie

Mrs. Foote[6] is at Rugby House— Shall go to see first day I can move—

1. Philip Fendall was a prominent Washington lawyer. His twenty-nine-year-old son Philip joined the Marines in 1857 and retired in 1878.

2. On November 8, 1862, EBL added: "Father thinks Franks election has got us out of the Frémont slough for all time— I must say I rejoice over the deliverance— They have given me many a heart ache."

3. The Union majority in the House was damaged by the election. In New York, the party lost the governorship to Democrat Horatio Seymour.

4. Blair Sands, son of SPL's old naval friend, Benjamin Franklin Sands.

5. Comdr. William B. Renshaw captured Galveston, Texas, on October 3.

6. Carolina August Street of New Haven married Andrew Foote in 1842.

Silver Spring   November 10, 1862

Dear Phil   The agony is over & McClellan is superceded—[1]   I am very sorry for it— Brother opposed it bitterly— Still he was slow too slow— to gather all the laurels for himself or benefits for his Country which were I think within his grasp— Secesh is jubilant— Burnside is his successor fortunately for us as he is not a whit less brave than Hooker & has more intelligence & character— Nothing gives me more trouble than to see men of bad morals put in positions to win renown & gratitude from our Countrymen— Persecution may do for McClellan what it did for Genl Taylor—[2] consequently I rejoice that he is a man of good character You see I cannot give up my General No he took a vanquished & demoralized Army & drove off the enemy from my home so I owe personal as well as patriotic gratitude & if his successor was not his true friend I would feel less assured as to his future successes.

Your's with extracts from the laws about the Navy came today I went to see Mrs. Foote today she was out— I then took Annie Lee to Maynards[3] to have her teeth fixed. He is in New York & will not return for some weeks & after their move to the Country I urged Ellen not to neglect her teeth— to let me make an engagement for the child when he returns— which Ill do & write to them— & I will have Annie out here with me to share my room & bed— "Uncle Phil's place"— to which Ellen agreed— I feel more & more the trouble of parting with Nelly— they dont *take* to Father's plan— much to my surprise   I talked as you suggested to Nelly she agrees with me entirely about things in P George—

Novr 11th Father went to the City today evidently apprehensive about the condition of the Army. Father wrote to Frank to come on to see him— as this letter dont go to you immediately I am sorely tempted to write of things as I see them through my optics— but last night when writing to Mrs Ingersoll[4] about Mrs Lizinka Brown[5]   Father stopped writing & said "My daughter *we* cannot write or talk too prudently now a days— I told him that on yesterday when in the City everybody asked me what I thought of McCs removal— I replied that I was sorry for it & there stopped invariably— except once— Mrs. Franklin & Mrs. Merrick were both exclaiming— & asked if I did not pity Mrs. McC. I said no— she had her husband— home safe & sound crowned with laurels at Atietam, & consoled with dreams of presidential grandeurs— for you know that every body over ten years old out of Washington dream dreams of such things— Then Mrs Franklin said she wished they would relieve her husband—

I asked if she thought he would ask it— No never in the face of the enemy! was her reply— I repeated all this here & Father remarked well there's no harm done yet— but it is best *now* to be silent— it is absolutely necessary— & then went on to give some good reasons which I cannot so well repeat—

I received yours of Sunday. I shall not write again as I expect this fair weather will have insured your departure— Your note to Mr. Smith I'll file— but dont expect to use it— as my purchases— grates— gas fixtures— nine window frames & etc cost me $130. So I have enough to get me along with my current expenditures during the winter—

Father seems cheerful to night— more so than for several weeks The President told Brother Franks gain of his state consoled him for the loss of his own & all the recent political reverses—[6] No thanks to S. or any of that ilk

I had a box with strong top & fixings generally to put my constantia in & I shall bring it out here tomorrow   I shall go to the City as I am strong & well again— & every body smiles incredulously when I mention my late sickness so I must look as well as ever—

Fox told Father that no prize money had been yet recd at the Dept & then went to tell how Lord Ad Cochran[7] was moved by his efforts to put down the land sharks who devoured all the Sailor's prize money & etc— I remarked it was matter about which you had & would make no effort— The enemy have escaped & are mostly now in Richmond— & this is the President's motive for McC removal

Novr 12 The excitement about the removal of McClellan is intense— the President I think will find one result— that is that it has given a laurel covered chief to the Democrats to rally under to the Presidency— without any further risk to him in any way— & that the Republicans in self defence will have to take one of our fighting Genls— whose laurels are yet to grow instead of the President— but oh how very anxious I am about the battles now to be fought— or actually now fighting— it is the times like these days when Pope an untried man held our destiny as it were in his hand— & then I had my husband by me & that joy uplifted even such anxieties from me until fears became facts but now when I feel certain that a battle must ensue *very* soon, I am oppressed more than I can utter— It is reported that McClellan offered to be an aid to Burnsides— but the later preferred all risks to grasp the entire renown of success— The enemy are obliged to fight now on the Rappahannock— bt. Culpepper & Gordonsville—

Novr 13.[8] I have busy out doors all day gardening— As I recd no letter from you I feel certain that you have gone to the Carolina Coast consequently I took a double pleasure in todays sunshine. The excitement continues in the papers about McClellan & his quiet manly course seems to add to the feeling— Many prophesy another Pope Campaign   the very idea makes me shiver— I forgot to say that it is believed among our people that the enemy are concentrating all their force on the Rappahannock— from all quarters— for another grand battle by which to capture our people want to fight them ere they all get together— McC told a council of officers the night before he recd the dismissal— that he would give Lee battle at Culpepper C. House— in 3 days— his removal has caused great delay & consequent advantages to the enemy— No news to night from the Armies—

Apo writes jubilant over Franks success his majority is bt. six & 1,600— Frémont rushed off to New York the night of the election when the result was ascertained— without once appearing in the McKinstry case— He went & took possession of Mrs Brants[9] house had the Carpets put down— & caroused the world (the dutch particularly) there for two weeks on old Brants wines & other large stores— Mrs. Brant returned two days 'ere the end— refused to go to her house & sent an angent [agent] to demand by whose authority he so used her home. Frémont's sudden departure was his only response— her rage is delightful to see— He brought a good deal of money which was used in the election & from Apo's & Franks accts was the hardest fight he has ever had yet— but our Brigadier won the day— Thank God—

Novr 14. I recd your note from Hatteras. for with the storms & your new battery— it was a relief to know you were safe so far as the Ocean is concerned— but these English iron clads are thorns in my pillow This is the way England intends to war on us. I hear that Geo Riggs has a letter from Elisha Riggs in which he says Mary has won favor with Empress Eugenie[10] & is trying to convert her to be for the Union— she is very secesh however & is well posted in our affairs— Boswell[11] has captivated the young Prince who says he will go for the Union with Bossy as he is a good American & knows best— Geo Riggs seems to be willing to claim kin with Mary since she knows an Empress—

I saw John to day he is looking better— He & Nelly are very busy & will leave their house for P. George on next tuesday— I would have spent the day but they were too busy— John thinks the removal of McC. taking another chance for *better* success to use Js words "he is not a great man— he only half did his work"

Novr 15. This has been the perfection of an Indian summer day— & we have had company all day & to dinner. Bettys young friends & as Alick has proved anything but a good house servant— I am a busy body on company occasions— It would amuse you to see Blairs enjoyment of the girls— & the music— in that respect he is Grandpa's boy— Nelly said yesterday that he looked badly when I brought him home from Phila but now he is a lovely boy & so hearty & gay & good— I took him there Wednesday to spend a day with Phil— & I would take him to see John & Nelly tomorrow— but I hear the diptheria is rife in the City & I am afraid— Mr Welles beautiful boy of four years old has it—[12]   there are some cases in this neighborhood of a violent character— which keep me on the anxious seat— but they are three miles off—

Mrs. Crittenden wants my house for five months— Father seems to think I have no right to deprive Mrs Thompson of a tenant (an eligible one)— Ive not settled the matter— Her daughter Mrs Cabell[13] is with her & says she never intends to return south or leave her Mother again— & asked me plumply if I did not prefer My Parents to my husband for quoth she I do— I do not, was my reply— Mrs. Crittenden said "Why to be sure she dont for Capt Lee is one of the most charming men in the world— so if Mr C. should pop off I must look out however the poor lady is wofully broken— & sans rouge, teeth & curls— I can hold *my own*

Capt Barton dined here & his dog Ned & friend Blair were very cordial in their greetings & welcome to him— Young Martindale[14] the Genl's son says McClelland has been broken down by his trio of dull cronies— Baldy Smith Fitz John Porter[15] and Franklin this junto ruled him absolutely— his devotion to them has created an intense jealousy which has worked great evil to him & I fear the Country— Still it is no misfortune to a powerful opposition who will watch over our "Constitution Nationality & personal rights—" they need care & I firmly believe it is all for the best

Silver Spring Novr 17. Yesterday I went to the city & left Blair with Mother to ride— but I feared he was not well from his looks when I made the arrangement but he was gay & bright— So I went he was well all day— & night & this morning he waked up complaining & has had a sick stomach all day. he has been on his mule but has hung the rest of the time about *Mama*— & yet he has no fever— & no other indication of illness— Capt Rogers who I met at the Church door— told me you looked well but *thin very!* So if I have been since *low* in spirits it is not without cause for you & my boy are the life of my life—

I saw John & Nelly & chatted a while with both— I promised to write often— which John more than intimated was a poor exchange as I am in his judgement a clever talker & "you cannot write at all" quoth he he says Fanny & I have gift of speech— but deliver him from our epistles— Well as I am not going to inflict them on him I will get Nel to talk cleverly— all that interests him in them— If Blair is well enough I go bid them good bye tomorrow but if he is ailing I cannot go

Novr 18th We were surprised by a visit from John Van Buren. He is wonderfully well again— but talks of a trip to California says he improved so much in he election tour— that it convinced him that gadding around was the best thing for him— he intends to take his daughter with him— he is very amusing & seems very happy in his late success— & poked fun at Father with a wit peculiar to him— his visit was scarcely agreeable to Mother until she heard him say that the Democracy would all fall thro again unless it vied with the administration in zeal— for & about the war— "Democrats have always sustained all the wars— English Indian Mexican right or wrong— go for it through everything.!! He says he will return here with his daughter during the winter— He gave an amusing account of his lectures to her about flirting— talked a great deal of his Father—

Blair is better today & went to ride even in the mists with his Grandma Still I could not go away from him all day so wrote a goodbye to Nelly & John— Elida Carroll[16] has been here some days— had a handsome beau— a son of Genl Martindales dancing in attendance— they leave tomorrow she goes to Prince Georges to go stay with her Grandma Sprigg— whose hopeful Osborn Sprigg—[17] died of whisky yesterday— The City is rife with rumors about the Movements of the Secesh Army in the rear— but I dont believe anything un-comfortable any sooner than oblige to do   John Van Buren says he knows that the solid men & a large majority of the people south are sick of the War I hope they will sicken to the point of seeking a cure for it

Novr 19. A rainy day— Spent by me mostly with Blair who is not well sent his ailments to Dr May— who has sent remedies for him to take— evi-dently thinks there's not much the matter— his old trouble with worms— Mr Martindale & Miss Alida Carroll went to the City today to finish their flirtation there— the storm of last night the excuse for his staying here all night after his ride with her— he is in love— she not a bit— Capt Barton came out— & evidently wants to pay his devoirs to Betty— who treats him like she was forty & he a youth She is very patronizing— & she dont or wont see what he is here for— & thereby puzzles & confuses him so completely as to prevent all his approaches— It has been a study for me to solve B's feelings about her admirers She thinks herself fancy free yet but theres one of them who has piqued & won her fancy— but not her faith— I am a listener in all these matters as it is the only thing in the world from which I would shrink from the responsibility of advising— But I must not tell you any of these secrets— lest you tell on me— but it is the only thing passing around me which takes me today from what I know is a useless anxiety about my child who plays about the house— tho more languid than is comfortable to me—

Novr 20 Father, Betty & Capt Barton went to the City this morning & the storm has prevented their return tonight— My occupation has been to amuse Blair & reconcile him to the house— the Dr's prescription proved his supposition the right one— which amazes me as the child has been so robust until friday last— but seeing is believing— & it is a comfort to see how much the little fellow is relieved already—

Mother & I have no news but suppose that the rain will stop the Army consequently news I hoped to hear from you— As Burnside is rushing on to Richmond[18] I have thought the movement would hasten your return to the Roads before the end of three weeks— which are now over half gone— I miss your letters & count off the days as each one passes that brings me nearer to the time when I can hope for them—

The Crittendens took possession on Monday last. I was sorry to let them have it as they are not tenants after Mrs Thomson's style— I see Mrs & Secy Welles has lost their little boy of 4 yrs old— with diptheria he was a beautiful child— they have lost a great many children so she told me once— & it must a terrible trial to them to lose this little darling—

Novr 21. Blair is quite himself again & delivered of what must have soon made him ill— if he had not received such prompt relief— Gist had a convulsion last night & I have always had the idea that these convulsions which he & little Maria have had were from the same cause which gives Blair trouble. formerly twice a year— but he is getting stronger I hope & it is nearly a year since he has been so annoyed until this attack—

Father says Frank is to go down the Missipi with McClernand & finish up that job which you all were not allowed to complete There's a big army assembling in Memphis— to join and cooperate with David Porter— We had a letter *here* from Alfred the brother Laura & Clem the advance Corp of the Army of the Potomac which says they had information from one just deserted from Jacksons who says the Rebels have stores of food to last at least two years— at Charlotteville Danville— & Linchburg— this seems to be carrying out Jeff's idea of keeping up the war for 20 year in Virginia alone— They have concentrated all their treasures— at these places also— Danville is so near the North Carolina line that it looks like a last stand place in Virginia— McClellan wrote a month ago to have the railway at Aquia Creek repaired it was not done— & consequently the army has now to stop whilst it is done I hear they have appointed a court of Volunteer Generals some of them have been denouncing him on Buells Court Martial— his friends are outraged— altho I think he belongs to that class on our side who wish our erring sisters to go in peace—" Still such injustice will react on those guilty of it—

Novr 22 I went to the City today to market for Mother— & to go to the Asylum & to see Mrs Trumbull— Her greeting was kind & her inquiries for you most affectionate— she gives a good account of Walters studies but he gets marks for *small matters* of discipline— She pitched into McClellan I did a little by way of weak defence she laughed at me— was evidently delighted with herself for so overpowering me. She put at me about Mrs L. of course I was not to be caught there & made no defence because I was to unskillful & feared to damaged my friend— Our Army seems to be as much infected with the "*Slows*" under Burnside as McClellan— Mrs Trumbull has a very pretty young sister with who Ill take Betty to see— She begged me to come often as no one was more agreeable!!!

Novr 23— My horse tired & lame Cupid lame— Hickory too new for me to venture with— the old carriage at the Shop— the carriage horses out in pasture so nobody got to Church today. Alick had his holiday— Mother not well— so I played dining room Servant as I wanted Blair to be out & Becky with him— He is as well as ever & not much pulled down by this late sickness—

Novr 24 Father went today to the City on Trifle for news & came back with your letter from Beaufort N.C. which was joyfully welcomed by me— I am so relieved to hear you are better for the trip. John Roger's report of your thin condition has followed me—

You & Frank agree about McClellan more— he wrote a very clever letter about that & gives details of the effort to defeat him by— S. C. & Co—[19] says he sometimes felt determined to protest against it— to Uncle Abe— but felt he had enough to plague & worry his heart out of him— Says he had a telegraph from the President to know the result of his election about which he expressed great interest— & says— the results in Mo (where they carried the emancipation ticket— for legislature & for all the Congressmen but two) has more than compensated him for all defeats elsewhere—

I have written a long letter to Nelly this evening— I have not heard from her since they left— I saw strange faces at their windows when I passed Saty   Blair had his ride with Grandma today— & is blooming & bright again & has lost no strength—

Novr 25 Mother not very well so I persuaded her to let me look after the house so she went off early with Blair on Jenny Lind— Sam Jones as escort to both   her head is better for it. & our darling eats, sleeps & plays & looks as hearty as our hearts could wish   he wrote you a letter but it will have to await (like his Mama's) your return. We had no mail or news from the City today   Betty & I had our usual walk on the highway— which is like a street— & I finished the day by helping to rake up leaves— & Blair helped Sam Jones to load & unload the Donkey Cart— & we were as merry as we were busy. Father went all over the Wilsons[20] land today— some of them want to sell & invest in Missouri as that will soon be a free state. they are offered by some northern people 30 dollars an acre— there are bt 2 & 3 thousand acres if sold to northern men in small farms it will be a good thing for this region

1. McClellan was relieved of command of the Army of the Potomac on November 7.

2. During the Mexican War, Gen. Zachary Taylor's popularity soared because of his victories in northern Mexico. He became a political threat as a potential presidential candidate, and that situation affected his military career.

3. Dr. Edward Maynard, the Lees' dentist, had offices on L Street at Pennsylvania Avenue.

4. Susan C. Brown of New Orleans was married to Charles Ingersoll, a Philadelphia lawyer.

5. Leczinska Brown was the daughter of Judge George Washington Campbell of Tennessee, a personal friend of Jackson and Madison's secretary of the treasury.

6. On November 8, 1862, EBL wrote: "It is now quite ascertained that the President has a good working majority in the next House of Reps— anything more is

hardly desirable— a strong opposition is a healthy condition of things for the Countrys well being."

7. Thomas Cochrane, tenth earl of Dundonald (1775–1860), spent a good deal of time blockading, made enemies, and caused jealousies. He was a good commander but never great because he was never in the appropriate situation for daring action.

8. A notation added in SPL's hand: "1839 one of our anniversaries." November 13, 1839, was the date of the Lees' secret engagement, and they always considered it an anniversary.

9. Sarah Benton Brant, wife of Joshua Brant, was Jessie Benton's cousin and Mrs. Benton's favorite niece. Her husband was an army officer and an old friend of Frémont. Their St. Louis home was on Chouteau Avenue.

10. Mary Boswell Riggs was the wife of Elisha Riggs and the ward of EBL's uncle Benjamin Gratz. Although distantly related, she had always been considered part of the Blair family circle. In 1852 Eugenia de Montijo, Condesa de Teba, married Louis Napoleon, the newly crowned emperor of France.

11. Boswell Riggs, born in 1850, was the son of Mary and Elisha Riggs.

12. Hubert Welles died November 18, 1862, of diptheria.

13. Mary Cabell, daughter of J. R. Thomson, was Mrs. Edward Cabell.

14. Capt. Edward Martindale, son of Gen. John H. Martindale, served in the Twenty-sixth New Jersey Volunteers and in 1864 became colonel of the Eighty-first U.S. Colored Troops.

15. William "Baldy" Farrar Smith commanded a division of the Sixth Corps on the Peninsula and led that corps at Fredericksburg. A good friend of McClellan, he was outspokenly critical of Burnside. Fitz John Porter, also devoted to McCellan, had fought with distinction on the Peninsula. Critical of John Pope, he was brought to court martial for actions at Second Bull Run and relieved of command in November. Stanton was behind the scheme to discredit McClellan through Porter. Porter was found guilty and dismissed from the service January 21, 1863, although eventually exonerated.

16. Alida Carroll, born 1844, was the daughter of William T. and Sally Carroll.

17. Grandma Sprigg was Margaret Weems Sprigg, wife of Joseph Sprigg and mother of Samuel, who was governor of Maryland (1819–22). In 1840 Samuel's son Osborn married Caroline Landsdale Bowie, daughter of Gov. Robert Bowie.

18. Ambrose Burnside, as the new commander of the Army of the Potomac, had begun his march toward Richmond and was moving toward Fredericksburg.

19. Stanton, Chase, and the radical Republicans.

20. John C. Wilson and R. T. Wilson owned land on either side of the railroad, northwest of Blair's property.

Silver Spring   December 2, 1862

Dear Phil   I started early this morning went directly to see Nelly who I found watching her Mother, our poor sister seems just now to be giving utterance to her long pent up grief about her Mother— who now lies with a raging fever insensible to everything & every body— Ellen is comforted by thinking her Mother recognized her on her arrival Sunday. Says she smiled when she asked her if she knew her— & that she followed her with her eyes as walked her room weeping— I was touched by the reiterated assurance— Oh Lizzie I am sure she knew me— Nelly left her children with Eliza Graham to whom John returned yesterday I then went to the Asylum & got there before some of the City Ladies— I forgot to say that Mrs. Young[1] was considered better— Mrs. Hill & Mrs. Young were both taken ill on Thursday & Ellen seems to have no hope for either—[2] She says they tell her it is a release for her Mother but she cannot yet feel so—

Mrs. Harris gave me a long sad story of an affair of Majr Russell who it seems was to be married on the 17th inst to a beautiful rich young lady of Syracuse— He had just returned from a visit to her & left his youngest boy in her charge Mrs. Harris thinks she succeeded in making her feel that God has delivered her from a frightful fate— Miss Coleman[3] returned today & was full of compliments on our improved condition at the Asylum We had seven hundred & 50 dollars sent to us today— which is comfortable when we have our fuel all stored & paid for— & no debts— & all our children well clad— & our premises improved— House newly painted & everything clean & children all well— a pretty good report to make of so many children in a camp town like Washington—

I met Govr Dennison who says there is considerable discontent about the Message[4] among the Ultras— who call it a let down on the question— We met Mr. Sumner who said Massachusetts was satisfied— & all reasonable men ought to be so if we could get rid of slavery at the end of this century & that without any more fighting— he did not believe this olive branch would be accepted altho' it was Mason's proposition to the British Cabinet—[5] Still if accepted— who would be fool enough to refuse it on our side no *real* abolitionist certainly— I said well if Massachusetts was content I am sure the rest of us ought to be— He seemed well & in good spirits which was the aspect of things today in our political horizon— Blair rode with mother today & we found them by Grand fires & bright faces— on our return home— All well— including— Your affectionate Lizzie

1. Barbara Smith Young, wife of Ignatius F. Young, was Ellen Hill's aunt (her mother's sister).

2. On December 4, EBL reported that Mrs. Hill "died a few hours after I left Ellen." She explained her affection for her relative, writing: "I could pay no more visits after hearing this & came home sad for altho I have long mourned & missed Mrs. Hill— Today I realized that there was yet a hope in my heart about her & I thank God I shall hope no, believe she is now enjoying all her faculties in the highest happiest sense in that Home where all who are as faithful as she was here— have unending joy."

3. Sarah Coleman, a member of the Orphan Asylum board, was related to the Crittendens.

4. In his second annual message, Lincoln suggested constitutional amendments to provide for compensated and gradual emancipation by 1900; he also called for con-

gressional support of colonization programs. On December 1, EBL wrote: "Father read tonight the message— thinks it an able paper— but thinks the result can be obtained by legislation— it makes the abolitionists wrathy   he did not read it to or consult Father about it— He wrote it himself Preston King dont like any constitutional changes— & has resisted all infringements upon the Constitution for any purpose whatever He has no chance of a reelection   Chase is going to try for the Senate."

5. In the fall of 1862, several foreign nations, including Great Britain, toyed with the idea of mediating the American dispute. Southern diplomats encouraged them because the plan called for an armistice during mediation, something that could have been beneficial to the South.

Silver Spring   December 9, 1862

My dear Phil   I went to the City chiefly to go see Aunt Kitty & do Mother's errands & Betty's who has in her efforts to get ready to go with Govr Dennison made herself sick & thereby will prevent her journey— for she is really sick tonight— Blair got his hair cut— & I paid two visits— but not to Mrs Hale[1] as I intended   I find Mrs Trumbull & others who have young ladies offended because Betty dont call with me & as she is absorbed in the Ohio trip I cant get her on duty at all So Ill await her departure— or until she give it up— day after tomorrow decides it— & then pay my devoirs to Madame H.

Father has seen the Senator—[2] & Father thinks *he* dont intend his move but to get his *own* way on some points— Father began by saying Hale I hope you are not serious in this raging business— for I want you to take care of my Admiral thro the Senate— yours & mine are in the same boat you remember— "I know that pretty well" was his reply— & they evidently parted on excellent terms Fox says there will be no trouble about the matter—" Father remained in the City again tonight he is very busy— getting compensation for the emancipated in the Middle States— his plan obviates any change of constitution— a thing impracticable— McClellan is in the City & gives his evidence tomorrow in McDowells Court—[3] Govr Dennison follows— he wanted my Father in the City with him— I left them at Brothers— There is no news or excitement in the City— I saw Clem Hill who told me that "they were bothering William again— but that my Bro— came to his rescue like a true "brotherly friend—"

I had no head ache today & am well in every respect— Blair & I sleep soundly— after once I get to sleep & as we indulge here in late hours— even I do lie awake long— I can bring up arrears in the morning hours— but I have often wished that Blair & I had been in our usual good condition when you paid yr flying visit— Still it was & is a bright spot to me, and as your post is near I can hope for more

I must write Ellen a few lines about Aunt Kitty— and the Youngs— Molly talks of the nunery— the refuge of desolate women— Clementina[4] will go "to some friends *after* a while in the West where her health improved during a recent visit to them—" Aunt Kitty returns to Dick Hill— Clem's Dick[5] is the chief of Ordinance in Bank's Staff— Mrs. Clem is delighted!!— So wags this world of ours

They have Mary Riggs & Mrs D's old coach man Edward— a free darky— after all— their determination to the Contrary— You see I cant write you politics so I am obliged to talk gossip   Ever your affectionate Lizzie

1. Lucy Lambert married Senator John P. Hale in 1834.

2. John P. Hale, Republican senator from New Hampshire, chaired the Naval Affairs Committee.

3. On December 4, EBL had explained: "Govr Dennison is still in the City awaiting McClellands coming— who is expected tomorrow to testify in McDowells case— this & Fitz John Porters will probably bring out all whys & wherefores— of McC's removal & other things oft discussed— There is a great deal of comment on Hallecks report— which is called a studied & rather cunning attack on McClelland."

4. Molly and Clementina were Mary C. Young and Clementina S. Young, daughters of Barbara S. Young.

5. Richard Mason Hill, major in the Ordnance Corps, was the son of Clement Hill, Ellen Lee's brother.

Silver Spring   December 12, 1862

Dear Phil   I cannot say that I was sure of seeing you today— but I thought about it all the time until I ascertained that you were not here— but when I found I had no letter I had a hope to grow up in me which I shall follow up in town tomorrow when I can go to church if I have to seek consolation— Betty did not get off as she expected— Govr D— wants another *talk* til 2 olk at night— there is great excitement in the city   the battle has opened on Fredericksburg[1] which I heard was in flames this morning

I cannot tell you how cramped I feel that I cant write you just what I hear— but it is safest not to do so— I want you to read an article on foreign affairs in the Balt American of to day *Thursday*—[2] & you will see some Silver Spring handywork— by the *best hand* on the place—" Uncle Abe read it & when Brother went to Cabinet— he was cornered to hear it read & the cut piece was taken out of his pocket & duly enjoyed by both— under the circumstances the P.G. was charmed— I expect to have some copying to do— So you may look out for it—

Govr D— goes off at six in the morning takes Betty with him who I do not think well enough to go— I was very busy with her affairs— still I called to see Mrs. Hale found she will not be here until Jany— left cards for Hoopers—[3] who Mrs Govr Andrew considers "the nicest the very nicest people in Boston—" I heard Mrs. Welles received calls so I shall go there tomorrow—[4] they have lost seven children—

George Alexander came out with us tonight he is wonderfully improved &

is still on the cartridge hunt— Blair came running out to meet him— hoping to see you— he was sorely disappointed— stopped short & eyed George— then after some hesitation— Said "I am sorry not to see Papa— where is he Mama— Cousin George I am glad you came anyhow— George picked him up in his arms saying— well you are a great boy— he seems struck with his warm heartedness & to console him read stories— told them to him for over an hour— Blair had his ride on Jenny Lind today— & had a "bully time with Sammy"

Everybody talks Court Martials— Congress is quite deserted & these court rooms are so thronged that it is scarcely possible to enter the doorway from the Street Father went there in search of Govr Dennison today— McDowell is coming off in flying colors & Porter will so too all the evidence will I hope open the eyes of the Country & Congress to our true source of difficulty & help to remedy it I heard a revelation about Banks & the south Mountain fight— he desired to fight it single handed to get the glory & the White House so says Pope— Who I never believe— Still I repeat it to show you the style of the table talk now in vogue— Genl McC. had a grand dinner at *No 4.* yesterday Ever your devoted Lizzie

1. On December 11, Ambrose Burnside's Union troops began crossing the Rappahannock River and occupied Fredericksburg, Virginia. The actual battle of Fredericksburg occurred southeast of the town on December 13.

2. The Baltimore *American* of December 11, 1862, contained an editorial on compensated emancipation and its relationship to foreign affairs. It suggests that the French interest in our Civil War stemmed from their desire to control Mexico and expand their influence "round the Gulf." It points out that England has freed all slaves in her dominions and Russia has freed her serfs, thus those nations will refuse to be allied with a "lawless power which avows the design of destroying liberal institutions for the express purpose of extending and perpetuating slavery." The article also lauds Lincoln's emancipation proclamation, "his humane, healing, redeeming plan," which should "appeal to the hearts of men wherever opened to human sympathies."

3. Samuel Hooper, Massachusetts congressman.

4. In another December 12 letter, EBL fulfilled her promise and "paid a visit to Mrs Welles one of the saddest persons I ever saw— she asked me to visit her often which I will do—."

Silver Spring   December 13, 1862

Dear Phil   We are in considerable perturbation here tonight— just before we left the City we heard through Mrs Seward that there was a fierce battle going on at Fredericksburg that Sumner had taken one redoubt— & all our army was across the River— I thought from the fact that our troops got over the River with so little loss & opposition the Rebels had retreated to Richmond— &

only kept enough for a show at Fredericksburg— but *it is said* they took their heavy artillery 15 miles below— to attack when our forces attempted to cross under the cover of the Gun boats lying there   if this is true— for once we outwitted them— which will be a great comfort after frequent blunders

I recd a letter from Sara Moses today saying her husbands health was failing & expressing great unhappiness about it— the Doctors ordered him to go on a trip some where either over the Ocean or to the South some where— My Parents asked them to pay us a visit here—[1] so I hope to have my old crony with me— the most loved of them all— & just as true & warm hearted as in the days of our youth— I have never left here in these troubled times— that she & her husband have not offered— to come after me & take Blair & I to their home This last fall she was extremely urgent for us to spend the winter with them— I have written to her & to Fanny tonight— for last night I was too weary write—

I went to town in Marys little waggon & it is as rough as a ride on horse back nearly— but I slept all the better for it— & it is too sloppy out here to get exercise in any other way than by a drive— the weather is perfect for this season— I visited Mrs Clem Hill today saw Aunt Kitty who told me she saw John when he brought the boys up They have now moved to their own house & are all very well again— I went to the Navy Yard to see about the oysters— found they had not arrived— made arrangements where to have them sent when they did arrive— I paid Mrs Hammond[2] a visit and your good friend Mrs. Harris—

I got a directory at last & can now go see my congressional acquaintance   I have had a search for the womankind of the M.Cs— but got thro ten visits today not MC's however— but all I could find out & just as I left town— I heard Mrs Doolittle[3] was in a house where I called yesterday— No fault of mine   Ill soon amend that matter When Govr Dennison bid me goodbye— he told me if I saw any trouble about the Admirals— I must telegraph him & he could come & do all he could for my admiral— he had spoken to Mr Grimes & other & there seemed no difficulty— I see none but this delay to act— & that annoys me & yet so far I have not rested quietly under it— Blair enjoyed the sunshine on Jenny Lind & with the Donkey & wheeling wood down to the house— Father said today "he has all of Phil's industry & activity."   Ever yr own devoted Lizzie

1. Jacob Henry (Harry) Joseph of Montreal, Canada, was the husband of EBL's close friend and cousin Sara. When it appeared certain that Joseph would visit the Blairs without his wife, EBL complained in her December 26 letter that Sara "knows of yore that he was the greatest bore on terra firma to me—." Admitting that "he is an honest true hearted man," she groaned, "except *Tish* McK— the least interesting

human being I ever met & only won Sara by persistent devotion of seven years or more."

2. Helen Nisbet of Philadelphia married William A. Hammond in 1849. He was presently surgeon general of the U.S.

3. Mary Lovina Cutting married James R. Doolittle in 1837.

                                        Silver Spring   December 16, 1862

Dear Phil   I did not utter my apprehension about the Army yesterday that it was sorely cut up—[1] in the retreat over the River & the rumor that 20 thousand would not cover our loss confirmed my apprehension— but from all this we are relieved by the fact that Burnside recrossed his army during the night & that the storm aided to conceal the movement "a folly from its beginning to its end' anybody at all acquainted with the point d'appuis—[2] would see that the enemy could make themselves impregnable except by army able to surround them— Why Lee did not slaughter hundreds in crossing amazed me— for the hills command the River— & were filled with rifle pits— If it reverses some things going on here it will be a national blessing—[3] instead of misfortune but to the bereaved families who mourn their dead— whose lives were apparently so thrown away— it is hard to endure— poor Bayard[4] was to have been married the day he was buried— the cards were issued— Many is the young heart that is broken by this woful war—

We had a letter from Betty who was safe & well & most kindly recieved at Columbus but they were all in great trepidation about the Army of the Potomac— Govr D. assured Betty in a note no battle could take place at Fredericksburg— the situation of the enemy made it impossible— for us to attack successfully"— so she went free of terror of Bull Runs & etc— I had the Rockaway brought home today where I have kept very quietly— for altho unhurt my nervous temperament makes me feel *let* down after such an ordeal—[5] but I am quite well in every respect— Father went to see the P. had a long talk— & is cheerful tonight—

Mother & Blair rode on horse back— he wheeled his wood down to the house— & is a busy gay— hearty boy & full of demonstration of affection to me— the only way he has noticed the accident of yesterday— He has great disputes about the Alphabet with little Henry— who is now regularly taught by old Henry   Blair knows all of his letters as well as I do— but never learn them AbC fashion— has picked up his learning from his blocks & picture books & knows dog & many names of animals & other words when he sees them— & evinces great aptitude for such things & if a sendentary child would soon read— but I keep him out doors even in the cold weather we have had & try to find active occupation for him hoping it will make him physically strong— I have a steam engine which I am going to give him from you for Xmas— it winds up & runs about the floor— & I hope the oysters which he likes will also come for that season I always make it joyous today to the little fellow consequently he is full of bright anticipations—

Father is very busy writing tonight— goes in tomorrow again & if the carriage goes I will go with him— if Mother is well enough— she has not been in her usual good condition this week— Ever your devoted Lizzie

1. In another letter of December 16, EBL told of her conversation with young Dennison: "I asked him if the enemy were entrenched in the rear of Fredericksburg 'Yes'— 'Well if I remember the locality none but mad men would attack them there— No, was his reply none but mad men & bad men would think of it'— & so it proved to our sorrow—."

2. Point of support for a battle line.

3. Also on December 16, EBL reminded her husband, "Your prophesy that things will get a great deal worse 'ere they mend is surely being fulfilled— & if this reverse delivers us of some cormorants well known— it will eventually be no misfortune and we are at the mending point I hope at last."

4. Brig. Gen. George D. Bayard died December 14, 1862, of wounds suffered at Fredericksburg. He had led the cavalry brigade.

5. In her other letter of December 16, EBL described her accident: "I was coming home Jimmy Byrnes driving— when passing a waggon & four horses— Canada— doubled her pace as usual when he passes anything— when the driver of the waggon turned his horses right in front of him— He got entangled in gear single trees & etc— plunged frantically & all set of in a run— but the waggon was too heavy— the Rockaway got hitched into the waggon— Canada wrenched the front wheel off— & down we tumbled & he would have dragged us to death but for the wagoner catching & holding him— I crept out thro the torn curtain— without a bruise even— crawling between rockaway & waggon wheels uncomfortably near a horse's heels— & yet unhurt & with a heart full of thankfulness—."

Silver Spring   December 20, 1862

My dear Phil   The process of cabinet making or reconstruction has not yet begun save that the member of the Cabinet who has been so longer eager to quit has been requested not offer a resignation when it was proffered—[1] Chase's resignation has been accepted— no harm to mention the fact as I hear it is published— It seems now that caucus began its war on Stanton— but concluded to hit the whole Cabinet by a blow at the head & his— I would be sorry for Mr Seward but for his course in the beginning of his Cabinet career & a sort of conviction that he is too old to change his convictions— for altho I dont agree with Landon Carter[2] that a man after 40 does not change his opinions— having reached that age I know better, still there is an increase of rigidity of mind & body with age— so I could part with him & Mr C in the faith that Separation is with them is a fixed policy & so they may go with even all Mr. Cs asseverations to boot   I felt it in bones that this democratic upturning would bring good to our country & that faith is now being hourly increased   how you will find by reading the papers.

I am afraid you felt the cold last night— & tonight— I felt very lonesome until I took myself for feeling so— why— because I had 24 hours of happiness in seeing my husband an altogether unexpected pleasure— concluded it was no reason for being particularly lonesome— so tried my hand cabinet making & went to sleep at the work—

Father went to the city on Trifle this cold day— returned early & in good spirits— Mother Blair & I had a long walk   Mother dont wish the carriage to go in tomorrow so I am deprived of Church so much for Canadas misbehavior— which will be all arranged when Father is less occupied with things of greater import— Ill wait to close this after Brothers visit tomorrow & give you Sundays news—

Sunday   I am going to send this in by Brother— the situation is unaltered as yet   Halleck is trying to supercede by Sherman— McClernand in the Missippi Expedition[3]   this will make the Trumbull uproarious   Brother seems in excellent spirits— So things must look promising thro our horoscope   God grant us some honest men to guide our country in its present troubles is my constant prayer—[4] but first thought I must confess is for you it may be selfish— but your welfare is now— I think that of the Country consequently I feel very patriotic even when I pray only for my husband

Blair is very well & merry out gathering laurels— Some of which I will take in to deck St John's tomorrow for Christmas   Blair is busy putting some around Papa's picture— He & Becky will I expect deck all my pictures— God bless you   Your affecate Lizzie

1. Secretary of State William H. Seward came under attack by radical Republicans who demanded his resignation and a general reorganization of the cabinet. Seward sent his resignation to Lincoln, and in the political maneuvers, Secretary of the Treasury Salmon P. Chase also offered to resign. Lincoln refused both, and the cabinet crisis ended. Throughout the first two years of the war, there were numerous rumors that Seward might resign.

2. Landon Carter, a rather distant but oft-quoted Lee relative.

3. In October 1862 McClernand, a political general from Lincoln's home state of Illinois, offered a proposal for opening the Mississippi River. Although Halleck was skeptical, McClernand was authorized to recruit men for the expedition. Orders to all concerned were vague and confusing: Grant thought McClernand was to be a part of his command, and McClernand thought he had an independent command. When McClernand arrived at Grant's camp, he found Sherman in charge of troops he thought were his and complained to higher authorities. Ultimately, McClernand commanded the Thirteenth Corps of Grant's army.

4. On December 23, EBL wrote: "We have a calm after the storm & there is a truce

among the politicians— & one stamped by the characters of those who have made it—
I still cling fondly to the belief that my Country & its noble Govt will ever survive all
this— altho disappointed that the secret separatists are yet unmasked."

Silver Spring   December 24, 1862
Dear Phil—   Yours of blue Monday reached me today— I wished things
looked less blue— but we must hope for the best— certain it is that the Congressional report[1] makes out our Generals— the most brainless— inert set
that ever the world saw— & Halleck is chief of Imbeciles— His own evidence
is enough to hang him— but you will read it, I have just laid it down— & feel
so hurt at heart that so many brave men were so cruelly dealt by that I may
not be just— & am disposed to blame most— those I like least— I rejoice in
these investigations they must end in the right way

I received a letter from Fanny today— she is full of her politics but says one
thing true I have no doubt "Robt Lee says McClellan is our only great general
& he thanks God he is shelved" so no wonder secesh rejoices in the course of
the Powers here From all I hear the Army are not likely to follow its present
leaders willingly— the chiefs want their rewards— & then will talk plainly—
I know of several Genls in town today— indeed I never saw such a swarm of
people in my life as filled the Avenue today— never saw anything like it last
winter—

I recd a note from Susan Preston[2] alias Hepburn she wishes to see me, I'll
call— tomorrow when I hope to go Church I wish you could have seen Blair's
bright face tonight— & heard his odd surmises about Kris Kringle— I have
come to the conclusion to cut that thin disguise after this— he asks so many
questions that I can only escape story telling by refusing to answer— Mary
Blair has given him a pair of parlor skates which will enchant him & be great
exercise on the large porch in bad weather— Ill not let him go alone until he
has learned to use them well—

I sent off my letter to Horace— today mailed it myself— I spoke of it as
something I wish him to do for me— because I think it best to do so— & made
no excuses for my wish— save the state of things reiterated my request about
the change of draft into notes—all of which is literally true— as it was not
necessary to mention that your wishes were mine the letter will however accomplish the wish of both & bear inspection anywhere— Capt John Ro[d]gers
is here today he has a daughter three days old—[3] his wife told me she did not
wish his visit until after the little one's arrival but was vastly tried— about
it, as it was slow to come— & she feared he might be ordered off— Still she
would not have him here— "no true woman ever could willingly do so—" He
is to leave at the end of this week as he expects his vessel to be ready for sailing
next week—

I wish our Christmas could be happy together— which is fondly echoed by our loving boy— but he is still joyous & happy— "like a little child—" so often that example is given me by him— God bless you both— & in each other— Ever your devoted Lizzie Fanny says all well with her

1. Joint Committee on the Conduct of the War.
2. Susan Marshall Preston, daughter of William and Caroline Hancock Preston, married Hiatt Park Hepburn in 1860.
3. John Rodgers's new baby was Frederica Louisa Rodgers, born December 21, 1862.

Silver Spring   December 25, 1862
My Dear Phil   So far as we can share Blair's joys this has been a merry Christmas. He was awake before daylight— & had to take a look at his gifts by candle light— it was six— but you know that is not daylight in my room— Of all the toys nothing so pleased him as the Engine & railway Cars & Mary Blair skates— he told me— to say to Papa this is the best Christmas yet—" & I do wish Goverment would just let him be here to this time—"

I went to Church then to see Susan Preston— who is in love with California says if the Union cause fails we must come live there— tis the City of refuge— & one of immense prosperity— & thoroughly allied to the because of its Navy— She says there are immense numbers of southerners have gone there— Union people who still did not wish to take part in this war— the draft sent many of these to Europe Still they are daily flocking there from New Orleans & by land Susan says she is going to get some of her nephews who are paroled & wounded— all secesh to go with her— & get transplanted into free soil— it is a good cure that madness I enjoyed my visit—

Father and I then called to see the Footes but they declined seeing us— so I left cards— & then came home Your Genl Foster[1] *was here* in Washn today   I do hope he will be supported & shall not fail for want of asking— You see by the papers that Frank has gone to Vicksburg under Sherman— I hope they will get along together— John thinks S. able but I have watched his career closely— he has weak nerves— fights desperately— so will a woman when cornered, or fighting for her children   it is not that calm courage which can direct well in the Storm— this was evident at Shiloh—

Things are in a turbid condition here—[2] but by reading the papers with your knowledge of men can see the drift— the Intelligencer & American— the World are evidently leaders— There is a resolute purpose to resist by all legal power the Military Heads— Which have also got into deadlock with Navy Dept— where we all hope there will be no changes— but All is at Sea yet and the storm brewing

We are invited to dine at Sewards on New Year   Father has accepted for us all— Mother declines says she wont go— but I hope will be persuaded to go & let me stay at home   I shall keep quiet but am not going as I expect ample excuses ere that time— We had a letter from Betty She has gone to Cincinnatti & she is getting quiet satisfied with her trip enjoys it— and the Govr speaks of her in very flattering terms— I hear the Passaic is ready— & two other Iron Clads I confess to watching them very closely— George Alexander says he may join Frank he left the day after you did & writes to Father—

Virginia Fox— Minna— Mrs. Sands & Mrs Beale gave Blair beautiful books— Minna wrote for Blair Lee from his Aunt Minna We are well Ever your affectionate Lizzie

1. Maj. Gen. John G. Foster, military commandant at Fort Monroe, was planning a combined operation with SPL against Wilmington, North Carolina.

2. The next day, EBL described John Crittenden and Montgomery Blair as "The two most depressing people in the city at this moment."

Silver Spring December 30, [1862]
Dear Phil Father went today to help the deportation plans[1] the Alabama[2] makes everybody call for convoys! I think Capt Rockendorf's[3] ill luck most unenviable to let that craft escape him—

I did not go to the City as I gave Becky an extra holiday so as Blair objected to going to the City I remained home with him— She got back tonight & brings some Lee'sburg news— when may interest you— Maria—[4] Harrison's house servant left there for freedom a few days ago— She says Miss "Kate is about the same in her ways"— & keeps in her usual health— she was once very ill from remaining so long on her knees— has given to her sisters her watch & all her trinkets & fineries & wears the plainest calico all the time— She told Maria— she might just as well go as the rest of them were gone Sy & her other man are in Washington— She says she wants to see "Uncle Phil more than anybody—" her little sister said "Why dont you want to see yr Uncle John Yr Uncle Phil is a Yankee—" Kate replied— I want to see both of my Uncles but Uncle Phil most— he is the best Lee"

Robt Lee made Harrisons House Headquarters when on his way to Maryland & after his retreat— remained there a long time & was near being caught & left behind him all his luggage and papers— that same day Siegel "the french Genl" came there & demanded Rooms— Mrs. Harrison gave him the parlors— & was "dreadful afraid" he would find Genl Lee's things in his room upstairs (the one we occupied)— His papers were carried off to him that night by Harriet Jones husband[5] who tho' he has taken the oath of Allegiance to the U.S.— is Genl Lee chief agent for getting news of the enemy who R Lee said one day that he heard more regularly from the War Dept at Washington than from the one in Richmond— Henry Harrison wont talk about the war— "but gets all the best for nothing for Rebel generals—" & the Union Generals *pay* for everything they get from him" Mrs. H.[6] & the children are all violent Secesh— except Kate who is silent about every thing— So much for this intelligent Contraband who you remember is a bright mulatto

All of Mr. Harrison's servants have left him except the cook & two of her children— Maria says colored people was at first as hot secesh as the "white folks—" I outdid Mrs. Harrison—" but since the Union Army has been there "we know better—"

Father saw Ada Douglass[7] today who denies being engaged to Mr. Chase— which is reported & believed in the City— L told Brother today he was right about *the point* on which they differed this fall— So tho it is to acted on Thursday— he is not of your or Capt D's opinion— Nor am I— I hope he will see wisdom in some other good advice lately given— Father brought my last nights letters to & Mrs Seward back in his pocket— which I think shows my going is unimportant— I was sorry about the letter to you— I must write to Betty to night— I hear that Mrs Joe Johnston says that when the Rebels get out lead they may melt her husband— She has grown zealous & not lost her wit— devotedly your wife Lizzie

1. In her December 28 letter EBL had written: "Father met by appointment a Haytien envoye— *whitish* 'to talk emigration to the President—' who authorized an arrangement for carrying several thousand Countrabands off there in a few weeks— joy go with them—."

2. CSS *Alabama* was commissioned August 24, 1862. For two years, under Capt. Raphael Semmes, she raided, captured, and caused general havoc in Northern shipping.

3. William Ronckendorff, commanding the USS *San Jacinto*, had blockaded the *Alabama* at Martinique. On November 19, under cover of bad weather, the *Alabama* escaped.

4. Maria was Henry Harrison's servant.

5. In 1851 Anne Harriotte Jones, daughter of Gen. Walter Jones, married Matthew Harrison, a Leesburg lawyer. She was a sister of Henry Harrison's wife.

6. Elizabeth Mary Jones, daughter of Gen. Walter Jones, married Henry Harrison in 1841.

7. Adele Cutts married Stephen Douglas in 1856. She was the daughter of J. Madison Cutts of the District and a great niece of Dolly Madison.

Silver Spring   December 31, 1862

My dear Phil   The papers announce the departure of the Iron Clads on Monday for where they only surmise—[1] In this last day of this year of sorrow to our Country I have not forgotten my blessings— & recount them often times to cheer and chase my fears away— for the future   your escape at New Orleans & return in August to me Those three weeks— so portentious to the Country— & yet so enjoyed by me are my bright illuminated day which still cheer & comfort me Then Blair is evidently much improved   I mean physically—

& I do pray and hope he will be a sturdy strong man— He looked so gay this evening after being out in the raw weather from 9. until 2 olk— playing & riding— & then after dinner out again until driven in by the snow in which he was delighting— but I am not brave enough to let him stay out in falling weather—

Father got home about that time bringing me no letter from you— but one from Sara— who tries to impress me that "Harry needs society—" a cure he could never procure for himself & one I cannot attempt now a days— I shall do all that politeness can do— but I wrote her our house had not a visitor once in a month during the winter & I visited only in the morning but the idea of a man of 55, whose nose has been in his ledger for 35 years requiring "gay society" is absurd besides there is no gayity in this part of the world— it is all grim war— The Caswells[2] told me there would not be a dance outside of the Hotels this winter in Washington I enclose you Horaces letter recieved also today— as it is a receipt & an account too take care of it— I would not send it if I had seen the arrival of the Minnesota announced—

Father says the Contract was signed & sealed today for taking 5000 contrabands to Hayti— rather an adjoining Island— Des Vache[3] or some such name He & Mr. Doolittle think it the beginning of the 2nd great Exodus Father wishes me to go with him tomorrow & call on all of our Senatorial acquaintance & etc— I will go & begin the year in obedience & long before the end of it hope to enjoy your return home as my reward— I send you Dr Hays extract— I agree with him entirely & told Mother at Breakfast today— that I never saw a slave in this country half as degraded as all the Africans I saw just fresh from Africa in Cuba—[4] with their sharpened teeth— & I saw thousands— but I am an abolitionist for the sake of my own race— Contact with the African degenerates our white race— I find the association with them injurious to my child— keenly as I watch to prevent it & his faithful nurse to help me— but she insists pure blacks are not so bad as Mulattos— She is a good woman & so are many of them— Still the race is a degraded one— May God Bless & give *us* a happy New Year Yr devoted Lizzie

1. The ironclads were bound for Wilmington, North Carolina. After EBL had first seen the *Monitor*, she had commented on October 13, 1863: "It is a modest little thing to achieve such results."

2. Possibly John and Mary Caswell.

3. Isle a Vaches.

4. EBL had spent several months, from November 1840 to June 1841, in Cuba, attempting to regain her health.

9

"I feel upish as gold tonight—"

January 12, 1863

THE NEW YEAR SAW A RESTIVE NORTH, uncertain of the meaning of emancipation, discouraged at the lack of military success, and reluctant to consider
a draft. It had been a disappointment to the nation when the *Monitor* went
down off Cape Hatterras on December 31. The failure in early January to
close the remaining gap in Union control of the Mississippi at Vicksburg was
a further setback. At least Northerners could take heart from the repulse of
the rebel advance at Murfreesboro, Tennessee. Lincoln, still searching for a
winning general, replaced Burnside with "Fighting Joe" Hooker.

Elizabeth Lee's concern in the Vicksburg campaign was heightened by her
brother Frank's participation. Although disappointed in the Union failure to
take that stronghold, she was immensely relieved by word that her brother
was safe. A continuing goal for Elizabeth was gaining a congressional vote of
thanks for her husband and an attendant promotion.

Silver Spring   January 1, 1863

Dear Phil   After paying with Father 18 visits— seeing people every where—
then dining at Mrs Sewards, & driving home I am a weary woman— Still this
first day of 63 cannot pass without thanking you for yours & its enclosure from
Capt Parker—[1]

The city is full of rumors & excitement   Rosencrantz is giving the enemy
battle at Murfreeboro[2] which I know is true & the other talk is only the utterance of peoples wishes in the shape of on dits— There was only the Sewards
Brother Father & myself at the dinner to day— the dinner was in exquisite
taste My only enjoyed visits today were at the Pleasontons the Carrolls—
where I was surrounded by familiar faces At Trumbulls— there were only two
other guests besides ourselves— Nobody at the other senators— Chases had
the roughest set— & among them Miss C. looking like a fairy queen— in her
light draperies of lace—

Blair kept awake until 9 olk & then concluded— he had "staid out here many a night without Mama & could do it again— Told Becky if I did not return not wake him up— but put him in my bed & bring her bed down stairs— "if you wake me up I might not go to sleep again all night—" Still he was very sure of my return—

Father recd a letter from Frank dated 20th at the moment of departure for "our expedition—" Apo writes that his letter to her of the 19th was very cheerful— She is full of Dix cares— ie secessionist in St Louis—[3] You see by the papers that the President has exempted all states & part of states— not under rebel control— Brother opposed that part— which included Norfolk & a few Counties or County of *one state* it ignored State lines too much & etc— You see it reported he opposed it   Seward laughed at him today— & said he went for the proclamation *& a little* more—" certainly than those who originated it— He therefore now is reported as opposed to it all the time— I think he was right— all the time & if the pieces of states were left out it would look more in Earnest Louis Napoleon has given recent & most earnest assurances of having no purpose to recognize or interfere in any way in our affairs

Good night— I must go rest but if I could only rest & chat to you the small hours even would not catch me napping— Jany 2nd I am hors de combat with head ache today. so cannot talk much or write   a day of rest & night of sleep will make it all right again No news— All well— Ever your affecate Lizzie

1. Capt. Foxhall Parker, old naval friend of SPL, was captain of the USS *Mahaska* in the North Atlantic Blockading Squadron.

2. On December 31, 1862, Braxton Bragg's rebels forced Rosecrans's Federals back to Stone's River where they held near Murfreesboro, Tennessee. On January 3, Bragg's Army of Tennessee withdrew.

3. In Missouri, the military commander Gen. Samuel R. Curtis and Governor Gamble were involved in a wide-ranging dispute of authority. Part of their disagreement stemmed from Curtis's harsh treatment of Southern sympathizers and marked the beginning of the break between Radicals and moderates in the state.

Silver Spring   January 4, 1863
Dear Phil   I have just heard of the fate of the Monitor, & feel as if I could fly to comfort you—[1]

Our hearts almost stand still with breathless anxiety about dear Frank who is leader of the Centre in the battle waged at Vicksburg   the last reports from Sherman— the battle was still in progress—[2] But we all must possess our souls in patience & prayer— & trust in God— I believe firmly our Country will ride thro' all these storms it has been too mercifull & good a government not to find mercy in this its hour of need— We are all well & hopeful— Ever your devoted Lizzie The War Dept Reports from Tennessee are favorable— our loss in officers however is frightful— Saw Fox Our Secy is au des espoir The City is full of officers from the Army of the Potomac—

1. The *Monitor* sank off Cape Hatteras on December 31, 1862.

2. The day before, on January 3, EBL had written: "I see by the letters to the Union that Sherman is going to Vicksburg & has gone up the Yazoo 20 miles & intends to take Vicksburg in the rear—." On December 20, Sherman had moved down the Mississippi from Memphis toward Chickasaw Bayou north of Vicksburg. On December 26, his army arrived at the Yazoo River and moved up toward the bluffs of Vicksburg.

Silver Spring   January 5, 1863
Dear Phil   Your's of yesterday & Saturday received today— as to the case of friend Diggs—[1] Father & I having consulted over the case advise you to say "that upon inquiry that the Post Master Genl at the requests of Members of Congress has displaced every clerk he can conscienciously turn out & filled their places by MC's recommendations & they demand this upon the ground that Maryland which Brother is anxious to provide for has more than her share of appointments— & that their Constituents complain if they are not put upon an equality with the State who the P. M Genl is supposed particularly to represent— Mr. Digges will therefore apply in vain— & as a friend you can just suggest a postponement of his application— & you might intimate that you had heard Dr. Fairfax had said that Mr. Blair of Silver Spring was agent for all Montgomery County— & he might be more potential than any other you knew" & etc— Father did not say this last point but I think it but fair— that he has done so much for others that our kin of the Digges Clan might be treated civilly at least— Horaces & the St Louis letters I will put in your business file— which I keep with great care—

We are intensely anxious about Frank— Genl Grants telegraphs the Capture of Vicksburg— after hard fight— no details— as this comes from Secesh sources— Mother bears up bravely but I can see in her countenance a constant tremor to which my heart but too keenly responds— Yet each tries to be cheerful & over dinner & tea talks were this day as animated as ever you heard it— I read out every item I can find in the papers— & as I say any mishap to Frank would fly thro Secesh So no news is good news—

Blair wrote you a long letter which is up stairs— he heard the loss of the Monitor regretted & soon after wanted to write to you about it   he has not said one word to me on the subject He rode out with Mother today & he is a great source of talk & pleasure to her   Woody ask her the other day "GrandMa— I think you love Blair Lee better than you do any of us?   Mother said "I always love the Babies the best— & when they get to be men— I shall care most for the cleverest & the most honest of my grandchildren—" She told me this talk— & thereupon warned *me* to be careful not excite jealousy & ill will towards my boy. I told her I rarely talked of him save to you & your family— & I was happy in knowing he was a pet in all the family circles so far Nelly & Fanny are satisfied with a letter from me with Blair left out— & you know I am not stingy on the subject when I can indulge without prejudice to our boy—

Majr Isaac Moses[2] came out early today & told me of Capt Bankhead's[3] arrival I do hope you will never go to Sea in one of the Monitor Ships— I read tonight the account of Capt Bs report to you with great distress— & yet how many noble beings are swept off by devouring cannon We live in an awful era If you go off in the Minnesota on Wednesday this will be the last to get to you ere you sail So forget *not* my parting injunction "take care of my husband" amid all your other cares as he is the first of all earthly feeling of the heart of yr affectionate Lizzie

1. SPL's grandmother was Jane Digges Fitzgerald, thus the family tie to the Diggeses. In her January 9 letter, EBL tried to explain the lack of influence of her brother and father when she told an applicant: "he will have yet more powerful intervention as Mr. S. does not feel & has no reason to oblige the backers he appeals to— I told him that I did not know two person more out of favor with the Military officials & more certain to damage his application—." In the same letter, however, EBL's retelling of "a sort of joke upon Father" belies the Blair political influence: "he in late talk— spoke of the entire want of drill— & activities in a military way— of the Army in these part to the P.— two days after the pickets were increased *here* from four— to 20 men— & the officers called to intimate how very watchful they were over *us* You can imagine somebody's disgust tho' he wont see or admit the point."

2. Isaac Moses was a first cousin of Sara Moses Joseph, and the Lees considered him their relative.

3. Capt. John P. Bankhead was commanding the *Monitor* when it sank December 31, 1862.

Silver Spring   January 6, 1863

My dear Phil   I have had a busy day & sat like "the king in a parlor counting out money—" given by the charitable to the Asylum— we received today a thousand dollars— there Mary Merrick & I sat in charity & kindness when our Brothers are in mortal combat at Vicksburg— Corcoran sent us a hundred dollars & our subscriptions are mostly from our old regular subscribers—

I was happy outside of my own aching cares for oh Phil I am so anxious about Frank—[1] & tonight when I returned home & found Blair was hoarse I had difficulty to keep up my calmness The picket of soldiers are amused with him— & since not allowed to go in their house they come to the swing & play with him to which I did not object— but they seated themselves on the ground & he followed their example & Becky found him sitting with them yesterday— when she left him alone for a half hour yesterday— this gave him cold— & this morning I ordered him to remain in the house today & tonight & he is hoarse— but no sore throat— & if I had been light hearted would have thought little of it— Mr. Joseph who came out with us today says I am even more anxious than Sara but Blair does not often have a cold & this open weather has been the cause of two when you were last here— & this one— he gets heated with his overcoat— & I am afraid to let it be taken off— he wears it without a cape Still it oppresses him— consequently lounges & sits down after a run or romp— but you will tire of this nursery talk— but tis my vocation—

I had a little talk with Sarah Coleman— I wish you could hear her speak of Nelly— it would have made yr heart warm up for Sarah We had another visit from the Haytien projector— the jobbers are in a hot intrigue against him— Mr Joseph does not look ill— says he feels better tonight— Gives good accounts of Aunt Becky & Horace— Says the Secesh in Montreal— often of late lament the futility of the Secession movement— how they mistook the real grandeur of their country & exclaim at the power evinced by both North & south combined— what a Nation!!— This is a good seed— & oh watered with many tears of sorrow & I hope repentance too—

Mrs. Washington was in a fine humor today— so elated with our prosperity & the harmony & good temper of the Board which certainly is a better one than we have ever had before— I make it a point as the Senior member there to give all the precedence in my power to her— I try to divide the duties too— & that makes them more content— for occupation is happiness— Young Mrs Stone[2] has accepted— I nominated her & that set are good humored again— We took a little one in from Fredericksburg— made destitute by the war— two soldiers orphans— & 3 sailor's orphans— so tis well we are so generously dealt by—[3]

I heard no news— save that in the papers— & our hearts jump at the sound of the word Vicksburg— from whence we got no further tidings—[4] It is an old story with me torn in thought over that place— Our darling is sleeping quietly— & Ill keep this open I hope to say he is quite well in the morning—

Jany 7. Wednesday Blair is whittling sticks by me looking bright and well— but has a bad cold which his hoarseness made me fear croup last night but he never had it in his life— & there is no trouble about him except my useless fears— at which I smile *in daylight*— & every body else laughed last night— No news— today— the wind blew high last & I gave your iron clad some of my wakeful thoughts   in haste   Lizzie

1. On January 7, EBL wrote: "Frank is my present anxiety— the heaviest on my heart— & I feel scarce able to bear any thing more—."

2. Margaret Fouschee Ritchie Stone, wife of Dr. Robert K. Stone, was the daughter of Thomas Ritchie, who founded the Richmond *Enquirer.*

3. On November 17, EBL reported: "I took in the Asylum a Secesh baby— whose father was killed in the Army south & the Mother died & left it destitute so I shall call it Secessia— The Army generally take care of their own people but Sailors & refugees give great scope to our charities besides our local calls—."

4. On January 8, 1863, EBL proposed her solution for Vicksburg: "it strikes me that with our forces— 'safe in the rear— & the city surrounded front & rear— why not beseige the place— & starve them out— without such waste of life— I fear political ambition to make haste 'ere Banks arrives— has something to do."

Silver Spring   January 11, 1863
Dear Phil   I received yours of the 8th today in the City— where I went— dressed in my best gown to visit— it rained so much that the visits were give up— I did the marketting— & saw Mrs Sands and Genl. French who took a good laugh at me he said stored up for 20 odd years— then went on to relate the scene which occurred when Berty Young told me of the newspaper version of your Salt River row[1]   he says he never saw any body have such a struggle before or since for calmness— but he quoth he— "You succeeded— & eluded her observation— but not mine— from that hour I knew who had won you"— I had forgotten who was present besides Berty— but I remember the scene perfectly— & also my intense grief afterwards at the idea of your having killed a man— but you did not & your letters from Nashville gave me great relief— Some letters you wrote to Miss Violet Gist—[2] Oh how often I have regretting sending them back to you— Stolen joys were very sweet— so I remember those letters with not half the repentance I ought—

Genl F was full of the Fredericksburg fight— There was a canal— about Six hundred yards from the stone fence & it was in crossing that narrow bridge— he lost six hundred men— there was no reconnaisance & he protested against the proceeding— but was told "a brave & intelligent officer" ought to do what he was ordered— then an orderly was sent to know where he would be— he replied with the leading Brigade of his division— as officers ought to lead a forlorn hope He says— there were never better troops in the world— & that two Rgts of Jersey men joined him 3 days before the fight— & fought as well as his Western Veterans— who made secesh afraid to show their heads above the stone wall— only lifted the gun— on their heads & fired— He told these things as facts— but expressed no other opinions save sneers at Hooker who was their Buncombe Genl The Army en Mass want McClellan— who says Fifth Avenue— is a comfortable exchange— for Falmouth— His wife Genl F. shows the campaign more than he does— she looks as old as Mother— Col Dutton[3] was there— too confused to know anybody—

I recd a letter from Betty she has had a gay time in Cincinnatti— Met Charlie Pettit[4] who wished her to go Louisville with him— that Fanny told him she expected her— wants me to say whether she can go— Fanny you

know will be happy to have her visit but not to frolick— & so I'll tell her—
as Fanny wrote asking her to come to Louisville— Mr. Joseph wants her to go
Canada— I will give her choice of places & get her home—

I shall remain home tomorrow & take care of Blair— as tis Beckys Sunday— & the weather wet   he has had a cold too lately to be out all day— He
and Mr Joseph have great plans for the Donkey & his boys next summer— he
wants me to go to Canada to see the snow "as nothing is as good as snow"— I
do not think so— so shall not go— Your affectionate Lizzie

1. In 1839, near the confluence of the Salt and Ohio rivers, SPL had shot a river-
boat pilot in the heat of argument. The man did not die, and when Lee appeared before
the court, charges were dropped.

2. For four years before their 1843 marriage, EBL and SPL courted, despite the
opposition of her father. To hide their continuing courtship, SPL sent letters via Sarah
Moses in Philadelphia and addressed them to Violet Gist, using part of EBL's mother's
maiden name.

3. Col. Arthur Henry Dutton (USMA 1861) led the Twenty-first Connecticut at
Fredericksburg.

4. Charles Pettit was the brother-in-law of SPL's sister Fanny.

Silver Spring   January 12, 1863
Dear Phil   No letter from you today. & yet it brought us relief about Frank—
he is safe & mentioned with praise even in the short telegram I send you—
Poor Renshaw—[1] I know you will sorrow for him   I do— because no matter
how brave a man acts if he is ever *surprised*— there is no public feeling but
disgust for him— I judge this from the universal talk about Genl. McCook[2]
who has won so many laurels— then lost them by the mist which covered
Hardee's[3] approach— Still I hope as this is Rebel accounts of Texas affairs that
it is not so bad as it now appears— as I have not quite so much faith in their
versions of things as Genl Halleck— did you read his letter to Rosencranz—
nothing could be in worse judgement & taste

We went to the City today   I did as usual some buying for Mother & then
went to the Capitol with Mr. Joseph— no debates of interest going on—
looked at the new pictures chatted with some acquaintance returned for Father
& Blair at Brothers & came home— Mr. J. is weary of our dull routine &
talks of going home in a few days— he says he is much better— he has never
looked ill to me— though thinks him an invalid— He wants me to go Fortress
Monroe— & take a tour to Norfolk & to see you— I told him you would
be glad to see him— but not me— You thought ships & Forts no places for
womankind— & I no fancy to go where womankind were out of place— Sara
evidently thinks it important for him to keep out of his business atmosphere—
they are evidently a happy, home loving couple & he has given me a very
pleasant insight to their domestic life & the characters of their children for
whom I feel great kindness

I am off again in the morning to the City to the Annual Meeting of the Asylum & shall spend the day very busily & consequently more happy than usual— but I now have a light heart tonight— in spite of repulses & mishaps Frank is safe— & the Rebs are repulsed again in Missouri for the fifth or sixth time— I begin to feel as if that state was getting out of these troubles— for a full due— as you say—[4] Besides it is quite clear that England does not intend to interfere any fashion even the London Times has dethroned "King Cotton"— Louis Napoleon has given intimations unmistakable that he has done all he intends to do— & wants food for his Army in Mexico— So for the present that bugbear is out of the way & the little time I was in the Senate I heard *an ultra* say some *whole* some things as to Military Matters & I feel upish as gold tonight— which may be the whole dollar— When the new shin plasters are issued— when we will be able to get bread & meat & thats all as everything now is double price I dont care— Blair has clothes for a year— you shirts & I always more than I wear— so we can be cannie if not coutr*e*" & so I have no sorrow in my heart this night save for poor Renshaw— because you like him— Ever your own Lizzie

1. Comdr. William B. Renshaw was killed by the explosion of *Westfield* in the surprise and capture of Galveston, Texas, by the Confederates January 1, 1863.

2. Gen. Alexander M. McCook had fought well at First Bull Run, Corinth, Nashville, and Shiloh; he led a corps at Murfreesboro. The early-morning rebel attack had once again surprised the federal army. After initial success, the rebels could not dislodge their opponents and had to retreat.

3. Confederate Gen. William Joseph Hardee led a division at Stone's River.

4. In her January 8, 1863, letter EBL had commented: "Father is very happy at this moment in the prospects of Missouri over which he & Mr. J[oseph] are discanting very much to our satisfaction it is a great thing for us personally that this state which has all your material interests should take our side in this war— it alleviates the appearance of the future— come what may—."

Silver Spring   January 14, [1863]
Dear Phil   Father & I went to the City this morning Mr. J. preferring a country day— I went after getting the news— to Church & then seeing our carriage at the Presidents— went there & got in. Mrs. P[resident] asking me to wait until she was dressed— We had a pleasant chat which Father joined & (whilst I was in tete a tete with a Mrs. Crosby[1] an old denizen of these parts) they chatted on politics— & she said very loudly to be heard every where in the room— she regretted the making up of the family quarrel— that there was not a member of the Cabinet who did not stab her husband & the Country daily except my Brother— she did not know anything about Politics— but her instincts told her that much—

Your letter about the vote of thanks would have been answered tonight but for my engagement with Violet Jones—[2] & I put the query to myself which you would like me to attend to first I thought Violet— so called for her— & took to the patent office & after long waitings in the commissioners anterooms attained an entre & a profession of promises of work for her— she seemed very grateful & sent you a profusion of compliments to your wife— She looks & talks very well— says they heard a few days ago from Leesburg— all well Mrs. Knapp was here lately to get her rents and other comforts of life Mrs. Cazenoe [?] was with her & as they passed Chantilly[3] found it burnt to the ground— but bore it quietly saying so many were worse off in the deaths of husbands & children that they could only be thankful as all of her brothers so far had been spared to them— Violet asked me to go see Revd Mrs. Style as she was a widow Washington—

I got the enclosed from Nelly & as it gives a pleasing acct of the children— I thought it would gratify you to see it I always get more thanks than I earn— No letter from Frank— as the accounts are telegraphic we have no right to expect a letter before Friday or Saturday— Minna gave us an account of a Rebel Mail taken by DuPont & sent to the Dept— Mrs Davis & Jeffs photographs were in it— she looking more coarse & ugly than I thought it possible for her to grow— thick lips gross nose— looked almost *contraband*— Jeff's emaciated & thinner than ever— she Mrs D writes for laces patterns & etc— & Mr. Benjamin tells his daughter to tell Mrs. Slidell[4] to write to Mrs. Davis— as "she sighs for her letters—" many letters in cyphur & to Prince Murrat—[5] it seemed to have been gathering up at Charleston for a chance a long time as some business letters were dated 12 Sept & down to the day of sailing— There were great quantities of business letters— Tilly Emory was sent for at No 6 to enjoy the insight in Dixie Many letters containing news of friends were sent to them— Mrs. Sumner[6] got one from her daughter— I wrote to Nelly last night & always write regularly once a week

Blair has been helping Uncle Dick dig in the grapery today got mad with Becky for saying this was not his home— any how til my Papa comes back He squeezed me with all his might to wake me this morning— & laughed when he said— I meant that for Papa I want to see him so much— so does yr Lizzie

Your assurance about the Minnesota was comfortable I dread Merrimac No 2— never *never* be suprised

1. Catherine A. Beale Crosby was the widow of John Crosby, whom she married in 1820. She lived on the southwest corner of Third and C streets.

2. Violetta Lansdale Jones, unmarried daughter of Gen. Walter and Anne Lucinda Lee Jones.

3. Chantilly, near Fairfax Court House, was the home of SPL's cousin Cornelia Turberville Stuart. It was only a mile from SPL's boyhood home, Sully.

4. Mathilde Deslonde married John Slidell in 1835.

5. Probably Prince Lucien Murat (1803–78), first cousin of Napoleon III and son of the former queen and king of Naples, Caroline and Marachel Joachim Murat.

6. Hannah W. Forster married Edwin V. Sumner in 1822. Their daughter Mary Heron Sumner married Armistead Lindsay Long in 1860. Long resigned from the U.S. army to join the Confederacy and was R. E. Lee's military secretary.

Silver Spring   January 17, 1863
Dear Phil   Father has been in such agonies about Frank & affairs generally that I have not pressed on him our personal matters as I would otherwise have done but I think I can do so now as he is from under pressure now about Frank— from we got letters— they are meant for *use* & are written in excellent temper but shows up *the management*— ably— Morgan was ordered to lead his division— but was nowhere consequently the Rebels who seemed to know the orders not seeing Morgan reported him *dead* but this is not in Franks letters—[1] to Brother or Apo but she seems to have other informers— & they are all down on Sherman for every thing bad— treason inclusive Frank does not mention anything about him save the orders given by him to his Chief of the division— Franks whole correspondence report & letters are written in the most able effective style— He wore his Generals uniform & all give testimony to his intelligent courage— I must say I think that uniform was a paradful pride of which I hope he will never again be guilty I never saw my Father more absorbed in public matters— or wear a more anxious face & Yet he always speaks hopefully Mother is well again— but she too shows burden under which she moves about
I recd your No. 14— today— the first letter in 3 days— I have not been out today— the sudden change of weather gave me headache yesterday & today Blair revels in this north western winds with the zest nearly equal to that of his dog Ned— Mr. Speakman was here today & says our neighbors have again rallied to the unfinished church which is to be completed by April—[2]
I forgot to tell you that Joe says Stewarts cavalry in their late raid had a fight with our men at Chantilly— lost a Col— & a Lieut— & a shell during the fight hit some of the buildings & eventually consumed Chantilly— His Regiment is stationed at Halls farm not far from the place & some of them were in this fight— I got a note from the City about the Army of the Potomacs movements— but you will hear— by telegraph results— Mother makes me write to Betty tonight to come home She needs her children around her she says now— this is a rare confession for her tho' I have seen what a constant pleasure our Boy has been to her We go to Church tomorrow as it is my Sunday Ever your devoted Lizzie

1. Brig. Gen. George Washington Morgan had not been killed, as EBL explained on January 20: "Father got a long letter from Frank last night— Morgan was ordered to go with him— but stop short at the first rifle pits— & Frank had only 28 hundred men who followed him— He says since the concentration of Rebels they will require—

more troops & until they are sent— they will clear out the Arkansas & White Rivers— which you see they are doing finely—."

2. Grace Episcopal Church was located north and west of Silver Spring on land donated by Thomas N. Wilson. Additional land was later purchased from his son John C. Wilson.

Silver Spring   January 24, 1863

My dear Phil I enclose you a scrap which verifies what you say. it seems to me I would put the whole onus on Genl Dix—[1] and report the state of things to the Dept & so let it be You cannot fight our own Army & the enemy too— the root of the evil is in the War Dept— [2 words marked out] to Jeff if one may believe the report & commendations of Robt Lee— who says— his dispatches are sent thence more promptly than from Richmond— So says Harrisons intelligent contraband & that is orthodox now a days

Father is still in the city I suppose kept by Army News about which rumors are thick & I fear not good or they would not be suppressed— I had hoped to have gone to the city— but I took cold nursing Blair & was not well enough to go away from home today with sore throat as the morning was rainy & damp. but it cleared up finely afterwards & I could have gone without a penalty afterwards— Blair is very bright and well today— & has now gone all about the house— the eruption[2] is still on him thick but for that he would have mounted his good friend Jenny Lind— After the measles he seemed even stronger than before so I hope it will be now—

There are reports of enormous desertions in this neighborhood— Graves has been arrested— as conniving & aiding— also selling liquor— There is a nest of Secesh just around his shop which is indicative of his surroundings— Our soldiers all disgusted with seeing negroes pampered & in idleness & they kept with the shovel & axe in hand instead of the guns & cannon the officers with Fathers help leave protested in vain— But it does no good to growl as Frank says but we are in earnest go on to our work in good faith and the result must be right— He rejoices that he is not in this Congress— & feels it a relief to be even with Sherman—[3] Betty says it is reported generally that he is crazy in the West she travelled east under his Brothers care— who was very civil—

Marion got the news that Senator Hicks[4] went to the War Dept to claim promotion for Genl French as *a Maryland* man & *got the commission*— & took it right up to the Senate for confirmation today was eloquent about the *over-slaughing* of the middle states men— I am going to get Father to go see him about your promotion— they say he is the devoted friend of all who claim to represent Maryland— I enclose some speculation about the Missouri Senator Apo says Frank has only to say yes— to get it— Your devoted Lizzie

1. Maj. Gen. John A. Dix, military commandant at Fort Monroe, had a different view of trade regulations from SPL's. Lee's purpose was blockade—cutting off trade; Dix favored a liberal policy of allowing permits for trade.

2. Blair had the chicken pox.

3. In her January 23 letter, EBL wrote: "There is a great deal of feeling among Franks friends that Sherman exposed him intentionally & maliciously— & when I ascertained that he was selected to attack the Fort on Haines bluff & storm it I felt that it was some reason McClernands arrival change the orders & a dense fog of 24 hours delayed the attack for that time & until the arrival of McCle— who dallied on his way with his new wife Frank mentions none of this in any of his letters to St Louis or here The facts above are narrated in the St Louis papers—."

4. At the end of his term as governor of Maryland, Thomas Hicks became a Republican U.S. senator for his state, serving from 1862 to 1865.

Silver Spring   January 25, [1863]

Dear Phil   Father has returned after several days sojourn in the City with a conviction that no vote of thanks will get thro the Senate except Separately & for special acts of merit— The Committee will not report any of the names sent up from the House— now before them— This thing of Dalghrens & etc   it defeats the object of making the Admirals & makes it too cheap so say the Committee— Your chance depends upon the Capture & conduct of affairs in yr department— so far you have shown considerable administrative talent— this is the purport of the talk to Father at the Dept & in the Senate—[1] I told him what you said about the trade— And he says he will begin the attack & go right away to the P. & the Dept— & Congress   that it is an unpardonable crime to have the blockade defeated by Army management— & etc— So you had best write him something explicit— & short— if you approve of his proposed course—

He blesses the storm that stopped the late military moves instigated by Halleck & without anything feasible in the plan— & countermanded here— Father is very cheerful— says Frank was with Steele[2] in the capture of the Arkansas Post— The condemnation of Porter is Father thinks a blow at McClellan who is very clear of blame by his telegrams & subsequent urgent letters to Porter— whose bad temper betrayed him— & has made him odious to the whole Army of the Potomac & did much to impair the usefulness of McClellan— to whom he was a very incubus— He has the power of making devoted personal friends— & many many bitter enemies— Nothing achieves the last like the imperious bad temper of which he is possessed—

Today is my day home— Since Blairs illness I cannot be far away from him He enjoyed the sunshine of Saturday morning on horseback the first time he has been out & my first walk & I took it with a gratiful spirit— in every sense— for I never have been so alarmed about Blair since his birth as I was all day Monday—

I see the Secesh report Merrimac No. 2 a failure so they said about No 1— Merrimac— I sincerely hope it is a failure & has to be kept afloat with the help of scows for I only pray you may have no no more dangers to encounter & if you could now come back to me well, & contended in your feelings, my heart & pride will be fully satisfied & God spares to us our boy in vigor & health we will be joyfully happy— This morning— he is full of song & has now no trace of illness save some of the eruption on his limbs & face— He has written to you almost daily— but I had misplaced his billet doux they are hurrying for church Ever yr devoted Lizzie

1. In her January 27 letter, EBL commented: "I see no chance for your promotion— without further exposure & so far as I am concerned promotion cannot pay me for that—." Two pages later she explained, "I do not intend by what I have said any affected depreciation of honors or promotion— for you— I would & will do all I can to get what I feel you have earned— for I know it will add to your & my enjoyment of life— Still I will not *risk* either life or health for them—& my husband at our home & happy fills up all my dreams of enjoyment for the future."

2. Gen. Frederick Steele commanded a division of Sherman's army and captured Arkansas Post or Fort Hindman, Arkansas, fifty miles up the Arkansas River. Frank's brigade was part of the expedition.

Silver Spring   January 28, [1863]
Dear Phil Blairs sympathies are excited today for little Henry who has taken the Chicken Pox from him— & he is as ill tonight as Blair was on Monday. altho' I had all the remedies at hand & induced Nannie to apply them promptly which was not done in Blairs case as we did not know at first what was the matter with him— this disease is as severe as the measles but Blair has got over it well So we have reason to be thankful not only that he is well again but that he gets over these childrens ailments so sturdily— It is a great comfort to me & but for some imprudent eating on the day before he was taken I believe would have had not even one day of suffering I got him a real wood saw today— the one you bought is used by one hand & I fear using one hand will enlarge the right shoulder as is often the case—

Hookers appointment is the theme on the topis today— I find consolations in it—[1] one is that— altho Sumner & Franklin are both brave & good they are good soldiers— but are not poets or generals— so a turn in the wheel may as in lotteries turn up a General— we are certainly in search for one— Hooker may surprise the world as did Genl Taylor & Jackson— secesh one I mean who was considered in times past a stupid bore— beyond endurance— But he like Burnside— McClellan— Franklin & Lee was always religious— Burnsides gave our little Church a hundred as he passed & said its unfinished condition which has shamed the people so that it is now in the hands of the workmen to be finished by the first of April— I hope Mrs. Crittenden will pay up by that time & enable me to pay my quota as well as my dues to Dr. May & etc—

I met a Miss Dunwick today she had dined on board of the Minnesota &

seemed surprised & made big eyes— when I claimed you for my husband— She assured me you were charming & etc & she had tried her best to get a bouquet to send you when she returned your wifes cloak & she evidently pitied you in your choice of a wife— but she need not pin any hopes on my pale wan face of today for the anxiety I had about our darling has added to the wrinkles— which fresh air & exercise will soon flush over tho they never go— She is staying at Brothers— Mr. Joseph leaves tomorrow— Betty will not go I think & hope

29th As you have seen more of this huge storm than I have you know just that much more of what has been *going on* We are all well & snow bound for the next week— I have just a chance to send this & say we are well & that I hope the iron clads are not off 'ere the storm commenced Your own Lizzie Father said to Virginia Fox today that he put all his hopes now in the Navy & she says Fox feels beligerant towards Greely for his attacks on the Navy— Ever yr affectionate Lizzie

1. On January 27, EBL commented: "I regret Genl Hookers appointment still it may do— for he has the gift— of appreciating clever men & maybe to use them— if so he will get along & well— but I think he lacks every thing but courage—."

Silver Spring   February 5, 1863

Dear Phil   It snows again & that is our only event of today— except that our sick are better— Alick is out of danger— I do hope the M.Cs who want Negro Soldiers would undertake to make them They are however the best population to give over to be food for gun powder if it saves better men it is something gained—

Blair is quite well— but looks pale— & shows in his face the sickness from which he has suffered more than ever— but his spirits are fine & so is his appetite. He watches at the window his dog— & tis pitiful to see by his face— how he yearns to frolick out doors— but for some days he has not asked to go out— Father is more than ever devoted to him— thinks there never was "a fellow with a better head or heart—" I am afraid to let him go out in this bitter weather after his cold which he took in my eagerness to get him out

I feel sorry for Mr King but have expected it[1] these Northern people will never send men here as Senators again unless they live in a way to support the dignity— I hear a great deal of about the Southern Senators style of living— aiding them to carry out their policies of treason procuring for them foreign sympathy Gen Morgan[2] is enormously rich & has lived in grand style in Albany— besides he is not ultra— on the negro— he says he is for white men— & any benefit the black one may get is only incidental in the efforts to serve his own race— his politics are more in unison with Fathers if it were possible than Mr K who for the last year has associated with the Ultras—

& I think fatally for himself   Mother says Henry waits so good morrow to you   Your affectionate Lizzie

1. On February 4, EBL noted: "I am sorry to see our friend Preston King is laid upon the shelf— It is a sad fact that our ablest & purest men are thus treated." On February 12, she reported: "Father says Preston King is very cheerful— knows he was defeated by Seward & Greely factions as he was an appendage to neither—."
2. Edwin Denison Morgan of New York was a wealthy merchant and financier. Governor of New York, he was given the rank of major general so that he would have political and military authority. Resigning as governor, Morgan took his seat in the U.S. Senate in March 1863.

Silver Spring   February 10, [1863]
Dear Phil   Instead of rest I expect you will be pushed into more active duty— Cannot you now be relieved for a little leave just to get rid of your cold— from which every body has been suffering— Blair had really a month of sickness— with about five or six days of out door life— I took a cold nursing him— & I am yet affected by it & every servant has had a turn two of them quite ill— but Alick was result of a drunken frolic— Nothing helps to shake of these influenzes like a change of air—

I know as you do by this time that the 9th Corp of the Army of the Potomac are now in your waters— if Col Dutton of the Connt 21 Regt in command of Brigade calls to see you be civil is a special crony of Marions & Bettys— Genl French is also in that Corp. I hear of these movements actually taking place through these sources   there is no mention yet in the papers of it— I have no doubt that Hooker will take to the base I mentioned in my last to you—[1] & this is a complete triumph for McClellan—

Hales programme is not Fox's & he has warred on the Dept. & the Administration from the beginning— Father made no application— simply an application for "information—" I took instantly your idea— that if you were to be relieved— the sooner the better for your health tho I did not say a word of the sort & only expressed eagerness— to see & have you home which as an utterance of my own feelings I have a right to speak out & to get my hope realized was the information I sought—[2] it is going deep into three years since we took up our home & it is a weary long time to me— tho there is much in my surroundings to make me bear it without complaint I know few in this wretched war have as much to be thankful for consequently I scarcely dare to murmur— It would delight you to see the zest with which Blair enjoys out doors again— he is very well indeed & I look at his bright face with great thankfulness & joy—

I have read the pastoral Letter of the Southern Bishops with great delight— Dupont report is a little let up—[3] Father says the Bishops talk for European

Buncombe— but I believe they are beginning to see the truth— Violet Jones says that there is no watchfulness about intercourse— personal between here & Leesburg & Winchester but goods are stopped— I recd a letter from Apo— She growls hugely— against the Cotton Speculators— German & Curtis— Frank writes from Vicksburg— & cheerfully— But Apo is now dreadfully troubled now he is not kept at Arkansas Post where I hoped he would be kept   Blair sends his love & says he is going to ride Jenny Lind to day   Ever yr affecate Lizzie

1. On February 9, EBL had written: "There is a talk of gradually moving the P. Army to your region— & from what I know of Hooker via Alfred Pleasonton last summer I think it very probable—."

2. On February 8, EBL wrote: "I read your letter to Father— & then gave it to him to read— (I believe the first time in my life) He went immediately to the Dept— & Mr. Fox told him that it did not & should not be applied to you— saying civil I think just things about you. But— for your information & my own hope of getting an honorable discharge I asked Father to go & inquire about this matter."

3. In a letter to Welles, January 28, 1863, Du Pont reported on the attack at Fort McAllister, Georgia, by the ironclad *Montauk*. He reiterated his belief that despite their imperviousness to attack, ironclads were not good offensive weapons and could not capture a position without the aid of troops.

Silver Spring   February 11, 1863
My dear Phil   Your's of the 9th is recd endorsed "acknowledge reciept of this—" Your advice about collecting from the Crittendens[1] I dont know how to follow for the Thomsons deposited their rent & announced to me the fact always— I never asked for a cent or jogged them in any way directly or in-directly   fortunately for my comfort   I did not need it— I suppose they the C's will pay up when they have next month— & I can get along— without jogging them until then— It has struck me they will expect me to take their furniture— which I will not do— for I dont want anything they have got for when I do furnish a house I want all in keeping— & even if of a cheap kind— it looks well so I shall not go in when called to inspect I have an experience— but I do not repent my purchases of Mrs. T. (save that it has thrown me little behind hand in my money matters) but they are simple & just what I like—

As to the Acting appointments— you know all about that long 'ere this— No application of any sort was made by Father or me— I would as soon cut my hand off as to interfere with such matters without distinct written orders & all the applications written out by your self— such as you made out when going to the East Indies— when I asked you to write down exact instructions when & what to do & say   I have no fancy for responsibility which affects others— & never under take them without very many sober second thoughts—

Betty has just been pitching into me to take her out to Balls & parties with Miss Gibbs— They are another sort of responsibility which I decline quite as positively— Nothing so disgust me with these women as to see them on the pad for pleasure seeking— with husbands, Fathers, brothers in jeopardy of life & limb every hour of their lives— on the land or sea— They say it is very selfish in me not to sacrifice myself for their pleasure— I think so too if it was a decent sacrifice of self— to perform some duty of charity & necessity but to join the grassy, fast, crew in Washington is not to my fancy— or feelings.

We had a visit today from a Mrs. Beck— the widow of Dr. Beck who so persistently sought Mary Boswell— He died his estate to his own family as he had no children— & her an annuity of $5000 a year She leaves tomorrow to join the Army of the Potomac as a nurse— she is plain & robust— is full of energy & says one cannot expend strength or money in a more noble cause— her zeal was really cheering— I told her if she needed comforts for her sick— that she must let me know how I could help her here— but could only do second hand duties for the cause as my duty was at home to my husband child & Parents but I was too feeble a woman to be a nurse— but I gave her all my experience derived from the Orphan Asylum— where we have had bt 20 & thirty sick at once— for abating illness— by systematic cleanness & order— & for which the City Doctors pay us great compliments we had— the small pox— you know last winter & they say managed it with great success— out 17 ladies three volunteers to go there & carry out the orders of the Board— which they did for three months Mrs Harris Mrs Merrick & Mrs Brown[2] & I think them heroines—

No news save the Newport news movement which is known to every body in Washington & yet not in the papers[3] Since it is only the 9th Corp to operate in N.C. & to be commanded by Burnside But another corp was shipped Monday— but you dont like cross letters— so good bye Blair is a gay fellow among the girls— Ever yr affecate Lizzie

1. On February 6, EBL discussed the problems created by the Crittendens' failure to pay their rent: "After this month if the Crittendens do not pay up I shall need money for my current expenses of washing & servants wages— & this month the Taxes & insurance will be due on the city house— I have recd no notice yet of either— I paid them I think in Feby last year."

2. Mrs. Charles Brown, wife of Dr. Charles Brown, lived at 275 Pennsylvania Avenue.

3. To aid in threatening Richmond, on February 6 the Ninth Corps under W. F. Smith was moved to Newport News from the Army of the Potomac.

Silver Spring　　February 17, 1863

My dear Phil The snow storm blockaded my movements— so much that I cannot flatter myself with much hope of seeing you when we reach the city but

I know that if I wait the roads will only grow worse—[1] & besides the sooner Father does his part of looking after the vote the better— I feel both hopeful and anxious about & spent a very disappointed restless day for it was a struggle to leave you even with the thought that my presence would only embarras your movements and that I ought not to risk the care of Blair with anybody— with this croup tendency which I hope he will grow robust enough to throw off before another winter—

We had the Quaker & I believe that nobody rejoiced at his detention but Blair who he amused with hunting yarns— for which happiness to the boy I am thankful   besides— I am so afraid of being a "*respector* of persons that I always require of myself more scrupulous politeness for the plain rather than those of the loftiest pretensions— & even in this I fear there is some pride

I have got a list of the Senators & I will give it to Father & get him to speak to a majority of the Senate—[2] if you are hopeful in the matter which I expect a note from you will indicate today— I think Father from the snatches of the talks I have had with him today is *very* hopeful of his plans. There is one small point— which is agreeable to me— Frank does not blame Sherman for the Vicksburg failure— I see that Porter blames Col De Courcy—[3] the man who Frank so indignantly rebuked on the field— & who volunteered to lead the attack— so said Frank in his letter— He is a foreigner— of vast pretension & Gas— but it seems it gave out when it came to the battle field   Father talked over the vote today before Mr. S. who wrote *a good letter* to Govr Hicks— who he knows well   I must write to Nelly & Fanny to night as they will expect their bulletins— Your own devoted Lizzie

1. The next day EBL wrote: "I went to the City today over bad roads & etc to get another look at you but you had gone & was on your ship again 'ere I started on my fruitless errand— & when on my return home I '*weathered*' an easterly storm of rain & wind I felt provoked that I had not persisted in my purpose the day before & had better roads & a better time altogether."

2. Naval law required a specific vote of thanks by Congress before an officer could be promoted. Elizabeth and her father were unflagging in their efforts to lobby members to support a special resolution including Lee. On February 24, 1863, EBL stated: "I will write to Mrs. Trumbull a note saying all I can to get her to interest her husband in your behalf since I am blockaded by snow & you are returning the compliment to the Rebels—."

3. Col. John F. DeCourcy led a brigade in George Morgan's division. Blair's brigade had been detached from Steele's and ordered to Morgan. Both DeCourcy's and Blair's troops led the assault on the Chickasaw Bluffs, and Blair felt DeCourcy's troops had not performed well. Sherman agreed.

Silver Spring   February 20, [1863]

Dear Phil   Father is still in the city so I cannot report progress of "the thanks" he said when he left that he meant to see *all* the Senators & give each a talk with whom he had acquaintance or influence Mr. Thompson called to see about Morris Clagetts case[1] but Father was off & on his return at eight olk at night— he found Father still in town by him we got the evening papers so Mother & I are posted without the mail except I recd no letter but that I did not much expect until tomorrow— I see the Nahant[2] sailed just before the storm which was a great folly in any sort of a vessel

Our snow is nearly gone tho ten inches deep two days ago— but we have had as much rain since as snow— Mother and Blair growl at the confinement to the house— but he is merry as a cricket & ranges from the garret to the cellar

You see the program in the Herald—[3] some people dont keep secrets well— There were eight or nine persons at dinner with Father on Sunday last who after the talk sent Father to bring Brother to dine with the party Govr Dennison is expected to day or tomorrow— I shall go right after him & if you second thoughts are at all helpful you had best give the benefit of them in a letter[4] to him which Ill present & tell him how much we were tempted to take him at his word— & I to redeem my promise to call for him whenever we thought he could help us— & etc— Father says he has a great mind to tell him he needed him on this point as well as for others— Father had an appointment at 12 today in the same house as that of Sunday.

I wrote to Fanny today & to Horace about the wine— Dont take fright at my newspaper scraps— but I have no fancy to have you behind hand in political men or facts— a la Halleck and yet I hate to have you weary yr eyes over newspapers— I hope you will use some younger eyes about you at any some that have taken fewer observations & done less work— Never were a pair of grey eyes more taxed than yours have been— the day is bright & clear & our little one is all joy at the idea of out doors Ever yr affectionate Lizzie

1. Morris Clagett was a private in the First Virginia Infantry and son of Darius and Providence Clagett. Maurice's sister was Mary Ann Clagett, wife of Smith Thompson of New York. On February 13, EBL reported: "Mr Thompson came too to get Father to help him to [get] a permit for his wife to go see her Brother Morris Clagett who was taken prisoner— he says he returns a prodigal son— certainly from all accounts he is naked enough to look the part— His sister seeks to see him & to give him clothing—."

2. The ironclad *Nahant* arrived at Savannah on March 3.

3. On February 20, the New York *Herald* reported on its front page that there was expected to be an attack on Charleston and Savannah.

4. On February 25, EBL explained that she had another use for her husband's letter: "Govr. D. is not here & not a word of response from him but I have cut off his name at the bottom of your well written letter & will take it to the Senate now & use it to the best of our abilities—."

Silver Spring   February 26, 1863

Dear Phil   I would have gone to my rest last night more content if I had written to you after I got home but fatigue & having naught to say particularly
encouraging reconciled me to do so & when waked in the night by the storm
still going on— I felt it was just as well—

I went with Father to the Capitol & he was so *bitterly opposed* to my seeking
conference with the Senators— that I gave it up upon faith & not conviction.[1] that is, it is right for a woman to obey— at the same time I was egotistic
enough to think I could get things done he could not— Still my going had this
effect he saw & had long talks with Grimes— Sedgewick— Doolittle to whom
he gave the paper intended for Gov. Dennison & who is keen for the thanks.
Hicks to act on Kennedy— Olin[2] & others in the House— & I never saw
Father more active or earnest about anything— Grimes on the thanks first said
that he was entirely governed by the Dept & that is utterly opposed to them—
then said Father here is their voice showing the recommendation & I have just
talked hours with Mr Welles— & he is violent on the Course pursued by the
Committee— He smiled & said in spite of all that— he must reassert what he
had said when Father said he did not like to contradict him— but there was
certainly something very unlike fair play about it all through & then went on
to urge his own views & closed by asking him not to let Farragut swallow up
all the Missippi   it was rather much for one little man when the Sounds was
thought enough for 3 bites altho it was but a cherry when compared with the
others— Father had an audience of Senators— who joined him & told Grimes
he would have to answer that on the floor for it seemed to them conclusive—[3]
Father said it was all good humored— & he thought G. looked less grim— &
as he *runs* the thing (so said Sedgewick who he consulted)— who said it was
impossible to get at the matter save thro him— So Father & Trumbull & King
have done their best on him

Father is sanguine of one or the other plans getting thro' & has men pledged
in both Houses to help it— The storm makes it impossible for him to go
in again today as he is not well he always gets a back set when he stays at
Brothers either the furnace fires or something makes him invariably sick— He
is now writing a statement for Govr Hicks who requested it which Ill pack off
with this—

Blair & I are very well My jolting did not hurt me indeed I took to the Cars
& my feet over the worst of the road on our return for if my back could stand
it— my nerves could not for frequent upsetting has upset them completely— I
got a letter from Horace who says Edward Etting has none of Uncle Joes wine
But there is "*some very* good in Horatios hands for sale   Your affecate Lizzie

1. On March 10, EBL wrote: "I have not spoken to Mrs. Trumbull save to know
what had been done   Father has objected to all my projects about which I have always

consulted with him— I have visited people— & that is all I have done— & if able Ill go see Mrs Lincoln tomorrow after church."

2. Maryland Unionist senator Anthony Kennedy (1857–63); Abram B. Olin, Republican congressman from New York (1857–63) and justice of the Supreme Court of Washington, D.C. (1863–79).

3. On February 28, EBL wrote: "I hear that Mrs. Grimes is very ill— or I think I would quietly get at her altho' I hear she is a nobody with her husband which has made me pity her vastly— to be childless & & unloved by ones husband is to my mind the worst earthly poverty—."

Silver Spring   February 27, 1863
My dear Phil   Yours with Nellys enclosed— which I thought would give you better than anything a peep into Johns home came last evening— I luckily forgot to take the check with me to the city the last time I went or it would have been converted into yellow jackets[1] at the present high rates— just when Horace suggests a sale of those you have for he thinks the late finance measures are very sound & will produce a sound condition of affairs in a few months & you know he is not one of the sanguine sort— & there is plenty of money north which as yet— has been unhurt by the war save in loss of life— for laborers have come from abroad who more than fill the vacant places of the soldiers in the field— He employs a great number of men & is among those who hire thousands— so is posted on these points

Father says the Wilson track between the Carrolls & the Wilderness track is for sale & is well covered with timber   he will see what is the lowest they will take for it   he thinks the other place too far off & evidently is anxious to get that tract for Blair but fears they will not part with so few acres but he will see about it. George Riggs has bought the Wilson tract which lies along the road opposite to the Ross place— thence to Batchelors— gave $48 dollars an acre & is trying hard to get the Carroll track through Bonifant & will give $150 an acre   the Wilsons offered theirs between that place & Wilderness to Father for $50, & say George Riggs will be likely to take it— as he has not the money to buy—

I am not eager for any country place— for I want keep my room here always & cling to my Parents all the time that I can be in the Country, your profession may take you elsewhere than in this part of the world— then I follow you as long as you are not on shipboard— but a country place of our own would prevent my coming here— and as my parents are both 70 now— you can see as I have so long clung to them that I am or fancy I am very important to them they are to me— & six miles is as far as I would ever choose to go from them— but amid the uncertainties of the future which hangs over us all it is almost absurd even to utter ones dreams & hopes for the future— & my prayers have long been limited to the preservation of life & health of my dear ones— &

until Blair was sick I half forgot everybody but you & Frank to whom I must write today as he complains of being neglected by Father & Brother, so I concluded I would send him a weekly bulletin from home just as I do Nelly— Blair is playing soldier with Jim, is well & merry. in spite of the bad weather— The carriage takes this. Ever your affecate Lizzie

1. Yellow jackets were gold coins. On February 25, 1863, Lincoln signed the National Banking Act designed to create a uniform currency and national control of banking.

10

"I have thought him [Stonewall Jackson] a sort
of Cromwell only a far better man & in times to come
I think we as Nation will take pride in his heroism
even in spite of the miserable Cause
which won his heart—"

May 13, 1863

THE NORTH IMPATIENTLY WATCHED AS HOOKER prepared for the spring campaign. When it began, there was once again little reason for rejoicing. The Union defeat at Chancellorsville was only partially offset by the loss to the South of Stonewall Jackson; Vicksburg still remained untaken; an attack on Charleston failed. In S. P. Lee's command, a rebel offensive in North Carolina was beaten back, but the effort demonstrated the difficulties of army-navy cooperation. The Blair and Lee families concentrated their worries on their absent members. Frank, promoted to major general, led a division under William T. Sherman at Vicksburg. Elizabeth and her father continued to press for Phillips's promotion.

Silver Spring   March 2, [1863]
Dear Phil   Yours acknowledging the receipt of Fathers came with him on his return from the City fagged & disappointed He could not get any thing done with the Resolution because Sedgewick as well as G. was opposed to it— but he seemed relieved by your letter— I think he feels he was misled in the beginning & now that he has tried to bring up arrears he is not pleased with the result— But after much confab— he thinks his moving in the matter will show some people a thing they did not know & that these late movements will not be in the end fruitless—

The *Democrats* have taken excellent care of Franks— two commission in the Senate— Brig & Majr Genl the first has been kept back in committee by the Chairman *all winter*— There was a trap fixed to defeat him— but it was all put hors de combat— by Latham Rice Nesmith & King.[1] I rejoice in these things it convinces father of facts which I have long ding dong— in vain— & Now things are getting out— the West is the same— light[2]

A letter from Dennison saying he will be here tomorrow— he was at Cincinnati— looking after the Winter meeting[3] he writes in a glow of satisfaction— he says the people are unbroken in their spirit & purpose (He was desponding in the last visit here) & says Secesh in all its shapes here and at the south is now perfectly found out— & they are chiefly northern presidential candidates & Northern owners of Cotton estates— & are generally understood & will soon be put down— He has just come back from a tour through the state— His letter is comforting— Father did nothing in Franks matter & was ignorant— until Latham came & told Brother

I read your letter or the copy to Father— It is all right but I think its motive is little too apparent— Father did not object to that— as you ought to be on record as Old Hickory said— especially when so good

I am still nurse— send this by the messenger— the carriage can only go to the College[4] as the swamp below it is impassable— All well   Your affectionate Lizzie

1. Democratic senators Milton S. Latham, California (1860–63); Henry M. Rice, Minnesota (1858–63); James Nesmith, Oregon (1861–65); and Preston King, New York (1857–63).

2. "Light" lined out.

3. By early 1863, the peace movement in the North had gained momentum, and the label of Union party was used to unite Republicans and War Democrats. On February 23, 1863, there was a Union meeting in Cincinnati.

4. Columbian College, later George Washington University, was located on Fourteenth Street beyond the city boundary.

Silver Spring   March [3], 1863

Dear Phil   Yours enclosing Mr. G's is recieved I send it back— very satisfied with your share of it— I will take the rest of the enclosure tomorrow & go see Mrs. Trumbull & we will talk it over as to what is best to do— The weather & roads are good besides if it is not sunshine— I can stand bad weather better than anybody I know among womankind Tomorrow is my Asylum day so I will have two things to go for— which is just as much as I can accomplish— for the carriage can only go as far as the College & from there we have to take the cars— & when it has stormed— the roads along that lane are dreadful also—

Father says that Fox & Welles both together told him— that they intended to keep in your present position— & that the Resolution repealing the qualifying thanks would give you a hundred competitors where you have now none— if you take Wilmington & none other will have the opportunities of doing so but you— that done & you are without a rival— I can see that there is a good deal to be considered that reconciles me— when these people are so plain spoken to Father— & that is the good result of these late movements on your part   I have read your confidential letter to Gideon— only to my Father & he will keep our council

There are rumors about Vicksburg which make me shiver & shake but I keep up a stout look here— for Mother's anxieties about Frank are hard for her to bear— I never saw her struggle more with her feelings She said to me "dear child I now better appreciate your agonies last summer—" Then I thought if I ever could see & have you near me again I would never murmur anymore— & I will not if you will only take good care of your health— go ashore & walk about on deck regularly. Nothing in country & all this world offers compensates me for your health— it is far more essential to my happiness & enjoyment of life than my own health & this I say from experience for I have been ill & yet happy   I believe there never was woman more happy than your invalid wife except your well one— when my husband is home with   Your affecate Lizzie

Silver Spring   March 4, 1863
My dear Phil   Your's & G.V.F.'s[1] confidential are received & I keep it to read to Father, who we expect home today   he went in yesterday to give a last try in our affairs— Franks affairs are through winningly last week & that without difficulties from any but *our peculiar friends*— about whom they got warning via the Democrats who with the aid of Mr. King was put right 'ere Father knew about it— Mr. King & the those Democrats making a majority of the Committee. Old Wade too is devoted to Frank—

As to our affairs— let come what you seem to think the worst & it will be no ill wind to Blair & me— at the very idea of getting possession of you again we are fixing up our home— he promises to saw all our wood, to plough with his Donkey— & to do divers other useful things— he went to bed full of our future domestic joys & plans— & no matter where you locate them, with you & him well & contented I shall greet my 20th wedding day rejoicing in the good gifts I recieved on my first one Whatever you decide to do will have my hearty sympathy & assent for I know it will emanate from the truest sense of honor & duty—

I went to the Asylum & to see Mrs Trumbull she looks badly had no news to tell— I talk our affair over she was all cordiality but— the storm started me home as I was in an open carriage. but I did all you desired— but not all that I had planned— Walter has been sick— but is now recovering— has leave until 18th inst when they start for their abode in Chicago which will hereafter be their home— they give up their residence in Washington—

I find everybody blue as indigo about the Indianola—[2] if DuPont fails now— our navy will fall into the Army rut I might almost say disgrace with the Country— Mrs Merrick burst out on me with politics today & declared I should not have a servant I was enquiring about because I was an abolitionist I did not deny the impeachment & accepted it as a compliment. However when parting with the Board she said please Lizzie call to see me next time you are in the City I want to talk a long one too with you— I dont have half the amusement in the Board as of yore for I have to attend to business every moment of the time—

This is my night for writing to John & Nelly for he insists my letters are to him too— which is very kind in him— Ever your devoted Lizzie

1. Gustavus Vasa Fox.
2. The Union ironclad *Indianola* surrendered to rebel forces on the Mississippi River. On February 26, she was sunk.

Silver Spring   March 5, 1863

Dear Phil   Father says the resolution has passed so there is no limitation about Admirals— but according to Fox that gives you a hundred Rivals where you had *none* before—[1] Now I must get your appointment if I can and shall go to the City today to see about it— I think I will go straight to the President & Secy— altho Father & you both will be angry with me for doing so—[2]

Father says there are forty cords of wood on the land per acre— which sells on the ground for $3 a cord— there are two lots of land between the Wilderness & Carrolls land 160 acres each— which can be bought for $50 an acre— the pine wood cut off— stumps & brush rot in three years— One of these lots is partially cleared— Bell's old cabin is on it— the other is entirely woodland— both lie on Sligo— & they belong to Mr. Wilsons daughters— & was bought by Old Wilson from Roberta Youngs Father or Mother I do not know which— for $3 an acre There is all I know about the matter and I only mention it as I knew it was for sale & you wrote about buying land above here—

I have no desire to accumulate for Blair for whom I have but one fear that he will be good for nothing if he is not reared to rely on himself & it is my daily lesson that he is to do so when he reaches manhood & to serve me & work for us in his boyhood I reverse all of John's talk I am proud of the wood which he now saws for Mama which warms me in spirit as well the body— You may see in this selfishness— & self-indulgence— & may be I deceive myself about the matter— but I think I am honest & earnest in my desire to make our boy a good boy and man as far as it is my power— & not to spoil him by too much care— notice or money. but still to let him see & believe in the devoted love which I think we both feel for him— I do not [think] it makes children either good or happy to be unloved— Brothers idea of wholesome neglect is not in my theory at all he has thrown away the heart of one child by it—[3] to me such a loss would be irreparable

Father says the roads are dreadful Still I must go see about things but will act only after consulting him for I know his heart is entirely with me— Frank as I told you was sent to the Senate last week as Majr Genl

A letter from Cousin Anne gives us dire accounts of things in Ky— Wright is absorbed in the luxury of his position— lives in Cin[cinnat]ti & takes it easy—[4] West Point seems all the time on the enemy's side as that is the side for an aristocratic Govt Your affectionate Lizzie Aunt Becky is 82 today

1. On March 3, Lyman Trumbull argued against the necessity of a vote of thanks from Congress in order to attain the rank of rear admiral and offered an amendment to that end.

2. On March 10, EBL wrote: "Now I want to ask them [Senators who are friends] to go do it— but Father & you both have objected to my doing so— I intended to go today to see Mrs. Lincoln— but cant go in a storm— . . . . I hate to lose a thing deserved by mawkish pride—."

3. When Montgomery's first wife, Caroline Buckner, died in 1844, he allowed his parents to adopt his daughter Elizabeth (Betty) Blair.

4. Horatio G. Wright commanded the Department of the Ohio with headquarters in Cincinnati.

Silver Spring　　March 7, 1863

Dear Phil　I was too tired to write last night— The efforts I made to get a copy of the bill for 2 days were futile but they all say the resolution is passed. Father went to see Mr. Welles & asked him if the amendment had passed which allowed him to appoint admirals from among those who had not recd thanks— He said he believed it had but was not positive　Father said if it had been repealed I hoped he would see that my son in law was not overslaughed as Admiral　Mr Welles replied I will take care of that— Other things passed between them in regard to your fitness for the place　yr claims for past service— yr political affinities with Mr. Welles & my Father to give adhesion to the principles of your grandfather— & the prospect of the service immediately before you— & etc— His manner was extremely cordial— friendly & assuring— The conversation was to Father very satisfactory & no one has your promotion more at heart— as he says— truly.[1]

Frank's Maj Genlship is a temporary thing—[2] politics being really the ambition of his life whereas your profession is yours　Father dined with Mr Dudly Gould [?] who remarked that there was a fine Whitworth Cannon in the Custom house at New York & had been for weeks bought by Americans abroad & presented to the Government— it was made for the Brazilian Govt & *some* of our people heard of it gave an advanced price & the owner sold it to them & makes another for Brazil　Father suggests that you try & get this gun as the rencontre with Sands shows they have one of them at Fort Caswell　Mr Baily[3] promised me to get a copy of the law for you   he may send it to you— if I get it I will forward it— I paid him my insurance which is out today   I thanked you in my heart that I had the money when I was called upon to pay— Ever yours affectionately Lizzie

1. On March 10, EBL informed her husband: "Mother & I have urged Father to go in & attend to things himself— which he refuses to do— he cannot beg promotion at the Bar of the Senate— for his children— he has done his part & what is better Frank & Phil have done their's well & faithfully— & if rejected & refused promotion it because of jealousy which his presence & perserverance for it, will only increase So— he wont go— He says he asked the Secy. for your appointment & he considers it promised—."

2. On January 31, EBL had commented on her brother's rank: "Franks was made by Mr Lincoln proper— versus underling and ultras—."

3. Mr. Bailey was part of the publishing firm of the *Congressional Globe*, Franklin Rives, Jefferson Rives, and George A. Bailey.

Silver Spring   March 13, 1863

Dear Phil   Father returned with a note from Mr. Sumner saying—

Senate chamber   Thursday 5 o'clk Frank is this moment confirmed as majr Genl on the ayes & nays—Yeas 28. Nay 7.

C.S Addressed to Brother & endorsed "Immediate—" & "Gallop"   Father would not come down one atom on the Frémonts— sent a letter in yesterday to Lane[1] saying that he shrunk from a court martial (which Frank courted)— if it had not been covered by the Dept from its investigation that his fate would have been that of his instrument McKinstry[2]

These Ultras then wanted to compromise on the Brigadier which it seems was not passed   Father said Majr Genl or nothing & so he stood— Lane came out to know if that was his or Franks words— "my own only—" for Frank was too far to consult— He thought Frank would not attempt to dictate to the Senate in that style— & etc— Father did [not] care to risk his son any more— he could do the Country even better service in Congress & save him great anxiety & etc this will show you "the style" of the affair He came happy in all things save the result in New Hampshire over which Miss Ellen exulted very much to his disgust— I tried to show him how good might grow out of the evil but— he is not satisfied even with that view of it— He says he wrote to you about your affairs which satisfies me very much as the election does him—

I shall try to get the comfort of church today so must close this & be off— Blair wants to go with me to have his musket mended but Ill send that by Becky as this is her week for a city visit— He is more than ever pleased with his musket since a soldier told him it was as good as his— (one of the Austrian guns & purchased by Frémont— He took his toy dump cart to be mended by Jimmy Reynolds— As Uncle Dick says its time be getting things ready for spring work Ever your affectionate Lizzie There was a big debate on Frank he was the last man confirmed so it is said

1. Henry S. Lane, Republican senator from Indiana (1861–67).
2. Gen. Justus McKinstry, while quartermaster under Frémont's command in Missouri, profited enormously from his office. He was dismissed from the service January 28, 1863.

Silver Spring   March 17, 1863

My dear Phil   Yours of Friday reached me last night— & there was one word of comfort in it— that is you were going on shore for exercise— If you would walk the deck for a little while each morning— say an hour or even half a one you would do your business quicker & better for it & then go later regularly on shore for some miles— & keep well— I know you so well that if I had but one motive & that to get your work done & well— I would give you this advice— You never work well with "cold feet & a hot head—" nobody can how I sigh to be at your side to take care of my husband whilst he is caring so little for what is most precious to me—

If the weather permits— I shall go tomorrow to the City to take possession of the house & to get somebody to put in charge of it— As I came out of church Juliana Gales[1] advanced from the side of the pavement with a smiling face & extended hand— greeting me as "Cousin Lizzie how glad I am to meet you again I am glad too she has recovered her good temper & a more Christian spirit— so my reception of her advance was cordial We walked a few paces when she inquired for you & John & Nelly with her old time friendship— You may remember she has cut me for a year past beginning by looking me full in the face— without recognition—

My letters will have told you the result of the opposition to Frank in the Senate— You see that Genl Wright is rejected some say because of an intrigue against him by Benham, Saxton[2] & Hunter— but the tone of the letters I have seen from Ky about his inactivity in protecting that state from Raids & devastation accounts more rationally for the determined hostility of all— the Western Senators to him— An officer & one of Genl W.'s intimate friends told me that he had no option about that— but only obeyed the most minute orders in that respect from Head Quarters here— Maria Smith is excessively exercised about this matter as they are her friends & good ones too—

I allowed Blair a little run in the snow— he begged so hard for it— he put the enclosed letter for you in this envelope himself— saying it is full of talk to Papa   Mother tries to make him call you Father but he wont learn— says Papa always says Papa & I think he likes it best We are all well & ever fondly your own Lizzie

1. Juliana Lee, daughter of Theodoric Lee, married Joseph Gales of the *National Intelligencer* in 1813.
2. The Senate rejected Horatio Wright's promotion to major general on March 12. Gen. Henry W. Benham commanded the engineer brigade of the Army of the Potomac; Gen. David Hunter commanded the Department of the South; and Gen. Rufus Saxton was in charge of the Sea Island reconstruction experiment.

Silver Spring   March 19, 1863

My dear Phil   I went to the City yesterday called at the Trumbull's & found they had gone to Old Point with a Senatorial party— So I am imagining you very busy entertaining them today as they are all your friends & all of them evinced great interest in you lately—

After Church I went to see about the House— found Mrs. Coleman[1] packing up the furniture which her Father had given her to fix her up in Baltimore   one of my earliest recollections in life was the talk about her marriage to an old man for money Now she is poor with a parcel of daughters to take care of. I did not go in the house but took the car & went to shop for Mother which I got thro & then with my arms full of Bundles took the Cars for the College— where I had left the Carriage— I was a tired little woman but slept sound & am very well— Blair came with a sorrowfull face telling me "Gardner had died— a boy soldier who had played with him— He is off now with "Beck" full play again.

The city is filling with paupers & refugees from Virginia & our people think it very fine to relieve the Secesh of such burdens Of course when they bring orphans sworn to as such to the door of the Asylum I take my share in, because I am pledged never to turn an orphan away under seven years old— but I have those older & am called very cold hearted— but some of our secesh managers take care of them in some way I know— I have no idea of aiding Secesh & giving them any help to make more widows & orphans among us—

I saw on the st Clem Hill. he spoke of John's robustness— says he has grown too fat "Sitting in the house all the time reading—" Says Ellen Annie Katherine— hate the Country as much as "the dear Sharer of all his joys—" ever did & no wonder for of all the horrid places Prince Georges is the most horrid this winter   Ever your affectionate Lizzie

1. Ann Mary Crittenden, daughter of John J. Crittenden, was married to Chapman Coleman, a Louisville merchant.

Silver Spring   March 20, 1863

My dear Phil   I send you today the debate in the Senate about the resolution got through by Judge Trumbull   I think he evinced real friendship— & managed it well— but I have just talked it over with Father & he sees where it affects you injuriously— & as Mr. Welles urged the repeal— & said it was opposed *always* by him & he was overslaughed in the matter— Father says he seemed fully determined you should not be by the same influence but Father told me to night it was a matter he meant to talk over with the President— & to *follow up* until the end he most coveted was attained— He now sees the *under*current which I never could get him to believe in— before & I do so shrink from attributing unkind motives— a thing only to be guessed— never known in this world— but as I told him tonight that a known enemy should never be ignored— or treated as a passive thing when we know it could act without any sort risk in the act— *I never have had so satisfactory* a talk *on these matters* before *in my life*— So I owe something to the debate which he read to Mother & I— & she took the most animated part in the confab & did you justice with tone of kindness that was sweet indeed to me— more than it ever can be from any one else as you are both so precious to me—

I only recieved yours of the 13. today a week old— last night— it was post marked the 13— the only excuse for the delay— is that it is marked *No* 154— so they may have thought it was the House 154 & not the box But I hope the Post Office here will be better managed hereafter tho' I feel sorry for Mr. Clephane[1] (who has just married a pretty young wife) should lose the office

Did you see Genl. Frémont proposes to take command of the Negro legion—[2] I feel sorry for both— think how it must hurt Jessie— for no Southern woman could fail to feel some bitterness— & yet they may do well— but it will surprise me if they do— who knows so well the material which will compose the Legion

Blair is well— eats & sleeps hearty & goes out now very much as he used to do— the only difference is— that now I allow him to go out— in raw, damp cold indeed all kinds of weather save in a hard rain or snow— but I require him to take active exercise & then come in the house in bad weather— formerly he played out all day save in stormy days & even the snow storms were indulged in very often but *croop* has put an end to that spartan folly   Your devoted Lizzie

1. Lewis Clephane of the *National Republican* was appointed postmaster of the District of Columbia. He resigned in 1863 to be replaced by Sayles J. Bowen. He then became collector of internal revenue for the District. In 1862 Clephane married Annie M. Collins of Connecticut.

2. John C. Frémont had resigned from the army in June 1862. Since that time he had continued to try to find a command and reenter the army.

Silver Spring   March 27, 1863

Dear Phil   I felt the truth of your observation when informed to day that some gentlemen & ladies desired to meet me tomorrow to arrange as to terms for the rooms— I immediately sat down & wrote the terms— & what rooms— (the entire second story) would be rented— & added the rest of the premises— were not for rent on any terms— I'll will only furnish the office for use of this family & which I will use chiefly for my orphan asylum business— Now that Ellen has left here I have no place for that business when there is an infectious disease there as at present— besides this it be a place for the use of the family for bundles and errands At the other house now I alone am *not snubbed* now adays— Father & Mother like this plan— & I shall take good care— never to come in contact (personal) with my tenants for I have desired "all applications for rooms to be made in writing to be left with servant in charge of the house with whom prompt replies will be left—" & as to my meeting any of them I never expect to see their faces—

I will make Becky my inspector of the premises to see that they are in good order— the yard I will again have sodded & planted with roses & vines— the parlors will be locked up— I will put a bed & wash stand in the dining room for your & John's use when you are detained in the City— I never expect to be at the house an hour at a time & rarely later than 3 olk— never at night except to be with you & in summer that will not be necessary— for this will be a better place for us both— I have paid a man eight dollars to clean out the yard & basement— the oak parlor doors have iron nails driven in them & the walls are so defaced that we could never make it our home until painted & whitewashed from the attic to the cellar— & that I will not do in these times—[1] If I find things work unpleasantly— I can just give notice that I will cease to rent the rooms & at the end of any month stop it—

The oysters are there tonight & the waggon goes in for coal— & will finish hauling off the dirt piled out the premises into the ally— There is no less than one barrel two bundles— a servants cot & basket of marketting ready at 9 olk— for the waggon to bring out tomorrow—

Since Joe left for the War— I have done or had done all of the errand business of this household & at present there are no bills— (save one for mending little waggon yet at the shop so I try to serve those who shelter & give me comfort in you long long absence which grows more weary to me with each day dear & kind as this home & its inmates are my husband alone gives zest to all to life the joys of life to me This I say fully conscious that few are as blessed with as happy surroundings for which I am deeply grateful—

Evy Martin came today & Mother is especially thankful for the oysters which are to her (Mother) the greatest treat— & of late she has been without appetite & thinner than I ever saw her in my life and yet she has not been sick— Your map of N.C. came to day too— many thanks Ever your devoted Lizzie

1. On March 25, EBL explained that she expected to receive "$120 a month for the 4 bed rooms & keep for my own uses & from damage the parlor floor— & if you could see the house today you would say never rent it again—."

Silver Spring   April 6, [1863]

Dear Phil   Blair & I were caught in the storm on Saturday night— but we got home safe— Blair not even cold & he thought it great fun All of yesterday the storm continued until evening with a fury I never saw equalled— The snow is melting very slowly— & our spring is just where it was the 1st of Febuary— Meats & every thing from this cause have become enormously high up here

The President has gone to Review the Army & I expect Betty & Evy have followed him this morning— But as to the On to Richd movement that is a physical impossibility via Fredericksburg for month or more now   it is— & has been hinted for weeks that there are going down your way Old Wade told Father Saty. his service on the Investigating Committee has made him put his Fathers way of thinking— *it had converted him*[1]

I think our Dept is intensely Anxious about D—[2] Fox has grown thinner in two weeks & I never saw him look as anxious as now   he seems feel that   [3] is entering at the service of the enemy— but still says the Navy will conquer the rebellion— but of course dont quote him   he never said this to me— We are all well here Blair & Wood had a great frolick yesterday catching snow birds it was the first thing I ever saw Blair catch & kill   I confess it made me sad— I did not however utter a word to stop their boyish sport— but our boy— has ever been so averse to hurting even insects that I did feel sorry that Wood had taught other ideas— Still your comment on the hog killing kept me mum— Blair is now busy shovelling off the snow from the porches & doors— Father says is there any opening (Naval) for Ross's boy. Father got him to Newport where he failed— for want of mathematics— he is wild to get in   in the service in any way. Can you suggest one— We are all well   Your devoted Lizzie

1. On April 7, EBL wrote: "Father is reading the Report of the Committee on the War its conclusions seem very complimentary to the Navy— & to all the Armies far enough away from the capitol to escape in part its malign influences—."
2. Samuel F. Du Pont, commander of the South Atlantic Blockading Squadron, did not share Fox's faith in ironclads. He thought they did not have the offensive power to subdue a fortified position without the aid of troops. The April 7 Union attack on Fort Sumter was a failure.
3. EBL left a blank space.

Silver Spring   April 8, 1863

My dear Phil   I had a busy day yesterday— had to walk in from the College— then went to the meeting at Mrs. Gillis'—[1] had some little rest & fun there— A mulatto came in to get her children into the Asylum. I bade her be seated— questioned her civilly— Mrs Merrick broke in evidently dreading my abolitionism— saying that such cases belonged to the Committee & read over their names— I dismissed the woman saying the Committee would inquire into her case & have an Answer for her with Miss Wannall— When she left I turned to the Board & said that as we did not foster Negroes at the Asylum we could have sent the woman away instantly but for the more dignified consideration which Mrs. Merrick had thought best to give the *case*" So I got the better of Secesh that time— She took in great merriment for all laughed & she could not well do otherwise— in the course of the morning she got an opportunity to say that her Brother who is in Braggs Army writes her lately that the Rebellion would have ended a year ago but for the courage and fortitude of the Southern women—

No late news from Frank or Fanny who owes me several letters— & I would be uneasy but I know she is well from the long letters she sends through me to John—

My House is fairly under way— looks clean & cheerfull— & I hope will work well— if it dont you know it can be easy stopped The back area is again full of Water— Can you remember whether in the end or middle the drain was put— it will have to be opened & cleared out of the coal ashes— with which the Crittendens filled the whole area— Mother finds the use of the house the greates comfort to her I have her marketting— & etc brought there— her hired servants wait there for the waggon— & it is rendezvous & saves a great deal of time in running around for things— On Friday I will complete your's & Johns bed & etc when I shall get all in order but the area— I have not unpacked the china gas fixtures & etc & shall not do so. I had a great deal done to the yard yesterday & will soon have it decent again Your affecate Lizzie

1. Rebecca Roberts, daughter of John Roberts of Alexandria, married James Gillis in 1838. Mrs. Gillis was a member of the asylum board, and her husband was the superintendent of the Naval Observatory.

Silver Spring   April 15, 1863

My dear Phil   I have failed a half dozen times to mention that I stood in the Hall & received each box & bundle of our housewares[1] & have gone over the list several times & find our things all right— & the surplus boxes are only more than you have mentioned— They are to themselves under lock & key but I am going to put it under a key of a stronger kind altho they are in the pantry where John R. kept all of his drinkables & they were not a few— Our furniture was generally in good order— some things were rubbed & tarnished still I never saw stored things carpets & all in such good condition— & I shall endeavor to keep them so—

The tenants are quiet & give no trouble— & I know not the face of one of them— & only the name of one— all I do know is that that they are West Pointers & the beaux of the girls of my acquaintance. My asylum meeting there was a great relief to me as I am weary of trotting around after things when

I can accomplish so much more by having a place where I can see these ladies at a fixed time—[2] this is only needful when we have a contagion at the Asylum which was the case last winter & this year also— Mother has her oyster safe in the Ice house & ordered some for breakfast last evening I think with considerable satisfaction

I think there was a great deal anxiety felt yesterday in the City— But Father says he was with Mr. L a great deal & he said there was a disappointment as to the attack on Charleston[3] but it was very much as he expected to to be— You remember yr idea about the letters of Marque—[4] it is in process of accomplishment in the most rapid way— I see your talk of casemented guns is *now* in all the papers—

Blair is well & very happy in this bright weather & his outdoor joys— & he certainly does not spend much of time in the house save when asleep— Mr. Beale says he will send you the Tribune with some attacks on D— I rather discouraged it saying— "You thought him eminent in his specialty" it seems— Comre at the Yard wants the Bureau—

Joe Cook has been home & joins in the praises which come from all sides as to discipline— that Hooker has got up in the Army & the wonderful improvement it has worked. Joe says his crew is now double the value it was when under Heitzlman   I have a bad pen & can scarce write at all with it Ever yr affecate Lizzie

1. On March 25, EBL had informed her husband that she was moving their belongings stored at the navy yard "where they are all getting spoiled— so George Beale tells me & he says— there is now such a state of things there he can hardly pledge to keep things safe So is greatly relieved at the idea of my removing our chattels which I will do next week—."

2. On April 14, she had explained: "I am off in a few minutes to the city to attend the meeting of the Asylum Board at No 4— You dont know what a convenience this arrangement is to me— We are just now full of a Concert for the benefit of the Aslyum as it was suggested by Mrs Washington we are going in to it with unusual zeal for she is the one to pull back."

3. On April 10, she noted: "We are all under the tension— we felt during the bombardment of Fort Sumpter—."

4. Letters of marque were official government documents which allowed private citizens to seize property or attack vessels of another nation.

Silver Spring   April 16, 1863

Dear Phil   The April showers proved an easterly storm & made yesterday a house day for us all except Father who suddenly made up his mind to go to the City with Geo Beale— who called in all the storm again to let us know that Father would remain in the City & brought our mail but no letter from you so I concluded you were doing your best to help at Suffolk & in North Carolina[1] Frank raves about this scattering our troops The rule seems to divide them that may be conquered in detail—

Father had a brush with Mr. Stanton a few days ago about one of our Montgomery people who is a kinsman of John Key & to whom he gave shelter & food for a night & who he received as was proved with reluctance as he was always a Union man Stanton wanted to have him hung— the P. commuted that sentence to imprisonment & as his health is wretched & Father wanted his imprisonment shortened & so arranged as not injure his health— Father carried his point & to attain it the skirmish was sharp & long— Mr. S. very bitter Mr. Bates sat mute— as all did all the Cabinet— but afterwards thanked Father for saving the life of his kinsman— Father wrote out last night that there was no news so I still hope that Genl Foster may get out of his bad box—

We consoled ourselves with oysters— books & work in the house during the storm over which the girls rejoice as it may delay the Army a little longer— which loses one third of its men at the end of this month I did not get your letter until I had given orders about the oysters to go to Mrs. Sands Geo Beale told me of their arrival out here— & I dispatched Sam Jones immediately for them— Your affectionate Lizzie A letter from Frank gives rather a bad account of his ankle— he is to have Shermans division the 15th Army Corp— seems sorry to part with his Brigade of his own people Gives no military news the letter is to his wife

1. April brought widespread rebel attacks within SPL's command: at Washington, North Carolina; and Suffolk and Williamsburg, Virginia.

Silver Spring   April 17, 1863

Dear Phil No letter last night This only reminds me of your being overworked & that too with your neck suffering— would that I (who ought to do something for you) could have all such troubles transferred to me I think I did know how to endure well— experience years past— tho' I confess that of late few have had more to be thankful than I in way of health— I ventured to let Blair go out yesterday in spite of the dampness & drizzle but I did not enjoy it if he did

Father has great hopes of his new road which is to start on St West of the city Hall go up Smith's Spring branch 'through by Corcoran's place— then along the line of the Soldiers Home through Ogle Tayloe's place through Mosiers just east of the House— then up Piney Branch to Grammers place— thence to our Gate on the Church road to the District line— it is to be Macadamized or paved with round stone!!!!— So we wont have to walk in & out of the City after this— All the court are in favor of this & have appointed a committee to make the Survey in conjunction with an Army Engineer— Father's plan is to get the assistance of the Govt US upon the ground that it facilitates trans-portation from the Railroad Depots, to the Forts & Asylum— He staid in the City— 24 hours on this business & returned last evening quite full of his plans for the future & the success he had achieved in the Court & Committee Roads were once a hobby of yours so I thought this would interest you— especially as it will if it is a success— add to the comforts of Silver Spring—

Father says there is no news in the city Fox says the Army had moved be-fore this storm which will arrest it— & may betray to the enemy the plan of the move which they generally know in some way There is intense anxiety about Foster.[1] I hope the feint at Norfolk will not prevent reinforcements being sent to him

Yesterday & the day before have been passed by me in house keeping— Alick has gone to the field & I have a new boy of 14 or 15 to drill as a waiter slow & stupid— but I think in a few weeks will make us content to forget Vincent & Alicks existence— for he is clean & reported honest of which I am not sure as he is such a light mulatto— This comes malapropos as I want to work my garden but it helps Mother so the garden must be patient Ever your own Lizzie

1. SPL and General Foster had been planning another assault on Wilmington, North Carolina, but Foster did not have sufficient troops.

Silver Spring   April 21, [1863]

Dear Phil   I had no letter yesterday from you this added to the fact that all the Regts this side of the River were ordered yesterday morning into active service & away from these parts bag & baggage gives token of the opening of the cam-paign[1] I confess to an aching anxiety still I believe that Hooker is brave & tho without an original idea— can like some people absorb & appropriate them with wonderful facility I mentioned this trait to one of his aids in half fun by saying he & McClelland were opposites in this respect— he subsequently told Betty that this faculty was Hookers only element of success— & it is a great one in a commander— an appreciation of men & their peculiar faculties & then to use them according to their gifts— I con these things over to you as to myself to get up my hopes & keep in good cheer—

The papers talk about Merrimac No. 2 until my back aches. There are two iron clads up the James River so says the "papers" & you have only one to keep them at Bay— I take mightily to counter obstructions particularly when the idea is to keep the Minnesota[2] from being rammed & jammed— We got the papers with nothing in them of our Army movements in them & as they are all moving it was some comfort— May be as some of our leaky people are just now away the movement may be kept quiet—

Father goes in to morrow & I feel quite eager to get Fox's report on his return from New York— I am to meet Mrs. Harris to fix up the Concert affairs but if the weather continues this bad I'll have to give it up—

My affairs so far move on quietly & well at No 4 I brought Mother out two bottles of Claret yesterday— & the oysters have really done her good Upon the feeling of getting well she is quite cheerful— more so than for sometime— Our new waiter does his work & that is a great relief to us all— & I hope in a few months to make him a good servant— The girls Marion— Evy & Betty take this storm hard since the beaux are all ordered off out of the neighborhood— Blair joins the grumbling for he says he "has lots of work to do out doors" Evy says he is a real "Blair— came & gave her violets with such a tender manner—" Mother remarked— he is not all Blair my dear— he has the Lee sincerity with the Blair manner." which was a hit at Fathers late visit to Mrs Douglas— who he found reading Cicero's orations in Latin to one of the Holy Fathers looking exquisitely beautiful— & charming— She says she cannot marry without *descending* to do it & is too proud for that— Mothers comment was witty but looks hard written so Ill spare it— Ever yr affectionate Lizzie   Marion & I are both looking to your part of the world for *our* news just now— Dutton is at Suffolk

1. On April 28 Hooker's Army of the Potomac began to cross the Rappahannock, the opening of the spring offensive.
2. The *Minnesota* was SPL's flagship.

Silver Spring   April 23, [1863]
My dear Phil   I recd no letter— but am hoping to get one today. I am vastly relieved by the retreat of the Rebs from your precincts—[1] We have been exercised over Stoneman. but hear tonight he was stopped by mud & finding he could not surprise the part he was aiming for he concludes to wait for the Army which will move some of these days[2]

The tower of the Monitors are weak in the joints— the bolt are driven in & by them we lost all of our men that were lost— but you know more than I of these matters— Worden was in town sick. Father talked to Fox sometime yesterday & we have had another congratulatory confab on the subject of the experiment No. 1— & are thankful enough that you did not have it to do— So much many extravagant notions are fostered by the Country about these iron clads that any man who handles them & does not achieve all hoped will be blamed for not doing things impossible—[3]

I must go see about Joe Cook (who is in the hospital) with Birney today. his knee is injured & he will be some time an invalid   the Doctor wont allow him to be moved home at all. Mary Blair is trying to rent the Moorings which is in the most delapidated condition   I fear the Porch will soon fall down—

I send you a letter which is a sample of some of Blairs rainy day vocations— He was digging & working hard yesterday helping Uncle Dick to dig a gutter— I had to be stern with him for the first in months past— but he disobeyed me— & he revolts against a nurse's attendance & yet I am afraid of the pond— the donkey— & these little negroes without her guarding & restraining presence— I more than ever dislike the race— when I see so much ill developed at so tender an age— I allow him to play alone— all about the house— in front or everywhere I can watch him without his knowing it from the windows but out of my sight or Beckys presence I am in torture so order to let him play with as little interference as possible so he is roughing it by climbing & all such plays more than ever before— He is very well

Miss Nancys farm was valued at $50 an acre   the Clagetts sell out soon— Ever your own   Lizzie

1. On April 20 Union troops captured Hill's Point on the Nansemond River and ended the rebel threat to Suffolk.

2. Hooker had ordered his cavalry commander Gen. George Stoneman to raid behind rebel lines and force a retreat. Bad weather turned roads to mud, and Stoneman could not carry out his orders.

3. On April 26, EBL wrote: "I think the warfare for the present is one upon the resources of the south & every means to keep them from being replenished is the one that will succeed best— just now— Ironclads I think—with all the bolts started are things that will take some months of consideration— & in the meantime if I could catch several English Blockade Runners in any net of Ropes— I think I would do it & that quickly— I would carry on the war against *all* their resources— internal & external & to war on their English Allies is the way to hit them hard *now.*"

Silver Spring   *April 27, 1863*
Dear Phil   When you took me for better or for worse— you never dreamed it would be for twenty years did you?[1] Well I am quite ready for twenty more with you so I was well pleased to hear by Majr Mosses today (who saw you last week) say you were looking remarkably well evidently absorbed in business. but that you looked animated with a "clear eye, head, & complexion" I had no letter today or yesterday I expect them now *when I get them* & will only acknowledge their coming & not note the missing days— I see that the Press is answered already by the American in Balt Still when I get your letter Father will make Mr. Forney correct his correspondant[2]

It is funny to see how greedy these Army people are for praise they are too recreant to deserve— I dont talk about them— being never any the happier for condemning people— so the less I say of these people the better Things look better in the West

I have been busy gardening— Father & I planted in the Circle in front of the house today. two Ivys the Melrose & the English to grow on one tree or standard (cedar) to commemorate today— Blair is full of fun & frolic, it is exhilerating to see how he enjoys this bright weather after the week of rain—which so dampens his out door pleasures— Our spring never was more backward & there never was more to do than now so I must go as I have no news—& only talk because I have nothing else to write & I give you great quantities of that you cannot hear— for you, & the past days of our life & joys together are uppermost today in the feelings & thoughts of Your devoted wife Lizzie

1. On April 24, EBL anticipated their wedding anniversary: "Last year it was Sunday & I will ever remember gratefully what a comfort it was to me to spend all of it nearly in Church— I was then so very miserable about you— & thro' that great tribulation I found out that you were as dearer to me than you had been for the twenty odd years before— if that were possible—."

2. In pushing back the rebel attacks in North Carolina, Lee and Gen. John J. Peck commanding at Suffolk had disagreed over tactics, and the interservice rivalry was publicized in the newspapers. Lee was accused of refusing to cooperate with the army. On April 27, 1863, the *Baltimore American Commercial Advertiser* printed a retraction. On May 9, the New York *Herald* reporter admitted that he had been wrong and that Lee had indeed fully cooperated with the army. Gen. John Dix, Peck's superior, wrote a letter of apology to Lee, acknowledging his cooperation.

Silver Spring   April 29, 1863
Dear Phil   Father returned without the dispatches but in fine spirits about you— says that Fox & Foote say you are all right & that the President maugre all that Stanton could say or Dix persisted that the Gunboats were to do & go just as you deemed best—[1] I confess to some sympathy (with some of the timid & frightened down your way) in their faith in Gunboats & the Navy— & feel sure if you can help & save that beleaguered— helpless— mismanaged Army at Suffolk— you will do in spite of their greed for naval laurels as the Country is more at stake than these mere men— The situation at Suffolk & all in front & about us gives me an intense anxiety.[2]

It began to rain yesterday & I some how became so low spirited & unhappy about things that I forgot most of my city errands & had but one thought that was the battles which I felt sure were being fought— I came home & took refuge in Blair's talk & frolics— He is sunshine the darkest day to me— always meets at the door so full of joy & now so well that often sigh to give you just a good look at him— Betty laughed at his patched knees one day he said, "I dont care for the patches so they keep my knees covered—" He crawls & rolls & jumps just as he chooses without a thought of clothing any more than a young Indian & still he does not wear out more clothing than other children— that are unnursed— I want the nurse to take care of him more than his clothing— she patches however & that her care on that score

All the girls took flight into the City to hear the news— now that *the Army* has moved. I think Marion & Betty looked as sobered by yesterdays news as any couple of damsels I know— Marion about her Col— & Betty has special care of "the whole army of the Potomac" I give her own words— I confess to a tenderness for the fleet some where on the Virginia waters— So am off soon to get the news & to make some arrangements about the Orphan Asylum— There is nothing to do in the garden it is too wet to work— but tis lovely growing weather   Your own Lizzie

    1. Gideon Welles voiced his support, both publicly and privately, for Lee. His letter of April 24, 1863, to SPL was reprinted in the *National Intelligencer* on May 23. On May 14, EBL told Lee: "Your letter to General D. was received last night & was vastly praised commended & enjoyed by Father & myself   he suggested a read of it to Abe but I concluded that if he could get it done thro the Dept it would be better— at any rate I suggested this— & only a mention of facts— in conversation— so it was decided   I asked him to get at these thro F. as I think it best to keep all things of that kind as confidential— to me— & often keep back things until I seem them in print— We think you have every reason to be proud of '*the* correspondance'— I am intensely—."
    2. On April 30, she wrote: "I sincerely hope nothing will go wrong at Suffolk— the newspapers will pitch all the blame on you if there is any loop hole for it— I try not to think of these people   I feel so bitter when I do."

Silver Spring   May 4, 1863

My dear Phil   They made such an early start this morning that my letter was not ready. He has an engagement about the road— he is also to have another talk with your Secy & Fox They want *the* facts put before the public but they think anything like discord between the two services would be unfortunate—[1] when it is not unlikely that will soon have to cooperate with them on a large scale Father takes a bolder vision of the matter— but thinks it important *to you* to act entirely in accord with *them*
    Last night I was brimfull of talk to you— but dare not write it as the things prognosticated may not happen & then you too will have a disappointment— It seems that *nobody* here knows or knew Hookers plans not even the Secy or President[2] The last told Father so yesterday & was in great glee that the ene- mies pickets were for once taken by surprise & captured   they were sent up to the City yesterday All the town was agog with rumors— The same course will be dished up to you 'ere you get the truth   Hooker has as usual his trumpeter along & has sent his blessings this time to the Tribune— in which several cuts are made at Halleck via the pontoons— that word will be his sobriquet yet before he dies
    I have been hard at work trimming my roses today & am tired. Mr Smith from whom I am learning gardening more thoroughly— gave me a good les- son— We have in one week parted with winter for May nothing can exceed the beauty of the verdure & I am so charmed that the house is irksome even for rest & I am now writing on the porch— where I would of all things in this

world enjoy most a good long talk but feel stupid to when I cannot write what I wish to talk about—

The Carroll girls are now visiting Betty I find them amiable & pretty but alas there is great lack of internal resources but they have some in the shape of beaux by whom I expect to get this to the Post Office for me or it will have to await my tramp to town on the morrow when the Asylum forces me to go in— then I have to go again on Friday when my Goddaughter Violet Blair[3] is to be confirmed as the Bishop visits our Church on that day— but this is an occasion when I would leave all my work pleasures joyfully to go see

May 5. The Carroll party remained all night kept by rain The Battle[4] & its losses occupies every tongue mind & heart— They have two brothers & a brother in law in & as yet are ignorant of their fate We go to City immediately— Your letter to Genl Dix recd. last night & the tone giving me a hope of soon seeing you is delightful to Yr Lizzie

1. Lee faced a major problem in resolving differences with the army over the enforcement of trade regulations within his command. The Navy Department intended that the blockade should stop all trade. The army commander in the area, John Dix, favored the issuance of some trade permits. The conflict reached to the highest levels and involved the respective cabinet secretaries in something of a power struggle. On April 26, EBL had reported: "Father says write out the case so he can print the facts & he will see Fox then under the authority of the Dept he will publish the truth He thought some time ago that the falsehoods of the army traders ought to be contradicted that promptly always— & as you military men dont like to appear in print— He will see that the facts are published just where the lies started—."

2. On April 27, Joseph Hooker, commanding the Army of the Potomac, had moved across the Rappahannock; on May 1, the Battle of Chancellorsville began. On May 3, he was withdrawing from Chancellorsville. On April 30, EBL had reported: "I saw hundreds of ambulances moving in the Streets— but could not find out where they were going so followed them a while & saw them make for the steamboat wharves I came home with a heavy heart as there was nothing of a battle in the papers even in the second edition which I got as it was issued on the Avenue— Silence is ever ominous for us."

3. Violet Blair, born in 1848, was the daughter of James and Mary Blair.

4. The battle at Chancellorsville, Virginia, May 1–4, which was a terrible defeat for the Union.

Silver Spring   May 6, 1863

My dear Phil I returned home last night after five hours of hard work desk work at the Asylum & my bones ached for myself & thoughts ached to think how hard your life must be to have 15 hours of such labor that even divided my thoughts from the War— which is the perpetual theme of every bodys talk— Hooker, Stoneman[1] Vicksburg. at home— on the pavements everywhere— I see that Robt Brown [2] is a prisoner & I am going to the City in this rain to see him & his comforts for the Fendalls have not such a word in their Vocabulary

Fox says that the Dept has assumed all your acts or ordered them & that for the present it will be best to keep quiet— Secy is less of that opinion— but Father advises you & *yours* not do anything more in it   Father likes your correspondence with Dix it is in good temper & "uses him up effectually—"

Nobody *knew* in the City what was going on in Hooker's army—[3] or Stoneman except the President— who they say excludes the War Dept— They is the mildest form of this matter assuming in the City circles— there is an evident breach— to city observers

I am off in a few moments to see after this Godchild   by the way it may make you feel very aged but I stood god Mother yesterday to the child of a girl I have had in the Asylum— since she was six yrs old consequently it my grandchild You need not feel so old— but I claimed to be a Grandma against which Mrs. Harris protest vehemently in her own & your behalf— Ever your affectionate Lizzie

1. Stoneman had attempted to cut communications between Fredericksburg and Richmond. On May 12, EBL reported: "Our late Cavalry Raid in Virginia was as successful as anything of the kind could be—."

2. Robert Brown, son of former Mississippi senator A. G. Brown, was brought to Washington as a prisoner on May 5.

3. On May 2, EBL had written: "We sit here with almost suspended breath fearing & yet aching to know the result of the late movements at Fredericksburg. The movement so far as I can fathom it seems only a repetition of last winter's blunder— with this difference— that the Army in far better condition— everybody gives a good account of that   Hooker is not a brave but a more audacious man than Burnside."

Washington   May 8, 1863

Dear Phil   I came in early this morning to be present at the Confirmation of my God Child Violet Blair & great is my joy to see her assume the vows I made in her behalf— She is a lovely girl— & I think will prove a great treasure to us— It rains hard— & I find this good fire comfortable to sit down by to write you a few lines

I do not find the people oppressed here— the Army are in a rage with the Commander & I hear it asserted that there are many to swear to the truth of what I told you about him Yesterday [1] He was drunk all the time & that after the first days battle was unfit for duty— I saw a letter dated Monday which has just this sentence "Hooker is stretched on the grass— the Staff standing around. & the Army perfectly quiet in the rear the enemy in front within sight a line of picket in front of us—"   draw you your own conclusions from this faithful picture— This is one of the staff—

Last night Blair reminded me so intensely of a speech you once made to me that I felt as if you had spoken it over again by his mouth He sat in my lap as usual warming his feet after saying his prayers & as I wanted him to quit talking I began to sing— in a few moments— I thought he was crying & found he was doing so— at first he would not tell me— then said— "Mama you sing so sorrowful it makes me cry—" I like Billy Barlow—" Now I never told him or anybody that you thought I was saddest always when I sing— because I was ever rather mortified that my singing was painful to you— So I am now mute as a singer save when alone then I confess I have either to sing or weap—

Everybody is full of Stonemans achievements & Even Secesh admit the efficacy & gallantry of his raid— Evy Martin is to return with me this after-noon she has been staying with Mary Blair The farmers are getting alarmed about planting corn & potatoes The season continues cold much longer— the prospect will be blue— for the ground has been too wet to plough ever since Jany— Ever your affecate Lizzie   Mrs Trumbull says her son wrote her last night that 10,000 will more than cover all our losses— & more than half were the dutch racers who had evidently made up their minds to run— to revenge Sigels wrongs— for they ran 'ere a gun was fired So much for Genl Hallecks personal quarrels—[2]

1. Hooker was either drunk or shaken by the near miss that occurred when a shell hit very close to him at Chancellorsville.

2. Hooker had replaced the popular Franz Sigel with Oliver O. Howard as head of the Eleventh Corps. Over two-fifths of the corps was German, and they resented their new commander. Stonewall Jackson routed Howard's corps on the Union right at Chancellorsville, May 2, 1863. Although victorious in battle, Jackson was unlucky in the aftermath; he was accidently shot by one of his own men. EBL commented in her May 13 letter: "I heard this morning that Stonewall Jackson is to buried at Rich-mond today— He was an able Genl & an earnest man & I hope is taken away to be spared the sorrow which I think the Cause he earnestly espoused is to come to— I have thought him a sort of Cromwell only a far better man & in times to come I think we as Nation will take pride in his heroism even in spite of the miserable Cause which won his heart—."

Silver Spring   May 8, [1863]

Dear Phil   I was put in terror last evening just before leaving the City by hear-ing from an official source" that the President had ordered Hooker to march back again over the Rappahannock— I scarcely think Hooker drunk enough to go— so went to sleep upon that conviction— Father has gone off with a purpose which will greatly affect us— so Ill not write it down until he returns, with it vastly modified, & I hope quieted down

Altho' I was almost amused yesterday at the violent gestications & rage in the manners & faces of the people everywhere yesterday men & women   I saw some secessionists smiling quietly & looking hopeful— I had just heard of Stonemans raid so did feel bitter— & when they put Hooker at me— I smiled too & said I was happy that it was not worse— that the disaster was far short of the extent my fear made them two weeks since— Father & Brother's prognostications have robbed me of sleep many a night— Yet every body else was so hopeful— Father had the longest & most urgent talks with the powers that *are*— last Sunday & the Sunday before— just on this point & Asked the P. on his return from Falmouth if his Genl was drunk or sober— when he inspected him— I heard this reason for his recrossing given from one end of town to the other yesterday & the letters I said from the Army breathe nothing but disgust   one from Hookers own staff which was recd out here last night discloses the particulars— & winds up & "thus we are disgraced." Others say they "envy the fine fellows who died on the field"

Saturday night Mr. King says he is my letter tonight— bulky & kind He finds us, as on another occasion full of tribulation Father says the Army is ordered back over the other side of the Rap. to get more Rapping—[1] God may help us & if it results in success to our arms I shall feel as if his interposition was as palpable as when the Walls of Jericho fell at the sounds of the trumpets— & if defeated again I can discern both mercy & justice—

Mr. King says things look look less gloomy from this stand point than your's   Father did nothing today There is a consultation here tomorrow— when Ill wander over this place or maybe go to our Country Church with our boy & the Young ladies   Mr King— says Blair is much grown & *stouter* than he ever was before— He received Mr. K— affectionately & ran to my garden to tell me of his arrival saying— "Mr King saw Papa yesterday— & he is very well—" the boy did look particularly joyous & pretty to his Mother— Mr. King says you are well in every respect except the news which oppresses you as it does everybody. Says you are growing a *new* beard!! but I am repeating *your* news & not mine— but mine is so harrassing that I want to run away from it—

Marian Sands told me she was writing to you tonight   Bet & Evy criticized her letter said it was sheepish & etc   I insisted it was just right & that you would do all you could to have her Father here to give her away to Col Dutton the day is not fixed as he is in the field— but the first week in June is the time appointed & for which he begs— so Marian consents altho I understood late in the fall— but I suppose he wants her out of Washington with his Mother in New England—

I shall stay here & in the City until I get yr orders to depart which will not I hope & pray be sent at all for I feel safer this near your ships than in Phila But I am writing too blue more so than those around me feel & I confess that nine tenths of the time my hopes get the better of my fears   Ever your own Lizzie

1. Lincoln met with Hooker at army headquarters on May 7 and urged, but did not require, immediate offensive activity.

11

"I think the 4th of July of 1863 will stand by that of 76 in the annals of Country"

July 7, 1863

AFTER A WEEK'S LEAVE AT HOME, S. P. Lee resumed command of the North Atlantic Blockading Squadron. The impending rebel invasion caused Elizabeth to abandon her country home and move into Washington. George Gordon Meade replaced Hooker as commander of the Army of the Potomac and almost immediately faced a major battle. Robert E. Lee moved north across the Potomac, and the two armies collided in Pennsylvania. The Union victory at Gettysburg on July 3, coupled with the surrender of Vicksburg on the next day, became the major turning point of the war.

Silver Spring   May 24, 1863
Dear Phil   After a week of the priviledge of hearing talking writing is scarce a priviledge— except to hear from the run away Yesterday was a busy day. Mother still complaining & the house full of company from morning until after one olk— indeed Andrew Alexander remained all night The others remained until the small hours— walking & talking *in the porches* tonight Evy got a reprieve from her Mother & remains to Marions wedding— Miss Chase & Govr Sprague were here this morning & I think turned a *restless* eye upon us all when she saw Father talking to the Govr & heard the last say— "I agree with you Mr. Blair entirely" I told Father of her impatience when he said she had reason— for he had Hooker & Stanton under discussion— & their entente cordiale could not be acceptable since Mr Chase is pledged & lately to stand by both—
    The talk & tone of the Army is encourage   General Mead[1] was called upon by Hooker to know if had said— he would never willingly go in battle under him again— to which Genl Meade pleads guilty— ditto Birney Sedgewick—[2] Birney resented the inquiry as a personal indignity desired to relieved— Whereupon Hooker apologized—!! There are others equally *demoralized*!!! so we may hope for deliverance—
    I must go to Church— with a heart full of gratitude for the good news from

Vicksburg—[3] but still with an aching anxiety about Frank— so intense— but you share the feeling with me so entirely that I need not dwell on it to get yr sympathy— Blair was grieved to find you were gone— He found your knife & bade me be sure to send it to you— He goes with me to the City to see Nelly & the children with your devoted Lizie

One letter from Capt Crossby[4] I will forward it if you but am in a hurry now—

1. Maj. Gen. George Meade commanded the Fifth Corps at Chancellorsville. Since that battle, numerous officers had expressed to Lincoln their eagerness for the replacement of Hooker. On June 27, Meade was made the new commander of the Army of the Potomac.

2. Brig. Gen. David B. Birney led the First Division of Stoneman's Third Corps, and Maj. Gen. John Sedgwick led the Sixth Corps.

3. On April 30, Grant's army had crossed to the eastern bank of the Mississippi River south of Vicksburg. On May 14, his army occupied Jackson, Mississippi; he then turned back toward Vicksburg, and the siege began on May 18.

4. Capt. Peirce Crosby, Fleet Commander of the North Atlantic Blockading Squadron.

Silver Spring   May 26, 1863

My Dear Phil   Your two first letters after your return to your Ship reached me last night. Your extract from the R Enquirer was news at our tea table— but since Andrew Alexander has come from the City & says they have in the City official news— of the same import there— with some additional details Apo sends us a letter from Frank dated from a plantation en route to Grand Gulf

I wish you could hear the talk of these officers now on a leave from the Army. Stoneman— has been *retired*— they say for going too near Richmond— & Averill[1] for not going near enough I was amused at a sarcasm I heard on the Street— After great exultation over Grants victory— some said Oh what a pity he is to be removed immediately— & his whole Army put on half Rations like Rosencrantz— & kept in penitence for not doing more— Minna announced here yesterday that Grant is the Naval presidential Candidate— even if he should be drunk for the rest of his life— so added her secretary   thereafter they left for the City

I went to work on my borders & it is an effort to leave them now— but this is Nelly's only week in the City— She said she would *not* now return to city on her own account if she could She finds *every* thing so changed This is not a bad political sign— for as I know some of her cronies who are vastly sobered in their views of late— She says they cannot build this year & I am not sorry— for with our ideas we would regret to have John obliged— by such an investment to make it his home This is however a severe trial to her as their present abode is painfully small & I fear will be warm during the summer but they all have got thro the winter so well that I hope that it will be just as kindly for the rest of the year— I shall go in certain, every other day whilst they stay here & help them all I can—

I am in a muss with Mrs Merrick & will have to go to see about that today— She is a trying Secesh & yet I feel that she can think tho I do not   she has wrongs & I must try to be patient & amiable. Ever your devoted Lizzie

1. William W. Averell commanded the Second Division of Stoneman's Cavalry Corps and was part of the ill-fated cavalry raid toward Richmond during the Chancellorsville campaign.

Silver Spring   June 3, 1863

Dear Phil   I was lucky yesterday in getting my affairs arranged *well* at the Asylum[1] We made five hundred dollars by the Concert & that puts us above want for the coming summer months Then I got family affairs into a decent shape— The treaty of peace suggested by me was accepted—[2] Now mind— *I* have not taken any part in these feuds save to preach peace in season & out of season. but peace for at least the courtesy & decency is so essentially the interest of all that all are made now— only too glad to accept it I have an easy role & for the rest of my life will conform to it— deference— kindness to all— but my heart shall be garnered up for the precious ones of my home & to attain a Heavenly home for them & myself— in that better Country for which all our hearts must yearn in this sorrowful Land— & dark days—

I see no apprehension here about Raids— S— may be galled by the feint of the Rebels who are concentrating all their Powers on Vicksburg & whither Jeff Davis has gone himself— Blair & I are busy in the flower garden today & as it is the first transplanting day we have had— I must hurry back to it A letter from Frank to his wife yesterday dated 21st well & in good spirits— his assault was a failure as no division was ready but his at the appointed hour—[3] Father & Mother go off on Saturday— Ill take care not to out here alone— Ever your own devoted Lizzie

1. On June 2, EBL had written: "I am here at the Asylum like a king in a parlor 'counting out' money. . . . This Concert puts this house above want during the summer which you know is a relief to my mind & heart— for really my heart is so much in this establishment that I can no longer call it a work— ."
2. There were numerous causes of tension between the residents of No. 6 (Minna and Montgomery) and those at No. 4 (EBL and her parents). For years Eliza and her daughter-in-law had had an uneasy relationship and were barely on speaking terms. In addition, there was the suspicion that Minna and Montgomery were thwarting S. P. Lee's chances for promotion. Montgomery was close to Secretary of the Navy Gideon Welles and Minna's sister Virginia was married to Assistant Secretary Gustavus Fox, who had his own reasons for disliking Lee. Eliza was especially fond of Lee and typically did not keep her opinions to herself.

3. Frank Blair commanded the Second Division of Sherman's Fifteenth Corps during the first assault on Vicksburg, May 19.

Silver Spring   June 6, 1863

Dear Phil   I went to the Cars with Mother & Father this morning at 6 Ock— saw them off comfortably— then went to the market & provided myself with a weeks supplies— did sundry errands for others & one for myself at the Orphan Asylum much to their amazement but found our good Matron as ready for company & inspection as midday She has been invited to go down to Norfolk— for an excursion— she asked me if she could go see any ships— I told her to go to the Minnesota— as she is really the best friend I have in Washington You would have everything shown I gave her permission to go as she is the hardest worked person I know except yourself— I have been seeking a chance to give her a few days of holiday.

From the asylum I went to the Sands— & I really shared poor Henriettas disappointment about her husband You can imagine that I felt more than I said for Sands has never intimated the Condition of his health in any of his letters shown to me & of course I was silent   he will never ask for a survey— I feel a sympathy in his pride still cannot approve any mans wearing out his life— care of his health is due to himself & then he is false to none

Father put no queries about your position— as he found it was DuPont & F[ox] in course of talk said yours was an arduous post— & that no one in Service could fill it more ably than you did— I should feel no anxiety about it if you took good care of your health— I will forgive smoking if the chewing is abandoned & the walks daily & regular are kept up—

Blair is in a frolick with Woody who stays here now altogether— I was *heartily* cordially received at No 6 this morning the first time in many years The children all prefer staying with me to going to see Aunt Frank[1] with Ma— Your affecate Lizzie   Blair says he cant do without you & Grandpa too— There was great stir in town today   I heard on Tuesday from Secesh Robt Lee has gone to West Virginia

1. Aunt Frank was Minna's sister Frances Anstriss Woodbury Lowery.

Silver Spring   June 10, 1863

Dear Phil   Blair and I are glad to get out of the dusty city. I never saw a little chap as impatient as he was to return to his accustomed range We still have cold & dry weather which is ruining the crops Many have ploughed up their corn & replanted

We are all excitement here about an expedition under Ames & Andrew Alexander to head off a raid on Maryland now concentrating at Culpepper—[1] They were fighting yesterday consequently my young ladies were in a high state of excitement Evy went off home last evening with tears in her eyes— I miss her for she is vastly congenial to me—

I have just done an act of doubtful hospitality— to some guests Capt Dutton—[2] brother of the groom— who is I think going to have camp fever— so I have arranged to send him to the City feeling if he was ill my utter incapacity to take care of him besides the horror of the disease in this helpless family of women still I feel as if it was more hospitable to urge him to stay— I must be off to see a work man & a soldier so must add only Your own Lizzie

1. Brig. Gen. Adelbert Ames, under General Pleasonton's command, was part of the greatest cavalry battle of the war on June 9, 1863, at Brandy Station, Virginia. Union cavalry had crossed the Rappahannock, and Pleasonton reported that the engagement near Culpeper Court House had stopped J. E. B. Stuart's attempt to move into Maryland. For the first time, Union cavalry appeared to be equal to Southern cavalry. Andrew Alexander was Ames's assistant adjutant general.

2. Capt. Clarence Dutton of the Twenty-first Connecticut Volunteers was the younger brother of Arthur Dutton.

Silver Spring June 12, 1863

Dear Phil Betty has just congratulated me upon taking my seat— as she says I tramp around like a troubled spirit— I am certainly a busy one— & yet I feel each night that I have not half attended to the many things with which I am charged Then I am troubled by the drought. I fear we will have famine added to War— & then will come pestilence if this Nation does not repent of its sins— Now you may think I say this carelessly but it is a fear which overshadows my heart a great deal— when I have seen vice stalking around everywhere scarce heeded much less rebuked—

I received no letter from you or Father yesterday I got a note from Mr. Baily at the Globe Office kindly offering to be agent for renting the upper rooms at No 4— I felt the force of your ideas when I had to get rid of the fast set who I had only to notify of my wish to have them leave— still it was disagreeable— & I devised this other plan— & shall try it— & then if it fails just stop & keep it empty. & do with less money which I spend here to fill up gaps made by others— & which for the sake of feeling that no accustomed comfort is missed— I enjoy to so spend it— but it is a luxury with some other I can forgo & Ill soon be equipped with 2 years clothing— (under garments—) one year of dresses— all black— I can get for daily use— for parade occasions I'll have to abide the coming season for— tis the fashion— which makes things fit for them— I do not know yet how much this wardrobe will cost & making it is all to be paid for— but will tell you & then draw as you direct me

Blair is very busy raking hay— & just now shaking the carpets He misses my Parents— & since all went off hates me even to get in the carriage— Ever your own Lizzie

Silver Spring   June 18, 1863
Dear Phil   Mr. Stabler went off too early to take my daily bulletin & the
storm this evening prevented us from going in as we anticipated so you will
get no letter from me today. Last night we heard the guns over in Virginia but
hear of no Rebels nearer than Harpers Ferry & Centerville but as our Army is
between us I am not nervous besides I cannot loose faith in that Army or our
Good cause & feel confident & sleep sound in spite of the Rebel approaches—[1]
Fox will send me an express notice— if we are defeated so that I can retreat
from this back door to our city if the enemy ever came a knocking at it— No
tidings from Father today   I expect them home at any hour since this Raid by
the Rebels

I heard Betty just now discussing to Miss Dutton[2] Capt & Mrs. Sands &
you & I   she said Capt Sands was the one in love of that Couple & that I was
the lover in our Match. that you were intensely cold mannered person & she
really doubted whether you ever made a pretty speech to me in my life— but I
revelled in my devotion to you & was so absorbed in it that I never thought or
cared about myself or anybody else much— Now is not that a character to go
Connecticut!! She told with some humor how complacently Mrs Sands would
listen to her husbands epithets of "beautiful lovely &etc. Listeners may not
hear agreeable things so I discovered myself & insist that you have said several
very civil things to me in the course of the last 24 years

I am rejoicing tonight in the showers of this evening   they are exhilerating
& oh how thirsty the Old Earth is— My Hay workers have done more today
than Old Stabler said they could & my house cleaning is finished, now if I can
get the grapery in fine order by tomorrow I shall be ready to abdicate my boss
ship & resume my own garden & Asylum duties

I shall take Miss Dutton to the Cars in the morning & as it has rained Ill
take my boy with me— He suffers from heat just as you do & was sweltering
today when bare footed— & with only his linen pants & shirt on over the
merest excuse of a flannel He begs hard for cherries & yesterday I relented—
but I fancied he was not so well today— & denied them to him today which
goes very hard— but still he is perfectly obedient to me & just as full of life
& glee as he had ate the hat full cherries which he saw Betty disposing of so
satisfactorily—

June 19—In Washington Father & Mother have just gone out home— both
much improved by that trip—[3] No news— so they say. Hooker in fog was
Fathers reply when I asked him the news— I have got Beckys investment all
properly attended to by Blair [Sands] but utterly forgotten by his Mother—
she says has had so much to excite & think of that she was confused & it was
a whole day & upon a second inquiry only that she remembered it— so make
my apology to Blair & my thanks also—[4]

I am very glad have Father— altho I have not been nervous in the least—

until today—[5] I hated to leave Blair behind me today— but I would not force him. Are you not sorry for Foote— Your affectionate Lizzie

1. On June 15, EBL wrote: "Yesterday there was a panic in town made by the ambulance trains— which were so large & enough to affright the people but it was the sick from Fredricksburg hospitals— & not the wounded from any battle as I ascertained 'ere I left the City— That entire Army is in motion— & it is a race between Hooker & Lee the first having the inside circle— the result— I think will not be brilliant but there are men enough & good genls enough to take care of us so with a heart full of prayer for us all & a perfect trust that all things will work for good to those who love God. Your devoted Lizzie."

2. Miss Emily Dutton, twenty-seven-year-old sister of Arthur Dutton.

3. The Blairs had been on a weeklong jaunt in New York and Pennsylvania.

4. Blair Sands, who served under SPL's command, had been given Becky's money to invest in a bond. He did so, giving the bond to his mother to pass on to EBL when she was in the city. Henrietta Sands evidently forgot about it, and EBL had written to SPL inquiring if Blair had fulfilled his promise.

5. On June 17, EBL reported: "I got a message from Mr. Fox today saying that the Rebs were not in Penny. nor was Lee's army in Maryland."

Silver Spring   June 20, 1863

Dear Phil   Our people are surely on the qui vive in the city—[1] Our trunks we taken out of the waggon & detained against all former precedent & the man having a pass also— So he has to return with a key & have them opened— for which purpose my man Sam goes & takes this

This is my birthday which I have enjoyed among my flowers as it is the first *planting* day we have had this spring or summer— I hear the Prince George farmers could make no crop of tobacco if they had all the hands in the Carolinas so I am glad John did not *sell* it will be a very high article in the coming years—

Father & Mother luxuriate in getting home The journey has had a good effect on Mother She is more cheerful eats & sleeps well— & seems in heart about Frank— She says she told them at the North that she could not trust your wife & child to be in reach of Rebels— for they were more bitter on you— than any other man in our army or Navy except Drayton—[2] *so she* would come home— Joe Cook was ordered away— just the day Father got home He has been *our picket* up to that day.

I wrote about the bond. Becky got it yesterday & evidently felt very proud & rich— She heard me say that John said there was no better investment & she has great faith in "*Major Lee's smartness—*"

Blair has been with Mother replanting the roasting ear patch— & it would have pleased you to see them enjoy each other He follows her everywhere & they talk by the hour— The cool day is a great relief to him he is covered with heat & lost his appetite during the hot days— but is now as merry & hearty as ever— Ever your own devoted Lizzie I have lost my desk key & have not sealed my letter for a week past—

1. On June 16, EBL announced that she had heard that rebels were at Hagerstown: "I do not believe they will come this way but will go to richer scenes for the greater devastation & retaliation without check they will avoid a fight & as our side cant get one even quickly Besides it will help the draft for which it was promoted so I *suspect*— they will riot awhile in the fertility of Pennsylvania— get fat & saucy then return upon the Capitol if unchecked & we have no better captains than now wield our destinies This move of the Rebels will bring Father home I think tomorrow— There are pickets many miles above us— & I do not feel the least nervous about the family here for the present— the moment I do so I get in the carriage— with market waggon & go to the City— where we can our chances with those who are more timid than I am & that is saying much on that score— ."
2. Percival Drayton, commanding the ironclad *Passaic* in the South Atlantic Blockading Squadron, was extremely active in the bombardment of Savannah in March and of Charleston in April.

Silver Spring   June 23, 1862 [1863]
Dear Phil   It is evident that these Cavalry fights no matter how *dashing* & gallant do not impede Lee's march to the Valley & down it, to Maryland & Pensy where his advance corp is already revelling in plenty—[1] The Army of the Potomac may hug Washington but that will make it secure for a while only— The President said today he got rid of McC because he let Lee get the better of him in the race to Richmond & he seemed to have it in his mind that if Hooker got beat in the present race— he would make short work of him— but— prudence forbids my saying even this much

Capt Sands is ordered to the Roanoke— I suppose to supersede your two Monitors which are to be sent elsewhere *I guess* this much & suggest that you look out in time to keep something with a thick skin to help in the defence of our Capitol. The day may not be distant ere it is needed—

Brothers family go north tomorrow   I think we are as safe here as at Philadelphia— where I shall go— when I think danger impends here— but Lee I think rather avoids this point at present— which is covered by our Army—[2] for a few days I must keep quiet for I have a cold which requires care—

Sands thinks the trip to Hampton Roads experimental only. I think it is an unwieldy battery for the mouth of James River Dalhgren— will gobble up everything Iron that has a casemate on it— Now I only say this from my knowledge of the man alone— for I have not seen— anybody in or out of the Navy Dept— & did not think of D. replacing Foote until your letter suggested it— Father did not see F.—[3] & I called to see Virginia who was too sick to see me— Now dont act on these suspicions of mine save to inquire about things—

I have written to Horace I will go to Aunt if he has to leave her & to let me know his movements   Blair is gay & well— Your own Lizzie Your gold thimble gave me 24 years ago is now my seal

1. On June 16, Lee's army had begun crossing the Potomac, in a movement which culminated at Gettysburg. On June 24, EBL commented upon Southern sympathizers: "I forgot to say when I was in the city last I met the Bayard Smiths, they are as rabid as snakes. I never saw such bitterness & have it to say of them that tho' they kept within the bounds of courtesy they were nearer forgetting it than any persons of their ilk I have ever spoken to— They are elate with this invasion of my Maryland."

2. On June 26, EBL wrote: "The Army is between us & them & we can hear every battle & can get out of the way if we are defeated— in which case this place— will be the next secen [scene] of conflict—."

3. G. V. Fox.

Silver Spring   June 27, 1863

Dear Phil   Yours enclosing the 2 Goldsborough letters were recieved last night   I have tried to give you all the light as to the "situation" which I could discern through our obscured vista but I really scarce thought it prudent to give vent to all my forbodings as to the managers of our affairs in town who reminded me of Neros fiddling whilst Rome was burning" Today it is reported that McClellan who is in the city is recalled   he once saved this state with a demoralized Army and I take hope again if anybody but that stupid drunkard has the command of our troops— Our troops at Winchester & every where & you know I believe intentionally are commanded by bad men.

We read here last night Franks report to Sherman— of his whole proceedings since May 1st & no man could have better troops except one Regt of foreigners— 38th Ohio I believe—[1] who laid down in their tracks in the assault of the 22nd— blocked up the road— & it was with the greatest difficulty Frank could rescue the 2 Regiments which had preceded this recreant crew & who had already got into the Rebel works when the Retreat was thus made unavoidable These two leading Regts had to be followed to save them from massacre— by a new route, which was done only in time to save 1200 out of two thousand—

Wright Rives is back & I enclose you Brother's note to me which is our latest news from town save the rumor of McClellans restoration which was first heard late last night—[2] Wright is ill & fears are entertained lest he lose one of his legs— the result of exposure after the typhoid fever

A gentleman by the name of Norris[3] has just been here & given me the big picture of his Iron Ship— which he says he wants you to command   he says it is to run 20 knots an hour & do other prodigies— All the scientifics— Davis— Henry, Bache— Haskell[4] & a dozen others say, it is a marvel of a ship— I told him you were not a scientific sailor— but a practical one— I could not refuse the picture— tho its dark frame & shape looks like the coffin of a ship— & I fear this idea prevented me being as cordially polite as I ought to have been

I am again outdoors— tho not very strong yet— I can move away now if needs be which could not have done a day or so since— Blair is well & happy in such times one realizes the glorious priviledges of childhood ignorance & happiness Ever yr own Lizzie

1. In his report to Sherman, Frank explained that the Thirty-seventh Regiment of Ohio Volunteer Infantry "faltered and gave way under the fire of enemy, which was far from being severe." *War of the Rebellion*, series 1, vol. 24, part 2, 257. On June 21, EBL stated that Frank had informed the family "that Banks has refused to co-operate with Grant— so much for political Generals— F. encloses a copy of letter & orders from Grant— nothing *could* be more satisfactory than their whole tone & purport— Franks letter is cheerful— altho, he says the battle which decides this war is being fought then & there— ."

2. The growing disaffection with Hooker led to some talk of bringing back McClellan; Lincoln turned instead to Meade.

3. William Norris of New York had offered a ship design for an ironclad in 1861, but it had been rejected as too small.

4. Charles Henry Davis, career naval officer, had worked on the Coast Survey and been director of the Nautical Almanac before the war. Professor Joseph Henry, distinguished physicist, was secretary of the Smithsonian Institution. Alexander Bache was superintendent of the Coast Survey. James Richards Haskell, inventor, had experimented with breech-loading arms and in 1862 developed a rapid-fire machine gun.

Washington   June 29, [1863]
Dear Phil   Here I am bag & baggage   Father & Mother staying with Brother who is alone— Betty, Blair & I & the servants are here in my domicil— which is very comfortable— The Rebels were at the Cross Roads led by the Nolands [1] (who Father got out of prison not long since— they took 600 horses— then instead of coming toward us— & *the forts* they went to the Quaker neighborhood But the Col in command of our troops (Col Benton) [2] seem to expect a fight first in our fields so all thought it safe & best to retreat & take shelter in the City— Father was at Silver Spring today all is as usual— Minus people— Our House key was delivered to the Sergeant in command of the Guard— near the House— I dwell upon these private details because my heart sickens when it turns to public affairs of which the papers tell enough—

Hooker is at last deposed. Mead has a good reputation & is a sober man & a good soldier— & may prove a lucky appointment [3] They are all people of talent & *intense* in all the undertake so far as energy & honesty can lead them a right— but they are not a well balanced race— Still I am more hopeful since the decapitation of Hooker & I take heart again—

We are very comfortable— laugh eat & sleep— hope & pray Still firmly trusting in Him who is our ever present help time of trouble— I have just recd your letter saying you were off to Wilmington it adds to my burden— Your letters are such a comfort to your devoted Lizzie

1. Probably Thomas E. Noland, who lived east of Rockville. J. E. B. Stuart crossed the Potomac near Seneca, twenty miles above Washington on June 27. His force then turned north, passing Rockville the next day, continuing to Union Mills, where he camped on June 29. His object was to pass between Hooker's army and Washington to relieve pressure on Robert E. Lee.

2. Col. James G. Benton served in the ordnance office in Washington as first assistant to the chief of ordnance. In September 1863 he gained command of the Washington Arsenal.

3. On June 28, Lincoln appointed George Meade commander of the Army of the Potomac.

Washington   July 1, 1863

Dear Phil   I feel as if I was regularly housekeeping— Becky house servant & I nurse Harriet Cook My Parents returned to Silver Spring yesterday morning to look after their affairs & found that there were no Rebels between there & Rockville— so remained out there last night— I shall go to see them today— they say Betty Blair & I shall not return until all things are in their usual condition but I think I'll break up my encampment here & go to the Country tomorrow or next day for I fear the City— for my child. I spent the day out home with them & him yesterday & shall do so today & every day until I can return. Col Benton the commander at the Fort is affectionately considerate of us & has a lovely little wife to whom we are kind

The force in the City is very much increased since Sunday. I do not feel frightened but on Sunday Stuart told Capt Duane [1] & others who he took prisoner "but for his jaded horses— he would have marched down the 7 Street Road— took Abe & Cabinet prioners" for the life of me I cannot see that he would have failed— had he tried it. until 3 olk at night there was only one hundred men at the Guns at Fort Massachusetts— Joe Cook had a narrow escaped— he & 400 cavalry were under Majr Fry [2] en route for our Army near Rockville— when suddenly on the rise of Hills they discovered 8,000 of Stuarts men— Instantly Fry ordered his 400 to charge those nearest to them— which was done & then they retreated— & as he intended they took them for the advance of our Army— & did not pursue— & Joe knowing the by ways of the County brought them off save thro' the country— they took 12 prisoners who were full of talk about the plan for capturing "Old Blair" One Georgia Capt said "Well if we could catch that Old Fox & his cub the Yankee P.M Genl we would have all the pluck out of that Washington concern & soon end the war" Jo came before day to Silver Spring to see if they had carried Father off but the party intended for that purpose Got no farther than Wilsons where they learned the "Old Fox" was out of their reach.

The servants returned home with Father & Mother— except Nanny's children— they leave their best *gowns* here— & seem happy in having a city refuge They have all behaved remarkable well— Alick got married last week— Stuck to his wife Sunday but on Monday went home & to work— Old Dick would not leave the place— but the Soldiers behaved as well as men could do— everything was in precisely the order we left it & that is something remarkable when we had 50 men at the House & 500 Cavalry from Sunday night until yesterday in Mary Blairs lawn— Bernie remained at home but you would laugh at the stories of scampering of the County people with horses & cattle— they let off all the Secesh— but were hard on the Quakers particularly the Brooks— Old Stabler had his cattle & horses secreted but they encampted at the Old Roger Brooks [3] place— & cleaned it out— so wherever they stopped— 60 stragglers or deserters were picked up yesterday— about the county & one in the Moorings woods—

Blair is well— but my Parents seem enfeebled & broke down by this excitement & it cost me great effort to leave them yesterday So I am now off to them again— our presence & the boy's prattle— divert them & cheer— Your devoted Lizzie Robt Lee's whole object is in my opinion Washington

1. Capt. James C. Duane, chief engineer of the Army of the Potomac, was among those taken prisoner when J. E. B. Stuart captured a Union wagon train en route from Washington.

2. Maj. William H. Fry commanded a cavalry unit of the Army of the Potomac.

3. Roger Brooke, descended from one of the earliest Maryland families, was a successful farmer living south of Sandy Springs.

Washington   July 2, 1863

Dear Phil   Mother sent the carriage for us this afternoon and I made all my arrangements to go waiting until the latest moment to write you & had pen in hand when Brother sent word for some of us to come to him 'ere we went out— He told me— for I cannot by entreaty or ought else persuade Betty to go in there He told me the Rebels were in force at Rockville & were evidently massing there— I then ordered out my trunks & Becky Betty & the children & was just stepping in the carriage to go after my Parents & insist on their coming here when they rode up— on their horses— much to my relief— I do assure

Since then I have been very much occupied with my Mother— who does not flinch at all, but she was exhausted by the ride & heat— She is now here & servants expected every moment & all her servants & looked very cheerful just now pouring out tea with her own tea pot & etc— I have but one room occupied with lodgers— who are officers— & off on duty so we see nothing of them— & I not admit any more—

Your's of yesterday came just now I read your ideas of public affairs— in which he concedes & says— the result you prophecy to the Administration is exactly what he told Lincoln a week ago— Betty got a letter from Grants Army— which speaks of Frank being well the 20th & most cheerful & confident of the result— This Engineer is not quite so much so but says time is as much a gain to as it is to Joe Johnston & as our dates are to 25th five days more is of vast importance to us— I think Kilpatrick[1] is chasing Stuart back on the track to Poolesville where I think he will meet French— who has evacuated Harpers Ferry & is ready to fight any of the retreating foe as they approach the [river]

I enclose you "full of love a letter from Blair he was rather indignant at me for not going home tonight— Ever your own Lizzie

1. Brig. Gen. Judson Kilpatrick, leading the Third Division of cavalry had skirmished with Stuart's forces on June 30.

Silver Spring   [July 3, 1863]
My Dear Phil   We are here still on tiptoe with all eyes turned towards the north West where I have felt all day that a mortal combat was going on for our Country's life[1] & I think our troops are more alive to the exigencies of the country ever before— besides Meade has just done what the Rebels did two years ago— ordered the instant death of the recreant— if this had been done by Grant we would have had Vicksburg. & saved many brave men by punishing the Cowards & preventing their Contagion from spreading— & that is one reason why the Rebels fight well Our political Generals are afraid to deal with our Army according to Military discipline— I have great hopes of Mead   the whole family are people of talent & energy & as he was born in Spain he can never be President— thus will not be warred upon by Politicians or get a tete monte himself

Letters today from Frank who writes confidently They know that Bragg's army are coming on them.[2] but says they have now means to cope with them— but Grant hopes to be in Vicksburg before they turn to fight Joe Johnston— Frank encloses a letter to him from Sherman giving the history of Genl McClellands dismissal by Grant

A letter today from Meade to the P says yesterday at 3 olk— he had all his Army concentrated but 2 corps were so prostrated for an immense march that he would not attack until today— Our Army lay in full view of the enemy   I think Lee will retreat if it is possible— Our two corps 1st & 11th got the best of the fight with Longstreet & Hill until they were reinforced by Ewell—[3] when it became a drawn battle— Mead says they got our field of battle & the wounded

which gives them therin the Victory in all else the battle was a drawn one—
I send you a poster which is cast on every wall in New York— Your devoted
Lizzie No news from Silver Spring today— Father rides to the Fort in a few
minutes— Mother is very content here—

    1. July 3 was the third day of the Battle of Gettysburg.
    2. Braxton Bragg's rebel army was engaged in the Tullahoma campaign in eastern
Tennessee. Rosecrans's Federals eventually forced Bragg to withdraw to Chattanooga.
    3. James Longstreet, A. P. Hill, and Richard S. Ewell were Confederate corps com-
manders at Gettysburg. On July 1, Hill and Ewell launched attacks against the Union
right, defended by John Reynolds's First Corps and Howard's Eleventh Corps. On
July 2, Longstreet attacked the Union left. Neither of the attacks moved the federal
position.

Washington   July 4, 1863

Dear Phil   Mother Blair & I have just returned from the Country where we
went after a 7 olk breakfast— We found everything in good order & as quietly
beautiful as ever— birds were joyous & dogs gave Blair a riotous welcome and
I think all three of us were heartily sorry to come back to the City— altho
entirely comfortable here

The news from the Armies is favorable but scarcely decisive enough for my
appetite but I confess to some relief about things for our Army was *not* concentrated as rapidly as the enemy & I feared bad results from the fatigue &
scramble with which it was collected— but Meade has only had it in hand 6
days— & in that time has fought three of them— he is in good position & on
the defensive to get his men rested & in hand for an assault— Betty says there
was an artillery train by this door today which took three quarters of an hour
to pass— I have just asked Brother for the news & he says nothing especial—

Blair is firing of his small artillery in the alley under the window where he
first realized that his Country had a birthday— & this one will long be remembered by the Nation & Lee's retreat will sanctify it anew in the feelings of
the people— He commenced his Retreat at 3 olk this morning—[1] Now I hope
Meade will show his energy of which none of his family I've known lack—
that is *the* trait of the race— especially in a quarrel or fight— but George &
Robt—[2] who was my friend always kept themselves out of the family feuds—

I recieved a letter from Apo inviting me most cordially to come stay with
her says it will be a comfort to her as well as of service to Blair & me— the
journey is too long to go alone besides I am loth to leave my mother who said
to me I cannot last long under such trials— & yet a little while after she was
amused by Blair I feel I am a comfort to her & it is a great one to your own
affecate Lizzie

Sunday July 5/63 I was too late getting in town to have this mailed yesterday, I went next door with it & there met your Secy with a dispatch in his hand— he said it was a matter of business— Dalhgren son[3] a Capt. intercepted a letter of Jeff Davis' to Robt. Lee which developes their plan of this perilous campaign out of which he is trying now to extricate himself— the plan was for Lee to lead off Hooker just as he has done— take Harrisburg & then strike for Phila & Baltimore & Cut off all our Railroad resources— when Beauregard was to strike in at the rear of Washington led by Stuart— but when Cooper[4] came to ordering off Beauregard— Jeff objected it seems that he had not been taken in confidence by Cooper & Lee— & his intercepted letter shows this fact— & he explains how impossible it is to part with Beauregard— that the Yankees are at the White House[5] & threatening Charleston from which place he has had to reinforce Johnston & through the mercy of God we are saved by Jeff fears— for if Beauregard had accompanied Stuart last Saturday this day a week ago— Washington would now have been in the hands of the Rebels— that you & I know—

Meade would pursue Lee instantly but has to stop to get food for his men!! this I heard the President say when we met him at the White House door— where we took Blair to see the fireworks in which he was disappointed— And he also said that Meade said he was not yet certain whether Lee was beating a retreat— or in search of a good stronghold— at which to have another fight—[6] You see the details of the battles so I need not dwell upon them I shall return home tomorrow— but Nothing is sure in this world. Your own   Lizzie

1. On July 4, Lee began to move his force back toward the Potomac; his attempted invasion of Pennsylvania had failed. On July 7, EBL explained: "The Retreat of the enemy is so rapid & our house has such a strong guard at the Wood House & a picket at the gate so that Father & Mother go home today— I shall linger here a day or two longer— until I hear that the Rebels have surrendered— or are on the other side of the Potomac."

2. Robert Leamy Meade, who died in 1841, was the younger brother of George Meade, who had been Montgomery Blair's classmate at West Point.

3. Capt. Ulric Dahlgren was an aide to Meade at Gettysburg. While in pursuit of the retreating rebels, he was wounded in the foot, which was later amputated.

4. Lee had wanted to create a new army under Beauregard's command and had made his request to Adj. Gen. Samuel Cooper. While on reconnaisance behind rebel lines, Dahlgren captured a courier carrying letters to Lee from Cooper and Davis stating that any attack or even a feint toward Washington was impossible. They both agreed that there were not enough troops.

5. The White House on the Pamunkey River in Virginia had been the scene of the marriage of George Washington and Martha Custis. It had been the home of R. E. Lee's son William Henry Fitzhugh (Rooney) Lee until the spring of 1862. On July 1 and 2, 1863, federal troops initiated secondary movements from the White House, causing uneasiness for Confederate leaders in Richmond.

6. Having been in command only six days, Meade thought his exhausted army incapable of strenuous pursuit.

Washington   July 6, 1863

Dear Phil   Troops are leaving here to go by Railway to Harpers Ferry & our people are apparently nearing here to catch Lee's Army. But I heard that the President was out done by Baldy Smith remaining two days after he was ordered to march to fall on the Rear of Lees Army.[1] but the true reason of our lossing the fruit of the Victory if lost is over the way— our army has nothing to eat, so the President told Father— in my presence[2] Today there is no news promulgated which makes me fearful the Retreat of the enemy is unmolested. I never want to let it cross the Potomac as an army again & then we will have peace—[3] I think you are right about Dix[4] as the P can do it if he will & ought to do it— & if they would only follow up thing right ere the people at Richmond get over their Consternation strike there & Charleston at once we might feel assured of our Nation's future— & Oh how I sigh for peace— which will bring you home & in that is the type of all my joy in it so it is a huge one—

I enclose you Genl. D's letter & think there is a sort of truce between you now & that it is not good faith to break it— besides theres no reward in doing the disagreeable errands of any body A lesson you once gave me in dear Jim's Phila Guilon matter—[5] but it took years of bitter fruits to teach me fully to appreciate your sound counsel which I rejoice you have followed—

We will return home tomorrow— by which time we will know which way the enemy is taking to Virginia— Mother wants me to walk with her— so good morning to you— Blair has pages written to you this rainy morning— but the Generals excludes them— Ever yr devoted Lizzie

1. A large portion of William Farrar "Baldy" Smith's command was inexperienced militia. Knowing his force would not do well on a night march, he had delayed moving until the morning of July 4.

2. On July 10, EBL wrote: "The Army of the Potomac could not catch Lee because they had no supplies all being captured by Stuart in his movement in that Army's rear—."

3. On July 20, EBL explained: "Meades mistake was altogether the want of Judgement here & there, They supposed Lee would attack them & he out *wised* them for he made all the appearances of an immediate attack & *thus* saved himself— Meade wished to attack him but was over counselled— here & by the generals of his Army. Cameron was there & wanted to fight & telegraphed to Mr. Lincoln to over rule the decision of the Corp Generals & order an immediate attack— if he had done so on Monday morning he would have found half of Lee's Army on this side & helpless for lack of cannon & easy captured   I fear we will never have such an easy prey within our grasp again."

4. John A. Dix commanded at Fort Monroe. He and SPL had serious disagreements over the issuance of trade permits, Dix being much more lenient. In July, he was replaced as commander of the Department of Virginia and North Carolina by John G. Foster.

5. In 1843, EBL had actively opposed her brother Jim's marriage to Elizabeth Buillon of Philadelphia, and the engagement was broken.

Washington   July 7, 1863

Dear Phil   I think the 4th of July of 1863 will stand by that of 76 in the annals of Country   I feel too full of joy to wait until the morrow to tell it over to you altho you may know it now & revel in the Good tidings— Mary Merrick & I were in a deep confab about Mattrasses for the asylum when the word Vicksburg greeted my ear—[1] I bought the paper & whilst I was getting the money, she read to me Porters dispatch with a firm voice— two of her brothers were inside & mine is outside of that town. We never talk politics & I believe together in perfect kindness She looked at me with a quiet sadness when my heart overflowed in thankfullness— and only remarked, "Oh the Sea of blood this dreadful war has cost. she may have said— will cost." for I turned the conversation to remark upon Genl Pemberton[2] whose family are such warm friends of ours & who got his West Point appointment thro' my father (I did not say to her this last thing) & then we soon parted she went home The City is quite excited by the Refusal of the President to recieve Mr. Stephens & his message in making *peace overture*" as it is called here—[3]

Monday morning I have just recieved yr yours asking who I had mentioned your communications about Stevens to— Nobody except Father & Mother— Until yesterday when a great many persons asked me if the publications in the Herald & Star were true when I replied that it was so far as the fact "Dragon" contained Mr. Stephens— who was ever a Union Man & men did not change much in opinions after they were his age—" this I said to Capt Cushing—[4] Betty— & when asked if by several others the newspaper story about the Presidents refusal to recieve Mr. Stephens was true— & replied I believed it— but I never mentioned even to Betty or anybody except Father your communication to me— Then Mother joined us & they then told me it had been under Cabinet consideration— Saturday night & Sunday— when Brother did not go to Church— I met the Secy of Navy at Brother's with what he called "Your husbands important business telegraph" in his hand— I wish hereafter you would just mark what I am to consider confidential— In this case I was lucky in only mentioning it to Father simply from habit of keeping your public affairs to myself— & what I said about *my belief* was just as much derived from a dozen others— as from you— still I now regret that I even gave out my credence in the Newspaper news.

Mrs. Reynolds[5] has your shirts & since the Raid I have not been able to communicate with her. I gave them to her— saying there was no hurry & all communication mail & otherwise save thro Cavalry has been stopped for weeks a week before my Parents returned from the North— We had to get passes to go Silver Spring & even with them our trunks were examined at the different points on the Road— I will as soon as possible get your clothing—

Blair S. walked in just now when I was closing this letter with our boy at my side— The Secessionists are arrested in our neighborhood Gittings & Tucker—[6] for shooting at the Pickets stationed at Graves Store—

There was a small ovation to Stanton last night claiming Vicksburg as his speciality— Ever your own Lizzie

    1. On July 4, Confederate forces at Vicksburg surrendered to U. S. Grant.

    2. Gen. John C. Pemberton commanded the rebel forces at Vicksburg.

    3. On July 4, Confederate vice president Alexander Stephens traveled down the James River to Hampton Roads with the hope of going to Washington to discuss a prisoner exchange and perhaps also an end to the war. Lincoln refused to receive him.

    4. Lt. William B. Cushing was serving in the North Atlantic Blockading Squadron under Lee. The intrepid Cushing was later responsible for sinking the rebel ironclad *Albemarle* in 1864.

    5. Mrs. Nanni Reynolds, a seamstress regularly employed by EBL.

    6. Probably Frank Gittings, who lived north of Silver Spring.

Washington   July 9, 1863

Dear Phil   Blair Sands will carry my note of today as well as yesterday as he was detained by the slowness of a clerk in the Dept— but Mr. Fox said he would telegraph the reply to your dispatches last night—

There is a universal revolt against Dix but as Father says we have done more than our share of fight against incompetent Generals never was anything more persistent & earnest than Fathers course towards Hooker— all *in vain* he re-signed— because the Army made him— I hear that Halleck gives out that *he did* it & yesterday to give his assertion semblance Hooker was arrested here day before yesterday because he ordered the evacuation of Harpers Ferry. Milroy[1] is arrested because he did not evacuate Winchester sooner— We have Harpers Ferry again. French made it useless to the Rebels ere he left it, & Genl Meigs told me that Johnny[2] his son took some iron clad cars thro up there on Monday evening—

I hope Father will send for us today— What they call Guerillas shooting out there is some of the Natives who have had quarrels with the soldiers & avail themselves of the cover of the invasion to get revenge So far I have not heard of one instance of enmity to us— but of some kindness from those we had little reason to expect it— As we have a guard at the door of several men— I think theres nothing to fear from stragglers who are being caught up very rapidly many of whom since the defeat give themselves up.

You would have laughed last night to hear Wise[3] *gas* about the Navy & with some truth so far as the jealousy of the army is concerned & the politicians at the War Dept ignored David Porter— tho all their rejoicings were based on his dispatch— but this is not a good spirit to cultivate between the services— for they are essential to each other in this war & may be in all we may have We are all well & are enjoying our first good day for a long time Ever your own Lizzie Lee is fortifying at Hagerstown—[4] Our whole army will reach there today—[5] Each day but developes the completeness of our victory— No letter or message yet from Frank   Father & Mother have been out home since Tuesday—

1. Against advice from Washington, Gen. Robert H. Milroy delayed evacuating Winchester until June 15, when Ewell's advancing corps completely overwhelmed him, capturing all of his artillery and 3400 prisoners.

2. Lt. John Rodgers Meigs, oldest child of Montgomery Meigs, graduated from the Military Academy in 1863. He was killed in 1864 behind Union lines by rebels disguised as federal soldiers.

3. George Douglas Wise, assistant quartermaster of the U.S. Volunteers. His brother Henry Augustus Wise and his son Frederick May Wise both served in the navy.

4. On July 10, EBL wrote: "Father has just returned from the city & brings he says no news— but I am certain theres a battle raging at Hagerstown & a desparate one— Our people feel as if they are ending the war— & the enemy are fighting for all they fancy is right— As you said Lee made a most desparate & false step by this invasion— & may be his best excuse is the calculation that Hooker was to be our general— & if he had been it would have been another thing for him & us but thanks to Him who rules all things for good to those who love Him."

5. Again on July 10, she commented: "I think I saw considerable anxiety on the faces of people as to the result of the fighting at Hagerstown   Meades Army if properly concentrated can completely overwhelm the Rebels— but our men have been starved & never was an army so used by— but I am too happy to grumble at anybody."

Silver Spring   July 11, 1863

Dear Phil   There is no war news this morning & I have been out trying to get the weeds out of my flowers which have got riotous since my run away visit to the City— All is perfectly quiet here now & will continue so if Lee loses his canon & all his warlike implements Then sick & food & etc they are welcome to & men too— but I want their cannon & shooting irons of all sorts

We are all well— but the absence of the pictures in the parlor & silver at our meals reminds us still of the uncertainties of this life— I confess to working my flowers with more heart today than at any time since the battle of Chancellorsville— Bennie Davis[1] was here lost six of his best horses— & that was the case of most of his neighbors— of all sorts— his wife is a Mason— & give her kinsman Fitzhugh Lee so severe talk & refused to shake hands with him they were 5 hours passing Davis' by two roads— Judge Bowie was treated with great indignity as were many men of high charater of decided Union politics who refused to give them aid in any form—

Blair is well— but these hot days & night wilt the wee one sadly the rest are all well Ever yr own Lizzie

1. Benjamin Davis lived northeast of the Blairs' Silver Spring home.

12

"Blair has looked up to yr picture so long—
that he knows it better than he does his Papa—"

July 29, 1863

THE THIRD SUMMER OF CIVIL WAR provided significant victories for the
North, but the end of the conflict seemed no nearer. Public discontent found
expression through a growing peace movement in the country and in resistance to the draft, particularly the devastating New York riots. Francis Preston
Blair anticipated an additional danger to his country. With French support,
the Austrian archduke Maximilian was crowned emperor of Mexico, and Blair
began to think war with France was possible.

While the great armies paused, attention focused on the need to capture
the major Southern port and cradle of the Confederacy, Charleston. Planning
and execution would take time, dragging into months, as Northern strategists
debated the value of ironclad ships as offensive weapons and struggled with
problems of cooperation between the armed services. Frank Blair returned
home safely from his military campaigns, and Elizabeth yearned to have her
husband join the family circle. For half of his young son's six-year life Phillips
Lee had been at war; in mid-September he spent a well-deserved week of rest
with his family.

Silver Spring   July 16, 1863
Dear Phil   Yours from the James River came last night with Mr. Dicks— I
think the undercurrent he speaks of will now soon quiet down since the Negro
question is settled & that too by a convention— called by a Secesh Governor— & elected under his auspices— that emancipation act is a great event I
think to property holders in Missouri— & tis a great point to have it settled
in such a short period—[1] & now that the Mississippi is open I take hope that
the war will be over before very long Nothing however will so prolong it as
the proceedings in New York— which any body but Wool would have settled
down in a few hours[2] Old Paulding soon took the Government's property in
his care & made that safe

Brother is here & getting well— He has no letters from Frank— who went off the day of the Surrender— to get at Johnston ere he could recruit himself with the garrison of Vicksburg which was paroled & afterwards detained by Genl Grant Our captures out there are about 50 thousand men— a huge Army. From the formula which Grant has instituted[3] & the fact that men seem glad to be thus relieved from future service— I hope but few will get back in their Army but the idea was that the men were required there to protect the women & children the Negroes— this is not promulgated

The rain has stopped, & it has turned cooler— there never was known such a season of drought & rain— but every thing is looking sweetly here & our garden & oats which was feared to be a failure have turned out finely There they are off— Ever your affecate Lizzie

1. Governor Hamilton R. Gamble called a convention to meet on June 15, 1863, to decide the issue of emancipation in Missouri. After extensive debate, the convention approved an emancipation ordinance which would end slavery on July 4, 1870; emancipated persons over forty would remain servants (lifelong); children under twelve would be servants until age twenty-three; all others would be servants until July 4, 1876. The ordinance also prohibited the sale of emancipated persons and the taxing of property in slaves.

2. From July 13 to 16, America saw the worst riots in its history, in protest of the new conscription act. It became an outlet for racial tensions and antiblack feeling. Predominantly Irish mobs lynched over a dozen blacks and burned the Colored Orphan Asylum. John E. Wool commanded the army in New York City and Hiram Paulding was in command of the New York Navy Yard. On July 18, EBL commented: "I think the Riot a plunder mob of foreigners incited by our Secessionist & Cooperheads."

3. Grant had paroled those captured at Vicksburg. They were pledged not to fight again until officially exchanged.

Silver Spring   July 24, 1863

Dear Phil   Did you lose at Ft. Powhatton your Ensign & men as reported by the Newspapers?[1] Fox says he has had no report about any thing of the sort & he does not believe it— He told me that Hunter was ordered to cooperate with Dupont— Now the shoe is on tother foot & Dalgrhen is ordered to cooperate with Gilmore—[2] I said it was not probable that Hunter would ever successfully cooperate with any body. His career never indicated in any act He said Dalgrhen had made requisition for an amount ammunition that would take the resources of the Dept. two years to make— He said also that D. had made an appeal for reinforcements for Gilmore— when the same mail brought Gilmore's report & requisitions— but he said he had from 5 to 10 thousand more men than he needed so Secy. wrote to D. that Gilmore understood very his own work & all he had to do was to look out for his end of the business— poor Capt. Dalghren is desperately ill since the amputation of his foot He is just 21— & if he dies he will be Dalghrens second child he has lost when just grown— Lizzie his beautiful daughter was 17 the year she died— I feel for these children as I knew & like their mother in my & her school days

I saw Mr. Beale & asked him to send the Sea Turtle to Mrs Welles with your compliments   I packed up in box & gave over to Mr. B. your shirts (20) to send you by next steamer from the yard— which he said would be tomorrow— Ill attend to the Vests promptly— You have a great many socks in your sea chest   do you need any of them now?

Brother tried to get a telegraph to Andrew Alexander— but they told him at War Dept. that the Hdquarters of the Army was *not* within telegraphic communication— Then I sent word to one of the Young Alexanders what I had heard about his cousin— & he will go up to Berlin today   Father had a letter from Apo yesterday. She writes that Frank will have a furlough for a few weeks before the Commencement of the fall Campaign— that G. ordered them only to push our lines to Jackson & the Pearl River— Frank was very well   She talks of Frank going to Texas but I think Father has no fancy for it— & that he wants F in Congress next winter— that over such year of fighting is enough— as it not to be his future vocation   Father mends but slowly   Blair is well & blythe— Ever yr own Lizzie

1. The newspaper reports were false. On July 14, the Union navy ensured control of the James River to Drewry's Bluff by capturing Fort Powhatan.

2. Gen. Quincy A. Gillmore, who had replaced David Hunter as commander of the Department of the South, unsuccessfully attempted to retake fortifications in Charleston Harbor.

Silver Spring   July 28, 1863

Dear Phil   According to your plans you are off for Wilmington tomorrow & the papers say Charleston too but I know that is not so, therefore will not be troubled about it— Such is the rainy season here that Blair was annoyed with muskitoes here last night for the first time. I can stand *a few* but one even torments him so as to keep him awake.

I heard Father tell Betty who wished him to do something about a sick leave for Genl. Griffin (Sally Carrolls husband) that he did not intend dancing attendance in the Presidents anti chamber any more   Apo wrote to Father to get the independent Dept. of Texas for Frank— & as it came only two days ago I take the above Answer to Betty as answer to Apo too— Indeed he told me that without we had by misfortune a prolongation of War with the South or a new one with France he did not wish Frank to remain in the Army longer than next Christmas—

I think for all I can hear that the army may draw near to Washn & get its recruits & get rested & start for a fall campaign— reinforced & reinvigorated— Lee has evidently got the road to Richmond open to him & if he cares for human life he will keep his Army about the Rapidan— & not kill in the swamps of lower Virginia—

There is great joy here in the Capture of Morgan.[1] you remember the big house on the same square with Uncle Ben Gratz there are but two on the square Morgan was born & reared there with the Gratz boys— & has done nothing but torment his own townspeople & state during this whole War— & from the state of matters West— he is not likely to be exchanged during the War— So Kentucky is to enjoy quiet & Maryland too I hope—

Mr. Crittendens death[2] has shocked & depressed my Father a great deal— Mother remarked— John Crittenden impaired a noble intellect & constitution by gambling all night habitually I wonder he lived so long— & this after some kind talk about him appears unaffected by it— I am off to the City to attend to some business. Col Alexander goes to the Army tomorrow quite restored to health but not flesh— Ever your own Lizzie

1. On July 26, John Hunt Morgan was captured at Salineville, Ohio, and imprisoned in the Ohio State Penitentiary. He escaped in November and again led cavalry raids in Kentucky in 1864.

2. John J. Crittenden died on July 26. Although a political opponent, Crittenden had been Blair's personal friend since childhood.

Silver Spring   July 29, 1863
Dear Phil   I went to the City to attend to some business for Mother & to have the Hermitage picture— Mothers & Fathers & Jims photographed— I would have had mine but I concluded it was not fair to your old to send you the face of a girl of 19 to look at as your wife then come home to such old wrinkled dame of forty four as I am— besides you never thought the picture like me I am glad other do— so that Blair can fancy his Mama was once young. I remember the beauty of mine & when I used to watch her & help to dress her & think nothing in this world was half so beautiful to my juvenile eyes Blair has looked up to yr picture so long— that he knows that better than he does his Papa— poor child— as tis now just one half of his life that this cruising has taken up—

Father is looks quite like himself today rode out with Mother before breakfast ate it heartily & talked cheerfully— but still of Mr. Crittenden— I heard yesterday that our Army is ordered to follow Lee over the Rappahannock but it cannot go far simply because they can not feed it. Still there may be a fight in the hills of the Rapidan— which is a very defensible country.

Andrew Alexander has gone to the Army today I paid all my debts yesterday & have all nicely put away the best outfit of garments under ones) for winter & summer I ever had in my life except— when I was married & these

are quite as good— only have no lace or embroidery on them— I got no letter yesterday— suppose you too busy getting off— I went to hurry your tailor
about yr vests   they wont be ready before Friday & go down to you that day—
Yours ever devotedly Lizzie

Silver Spring   July 30, 1863
Dear Phil   Father has been inundated lately with letters from Texas refugees
to get him to have Frank sent there— I am utterly opposed to it— Yet they
think the prospect of a french War so imminent that we ought to have an able
& honest man at that point— Father has enclosed these letters today to the
P. saying he can judge better in such a matter than Franks Father— I think
Brother wants it but thinks he had best not be eager for it— It is said that the
P. has determined not to send Banks— Stanton & Seward are in close alliance
& yet the last is out for the Union as it was maugre [despite] the proclamation
    Robt Lee has made an odd report about his rear Guard— there surely was a
fight & Genl Pettigrew[1] who commanded it was killed in his efforts to rally &
save it. Robert is sensitive & less exact than one was once disposed to think   I
have heard that from some of his former fondest Engineer corp friends—
Do you observe the discrepancy in the intercepted correspondence— which
Brother said here last night is a true copy of the originals— that Cooper—
says that Jeff knew nothing of the sending of Beauregard to Culpepper until
that day— & yet Jeff writes the same day of it to Robt Lee as if it was a matter
understood between them— The exhibit of their resources is comforting
    It is thought here our Army will follow Lee over the Rappahanock as his
men are very weary & disheartened   our men are tired too & are not strong
enough to attack I fear— besides our dutch corp in spite of the new officers
& all else is despicable run like sheep on all occasions altho shot down by our
own batteries for doing it   this occured in the battle at Chancellorsville &
Gettysburg— Reynolds's[2] first days retreat was entirely owing to this recreant
corp whose officers had foght their own men— Shurtz ran & was hid for 24
hours in a barrel in a cellar— where our troops to their great fun found him
fasting—[3] of late we have been quite posted in the Army talk— Ever your
affecate Lizzie

    1. On July 14, Confederate Gen. James J. Pettigrew was mortally wounded when
Judson Kilpatrick's Federals surprised the retreating rebels.
    2. On the first day of the battle at Gettysburg, July 1, Gen. John F. Reynolds was
killed by a sharpshooter while urging his men into defensive positions.
    3. During a brief period, Alexander Schimmelfennig had command of Schurz's
division, and while in retreat was wounded. He spent the next two days hiding in a
pigsty.

Silver Spring   August 3, 1863
Dear Phil   Mr. Lamson[1] came yesterday to breakfast with Miss Wright to en-
liven his drive   he seems very elate with his new command— which he told
me was altogether from your kindness to him— & he is grateful & etc Says he
grieves to leave the Minnesota which he styles "the happiest of ships—"

We have intensely hot weather So far Blair keeps well   he takes his daily
rides on horseback— eats, & sleeps well— as long as this continues I shall
hold on to Silver Spring— Mary Blair will not let Jesup sell Jennie to anybody as she was his Grandpa Blairs gift & that she would be miserable to see
him mounted on any other animal so my happy prospect in that direction is
closed— Mary starts today to the Seashore— Cape May   Jimmie[2] is better—
but still sick— Father & Mother are just returned from a ride— both looking
well & in good spirits—

I received a long letter from Fanny— She give a good account of her family
concerns; then begins a disertation on "Cousin Robert who I intimated was no
cousin of yours— She gives a family tree proving that Robert Lee is your sixth
cousin by heresay.[3] The letter is interesting on that account & proves just what
you said years ago   that your Aunts were claimed as cousin by their lovers—
but there is no blood relationship She admits one this Continent— but it was
the same family in England & two brothers ("it is believed emigrated. ." one
the grand- or great grandfather of Richd Henry Lee—" This is evidently a
matter she has sifted well— & gives all the evidence she can to prove up her
case— & fails to do so to my mind. there is such inherent difference in the
race— one so honest, & high toned. & the other even in its best specimens
so entirely the otherwise for instance—

this late report of Lees about Meade— Our cavalry did attack & take his
rear Brigade— killed & captured its Genl Pettigrew— a fact which can be
proved by thousands— so says Andrew— & every body— Meade's character
is just as reliable & any mans & all of the family are as noted for plain honest
speaking Blair sends best love is standing by me— very anxious to write all on
this. I object   Your own Lizzie

1. On August 7, Lt. Roswell H. Lamson was detached from duty on the *Minnesota* and given command of the USS *Nansemond*, with orders to join the blockade off
Wilmington.

2. Jimmie was Lucy James Blair, daughter of James and Mary Blair, born 1853.

3. SPL and Robert E. Lee shared a great-great-grandfather, Richard Lee; their great-
grandfathers, Thomas Lee and Richard Lee, respectively, were brothers, thus making
the two men third cousins.

Silver Spring   August 6, 1863
Dear Phil   I shall be off I hope soon to Church—[1] Our patriotic Old Bishop[2]

has urged us all to join in our prayers & thanksgiving and we who realize by faith the Divine presence "when two or three are gathered together" ever must joyfully seize this opportunity of praying for our Earthly treasures— & some how whenever Navy is uttered you are its representation in my heart & Frank the Army— My Country is both

Father received a short letter from Apo saying that she expects Frank in a few days. she will accompany him with the two eldest children— She says the death of Otis[3] has stunned them all but his Mothers anguish is dreadful She has borne six sons & lost three— a dear, tender, little, Mother she is too over her darlings—

Govr Dennison left us this morning to return home— He says the nomination Vallandigham[4] Morgan's Raid & now the result in Kentucky makes the defeat of Copperheads certain in Ohio— where the Conscription risked matters in the absence of so many to the Army. He says Lizzie & Mrs. Dennison[5] will come to Washington next winter I told them I was not housekeeping— but they could use Silver Spring Hdquarters as we did & have a merry time. he seemed to think so when he dined there with me on Tuesday. Father & Betty making the party— I had a good dinner which will be a satisfaction to you to know— And the house altho empty was clean & the coolest place any of us had been that day

Our weather continues intensly hot. so far Blair endures it well— cheerful as a bird— out under the trees all day about the Spring where it is cool from the dense shade & the cool waters, he makes mill dams, mud cakes & runs barefooted, but I cannot let him go wading in the water as it is too cold— too great a difference between it & the atmosphere— so he like his dog Ned— keeps out of it save with his hands in making his mill dams— He luxuriates in peaches & etc— I am so thankful he keeps well— for in going about for health one sometimes catches worse ailments than those they seek to cure—

Father & Mother are very happy in the hope of soon welcoming Frank home— Ever your own Lizzie

1. On August 7, EBL commented: "Mr. Pyne gave us a good discourse semi religious & political & so loyal & patriotic and clever that I sighed for Fanny as nothing convinces save it comes from the pulpit—."

2. William Rollinson Whittingham was Episcopal bishop of Maryland.

3. Otis Dick, six months older than Blair Lee, was the son of Mira and Franklin Dick.

4. Clement C. Vallandigham, leader of the Copperheads in Ohio, was convicted by a military commission of aiding the enemy by expressing treasonable ideas. He had gone to Canada, and on June 11, the Ohio Peace Democrats had nominated him in abstentia for governor.

5. Ann Neil, daughter of William Neil (a Columbus, Ohio, businessman), was William Dennison's wife.

Silver Spring   August 9, 1863

Dear Phil   This Sunday six years ago your son was born & a great joy and comfort he has been to his Mother   I sometimes wonder what would have become of me in these last three years of separation from you & bitter miseries of the War— I have been many times felt most gratefully that he was an endless source of occupation, comfort & joy to me & how often I pray he may be a prop to our old age— & that he may be to you— too a good gift— He rode Jinny alone today all about the Yard in a great glee— he is well full of spirit & frolic but looks thin & pale from the heat— Still he sleeps & eats heartily & is well in all respects— covered with prickly heat but dont complain of it at all— & as the old women say its a healthy sign— I am easy about it—

The wine from St. Louis & the Claret from Philadelphia all arrived today. for which my Parents send you many many thanks— I received an immense package last night from Mr. Keim— of receipts & a check for one hundred dollars— I shall retain these until you return from the Coast— in the meantime mention what you desire to do about it— I shall copy his letter to you which intended doing today— but have been busy & it is so hot— that I was lazy as could excuse myself by thinking that even if delayed it might reach you just as promptly

Father got a letter from a person who is position to know saying there a great feud between Robt Lee & Jeff Davis & that the Genl has proffered his resignation that there is a great change in Va about matters & they begin to fear they are bear the brunt of the War— & then to be left in the lurch by the Cotton States

I forwarded a letter from Fanny boys about business— & I fear they may do something wrong about the draft— write to them promptly. Fanny does talk such nonsense "about Cousin Robt" & yet is so right in her ideas that no success be ruled holy which forged fetters for man, black or white

I am not less anxious about Johns boys it does seem such a sin to stop the studies of such a boy as Johnnie & Willie & bring them near Prince George bumpkins & it is evident John thinks himself too poor to continue their education— I have often wanted to sound them about it but never had the hardihood & now as the commencement of a collegiate year approaches I really cannot resist suggesting that if possible without hurting your Brother you ought help him to educate his sons. tis the best way to help them in life— & I regard it as the best storage in life for our own child These are all fine children & they are the band of Brothers to which I hope our little one will belong & I hope with mutual benefit—

I am going to send your Secy a basket of peaches— this day ours are very fine— Mr Fox is sick & will probably be here today— Ever your devoted Lizzie

Silver Spring   August 10, 1863

Dear Phil   I was not smart enough this morning to get my letter ready to go with Brother as he started at seven olk to avoid the heat— & I had to dress Blair as well as myself— so as you well know I was not quite up to that time tho I did try for it— but had not Becky to help so failed— Blair had a severe stinging from a yellow jacket today which pained & fretted the little fellow this hot day.

Mr. Fox dined here yesterday talked very freely about DuPont & Dalghren & with some bitterness of both   said the latter's course[1] was uncomprehensible to him that he always regarded him as the *tallest* man in the Service— & his bitterness towards himself F. is undeserved & without the slightest justice for he was always his friend & admirer & that Davis was always his adorer & follower   is equally *nonplussed*— He says was more miserable after he was made Admiral than he was ever before— he did not deserve the place "tho *Lee* thought he did—" got it via the "Senate in spite of the Secy & Grimes. that he has molded all naval Legislation for ten years" & if he takes Charleston he will dictate for the rest of his life to the Service   Dalghren thinks in his latest dispatches that the Monitors can take Sumpter which is packed in the middle with cotton bales from Duponts fight— got these facts by a leak thro' french Admiral— who during his visit to Charleston got by *great* effort the official report to give the French Govt an idea of the power of the monitors a friend got a reading of this report memorized it & this added to the french Admirals opinion that that the Navy of the U.S. can take *any fort "almost"* convinced Fox that the Monitors can take Sumpter— Dalghren writes without knowing these things & says with the Lehigh Saugamon & two other monitors— he can take Charleston— the fleet now lies safely where Dupont said it was an impossible & already passed thro terrific storms & feel they can weather anything but a hurricane— Rogers has the Canonicus & is off in 30 days— Fox wishes for the Norfolk Yard— "in that hot place he could get ships off— but now it takes as long to repair as to build a ship—" has 40 ships repairing in New York— & they could be all finished in two weeks if honestly worked" I repeat this talk as some of it may interest you

I sent peaches to our good Old Secy— I have no chance for this today It is still excessively hot & I rejoice that you have sea breezes

August 11. Tuesday— I am in time today— Frank Apo Christine & (to Blair's great joy) Jim are all expected tonight. Andrew Alexander was here last evening— he is stationed now in Washington where there's to be a great Depot of Cavalry. right on Fen Young's[2] place at Geessboro   dont these poor secesh seemed to be fated— Stoneman & staff are fixtures consequently in Washington City— Alfred P. is to command in the field[3]   Andrew I think is just now quite content with this release I think there's a matrimonial dream in his heart

This is like last year the hotest day of all   you returned from New Orleans this day a year ago & now we hope for Frank this evening— I should enjoy it more if I could hope for 3 weeks of your company which I had last year— I wrote you some disconnected talk yesterday— it may be news professional news to you & it *may not* be— but I concluded to give the chance— Fox goes north for a week he is sick from a bilious cholick & needs the change— Ever yr own Lizzie

1. John A. Dahlgren, engineer and inventor, had been appointed in June to command the South Atlantic Blockading Squadron for the purpose of an attack on Fort Sumter. He had never before commanded a ship. On July 10, the assault at Charleston began with an attack on Morris Island, with ironclads cooperating with Gen. Quincy Gillmore's army force. It proved to be impossible to take Battery Wagner on the island because of heavy fire from Fort Sumter. Gillmore then wanted naval firepower turned on Sumter while Dahlgren favored another attack on Wagner, suggesting that he land part of Gillmore's army in the rear while a larger force made a frontal assault. Gillmore thought his force too weak for division and asked for sailors and marines to augment the army. Because his ships were already undermanned, Dahlgren refused the request.

2. Ignatius Fenwick Young, son of Nicholas and Sarah Fenwick, had a farm, Gisborough, in the District.

3. On May 22, Alfred Pleasonton had assumed command of the cavalry of the Army of the Potomac.

Silver Spring   August 12, 1863

Dear Phil Frank did not come last night but a large package of letters from him arrived— & we think he is very likely to be in town when Brother gets there— preferring to travel at night this hot weather— I think they may have stopped in Phila about Apo's eyes Frank did not go to Newport at all— but stopped in New York where Apo and the children joined him—

Brother says that Halleck says Robt Lee has resigned & there is a great feud between him & Jeff— I think that may be these rumors may be set afloat to tempt us into an attack but just now Old Abe is absorbed in the Charleston fight. has sent ten thousand men which have not been asked for by Gilmore Mr. Fox told me that Foster asked to have the Ironclad go up James River on a very useless (he thought) reconnaisance— lost two sailors & calls it very successfull!!

a friend of Franks was in Brothers office today & says the enthusiasm of Franks reception in St Louis is beyond the power of "pen or speech to describe— *Paschall* & Knapp[1] have come in privately to say they are "all Frank—" but this I think unreliable from its channel—[2]

The news from the South extracts from the Mobile & other papers show that there is a growing revolt to the Confederacy. if our armies were only in flight to follow up our military success against Lee— which is now the only rallying left— we might soon have peace— at home Father thinks a french War will be our next National *labor*— Says the destruction of our commerce & extension of French commerce is essential to a french Navy which is Louis Napoleon's Hobby— They are certainly marvellously curious about our Ironclads testing their power by the most minute inquiry here & among the rebels— & pay well for the information— Which I told Fox ought to be denied them he said if denied we would get the credit of fear & discourtesy & they would buy all the information just as they do in Charleston & elsewhere—

I must write to Nelly as this is my day for writing and if I miss one week she complains by saying I have spoilt & must now go on since my letters are a family institution & other kind things she always sends love to you & says all enjoy all my talk about you & Blair— Ever your devoted Lizzie

1. George Knapp and Nathaniel Paschall, along with Knapp's brother John, constituted George Knapp and Company, which owned the Missouri *Republican* newspaper. They were Union supporters but advocated moderation in military rule.

2. On August 16, EBL reported: "They are just now discussing Frank plans for the approaching winter— He has declined the Senatorship & will come to the House during the winter Nobody of his politics could be elected in his District where Charcoals & Democrats are his friends & when he was there the former thronged around him— He says he would have less influence in the Senate— He is at home in the House & prefers the House—."

Silver Spring   August 14, 1863

Dear Phil   I was too lazy this morning having sit up late listening to Frank talk & was surprised to find it was one olck 'ere I was in bed, consequently I was not up early enough this morning to write in time to go by Brother after breakfast I thought often last night that it would be to me the good*liest* treat to have you & Frank to talk your campaigns over together— it is almost impossible to write endless points which give zest to talk—

One thing will interest you to know that the plan of campaign was *Grants* alone— Sherman wanted to go to the rear of Vicksburg— by the Yazoo McPherson[1] wanted to go below & land at Grand Gulf— then go take Fort Hudson— take all of Banks troops & then invest Vicksburg in the rear— their plans & others were all considered in council & then Grant announced his own & his purpose to follow it. & nothing strikes me more in listening to Frank— than the minute care in every detail to avoid miscarriage— every precaution possible was taken & his own caution & prudence was amazing to his volunteer generals— but the results showed that in their execution of their plans it all told so beautifully that it has evidently uplifted their general in the hearts as well as heads that he should look ahead so much to prepare for their comforts as well as safety—

Frank was so close on Johnston that he ate a dinner just prepared for him
by a rich planter named Harris & just before reaching Jackson he had his tents
put in a fine lawn & when sitting at his breakfast after a nights march— he
saw a parcel of papers— it turned out to be John Breckinridges who left them
in hot haste at a late hour the night before— In the papers was the curl of a
childs hair & some orders signed by John & others from Joe Johnston— Frank
says Joe's fatal mistake to himself was to order Pemberton over the big Black—
Johnstons Army was just about equal in numbers to Grants— Who by his rear
movement just cut Joe in two— then whipped with his United Army first one
half of Joe's & then the other— Pemberton is thought brave— but not a great
Genl. & his best troops were from Missouri— many of whom have gone home
for a *full due* as you sailors say—

Saturday *August 15th* Frank & Brother are off in a few moments to see Abe
& others of import   Father has not been well & Frank is urging him to go to
Newport with him but I dont think he will go however for the weather is not
quite so hot & the nights are always cool after this   Blair rides daily & so far
has got thro' the summer better than any season of heat heretofore—

Frank goes to Newport tomorrow as he has not yet seen his two little children   I think the case of dyptheria in his family makes him uneasy   Ever your
own   Lizzie

1. Maj. Gen. James B. McPherson, commanding the Seventeenth Corps at Vicksburg.

Silver Spring   August 24, 1863
Dear Phil   The old Contraband went off too early for me today after Becky—
I dressed "the Baby" as he says I may call him when we go to bed at night—
but no other time

I direct a letter to you today from Nelly— who says in her letter— Please
send the enclosed to Phil who is the best brother in law in the world— if my
own were not so good— I would say he say he is the best Brother with which
any woman was ever blessed." I quote this mostly to let you know that her
family are attentive and kind to her— which is comfort to me to know— She
says she is busy fixing off her three boys to College which brings up very vividly
her own Mother who had to deprive herself of all her children for the sake
of education when they were her sole resource for earthly enjoyment— She
often writes & talks about her Mother of late— Kate Gaston cannot come to
her sister save under the pledge of remaining until the end of the War— I have
tried that well— by the cases of Becky Ellis—[1] who came thro' under that
promise & Mrs. Stannard[2] who would not agree to do it as she left her child
behind. Nelly's accounts of the running away of slaves will soon make Mary-

land a free state if they can be kept out of it— This enlisting has renewed the higera—[3] Uncle Charles daughter Laura[4] has lost all she had & she mentions others reduced from ease to poverty—

I have just got an enclosure from Fanny for you— which I forward today Betty expects Alida Carroll here on a visit they are sadly broken down by the death of their Father[5] Father is still ailing— tho not sick— but the heat is quite enough to overpower those who suffer from it— Mr. Vance told me today that all around Bladensburg the crop was almost destroyed by drought— Ever your own   Lizzie

Augst 25 Tuesday Had no chance to send this bulletin off yesterday— and now have to waylay Mr. Beale by times to get this off as nobody is willing to encounter the dust & heat of the city— who can avoid it & yet we are wild to hear the news from Charleston— for which all the Country is on the qui vive— How sorry I am for poor Capt. Rogers—[6] who I never knew but of whose history I He married somebody considered beneath him some say because of her beauty & other because she was in the house with him when he had smallpox & had courage to nurse him when all others fled— The poor little woman was always overpowered by the grandeur of her new condition

Those bolts seem to be terrific in their execution— please keep off those monitors— I see that they have now three Ironclads at Richmond & are building two more. we may wake up some morning with some bolts flying in Washington if all your Ironclads are taken away— those big ships could not follow small craft up the Potomac & could escape by keeping in shoal water— away from yr big ships— Excuse this talk but Ive nothing else to write which is very often the case with   Ever yr Lizzie

1. Becky Ellis, who lived in Richmond, was an old friend of EBL.

2. Martha Pierce Stanard, widow of Robert Craig Stanard, was a leader of Confederate society in Richmond.

3. In the spring of 1863 Stanton had ordered Adj. Gen. Lorenzo Thomas to begin large-scale enlistment of black troops. By summer the project was well under way. On August 23, EBL commented: "This *transition state* makes the *servant* department go hard with womankind in the south generally who are unused to waiting on themselves— I heard from Dr. Hall that George Graham had lost 14 or 15 of his slaves lately— which was his first loss of the sort— Frank said he had as many white people in this waggon train as Negroes when he left Jackson his empty waggon were filled with white women & children who begged for his protection—."

4. Charles Hill was Nelly's father's brother. Laura, daughter of Charles and his third wife Anne Elizabeth Snowden, was born in 1837 and married Samuel Brooke of Anne Arundel County.

5. William Thomas Carroll, clerk of the Supreme Court of the United States.

6. Lt. George W. Rodgers, commanding the USS *Catskill*, was Dahlgren's chief

of staff. He was killed August 17, 1863, during the engagement of Battery Wagner, when fragments of the interior iron plating of the pilothouse crushed his head. He had married Margaret Lane in 1842.

Silver Spring   August 27, 1863

Dear Phil   I received a letter of ten pages from Wright Rives trying to threaten us into getting him promoted to prevent him from resigning— He wrote me a short letter of this kind— & I tried to get Father to do something about it— but he is really not well enough— but I replied kindly & he thinks it little more of the same style— will give him the result— one we would gladly obtain if it were possible—

I got a notice from my quiet gentleman that he quits No 4 on 1st of Sept. He complains of the price so Mr. Baily informs me— I suspect Harriet of some extras & think it will be a good time to send her off— because nothing look better than all the arrangements— but I expect he only got a big room for the hot months— & it is an annoyance to have strangers about the house & Ill now drop as you suggest all lodgers— I can now get along very comfortably with $50 or 60 dollars a month— my washing— Harriet & Becky taking half of it $25—

The Sands came out, it was their first evening here since she lost her son I felt a great deal for her. She heard of his death out here— Sands looks wonderfully well says to his surprise— Blockading agreed with him— Fox got back— Charleston is the everlasting theme nobody talks about anything else— Capt Sands says Wilmington comes next— & hopes it will all be done up before winter comes around Oh how intensely I hope it for I am weary of this long long cruise— now near three years since you sailed in the Vandalia—

I got a long letter from Fanny about her boys— & the war— The Mexican capture by France,[1] & the talk of the Secesh about her who prefer the fall of Mexico to the old Union has taken the scales from her eyes in such a cause— she could even consent to fight "cousin Robt rather than to consent to "French" & "*Catholic*" dicatation" on this Continent!— Father apprehends trouble with France— I hope this fight at Charleston will save us from it— Fanny is at last a converted Union woman & if she sticks to it as she does her own church after her wandering she will be sure to keep her boys all right which has been a matter of some anxiety with me— in the last year and am now glad to be rid of it— Your devoted Lizzie

1. During the summer of 1863, the French army ousted Benito Juarez and established Archduke Ferdinand Maximilian as emperor of Mexico.

Silver Spring   August 28, [1863]

Dear Phil   Secy Welles, son[1] & Mr. Fox paid us a visit yesterday evening & brought me the news of your Capture of two guns near Fort Fisher— which tidings came via Richmond— also that they admit that Sumpter is no longer tenable— but add that Sumpter is but a *small* part of the defences of Charleston— forgetting that our Navy can destroy Charleston from Fort Sumpter

The accounts about you via Richmond are very meagre & I shall feel anxious until I hear from you— The Old Secy seemed vastly well pleased with even the Secesh account of your proceedings[2] thinks the reduction of Charleston is only a matter of time— Fox told me in reply to my suggestion that if Gilmore had been there DuPont & he would have reduced Charleston long since Fox replied No when Foster became ill the Dept urged Dupont to cooperate with Gilmore— & Gilmore asked his aid in landing on Morris Island— he refused— saying it was impossible—[3] in truth for all I hear of this matter impresses me with the fact that Dupont was too old for such continuous hard work & had grown too weary & dispirited for such a herculean labor— Some show age— first by a loss of spirit. & with others tis the last thing they do lose—

Blair has revelled in his young company for two days— keeps along with George Sands[4] who is a month two older than Phill Lee & they are very nearly the same size & weight— Blairs hands & feet are smaller— & features are more infantine The Sands want a naval apt pay masters place for their boy Blair they say there are 4 vacancies Your affectionate Lizzie

1. Welles's oldest son Edgar was a Yale student.
2. SPL had refined the blockading technique at Wilmington, using several lines of ships to make running the blockade more difficult.
3. Command disputes between Foster and Hunter, combined with army-navy disagreement over tactics, delayed any attack on Charleston. Foster refused to continue in his position, and the army was left to Hunter, who had never commanded troops in battle. Eventually, Gillmore replaced Hunter and Dahlgren replaced Du Pont.
4. George Sands, the young son of Henrietta and B. F. Sands.

Silver Spring   August 29, 1863

My Dear Phil   I think Fox meant it as a sort of apology & explanation to you— his complaint about the difficulty in getting thro' with repairs— he remarked one day of late that he had 40 vessels repairing & his mail was crammed with excuses for their delays in getting off. he was sick— & spoke in the most bitter & irritated tone & said that his spirit was almost broken with this kind of *"cheating"* which he had done everything he could to prevent—

There is evidently a desire on the part of the Dept— to Give Dalghren (who is no favorite— but has the ear & control so says Fox of Congress) no room for complaint on any score— & then DuPont is on the other side bent upon defeat of our operations at Charleston by way of self justification— so the Depart is in a tight place & evidently is oblivious of all its duties save those at Charleston as thro' these two Admirals it is on a sort of trial before the public— Brother made this remark to me some weeks since— & evidently thought that Fox's sickness was caused by his intense excitement & labor *over* this matter & he evidently feels slaked upon the issue which Dupont has made with him personally He never talks to me five minutes in the last two months without getting on this Dupont fight with the Dept—[1] in which it is evident that both he & Welles have become very bitter— I am not sure that is very prudent to write this all out— but as you go to the Dept personally before I see you— which I rejoice is to be so soon— it has been very long since you have been here & I began as you may see to hint modestly at a visit—

I am a busy & now a comparatively well woman & have a cheerful mein & I hope a grateful heart for the preservation of my dear husband & Brother thro' so many perils— but I am weary of this long long absence— & can never utter the fullness of my joy when I get you home again for a "full due—" as you sailors phrase it. I shall hope to see you from this night a week—[2] I have been busy all this day moving spinach & other gardening— it has been almost of October in temperature— which everybody enjoys rather more than I do especially Blair who has been very jubilant over his company— who all left us last night as Sands had to go to Baltimre to hurry up the Decotah— which he says will ready to go off in a week or ten days which means two or 3 weeks according to Fox—

I shall be off to church early tomorrow & will not have time to say a word until at night again— *Au revoir*   Your devoted Lizzie

1. As a result of Du Pont's conviction that monitors were ineffective offensive weapons, he and Fox were continually at odds.

2. On September 4, EBL wrote: "Oh how I do wish you may come home this next week   I want you to meet Frank— but first & most I want to see you— four long long months have passed since you were here in May."

Washington   August 30, [1863]

Dear Phil   Mr. F walked from church just now with me— I asked him if the newspaper story was true about the 4 war vessels of the enemy moving into Wilmington— he said he did not believe a word of it— which was some relief to my anxiety— He then began to pitch into Almy[1] who had no business on your side of the Gulf stream & was in your bailywick without any instructions & had destroyed the fastest gun boat by being there. that he was as usual just where he ought not to be— & was intensely bitter on Almy & Smith[2] about repairs & Navy Yards. that it is impossible to get along this way & he told the Secy. so this morning. that the Quaker City had been seven month repairing— that Farragut had sent home about half his squadron for repairs & etc

I write this hurriedly— but must add that he said that three vessel would be sent to you in eight & ten days & he had told them that they should go without paint & etc etc & just the moment the boiler was in— the Deco-tah is one & Mantanzas or some such name is the other[3] he asked when I thought you would come back— I said you had said "that depended on cir-cumstances— which is the closing part of your sentence of your letter that is you be here by tomorrow week if *nothing occurred to prevent* so I did not choose to indicate your movements as had not done so yr self— He remarked you had "held on there—" but you were right because you "had not half force enough to blockade that port—" He inquired about Lamson—"

I write in haste as Alida Carrol waits for me   Ever your devoted wife   Lizzie

1. In the first week of August, John J. Almy had sailed from New York in the USS *Connecticut* to cruise the outer limits of the blockade off Wilmington. After two weeks of frustration in not finding or capturing any runners, he came in to port to consult with SPL. On his way out of port, his ship collided with the USS *Quaker City*, making her unfit for sea service.

2. Rear Adm. Joseph Smith was chief of the Naval Bureau of Yards and Docks.

3. Both the *Dacotah* and the *Maratanza* had been repairing at Baltimore.

Washington   September 3, [1863]
Dear Phil   Our panic yesterday morning created by the removal of all the cattle in the county above us— which amounted to thousands & thousands of head but the drovers say that the enemy got 700 mules which were between Poolesville & Rockville— There is a strong cavalry patrol above us last night so we concluded to stay home— & shall do so until the enemy advance in force— which is not yet the case— we are too near the lines & within strong pickets consequently are for the time safe— & this is a deadly time to be in the city.[1]

I write at No 6 where my Yankee kin are expected today   I left Blair helping Sam to gather apples & about as merry a boy as I ever saw— he is very much better in color from this cool weather— has ate & slept well all the time— but grows fast & is very thin. Consequently if we have go from Silver Spring I shall remain in the city until I see you & then Ill go north for I cannot risk him in this atmosphere or odors— & shall not be scared easily from home   I see they want to leave cattle at Silver Spring which is an indication that the Contractors think it a safe place

Fathers teeth plague him again & he is not well today— the rest of us quite so— & I have much to do— so good morning to you— I delayed this to see if there was any news to send you but there is none I got as yet to send   Ever yours devotedly   Lizzie

1. In her September 1 letter, under the date of September 2, EBL wrote: "The enemy are again in Maryland— with some cavalry now at Rockville— we have not one man between us and the enemy—Father goes in individually & I shall set myself

to work & get ready for a move in later in the day— So you need not be anxious about us immediately but it is enough to make one bitter to have such miserable management in our affairs—."

Silver Spring   September 5, [1863]
Dear Phil   I have been a very busy woman ever since yesterday morning. Apo & her children & mother got here before breakfast— Mother was sick & I more than busy. Today there were ten to dinner beside our own family   Frank has always a suite of cronies & as we are somewhat short in servants— I was busy again today. Now that all are served & the children in a romp on the porch where the rain will keep them I hope until I finish this letter which I have thought of oftener than anything else

I had a long sad letter from Nelly— John had left home with the boys who enter upon their college career tomorrow. She encloses me two letters from Harrison about Kate[1] & John's reply which I think excellent for he declines taking the onus of advising Mr. Harrison to confine the poor child to an asylum which has been Mr Harrisons determination for years past— I think she cannot be worse off than in his care & often had the matter to hang very heavily upon my heart. But the case presented such endless difficulty & your absence made it impossible for me to undertake the charge of her— but I am convinced that a regular life— food— exercise— & above all occupation will make her a happy useful woman— & it may be the Asylum is the place to obtain these results— but if she recovers— her fathers house will run her mad again— I should have died in her place without occupation— or the love of those around. Starvation is nothing to it— no wonder she refused food   I have pitied that poor hungry hearted child more than any human being I have ever known in my life— Her morbid sensitive nature from her mother— linked with sordid coarse one of her father— is a comment upon women ever marrying to serve any but the law which God has put in our hearts— I will retain these letters until you come here when I will hand them with those of your St. Louis agent to you.

Frank is looking well but Apo is thin & looks sick— the children are looking well. Our boy is taller than Preston— but lacks his width & weight. I sometimes make great calculations upon yr aid in making Blair use dumb bells— his chest will be contracted if not expanded by some exercise   I have a fine pair of dumb bells but he is very loth to use them   Becky is all satisfaction   she says Blairs cloths just fit Pres & he a year older than Blair— who is certainly quite a half inch the tallest. They have talked of poor Otis' death until I have trembled will terror   his death was so sudden— Ever yr devoted Lizzie
The Dicks are in Phila at the Continental

1. Kate Harrison was SPL's niece, the daughter of his deceased sister Jane Elizabeth. Jane had married in 1834 and died in 1837, leaving her husband Henry Harrison with a young daughter. As Kate matured, her erratic behavior created distressing problems for her father and her two uncles, SPL and John Lee. All the family attempted to placate the young woman and find appropriate living arrangements acceptable to her. Ultimately she was institutionalized.

Silver Spring   September 10, 1863
Dear Phil   We have had nothing to vary our routine save rumors about Charleston & the Army of the Potomac of which I believe none at all— the Army near us is getting in fine order[1] & we hear good accounts of the con- scripts which are coming in sometimes a thousand a day so said young Seward[2] here last evening. They say it is now as strong as at Gettysburg. The best news I have had is that Capt Sands *is off* for Wilmington— is to take in some provi- sions at Old Pt. today & then goes to Sea— maybe this will go by him— I have heard that the conscription has made it very difficult to get Sailors They are bought up for substitutes There are stories of men being drugged & swindled into the Army by the substitute agents— & the desperate efforts of some of them to desert show that there must be something of the sort

It is now settled that Frank & Co are to go on Sunday next— at 6 olk. So I still hope that you may come ere they go— There is a great deal of talk of the Ironclads coming from England. consequently I am more than ever anxious to have you where you can have an Ironclad too— Still I have heard so much & so long of these crafts that I am getting incredulous about them— Father is convinced that when European despots find that this southern conspiracy has not extinguished our Republic that they will try to do it themselves— Then the real patriots of the South will join their Country's cause & we will be truly one people again— but I look at the idea of another war with utter dismay. cant & wont believe in it. Ever your affectionate   Lizzie

1. On September 9, EBL wrote: "You will take some satisfaction in knowing that their is a special patrol here at night— as the Post Master General is now enjoying his country residence— Mrs. No. 6 is cross & scared & I am rather prone to increase her alarms by relating my own— which may be ill natured but was unintentional."

2. William Henry Seward's son, Frederick W. Seward, served as assistant secretary of state.

13

*"my hopes greatly predominate over my fears—
besides tis my nature to believe the best
until I know the worst—"*

October 15, 1863

THE 1863 CONGRESSIONAL ELECTIONS WERE crucial for Lincoln's administration. Opposition mounted within his own party, and Salmon P. Chase
emerged as a leading contender for the presidential nomination. At the
same time, there were those in the Democratic party who wished to back
a peace candidate. In Maryland, the issue of state emancipation formed the
cornerstone of debate; radicals urged unconditional emancipation; moderates called for compensation and colonization; and conservatives resisted all
moves toward abolition. The Blairs, stalwart supporters of Lincoln, took up
the cudgels for their leader and stumped hard to retain a moderate balance in
Congress. Despite Radical gains in the election, Lincoln set forth the basic
principles of his moderate "10% plan" of reconstruction in his annual message.
Throughout the North citizens began to develop their visions of reconstruction
of the Union, and the lines of political battle were drawn.

On the military front, action concentrated in Tennessee. Because Frank
commanded a division under Sherman, Blair interest was especially high.
Victory at Chattanooga followed by federal occupation of Knoxville ended
the year's fighting and improved the Union position in the middle theater of
the war.

Silver Spring   September 29, 1863

Dear Phil   I had another day of perserving & with another in prospect for
tomorrow   I made some good brandy peaches for mine goode mon today &
felt happy that I could do something for him   I will pack them in a box & if
you will not eat them this year may be the time will come when you will   they
will only improve with the keeping— Then you can have Scuppernon Wine
& peaches too— for your home desserts

If you can pick up a good dining room servant, among your contrabands it would be a great benefit conferred on this domicil— We have a small house with two rooms where the man's wife can live if he has one, & she can do the milking & some washing— I mention this as you told me to remind you of this promise you made to Mother— who seems to look to it as a chance for a good servant— Also dont forget the letter about young Sands.

Blair has been busy driving his donkey cart & took his ride with Sammy. I have heard no news & been too busy even to read the papers as yet— We are all well— only I am very tired having worked more than I am used to of late Ever your affectionate Lizzie

Silver Spring   September 30, 1863

Dear Phil   I ought to be very sweet on you tonight as I have been *besugared* all day but I must say that in doing up sweets I have no pleasure save in the thought that it will be sweet some time other to you— or others dear to me— for like my chickens I cannot eat my own cooking— indeed care too little for dessert to enjoy it

Blair got tired of jogging around the door & went off with Henry to hunt nuts. Sam was a long time finding them so you see he is cutting lose from the apron string— I did not rebuke him— Frank left St Louis Monday— made a speech on Saturday night which Ill send you just as soon as I get it—[1] Mrs Phelps is in the City— I will go see her friday— Ludwell Alexander[2] came here today & from him I learned that they called here the day you & I went to the City— This poor boy looks desparately ill— & has grown to be six feet high & is only Arthur's age— I shall pay my devoirs in that quarter soon as Mrs L returns to rusticate— Maria Smith is on the Hill with our neighbors— went up to the Quaker neighborhood to enter Woodbury to School— who seemed rather to like the change— Hookers appointment makes a great row among the military Slocum, Howard,[3] & many others resign— because of his appt.

From what I hear of west End Gossip the North is coming down to Washington in fashionable force— & it is that fact that make houses rent so high— Mrs Bayard Smith has found Balt uncomfortable— & is now a house searcher in Washn & GeoTown Hoopers are building a famous Stable & other fine things on her old grounds— Geo Riggs has given in cash $25000 for the Digges place. "Green Hill" We are all well & busy— but even work— & hard work too— does not keep me from missing you all the time— Ever your devoted Lizzie

1. On October 2, EBL wrote: "We have been in family group around the fire discussing Franks Speech who has taken the course which I have urged for many weeks on Father When F. was here he was silent & agreed it was by others that the best thing to do was to do & say nothing in Missouri just now— I considered silence in active politicians as consent to schemes which seemed to me akin to Secession & so it seems I was not alone."

2. Ludwell Alexander was a Kentucky relative of the Blairs and also related to Thomas L. Alexander of the Old Soldiers' Home.

3. On September 23, Joseph Hooker was ordered to take the Eleventh and Twelfth Corps of the Army of the Potomac to reinforce Rosecrans at Chattanooga. These troops were commanded by Oliver O. Howard and Henry W. Slocum. The latter submitted his resignation, but it was rejected. At Chattanooga, Slocum's division was assigned special duty to protect the railroad and thereby was not directly under Hooker's command.

Silver Spring   October 3, 1863

Dear Phil   I was glad to know that the "*Old Box* recd—" at last & hope the shirts are still wearable— but as they are old ones, fear the keeping so long will make them nearer yellow than white, Still they are clean.

Mr. Smith stopped here en route from Rockville says the meeting was a success— but thinks both Brothers & Thomas' speeches[1] are meant for a different audience— there was a gathering of about 300 men which is enough for a County meeting—[2] All was going on fairly until a late hour. They hope to carry the emancipation M.C. in this District but I fear the Secesh will unite on Calvert who is proslavery Union Man— It is going to be a well contested election & if carried by Holland[3] will soon emancipate slavery in this State— for this District has some of the largest secesh counties in the State in it— Father puts much on their getting paid for their negroes & that is a point of much import— for they are fast losing them without any hope of recovery for loss in any shape Many that now stay hoping for emancipation & would leave if disappointed If I was a large owner of that property I would put them on wages now & be sure of my crops— Thomas goes for deportation & emancipation & made an admirable speech— Brother pitched into Sumners plan of making the Southern States a Territory.[4] thus depriving them of their national equality with northern States— that is Chase's & the ultra hobby upon which to split the Republican party & to get the election & Govt into the hands of the "Ultras" Read brothers speech— I think it will pay— from what I know of it *This* is a *crisis* in the political world— of no small import to us—

Frank went to Vicksburg. Apo wants to sell Rose Bank[5] has been offered $40,000 for it   thinks she can get better interest for that than for the place They are all well out there   I am glad you part in peace with H——n[6]   that his discontent is more with himself than you— Betty left here— but not Washn   kept very quiet there, for fear of not getting off— at all from here Went down with Blair Sands— as you know by this time

Blair is well but was really worn out by his riding & racing of day   I often think his spirit like mine overtaxes his strength— he sleeps sweetly   Ever your devoted   Lizzie

1. The issue of emancipation divided Maryland politicians in the 1863 congressional elections. On October 3, at a political rally at Rockville, Montgomery Blair

spoke out strongly against Radical abolitionists and advocated a moderate approach to emancipation. Francis Thomas, Maryland congressman from 1861 to 1869, was running for reelection and had shifted his position to favor emancipation.

2. On October 2, EBL mentioned the meeting at Rockville: "Frank Thomas & Brother are to speak— also Mr. Randall but I expect the affair is rather sudden to amount to much. From all I hear Calvert will be elected & he is a genuine copperhead. Still I have some reasons for thinking him honestly for the Union tho' pro-slavery—."

3. Charles Benedict Calvert, also running for reelection, opposed emancipation on states' rights principles. Part of the Union convention had bolted and nominated John C. Holland, an Unconditional Unionist who proposed ridding Maryland of slavery. Holland garnered the support of both the moderate Montgomery Blair and the Radical Winter Davis.

4. Charles Sumner subscribed to the theory that the Southern states had committed political suicide and should be treated as territories, subject to the jurisdiction of Congress. His ideas were not as radical as those of Thaddeus Stevens, who considered the Southern states as conquered provinces, nor as lenient as those of Lincoln, who believed that the Union had never been dissolved.

5. Rose Bank was Frank's home in St. Louis.

6. Henry Harrison, Kate's father and husband of SPL's eldest sister.

Silver Spring   October 7, 1863
Dear Phil   I believe Blair is more in a writing mood tonight than I am, choked up with a bad cold, for which I have kept close in the house as it was a damp day— he says one of his epistles is for Micheal—[1] he was vastly amused at the idea of your Irish boy Kicking Ned— "for you see he dont know Ned who would growl & open his mouth wide & would not Micheal foot it fast—."

"*Tish*" came over from the hill but I could not get an item from her of any kind   Brother stopped en route home laughing at the black looks of the Lord of the Treasury & the loud— high flown compliments— of the veritable "Premier—" about his speech   The Herald has wound up a loud panygeric with a sting because of a misprint rather the want quotation marks   The Intelligencer & all that style of papers have republished with compliments the speech & *nearly* right—[2] it is to be put out in pamphlet form from that office

We got yesterday the Article from the Atlantic Monthly— with Mr Sumner's name to it—[3] Wade is against Chase because he is for himself— Dennison is in control of the whole Republican organization in Ohio & will be here this winter— to spend some weeks with us & brings Miss Lizzie with him in Jany— Then I hope to get some things arranged to my satisfaction as they will be our guests here & in the City— But "mice & men" lay plans in vain sometimes— Good night   We had no mail today— Ever your own Lizzie

1. Michael Carroll was a cabin boy on the *Minnesota*.

2. Under the headline "On the Revolutionary Schemes of the Abolitionists and in Defence of the Policy of the President," the Washington *Daily National Intelligencer* of October 6, 1863, reported Montgomery Blair's speech given at an Unconditional

Union meeting at Rockville on September 31. Blair distinguished between loyal citizens and rebels in the Southern states and reiterated the presidential policy to save states, place power in the hands of loyal men, and allow states to resume their former place in the nation. On October 13, EBL added: "Father said the election would have been certainly been lost but for Brother's speech— he made it to save them— & joins in a hearty desire to keep the Republican party in array—."

3. In an unsigned article, Charles Sumner denounced the presidential plan of reconstruction and asserted that when the Southern states seceded, they no longer had legal existence, and therefore reconstruction should be conducted by Congress. "Our Domestic Relations; or, How to Treat the Rebel States," *Atlantic Monthly* 12 (Oct. 1863): 507–29.

Silver Spring   October 11, 1863

Dear Phil   I will go some day next week and see what I can get things for in the city. I have look at some of the furniture place & find that dining room furniture alone will cost four hundred dollars of oil walnut which is as cheap wood as oak. Minna reports that she can get carpets here as cheap as in Phila— She having employed Tish to enquire prices there— carpets like that in the office cost $150. the Brussells such as she gave for her parlors two years ago $150, is now sold for $225 by Barnes—[1] is the contractor— & Perry asks $262— for the same carpets— Barnes showed his bills at Ornes[2] in Phila— & he paid for these carpets in wholesdale $205 They are remarkably fine thick carpeting & one ply thicker than those for which she paid $150— She inquired for these things in New York— got Tish to do so in Phila and has concluded to buy here— & to take the cheap carpeting like that in our office— the patterns are beautiful & she says they will look as well now & when times get better she will buy a better one— This is her confab with me today—

Now about fixing up   it is expensive to you & troublesome to me— but Mother wants it   Father has never utter an objection to it— on the Contrary is after Vance all the time to put up a shed in which he intends to put his horses has sent wood daily there week until the cellar is now crammed— & Sammy will have go in Monday to pack it in the laundry for they say both cellars must be filled   I have never desired a stick to be sent there— When I took Laura & Hyman[3] there & had them taken care Father remarked— upon it with great satisfaction   I think the House is a comfort to them & I think Father never asks anything of his children which implies a pecuniary sacrifice— still he in this case has never discouraged the proceeding has by *actions* intimated that it was what he wanted. Mother goes in all the details— says she will take two of her servants— the waiter when she gets him— & her chambermaid Elizabeth an excellent servant— Harriet she will give $5 dollars more a month for cook and of the little darkies— (she has already spoken to Harriet on this point) She will provide & keep the house to which I assent as I'll never go there to stay without her & it a point upon which my pride is most gratified in pleasing her I have enquired about carpets & oil cloth— the latter is much the cheap-est for the Hall— the best quality costs $125 to $150 for *square* yard— a poor carpet costs that— & the dust make the oil cloth the best in other respects—

Mother was vastly pleased with your attentions to Betty— to whom she had to give all the considerations in her power since "the child has been snubbed because reared by me—" I use her own words— She wants Betty to come home & thinks when Marion leaves— it is good chance & Father immediately said it was horrid for individuals to appropriate for their own & family use the private property of anybody if confiscated— it was for Govt use—& they really want Betty to come home— & I have written their wishes to her—

Sunday morning I have just recd a letter from Nelly saying all the family are sick save John— & it is evident she wants a change of air for Annie & Phill— wants boarding in GeoTown & etc I shall woo & beg her to come to the house & I will go there & do all I can to make her comfortable & the children well— Chills & fever is the universal malady. I can fix it all very easy & I think it better than so much physic for the little ones— We are all well here Brothers mail will soon be by so I can only add Ever your own Lizzie

1. Barnes and Mitchell Dry Goods Store in Washington.
2. J. F. and E. B. Orne sold carpets, rugs, and floor cloths in Philadelphia.
3. Hyman Cecil Gratz, born 1824, was the son of EBL's uncle Ben Gratz. In 1857, Hyman married Laura J. Hamilton.

Silver Spring　October 15, 1863

Dear Phil Your's enclosing Andrews, Mr. Dicks letters & the linen samples came last night The linen is wonderfully cheap— Cotton of that width costs in the city $1,25cts & not of the best quality— that linen here would sell for $1,50 to 60cts I think if you are not as well off as you want to be in the sheet line you could not do better than buy two pairs— they will take about 11 yards— I have 12 prs of double linen sheets & two prs single— Becky says if it is not too much trouble she would like a whole piece of cotton a yd wide if it is to be had for 25cts a yard— & two pairs of Blankets— for we cannot get *any* blankets here for less than six dollars I would like one pair—

We are in a high state of anxiety here. The Sound of battle fell upon my ear & heart all day yesterday—[1] even after dark the cannon's insatiate roar continued— As yet we are as completely in the dark about the result as they are who live in England— but I am off in a few moments to the city to greet Nelly if she should come during the day— & to seek the news— Of course the telegraph will bear you the tidings— our Army is thinned by every means in the power of— & our men were in Pennsy voting— Still as the sound of the battle grew less loud toward evening— my hopes greatly predominate over my fears— besides tis my nature to believe the best until I know the worst—[2]

I shall have some little trouble with Dicks— When I go to Phila as I shall stay with Aunt— who is terribly out with them for their treatment of Dr. Gratz Moses however I shall see them almost daily & do my part in cordiality—[3] I am very glad that they are in Phila!! If Blair proves to have the whooping cough the trip will be a good thing for him but I still hope it is only a cold— for his eyes look well— & he eats heartily & plays ditto— looks very much better than when you saw him— Hyman asked him if you cared much for such a fellow as he is "I think he does & mama dont he? was his reply— looking as diffident as a girl ought to look— I need not repeat the reply of Mama & your own Lizzie

I have written to Betty tonight & sent it to Norfolk to Col Duttons care as you say they to move there

1. There had been skirmishing between the Army of Northern Virginia and the Army of the Potomac in the area of the Bull Run battlefield. On October 16, EBL wrote: "The sounds of the battle on Wednesday were so close and terrible that sleep did not visit my pillow with its wanted kindness that night—."

2. Despite her optimistic tone, EBL had stated on October 12: "Lee has just had time to bring his forces back to Virginia— & has now got all of our Armies on the defensive but I always begin to grumble when I get *scarry!!*" On October 19, she reported: "Fox said here yesterday afternoon that he advised us all to go to the City— at least Father & Brother Ladies never being in any danger For it was certain that yesterday morning *nobody* on this side of the lines knew where Lee was— He thinks that another raid over the Potomac inevitable from necessity The North Carolina prisoners say they have no meat— & it is now root or shoot pig or die—."

3. Franklin Dick had arrested the Confederate-sympathizing Dr. Moses in St. Louis.

Silver Spring   October 20, 1863
Dear Phil   Your draft for $242.67 (two hundred & forty two) came last evening also your letter of Saturday & the one enclosing the account of your's & Genl Foster "entent cordiale" which is peculiarly satisfactory to me—[1] as the world wags so everlastingly about the quarrels between army & Navy.

I think I can furnish the whole house (2 parlors excepted) as comfortably as we shall ever care to have it with the money you have sent me The Halls— office— dining room— & bed rooms. I have bought a beautiful carpet you I fear will object to the white ground in it but that wears as well as any other— & our dining room is rather a dark room & the curtains which Mother has given me for it are a dark green lined with a golden yellow— I think the combination will be cheerful & handsome— If you will observe all hotel carpets have white ground because soap & water cleans them perfectly I shall have the maple set of chamber furniture cleaned & varnished & I think it will make a pretty set for one of the north rooms

The Gratzs will go today— I shall dine them in the city & they leave in the 3 olk cars I feel intensely sorry for poor Laura— she feels doomed & it is so hard to leave her husband & little boy who she says is like our boy— he is riding Jenny Lind all around the Lawn— singing & shouting just from the exuberance of spirits— Sam went to the city to pack away the wood so as to make room for more—

I believe I mentioned that Nelly would be up the end of this week— Eliza Graham got hold of Father & they procured a pass for Miss Kate from the President. She will not be here to excite Mr. Stantons ire Father seems rather averse to asking these permissions for such avowed secessionists— Eliza's lonely condition however moved him up to it but he thinks the Upshurs such murmurers [?] that they deserve what they have so long sought for others & themselves— You knew the Judge was a most active Nullifyer Judge Gaston the truest Union man[2]

There is a profound mystery & silence on all affairs military Nobody knows anything— but there is a great increase of pickets & troops out this way— We expect Betty Thursday. Ever your own Lizzie Blair wrote & sealed the enclosed *"just as papa seals up his letters—"*

1. Gen. John G. Foster, in command of the Department of Virginia and North Carolina, had exchanged a series of letters with SPL in which they discussed their ideas of proper strategy.

2. Judge Abel Parker Upshur, a member of Virginia's Supreme Court from 1826 to 1841 and secretary of the navy before his death in 1841, had been outspoken in his support of the South and the institution of slavery. Judge William Gaston, father of Eliza Graham, was elected to the North Carolina Supreme Court in 1833; he had favored the eventual abolition of slavery. On October 17, EBL had explained: "Father & I have counselled over Mrs. U. he says if he were *to fight* a pass for her thro the Dept (the only way he could get it)— it would expose her to all sorts of petty persecution & that she is too open to attack to have it fail of its object— Her former position— known sentiments— & fine west end House so much coveted as almost every shelter is in Washington— would invite attention & attack— therefore some other chance of permission had best be sought."

Silver Spring   October 22, [1863]

Dear Phil Father thought my benevolence extravagant & he curtailed my autographs to one endorsement & a frank of the Old Hero— I want to do the kind thing by the Trumbulls as well as the sick soldiers—[1]

Father recieved a letter from Apo Frank has the command of a Corp— & division—[2] he is well & busy It is believed here that Grant has superceded Rozencranz.[3] Nobody know where Lee is yet— if they do they dont tell— It is evident I think he wanted give the last tag to Meade & claim the prestige of having driven him to his line & defences instead of being driven as was expected— to those of Richmond. but if he had not been too much he would had a general battle— Still even if whipped he has aquired European prestige— from Meades retreat— if he stay where he is long—

John yesterday read a moderate well written paper to Father about the outrages inflicted upon the people of Prince Georges— & he advised the Committee to present it to the President & Brother to present them to him in person— which was agreed upon when he left them— from all signs Calvert will be elected— in this district— The Ultras course being pursued is exciting an intense feeling in this State

Mrs Welles & Mrs Ripley[4] were here yesterday   I was caught in the garden working my roses— I gave them both beautiful bouquets & some chesnuts asked to remain for a lunch which would soon be ready but they declined having to visit Minna— she gave them a lunch when they went to the Old Soldiers Home— Mrs Cutts[5] (Richard) came soon after— I did the polite & so consumed the morning whilst Grandma & Blair took a long ride. Geo Beale is desperately ill with typhoid fever I go to the City to see Mrs Knapp meet Betty & see about sundries   Ever your affecate Lizzie

1. EBL donated items, including some Jacksonian relics, for a soldiers' benefit fair.

2. On October 29, Frank took command of the Fifteenth Corps of Sherman's army near Chattanooga.

3. On October 17, Grant received orders appointing him to command the newly created Military Division of the Mississippi. Rosecrans was relieved as commander of the Department of the Cumberland, to be replaced by George H. Thomas.

4. Sarah Denny married James W. Ripley in 1824. Ripley now served as chief of ordnance.

5. Martha Jefferson Hockley married Richard D. Cutts in 1845. He was serving on Halleck's staff.

Silver Spring   [October 24, 1863]

Dear Phill   I have just read aloud Frank phillipic against Mr. Blow & Mr. Chase in response to Mr. Blows attack upon him—[1] Frank will not let even a great man set his small dogs on him without kicking the dog & giving his master some share of his resentment who is in this case most evidently marked to attack Frank as he alone could furnish Mr. Blow with Genl Grants letter— & which helps Frank's case & hurts that of the Secy— They were bitter personally & I think an avowed enemy is less hurtfull in every way than a covert one— besides this will put all the other "aspirants in a good humor. Ill send the paper with Franks letter in it— as it may not be republished as it is very severe— Towards the end you will be reminded of some of your experience—

I received a letter today from Nelly saying if it did not rain she will come up with Annie & Phill to spend a week with me. I am prepared to go in rain or shine to meet her & the little ones. I shall talk carpets & furniture to Nelly & eschew politics most carefully   Betty got up safely & we are glad to get a good servant— one is vastly needed here Blair is entirely willing to go meet the children & seems full of plans for their enjoyment out here & in the city. I shall take Becky & Sam in with me— the latter to saw wood & white wash the basement & to clean up the yard— whilst I am there to have it well done— The basement needs a good purification & I think I can afford to give Sam his food & get the wood sawed— will of itself pay me— for they now charge $1.75cts a cord—

Mr. Fox will know & tell you more news than I can— I think George Beale has not been dealt by fairly[2] & dont you say anything *against him* until you *read* the evidence— besides he is now so low with typhoid fever that many fear he will not recover— I feel very troubled for them— I will close this in town— It rains so hard that I dont expect Nelly so will not take Blair & Becky— but will go have some made in the furnace so as dry the house & make it safer to go to Blair is well & I am over the whooping cough panic Your affecate Lizzie

1. Henry T. Blow served as Republican congressman from Missouri from 1863 to 1867. Frank thought Chase used his position as Treasury secretary to advance his presidential candidacy. His speech was printed in the St. Louis *Union* of October 19. In June, Frank had been accused of ordering liquor and tobacco at government expense, then selling it for profit. The unwarranted charges had been widely published and added to Frank's political feuds.

2. George Beale was replaced as the naval storekeeper at the Washington Yard by Charles E. Lathrop.

Washington   November 4, 1863
Dear Phil I received your letters today explaining your oyster trouble[1] & I wish I had mentioned before— that until I recd your dispatch I had never said *oyster* once—

Nelly received your letter & has a dozen times said well I'll answer Phills letter today but she has been so busy that she has had no time— I am very late too tonight for John came up— from Prince Georges & is very excited by proceedings there—[2] He did not vote and I am only too glad to have him here with us tonight consequently have been as kind & listening as I can be— & he seemed relieved in talking— & there are no listeners in the cosy corner room— he has exploded & I think feels better for it He says Ellen will have to do her own washing & cooking before Christmas— that it is now emancipation by force— & their region is being sorely visited, *because of its* sympathies— Still his crop is housed— & tobacco being packed— it is evident that he is beforehand in his affairs— I shall devote my every faculty to sooth & comfort them & it is a real comfort to find Nelly is thoroughly prudent. I lose no chance of suggesting a gradual change of things— but they are in no temper just yet for it

Miss Bell Becky's mistress has induced all of her Contrabands to return

home gather her crops & then return here— They are to go home at Christmas— the idea is to keep an ownership over them for future remuneration
This course evidently impresses Nelly & I think somebody else will get into
his head— I get this from the my servants all of whom enter cordially "*into
the plans of Miss Elizabeth*" & with such evident relish that they wont say what
they are even to me— I am late so must to bed as I am not as robust woman as
you would like to have me *but* am always   Your devoted wife   Lizzie

    1. A part of SPL's blockading duties was the restriction of trade on the rivers flow-
ing into the Atlantic. Because of jurisdictional disputes between the army and navy,
a great many trade permits allowed oysterers to ply their trade off Hampton Roads,
increasing the danger to the Union fleet.
    2. The November 4 election in Prince Georges was a vote for Democrats and slavery
in the House of Delegates. On November 14, EBL explained: "The Prince Georges
people are intensely excited by the recent election results in this state & what hurts
most is that in their part of the state they elected in the presence of Bayonets a
rank secessionist to Congress— so they can not say that the people could not vote
their views—."

                                         .

                                  Washington   November 10, 1863
My dear Phil   Last night I had such a crowd here— so much to do with an
aching head— & an anxious mind that I did not write to you as usual— Blair
has taken a bad cold which made him an anxiety for fear of croup (which he
did *not* have—) & Nelly was packing— Mrs. Hill & Clem— Mrs Blair Mrs
Churchill[1] & sundry others called to see Nelly— Aunt Susan & Mrs Coleman
were guests for the night— that added to our arrangements for Kate kept your
little woman busy until a late hour & up this morning at an early one to see
Nelly off at 7 olk— with a good breakfast served in a warm room She got off
most comfortably & was waiting when the stage called for them—
    Nelly got a room for Kate at Mrs Brents[2] & Kate is in great glee over the
arrangement— Now says if she could only get some writing to do she would
be entirely satisfied— I think John would feel a little mad if he could see how
she felt about going to his home which cost him such an effort to offer. I
do not know if John will sanction the arrangement— it will cost over $50 a
month— meals & lodging but that is the least any one can live for in this
city now   a whole comfortable room to themselves which she says she must
have— She says she will not live with anybody & wants to work for her living
that it will be good for her mind & body. I shall not seek to get writing for
her until I see John If she is deranged there are lots just such at large among
my acquaintance— for example— why cannot Maria Smith & her widowed
sister live decently together— simply because of bad tempered selfishness & I

can enumerate others— smart enough to smooth appearances in life to which Kate is stupidly indifferent besides— she never had much mind

I recd your letter & list of good things you gave yr guests who were enchanted from what I hear with their visit— Blairs cold may delay my visit to Phila until Monday— I will not go until he is clear of it— our weather has been wretched I must close this to get it mailed for today— Your affectionate Lizzie

1. Lucy L. Churchill was the wife of Sylvester Churchill, inspector general of the United States.

2. Kate stayed at EBL's home in Washington until arrangements were made for her to move into the home of Harriet Brent, widow of Robert, who lived at 450 Thirteenth West.

Washington   November 12, [1863]
Dear Phil Whilst at dinner today John sent for me to know about Kate. I rendered the account I did to you in all respects save that I did enquire of Father about writing for her— He told me he could not ask for it for her— as it was not a matter of poverty but— pride as he knew his son in law was able & willing to support— if her estate was destroyed— or mispent— by her Father or self— and thus he declined to seek it for her which experiment I would gladly have tried for the sake of giving her occupation— as I think idleness one of the many things which has combined to make her what she is— I did not expect John until tomorrow & had sent off your letter for him to get this afternoon I think he will just carry out Kates present arrangements he will be here in the morning & I will learn— what are his conclusions— I begged him to stay here tonight as I had a room for him— but he prefers Carlisle's[1] when alone they are congenialities— & for the nonce he is good company— for he is cautious in talk, & tho a *sympathiser*— is not *an actor* on the stage of these turbulent times

Betty & Father have returned from Miss Kates wedding—[2] Betty says it was a great display of elegance & riches— but the young people were not acquaintances— consequently the gayety was very lame— She danced but the Washington girls generally hate balls— a bore since the Yankee reserve about introducing is prevelant Mother & Father are here tonight & we form quite a family party in town. Father enjoyed the wedding reproached Sprague with have seen one of his flames & Betty says he was quite the belle of the occasion— Next door did not go— Nor would Mrs Lincoln— Maybe for the same reasons. Mary Meigs is said to be engaged to Hancock Taylor. Genl Joe's son[3] Blair is better today— I congratulate you on the captures at Wilmington

Friday morning Blair's cold gave him a bad night so I'll not go to Phila before Monday I let him stay out too long yesterday Rest all well Your affecate Lizzie

1. Probably James M. Carlisle, Washington lawyer, who lived at 436 D North.
2. Kate Chase, daughter of Salmon P. Chase, married William Sprague of Rhode Island on November 12.
3. Mary Meigs, daughter of Montgomery Meigs, married Maj. Joseph Hancock Taylor, son of Gen. Joseph P. Taylor. A graduate of the U.S. Military Academy (1856), he served as assistant adjutant general during the war.

Silver Spring   November 16, 1863
Dear Phil   Blair & I had a good sleep last night— he coughed but once last night & today is as bright & merry as heart could wish— I feel now over uneasiness about croup for the hoarseness is all gone this morning— I feel fresh & well amazingly relieved— for there is nothing that is so dreaded by me as croup— & any hoarseness gives me a panic as you may have discovered by my late letters— as it has been *my one idea* for this past week This would have been a delicious day to have gone to Phila after the rain— dust put down— but I confess to the timidity of a hare where Blair is concerned—

Andrew Alexander was here last night— took joking about Evy very happily is going up there Christmas & I suppose Evy will return the visit during the latter part of winter They are not to marry until the War is over so says her Father— Andrew thinks there'll be a battle this week between Meade & Lee A letter from Frank saying I have the 15th corp— given me by Sherman— approved by Grant— I wonder if the War Dept have as much discrimination? he is angry at one of Chase officials— forging a bill in which by the quantitites ordered makes him appear a trader in liquors— he ordered some for himself & the officers with whom he is intimate— This was magnified by an alteration of figures in the Custom House— to look very ugly indeed— & then published— Frank is furious— Betty and the carriage are waiting so I must close my talk feeling a very light hearted woman about our darling boy Ever your own Lizzie

Silver Spring   November 18, 1863
Dear Phil   I am off in the morning to Phila & shall drop this en route to the Cars. Blair is very bright and well & is very sorry to leave home now that Mary Blair is here with her children, "Mama don't go 'til tomorrow night & we can play all day & travel in the night—"

I recd your letter with the list of the Mt Washns cargo I think you load the Welles rather much for good taste— however shall not alter your orders— Now I am as apt to be mistaken as anybody & may be over proud— The Ws are *our real friends*[1] & you may be more judicious & right both on the pt of feeling & taste— Still I always utter just what I think to you & know you will take it as meant   a suggestion so that all views & sides may be well considered a la Mother who is ever for the same reason on the objective case

I have been visiting some neighbors— John Clagett has his Fathers place & a really pleasant lady for a wife[2]   Riggs[3] has sold his farm opposite to us & is centering his country tastes upon "Green Hill—" the Digges homestead   Beale is getting better after hanging between life & death for forty days. his poor little wife is nearly broken down in mind & body by this trial

Father says he will come after Blair & will be in Phila in a week— evidently dislikes me to go away from home again. He & Blair are very sympathetic & yet he cannot persuade Blair to remain home & let me go without him He and Mother have exhausted themselves on this point in vain—

By the time you get back I'll return home too— so I look forward to that time with some of Blairs joy— You will not be off I hope longer than two weeks— Now that you Genl. B. got together I suppose you hope for another New Orleans feat—[4] Wilmington is now of greater importance to the Rebs than New Orleans was at the time of its Capture—

Everything here seems now in abeyance to the meeting of Congress— when— the current of affairs will again go in a swift current   I must write to Fanny tonight— & to confess the truth I feel as if this will not reach you for a month to come— Ever your affectionate Lizzie

1. On December 24, EBL told her husband: "I am glad you have written to Mr Welles— he is your friend as I think the effect is good to confide in him your views."

2. John B. Clagett, of Clagett and May dry goods store, was the son of Darius Clagett, who died October 1, 1860. The family home, Pomona, was located on Clagett land which extended south from the north cornerstone of the District of Columbia. John Clagett married Margaret Gunnell, daughter of William Hunter and Sarah Duckworth Gunnell of Washington, in 1848.

3. George Riggs of the banking firm Riggs and Company had purchased Green Hill in Prince Georges County, Maryland.

4. Butler had led the army contingent, in cooperation with the navy, to capture New Orleans in 1862. SPL did not find Butler as congenial for planning the capture of Wilmington.

Philadelphia   November 25, 1863

Dear Phil   This has been the perfection of a thanksgiving day. so beautiful seasonable & the very air which we breathe so exhilerating so rejoicing— The good news from Grant[1] just overflowed the cup of thanksgiving which was already made full— Nothing strikes me more than teeming prosperity of this city wherever I go. the grand new buildings on the fine streets & the *new towns* on the outskirts for the laboring class— so well fitted for use & comfort— have grown up in one year— I went to Church at St Stephens where I sat in school days— met great many old acquaintances— Then I spent an hour or so at Mrs. Dicks— then a good walk— gave me just time & appetite for dinner— I am now quietly at home with Aunt Becky for the evening[2] wont send this as you are not in the Roads to get a daily bulletin—

Friday Novr 26 I am very anxious about Franks whereabouts— have no late tidings from him   Apo & etc very bitter at his being superceded—[3] he is expected in Washn next— but I doubt if he comes whilst his division is action as at present— I have just been to get my winter dress fitted at Miss Williamsons—[4] she insists upon tuning me up as I am an admirals wife   I shall have to wait till you get the rank which I think you fill so well— she is a smart english woman who delights in dealing with soft southrons— Yankees are too exact in dealing for her to make money fast enough—

I am to dine with Mrs. Dick— but I shall walk with Aunt before I do so as I find that she is no longer at home in the streets & is far more feeble than she appeared at home indeed more the old lady in her than ever before— one year has wrought a great change in her strength   She is going with me to get the rest of the carpets I need & as they go in the boxes with my furniture will not cost me anything extra— There is far larger varieties to choose from than in Washington but Mary Blair has bought there after looking here. The immense rents or from some cause they are the same prices there as here— & six weeks ago I bought cheaper there in Washington than I can there or here now I only wish I had come to this work earlier in the season but there was no help for it— Some person await me on a visit, so good morning to you   Ever your own   Lizzie

1. Grant had begun operations to lift the siege of Chattanooga. On November 24, federal troops under Joseph Hooker took Lookout Mountain, and the rebels had retreated to Missionary Ridge.

2. EBL renewed many old acquaintances, as she explained on November 22: "There has been a constant rush of people in the family circle here to see Sarah & me ever since our arrival— so we have not had much time for each save what we stole from sleep— & I confess the small hours have caught us as of yore, deep in our chats."

3. Frank's corps had been transferred to Gen. John Logan, but Frank remained and fought at Chattanooga and Knoxville. See his account of the matter in EBL's December 26 letter.

4. Agnes Williamson, a seamstress in Philadelphia.

Philadelphia   November 30, 1863
My dear Phil   The quiet routine pursued here gives me but small opportunity for news save what one gleans out of the papers & there is so much of import on the topis to us all that I confess to sharing no little of Blair's eagerness to get home which he announced was to be in 4 days at breakfast— altho I had given him a certain lecture just before on the impoliteness of talking about

it— I am nearly thro' my purchases & only now wait to know the amount for boxing (which counts up) ere Ill pay bills & be off home

I went to church yesterday twice with Midge[1] who still thinks it probable she may be recalled to St Louis by her husband who I think commits a great folly in leaving the scene of all his manly pursuits & business & social friends— he will never be happy here as he will feel the loss of occupation & social importance which he has attained in St Louis— which mere family connection does not give any where He writes that Apo is in very bad health— & that the children have been sick too so the summers at Newport are no guarantee against ailments

I am now off to get some cards to pay my visits which have accumulated uncomfortably Dr. Foltz & wife are among those who called— This city is full of southern people refugees from Southern discomforts & poverty— Mrs. Bell[2] is just as ugly as ever— & they say these really crowded the small tenement part of the City— Most are women & children some (very few) old men— These late tidings from Grants Army makes such people as Majr Mordicai rude as a sore headed bear— He has sunk down to utter idle good for nothingness living on the earnings of his daughters[3] if he was old or incompetent this would be no disgrace— but as he is neither— the reflection is irresistable— Sarah Moses had some of her brother Gratzs family visit her who were in this conspiracy to burn our lake cities[4] but since their failure in these attempts they have all embarked from Montreal to Nassau & expect to run the Blockade at Wilmington— They now ship all the coal they use from Montreal to Nassau— & the Secesh who are in force in Montreal & speculating a vast deal in this trade which Mr. Joseph says is very brisk— Capt. Magruders 2nd daughter has married Lord Abinger of the Guards[5] & is vastly pleased with the match— as the bridegroom is both rich & a lordling— We are all well here— Ever your affectionate Lizzie

Miss Clem Hill is here & already disgusted with her hotel & talks of a year in Europe & then returning to Washington

1. Midge was Mira Dick, wife of Franklin Dick.

2. Margaret Cabell Pollard married Henry H. Bell in 1851.

3. Maj. Alfred Mordecai had three unmarried daughters: Laura, b. 1837; Rosa, b. 1839; and Miriam, b. 1843. On November 25, Union forces had taken Missionary Ridge, insuring the safety of Chattanooga, and the rebels retreated toward Chickamauga.

4. On November 11, Stanton wrote to the mayor of Buffalo that the governor general of Canada had reported a rebel plot to invade the U.S., destroy Buffalo, and take possession of Lake Erie. There was an unsuccessful attempt to seize Johnson's Island and release rebel prisoners held there.

5. William Frederick Scarlett of the Scots Guards, third baron Abinger, married Helen Magruder, daughter of U.S. naval commander George A. Magruder.

Philadelphia   December 1, 1863
Dear Phil   The first day of winter has brought winter in earnest & Blair had
what he calls *"real fun* "skating on the ice— everything is frozen hard &
tight—
Your letters came from Beaufort today— Adl Shubrick is getting well so
Miss Mary McKnight tells me— Mrs. Stockton thinks him yet "a sick man—"
but says he has always been so temperate & etc that his days may yet be long
in the land. The papers say he is entirely recovered from his late illness I can
write more about this on my return home on Monday next— I think it best
not to rush on with the crowd at the end of this week— everybody will be
there to organize the House during the latter part of the week Your new fleet
Captain called to see me but I was out I met his wifes Mother & she says he
goes to the Minnesota tomorrow— his wife goes to his fathers in Norfolk after
Christmas they are all clever people & I am glad he has been ordered to yr ship
I had a long letter from Fanny about Kate— the synopsis of which is Mr. Pettit will soon have in his hands $700 of Kate's— the deferred payt. of her Ky
land by the Germans. He wishes to put it at yours or Johns disposition for
her present use— Then Fanny is dreadfully exercised because Mr. P. will not
now give Kate an allowance or ask her to his house— He has been obdurate
to Fanny on these points— I will send you the letter when you return to the
Roads— It only shows however that he sticks to his purposes in this respect—
for he told me— that he meant to put it his will that Kate was never to have
to live with Fanny— it was bad for both— consequently he would prevent it
in his life time— & forbid it when he was dead— I think he is right—
I had a letter from Father not in very good spirits as he is evidently most
anxious & worried about Frank— Gave me some commissions here to attend
to & wants us home— Mary Blair is still there— Today I went to Earles[1] to
get an engraving of Genl. Washington copy of Stuarts for— $1,50 cts— & a
fine one— I have a plan of matching it with that of your Grandfather & put
their antislavery sentiments on the backs of the pictures Fine models for us to
set up for our boy's study & example   Aunt Becky is well & spent the day out
at the Asylum made me feel as if I neglected my duties on this meeting day
Wednesday morning 9 olk am Dec 2nd 1863. Henry Etting has just left here
told me Henry Upshur[2] has been ordered to the Minnesota at your request—
as Capt of the ship— I replied that you liked Upshur but that I did not know
anything about the application for him but it would be I know a most agreeable
order to you   Henry says Barnes is too young for fleet Capt— I said you liked
youngsters— He said he was too green to be useful— I insisted that clever-
ness often made amends for inexperience— He admitted he was very clever I
thought you would be very well pleased with both of your new helpmates— at
which Paymaster departed   Mrs. Upshur is at Germantown Has been in great
affliction since her brother was hung as a spy in Tennessee—[3]
Blair is well in spite of a cake frolic he had yesterday. He went out with

Becky to see some of her colored friends & the family upstairs made great ado over Blair took him to the well supplied Pantry & crammed his pockets with nuts cakes & apples— He says they had Uncle Franks pictures in two parlors— Uncle Judges & Grandpas in one & they were very kind people— I do not know anything about them The deer & squirrils in the Square got the nuts & some of the cake— He is all eagerness to go home— counts the days but is easily put off as he has about as much idea of numbers as his mother I go home Monday— Decr 7th. No news about Frank Ever your own Lizzie

1. James Earle and Son sold looking glass and picture frames in their store at 816 Chestnut in Philadelphia.
2. Lt. Comdr. John Henry Upshur entered the navy in 1841 and was captain of the *Minnesota*, flagship of the North Atlantic Blockading Squadron.
3. Katharine Alicia Williams Upshur was the daughter of Capt. William G. Williams (USA) and America Pinckney Peter Williams. Her brother was W. Orton Williams, who resigned from the U.S. army on June 10, 1861. He was hanged as a Confederate spy on June 9, 1863.

Silver Spring   December 8, 1863
My dear Phil   I reached the Depot at seven olk having been detained by a car getting off the track   there found Betty, the carriage and the three blacks waiting for me— I had not been here a half hour 'ere I found it was fortunate I had returned home   all my family are in a tremor about Frank— he is with Sherman sent to Burnsides relief & the City is full of rumors about fighting going on in East Tennessee—[1] Mother & Father are very much excited. Mina told that a staff officer of Grants told him of Grant saying— "Well if I want a thing well & quickly done I always send Blair"[2] No one has had a line from him since or a telegraph since he telegraphed that he had been in battle 3 days but had escaped unscathed— this was the day after the battle from that day to this nothing has been heard from or about him— & there is a remarkable ommission of his name in all the papers about him, he commanded Shermans Corp & division from Corinth to Chattanooga & writes that he fought his way every day with Joe Johnston— & not one word is said of it in any paper— He commanded Shermans corp in battle, Logan gets the newspaper credit, when he remained at home to see the last days of his poor little one he buried 'ere he left his desolate home—[3]

The Radicals have organized this House to suit themselves— which Lincoln thinks Frank could have prevented if he had come here— but admits that he could not have done it as a soldier— His message[4] supports the Conservatives— one tenth of the loyal inhabitants can reorganize the State Governments & start afresh into the Union which annihilates Summners & Chase's territorial project but they now all subscribe to the message. I dont know what loop hole of it Lincoln has put in for their benefit but the principle of States independent in local law is maintained— & it is essential to the Union for such a wide spread Country as ours This is *our* specialty as it is a fundamental part of the Constitution— which the Conservative Union people of the country intend to keep inviolate

I came immediately home to Mother who had been all day alone— & rejoice to be here where I feel I can cheer & comfort them. She said to "Blair oh how glad I am to get you back. I have been heart broken & I wanted you—" & the little fellows extasy was charming to them at getting here— he never closed his eyes all day— or on the way out here— As we came in our room the fire blazed bright & high— he said "Oh— Mama is not this the brightest dearest little room in the world—" He is now off to feed "Papa's Turkies" with Ned, & Dice, & Henry— all in a caper down the walk He is very well now in all respects which is the first time in some months for he had cold affected his bladder & has made me anxious— but that is all well again—

Dont be worry about me talking "*Navy*—" I never talk about the people in it save in the kindest way— & as to what they are doing to going to do— I never know— to talk about to Henry E or anybody— & in such cases as the Shubrick matter— my own delicacy would make you sure on that point—

I enclose you a money article from the Ledger which I heard three or four Phila merchants comment upon— as "setting forth the simple truth" with great clearness. The prosperity of the north never was so great, Clem Hill said that it takes sight to convince men of the fact & of its enormous extent— He takes great comfort in it— what he looses in Maryland is more than made up in the improved condition & demand for his wifes Phila estate He thinks now the South will have to stop the War to spite the North as it grows so fat on it & it is not bloated fat— it is in emmigrants— manufactures buildings people & everything that makes material wealth— & no collapse is expected by peace for with it will come— Cotton— & a wider market for their manufactures— Labor is now paid for in cash at 13 dollars a week— consequently volunteering at thirteen a month is slow— Gold is kept high by the good harvests of Europe— our products are not now taken so much in exchange— still Cotton is going out gradually from New Orleans a million bales already of this season & that will help to keep the equilibrium & if we take Georgia— this winter the Cotton States will be tranquilized by spring— & the war confined to the Carolinas & Virginia—

I must hurry Sam off now for Becky & my trunks & then next day Ill go look after my boxes Blair will stay here & Ill return every night the small pox is rife in the City Ever yr own Lizzie

---

1. On December 3, Longstreet began to remove his troops from the siege of Knoxville; on December 6, William T. Sherman entered the city, ending the siege. As Longstreet moved east, there was considerable skirmishing along the way.

2. On December 9, EBL wrote: "We are still worried about Frank— Brother said today Mr. Ellard told him that he heard that Grant said he could not spare Genl Blair & would not detach him from his corp— Apo did not mention him at all in her letter to Minna which however only enclosed something but she had not heard two days ago— Andrew Alexander says he believed ["knows"—marked out] that he is with Sherman— I blurted out all our troubles today to Mr. Cameron & added I am only too sorry I have not you to go to who so kindly helped me in times gone by. He was evidently pleased—."

3. See EBL's letter of December 26 for Frank's explanation of the situation.

4. On December 8, Lincoln issued his Proclamation of Amnesty and Reconstruction, establishing his basic policy for reunification of the nation.

Silver Spring   December 11, 1863

Dear Phil   I had an uncivil note from Mrs. Thomson— I will keep the whole correspondence for you The truth is she wants to bully me into giving high prices for things I dont want— at last after in vain trying get me to appraise & buy. Sets a huge price— & says I may take it or— she will remove them charging me with a years use (Mrs Crittenden after my telling her the curtains were for sale used them)   Father dictated the following reply to her note which I shall send

For Mrs Thomson

"You propose to remove the articles you left in my house— I am gratified that it is your pleasure to do so   I will cheerfully pay for the use made of them

Yours truly

EB Lee

I was just as civil in my style as she & determined to avoid an altercation I staid away from her when she was breaking up just to avoid this sort of thing as her character for hardness made me conscious that in flight alone I was safe but as I alighted at Brothers when I thought she was gone & sold out she caught me & dragged into buing the chandeliers to permit her to leave the things which I would not buy for my incoming tenant   what a match she & Dalghren would be— Greek meet Greek   flint versus flint—

The only thing I ordered for the parlors was an English grate which is now in great vogue in Phila— & Henry Etting says he puts them in his houses (he has 2) for renting as the cheapest & best thing   they are good to burn coal of any sort— Shut off the dampers & they burn wood— I shall order two now— & as the man comes on from Phila to put up a large order in Washington I feel that the ugly gloomy grates are a riddance— tho I would have taken them for the sake of my new carpet but she (which Ill cover with Mothers large bureau)— charges two dollars more for each than I can buy better ones of that obsolete pattern in Phila

At first I concluded to send all my correspondance with her of which I kept copies— in most instances as I was afraid of her & send it all to you—

but, I talked it over to Father who remarked why pester your husbands head & eyes with such things when he has his hands & head so full. I then said if you will dictate after listening to all the details the reply— He will think be satisfied— & the above letter was the result   I wanted to put in that no one used her things but Mrs Crittenden— but Fathers feeling for his old friend made him omit this Still he says it is most ladylike not to make such points in such matters— particularly as I told rather admitted that I did not find them in the good order in which she left them against my wishes— He says if old Thomson was alive he would answer it differently but Ladies cannot wrangle & be ladies— so I submit to the injustice

Genl Ames made his appearance today looks thin & sick— still he has good looks enough left to make him welcome   I like him as there is something about his head & eyes which reminds me of dear Jim who lives so freshly in my memory & heart

No news from Frank & I feel loth to go even for one night away from Mother but since it is to get her room ready to stay in on Sunday night & that she & Father planned the trip to ensure our being at Church to join the Thanksgiving Sunday— I do as they wish They already enjoy the house & will spend most of the winter there— Mother will keep the house & I am as at Silver Spring Chef de Staff— Father said that it would be a good time to fix our conveniences here down under these front step— which is now worse than entirely useless & unused— Blair resist all entreaties to let me go for one night without him   I hate the old city but I cant do without Mama— Ever your own affecate Lizzie

Silver Spring   December 18, 1863

Dear Phil   Yours of the 16th & 17th came today— I never said Kate was an idiot— I say & believe her to be a weak minded woman   there is a world full of such but you rarely see it accompanied with so much temper & obstinacy   her heart in childhood might have been affectionate— but it has been seared by a want of love— I doubt if she has been treated with cruelty— save the cruelty of neglect & coldness   I pity her more than any woman I ever knew— simply because she has no power of inspiring love without which a womans life is to my mind the bitterest poverty to befall in this world

You Fanny & John have for her Mother[1] the most unfailing love— & would gladly endow her child with it— but none of you can come in contact with her without being embittered & alienated— The two last I have had twice in my time intervened to save her from actual harshness— It is this state of facts which makes me feel & believe the present mode of life is best for her— not that I hope to change or alter the character of a woman of thirty two or three years old, particularly when fixedness is the marked characteristic of the woman— there is another peculiarity of your's & Johns— you always talk of Kate as if she was a child— she is no more to be made or moulded afresh—

than you or I— indeed I am the most likely of the three to change my mind about things. but in matters of feeling I am unhappily tenacious for I do not cease to love those who ever maltreat me— Even Jessie & Minna retain warm places in my heart a fact Ill confess to none but you—

I have always been desirous of doing a kind part by Kate but during her visit on 13 Street I concluded never to seek to make her a permanent inmate in my home, which was my plan for her future up to that time— You of course, can do so & with my hearty consent if it is yr wish but it is my conviction that it will not inure to her or our happiness at the same time I feel sure I can get along with her there even better than you can— Now my only desire is make her comfortable physically as to any great change— or building up anew— which you so fondly hope— I never dreamed of it— occupation will stop many of her silly doings which are the results of idleness— but occupation added to her naturally taciturn habit— will give her a respectability which she deserves for she has one great power— that of silence—which covers as many defects— as charity— I have dwelt on her wardrobe & doings to let you see that she did not as John thought spend her money in some monomania— but in the one common to the sex— a love of fine clothing it has taken all of her money to get her present wardrobe— & I see it is her idea to get under clothing sheets pillow cases & etc When she feels she had done the *respectable* then she will do the vainer & mere externals— a contempt of which is one of her hobbys Now I infer this from observation *only* she *never talks* about her affairs save she wants money—

There is one correction I must make in the money items— I gave in cash $33— and the rest I spent in buying things she wanted & in altering the trimmings of dress but this last item she knew nothing about— she wears black— the dress was trimmed with blue— so it was altered before giving it to her— but I did not narrate any of these matters to be refunded only to tell you my daily doings & experiences with her all of which I think tend to show her fathers convictions about her are the results of his own avarice and impatient bad temper— John has adopted his views, consequently they may impress and distress you— I want to prevent this— and I will gladly do anything I can to give you relief & comfort about her— this has prompted all I have done in the matter about which I fear John has thought me officious— I fear I have also hurt you by speaking perhaps too freely of her traits of mind & character— I felt it was a time for frankness rather than delicacy & you have always overated her mentally & consequently expected *too* much from her She is as weak as Emily Lee as my Aunt Susan— as fifty other silly *talking* women I know, the difference is— she has but little to say— & a reserve which she gets from her mother's blood. You have it— even John with a stronger Irish cross— has it in matters which touch *his own* heart Blair shows it even at this tender age— & it will keep him from appearing Silly even if he is so—

Father & Mother are both better today— & I pray you may be so too— this trip to Wilmington— holds me uneasy Wily the servant the Duttons sent us says he is not willing to return to them— he did not wish to leave them— but they sent him here— & now he is just as happy as when with them & is a free man & means this time to follow his own inclinations & entre nous (interests) So we dont need the servant you propose to send who would be acceptable if he left us—

The St Louis papers papers say Frank is expected there to stay *one* day— when he will proceed to Washington Brother is seriously sick & has been so now for over two weeks— I have made up my mind to let my bills stand until the next year— and people in Washington will trust longer even than that I dont owe any in Phila as yet— The grates that are ordered are to be made yet— & the picture of your Grandfather has to be copied in crayon— it wont photograph it has so much yellow in it that it is one blur— I am going to get it for the good of our young set of Lee's I want them to go back to good examples— & first principles (& pals!!) in the family

Blair is very excited today over Hymans gift of sheep— he is well— his front teeth grow through & I hope will be beautiful— I will write Nelly what you say about Cousin Kate & Harr Goodbye as I hope this will reach you ere you sail— You are followed everywhere by the fond prayers of your devoted wife Lizzie

1. Kate's mother was SPL's sister Jane Elizabeth Harrison, who had died in 1837.

Silver Spring   December 21, [1863]
Dear Phil   You have a niece— & I have an old Aunt— *both* weak— silly bad tempered women— I would prefer the humblest log cabin with my husband & child than share a palace with either My Aunt has killed three husbands, wasted two large fortunes— driven to ruin the loveliest child a mother ever had— by her inordinate selfishness— will— bad temper & a want of intel- lect— Yet she is not an idiot— *only a talking* self willed fool— Kate is like her, only silent— she acts the termagant— drilled by sixteen years good practice— in domestic warfare—

I cannot live happily with such a woman in your absence I will not risk such an ordeal upon my temper & feelings— at present they are more kind than any body elses who come in contact with her— I resist with an honest zeal any outrage upon her from either Father— or any body & believe in my heart her desire to live among strangers & the restraints it imposes is a most wise instinct on her part— but I would rather than live in No 4 with her rent it & devote its whole proceeds to her pleasure & this if you desire it as an alternative I will take with joy— rather than to live there with her No I wrote to you some days ago that I would never seek Kate as an inmate of our home again— & this feeling is not only selfish for as John justly said she oppressed you far more than she did me but— this was the point in which she most deeply affects me—

not that she is not a skeleton behind my own door all the time— but it all resolved me never again to live three months with her in my home *save upon compulsion*— from which dire necessity I shall pray you and God in his mercy to deliver me

At present I feel no bitterness towards & can serve & watch over her kindly & cheerfully gladly sharing anything I have *but my home* but when a person brings a shadow over that, by natural bad temper— no meal, no hour safe from her grim countenance No hour of the night she may not startle you from sleep by her wanderings over the house in the pantry or after some other fancy— Many is the scare she gave me that winter & when last with me I caught cold in terror lest somebody was in the house— but my terrors never abated her tipping along upstairs— & so it is night after night— in a boarding house all this is stopped & she buys her supper & eats in her room— she inspected the closets, trunks of my house— but it is useless to descant on her ways— they are intolerable to a woman of my nervous construction & I never will struggle with her about anything— soothe her temper protect her from unkindness if I can— but you can as soon alter the leopards spots as her temper & she has no kindness save for those who indulge her— John is now abused without stint for meanness— but still I am as utterly opposed to dealing hardly with her as I have ever been to doing so to Aunt Susan— for whom I plead & get things whenever I can—

We ought to do what is just & kind to our unhappy or unworthy kindred— still in in doing that duty is it right to overshadow ones whole life & home by their vices or misfortunes? My Mother would not let her drunken brother live in her house she had a little room for him near her where she took care of him— Aunt Susan told me, no friend had been so true & steady to her in all her trials as my Mother, yet Mother never would live with her & she never quarrelled with Mother & she has with everybody else— Now Ill never forsake Kate as long as I live Ill share my means gladly with her— nurse in sickness— try to soothe be gentle always when she ungovernable angry— but dear Phil I do not want to live with her— so please do not require it of me, I implore you

I sent your letter to Kate because I will not deny her anything that is kind & affectionate from you— & your letter was so sweet & gentle & good that I had not the heart to refuse it to anybody— for I cannot help feeling that it must touch & soften her Still I shall say most honestly that I differ from you & agree with her as to her present arrangements & shall thus continue them— As to the writing I will look after & ask her to work at No 4 if she refuses will dole out the work & look after it most carefully— I agree with John that something unimportant ought first be given to her even make believe work— but you are on extremes about this poor woman— Ill do the best I can about it—for I feel that there is no preservation of her from her bad habits save by work for money for which she now has such an insatiate desire

Mr. Lamson is in town & called three times to see me today but I was out—[1] No news from Frank It is bitter cold but I have go in tomorrow about Kates matters as the Express had not arrived when I left town today. I got a toy for Blair from you & one from myself & there Ill stop as Ive more debts than money by a great deal— the man who fixed the fire places agreed to do it for $50— brought bill for $95— another some work in the pantry for $22 brought a bill for $42— so much for verbal agreements— so no wonder I am disgusted with my business arrangements I got a wheelbarrow for you— for Blair & one for Phil— for me They are strong & capable of good hard work— I got a velociped for Blair from me— He know Santa Claus "is all story—" but Papa & Mama are the real Santa Claus Good night— forgive this scrawl

I lost one pair of specs some days ago & broke my others today in the cold so have to go it blind tonight Still with fond faith in your unfailing indulgence— to your affecate Lizzie

1. On December 13, EBL explained her busy schedule: "I shall go to the City to look after things & pay visits Father gave me *an order* to call on every member & leave his card & his wife if they had any here & to put No 4 on all the Cards I could but think how much easier said than done— So I begin tomorrow the work— I got some cards but never dreamt of such a wide sweep with them."

Silver Spring   December 26, [1863]
Dear Phil I have not had a letter from you this week— & do not know whether you are off to Wilmington where you said you intended going on Sunday last I am much better today.

Blair is well— I enclose you a slip from the papers about the blockade I thought it might suggest a closer inspection of vessels under our flag— I also enclose you Kates last note to me & my response I have taken two long very cold rides over there to see her about doing the work at No 4 as I suggested— but never see her & I know she was in when I was last there so concluded this was my best way to reach her on the subject— I know she is mad about not getting as much money as she asks for from the style in which she slam the door when I last called— her room is over the parlor where I stood so I heard her movements

I have Franks letter in my hand he says "I should have taken the advice of the President but for the fact that the battle & pursuit of the enemy at Chattanooga came off at the time it did & afterwards the movement for the relief of Burnside in which Logan did not wish to take the command of the Corps, because he said to me, he did not get up in time for the battle & it was proper I should finish the campaign 'It was not his funeral' he said & he did not wish to take the command from me at such a moment— He behaved very handsomely & I was not sorry, as I had to relinquish the corps to turn it over to one who has shown me so much good feeling— Sherman also advised me to re[tain] the command until the campaign was completed for the reason that Logan was not acquainted with officers & men (never having served with the corps) & if we had had serious work at Knoxville as we expected to have it have made some difference in results I sent a copy of Shermans order relieving— by Horace Maynard,[1] from the command after the seige of Knoxville was raised, It was complimentary & I would like you to show it to the President by way of letting him know that I have not disgraced his commission— I was not much hurt by Secy Stanton assignment of Genl Logan over my head— Good fortune enabled me to retain the command through one of the most brilliant campaigns on record & altho the "Corps" does not get the credit it deserves in the newspaper accounts Yet I am *satisfied it will have justice when Grant makes his report.* we marched 500 miles & bore the brunt of the battle & it was only because the enemy massed against us that Thomas was able to Carry the Centre My command lost more men in killed and wounded than the rest the whole Army— but the Army correspondants who have been hanging around the Army of the Cumberland thought it proper to ignore us altogether— Grant I am certain will set the matter all right— I shall not therefore grieve myself about the correspondants or about Stantons conduct to me, I am well satisfied with having done my duty to the country & no discredit to the Commission which I owe to the Presidents good opinion—

After the campaign was over I saw Genl Grant & as the Head was already organized, I felt inclined to accept the command of a Divison which he offered me but I was so much pressed by letters from friends here to go to Washn that I gave way & asked a leave of absence— Grant said that changes would probably take place & that McPherson might get a better place which would leave his Corps (17) vacant & that Logan would prefer it (having served with it) to the 15th— He intimated he would like me to have the 15th if such a state of things occurred— I told him very frankly I would be glad to have it— or a Division if the War is protracted I do not want to have it thought that I left the Army because I did not obtain a command & I do not feel aggrieved at all on that score

I send you my leave of absence get the P. to order it extended permission given to visit Washington— When I there Ill make up my mind whether I will take my seat or not— If it seems likely that the war is to be protracted & I can get a command I will take it, but if I can be of service in Washn during the months of inactivity I will retain my seat, if the Rads dont turn me out as from appearances they are prepared to do— My family are all well & etc & etc"

The P endorsed the leave & extended it & it is now en route to St. Louis Ned Byrne waits for this So goodby in haste Yrs ever Lizzie

1. Horace Maynard, Tennessee American party congressman (1857–63). He was the state's attorney general (1863–65), and a Republican congressman (1866–75).

14

"I loved best the man who never flattered with words at all"

January 24, 1864

THE WINTER LULL IN MILITARY ACTIVITY gave time for concentration on domestic concerns. The Blairs devoted New Year's Day to their grandchildren, and Elizabeth worked hard to make their dinner special. The beginning of a new year meant a new social season, and the duties of calling upon the wives of congressmen and government officials consumed a good deal of her time. More than social convention was involved: Elizabeth Lee was intent on using her connections to push for her husband's promotion from acting rear admiral to permanent rank. The Washington City Orphan Asylum held its annual meeting, reelecting Elizabeth to another term as first directress. The Lees tried to deal reasonably with the delicate problem of handling Phillips's difficult niece Kate Harrison, who resisted almost all the help or control which Elizabeth extended in her husband's absence. The family was heartened by Frank's return from the war to take his seat in Congress until the beginning of the spring campaign. Although Phillips did not get home, Elizabeth and Blair went to him in the first week of February for their own brief reunion.

Washington   January 7, 1864

Dear Phil   The sight of your writing did my eyes & heart good today & set my blood to moving which this cold weather almost stagnates— in yr note you say you were not well. I have felt it in my bones that you were sick. I dreamed it at night & it stuck in my thoughts many days— It is snowing & as Ive no account of anything happening to the Minnesota I hope you are comfortably on her & homeward bound by this time.

Kate Gaston has not come yet so Mrs Washington said on whom I called today— Eliza Graham has been up to meet her in vain— I am paying my visits steadily & thoroughly[1] The Dennisons come here tomorrow to stay & I intend to have some confab with the Govr. & take council with him about our affairs[2] I read & reread your letter to Mr Sumner— it is well done— I gave it

as it was to Father as he says your hand is plainer than mine   I have locked up
the Secys at home— & concluded— from my own notions that it was best not
to give to Father as he knew all the points in it & they were not put with half
the tact as in your letter to Sumner— which is admirably written— Pardon
my criticism. I never do it save when an instinct prompts it, to protect you
from that of others—

Friday night The house is full tonight & the Governor is already posted
about Grimes who has asked him to do him a favor & with whom Govr D.
is very intimate now the thing is sure if we can only get him right— I have
invited Miss Woodrow to come with them & we are now quite a large family
and a gay one but the couples down stairs are rejoicing that they the old people
were sleepy headed but the old folks in getting up stairs spurred many a good
joke at the quiet arrangements of the young ones to get off together

I recd a note from Marian Sands today saying how good "the Admiral was
to her & how much she missed him when he went of to Wilmington So do I
miss him— I realize fully how much your bulletins are the event of my daily
life when I go day after day without any— Mrs Gooch[3] is our near neighbor &
gave me a pleasant account of the basket of figs you sent her by her husband   I
paid her a long visit, She put the negro rather strong, but my temper bore it
tho' my stomach sickened under it— Franks non appearance makes my Parents uneasy— from the terrific storm at the North— where the cold is greater
than for a generation past   Mother rejoices in & enjoys this warm comfortable
house   Blair enjoys his coaster & plays some hours daily in the snow— Ever
your own   Lizzie

    1. On January 9, 1864, EBL explained: "dont think me self seeking all the time in
these courtesies for I am not— but I confess I do & will do anything honest to have *our*
ambition gratified & your work rewarded as it deserves— which I know will gratify &
make you happy— the point I most care for."
    2. EBL and her father continued to use all their connections to push for SPL's
promotion.
    3. Mrs. Daniel W. Gooch was the wife of the Republican congressman from Mas-
sachusetts (1858–65).

                              Washington   January 11, [1864]
Dear Phil   Frank's arrival was the event which roused me this morning &
soon after I heard him talking in the next room with Father and Mother—[1]
in a very joyous tone He breakfasted next door— & then took up his abode
in the room over the dining room— & had quite a levee tonight among them
Mr Rollins of Mo— & others of his friends.

The Dennisons went off to the Hotel about midday with their young lady
friend who wants to see Hotel life in Washington as it forms a prominent fea-

ture I said & did all I could to keep them here— but this damsel dragged them off and rebelled against their coming here— besides Mrs Dennison expected her hopeful heir from the Army tonight— who has won here no enviable name for himself— & the girls suspect that he is engaged to this rich merchants daughter travelling with the Dennisons

What do you think of Genl Dixs calling here to see us— seeing Mother & Father if they would take charge of his daughter Kelly for a few days? I was glad I did not go in to see him They answered him yes civilly but it was with such great reluctance on Mothers part— so Father think he wont send her— I took the carriage and paid a great many visits Congressional after lauding the Dennisons I then came home to take a rest from a bad fall I got in getting out of the carriage— was a late dinner time

Kate came to say she could [not] do any writing today but would come in to work tomorrow I said I would wait until 12 olk when I would go out— & after some chat pleasantly enough she started off to GeoTown where she might get in at proper hour if she road but will not ride in anything but a hack— which I now dread as they have had a smallpox case the last time employed— I think she will come to work tomorrow— she is very anxious about your return to Hampton Roads— I give anything she asks for but money. paper needles, thread— & each time she asks for just little things she fancies of this sort Thus you see we are on very amiable terms & I make it a point to eschew all control of her. this being her present hobby—

Blair is well— little Gist next door has measles all well here— but me & I am just a little jarred from my fall— Marion Sands is here tonight returns to her Mother tomorrow all well Yr affecate Lizzie

  1. Frank had arrived in Washington to take his congressional seat.

Washington   January 12, [1864]

Dear Phil Kate did not come to her work and this is one of several days she has appointed to come— I showed her the work & all the arrangements & she seemed pleased with everything but that all the doors upstairs here were open I told her that none of our family ever sat in the bedrooms & they were opened all day— to be aired & healthy to sleep in— my Mother & my grandmother had so trained their families. She said nothing but seemed un-convinced that it was right to have bedroom doors wide open all day— This may serve as an excuse for her indisposition to work but I think she wants to take the work to her own room tho she has not proposed since I said you concurred with me in wishing her to do it here— but this I'll not permit until you say so—[1]

Frank takes his seat in Congress tomorrow under orders from the White House— & will go to the field in the Spring— by a restitution of his commission— this was offered not asked Frank simply saying he was here to obey the wish of his Chiefs letter to him & would now do what was thought best by Mr L— & it was promptly settled— The P. thinking this session one of vast import to the future of the Country— So I expect this arrangement will keep this concern agoing all of the winter— to March Father is in a whirl of visits & visitors— & nobody thinks of or regrets home but our little one who wants to know when we will go out of this old town every day or night when he gets in a long confab with father, Mother or me

After waiting for an hour beyond the time I appointed to see Kate, I went to the Asylum where I had a good report to make to the public who met us there in large numbers I was reelected as 1st Directress nobody voting against me but your wife— we had a most cheerful, happy annual meeting— Our children's ruddy faces & good behavior being the source of many compliments & I think it is a good work to better the condition of 72 children— some of whom we had to use great skill in weighing & measuring out food— to save them from death of too much food after a long process of starvation— Now fat & rosy. I confess to great delight in cultivating & watching over children— which I do not feel in extending benefits to adults— for the first there is a future— to the last it seems to me it is only a struggle to prolong a bitter or profitless present—[2]

Genl Ames is off tonight & Ill now do get some hours more sleep than Ive had of late— Gratz Brown was here tonight & says he will go down with me to see you— I felt badly at the risks you are exposed to in that miserable little vessel Fahkee[3] yr doings of the 3rd sent cold chills down my back & made me more than ever sigh to have my husband home— Devotedly your own Lizzie

1. On March 7, 1864, EBL made her attitude clear in regard to actions toward Kate: "Ill not act in the matter save under your orders— the only matter in our affairs in which I ask *for orders*—."

2. On January 4, EBL explained part of her asylum work: "I have been at the Asylum today preparing for the annual meeting— had some disagreeable duty to do in taking away two children from some people who treated them with cruelty— . . . . The girl is a beauty & I hope we have rescued her in time to save her— They are entire orphans— Mrs. Washington was the most excited person I ever saw— she & I put them there— & she has worked & investigated the matter with a zeal that greatly elevates her in my mind— Mrs. Merrick resumed her duties today— very sad & yet very much touched by the kindness of her welcome among us— We have Mrs. Mayor Maury now among us— & I shall try to get Mrs. Har[k]ness in on Teusday so you see I am getting a real worky set & as proof of it we counted up only 12,000— today as donations—."

3. SPL was aboard USS *Fahkee* off Wilmington. On January 3, they discovered the blockade runner *Bendigo* aground. After considerable effort to get her afloat, while his men were exposed to artillery fire from the shore, Lee finally had to scuttle the prize.

Washington   January 13, 1864

Dear Phil   Yours of the 4th brought me the glad tidings that you were no longer on the "beast Fahkee—" but on your good ship the Minnesota—

Its enclosure for Kate I will give to John to whom hereafter I will refer your for all that concerns her— I confess to being much hurt by the ignoring of all the statements I have made about this unfortunate woman— over whom I have no more control than a West Indian hurricane— & now I regret that instead of writing out my own feelings which I am prone to do to you I had not confined myself to simple statements of events as they occurred— for example, when you wrote that you wished her to come to me— I sent her the letter— then went to see her— & did so without getting in, & never did see her until I wrote I would not agree to her Uncles ("interfering") her own word "propositions"   then she was in a good humor— & ever since our relations have been perfectly amiable & so they shall continue— I will give her anything I have from my gowns down to needles & thread— & share gladly ought that I have— *but my home* and that I honestly believe I refuse more for the sake of my husband & child than for myself— In this I maybe mistaken— as we do not always know ourselves— but so far— I might have spared myself this scrutiny— for Kate most positively declines to share the homes of any of her kindred— But hereafter I shall confine all my letters to stating only when I saw her & how she is— which will give you an account of my proceedings only in reference to her— All else look to John whose nearer relationship will give you more confidence in the truth of what he says— & to the right feelings also— for you do not feel any more for your sister or her child than he does— this much I can say for him— when I am dead & gone & he should outlive me I feel assured that my boy will have a noble friend in his Uncle— & if he ever extends to him half the tenderness & patience you and he[1] he has given to his niece I shall be gratefully satisfied—

I have no faith in harshness in the guidance of the young— but Kate is too old for that Category & I really find her unimpressed by my kindness save when accompanied with means to attend some whim of the moment She promised me day after day to come here to write & day after day I have spent my mornings waiting for her with pens, ink, table, book, letters & room all ready with all the little appointments in it to make it attractive to her but she has never entered the house since, other than three olk & then to say she did not intend to write until next day & etc— I write this whilst sitting waiting for her— instead of going out in the carriage & paying the visits which you & my Father wish done— Of which I have paid 150 & now have as many more to pay In this matter I have followed no instinct but fidelity to you— I cannot claim credit for any higher principle of action— with that I am serious & with it I am content— until I take up Miss Nightingales vocation & devote my whole life to works of charity. which Ill not do as long as you, my Parents & child are my first duties & happiness in life— When I become useless to all of you— if the flesh holds out under such a killing contingency— the world is full of work for those who believe we must work for "salvation" hereafter— Ever yr devoted wife Lizzie

1. The words "you and he" are marked through.

Washington   January 13, 1864

My dear Phil   As I received two letters from you today I may be excused for writing two to you— I asked Govr Dennison to send & find for me the policy of the Dept about the promotions   he talked with Fox who said he believed the Department meant "to adhere to that heretofore pursued— I then intimated that he had not got Grimes views— that I did not want him asked as to you but simply to know if these small specialties like Dalghren's[1] were to be the style— of getting the vacancies filled— Govr Dennison entered fully into my meaning & I think now understands the scope of the matter better He dwelt a great deal upon Fox's expressions about you— he said "Fox talks of him like a brother with both pride and affection—" I said I knew that the Dept— had the very kindest feelings for you & that the feeling was warmly returned by us— I liked your letter to Sumner— it was well written—

I paid seventeen visits today[2] besides a long one to Mrs Dennison who finds lionizing a young lady about very fatiguing— it is especially so to Govr. D who is not well— & told me tonight that he missed the comforts he had here & came to get a mixture which gave him some relief yesterday   Ned is here & he I expects is part of the Hotel attraction & he is I assure you a fast specimen & I fear gives his Mother many a heart ache—

You appeal to me to be kind to Kate— I assure you I have done everything she would let me— & now only hesitate to give her your letter and money because I think John may need it for her expenses— at any rate I think best to refer the matter to him and I am sure no heart is more tender or true than his— Ill trust him I believe next to you & my father— There has been uninterrupted intercourse between Kate & myself until I sent your very kind letter— which she misconstrued into a plan to put her under my control. Just as soon as I saw she avoided me I put the matter all right— being just as eager to avoid to have control as she was loth to let me have it, She however will not now let me provide a washerwoman— I may pay for it, but she can, she thinks get one to suit her better than I can— She did not come to do the writing— I waited until 2 olk

Jany 14. Betty came home from the Hop at Willards where she went to be civil to the Dennisons very sick so I infer very late— She fights off low spirits bravely but they were victorious last night— She will not admit any engagement to A— but I have no doubt as to his place in her feelings— Frank has crowds of people here to see him— I think he looks well & is in good spirits—

The Presidential question is rife—[3] & Abe has the inside of the track & he has the other candidates— they think so fixed that they will have to make a break from him & against him to get on the track even tis for that emergency F is here— it may occur soon— & then after this lull will come a big muss— it is evidently the purpose now to hold on to the Niggra— & as all agree to making him free— the next point is equality & fraternity & there the fight will be—[4] I dont doubt the result— The State lines also are to be rubbed out by the Radicals— but that is too unconstitutional & federal & will never be. Your affecate Lizzie

1. On June 24, 1863, John A. Dahlgren replaced Du Pont in command of the South Atlantic Squadron. A technical expert, he had developed the Dahlgren cannon and had been promoted to rear admiral in February 1863.

2. On January 26, EBL explained her social duty: "I have called on about half the Ladies— & found since the publication of the Directory that there is about as many more to go to see Where there are no ladies I have left Fathers & Franks card— but it is more tedious than of yore as they are scattered about— & very few are in houses or at the Hotels even."

3. In the final year of his first term, Lincoln was not at all certain of his reelection. Under increasing pressure from the Radicals, Lincoln faced challenges within his own party from John Frémont and Salmon Chase; at the same time, Peace Democrats had become more outspoken in their opposition to the continuation of the war.

4. On January 23, 1864, EBL remarked: "The Radicals will throttle him— if he does not soon take them by the throat."

Washington   January 22, 1864

Dear Phil   I went out to the Country with Father today after Kate failed to keep her appointment— We found everything in its usual winter condition   I had the fire made in the parlor & in a few moments you would not have known we had been out of the house three hours much less weeks & over This is a great satisfaction to Father that the house is not broken up— Blair and the dogs rolled over the lawn   I heard Blair telling Dice not to be too glad dont shake your tail off Old fellow— Yesterday Mr Van Brunt[1] said he did not look delicate at all—

Mr Fox reported to Betty last night your return to the Roads—[2] which she forgot to tell me until today   I was really angry with her about it but she plead her violent sick head ache as an excuse & as she has been sick all day I have quit grumbling— tho she would have saved me some worry about you for your protracted stay off Wilmington made me very anxious about you & last night I was really low spirited— I asked Mr. Fox when he was going down in the Steamer he said the Steamer would be ready in a week— but the next time he went he wished to take his wife— for whom he goes tomorrow & who is still in New York kept there with sickness he said I could go on the boat whenever she went   I have a great mind to get Gratz Brown to go with me— altho he & Frank are locking horns— about nothing ie Schofield[3]

Judge Trumbull spent this evening with us— he is very affectionate in his tone about you & bid me tell you that Walter was doing well— for which he owed much to you— One of their little ones (Arthur)[4] is in almost a hopeless condition a sort of consumption— They were discussing the Military condition of things & F. to show how dead the War Dept was to all activity— said your proposition about Wilmington was cordially & fully endorsed by the Navy Dept. & *others* was sent for consideration to their military neighbor— & they did not even extend to the Secy of the Navy the Courtesy of a reply— to his letter

Fox spent the evening here   he and Blair are great friends My long ride makes me sleepy— besides I feel I am off guard duty tonight the girls beaux have all gone to the Army   that is Ames & Andrew Alexander the last went west today   Ever your own   Lizzie

    1. Mr. Van Brunt worked at Silver Spring for Preston Blair.

    2. SPL returned from Wilmington to Hampton Roads on January 21, 1864.

    3. John M. Schofield commanded the Department of Missouri from May 24, 1863, to January 22, 1864. Schofield used his position and influence to press for gradual, compensated emancipation in Missouri, a position offensive to the Radicals. Gratz Brown actively sought his removal.

    4. Arthur Trumbull was Lyman Trumbull's young son.

                           Washington   January 24, [1864]

Dear Phil   Your's with check for a thousand dollars is received. I will send you a list of all the bills I pay with it or the bills themselves if you prefer them— I do not feel any satisfaction in my lack of business talent and give you no better proof of how much discontented I feel than to tell you that I attributed much of this deficiency to not keeping a regular daily dairy of each days expenditure which I have not done for some yrs So with the beginning of the year & in turning over & beginning the Bible I resolved each night ere reading it I would settle up my worldy accounts & thereby ensure better sleeping afterwards— So far the book has been well kept—

As to reading your letters off alone— I have done so ever since girlhood when Aunt Susan came on tiptoe behind me & I first knew of her presence by her assuring me— "that page was well written—" Maybe I enjoyed my stolen fruits then best all to myself   I have had no change of feeling about you or your letters since, save be more dependant on both in every way. I am not a sad person— generally & naturally sanguine & cheerful— but sometimes I feel my burdens crushingly— I dont mention them for it might be called complaint which I hope never to make & it seems to me when I get you home again Ill never complain again whilst I live— for in these years just gone how many is the time I have prayed that your life might be spared— and Franks too— through so many many perils No if I am ever a grumbler I shall be certain I am ungrateful & wicked   I will think more about my writing and try to give you less trouble with my letters I know I made them too long— but I must talk to you & oftentimes when with you you do not hear— still I never stop when I have desire to talk to you rather think aloud— I am entirely satisfied with your letters— never evinced any other feeling to you or anybody— To op-press you with any more labor when you are already overworked— would hurt me— Betty and I are not alike & one night lately when discussing her affairs I took a view of them which was altogether opposite to her own— When she exclaimed— "People say we are alike never were two people so dissimilar on all things great and small" She may be the best & cleverest woman I perfectly willing that all the world may think her so— but you & I know she never did understand or appreciate you— until all the world through circumstances & your conduct in life proved to it & her what you are— no not half what you are according to my knowledge and faith— But Betty has very little knowl-edge of men Her friends among them are intelligent & good characters— Still any clever flatterer impresses her in that she is almost masculine— Whereas I loved best the man who never flattered with words at all that is as compared with the talk of other men— But I am prosy this Sunday morning & if I had six miles to go to church you would have escaped this long scrawl

I was fully repaid for my long yesterday to see after Kates affairs to learn thro Mrs. H's[1] complaint of her late walking (evening that she had never been out later than bt 6 & 7 oclk except once or twice when she returned in a hack about 9 olk— but Mrs Hs terror about these late hours has had a good effect— & she gets in now by dinner time—

Monday morning We are all well but Blair   the return of warm weather & some imprudent eating gave him a bad night— but he is out doors now merry & better— He takes some of his meals at the table here— breakfast & dinner on Sunday when it takes almost fighting courage to protect his little stomach from his indulgent friends around him & yesterday I protested but in vain Strange feeling in people to imagine that I who delight to indulge him should deny him unnecessarily   Ever your affectionate Lizzie

1. Eliza S. Hepburn, the widow of John Hepburn, lived at 113 West in Georgetown.

Washington   January 28, 1864   *12 ock at night*
Dear Phil   Your enclosure from Mr. W[elles] came today— who I met for a few moments next door this evening where there was a great gathering of people I matronized Evy Martin for an hour— as both Frank, Father declined

going & Mother could not go from Betty who continues quite sick   I have got thro my winter's dissipation— Nothing tires me more than these parties altho' vastly amused whilst there   Capt Walker[1] bored me— he is the worst mannered man I ever knew who had seen as much of clever & refined people— He followed me with his case & at last I took Baileys[2] part— & found it was a great mistake as that put him on the defensive when of course there was no end to his yarn

I received a long letter from Fanny today enquiring about the tax on tobacco   I replied to the boys letter the day I received it & answered fully their enquiries but I will reply to hers tomorrow— She says they are well and working hard— & so far have succeeded beyond their expectations— They are now anxious about the amount of tax to be paid on the manufactured articles which they must manage to put on the consumer   I expect they will be more lenient to tobacco than whiskey as the soldiers take so much comfort— & sailors too— much to their injury I think—

There were an immense number of magnificently dressed people next door among them Mrs. Davenport[3] in laces quite regal & beautiful— Mrs Foster & others had diamonds which exceeded anything I had ever seen before— The Congressmen are of a different class of people from those heretofore sent to Congress— far more of refinement in manner & appearance than ever before seen here— & many take houses & entertain   Johns house is open tonight in a style that quite eclipses anything ever heard of. Corcoran is thrown quite into the Shade—

Blair is well wants to go home so Mama wont go to parties altho he was put to bed & sleeping 'ere I left him   Your affecate Lizzie

1. Capt. William M. Walker who was serving in the Western Gulf Blockading Squadron.

2. Rear Adm. Theodorus Bailey, Walker's immediate superior in the Western Gulf Blockading Squadron.

3. Jeannie Brent Graham, born 1826, married Henry K. Davenport in 1847.

Washington   January 31, 1864

Dear Phil   The old Signer—[1] and Genl Washington are very much observed & approved   I got them on the Wall last night. Father thinks both admirable— & sees your face in that of your Grandfather   Consequently has faith in the likeness— I must say privately that I think the old fellow far from being as good looking as his descendant— They (except Father) think I put Old Bullion[2] in too grand company but I think he loved his Country— his wife & then when few were kind in their words about you in my home circle he was— & never lost a chance of commending you— once I'll never forget he said you had head & a heart & besides that you had good manners— particularly to old people a thing left out in the manners of most young people now a days—" these things have given the old fellow a place with me which is abiding

I have spent the day at church & at my asylum Sunday School & as it is the work which I began in that place its present really good condition is very delightful The children have had several hundred good standard books given to them for their school

Mrs. Dennison introduced to me a clever lady to me whilst here— Mrs. Witmore a very intimate friend of Mrs D & I have asked her help (which was suggested by Mrs D) & she commenced her work today— she is a charming woman— to go with her was my errand today—

Many thanks for your little note of the 29. it is all I need to make me happy. Ned Byrne has played with Blair after Church today— & they walk with Grandma whose love for him grows with his growth— which saying a great deal   Ever yr affecate Lizzie

1. Richard Henry Lee, who moved for a declaration of independence on June 7, 1776, was SPL's grandfather.

2. Old Bullion was Thomas Hart Benton, who had been Blair's political ally and close friend.

Washington   February 2, 1864

Dear Phil   I have wondered why my letters are so long getting to you as I have taken so much pains to mail them before 12 olk ever since we have been in the city & conclude that one reason they appear to long coming is I write in the evening always when I go up to put Blair to bed to be sure to have a letter ready to go by the mail carrier who comes at 9 olk— I close the letter often in the morning— with the date of the night before The Wines were all delivered today— I shall open them tomorrow morning & give the test you desire tomorrow at dinner—

I have spent most of this day at the Asylum. where the throng of poor makes the first Tuesday in the month a doleful duty day. The orphans of soldiers and sailors we never turn away but I had to beg hard for a poor little Virginia boy whose father is imprisoned & his mother dead. his curly head & little touch of Irish look put me in mind of you & John

Frank is in great spirits tonight— he has managed to split the Radicals & to unite the entire democracy with him in the Legislature of Missouri— He thought last night Foy's[1] letter was over Sanguine but today when he "Saw" Hall & old King[2] sitting looking doleful over a letter, he walked near them & asked the News Why you know it and made it before you quit Missouri" Frank plead innocence & ignorance— so they then read a letter from King's son saying Willard Hall[3] had presided over a caucus of Democrats wherein it was settled that every man would go in for the Lincoln resolutions now before the

Legislature & (it seems *entre nous*— Frank's whole programme which he had arranged when home Hall is now acting Govr in Gambles place— I relate these things in full— as they are of import— Frank says he will go down to the Roads with me— when he gets back from Newport where he goes on friday to see Andrew whose good conduct deserves the visit from him—

I took a long walk after sitting four hours in the Asylum today and feel very tired tonight— The new Cook does well so far & is litterally a new broom[4] for the cleaning up in the kitchen gives it a new aspect & makes me feel more than ever what an infliction Harriet was in every way— save the cooking & that she did well— a great improvement on Nanny who has cooked for us at Silver Spring— Blair is glad to get Becky out of the kitchen she cleans the bed rooms— & attends to him— & generally starts out at 12 olk for a walk & does all my errands in the distant parts of the city— Good night Your affectionate Lizzie

1. Peter L. Foy, St. Louis Republican, was editor of the moderate *Missouri Democrat* and St. Louis postmaster (1861–67).

2. William Hall and Austin A. King were both Missouri Democratic congressmen (1862–65).

3. Willard P. Hall, brother of William, had been a Missouri Democratic congressman (1847–53). He was lieutenant governor (1861–64) and governor for a year after Gamble's death on January 31, 1864.

4. On May 9, 1864, EBL qualified her opinion of their cook Mary Ann "who Mother says is the best servant she ever knew— I dont like her manners— Becky says she has lived with Quakers— who dont make any servants know their places— & there is some truth in this, but it is a drawback easily borne— as long as she has Quaker cleanliness & honesty—."

Washington   February 8, [1864]
Dear Phil   We reached here after dark tonight—[1] found Mother in extreme distress about us as they had expected us to breakfast— After we parted all went well until about one olk when our boat stuck in the mud & there we kept stuck until eleven olk today— when we were rescued by an Army steamer with 300 soldiers on board— it brought us to Alexandria— from thence the Thomas Collyer[2] brought us to this city greatly to our friends' relief There was nothing disagreeable in this detention save the felt anxiety here—Mother was sure I was ill as I suffered from my arm— & was worried but it is all well passed   I rejoice & take great comfort in having seen you & Marion who is by me bids me say that your hearty kindness & sympathy for her was— & will always be, a real comfort to her—

We had scarcly finished our dinner when Uncle Ben walked in— I have since been doing devoir to him telling of our trip & putting Blair to bed— He told his Grandpa he would have liked to stay but he knew when *"night time came*" he could not go to sleep good if Mama was not there— He said he liked his trip & very well but it "would been great deal better if Papa & Mike had come back with us—" He gave your message very exactly to Mother— I must go to bed— as I am your weary little woman & ever your devoted wife   Lizzie Uncle Ben looks unaltered

1. EBL and Blair had just returned from a brief visit with SPL at Hampton Roads.
2. The army steamer *Thomas Colyer.*

Washington   February 10, [1864] Dear Phil   This has been like a Sunday with me. I have been to Church twice & quite occupied with myself— When home after morning church Uncle Ben came for me to go to the White House with him   I soon dressed & we went, but after detaining us for over an half hour Mrs. Lincoln sent word she was so weary that she begged to be excused & asked that we would come in the evening at eight olk as she really covetted the pleasure of a visit from Mr. Gratz— So they are now over there I could not go from Blair at his bed time at this hour & I was not needed as Betty and Mother went—

I was stopped by the cry of fire. They soon returned from the White House announcing the burning of the stable & the loss of all Mrs Lincoln's horses & the ponies of her little boy who took his loss sorely to heart   The soldiers stood around and did not take their hands out of their pockets[1]   Uncle Ben came back very much disgusted with the fire Department of Washington   Mrs Lincoln told them that they went out to see the Alexanders & found that the Col[2] had been ordered away much to Mrs Ls disgust she showed great irrita- tion about it— The Kings[3] were such *Secesh* that she was glad to have them removed but the Alexanders were her friends & she was angry—

Frank telegraphs that he will not be here before Saturday   I have been sad today from sympathy with Mrs Geo Bache[4]   her only daughter died this morning at seven olk with typhoid fever— She was born two or three months after her Father was drowned & has been her Mother's solace in life ever since & was a lovable sensible girl who was very dear to all of her kindred. I heard yesterday of this and went to see if I could serve her in way— but the Mothers message was one of hopelessness then. She has been ill only a few days—

Mrs Stone's Richmond letter[5] brings the tidings that Joe Johnston has the prospect of having an heir born to him—[6] Mrs Falkner[7] says Mrs Davis wears a "*levy* calico—" & has grown grey & forlorn— is very unpopular & never has moved "*in any style*" in Richmond— has quarrelled with "the Lees and almost everybody." & talks of the pleasures— friends & etc she sacrficed "in having to leave Washington" This looks like a true picture to me—

Blair is sleeping sweetly and we talk over our visit to you— & hope for another sight of you as he says "before *bery* long" Your devoted Lizzie Genl Pleasonton dined here— & seems hopeful that the war will end this year

1. During the evening of February 10, the president's stable burned and all six horses were lost, including two ponies used by Tad Lincoln. On the following day, the Washington *Evening Star* reported that "owing to the combustible nature of the material within the stables," fire fighters could do nothing except prevent the spread of the blaze.

2. Lt. Col. Thomas L. Alexander was deputy governor of the Old Soldiers' Home from 1858 to 1864.

3. Assistant Surgeon Benjamin King was the attending physician at the Old Soldiers' Home until 1864.

4. Eliza C. Patterson married George Bache in 1837. A brother of Alexander Dallas Bache, he had been lost at sea in September 1846.

5. Margaret Stone, wife of Washington physician Robert Stone, was the daughter of Thomas Ritchie who founded the Richmond *Enquirer.*

6. The Johnstons had no children.

7. In 1833, Mary Wagner Boyd married Charles J. Faulkner, who served the Confederacy as minister to France.

Washington   February 11, 1864

My dear Phil   Mother started me off early today with her to Brentwood to see Mrs Pearson[1] who is anxious to hear about Kate & as I had a recent talk with your boarding officer they thought I ought to give the Old Lady the benefit of it in present sad condition— After my return here— Betty & I paid a good many congressional visits & etc Mrs. Morris sent you many kind messages but bid me specially reminded me to say to you— that you are one of her *"boys"* & as life wanes she cherishes peculiar tenderness for those associated with her children & husband— I have been attentive to all of the old Naval Set since I have been in the City—

Here I was stopped by Father and told to get ready for the party next door where I was to accompany Uncle Ben I tried to get off, in vain so I have spent the evening in chatting away to people & am now very tired after a day of visiting Preston King was there. I invited him here but he says he must stay a while in his old haunts on Capitol Hill he dines here tomorrow & I told him of your invitation to the ship— He was very much surrounded by people all evening. He was affectionate in his talk about you

I met nobody there Naval but our Secy who was very kind— They all laughed at me wrecking Wise's[2] ordinance boat— I had but one regret that it did not stick somewhere nearer to the Minnesota— Capt Wise said you were not as civil to me as to his wife & then told of the oysters & etc you put on their returning vessel I said you were a law abiding man— & it was a naval law for officers Capts to be civil on ship board to the wives of other people— & I assured him I could forgive all your neglect of me & as proof of it I would go again on an ordinance boat whenever I was asked The Secy said I had permission to go whenever I pleased he is too stately for fun— It seems that Capt Fox had no confidence in the pilot so he was on the watch nearly all of both nights we were out— & the only time he took respite on a sofa he heard the Steamer gradually *grating* into the mud— He certainly was very kind & thoughtful of us in every way—

Blair is well and enjoyed his race with the little Pattersons[3] on the lawn at Brentwood he is less shy of people since we have been in the city— Your affecate Lizzie

1. Mrs. Pearson was the mother of Eliza Patterson. Carlisle and Eliza lived at Brentwood; their home was located at Florida Avenue and Seventh Street. The Pearsons were related to the late North Carolina congressman Joseph Pearson.
2. Capt. Henry A. Wise was an inspector of naval ordnance in Washington.
3. Both Carlisle and his brother Thomas had several children.

Washington   February 12, 1864

My dear Phil   I went to market, then to Church, then the Asylum— & then to see Mrs. Grimes—[1] who I really like— we had a very long chat about people & things, she seemed quite loth to part with me— Met Mrs Winter Davis[2] there— who I meet everywhere— & she gives me very knowing looks to which I respond innocent ones— feeling in that condition at least so far as she is & hers are concerned for I have been civil to her— always— When we get a good waiter Ill ask her here to dine so our debt in that way may be cancelled—

I found Mr. King here on my return from evening church & he seemed to enjoy his dinner & company hugely— He & Uncle Ben agree in the purpose & results of this war— & he seemed delighted to have met Uncle Ben & both enjoyed your oysters which are still abundant & excellent— He says Blair grows well— the boy gave him a hearty welcome which he described to me with evident pleasure— Mr & Mrs Foster[3] of Cont. spent the evening with us most socially & without invitation— Frank is still in New York— Gratz Brown is quite sick threatened with typhoid was invited to dine here with Uncle Ben the first day of his arrival— but was & is still too sick to come here

I have not heard from you since we parted on Sunday which makes it a long time to me— Ill make all of my letters short and as plain as print— if you will just give me a little recognition of my existence & quit chewing tobacco— Now you will think this no self denial on my part but you are mistaken for there is nothing I enjoy half as much as just scribbling to you— thinking aloud— & never thinking how I am saying or writing my utterances— a habit you gave me 22 or more years ago— when I promised you never to read over what I had written— but you are now too overworked for such trespassing nonsense Your devoted wife Lizzie

Uncle Ben sends you kindest greetings & says you are the greatest favorite he has among all who have married into his family circle he will not except even any of womankind Mrs Sands sends love to the Admiral for his kindness & sympathy for her "disappointed child—" Had a letter from Fanny all well with her, & hers—

1. Elizabeth Sarah Nealley married James W. Grimes in 1846.
2. Nancy Morris of Baltimore became Henry Winter Davis's second wife in 1857. In the House, Davis aligned with the Radicals and became an opponent of the Blairs.
3. Martha Lyman of Northampton, Massachusetts, was the second wife of Lafayette Sabine Foster. They married in 1860. He served in the U.S. Senate from 1855 to 1867.

Washington   February 16, 1864
Dear Phil This is only the third time I have sat down to write to you this morning and now I fear it is too late to get it off in time for todays mail. First Birnie & her husband came & they are the kind of people I must be civil to. They are now well fixed in their own home they came in answer to Mothers message about Neddy— who wants to live with us— I shall try to make him a gardener— in the meantime it is really a comfort to have about the premises an intelligent & affectionate white boy Many times we are at home all day alone & many nights too without gentleman— This boy is honest and good very much attached to us & so very deaf that he is unfitted for any but some pursuit like gardening— he reads remarkably well & his access to books makes our house a happier place to him than his own home & his deafness makes him very solitary without books. he writes well & ciphers & I shall make him continue his lessons & make him read gardening books under Mr. Smiths direction— Sam wont learn to read so Ill have to give him up as a grape cultivator— I feel more attached to Ned as he has been my charge ever since he was three years old Last not least Blair is devoted to him for whom he is a safe companion— about home he uses good language & tells the truth—

Your gift of oysters came yesterday whilst I was at the Dentists under whose hands I suffered two hours & a half— after trying for over six months to separate two teeth Maynard decided it could not be done— then one tooth must be cut away or I would loose both the decay was getting so deep. I resigned myself to the fill— fortunately the nerve was too dead already to take much to finish it— Still I was too used up to enjoy the party which father invited on coming of the oysters— You would have enjoyed seeing old Preston luxuriate on them & the terrapins we had some good singing & a very pleasant evening for Uncle Ben & Mr. King there about 18 persons & the supper was ample & pretty— almost entirely your providing— & I pressed Mr King to come stay with us— but he declined saying he was on business with a party who desired to be with him— he says he will be here in early spring— when he will stay here & seemed intensely pleased by our attentions

Mr & Mrs Lincoln have not let a day pass scarcely without extending some civility to Uncle Ben— Last night sent for him. Betty & Me to go to some entertainment at Willards Hall. Blair is enchanted with your photographs— I prefer the old ones which are without the grey beard & looks more like my husband This is too late for todays mail

EBL and Blair Lee at age four, 1861. Photo courtesy of the P. Blair Lee family.

SPL in 1863. Photo courtesy of Princeton University Library.

Blair Lee in 1861. Photo courtesy of Princeton University Library.

Blair Lee in 1866. Photo courtesy of Princeton University Library.

Francis Preston Blair and Eliza Gist Blair. Photo courtesy of the Blair Lee III family.

Francis Preston Blair, Jr.
(Frank). Photo courtesy of
the National Archives.

Montgomery Blair.
Photo courtesy of the
National Archives.

Blair home at Silver Spring, ca. 1864. Photo courtesy of the Library of Congress.

Blair-Lee House today (Lee house on the left). Photo courtesy of Andrew F. Laas.

Gun emplacements at Fort Stevens, protecting Washington, D.C. Photo courtesy of the Library of Congress.

Abraham Lincoln. Photo courtesy of the National Archives.

Mary Todd Lincoln in 1861. Photo courtesy of the National Archives.

Jefferson Davis. Photo courtesy of the National Archives.

Varina Howell Davis. Photo courtesy of the Library of Congress.

Assistant Secretary of the Navy Gustavus Vasa Fox. Photo courtesy of the U.S. Army Military History Institute.

Secretary of War Edwin Stanton. Photo courtesy of the National Archives.

Jessie Benton Frémont, ca. 1863. Photo courtesy of the National Portrait Gallery, Smithsonian Institution.

John C. Frémont in 1861. Photo courtesy of the National Archives.

Andrew H. Foote. Photo courtesy of the
Library of Congress.

David D. Porter. Photo courtesy of the
U.S. Army Military History Institute.

David G. Farragut. Photo courtesy of
the U.S. Army Military History Institute.

Secretary of the Navy Gideon Welles.
Photo courtesy of the National Archives.

Winfield Scott in 1862. Photo courtesy of the U.S. Army
Military History Institute.

Robert E. Lee. Photo courtesy of the U.S. Army Military History Institute.

Ulysses S. Grant. Photo courtesy of the Library of Congress.

William T. Sherman. Photo courtesy of the National Archives.

Thomas J. (Stonewall) Jackson. Photo courtesy of the Library of Congress.

Andrew Johnson. Photo courtesy of the U.S. Army Military History Institute.

Secretary of State William H. Seward. Photo courtesy of the National Archives.

George B. McClellan. Photo courtesy of the U.S. Army Military History Institute.

George H. Thomas. Photo courtesy of the U.S. Army Military History Institute.

Joseph Hooker. Photo courtesy of the U.S. Army Military History Institute.

Henry Wager Halleck. Photo courtesy of the U.S. Army Military History Institute.

George G. Meade. Photo courtesy of the U.S. Army Military History Institute.

Joseph E. Johnston. Photo courtesy of the Library of Congress.

15

*"We are all well & in good spirits
& not at all afraid of being
demolished politically—"*

March 3, 1864

AT LAST PRESIDENT ABRAHAM LINCOLN found a general, with his appointment of Ulysses Grant as general in chief of the United States. His elevation and consequent reorganization brought optimism to the Union cause, while radicals and moderates fought to control government policy. The Blairs promoted Lincoln's moderate plans and attacked their opponents at every opportunity. Frank's return to Congress brought verbal fireworks to the floor of the House and enmeshed him in two congressional investigations. His attacks on Secretary of the Treasury Salmon Chase contributed to Chase's decision not to seek the presidential nomination. Montgomery contributed outspoken polemics against the radical position, and his father became a candidate for election to the Maryland Constitutional Convention. S. P. Lee, meanwhile, continued to plead for combined operations against Wilmington, North Carolina, the weak link in his blockade. He was convinced that the only way to close that rebel port was to capture it.

Washington   February 23, [1864]
Dear Phil   The nerves are getting over their nervousness & I hope tomorrow I'll get thro the ordeal of Maynard's— Today three orphan children forced me out & after I once got out & doing something I got over my sore nerves & tooth & have been better ever since   from there (Asylum) I strolled by Franklin Row & was reminded that I had never called on the Goldsboroughs since they lost their only son. so I went in & had anything but a sad talk— & when I came away she said, I feel the kindness of this visit—"

I sent Blair to George town with some things I had bought for Kate & she sent word to me by Becky that you had written that you had sent her some money in a letter to GeoTown but that she had never recd it— What direction did you put upon it? Becky and Blair say that she was very well— but that Mrs Hepburn was ill with pneumonia I must go soon & pay the board as they may need the money— Mrs. Hepburn looks like a delicate woman & I fear the result for her— I think her a very good & ladylike person— I feel very sorry for her & her daughters— Kate says the house goes on as usual as she has several unmarried daughters to assist in house keeping & to nurse her These are her messages to me by Becky—

This evening at seven olk there was a musical gathering here— to concoct a concert to get an Organ for St Johns Church— I helped to get the old one in my girlhood— they all agreed upon their parts— the time & place of having it & then went off to the Theatre which is very fashionable & good here this winter— I never go in Lent

Mr. Kennedy[1] the English Secretary told me that you had caught about 30 Steamers in 6 months but that about 60 had got in safely— I see letters from a certain Charleston General who made a drawing of the steamer which was beached & unloaded by the Rebel which he said was a disgrace to Ad D. that he would not allow officers to go set it afire who were panting to do so There has been a signal book captured— which had all of Dalghrens signals to the most minor details up to the 6th of Feby— he copied many of them out of the captured book before him— "for Mrs Lee's amusement"!! I always *took* up for Adl Dalghren this winter & he pronounced him "a failure—" & "no sailor—"

Frank speaks tomorrow— answers Blow— *tis a hot fight—*[2] but I cannot well write about these matters— & it is not prudent to write these Charleston items *they strictly confidential—* & so you must not mention them to anybody—

I have concluded to let Mme Dorman teach Blair french orally Violet speaks it beauti & never learnt from anybody else— & now scarce remembers when or how she learnt— tis the next best thing to a french nurse which I cannot get Yr affecate Lizzie

1. John Gordon Kennedy was filling an appointment in Washington as a third secretary in the British Diplomatic Service.
2. Henry T. Blow, a Radical, and Frank, a moderate, represented opposing viewpoints in Missouri, and they exchanged insults on the floor of the House.

Washington February 25, 1864

My dear Phil On Thursday last when I first mentioned our affairs father & Frank took the livliest interest in them— & Father went immediately over to the Dept with my notes— but unluckily the Secy was off for the day that day Mr Blow made his attack on Frank— & since then it has been followed as you may see by others— today Winter Davis made an onslaught on the whole concern beginning with Fox & Mr Welles as the outposts— Frank defended these & was the only man in the house who did   Mr Rice[1] made a weak effort & said he would print his statistics & remarks— but did nothing there— I am going into the Country for your notes of last winter   I have most of your letters and papers here— but I put some for ready access in my bureau at home & I think they are there as I have not found them today— for some days now there will be some political excitement & then I will again push our matters—

There is another & the last reception next door— & there has never been such a throng before which will be a consolation under Winter's assault which Frank describes as one of marked ability— His attack on the Navy Dept— Fox in particular was savage—[2] Frank says that he said "he had only passed the complts of the season with him   Capt F.— so was not posted in the Departmental facts—" I think he will be posted after this— there has been a decided shyness— which F. has commented on to me— There will good come of it— & *honest* men & working ones will I hope get their rights— did you observe the thanks got by Rogers at Annapolis?— he is here busy as a bee— goes to NY for a day now & then—

I am better & do take great care of myself— ride altogether when I have far to go— the carriage comes in every other day & I think that often enough— to go out on a real visiting tour— lately I have had to use it to go to the Dentists— & then was not able to visit— suffered too much— but I declined any more Dentistry this week & feel much better today— will go to Silver Spring in Brothers P.O. carriage who loans it to Father & to me whenever I want it— But I am a great deal stronger & better in every respect than I was last week— the truth is I rarely have accute suffering & in all my life— & when it does come— lasts any time it is sure to hurt my weak points no matter how removed the part or cause may be from them—

Blair rode today out beyond the College in one of the country vehicles— with Becky and Ned— Then walked back home nearly three miles   that after he had worked & run about all morning & was as gay as ever this evening— Ever yr own   Lizzie

1. Alexander Hamilton Rice, Republican congressman from Massachusetts from 1859 to 1867, was a member of the Committee on Naval Affairs.

2. The 1863 congressional elections in Maryland had been particularly bitterly fought, with the Blairs on one side and Winter Davis on the other. In Congress, Frank defended the Navy Department against Davis's attacks over the failure to take Charleston.

Washington   March 1, 1864
My dear Phil   I went to the Asylum as it was meeting day & one of some importance— & there was a full board even Mrs Merrick from Baltre As Sarah

Coleman gave me the benefit of a ride I went & got the rest of the bills— & I find in counting it all up— it will take yet $500 to put me out of debt— & once more out of making bills— I feel as if I would never again get anything that I could not see the money & count it down— when I bought the comfortable habit of nearly all of my married life— which Ill resume with a sense of relief never before fully appreciated—

I have this evening been clerking for Frank whilst he is correcting & revising one speech at one end of the table— I am looking over his correspondence— to get names from among them to whom he wishes to send all his speeches of which I have already directed a goodly number The most tedious work possible In which Betty helps me with a very good will.

Blair is in great glee over Neddy who stays here at night & then works at the Capitol Garden he is too deaf to make a clerk of— or any pursuit where alertness is required & yet he writes well & none of my nephews are more advanced than he is for his age— he is just in his 13th year— Blair is very sympathetic with him for "making his living" & is very proud of him "When he was lame & sick so long—" Our boy is full of talk about going down in the Mt. Washington—

I am full of Asylum business today it is strange how much the responsibility of things keeps your mind bent on them— I have ceased to have any comic byplay since obliged to take charge of things generally— but of one thing I do keep entirely clear— that is all accounts & buying & etc that I have turned over to some very working smart, Northern women— & have their reports read at every meeting— & never buy a dollars worth on Credit— I have Mrs. Mayor Maury—[1] as one of the buying committee— & have the whole Board now *in working parties*— in committees & hope soon to get them really doing the work well by dividing it up among the whole Board— Tomorrow there is a public examination of the School of which I am very proud— it is that which took me out in this bad weather but I am much better so could venture out— I did very little else this day— Ever yr affecate Lizzie

1. Isabel Foyles married John W. Maury in 1831. He had been mayor of Washington and died in 1855.

Washington   March 3, 1864
My dear Phil I have written you one letter today but that was for Mother who discharged her gardener— Tom Jones— & now wants your little man & his wife to help in our domestic concerns

Frank was before the Committee on elections today— Seems to feel very little concern as to the result— & whether from his own sanguine nature or the goodness of his cause he certainly has none of Mr. Dick's fears on the

subject— & insinuates that Dick's wish is father to the thought— I see in one
of Apo's letters she says all of Dicks associations are with the Radicals— Still
there is a very kindly note from him to Frank today— I think his feelings have
got soured by something about the Provost Martial business— where I know
all his severities were not the most agreeable things in the world to Frank— In
truth there is growing up a rancor at the North which quite surpasses anything
I ever dreamt of in my phylosophy

I had a letter from Phila Aunt thanks me for some Brandy peaches—
which I sent her for her 83 birthday gift— which is today— Mother & Blair
wanted to ride today so I went to the Navy Yard to give them a long drive Blair
was delighted to point out things to Grandma they walked home from the
Capitol. I stopped to see Mrs Winn who is failing I fear rapidly. I paid visits to
all the Naval people in the Yard— & met a very pleasant set at Mrs. Harris'
who always has some special speeches for you— Was surprised to hear there
from Mrs. Welles that Adl Dalghren has come to the City last night—

We are all well & in good spirits & not at all afraid of being demolished
politically— & if we are, we have home resources wherin to be happy— if
all goes well with the Country which I never doubt whatever may overtake
individuals— Ever yr devoted wife Lizzie

Washington   March 4, 1864
My dear Phil Our streets have been filled with exciting rumors all of which
have been condensed in the truth of a cavalry ride thro Virginia after due
notice to the enemy to be all ready to defeat its object—[1] I take some comfort
that Grant is now Lt General[2] & that from a letter received & shown to the
President today there is a perfect entente cordiale— & my hope is that his
counsels will prevail over the stupid ones heretofore so much heeded—

Majr Moses came here tonight from Columbus Says that the quotas are
being filled rapidly with the best class of men for sturdy soldiers. he has been
our mustering officer at Columbus & also in Philadelphia He thinks there will
be but small part needed to be filled by Conscripts

You have caught a cotton ship at last. I hope Capt Sands was there for
his luck seems bad to be always off his post when a prize is taken— I heard
that the Court of Inquiry on Capt Wilkes called for a Court Martial on him[3]
& his family & friends are very unhappy about it I have taken a long walk
today & feel much stronger than for sometime past but a cold in the head is
rather stupifying— It is believed here that young Dalghren is a prisoner— The
Admiral is unfortunate in his children this young man loves him not. thinks
like Betty that he was harsh to his sister who died— Now the fate of this very
clever young man is very doubtful— the second daughter[4] is as ugly as mud &
stupid— his sailor son however promises well— Throop Martin has found it

best to resign his chances at Newport— since his last examination— Andrew stands well & so does Walter— Good night Blair & all of us well— Ever yr affectionate Lizzie

　　1. On February 28, the Union began a cavalry raid on Richmond, led by Hugh Judson Kilpatrick. The rebels were well informed of the attack, which came to naught on March 1.

　　2. The Senate confirmed Grant as lieutenant general on March 2.

　　3. Charles Wilkes was court-martialed for disobedience, disrespect, insubordination, and conduct unbecoming an officer. On April 30, he was found guilty and sentenced to a reprimand and three years' suspension, which was later reduced to one year.

　　4. Eva Dahlgren was the sixteen-year-old daughter of John Dahlgren.

Washington　March 16, 1864

My dear Phil　I was glad of indoor duties today to avoid going out in the cold wind & dust but nothing kept me from missing you. one gets quickly spoilt & Blair evidently had great sympathy with me for without having even mentioned your name to him— when playing with some toys on the floor— he suddenly looked at me & said "Mama dont you wish Papa was President— or something that would keep him home with us all the time."

　　Betty's frolic kept up until two olk & was very gay & pleasant altho many staid away— from fear of Varioloid[1] which seems to have been very thoroughly impressed on the minds of even those even who came— I did not let Blair see anybody— put him to bed 'ere the company came but I had to stay with him a great while after the music commenced to reconcile him to his bed— he heard Capt Smedburg's voice & sent for him to come see him in bed— The Captain boasted of being so kindly remembered as he had not seen the child for 18 months. Father thinks it another proof his being "his wonderful boy." I heard him telling it several times— Betty went of with a large party to a Ball given by the "Regulars" in the Army of the Potomac. We are all full of regrets that Mother let her go since it has grown so bitterly cold as it is tonight— it was freezing at midday.

　　Frank is still hard at work & very sick　both last night— & this evening I have had to bind his head with chloroform— which he says gives him temporary relief I think it may from his teeth this thought is suggested by the fact that since the cavity of my tooth has be filled & the exposed nerve gone— I have had no overwhelming headache— & yet had but very little sleep during the past week save the night before you left last night I did not go up stairs until after 3 olk as I had to see things put in some order & the house shut up as I induced my Parents to retire which I'll do now with a right good will.

　　I saw Mr. Asta burnagua[2] today, he was let in against orders— he told me

Riggs was making money fast & settling the property he bought on his wife—[3] he gave her whilst he was lately in New York a home— which cost 22,000 twenty two thousand dollars— I mention this as it shows that real estate is more affected by these Bankers than stocks as in his fathers day Yr affectionate Lizzie

I had a letter from Aunt Kitty today. All well but says nothing of John's family—

1. A mild form of smallpox.
2. F. S. Asta Burnaga, chargé d'affaires from Chile.
3. Janet Sheddon married George Riggs in 1840.

Washington   March 20 [1864]

My Dear Phil My thoughts have been Sunday as it is— almost wholly yours this day through I recd your letter & before breakfast had it thoroughly & carefully imparted to Father. He, Frank, & I, have discussed it frequently today Frank takes your view of the matter & says he will do his part now— best done promptly as he will have to go away— that your cases dont clash at all— & it is settled that *Father* will write your case & present it tomorrow to the Secy— as his own matter & then both will urge it thro' to Congress— where Frank says it will pass without any difficulty— Father has his whole plan arranged will carry it out tomorrow they will not consent to my doing anything at all Your chance in Congress does not need any such effort— I will watch & report all I see & hear & then do what you wish

I spent the evening at the Gooches. They called to see you on Tuesday after you left when I was up stairs with Blair— They speak of you with ever affectionateness— I met Adl Paulding today— Father bade me ask him to dine— if our new cook is what I hope I shall do so— very soon— Charles does very well & his wife better than at first— He takes my letters by eight olck every day— He goes for water with which to make breakfast— & then takes my letter & Becky thinks never later than half past 8 olk— He is a good servant & will improve & seems very well content to be with us—

Frank says that absurd Bill 303—[1] will never pass— but says you best try to pass now— His heartiness has given me great cheer— I cannot offer the money *now*— besides dont know what amt you would like to give for the purpose you suggest Blair & I are both well & the first delighted to be out doors again— I was surprised to see Capt Fox today he said he did not care to go "Gin" could not go— I heard no news today save that Mary Blair is very ill— I have been there twice today & shall go tomorrow very early to see how she is & maybe to stay. Ever your affecate Lizzie

1. House Bill 303 concerned naval rank. It provided for mental and physical examinations before an officer could be promoted, a regulation which dismayed SPL because he did not think he could pass the physical. On April 25, the president signed the bill into law.

Washington   March 23, [1864]

Dear Phil   Your's enclosing one for the Sub Secy. Mrs. Yulee[1] & etc came this morning— We are not likely to get out to Silver Spring for some weeks yet— the painting is unfinished and the smell is pernicious to mother— that it will take sometime to get that out even after the painting is done— then if Father is elected to the Convention[2] Ill stay here with Frank until he goes— But he thinks the Committee will soon report—

Govr Vance's[3] brag about the dependance of Lee on the N.C. Railroads & about the open port of Wilmington— hurts us— & seems to me far from the truth or the Gaston women would not have needed everything as they did I understood that Genl B[4] was very strict as to their luggage on their return went as they came— Cant you find out the author of this Newbern letter & get Vance's report? It quite puts me down tonight— at the same the signal lights & etc looks like blabbing—

I went to the Hotel to see Mrs. Grant[5] with Frank & Betty— the last says the Genl looks like you— he does in the lower part of his face— has quiet good manners & is about your figure— but is thinner even & more worn— in the expression of the face but has the same quiet, resolute bearing which denotes a man of Will— I heard him ask F about his late telegraph to him— to which F. answered in the affirmative all the way *through*— He then remarked the ladies around all chatting with each other) to F as they stood somewhat aloof— I think they will fight harder this campaign than ever as it will be the fight of desperation— & he soon after arranged with F. to manage his retreat from the parlor— as he had "an engagement for the evening" & he was gone some minutes 'ere the party of Ladies remarked upon it— I then paid a social visit to Mrs Senator Foster & came home found my boy sound asleep   he has been very good about not playing in the snow today of which I was afraid it would give him cold so soon after the Chicken Pox

Frank is delighted at getting a committee to investigate this fraud—[6] I heard him say to one of the Radicals— you see I am not afraid of a Committee— It is just what I have been trying to get all winter & was too modest to make so much of myself— & etc but thanks to my enemies for this good turn   I watched the mans countenance & it admitted a loss of a point in the game I thought— F did not tell me his Radical's reply. I confess to some nervousness about the outrageous insult F gave his colleague—[7] bad temper is so very unprofitable— if there was nothing else to be said against it— I wonder men & women of the world dont appreciate the point

I must close this & a huge carton of collars & seed & talk to Nelly tonight John did not refund my sixty so it was lucky you gave the forty— as I had to get coal & etc today— Your affecate Lizzie

1. Senator David Yulee of Florida married a daughter of Charles A. Wickcliffe of Kentucky in 1846. The subsecretary refers to Assistant Secretary of the Navy Gustavus Fox.
2. FPB wanted to be a candidate to the Maryland Constitutional Convention to be held in Annapolis in April 1864. Supporting a plan for emancipation with compensation, he was defeated by the strong Southern feeling in Montgomery County.
3. Zebulon B. Vance was elected governor of North Carolina in 1862. Until secession, he had been a supporter of the Union.
4. Gen. Benjamin Butler.
5. Julia Dent married Ulysses Grant in 1848.
6. On March 23, Frank succeeded in getting a congressional committee to investigate charges that he had ordered large quantities of liquor and tobacco, charged the cost to the government, and made immense profits by the resale of the goods. Radical Missouri congressman Joseph W. McClurg had brought the charges of fraud.
7. On the House floor, Frank had declaimed: "I pronounce his allegations from beginning to end a base and miserable falsehood. He has taken the place of the forger and falsifier, and I pronounce him an infamous liar and scoundrel. (Great Sensation.)" *Congressional Globe*, 38th Cong., 1st sess., 1863–64, 135, pt. 2:1252.

Washington   March 27, 1864
My dear Phil   We have had the loveliest Easter day. I went to church & then after dinner to School at the Asylum & to church & then to see Mary Blair's to see her so much improved was making the day close most happily & I was entirely satisfied with it— Until tonight. Mr. Gray & Mr. James—[1] of Frémont memory spent the evening & I am more than ever convinced that the last is not a gentleman— Mr. Gray told us that after paying all *dues* between him & Genl Frémont the Genl had settled on Mr James & his wife as a present $50,000 & yet he sat in our parlor & sneered at him & Jessie this night—

I was interested in much they told us about them— as I said to them— I only feel sorry— when I think of them— I have no bitterness or ill will towards them— & for their children— great interest as my God Children— & yet I hope never to encounter the Parents again— but I did not say this I was glad too to see that Father & I agree about this— for they had talked to Father 'ere I came in— & they smiled & said you & yr Father are agreed in this matter— Yes said Mother they were both fooled by Jessie & etc— They say Genl Frémont paid all his debts & bounties due on the Mariposa & then had 12 millions & that was one year ago Now he has less than one half a million left & that is going fast in presidential electioneering I was glad to observe great & unusual discretion in *our* circle during this visit— Mother was sharp but talked just as she always has done of these parties— They are evidently no longer Frémont men—

Frank has has had five or six & once seven gentlemen in his office today— & went out this evening for the first in many weeks— so you see he is well again— Ever yr affecate   Lizzie   Mr James says he has heard Jessie abuse almost every body she she knows— *but me* rather— "Lizzie Lee—" They say she has grown huge & is in bad health

1. Probably John C. Gray of New York. Charles James of Wisconsin had been active in Frémont's 1856 campaign.

Washington   March 28, 1864

My dear Phil   I went to the Country with Father to keep him company in his long ride to give a chance Blair to stretch himself over the lawn— with Henry, Ned, & Dice— & finally to give orders about getting the old domincil in order— It begins to get in ship shape— & I worked for some hours in the library to get the books in their accustomed places. The carpets are down & it will not take long to make it home again—

Father wishes to go out there for a while 'ere the election takes place so that he can see his neighbors— he saw about twenty today & they are all for him & even our most pro slavery man Dr. Hardin[1] & others *say* they will vote from feeling he has their interests more at heart than any other person of his persuasion— I heard today that he would be elected but the others on the ticket will be defeated—

When I got home I found Betty, Julia & Miss Ward (a niece of Hon Mr. Freeman Clark—[2] half brother to Mr Isaac Sherman)— waiting for me to matronize them to the Opera— Frank too sick to go— Mother would not— & Father of course was too weary So I went the first time since I enjoyed Burton[3] so much in New York. I am— to say that the illusions of life still cling to me— & I confess to have enjoyed Faust (Goethe's) with all its wickedness & as it was rendered in the most exquisite music— I did understand the music & the story— but not the German poetry— so I am *not* perverted by the last. can condemn the 2nd & enjoyed the first hugely. & really enjoyed to see a woman resist thro' prayer— the temptations to evil tho persuaded by her lover— & the spirit of Evil in person— They left out all that is most objectionable in the original play & in its present appearance is respectable— even moral—

Blair did revel in hunting a turkey's nest— seeing the two newborn Lambs— & his new dog— & now I shall & enjoy by his side some sleep The theatre is just over the old ground— & in spite Senator Sherman sitting by me & being very agreeable my thoughts did wander back to days now more than 21 yrs old   Ever your devoted   Lizzie

I recd yrs enclosing Capt Case's & $20

1. Dr. Josiah Harding of Sligo was married to Mary Valdenar in 1846 and lived in Carroll Cottage.

2. Freeman Clark, a founder of the Republican party, was a New York member of Congress from 1863 to 1865.

3. Actor William Evans Burton (1804–60) opened a small theater in New York in 1848, and it became one of the most popular and well-known theaters in the city.

Washington   March 31, [1864]

Dear Phil   Mother sits by me and says tell "Phil if he can conveniently manage it I wish he would send me some more oysters—" You said something about sending her some by Express— She wants them so much that she will gladly pay for them. Those we buy here are so poor after those we have been feasting on that they are not at all relished

Frank's neuralgia returns every evening & seems to have the intermittent form— but I thought he was quite improved over his condition of yesterday until his aids arrived from St Louis without Apo & announcing her purpose not to come— He takes it bitterly— The case of forgery about the whiskey case be completely proved & by Mr Howard[1] the Collector of the Port— & three other witnesses   I have asked Frank to ask Mr Howard to dine here as he is always civil to you—

Father is still up in the Country electioneering & as we have not heard from him I hope he will report himself home soon & in a good condition   I have been anxious about his being exposed to change of rooms & etc during this season—

I heard that Genl Grant has gone with Mrs. Lincoln & Mrs. Grant to your part of the world   Col Comstock[2] was here but I heard nothing of this movement until the hour after their departure or I would have sent yr stocks by him as I know him so well— I hope you will see the Genl. I would telegraph you but everything that goes is put thro' the War Dept. & is inspected by the Secy— I went out and paid some Senatorial Calls today— The weather is uncomfortable as its uncertain character keeps one a little anxious about their best hat.

Nelly will feel the death of old Mr. Ricd Smith[3] whose extreme feebleness has long since made his friends daily apprehensive of his death. He was a true, kind, friend to Mrs Hill when she needed assistance when her children were small— & she had to struggle along with a bankrupt estate   He was her lover in her youth— then her friend when she was a heart broken widow— Old Dr. Hunt used discant on this to me— for he too had "wooed her in vain" so he told me   & still thought her the finest woman in the world" Now they have all gone

Blair since yr visit has constantly called me Lizzie & Miss Lizzie & imitated you in divers ways   I told him if he did not want me for a *Mama* he ought call

me Mrs Lee— He was very cut— & has never since called me Lizzie— He is at
his french again & Madame says he is very smart— Your affectionate Lizzie

   1. Richard J. Howard was collector of customs at St. Louis.
   2. Cyrus B. Comstock of the Corps of Engineers was on Grant's staff.
   3. Richard Smith of Washington was the father-in-law of Ellen Lee's oldest brother,
William B. Hill.

                                      Washington   April 2, 1864
My dear Phil   This has been a continuous rainy day. the redeaming features
of which are that father is sitting by his own fireside with wide spread hands
enjoying it without any cold or sickness— Frank enjoys of all things to poke
fun at him about his campaign— upon which the destinies of his progeny all
depends.

   Blair is by me & insists on my writing a letter for him   he rejoices to have
Grandpa back— today at dinner Mr. Dick Howard asked him about you— he
told where you were & somebody intimated that he had seen so little of you
that he would not know you if he met you on the street— he was indignant &
said he knew you as well as he did Grandpa— who had home all the time. &
that if you did stay away it was not your fault but that Grandpa was home all
the time   it was an earnest display of affectionate zeal   Mr Howard says he is
like Franks children and that Betty is altogether like ———— [1]

   I rejoice to see Genl Smith is to go down your way.[2] I think there is great
wisdom in some of Genl Grants movements & removals and of none do I approve more than some *my own* friends— who tho good fellows had been for
courage & good conduct put up beyond their intellectual depth—

   I received your No 9, sending me Mr. Kiems papers which I file to themselves— I believe you have put in your box the rest you have received. I cannot
imagine what has detained my letter & the seal is all perfect a rough anchor
which I sometimes seal with when my squirrel is not near me   for a few day I
have been out of wax—

   Blair has some little stomach derangement but that I have expected for
when he is confined to the house as of late by weather & a week by chicken
pox— the weather has been so bad that I have not exposed him much to it
& then with some anxiety for the Cutaneous diseases always leave children so
tender about the skin that they are liable to cold— He looks bright & sawed
wood & said tonight that he felt as if he had worked too hard today— Grandpa
is enchanted to get back home & to "his boy" whose charm seem to be always
on the increase with him— Every morning his first talk when he creeps in my
bed is "Now Mama when do you think Papa will send for us—" but I must not
write any more about him or you will think him sick for if the least thing is

the matter with him I confess he is but little out of my thoughts but tonight he sleeps well & has no fever— & will be all right in morning—

Frank is the worst sufferer I almost ever saw— I am anxious about him & more so because he takes no right care of himself Ever your own Lizzie

1. Name not given
2. Grant gave Gen. William F. Smith the command of Eighteenth Corps of Benjamin Butler's Army of the James.

Washington   April 6, 1864

Dear Phil   Yours enclosing me $100 was received this morning I sent Kate fifty & with my part will buy me a summer silk gown which I want very much but could not afford it under present circumstances until this unexpected addition to my means came for which I thank you— I went to pay gas bill & other business delay by the storm if delayed longer they will not discount for prompt payt at Gas Office

Father returned home to dinner sick & worn out & went to his bed after drinking his tea he says he is more fatigued than sick— I hope so but he looked badly very— Late this evening Mr Randall[1] came next door to report that the chief man of the acqueduct works had sent him a courier to let him know that he took Rockville the laborers who were qualified to vote by a residence in the state of a year— when the secesh there objected & that involved a contest in which Secesh got whipped & then the Judge being Secesh closed the polls this cutts off the precinct, where our side feared defeat thinking as Judges & the chief people thereabouts were all Secesh— they would fix things to suit themselves— it has been their plan not vote at all— when they are outvoted— so as to make the aggregate vote of the state small— In Baltre for instance t'was known here they would not vote— but in our precinct they came out in force— so as to carry the County by the Rockville vote. that closed by their own act— makes Father's election a certain thing

Our neighborhood turned out en masse for Father Old Bell & other men there who have invariably voted with the Secesh— voted for him today— Thompson[2] Hardin & that set all but Batchelor & Taylor—[3] are the only persons who went against him that we know of— There was a full vote— & just as peaceable as before the war— & no soldiers at the polls at all—[4]

Blair & Becky took my note to Kate who sent me one back by him acknowledging the receipt of the money. She bade Blair tell me that he found her sewing & that he paid her "a nice long visit & she wanted him to come soon again" The little fellow you see fulfilled his errand well Becky says her room was warm & in order— & that she looked better Franks spirits seem to have helped his head. he is much better today His election case coming up hard Ever yr affecate Lizzie

1. First Assistant Postmaster General Alexander W. Randall, former governor of Wisconsin (1858–61).
2. Probably William Thompson, chief judge of the Orphans' Court; in Montgomery County he had a farm near Sligo.
3. William A. Batchelor lived north and west of the Blairs. His neighbor was Dr. W. Taylor, across the road to Mitchell's Cross Roads.
4. In January 1864, the Maryland legislature called for an election on April 6 to decide upon the question of a constitutional convention. At the same time, delegates were to be elected and FPB was a candidate. Although the question was defeated in Montgomery County, it carried statewide. On April 9, EBL reported: "Father bears his defeat with great philosophy. It has saved him a vast deal of trouble as the Maryland slaveholders would have regarded him as a permanent agent to get their pay for their slaves— Now he will be saved this trouble & the state will soon be a free one."

Washington   April 10, [1864]

Dear Phil   We have had a sad loss in the death of our friend Mr. Rives[1] the best friend my father ever had— & I believe anybody ever had— He died last night about three olk— About two weeks or more since brother met him at the Capitol & he seemed so much exhausted he urged him to go back to his room— & after some hesitation he consented & came with Brother in his carriage back to his office— he went home & has never been out since & seemed gradually to sink without any apparent disease or suffering— & as I told you yesterday was low spirited— Father was to have gone out to see him but the storm prevented yesterday. His illness increased & an great difficulty of breathing set in. & he died with a congestion of the lungs—

When I saw him some weeks since I told him he looked strong enough to fight rheumatism 20 yrs in his extremities— You have so long shared my feelings for this noble man— that I know how truly you will mourn with me now— I have heard he was annoyed about his business affairs in the Congressional Globe— but he has left a large fortune & had intended to be his own Executor & I think the Congressional Globe business has been done in Frank Rive's name for some months past— how far he carried out all this I dont know exactly but I know he had taken up and was carrying out the plan adopted by Father towards his boys— only he used to hint to me at "our King Lear" as a joke only— & say he never intended to let me be Cordelia as he meant always to play that part himself—

He intimated more than once that your business habits added to other good qualities were the greatest thing for "you all—" I cannot tell you how often he has described his effort to dissuade me from marrying you— told the story & then add— "but she was right—" "she knew better than we did" & etc I shall go out to see the family tomorrow.

My head & heart are full of this great loss— to us all— & Ill not oppress you any more with it   Your affecate   Lizzie

1. John Rives died April 10, 1864. On February 13 EBL had reported: "Today Father and I went out to see Mr Rives who is very ill with inflammatory rhumatism— he saw us both in his room- & it is a sad sight— such a huge man so prostrate & just as helpless as an infant— he can move his hands only He tried to joke & his lame efforts were just as sad as his utter helplessness, he was however unfeighnedly glad to see us—."

Washington   April 12 [1864]

Dear Phil   I could not induce John to go see Kate— He says he has written to you that he does not approve of her present mode of life & will not contribute one cent to continue it— for he regards it as neither humane nor respectable—" If her Father had outraged her, he had not   he had offered her a home & she replied she would not share it, or that of any of her relatives   This she has said to me— & added "relations make themselves disagreea[ble] by giving unasked advice—" I gave John Dr. Millers letter & he said he would write to you fully about it.

You may not feel it right in me to suggest anything on this subject but I have none but kind feelings for her & with that consciousness will say this one word of counsel—[1] You or John now that Mr Harrison has proved so delinquent in his duties, ought to take time investigate about these night walks & etc & then make right arrangements for her— there are places of less restraint & horror than Asylums— but I dont pretend to say what ought to be done— I am unfit to judge that, as I am to take charge of her— which I do not seek to do because *it is not my duty*— if it was, I would try to do it— if it cost my life— Now if you cannot leave your post and attend to this in person, let John have the *whole responsibility*— but while this responsibility has been cast first on John by her Father (with whom it was a duty)— then on you by John— you absorbed in public duties— are only oppressed & greived without the opportunity to act & investigate these matters personally which is the *only right way to do it*

I did not act carelessly in giving Kate $50— if you look at the bottom of her letter you see that you say $50 & mention that you have written to her so altho' you say $40 in other parts of yr letter— this seemed yr lastest wish & the one you had written her—

John spent last night here & sat up after one olk talking with Frank— seemed happy, & very full talk & clever talk too— & was vastly enjoyed by all of us— He promised Father and Mother to send Annie up next week to stay & get rid of her chills in the pine woods of Silver Spring where we are to go about the 1st of May

The Torpedo shocked me[2]   I hope your orders will be better enforced after this— You will be gratified to see the honor done Mr. Rives by Congress. it was unexpected by us   Frank thought it could not be done— as his long sickness had prevented his making the acquaintance of the New Members of Congress

Blair was very intimate with Uncle John tho he will not say he looks like you He was vastly pleased with your letter today— & has scribbled some for you but I misplaced them   Ever your affecate Lizzie

1. EBL offered her counsel despite her vow made only weeks earlier not to give advice to anyone: "Nonintervention is a good rule you gave me once in Phila & even some severe lesson since has not quite cured me—" (April 4, 1864).

2. On April 9, the rebel torpedo boat *Squib* made its way through the crowded waters at Newport News, Virginia, and hit SPL's flagship *Minnesota*. Damage was not serious.

Washington   April 13, 1864

Dear Phil   We left here at ten ol'k— & got back at five from Mr. Rives' funeral   I need hardly add that I had to go to bed with headache from which I roused myself to received Apo after nine olk— I have not seen a funeral like this since we buried Genl Jesup— the difference in distance alone preventing this from being twice the magnitude of the Genl's—[1] When we neared the City boundaries we were joined by what appeared to me to be a thousand men on foot— Those at the house were about two thirds of the laboring class— but many plain but well dressed women seem deeply grieved & some men were more moved than ever I saw in a throng before— the Service was well ordered beautifully read & Father remarked he had never attended a scene where there was such perfect order. it seemed a sympathetic host— his bier was laiden with flowers brought by the throng— though proud of this ovation I realized more than ever how terribly he will be missed

Mrs. Elliot[2] asked him if he felt ready to die— he said when first taken ill "I was haunted with sorrow about my young children But I have since learned to put my whole trust for them as well as myself in Jesus my Redeemer— He died as calmly & consciously almost to the last sands of life— At first Father bore this blow badly— but has rallied is cheerful tonight. I think it hurts me more than the rest— we were always good friends— & after my father he liked me best of our family— Said I was like father in everything but intellect of which luckily I had not as much as he luckily as I was a woman This has been lately repeated to me He has left a will full of minute details about his property & children— has given his home to his daughters— & as "women are always true to their own blood" I suppose he wished his boys to spend their holidays in their old home & precincts & out of the City

Apo has brought Pres— You may be sure I watch Blair's *new* front teeth Pres is a very cross fighting boy & Blair tho good tempered once in a fight sticks to it— Good night Your No 3 has just been given me by Betty   she had it in her pocket Got it when I was away— Your affecate   Lizzie

1. Rives's funeral was held at his home near Bladensburg.
2. Probably the mother of John M. Elliot, former clerk at the *Globe* office.

Washington   April 15, [1864]
Dear Phil   It is very probable that I shall see you ere this reaches you as
Mr. Wise wrote me a note saying that the Baltimore was going down to Hampton Roads at 1 olk tomorrow & if it does not storm I shall go to you as I want
to see & talk to you— even for a few hours— I have been sick & think the trip
will do me good— as I think there is much of nervousness in my ailments—
You see I am ingenious for excuses to do what is agreeable to me— and nothing will prevent but a storm that I will not risk my child in, for a pleasure to
myself   I dont think these short trips give you any satisfaction still to me they
more than repay me for the trouble many times over—

Blair is wild to go but wants me to bring Preston but I cannot take the
responsibility of such irrepressible genius— he is a great delight to Blair & I
think it would suit him to wait for Pres' departure so as to spread his joys— I
shall give a letter to you to Mr. Sheldon Stephens[1] a Canadian gentleman—
introduced by Sarah Moses as her near neighbor and friend— I cannot ask to
go down on the Baltre as dont want to be encumbered with anybody. So shall
only take Betty— Blair & Becky   a party which will take care of itself in a
social way at least—

I have had Miss Hamlin[2] to dine with us today & in a quiet have done
a great of that kind business of late Good night I have many small affairs to
attend to as I have suddenly made up my mind about this matter as I got the
note when going to dinner— & have just bid our guests good night— Yours
ever affecly Lizzie
I had a letter from Fanny today   all well

1. Sheldon Stephens was described by Sarah as "the son of one of our most influen-
tial and wealthy citizens."
2. Sarah Jane Hamlin, born 1842, was the daughter of Hannibal Hamlin.

16

"Grant has moved & moved Lee—"

May 21, 1864

UNDER THE LEADERSHIP OF ULYSSES GRANT, the Army of the Potomac crossed the Rapidan River to begin the final and decisive campaign of the war. At the same time Benjamin Butler established a second line of attack by moving his Army of the James upriver. With naval support under the command of Phillips Lee, Butler was to move against Richmond from the south. In the West, Sherman began his advance on Atlanta. Frank Blair, cleared in the liquor-fraud scandal but denied his seat in Congress, left Washington to rejoin Sherman's army. With both husband and brother directly involved in the two major Union campaigns, Elizabeth followed the events of war with even greater anxiety.

Washington   April 20, 1864

My dear Phil   Father says your views about a certain Secy—[1] are unjust— wholly & it does you harm to write & persevere in this opinion as no good can come out of it— & taking your view tis well know & readily recognized (& counteracted as far as possible)— when even brought to light in any way— I am sorry to admit only to you— that in writing this point you are imprudent— it reminds me of a time when you would persevere in your views about the female prototype. Your views are right— but fixed as we were then— & as we are now tis best ignore an evil when by recognizing it we *hurt* ourselves— Let it alone & try with all our might to do justly & earnestly our duties in life & I believe God in his mercy & goodness will protect us from evil doers & wishers— & tis by our own acts only that they can really hurt us—

This thing makes Father absolutely nervous & I believe has infected me— He says he will manage your affair with all his head & heart if you confide it to him— that he will do his best about it this session— and as you are not here to attend to it yourself I think he is the best person for us to look to as pilot through this affair— but my faith is a natural one & therefore this advice must be seen through this vista

I went to see some Congressional acquaintance— & felt like doing my little, with all my might so indulged my inclination & paid over a dozen calls on foot— got home to dinner & your letter without *No*— [number] and yours to Father out of which I have just erased *thoroughly* every allusion to our friend with middy recollections[2] please dont put any more on paper— Father says your letter will be useful to him— I had as very long talk about matters this morning & he strikes me as being quite as well posted as you are— & I listened to both with my every faculty

Apo goes Friday to see Andrew will be joined in New York Monday by Frank on Monday when they take up their line for the West & south—

Our mishap in the Southwest[3] is another Ball's Bluff at the hands of Genl Stone— who married a secesh wife[4] six months after losing his first one the mother of his children

John was here Monday— asked for me— & then only enquired how the rest were— & did not come in We are all well— No news to tell— Ever yr affectionate Lizzie

1. Secretary of the Navy Gideon Welles.
2. Reference to Assistant Naval Secretary Gustavus Fox.
3. Charles Pomeroy Stone served in the Red River Campaign under Nathaniel Banks. Their expedition into Louisiana began on March 12, and by the first of April had encountered a host of problems, from falling water to strong rebel resistance. After the Battle of Sabine Cross Roads on April 8, the Federals began their retreat. Stone had been blamed for the Ball's Bluff debacle in 1861, and had been imprisoned for 189 days before his assignment to Banks in the Department of the Gulf. After the Red River Campaign, Stanton took away his volunteer commission and reduced him to colonel in the regular army. Stone eventually resigned on September 13, 1864.
4. In 1863 Annie Granier, daughter of Dr. John Harce Stone, married Gen. C. P. Stone.

Washington   April 23, [1864]
My Dear Phil   I had to see about house matters this morning as Becky is still sick Got thro' in time to get to the House just as Frank began his speech it was a complete triumph— he made his opponents pop up & down in their seats— & they were voted down in all the points of order— & when Mr Colfax found he would be voted down he withdrew his point of order— & then Frank went on & made I think an excellent speech—[1] but he is now writing it out as hard as he can & you will judge it for yourself—

Tonight when I was putting Blair to Bed a great many carriages drove up to the door— & a troop of M.C.'s came in & made a speech & presented Frank with a superb sword sash— & spurs— on it is engraved— from his friends as a token for his gallant support of "*the Union*—" They were mostly Democrats— & western men— One of his M.C. friends gave him a beautiful seal ring— &

Frank asked him if there was an *Copper* in it? he could not stand copper— & there was a great deal of joking about it— The Committee on elections have agreed upon a Report— but his friends say after this speech it will be voted down in the House— Chase will leave no stone unturned to get that end— Father does not agree to this as he was so handsomely maintained by the vote of the House today.

Betty says she likes a serious answer to a serious question— & this is a serious question "Is Genl A Ames at Hampton Roads? or expected there or anywhere in your Ken?— She saw some troops in transports the evening she was at Old Point & thinks that this individual may be northward bound— He was at Jacksonville Florida It is rumored here that after a few days all correspondance with the Armies will be stopped for thirty days & it is also said that Lee is trying to flank Grant & etc

I forgot to say that when I went over to pay Kates Bill she would not see me   I knocked at her door— myself & called her— She is well & been out often but I am rejoiced to say *not* at night— not *even* after *dinner*— I feel with John & for him   I would never put her in an Asylum if she was my child but I would under surveillance night & day *Control* is essential to her character— to her health mental & physical of this I am now convinced. tho' most reluctant to think so— & am still of the opinion that it is a perverted temper warping a feeble mind— rather than a diseased mind   a good mother or kind steady husband could have made a happy & useful person of her

Blair is well— Mother depressed as Frank leave us tomorrow Ever yr devoted Lizzie

1. The committee investigating the charges of liquor speculation by Frank had reported that Michael Powers, a Treasury Department agent, had altered the original order. In his speech, Frank attacked Secretary of the Treasury Chase, accusing him of misusing his authority to war on the administration. On April 5, EBL had explained: "Tonight the Radicals called up the man accused of forging the increased amount of liquors & they looked very triumphant as they marched him in the Committee Room. When they began to cross examine him, he stopped & just confessed to the whole thing   Frank says he never witnessed a scene of so much painful humiliation— The man said he did it *first* to make money as he could give the officers the portion they ordered & then sell the rest for enormous profits & no one be the wiser & he only the richer for it— . . . . he had no intention of injuring Gen. Blair when he *first did it*   Frank now intends to prove that [Joseph] McClurg— [Missouri Radical congressman] the Union paper all knew that this was a forgery when they promulgated the slander— he says he has means to prove this—."

Washington   April 24, 1864

Dear Phil   Frank started this evening for home & then Sherman's Hdquarters— Mr. L[incoln] sent for him late last night & in the small hours Frank stopped at my door— he wrote out his speech last night— to get me to call him when Blair roused me— as he had an early appointment it is evident the talk was not a disagreeable one— It seems Sumner lately complained in that quarter of "*the Blairs*—" when the P. told him that "*his set*" began the war on the B's that when Frank was put under arrest by Frémont "S.'s whole set" warred on Frank long 'ere the merits of the case were made known & when "*they*" knew just as well as it is now known that "Frank was the most honest & best man of the two—" "Now Mr. S.[,] the B's are brave people & never whine— but are ready always to fight their enemies and very generally whip them—" The rejoined was not repeated I thought this conversation would at least amuse you—

As Dawes[1] is anxious to be Govr of Mass. & as he may want "to molify this "set" some anxiety is felt— about the election case altho it has been voted in Committee in F[rank]'s favor one man only voting against him— Our neighbor said F. put him in mind in his treatment of C[hase] & Co of a man who killed a dog. & then went out after breakfast & kicked & cut up the animal— this was repeated after every meal for a whole day— & when asked why he did it— said he was determined the vile thing should feel punishment after death— You must not repeat this— if you *do* decyphur it—

Mr. Pyne gave us a touch of politics this morning— text 18 verse 1st chap of Saint James—[2] I do not think it would console a secesh to have heard it— He alluded to political cauldrons in which we live— & said it was of import that even the humblest should eschew association with those harpies preying upon the vitals of the Country in its struggle for life— one characteristic among others by which these Harpies might be known was forgers who not only forged for money— but to rob honest men of their good names— & etc &etc he begged us to avoid all such association— not even to sit at board with such—

I went to the Asylum to attend the Sunday school— which I think I have helped by going there this winter— I started it & feel anxious it should be of use to the children— Mrs. Davenport came from New York to nurse her brother & has taken the small pox from him & was dangerously ill all of yesterday— but is better today I got a letter from Nelly today which I'll enclose I will write and beg her to come up with John & Annie I feel worried about this dear child— Your affecate Lizzie

1. Henry Laurens Dawes, Massachusetts Republican congressman (1857–75).
2. "Of his own will begat he us with the word of truth, that we should be a kind of first fruits of his creatures."

Washington   April 26, 1864
Dear Phil John & Nelly have not come— & there is a telegram which I imagine is from you awaiting John— Today I was tempted to send it to him— Yet I felt so certain that they would come that I went out early & returned

home so as be here whilst Mother took her walk to be sure to have some body to welcome them on arriving—

Genl Sherman telegraphed Frank that he wished him to join his Corp immediately at Cairo— or he would be too late for this campaign & "*you are needed*—" I took it to Brothers to forward immediately to him in New York—

I went to Genl Tottens[1] funeral as he was a man for whose life I had the greatest admiration He outlived his wife two years, & when the Doctor was nursing & trying to prolong his life he remarked "Oh Dr. let nature takes its course   tis all I ask— for you know I am going to more than I shall leave behind me." I never saw an old couple except my Parents who were so dependant upon each other & whose lives as far as I can judge were so lovely to each other—

Mr. Smith has been here this evening He gives me excellent accounts of Neddys industry & intelligence— He tells us that Mr Rives has willed his place to all of his children— as a *home* & if they sell it the proceeds go to the General Government— None of the children want to live there except Frank he alone is attached to it— & I am glad to say— since called upon to act for himself has shown a great deal of character & intelligence— & so far is equal to the part his Father has desired him to fill in life & just now this reporting business is an awkward position & it filled Mr. Rives with great anxiety & trouble during this last winter—

I have been fixing my affairs in condition gradually to move to the Country— beginning with my clothing & Blairs— We will not go until next week— I went to see Mrs. Gooch she & I are becoming great friends   she has been quite sick & it gives an opportunity for neighborly attentions— Mrs Welles was here today but I was out   she told Mother that troops were passing thro here last night—[2] & I have seen several companies going by today for passes in the office above where they are given for the front Blair is well & so is his Mama   Your affecate   Lizzie

1. Brig. Gen. Joseph G. Totten, chief engineer of the U.S. army, died on April 22.
2. On April 25, EBL wrote: "I watched Genl Burnsides Corps for an hour today— counted five full negro Regts— two Batteries of horse Artillery— & two full Regts of real soldiers— Others stood & watched them from one to four— some 12,000 passed others— 45,000— eight thousand I can speak for as I sat counted the companies as they filed by me— the Negroes were clad in new clothing marched well— every Regt had a good band of music— & they looked as well as Negroes can look— but Oh how different our Saxons looked in old war worn clothing— with their torn flags— but such noble looking men—."

Washington   April 27, 1864

My dear Phil   John came about 10 olk. & went to see Dr Miller— I went to church   it was my 21st wedding day & as it is ever a day of thanksgiving— I always go to church if possible— When I returned I found John here waiting for me— said he wanted me to go with him to Georgetown— I did not want to go— but he looked depressed & I agreed to go provided I was not to share the responsibility of his actions   he said he had made up his mind what to do   he wanted me only for his own sake— I went— Kate refused to see us both— but he would see her— I did not— she agreed to go with him to Balt most cheerfully— He said he must go to Balt to make arrangements & inquiries— I got him to stop & eat lunch— & when nearly done eating he said Lizzie I wish you could go with me— but it is too late & too fatiguing—" I said no— so ate a little, told Mother to look after my boy & was on my way with John in ten minutes— We went & he saw the Doctor— Mt Hope [1] & etc & Got me to give the room a close inspection— & he has made all his arrangements— I have done nothing but talk to him— divert his mind & tried all I could to cheer & comfort him when performing a painful duty

He goes there tomorrow with Kate— I shall go out home & get some flowers for Nelly. I would go with John tomorrow if he desired it— Ive not suggested, only evinced an honest willingness to do anything he wished— Mt Hope is a beautiful suburban place like *Uncle Charles'* near here— only ten times as handsome— I saw nothing within or without— that was painful, nothing gloomy but the nurses in their horrid dress— & but for that you would take it for an elegant residence of a gentleman— the room is about as large as Bettys at Silver Spring— perfectly comfortable   John will write you what medical men say— I did not talk with them or him—

I need not tell you that you have been in my thoughts every hour of this day & I have blessed & thanked God for giving me a true loving & more than ever dear husband for to love truly is even a greater blessing than to be much loved— Thank God I rejoice in both good gifts   Yr own   Lizzie
I find Govr Dennison here to stay— accepting my invitation given weeks ago—[2] Of course Ive a purpose in my invitation

1. Mount Hope Hospital in Baltimore was located on Bolton near Northern Avenue.

2. On April 22, EBL commented: "Govr Dennison is here tonight just from the Front and a visit to his son— speaks in great spirits about our Army the condition of which has altered amazingly for the better of late— since his visit in Jany—."

Washington   April 28, 1864
My dear Phil   Your Nos 23 & 24 came today   I had a letter yesterday No 22. It was my wedding day & Blair got the mail & brought your letter to me which he always thinks is partly his sometimes when he is omitted I take the liberty being a half of you to improvise a kiss or some token of remembrance

John has returned from his errand to Baltimore with Kate— She said she liked the place it was pretty & had every comfort   she objected however to his deception in taking her there— he never said where he was going to take her only saying as she preferred Baltimore— he had no other place to put her but that no other person would receive her (which was true)— & she had to stay there or go to her father   this she said she never would do— he was a "*bad man*—" & she never would live under his shelter again— that none of her relatives had treated her properly but "Aunt Ellen" & she had let her alone & never interfered & etc as you John & I had— The truth is Ellen has studiously avoided her— & last fall only sanctioned her husbands invitation— but as Kate said to me "was polite only & honest—" John when first returned tonight he was depressed— but I had some good hot coffee & a nice supper for him & a cheerful fire & surroundings & he is now talking as brightly as I ever heard him.

Miller went along in the Cars— & was of no use but to give Kate another grievance From what John tells me Kate had *no shock* at the place which she was taken to— said "I like this place" & think I shall be very happy here—" but then vent her anger on John & that was her only excitement— no grief— no mortification— no horror— would have come very willingly if he had not been false— & etc— for which she refused to write to him— he argued with her & tried to palliate & excuse his course— pointing to her present anger as the scene which had to take place & best to be there— The Doctors Miller & Stokes[1] who heard the whole conversation told John it was of itself quite enough to convince them she was exactly where it was best for her to be, & it was evidently essential to her health in every way— She looks wretchedly. has lived many weeks on ice cream & cakes & of late has been 48 hours at a time without any food at all— & that was her condition today The Sisters promised to write to me regularly about her condition— & I will try to correspond with her— if not with them— as it may at least make them attentive to her, to know she has watchful friends & I will offer to go see her whenever she wishes it or they advise it.

I went out home today & packed up some Roses I had in the pit for Nelly— got some other plants & this evening have brought a few others— which I will send to Annie from you— I wrote to Nelly today as I thought she might feel sorrowful about her husband when doing such a bitterly sad duty & said all I could to cheer her—

Tonight there are some of Franks speeches to direct & that Ill attend tomorrow. The papers all refuse to publish it & I told father that he might double his subscription $25 to $50 & I would pay the other half You may see by the papers that Chase & friends are going to roar about Franks appointment as Majr Genl— there is great deal of talk of Mr C. resigning   Mr Sherman said today— he would never speak to him again until he did but Govr Dennison who is still here says he will not resign— the *parting* speech has made a *big fuss* & it has a parthian arrow to those it was meant to hit— if one may judge from appearances— Goodnight I am weary & stupid— but always Yours fondly Lizzie

1. Dr. William H. Stokes was the attending physician at Mount Hope Hospital in Baltimore.

Silver Spring   May 2, 1864
My dear Phil   Your No 26 came today   talked over Matters with Father about you & Frank   he says he feels perfectly easy about the result— & that these Ultras are more partizan plunderers & he does not fear them— many honest men heretofore acting with them are having the scales to drop from their eyes

I hear Genl Schenk[1] is denouncing the President & making privately a point of unity with the President who mentioned the arrangement with Schenk & was from all I heard glad to have Genls S— & Garfield[2] in the same box— they dont venture to contradict the P except in private— but they are devoted Chase men— whose Congressional party held caucus on friday to consult about resigning— & you see that they could not make their minds up to that & Saturdays proceedings is the result— They cannot take Franks commission from him. they may pass as many resolutions & *acts* as they please but they are not laws without the Presidents signature— Mr. Dawes is trying to bring up his forces to make him Governor of Mass— but they have already voted in Committee on Frank's case— So he has to make up on the Genl— There is great fermentation among these politicians— & those who are honest dont want the *stain* of these times to hang over their names are really in much trouble— It is a great pride in my heart that all of mine will pass through with clean hands & untarnished names & yet never flinched in support of their Country—

Blair has been joyously happy all this day & is vastly pleased at the non-arrival of his bed so he can sleep with me

Father asked me tonight not to alter Franks office but leave it as it is as he wanted it to write & meet people in— I hope to meet John & Nelly tomorrow & will take asparagus & etc in for a good dinner   I have all my affairs fixed out here & shall be busy in my garden after this. Have 3 Turkies setting on 38 eggs— & expect to start a hen house soon— Olivia has given up that vocation   Ever yr own   Lizzie

1. Gen. Robert Schenck of Ohio had been elected to Congress and was chairman of the committee on military affairs. His agreement with the president was the same as Frank's: he could resume his military commission whenever he wished.

2. Future president James A. Garfield had seen active duty in the army as a participant in the battle at Shiloh. Poor health forced him to give up his military position. He then served as Republican congressman from Ohio (1863–80).

Silver Spring   May 3, [1864]
My dear Phil   I received your letter *No 27 & 28* today— the first containing
the letter for John & Mr. Keims vouchers & etc   I wrote to you the amt of
Tuckers Bill— $80. for two coats & $6 for some silver stars— are the items—
I will send your summer Panama hat my next chance & would have sent it by
Mr. Wise last week but I was out when his note came & until after he had
gone according to his note— John came to the City today & got your letter in
a half hour after I did— later on my return from the asylum I got your No 28.
but I could not go see Upshurs it was too late— John did not come to dinner
as he promised— told Betty he could not be as late as half past three— Had I
known this I would have ordered the dinner earlier

We were surprised to find that Mr. Lincoln had published his letter to
Brother calling Frank from the Army & *intimating* his wish to have him
Speaker—[1] He wanted Chase exposed as you see the St Louis speech was in
his mind & *yet* in good temper— & he takes this way of throwing off Chase's
corruptness— without *splitting* party— tis a personal affair— & yet he so endorses F. in all things *save* in a matter of *temper*— He could have avoided all
this *muss*, as I told you Frank gave him a graceful opportunity— but he did
not think it well "to back down—" best "*meet it*—" Now they war on him over
F's shoulder— but of course this makes the breach personal— & on the point
of *corruption* & *not negroes*— I have not the least idea that Mr. C. will resign
his greenback powers & thereby his hopes of a nomination—[2] for which he is
striving in an an unseemly way

John did not bring up Annie as I hoped but Nelly says she shall come   I expect she is fixing her spring clothing— Father talks of going to the city in the
morning— but I scarce think him well enough— he & Mother are both ailing
since their return home I think from overfatigue— Father is worried on the
finance question— Harvey is by far the worst of all his managers— I never saw
such bare faced plundering— I have paid the house servants for gas & coal &
a great deal of marketing— with their present income which is really plenty—
for them but not the farm— at least— that is Fathers conclusion tonight—
he has rented the Wilderness— & if this place was worked on shares outside
the gardens it would pay well— yr affecate   Lizzie

1. Lincoln wrote to Montgomery Blair on November 2, 1863: "My wish . . . is that
he will come here, put his military commission in my hands, take his seat, go into
caucus with our friends, abide the nominations, help elect the nominees, and thus aid
to organize a House of Representatives which will really support the government in
the war. If the result shall be the election of himself as Speaker, let him serve in that
position; if not, let him retake his commission and return to the army."
2. As a leading Radical, Secretary of the Treasury Salmon P. Chase aspired to challenge Lincoln for the Republican presidential nomination. Lincoln had refused his offer

to resign from the cabinet in March. In addition to Chase's opposition to Lincoln's policies, the Blairs worked to force Chase to resign for the manner in which he handled patronage and trade permits.

Silver Spring   May 7, 1864

My dear Phil   Your letter of the fourth & the sixth came together altho I watched the mails yesterday & had two couriers handing me letters today. I am comforted to know "All is well so far—" & keep these words on my tongues end to quiet the anxieties of my heart which for some weeks past have been intense— Indeed what I saw when I was last with you convinced me that marching & moving orders were soon to be given—

I am glad to be here— I get the news promptly & can keep quiet— & or work out doors following Blair about all day— to forget my aching anxiety & hush my fears in his joys & by looking at his healthy happy face— Consequently this day has been chiefly spent with him driving the Donkey who has pulled out of the lawn all the leaves & trash formerly done by Comanche— Grandma is delighted with both Boy & Donkey—

Frank has met the fate he expected in the Committee of Elections which has reversed its decision since he went away—[1] A member of it told him the vote before he spoke— I suppose they will say he was all the time a Maj General & therefore inelligible— for an election Since the other two Generals in Congress have preferred Congress to the field (Schenck & Garfield we have concluded that this would be the result— they are bitter in propotion— We are to have a fight with the money power— but since— Biddle—[2] with all his talent failed I do not grow faint hearted with the prospect. I think it has already passed its zenith—

We are suddenly in Summer   Mother is oppressed by it—Father & I physically enjoy it— but could easily gladly forgo our enjoyment to have cooler days for our marching armies—

I got a letter from Apo she says Frank is at Huntsville by this time or on the road to that place Even *she* is pleased with Franks reception in St Louis— She says that Walter Trumbull has "an inveterate itch—" which he is too careless to take the trouble to cure— & is consequently avoided by everybody as it is the most contagious of ailments." This will exclude him from your ship as no Doctor would admit him with that disease— I will send her letter when I feel certain of mine going to you promptly— I shall close this in the morning as tis Henrys Sunday & I have but a poor prospect of sending it in the early mail

Sunday night May 8th Brother did not come here to dinner as he was expected consequently I had no chance to mail this letter today

Our whole thought has been hanging over the military movements of Our Armies & Fleet— in a breathless suspense— with scare rumors enough to make one take a long breath— The Dept had no dispatches from Grant[3]

Newspaper letter writers say there has been 3 days fighting on the scene of Chancellorsville battle field— We scarce know what to believe— so hope & pray I may say literally obeying St Paul— & do it not these days "without ceasing—" for I dream over my daylight thoughts when asleep—

Our weather is very dry & warm— thermometer at 72 in the shade this day a week since & the trees between the house & spring were as leafless as at Christmas. Today their shade was comfortable & their verdure beautiful

Our sabbath was without an event save a visit from Col Benton to learn the news from Brother who disappointed him & all of us My conclusion is— that he had no news— Col Benton was at a collation given by Speaker Colfax last night on the occasion of some presentation of silver— by his Indiana friends,   Mr. Wade boards at the same house— & went at nine olk to the Secy of War for News— & got none & became convinced that *they really* had received none & there was an indignation meeting over our Lt Genl for failing to report— I suppose he is busy— too much so to think of such people's curiosity or solicitude   Col Benton is under orders to move the Garrison of Boston Harbor is to take charge of Fort Stevens When Col Benton leaves it— & there are to be a thousand men where there are now four hundred. Woe betide our orchards & garden when they come—

Father has made up his mind to defend Frank in his election business as soon as he gets the Report over his own signature He goes in town very early in the morning—

Monday morning We are all well— Yr affectionate   Lizzie

1. The Radicals, angry at Frank's attacks on Chase, turned their wrath on him. The Committee on Elections decided that Samuel Knox and not Frank Blair had won the contested Missouri congressional election in 1862.

2. A reference to Nicholas Biddle, head of the Second Bank of the United States, and his fight with Andrew Jackson.

3. On May 4, the Army of the Potomac had crossed the Rapidan to begin Grant's campaign against Robert E. Lee. On May 5, the Battle of the Wilderness began. EBL reported on May 6: "There is no news from the Army— Grant is off & across the River— & that is all that is known here— & that he keeps up no communications with these parts— so I expect they are all off for Richmond— There is an intense anxiety felt here & nothing can exceed the exalting confidence of the Secesh *all sorts & shades*— they talk with an openness & confidence that amazes me & what surprised me most is their bold utterance everywhere."

Silver Spring   May 10, [1864]

My dear Phil   I received today your letters of the 7 & 8th and it is marvellous even to myself to know the difference that they make in my condition of mind & body. I have seen & heard & felt nothing of late but Fort Darling—[1] Add your agreeable confab with Genl Butler to the destruction of the Rebel Ram Albemarle—[2] & there is no telling how relieved & thankful I feel tonight—

I made a hunt for the Upshurs today & found they have not reported themselves to their friends here at all I saw Lucy Jesup[3] today who looks about fifty— Says Maj Sitgreaves has been summoned for the second time before the retiring board She reports his health perfect & his labors unremitting— & his applications for field duties frequent— I suspect the talk of Julia of loud secesh has hurt the quiet & best part of the Jesup family Her sister arrived last night after nearly two years absence & Julia started for New York in the early train of today to go there to take music lessons— lives in boarding to enjoy this high priviledge when she already sings almost too *artistic* for a lady— I went to see Mrs Marion *Dutton* today she is very a *portly dame*— but just now anxious about her husband who I suppose is in your region if you should hear he was well— just suggest the fact for my fat friends benefit— She comes here for a visit next week—

Brother repeated Genl. Grants Report or telegram to the President recieved today dated on Sunday (8th)— This may be in tonights papers & yet I'll repeat as you may not see them— He regrets to say he has failed to achieve much he intended doing— & was *prevented* by "*the immense train*" (15 days rations) he had to protect & the "*formidable*" "*entrenchments*" of the enemy— who are however forced to retreat & are whipped.[4] I underline the only words I remember brother using— & give you the purport of the dispatch as it impressed me Capt Smedburg is wounded— so is Col Sprigg Carroll[5] & many of Bettys friends— & there is an intense anxiety in all the faces I saw today. Genl Grant did not say where the enemy had gone— or what he intended doing— & I dont believe it is known yet which way Lee retreated— All surmise Richmond but *that* is doubted by some who seem wise in military lore—

We are all well. Blair still rejoices in his turkies Your devoted Lizzie

1. Fort Darling, or Drewry's Bluff, was eight miles below Richmond on the James River. Grant had ordered General Butler to move up the James toward Richmond, and Drewry's Bluff was the last major Confederate defensive position on the river. On May 5, SPL and his naval force started up the James.

2. The rebel ram *Albemarle* was a constant threat to the Union navy. On May 5, she had engaged Federals in Albemarle Sound and then retired up the Roanoke River. It was not until October 27 that she was finally destroyed.

3. Lucy Ann Jesup, sister of Mary Blair, married Lorenzo Sitgreaves in 1854.

4. On May 5, the Battle of the Wilderness began. On May 7, federal forces started toward Spotsylvania but could not move fast enough to flank Lee's Confederates, and the two armies established new lines.

5. Col. Samuel Sprigg Carroll was wounded on May 5 during the Wilderness battle and again on May 13 at Spotsylvania. His father was clerk of the Supreme Court and his sister was the wife of Gen. Charles Griffin.

Washington　Silver Spring　May 15, 1864
My dear Phil　Just before going to Church I wrote you a hurried line which
did not express exactly my meaning— I believe B. & A[1] are really attracted
to each other & I fear that I have already said more than I ought & may be if
I had said *nothing* both would now have been happier— I ought to have said
interfere instead of *control*— I concluded after you were here to act on your
suggestion & sit up no more. the result has been *just right* as Mother took the
part of sentinel & worked an immediate reform— & I mean to carry this system all through & you may be sure that it will all come right— I shall not stay
here under any circumstances & I know Mother will not be so Betty cannot be
here "constantly" for Father will not let her come without one of us— I hope
therefore you'll not detain the tender bulletin any longer than possible

It is a matter of doubt whether Lee has retreated to Lynchburg or Richmond— I expect the first as that the great Rebel Depot of provisions— that
& Danville beside— these Ring leaders will naturally take to the Mountains
as a refuge— it will take high ones to cover the infamy of this rebellion— or
one tenth of the misery it has inflicted on the innocent

I recieved a letter from Nelly this morning　she writes most lovingly about
you— & begs me to writen oftener as tis not only a relief to all but evidently
a comfort to John to hear from you. I shall write tonight to them & Fanny—
Nelly gives me the purport of Sister Helens letter. I do not agree with them
about Kate never have— Her physical health has been good & is so strong
that even her irregularities has not broken her constitution— I hope to see her
get fat where they will not be indulge them. A part of last winter she looked
almost beautiful & until she got a great deal of money to buy trash to eat kept
pretty well But I found her beyond any more relatives control last December—
My greatest fear for her has proved unfounded. Knowing the intense pride of
many of her race I feared the shock upon of Johns plans for her & this deterred
him as he agreed with me— but as he remarked— She suffered less than any of
us could imagine certainly far less than he did dear fellow for God never made
a nobler nature than his— Ever your affecate　Lizzie
The misspelling is carefully watched— She rarely writes without me or a Dictionary close by— & tis that lack of confidence which betrays her but many
people never learn that gift— never did a child have severe training on this
part— tis the same way in french— which she speaks fluently & with good
accent

1. Betty Blair and Adelbert Ames.

Silver Spring　May 17, [1864]
Dear Phil　I have just tucked Blair up in bed & whilst he sleeps will thank you
for yours of Saturday 14th at 10 am— I had seen by the papers that you had

gone up the River— but did not know you had left the Malvern.[1] the papers say the Rebel Ironclad gave battle on Sunday but was driven back— this is rumor & not official I look anxiously for tidings from you about it—

Grant has been reinforced twenty thousand troops have been sent from the fortifications of Washington alone— troops from the North have taken their places There are troops coming from Ohio— passing thro the City yesterday & the Governors are calling out the Militia to do their duty— From what I hear & have seen I think Grant must be fully as strong as when he started out on this campaign— & he has his rear *in hand*— Stanton sent Miegs down to Fredericksburg on Monday to have things there carried on with more promptness and order Nothing strikes me more favorably than the earnestness & energy with which *work* is done now a days as compared with the past— The fighting seems to have changed *style too*—

I have been busy out doors most of the day looking after Blair & my outdoor occupations— tis fine weather for putting out my flowers consequently we are very busy in that way— I have a great many fine plants from seed— & hope to have a pretty garden this year & plant it with more hope of enjoying it, than for several years past— & there is another hope too which looms up often & gives zest to my occupation— but my most ever present thought is prayer for your safety in these days— little else fills the thoughts & heart of Your devoted Lizzie

1. On May 14, SPL had moved his flag to the light draft *Agawam.*

Silver Spring   May 19, 1864
Dear Phil   Your's of 16th (Monday morning written in pencil)— & the letter of 16th were both recieved tonight Neddy came out this morning without anything for me— But Mr Barnes[1] who gets the afternoon mail brought these letters to me— I shall never believe anything about the Rams that you do not write— Every paper reported you had had an encounter with them on Sunday morning— They all say now that Butler has been repulsed within *his* fortifications & with "great loss—" some call it a severe defeat but that he still holds the Railroad from Petersburg— to Richmond & that Kautz[2] has returned to City Point with his command in good condition[3] These are important points so I take breath— & heart

Grant has been *largely* reinforced, and has now as good an army as ever with a large weeding out of bad officers & promotion of good ones— Our loss has been terrible— but the wounded tho large in numbers are not badly hurt— the ammunition of the enemy much to be thanked— buckshot & old fashioned ammunition— Every account speaks well of the tone & spirit of the Army it is cheerful & hopeful— Our Army reports are all true save Hancocks success was hurt by the retaking of some of the guns—[4] but "Our *men*—" if driven from a point— "never rest until it is retaken— & what is remarkable the spirit of the men is even better than that among the officers & in every instance where there's been a want of conduct— it is traced to the officers. This coming from the *staff* shows that Grant is beginning *to know* practically his Army—[5] An advantage which Lee has had over him in this contest so far— There is a stream of reinforcements— gone going— & still to go— to Grant & he is backed up with all the energy & power of the Administration

Blair is quite well again & as I have to go to the City in the morning to see about the progress of house cleaning there— He promises to stick close to Grandma if Ill not take him to the City— We are all well except Betty who really excites my tenderness & intense sympathy by her sufferings— she has looked sick for two weeks— but gave up yesterday & today— I have given her some of Dr. Mays remedies & tonight she is better— I keep well— am out doors all day long doing something— & at night am tired enough to enjoy being still— & sleep better than usual under anxieties— Father has been delicate since his return to Silver Spring— & it makes a good joke on him that the City agrees best with him & last night talking I was talking domesticities to Mother & said something about the mattresses in the city, Father spoke up— told me not to alter his— twas "excellent—" & not to let any body else use it—" Blair got uneasy & declared he did not like any "*town bed*" & seem to feel that Grandpa was recreant to country joys tis the place for boys Good night Ever yr devoted Lizzie

1. John T. Barnes lived up the road toward Sligo and worked on the farm for Mr. Blair.

2. Brig. Gen. August V. Kautz commanded a division of cavalry in Butler's force raiding rebel supply lines.

3. On May 12, Butler had begun to move toward the rebels at Drewry's Bluff on the James River, and on the sixteenth the Federals were repulsed and began their retreat to Bermuda Hundred, where they established a defensive position and did not threaten Richmond. On May 20, EBL observed that she was "glad to get anything to do to get the din of '*repulse*' out of my ears— Nobody seems as sorry about Butler as they ought to be & as to Sigel no matter where he is or how many troops he has— the race will commence with appearance of the enemy— this seems the universal opinion— Such a general ought not have a place."

4. Winfield Scott Hancock, in command of the Second Corps of the Army of the Potomac.

5. On May 18, EBL wrote: "I expected it Grant will have some bitter duty to do— on those who have run away to fight another day. *some* regiments have been returned to the front this week— 30 officers *in irons*— We have comparatively few badly wounded 9 tenths so some one told me from the Hospital are slight wounds—."

Silver Spring   May 21, 1864
Dear Phil   Your's of the 18th came this evening and was gladly greeted. These
terrible times makes the very sight of your handwriting a comfort as lately
from yr hand— Ever since the repulse of Genl Butler I have felt very uneasy about your position & that of the Army with you— But my hope is that
Grant will soon give by his movements the Rebels something else to do—
but he very rightly keeps his own counsels to himself— Tis evident that he
has delayed because Lee has fallen back in a thoroughly fortified long ago—
embankments grass grown place— stronger than Richmond— & he awaits
his reinforcements— he now has them & is stronger than when he started
over the Rapidan. I hope he will not commit the folly of storming this stronghold the useless experiment having been played out for public appetite at
Vicksburg—

You bid me be of good cheer— I strive by constant activity to overcome the
intense anxiety which oppresses me— & you be sure standing on guard— &
following up Blair all this week keeps me busy & interested too— I did wish
for you today to see him & Jesup trying their hand at ploughing I got for Blair
a little garden hand plough for the Donkey & he is wild over it— They did
some wonderful ploughing today Blair has his corn patch & is *now training*
the Donkey so can work it himself— He is busy all day & in the evening has
fine fun playing hide & seek or "hy spy—" as he calls it & other plays with
Ned & Henry— I will not let him know that I am anxious about you & keep
him away from War Talk he is too intelligent & sympathetic not to be affected
by it—

Good night— I will close this in town tomorrow— as I may hear there
something to tell of more import to you than my country routine— Mrs Dutton
has come & will be here for sometime— looks very well & handsome

Sunday morning Washington All well at home Grant has moved & moved
Lee—[1] They are both marching toward Hanover in paralel lines— the nearer
G. gets to the James the better for you thats my comforting thought I find
Capt Almys card here this morning— the bell for church Rings & I must
close— to pray where more than two or three are gathered together— the
prayers ever in my heart for my dear husband. Yr devoted Lizzie

1. On May 25, EBL wrote: "Mr. Fox & all of No 6 were out here this evening &
report that our progress was all that we could wish so far— they do not intend to fight
every step of the way for they have now moved 25 miles without any serious fight I
suppose the Base of operations will be changed from what I hear—."

Silver Spring   May 23, 1864
My dear Phil   Yours of the 17— & 19th came this evening— It is the latest
news from your quarter but all you say to me is in the papers— its publication

looks like "a movement here—" I cannot see how the navy part of an expedition can be blamed for the Army part being *"taken by surprise & in a fog—"* as is reported in Mr. Stantons dispatches to Genl Dix— this I am sure put the *misfortune* where it belongs— on the party taken by surprise[1] Now if the Rams from Richmond take you by surprise— then the Navy part of this expedition are unlucky! & you know what Nelson said of that sort of ill luck too well for me to suggest the *qui vive* to you who are always quoting Nelson—

Father has returned from the City in fine spirits Judge Trumbull has found *so many precedents* which justify the Presidents cancelling Franks resignation that he says any action of the Senate must be for the *future* & not the *past* acts of that kind There has been such discoveries made about a certain Ohio politician[2] (who gave you the cold shoulder about 5 years ago in Columbus I think it was there)— but all that Frank has said about him— as the merest petty larceny comparatively with what is now *proved* on— this is from a member of the Committee— but this sub rosa committee talk has rather disgusted me of late especially since we were informed (by one of them) that every man in the Elections Committee had voted Frank in his seat but the man from Delaware— & the same Committee— next week vote him out & his opponent in—

Col Daingerfield[3] is here wants Father to recommend Majr or Capt Dulany[4] for Col Harris' place— & I hear that there is a scandal upon his past life which will prevent the Dept— from promoting him— I never heard of this *until two days ago*— & when at the Navy Yard & I proposed to make inquiries about him I was deterred in my purpose by the utter astonishment I saw in Comre Livingstons face— to whom I then mentioned my attachment for Mrs Winn & thereby an interest in her Brother— He replied that I might say to Mrs. Winn that her brother was in excellent health & there the subject dropped— & never recurred to my mind until I heard about him from the Nicholson's who have a fancy for that fine Mansion at the Barracks

Betty tells me you right in not delivering her letter— "I have written to Mr Lee not to deliver it just now—" She is desperately hurt that he does not write & come Marion gets "Army letters has gone to bed sick today she is better I feel guilty of this *breach* & sorry to know that it gives so much sorrow— & yet I did but say what was really right

I have a long letter from Fanny. she knew Capt Flusser[5] family— & grieves his loss & wants you facilitate any thing in their behalf— as they are poor & the best of people Ever yr affecate Lizzie

1. On May 16, under cover of dense fog, rebel forces at Drewry's Bluff attacked federal troops, and Butler ordered a retreat. His chance to capture Richmond thus ended.

2. Salmon Chase.

3. Marine Col. William Henry Daingerfield was married to Ella Johnson, daughter of Reverdy Johnson.

4. Col. William Dulany of the Marine Corps was Mrs. Winn's brother. Col. John Harris died on May 12, 1864, and was followed as commandant of the Marine Corps by Col. Jacob Zeilin.

5. Charles W. Flusser served under SPL in the North Atlantic Blockading Squadron. He was killed April 19, 1864, while attempting to destroy the rebel ram *Albelmarle* in the Sounds of North Carolina.

Silver Spring   May 26, 1864

My dear Phil   I recd. yours of the 20th & two dated the 24th— I am so glad to get them & yr mention of Col Dutton made Marion say I am glad to know that he was even alive on the 24th— her last was the 17th— I'll try not to get puffed up too much in my pride— at being oftener remembered than young handsome wives— But I will confess that there is nothing in this world that I am so proud of as (well it is school girlish to use the exact word) so Ill say yr *attentions*— that will do for forty odd— I have written very properly even to pass a cross eyed examination— besides my letters are sealed so that they must be torn to be read— & they are all numbered except some hasty notes.

Father returned from the City vastly amused with an account of a Row among the Radicals They all dined & drank too much   Govr Sprague & other got to fighting & it was quite an undignified affair— but some of the speeches & details were amusing as it was not among our friends   Mr. Wade has urged that the District be *let* off with the Negro voting   I mention these symtoms as evidence that there is a reaction reasonable coming about—

I have been busy this rainy day directing some of Franks speeches 400 more— accomplished today & that completes a big bundle to go in with Mother who goes in to see after some wounded acquaintances   Capt Rice & Smedburg— she will bring either of them here if able to come as the hospitals are so crowded by the change of base that private families are taking care of many officers— I shall stay home & do my directing as there are several thousand yet to go   Blair is quite well— but is thinner— he runs his flesh off never did a chap keep on the go so constantly—

I wrote to Nelly & must now give Fanny a store   She thinks Goldy may pay me a visit soon if he comes next week he will see us all at No. 4 except you— I wish he could just get a little *national* sense put in by you— but Ill not touch these points— Ever yr devoted   Lizzie

Silver Spring   May 30, 1863 [1864]

My dear Phil   Yesterday whilst I was at Church Capt Smedburg was brought to No 4 He was too ill to go farther & he said he found the Hospital dreadful— "my own pain is enough to bear—" & Oh how thank your Mother & you for delivering me from the sorrows of six others"   Mother had made [e]very provision for him when in town on Saturday— so I bade him welcome & ordered the servants to admit no visitors until today & go strictly by the orders of the Doctor— Brother Minna— Mr Pyne— & other promise to cheer him when he needs it— but his excellent nurse (man says he needs repose & good food— that he gets so I left him— I shall go to stay for a few days when John & Nelly come up on Wednesday— I put the Capt in the back parlor— consequently our privacy & comfort upstairs— & in the Library is undisturbed—

I was glad to get home out of the City the lines ambulances & the moans of their poor suffering men were too much for my nerves[1] I had terrors enough about you before but these scenes seem to add to them ten fold Certain it is I would be a poor Florence Nightengale whilst you are in the field—

Goldie[2] is now out gathering flowers— asparagus & etc to take these poor men He has his Mothers warm heart & is a charming boy— Father thinks very much of a Lee He comes back on Wednesday to meet John & Nelly— He is pretty well cured of secesh— he said— the Success of the Rebels would now only ensure ruin to the whole country— which now is mostly[3] felt south materially— but at the North only at the firesides in the death & wounds of her men— I enclose you Arthurs letter— keeping the receipt which I may have to give up when I receive the money

Blair & Goldie look like brothers— & are very well pleased with each other— the Carriage waits so I must close this as I have to seal it well Marion [bore] her trial well—[4] wept— but thanked God that her husband was spared to her— Is now in Washington with her Aunt & Mother— No news from Grant last night— Ever your affecate Lizzie

1. On June 9, EBL wrote, "Our hospitals cannot accommodate any more— They will take the Churches again and urge the Citizens to open their houses to those too ill to go farther."

2. Goldsborough Robinson was the son of SPL's sister Fanny. On May 27 EBL described him: "The boy is well grown fine fellow but with delicate features & gentle expression He says an urchin at Barnums looked at him yesterday & said 'Be'nt you a young gal in mans clothes' He says he is full excitement since he reached the atmosphere of Washington."

3. Line drawn through "mostly."

4. Dutton had been wounded while on reconnaissance near Bermuda Hundred on the James River. On June 4, EBL commented, "Our tidings from poor Col Dutton is woful— he is bleeding & starving to death was very uncontrollable until joined by his wife who is now at Hospital in Baltre with him."

Silver Spring   June 1, 1864

Dear Phil   You have two letters of this date— but I forgot that May had 31 days— I have to go to the City today to meet John, Nelly & Goldie— I shall take Blair with me to see them but will send him & Becky home after dinner as I really do not wish to keep him in a city containing so many afflicted people or in any city in this hot season   I shall have to stay all night— to be present at the Wedding of one of the orphan girls— this evening at 8 olk— I am glad this so happens as Nelly said she would not let me stay on her account   Blair says he intends to try & get Phil to come home with him— & has a great many plans "for fun—" all arranged— they are to sleep in my bed— & are play all sorts of tricks on Becky & etc So I shall help him (as he phrases it) to beg Aunt Nelly—

Yours of the twenty seventh dated Saturday came duly to hand & had a very hearty welcome— I have been nervous about the troops leaving & feared it might increase the dangers about you but you speak of the movement in a tone that indicates no anxiety & if the Rebels are to be taken as evidence you have only less to take care of— the Rebel evidence is that on James River— they could stand the soldiers— shooting— but when the Gunboats began to throw shot & shell— Blacksmith shops" & all— they had to back out

I hope you will send some Gunboats up the Pamuncky to take care of the Army. I told Genl Barnard[1] when he got back & said the Butler situation was "*safe*"— I said Oh yes well under cover of the Gun boats— he laughed & said yes— but I doubt if he will say so to anybody else tho tis literally true— he is our neighbor in the City & I think I shall have his wife[2] put on the Asylum Board in Mrs Harris's place who has gone to her brother in New York & we must have some one of Army ties in the Board particularly as we now have so many Army children We have 16 orphans of the Army & Navy— four only of the latter— two beautiful girls were the children of a pilot— on of NA Block Sq—

Did some gardening today— my flowers are getting very pretty Mrs Beale came this evening & I had to leave this hobby   they seem just as happy as *ever*— I must now be off— will close this in the City— The old carriage will last this summer I hope tho it goes along very noisily— I read your letter to Mother who was vastly pleased— & said you were a good child to her, All send love In the City   Capt Smedburg doing better— All well in haste Ever yr own   Lizzie

1. John G. Barnard, an 1833 graduate of West Point, was the chief engineer of the Washington defenses. Grant appointed him chief engineer of the armies in the field.

2. EBL succeeded in getting another military wife on the board, but it was not Mrs. Barnard. The 1865 list of managers includes Virginia Freeman Zeilin, wife of Jacob Zeilin, commandant of the Marine Corps.

17

"I believe there is but one remedy
for our national woe— that
is hard fighting—"

June 25, 1864

THE GRIM, BLOODY, FINAL CAMPAIGNS of the war moved inexorably forward: Sherman pushed steadily nearer Atlanta and Grant fought doggedly toward Richmond. After the terrible carnage of Cold Harbor in the first week of June, Grant decided to flank Richmond by moving his army south of the James River and attacking the railroad hub of Petersburg.

A coalition of Republicans and War Democrats met in the National Union convention to nominate Lincoln for reelection, while the regular Democratic party backed peace candidate George McClellan. John C. Frémont was the choice of many Radicals.

In July, the war quite literally came home to Elizabeth Lee, when Jubal Early's raid on Washington reached the outskirts of the nation's capital. Confederates camped at Silver Spring, ransacking the Blair home and burning Montgomery's country retreat. Phillips incurred the acute displeasure of the Navy Department by steaming up the Potomac from Hampton Roads to defend the city.

Silver Spring   June 6, 1864
Dear Phil   I came home last evening had hoped that Goldie would come out with me but he said he had a great many letters to write & he would not do it if came here— & he was to go Balt at an early hour today— I would not have asked for the carriage to return here yesterday but I thought he enjoyed the place so much last week that he would like another visit— Annie[1] is quite at home & well— out now with Blair feeding the turkeys & very happy

We were all grieved yesterday to hear of the death of Col Dutton—[2] Poor Marion a widow & a bride in less than a year— for tomorrow is the anniversary of her wedding— and so soon to bring into the world a fatherless child   but this last is now her best earthly comfort

Mr. Fox was here yesterday and showed me your telegram of the 3rd & said that the Ironclad fight which has been in all the papers is untrue as you have made no report of it to the Dept— or to me— There was no news from Grant yesterday— I heard he had sent for Genl Barnard & all of our best Engineers to go to him— tis said to consult as to the best mode of besieging Richmond—

The delegates are flocking & there seems no doubt of Lincolns renomination[3] I think our Star must be getting up again Johns old neighbor & now our next door one[4] officially came to spend the evening— & supped with us— first time in three yrs Brother wants Father to go to Baltre— he is not going— he has no official position— & to beg it thru as a lobby member— to get Foy & that set in as members— is I think beneath him calling indeed tis not dignified & so he dont go   Mr Dennison wants to be chairman & altho I would do much for him— that even will not make Father go— but he has written to Mr Preston King & others on the matter which is enough for him— Whenever he has attended these Conventions before he has been a member & as long as *he* managed Maryland matters he was not defeated in them This is a much mooted matter & Father & I are alone in this position   the rest— & intense about it

I got another letter about the Lee pedigree from Fanny— the one alluded to in that I sent you— I must write to Nelly about her little girl & so can only add yr affecate   Lizzie

1. Annie Lee, daughter of John and Ellen Lee.
2. On June 7, EBL wrote: "I have felt the sorrows of poor Marion very keenly & now that it is decided that she is to stay here for some weeks— I confess to almost wishing to run away— but tis a selfishness I shall conquer & only feel thankful for the opportunity to cheer & comfort her all I can— Dutton was baptized by a priest having written that he was willing to die & go to his God & Redeemer— & would do anything that which would give his wife comfort— who was his only earthly regret— He suffered & died from a suffusion of the lungs by bleeding from the throat— He was buried from the Catholic Church— & now lies in the Catholic Cemetery— & his poor old mother goes home without her "boy" as she calls him— saying his wife has the best right— even to make his grave among strangers I think she ought to have sent him to his home— where his people have dwelt for over a hundred years— & then followed him— but I suppose her religion made her take a different course She knows but little of his kindred having spent but a few days among them—."
3. The National Union Convention, including Republicans and War Democrats, met in Baltimore.
4. Montgomery Meigs had lived in the same block as John Lee, on H Street. Meigs's office as quartermaster general was next door to EBL on Pennsylvania Avenue.

Silver Spring   June 8, 1864

My dear Phil   Now that I have finished my report of Annie to her Mother— Ill thank you for your's of the 4th inst I had an uncomfortable day yesterday— Took Annie in the City to have a dress fitted— & this sudden change of weather made me fearful of having her to sit in front with Henry— but she is so sick inside that I consented after covering her with a shawl & etc— Still a half hour after we reached the the city a chill came on— I did everything I could think of to check it— & in two hours it was all over— & she had no fever— headache & etc & she said it was a very slight attack— but it seemed to me dreadful— & to come home without advice or medicine was impossible so I sent for Dr. May and he questioned her about the treatment she had had & he said answered very intelligently— & he has continued it— with some slight change but *he says* nothing but a *continuous* change of air & residence will cure chills— He desired me not to to take her to the City again as the air there in June was but little better than that on the Patuxent

I went in for Asylum business but of course gave all that the go by— & old Mrs Gilliss is such a nuisance that I was glad of a good excuse not to see her— I went to see Marion— she was not able to see anybody the Dr forbid anyone going in to see her— Her mother told Betty that she felt death would be a release from what she now suffered— I was grieved at this heart broken Mothers wailing over her poor daughter How strangely her talk reminded me of poor Mrs. Upshur's—

Capt Smedburg is still very ill Dr. May's visit to Annie was seized by his family for a consultation with him— which from the suggestions he made will I hope result in an alleviation of his suffering—

Gratz Brown was here to tea— with Brother & Minna enjoyed Cream strawberries & etc hugely— told me he had heard Mr. Grimes extol you highly yesterday— when pointing out the use of the Navy— & its work *over* that of the Army— I replied you had fought & worked hard— & longer than anybody else— but I suppose that was a good reason for keeping you an acting Admiral & making your juniors real ones— he said you had been dealt by "*unjustly*—" I told him you thought all Admirals appointed had earned their laurels— & but I felt you had more than earned your's— & I suffered my share too— he grumbled at leaving his wife a few months, what would he say to 4 yrs I find them long & weary— & dreary— each longer than the last— but if you are well & keep so tis my ever present fervent prayer while you are so beset with danger— I scarce dare ask for more Your own devoted wife Lizzie

Silver Spring June 11, [1864]
Dear Phil Yours of Tuesday (7th 11pm reached me— Friday at one olk— Sent for it by Neddy on horse back— Mary Ann sent word by him that Becky's Sister (Sophy) was ill— had convulsions so she had to go to her Capt Smedburg still very ill— bad amputation on the field tied up tendons & all with the Artery— Dr May when called to see Annie was called in on consultation & finds out that his illness is from these causes & he will be long The nerves

terribly racked & etc   as soon as he is better in that way he advises removal to Mountains somewhere All fear of nervous fever is now over— & that is a great relief to his friends—

Annie is very well and wants to go to the City— to fit her dress— I shall wait until after the Chill hour if I make up my mind to take her with me if she dont go I stay too   Andrew I hear has written to you to advise about his visit to you His Mother just wrote to Father that she left it to his judgement but since writes to forbid it altogether—

Mr Ellard[1] & Foy Col Peckham[2] & etc took tea here— I find them very sore about the Convention— I am glad that they no longer talk of Frank as a candidate for Governor Frank has joined Genl Sherman—[3] Tis rumored that Grant has crossed James River (he had Pontoons sent a week ago) & again flanked the enemy I do not think he expected to make *a short* campaign— I heard differently directly from his own lips & with my own ears he told Frank that we must expect a "long hard desparate fight—" he & Frank both thought it would end the war— consequently that Rebs would fight with their all usual desparation "but with obstinacy than ever before—" they then discussed the characteristics of Northern & Southern fighting— Frank thought the South were french in their tactics & everything— & the North English Genl Grant shook his head saying both "were American—" which we think is little different from the rest of the world— there was a half serious laugh in his face the only words I at all remember his using I quote— the rest is merely the impression left on my mind by the talk— which was half whispered near me— but the fact of his idea of the obstinacy of the enemy was written by me to Nelly who I repeat things that wont hurt to repeat— to prevent the feeling that any theme is excluded between us—

All well at the Lodge yesterday— Annie heard today Father still in the City Do be prudent in yr diet— these cold soups affect the bowels— rub with turpentine I dread the Malaria of the James River Indeed tis hard to say what tis I do not fear in these fearful days— Ever yr affecate Lizzie

Tis said that G. insists upon the removal of yr General[4]

1. Charles M. Elleard, soda water manufacturer and ice dealer, was a strong St. Louis Union man.

2. Col. James Peckham had managed the *Evening Bulletin* in St. Louis. He joined the army when the war started and served in Blair's Fifteenth Corps.

3. On May 29, EBL had reported: "Father brought a letter from Frank he is now with Sherman— he writes very cheerfully— He says that much of the country he marched over last fall following the Secesh Army & which was devasted by the two Armies & was already revived since delivered from secession thraldom & the tramp of both Armies—."

4. Benjamin Butler.

Silver Spring   June 13, [1864]
Dear Phil   I am off in the city in a little while for Sundry errands with Annie
& for her & Mother   I shall not go until after twelve as I dont think it save
to go out until her chill hour is past this cool weather consequently keep her
snugly by the fire in the library   she has had no return of her ailment— I
have stopped all medicine & shall for a while rely on nursing & the change
of place— & a good lunch & brandy instead of quinine of which I an intense
horror—

Andrew is here & got your permit to come to the James River but his
Mother has vetoed the movement so he is importuning her vows he wont go
to St Louis & is restless as a young Cub and finds no congenial spirits except
Blair & the dogs— Annie is rather shy of him & his roughness—

Yesterday Mr. King said a friend of his & a Dr was going front & as all people
& things are now sent to James River he meant to give a letter to this friend to
you   I assured him of all your best attentions— & told Mr King you hoped to
have a visit from him   he said he meant to have gone to see you but feared he
would be an encumbrance but if he was here again this summer which was not
improbable he would go to see you We talked over the Convention & he said
he was glad I had spoken out "*in such right spirit*—" when he was here some
evenings since & with persons who had voted agt "*us*—" I repeat this as much
for your satisfaction as my own

We are anxious about Frank— at this moment— not abt what others may
do— but abt his course— As we are firm in the faith that none can really
do us great harm— as long as we earnestly try to do what is honestly right—
but anger is the poorest of counsellors— & revenge is suicide—[1] I have a
long letter from John about the Lees but Father wants to use the facts— & I
delay sending it He is not well— has a swollen face & when discomforted— is
always sick He has said several times he hoped you had delayed putting down
obstructions until Grant was consulted by you—[2] for my part I am rather of the
military way of thinking— G[rant]'s officers do not think much of his courage
personal or moral— but he is an excellent Engineer—

Betty has had a letter from her Genl but I think their affairs are *very*
awry   he is I think hurt beyond cure & I think it unfortunate for them that
the letter you have was not sent— but Ill keep my tongue out of the matter—
& wont say even to her— that I think his course natural & manly & right all
the way— Capt Smedburg is very ill & I have great doubts of his recovery—
he was badly cared for until I telegraphed for his sister who is a fine woman &
one of the best of nurses— I sent for Mrs. Adams the day I went in to meet
Nelly & saw how things were managed about the Capt— & thro' Mary Ames
reports the Doctor since asked Betty by what instinct had I found out in as few
hours what was needed We are off to the City   Yr own   Lizzie

1. The Radicals, angry at the Blairs, questioned whether Frank could be both general and congressman. The House of Representatives unseated Frank Blair in favor of his 1862 opponent, Samuel Knox. On June 10, EBL had written: "Father is home today— cheerful bearing the licks at Frank with great equinimity— saying they are forced to take our man & platform & persecution never hurts an honest man & etc Our only real trouble is Frank will give vent to some of his wrath which will only hurt himself & help his foes—." A week later, on June 18, she explained Lincoln's attitude on the matter: "The No 6's were here tonight— report the P— very steady about F— intends to let Congress make itself just as absurd as it pleases— it is all aimed at 'me—' & that is self evident as he not only *did it* but suggested it first & held on to it— when it was evidently to be handled as it has been by the personal & political Rivals— when F— thought it best *not* to return to the Army & the reply was— 'we must not back down—' Of course tis a thought too personal for any interference by us & therefore— tis not even noticed in conversation by any of us save to each & that only in our trio— Father Mother & your little woman."

2. In May Benjamin Butler had urged that obstructions be placed in the James River, but SPL had objected and delayed any action until Grant ordered him to do so. On June 15, the first obstructions were laid down.

Silver Spring   June 14, 1864

Dear Phil   I recieved your's of the 10th & 11th on the 13th— From what we had heard here we thought "*the situation*" was changed— for we have reason to believe that supplies & reinforcements & etc have been sent up James River ever since Wednesday & that Grant is moving over that way—[1] to make that the *base* thinking it best to get the Navy to keep open his line of communications & it has always seemed to me the simplest problem of this war— I feel eager to have an Army on both sides of the River & then I shall fear sharpshooters less & have more time to think of fireworks & etc which are so formidable to me & the military   I know you all feel able to fight anything in your Armor & water but I am afraid of all— those close iron ships may be good in a fight— but, all the rest of the time they are dreadful places in hot seasons—[2]

Annie & I went to the City with Mrs. Rochester & Baby[3] & did sundry errands for Mother. Brought Becky home who no sooner gets in distress— than she begins to quarrel— I sometimes fear I shall have to part with her— but she is so honest & useful— then so devoted to Blair— that tis hard to do even what is right— She is at war with Charles & his wife & with my new cook who has been for years her most devoted friend— Charles & his wife are invaluable to Mother— & I'll have to hold on to them We have plenty of cream & the best of butter out of exactly the same cows which could scarcely provide us milk & cream for two or 3 yrs past— All the washing & house work are admirably done & we have never been so comfortably served since we lived out here— The moment any of us praise or like a servant except herself or Nannie— she begins to be jealous of them & her jealousy of Blair is really funny— & she looks like a grown mastiff all day & at night she always tries be present when he says his prayers & when he includes her— which he generally does she becomes all good nature— but wo betide us if he leaves her out— I generally ignore all this & on the surface things go on smoothly— but they come to the surface & ruffle me up a little— as was the case today but all is en routine now— & I think with management I can make all get along without parting with anybody who have proved to be honest & useful—

I got Bishop Mead[4] on Old Churches & Families of Virginia & today Father is deep the lore & he will read talk many hours about the Old times & people whose names were household words in their young days— Annie & Blair are joyous & well— Andrew has taken to work— so that he can have Ned to go play & go a fishing with him— He is still a *true boy* & a fine one   Yr affectionate Lizzie

1. On June 12, Grant began to move the Army of the Potomac toward the James River.

2. Weeks earlier EBL's concern for her husband increased after she had sent him his summer hat: "I am full of regret since that I did tis large & white & will make you conspicuous to sharpshooters— & I feel in terror about having sent it So please dont wear it on the James River—."

3. The first child of Anne L. Martin and William B. Rochester was Annie Townsend Rochester, born February 11, 1864.

4. Bishop William Meade, Protestant Episcopal bishop of Virginia, published *Old Churches, Ministers, and Families of Virginia* in 1857.

							Silver Spring June 19, [1864]
Dear Phil   Your letters came perfectly well sealed— intact— it is impossible to open them without tearing or defacing them   I hope you will not vote me unsympathetic— for strange as it may seem I regret that the Army has wounded the naval pride— & yet it is a world of relief to me to have no naval fight[1]   I did not fully realize how intense were my apprehensions until I felt even physically & mentally uplifted   a shout of joy almost escaped me as the burden fell off of my spirit & body too— Since I heard so much of late the agonies of the wounded— I have become so nervous about my husband that— well I am very thankful to Genl Grant— you have done your part fully & with spirit that satisfies my pride as you always have done brimfull— & midst all the din of war around you   I shall cease to quake all night with terror— & run & work all day to drive away anxieties which made me miserable—

I found the Receipt for taxes in a few minutes copied & sent it to John— about lot No. 4— in trust to Mr Rives   I did shopping for Mother— & then went to see Miss Cameron staying at Mrs Douglas' Father seems to have made up his mind to go off on this trip to the Mountains of Pennsylvania with Mr. Stabler & Cameron— Mrs Douglas was very civil in her talk about you & look very handsome— Miss Cameron too seem to remember you most kindly— I must write to Fanny & give her the comfort of the "Army obstructions it will be a great one to her Goldy left his pistol at No 4 he put on the bureau in Blairs reach & Becky had no fancy for that so put it on the shelf in Wardrobe & he went off without it altho shown where it was put— The Sands are gone— I think Andrew will soon join you *now*— All well— Yr affecate Lizzie

1. Obstructions sunk in the James River effectively separated the Union and rebel navies, foreclosing any possible naval engagement.

Silver Spring   June 21, 1864

My dear Phil   Your's of the 16th was my birthday gift & greeting—[1] I read it to Blair & he watched me putting his fingers along the lines & when I finished he said— "Well all of it is for you— not any for me—" dear little pet I felt like making a message for him but he knows him own name besides I never decieve him even in things so unimportant— I mention it to get you to say that your letters are always meant partly for him— to let us both know you are well & think of us—

Father came home looking very grave & anxious— to hear of Frank assaulting the "enemies works" on the Chattanooga as was reported in the Star over which River he has crossed always brings over us all an anxiety— which you can well appreciate—[2] Andrew went to the City en route for James River— trunk & all— but there encountered positive orders from his Mother in a letter to Minna forbidding either the Blockade or James River— tis evident to me she intends to make him quit the Navy when he graduates but I think in that she will fail— but 'tis her present plan—

We have almost cold weather & when you remember the season & the drought— tis a very remarkable thing— a hot day is almost sure take off scores of our sick men in the Hospitals— we feel blessed in this weather it makes my chief work in the garden watering— & is fine for haymaking which the only profitable crop of this place— I have a plan for getting the benefit of our peaches which are most promising but may drop off as they did last year—

Brother went to Baltr to get two of (Mag Wooley's) Mrs White brothers out of jail— boys at boarding school— who talked & refused the oath—[3] This has been a terror of mine about Emmetsburg— as well as St Jame's College— but our Bishop is a Union man—[4] & the Jesuits— so far keep dark about their politics— tho tis known to me that every priest is Secesh but two— I feel more about this as William is 18. He goes to Louisville— and I hope &

pray that Grants success will end the War— & all this & greater anxieties—
I sleep soundly— & so much that Ill soon have an average   I am quite well
consequently— Andrew & Annie send love   Yr affecate   Lizzie
Blair is not by me

    1. On June 15, EBL commented on her age: "The 20th inst my birthday, six years
your junior & getting as grey & wrinkled as if I was ten years your senior—."
    2. On June 22, EBL explained their fears: "We are terribly anxious about Frank—
If captured by the Secesh on the other side of the Chatochee— [Chattahoochee] they
would be as eager to kill him physically— as the Radicals are politically—."
    3. Margaret Woolley White's brothers Frank and Aaron Woolley were students at
the Maryland Military Institute from 1861 to 1866. They had been arrested and spent
five months in prison at Fort Delaware. Montgomery Blair arranged their release.
    4. The Catholic bishop of Maryland had been Francis P. Kenrick, who died July 3,
1863. There was a year's delay before Martin J. Spalding, whose loyalty to the Union
was questioned, replaced him on July 31, 1864.

Silver Spring   June 25, 1864
My dear Phil   Yours of Tuesday 22nd midnight by Walter reached me safely
at No 4 friday 24th— when I went there to see Annie off   John came about
twelve begged me to have every thing ready by two olk— he must be off as it
was so hot he would be obliged to drive slowly— Annie had dined & all was
ready at the appointed hour— but John was an hour behind time He said that
there was no taxes paid for 1862— He would come up on Monday en route
for the boys to bring them home when he would investigate the case fully—
& pay all dues & redeem the lot from all jeopardy— that it was sold a year
ago   I went to Mr Caton[1] who says you have always paid the Taxes and that he
has the Insurance receipts but not those for taxes— I did not look thro' your
reciepts before sending box— indeed I did not even think of looking to see
if you kept receipts— in the boxes— only put in the papers I had— & that
made it quite full— & sewed a strong cover over the box & sent it off—
    I wanted to go hunt for Walter— to have a long talk with him but the
excessive heat added to a headache made me a prisoner— Blair has made me
anxious of late & that hurt my head again— but both are well now— I shall
fix out the key today—[2]
    F[ox] & his party returned entirely *content* with the situation "the murder-
ous assault—" so barren of result & full of woe to us was made by the *Genl*[3]
who endorses the Rebel reports— & is considered a grievous mistake in high
quarters— He is too passionate to be judicious— Your letter was full of intense
interest to me and there is much seen at this distance that makes it true—
Still— I believe there is but one remedy for our national woe— that is *hard
fighting*— Still I do believe the worst of it for this year is done & it is the last
year too— of this heartbreaking war— this is my firm belief rather hope—

You will be glad to learn that Fox has given to newspapers— Grants order about the obstructions— & other points— which refutes the Heralds attack upon you—[4] He is evidently pleased with *"the naval position"* in this mat- ter John looked well Saw yr long letter to me in my hand— asked me twice what you were writing about— I said only about our confidential matters— He said I must write him often & let him know promptly all *"things personal to you—"* He was very kind— Nelly & Phill have had chills again & badly. Ever yr own Lizzie

Blair became quite jealous of Annie over which she had great fun— I am really very sorry to part with her, but to go to that sickly place it is grievous— Annie was *much* improved in her appearance so John thought—

1. Michael Caton was cashier at the *Globe* office.
2. The Lees sometimes disguised key words in their correspondence as a precaution against others opening their mail. The "key" was the cipher to decode their messages.
3. Gen. Benjamin Butler.
4. The New York *Herald* noted on June 24, 1864, that Grant, not SPL, had ordered obstructions placed in the James River. On June 28 EBL informed her husband that her father had told her "that Fox had furnished the Republican with Grants order & other official data about the obstructions & an article was prepared at the Dept on the subject— Ever since I have looked out for this article in vain— The Herald now ad- mits it was Grants order— but continues its mean abuse I suppose [James G.] Bennett [owner of the *Herald*] has heard the exaggerated accounts of your riches by prize money & wants to levy black mail— or you have snubbed some of its correspondants."

Silver Spring   June 30, 1864
Dear Phil   Yours of Sunday— 26th inst came last evening— Father thinks it is the Vanderbilt interest that attacks you rather which pays to have the Navy attacked on all occasions— I thought some days ago that G[rant] ought to refute that imputation of the Herald as an opinion of his— but Betty says— that G— never reads the papers— Father said tonight when I talked this *as my own* feelings & tis truly so)— that G. did not read papers— said they annoyed him so quit reading them— I never heard this but this I have heard it observed that he ignores the papers always in his own affairs— This was Franks view of him when with him— You know F. had some muss with Sherman about the report of a correspondant & it was in this discussion I took this impresse of his views from Frank— G would like to banish every letter writer out of the Army if it were possible— & I think that is the general Army feeling when they are not aspirants which *happens* just *now* not to be Genl. G's condition— Father thinks it *naval* purely the malice evinced towards you— I think it is trade & traders— & in that the General is in full sympathy with you.

Father had a long letter yesterday from Mary Riggs— full of patriotism & national pride— says *the people* of Europe keep their governments from recognizing the South— She hopes to see us all before very long— It is seven years since she left her country— I expect she is now purely french— I wish my boy spoke that language & German as her children do— but I could not endure seven years banishment even to attain that. She writes from Pare— where she has lived for five years "pushing the education of the children—"

As to politics— & etc All national interest & etc seems to me as if every other interest was just centered about you— Last eve— Mr. Stabler came to stay all night & when asked the news— he replied nobody thinks or feels any-thing— but Army news— One would never dream it was the year for electing a President— Brother suggested publishing some thing in reference to that matter— when he was told *all* such things at this hour would irritate the public mind— when so absorbed in the more vital business of life & death—

Andrew talks of starting on Saturday for yr Flag Ship— went yesterday after a pass— but he could not get *that* until he went up after Wood & saved the stylish horses that trip— There have been some gentlemen? arrested above us for *stealing* horses— Have not the Chivalry come to a sad pass in Md These arrests give the comforting assurance that the War Dept— has it eyes open as *to its* surroundings & this time it has arrested the right man— those long suspected by some wise acres I could mention—

I read what you said about the 48 hours to Blair he said you were right— he would not forget that 48 hours soon— he told Mr. S. about it soon after he got here— Your affectionate Lizzie

Silver Spring   July 2, 1864

Dear Phil   This makes the third letter I have commenced to you in the last hour— but 'ere I get half thro— they have got covered with blots from this miserable pen— but I have no other just now so must run the risk

Father will write his his own response about Mr. Mann— I think notice will give it importance Still I feel very much exasperated— I scarce trust myself to speak about it or to write for I would not add anything to yr resentments— when tis best to be patient

The news of the change in the Cabinet[1] took us all by surprise I think from all I hear our condition is bettered by the change—[2] altho he very ill tempered— but he is honest & as Mrs Jeff once said the ablest of all the Republican Senators—

Andrew has concluded to stay here with his young cousins until after the fourth, it is odd to see with all his boyishness how Violets beauty attracts him She is certainly very lovely There now seven of the grandchildren here & it makes a noisy house & I think it does Marion good for she is accustomed to children & *the sounds* are not oppressive— She is stronger & will I hope do well after this Still I feel very anxious about her Mrs Sands comes next week to make arrangements for her— Yesterday chiefly spent by me *cooking* Current

Jelly— I had a letter from Nelly last evening— full of thanks for Annies improved health   at the same time yours of Tuesday 28th— The enclosed from Father replies to your query about Mr Mann in it

Blair is riotously happy among so many youngsters— Wood wont go home even to show his prize or to say how do you do— He is a huge boy— taller than Andrew & yet 3 years younger—

I must hasten to close— but must tell a piece of gossip related by Mr. Grey— He says Jessie never was in such feathers— that Coxe of Ohio— Richardson[3] & others of the Democrats have been to see her— & make them believe that F. will be nominated by the Chicago Convention as a "*political necessity*" & etc[4] That there is no end to the nonsense she talks on this text— He Mr G. & others were to get Father to go for Morgan of NY— as Secy Treasurer We are all well Your affectionate   Lizzie

I had nearly finished indeed had only to sign my name when these blots lit on my papers

1. On June 30, Lincoln accepted Salmon P. Chase's resignation as secretary of the treasury. On July 1, William Pitt Fessenden, senator from Maine, was confirmed in the post by Congress.

2. On June 27, EBL gave another indication of her hope for a brighter political future, writing: "There was quite a party of Congressional visitors out here last night & strange to say the *extremes*—" who avoided us all winter— are now getting quite courteous—."

3. Samuel S. Cox was a Democratic congressman from Ohio (1857–65). William A. Richardson, Illinois Democrat, served in the House (1847–56, 1861–63) and in the Senate (1863–65).

4. The Democrats met in Chicago in August and nominated George B. McClellan. Frémont did not give up his challenge to Lincoln until September 22.

Silver Spring   July 3, 1864

Dear Phil   Yours of Tuesday night (29 came last evening   I sent for the mail early— & then Mr Barnes brought out the late mail so it did not reach Washington until after one olk— Would it not be well to let the world know that you put the correspondant of the Herald in Irons   I think so— It would account at once for the malice with which you are pursued. As a newspaper the Herald alone is valued so when an officer cannot be bribed into facilitating its trade in news— why they bully & brow beat him into it

I wrote to you last night that Mr. Chase had taken us all by surprise it now seems— that he was surprised himself the Tribune gives the true account as far as I can gather— Now F[essenden] & my opposite neighbor [Lincoln] will soon quarrel if my next door neighbor [Montgomery] will only keep quiet— There was a desparate effort made by Chases friends to save him— & they now try to put on Frank the onus of the muss— When all of his dishonesty comes to light Frank's denunciations of it will not then deprive him of his places— You see Mr. Garfield has declined investigating that branch of the business being a military & a western man he did venture to look into that ticklish matter

Mr Fessenden is reputed ambitious— & honest & in bad health & generally a bad humor— in years past I found him very agreeable— but he has been running a race with Mr Hamlin similar to that between Jeff D— & Brown— but since the defeat of Mr H—[1] I think his politics have bleached— he quarrelled with Mr Sumner— about some of his abstractions— & is really the great man of down east The Ps appointee declining— he took the one most acceptable to the Senate—

Marion goes to the City with me when I go to church She is stronger than when she came to us two weeks ago Her grief is intense & hard even to look upon— She thanked me yesterday for telling her to go to her husband when her mother urged her not to go She says she would have gone— but she felt my opinion when so opposed by others helped her to do what is now her last earthly comfort— The accounts today from Capt Smedberg are again bad— I fear the result— Father goes on a hunting trip on next Wednesday to the Mts in Peny— with Mr Cameron— Brother Mr. Stabler & others go— Wood— & Andrew Blair is eager to go— & I would gladly indulge him— but we cannot all leave Mother besides I fret when leaving home as you— when I cannot get yr letters Our long separation makes me grow morbid & miserable

Blair is well— I think the quiet of a weeken & the restraint from running so much much has improved him in the way of flesh Ever yr affecate Lizzie

1. Hannibal Hamlin, former governor of Maine (1857), U.S. senator (1857–61), and vice president (1861–65), was replaced on the Republican Union ticket by Andrew Johnson.

Silver Spring   July 6, 1864

Dear Phil Last night I returned home bringing almost consternation with me— But 'ere I left the city I waited to see Father & Brother & gave them a full benefit all my Secesh rumors— strange to say— Father had been so occupied with his plans for his hunting expedition that he had not even heard of the Attack upon Harpers' Ferry—[1] However when I told him about it he went to the White House— but the P. was at the War Dept— Brother soon came in & saw into matters better— but said that the Rebs were checked & held at Harpers Hunters command was now in cars en route to face the foe[2] So Father & Brother go off— & I am not sorry for that leaves us womankind here more free [to] skidadle into the city.

I met Mr. Fox at No. 6. asked him to come take care of us at Silver Spring was as civil as possible— but I observe he is far more cordial to me anywhere else than at that locality. & tho pleased with attentions would give offence by accepting— so I rarely anything but *merely civil there* His *entent* is completed there & he evidently dont want to complicate it— He told me he intended sleeping at the Relay H Father & I laughed at the idea— of being good for anything save a cheap good ride— & in that respect tis a good arrangement particularly as I am quite sure *free tickets* are plenty—

I met John soon after I closed my letter he was in search of a tobacco item meant to go home or to Baltimore at 3 olk— to the last place I believe— to sell as he feared *confiscation*— You can see how— I hope he will make no sacrifice under any such pressure but *Secesh* were in high glee—

Tis rumored that Petersburg was taken on the 4th[3] We have no news today & may be will get none until late in the day— F. seemed to think you would go off to Wilmington I confess to great satisfaction in having you out of the James but if this news about Petersburg is true I doubt if you leave there as you will not have them march to Richmond in your absence—

Mrs Hassler[4] is one of the Asylum Board now— told me to tell you that her son[5] wrote that the Oneida had had eleven commanders & *never* caught a prize She expects him home next week— She seems rather amused with me— Sits & looks at me— & says— well— tis an odd change of occupation for the gayest of the gay—

Johnny [Lee] took 8 prizes— for his studies— & the medal for good con-duct The P[resident of the College] said he was boy of the best character since Wm Hill & with vastly more talent In 30 yrs the College had no boy of equal character & ability John says he looks in bad health— I made them laugh at my old friend Mrs. Gilliss— when she said I had not lost my love of fun— I have not been associated with her since we were both about 18 yrs old— when she married— she looked then ten yrs my senior— but has not grown much older since Blair is well Mother busy house cleaning— & all seems very quiet with departure of so many person— 7 in all Yr own Lizzie

1. Jubal Early's Confederates had been involved in skirmishing around Harpers Ferry on July 3 and 4. He crossed the Potomac on July 5.

2. David Hunter, in command in the Shenandoah Valley, was supposed to neu-tralize Early's force, but he had retreated to western Virginia, and Early seized the opportunity to march north.

3. Petersburg, Virginia, had been under siege since June 23, but it was almost ten months before the city was surrendered.

4. Anne Josepha Nourse married Ferdinand Hassler's son, Charles August Hassler, surgeon in the U.S. navy.

5. Charles William Hassler, son of navy surgeon Charles A. Hassler and grandson of Ferdinand Hassler, was a paymaster on SPL's old ship *Oneida*.

Silver Spring July 8, 1864

Dear Phil Oh how busy I was all of yesterday— with Fathers Mothers & my own affairs getting things ready to go away We are all packed— & save the endless little matters are ready to go Yesterday Cannon was heard here all day by some of the family Others say it was thunder I received a message from Mr. Fox saying the Enemy had retreated down the Winchester Valley— & had given up— Maryland— Others insist the enemy are 40,000 strong—[1] The Silence of the officials is ominous to me & I am glad to go where I can sleep more than I can here—[2] I have still much to do— was up late & early. Blair is quite willing to go to play in the water for a little while—

Apo[3] Frank has sent a poney to Jesup   Mary declines taking it as he has Jenny Lind which is worth all the ponies in the world this disappoints me as I had a covetous eye on Jenny. Apo says she intended to sell the poney— I wont offer to buy until I have seen that it is a poney without tricks the rarest of animals Apo has sold Rosebank[4] for $20,000 a mistake I think— land is better than paper in any form these times— particularly when own by women & minors—

Blair is very bright & well— tho pale & very thin— but is better of the weakness of which I wrote— He is sore put to it about his turkies & chickens & Donkey— would like to take them & Neddy too— Ill write from Phil when we stop tonight yr own Lizzie

1. On July 9, the opposing forces met at Monocacy, Maryland, where the Federals were routed. Early's continued advance in the North spread fear in both Baltimore and Washington.
2. Because of her mother's ill health, EBL had decided to take her to Cape May.
3. Line drawn through "Apo."
4. Rose Bank, variously spelled by EBL, was Frank's St. Louis home.

Cape Island, Atlantic Hotel   July 13, 1864
My dear Phil   Mother is very much overcome by the burning of Silver Spring & the terror felt about the safety of my Father who we learn had returned to Washington—[1] It is very hard but as long as God spares our dear ones & covers their precious heads in battle I cannot grieve even for a home where everything is as dear to me as at Silver Spring. each bush & tree— having had my care & watching in that lawn— Still if our Capitol is not dishonored— My Husband & Brother brought safe thro all these hardships & battles— I shall be thankful— & will try let no other feeling come in my heart—

I have written to father that he has provided another home for us— & never had a man children more eager to comfort him & help repair injuries of our enemy— We younger people can bear such losses with more quietness however than the aged. Mother is terribly afflicted— had a bad night & is now lying by me with fever & great suffering in her back— fortunately Dr Stone[2] is here & Betty went for him at daylight this morning— I feel thankful we are here out of the distress & heat of the City with her— Dr. Stone agrees with me in thinking her general health needed care & change— So tis after all &

ought to be thankful even in being here— as it is so good for her to be here   I must hurry— to save the mail—

Blair is well— but terribly excited about Silver Spring affairs Your devoted   Lizzie

1. On July 11, Jubal Early's force had advanced to the outskirts of Washington, ransacking the Blairs' Silver Spring home and burning Montgomery's.

2. Washington physician Robert K. Stone was the Lincoln family doctor.

Cape May   July 14, 1864

My dear Phil   Even the suspense about Washington is grateful, as it is delay & in that, we may hope safety for it— if the Rebels had massed on it as we left it— they had little to do, but walk in it[1] The total blindness & stupidity about this invasion was extraordinary Any hint on my part of such a possibility was met with a scorn that withered my courage for any action— but to get away with my sick mother

I got nearly every article of clothing and all that was my own except my writing desk & work box— which have nothing in them— & as I came down stairs with them in my arms I met Mother & again urged that the silver at least might be taken to the City— No she would not have the house pulled to pieces— then I said well I'll send some plated ware— in its place to which she assented. I put down my boxes & went to work after the silver— & then was hurried off as we were late as usual— & in my haste left my dear old boxes— Your letters I had taken in the day before— the bulk of them always kept there by me   I shrink from being an alarmist but under the derision & even secession cast up to me I had not the whim to rise— I think Father Mr Fox & Brother will recollect with some pain my entreaties to them not to go away The truth is the fatuity is not yet over— for the Times of yesterday is out with the meanest article precisely in the same contemptuous tone as to the enemy & their force in Maryland & that in the same columns announcing the capitol cut off from the rest of the Country Such people are good Allies of our foe—

Mother is better but still has very bad symtoms. the Dr saw her three times yesterday & each time remarked how fortunate we were to have her out of Washington— I feel easier about Father & Brother   Horace telegraphed me— that they left Harrisburg for Washington on Sunday & the communications were not touched until Monday. I believe if there was no battle until yesterday the city is safe— as troops were [in] movement going up the Potomac Even the boats arriving to this place were taken by the Govr to carry troops there—[2] This all revives & comfort us— but Mother is for the first time in my memory *cut* down— I hope it is sickness & that her spirit will rise— but moans over an old age in poverty homeless & etc til it make my heart ache to an agony— Blair cheers her better than any body else   his fighting prattle & talk about his dogs turkies & etc— really touch the right chords of her heart & soothe with their loving sympathy— He is perfectly well— So am I— had no head ache & can sleep sitting my chair by Mothers bed— & feel today as well as ever in my life— Mother slept most of last night & is now dozing— so I hope with rest Good care & good news— she will revive & be herself again Horace is very attentive to us & is really a kind friend— sends papers & is ready to serve us in any way possible Yr affecate Lizzie

　　1. Grant had removed most of the troops from Washington for the offensive in Virginia, but the forts surrounding the capital were quite strong.
　　2. Grant quickly sent reinforcements to Washington. On July 11, Horatio Wright's Sixth Corps arrived to counter Early.

　　　　　　　　　　　　　　　　　　　　　　Cape May　　July 16, [1864]
My Dear Phil　To our surprise Father arrived here to dinner yesterday He was en route north again on some business Agwsfsnlw[1] but hearing mother was sick at Aunt Becky's came here immediately & is more full of rejoicing over her escape, than over that of his house— He left Washington Wednesday— in the Baltimore with Minna & children— Mary Blair & do— David Porter & family Sumner & some others— they came to Perrysville & reached Phil Thursday eve— in the special Car with Mr. Chase with whom he had some good natured chat They seemed to have had a merry time en route
　　Our loses by the Rebels are so small that can never think of the invasion without a sense of escape & thankfulness—[2] All the crops were left just as they found them　that is at least $6000— to us— then all the horses are saved but two thro Mr. Harvey the servants saved the rest— the mules— Jesups poney & Woodys & Blairs donkey— cart & harness & the light farm waggon gone— the book terribly scattered— papers— ditto— All the servants ran away leaving their clothes— found the lawn strewed with dirty rags & every article of clothing gone Thanks to Minna Andrews too　Mother sent his clothing to the city & she packed them back instead of next door as she might have done— & where she sends both Wood & Andrew— but they have lost their house— which cost them $14000 & the water work & out houses & grounds improvement makes a loss to them of $20,000—
　　Our Grapery was untouched & not a tree or shrub was injured & on the mantle in Library where a lately received picture of Genl Dix was put just below the Genl's figure is written— "A confederate officer, for himself & all his comrades, regrets exceedingly that damage & pilfering was committed in this house, before it was known that it was within our lines, or that private property was imperilled— Especially we regret that Ladies property has been disturbed, but restitution has been made, & punishment meted out as far as possible. We wage no ignoble warfare for plunder or revenge, but for all that

men hold dearest, & scorn to retaliate in kind the unmentioned outrages committed on our homes by federal Straps— of which the burning of Govr Letcher's,[3] Col Anderson's & hundreds of private houses, are but light matters in comparison with the darker crimes that remain untold—" On a photograph of Annie Mason[4] (Genl Buels stepdaughter) was written— "A confederate officer has remained here until after eleven— to prevent pillage & burning of the house— because of his love of (Emma Mason Mrs Wheaton)— who found in this home good & true friends—"

Mrs Beale told Father that the officers who ate at her house told her that John Breckinridge perserved Silver Spring— & made more fuss about things there than if they had belonged to Jeff Davis— It had been his place of refuge & of rest— & etc— Thus bread cast upon the waters came back to us to which I can say they were welcome in return for their good offices— Blair is well but dont like to part with the Donky & ponies is in a hurry to go home— All send love   Yr affecate Lizzie

Father left Mr Smith in charge of the house & farm & my conclusion is that if our own Army had swarmed over us & encamped there for two days— it would have been quite as bad for us— Consequently we may well congratulate ourselves— Mother has brightened up & this morning Father says looks better than she has done for some months past— We will not return home for a week or ten days more— on Mothers account who the doctor thinks ought to bathe for a more as soon as strong enough— this may detain us two weeks longer from home—

Mary Blair came down from Phil last night so we have quite a family party here which makes it more cheerful for us all   I got a very kind note just now from Mr Cameron assuring me that affairs were all getting right— I shall answer it today— Father says the President went to the front where the shot & shell fell thick around him— the battle was fought along the ridge from Munsons house— by Cousines Colclazers— Moorings Up to Wilsons where they left their dead & wounded— not in our house as reported but at Graves & that village— They were all removed to Hospitals— Silver Spring was HdQts— & they left the demijohns of good Old Bourbon empty under the table— & cleaned out the larder & poultry

1. Private cipher.

2. On August 5, EBL described the scene of their home: "that blackened ruin [Montgomery's home] on the hill before us— the empty Barn— lawn cut— Six thousand dollars will not cover all of Fathers losses & would not now replace them."

3. Robert P. Letcher had been governor of Kentucky (1840–44).

4. Annie (Emma) Mason was the daughter of Margaret Hunter and George Mason. Her mother's second husband was Don Carlos Buell.

Cape Island   July 18, 1864
My dear Phil   Father left us this morning as the Dr. said last night that mother was only nervous— not sick save an oppression of bowels—I feel this mental depression   tis something so unlike herself that I am more anxious about it than if she had more positive sickness physically. This morning I went to her bed when Father started off— at six— & she began to talk of the bad condition of our home— "so many dead buried near our front gate— & others on Mary Blairs place— said she could never go there again until it was all made to look as it did when she left it I proposed to go & have all her orders executed— She "would not part with me— would never have any peace if I left her alone—" with nobody but Betty & Blair & etc— So it is all uncertain what we will do— but as she is really bitter I am in hopes she will remain here until she gets stronger & then go home sometime early next week—

I have no letters from you yet— but will keep this open for a later mail— with hope of getting some letters from you. Mary Blair & her children are now with Mother & I shall go off to take Blair into the surf in which the little fellow revels coming out as red & hot whilst I am cold— & chivering & yet it has made me stronger He digs in the sand— makes forts— & fights the Rebs daily   still counts over his losses. his 20 odd young turkies is his latest grievance— as he wanted you to see them   they were so pretty & tame eating out his hands & etc—" I heard some grand music (sacred last night)— & meet daily some of my Phila acquaintance. but Mother absorbs me so entirely that I am not interested in aught else here—

Monday afternoon— I received your two letters of 8th & 9th inst by the 11 olk mail today— Left Mother after reading the newspaper to her in bed & went off to bathe— who when I got out of the water I found to my infinite surprize in the bathroom prepared to bathe— She took two breakers came in was dressed quickly & went to bed & to sleep & has waked up very bright It certainly has done her no harm The Dr. says now her tendencies are to a violent sort of rhumatism & not paralisys— Truth is he dont know— & as she has a hereditary right to both from her Father we must take the tenderest care of her

Letters from No. 4 today say a fourth amputation is to be tried to save poor Smedburgs life— Is it not the saddest case   Mrs Sands could not return to Silver Spring or Ellicott's Mills— & she with Marion are now there— & M. expects hourly to be confined— She was with Mrs Hoban— but *felt constrained* to leave from lack of room & etc If Marion can stand Smedburgs groans tis more than I can—

Mary Blair says Blair improvement in color & flesh in one week is wonderful. He is just as full of life & fun as he can be My only fear is that he is too much noticed & carassed by the boarders here— He is at home with every body— He runs away from Becky about half the time. but keeps within the limits to which I bind him— I never was stronger in my life & sleep all night & nap in the day sometimes Ever yr affectionate Lizzie

Cape Island   July 19, 1864

My dear Phil   I received yours of the 16th last night— those you sent me— between the 11th & 16th are still finding their way here— I read Blair what you said about reprisals. "Bully for Papa—" was his answer I think the regulation 100 is the best way— but Blair is quite sore under his losses as the little chap really loved his pets— & they were his playmates & chief occupation—[1] Mother went to dinner— yesterday slept well last night— so her unexpected bath did her good in spite of the Dr.'s opinion to the contrary— She is better decidedly in every way

Father got a letter from Mr. Cameron who proposes to meet him here some day this week I shall forward it to him in New York I must write to him & let him know that Father has gone to New York He is anxious about the election in Pa—[2] thinks this gubenatorial contest a very doubtful one—

Mother says she intends to claim of you a piece of sheeting which you promised her when home in March like that I have— We have sheets towels— & all things under the weight of a mattrass to replace in Silver Spring— All things wearable *usable* in a household were taken off— except some blankets which escaped I suppose because in the room used by Breckenridge— There were quite a number put in a pile in the room which he occupied when he stayed there to be washed— these from what I hear are left & are very good ones Mother has even her best blankets washed once a year— & these are her best ones

Henry told Father that Olivia would not return to the Country— if we gain as much in her loss as we did in that of Vincent— it will be the value of several servants— I am afraid Henry will follow her— altho he did advise Father when he bought her not to buy her if they put her in the jail to extort a large price for her— she has always been a poor bargain but Henry has made up for all her defects & in these late difficulties he has shown great fidelity— & would have saved every horse but for Mr Harveys interference as is he saved all that was left in his charge— Blair has gone to fish in the Inlet with Becky tis perfectly safe he is very hearty Ever your devoted Lizzie

1. On July 17, EBL wrote: "Blair wants to go home bears his losses sorowfully— a rebel shot his Dog— & stole his Donkey Cart— & Harness— & feels like an injured boy." On July 22, she reported that she had watched Blair "gathering up a huge quantity of pebbles large whole ones— I said you cant take all of them home Blair 'Please let me Mama I want them to put on old Ned's grave I know Uncle Dick has buried him & he was a brave old dog— fought the Rebs to the last—."

2. Because Pennsylvania had been McClellan's home state, it was anticipated that the election would be close, and it was.

Cape Island   July 20, 1864

My dear Phil   Yesterday I went to the Post office & made search for your missing letter At first the PM gave me the same reply— "All your letters as they
come are sent directly to you Mrs. Lee—" Well I said let me see all your letters
for The Lees & Ls— may be there are others here by that name— He did so—
& the only Lee among the whole package of L's was yours containing the copy
in your's of the 14th These people showed intense stupidity—

Our fat friend[1] smart as he is was among the rest   he never would have
let some new mattrasses & books & etc about which I know something, get
burnt up if he had known the force of the invasion— They were all taken by
surprise & saved by the mercy of God— or as you may call it— accidental
arrival & embarkation of the New Orleans troops But tis the policy of these
friends of ours *not* to admit this— & to pass over things as all prearranged &
etc— So let it pass— it may be a good thing for the Cause that this phase can
be presented—

This same person was mighty far from taking I think proper views of the
matter when I present it as the news from Secesh quarters & tried to keep
Father from going north— Father says— now I did not urge it sufficiently—
I did so enough to induce first him & then Brother to go over to the White
House & whilst I waited for the return of both I had to call up considerable
self control not to resent the fun poked at my timidity when in real danger   I
believe my courage is as good as any of the men in the room— so I had the
courage to be quiet— But we must be patient— Especially as Mrs. Lincoln
said once to me— with these "little brief authority people—" She was speaking to me as one connected permanently with the Govt— I remarked in such
things tho' they seemed to go wrong to her & my vision Still I believe it would
all work out right for the Country— & for those truly honest & earnest to
serve it— She was particularly mad that day with Stanton & Chase—

We have a report here that Sherman had captured Atlanta—[2] I hope tis
true— I got a letter yesterday dated 10th inst from Nelly— Asking question
abt coming here— I posted her with every detail & hope she will come—
Mother is now out riding with Mary Blair & children— She picked Blair up on
the beach— they went fishing together yesterday & make a very gay party—
Blair however has a facility of knowing people & is never at loss for amusement
There was an excitement on the beach last evening— 3 war steamers by in
sight & one fired several guns Of course everybody thought the one ahead was
the Florida   no colors on any of them except the last— Your affecate   Lizzie

1. EBL derisively referred to Fox as "Fatty."
2. Not until September 1 did the rebels leave Atlanta.

Philadelphia   July 24, 1864

Dear Phil   I am afraid I have not kept this Sunday as a day of rest— for after church I went to see all the family circles fine houses & called to see if Mrs Barnes was in town   found the house shut & my ring not answered So went off with the conclusion that they were out of town— did all this & reach this house in time for a 2 oclk dinner when Mother & Father joined me— They are staying with the Dicks— who are very kind. They still talk of remaining here the rest of their days but when the business season comes they will again their flight west— I find them both looking well—

We are very anxious about the battle before Atlanta   Frank was with McPher wing of the Army which was the one engaged & tis reported here that Genl McPherson is killed[1]   it must have been a very desparate fight & it will be no small relief to hear of Frank We go home tomorrow & as there is still great talk of repeating the Raid we must hurry— it was found not so profitable— the long postponement of the draft is considered a great mistake[2] Still I hear of people seeking to find a substitute before the draft as one will be an expensive luxury after that— It now costs 800 to get one— So the poor will have to go which will make an unruly arm— There is very little volunteering— now so says Horace—

I find Aunt Becky well but failing sadly in memory— it is sad because she conscious of depressed when with people about it— is very silent— with Father & Mother— but annoyed with me for going home so soon   remembers things which touch her feelings by asking about it over & over again

Blair is off feeding the squirrels his old resource when in this City— Becky is off to church as cross as ever so says Blair   I dont speak to her save to give an order— All quite well   had no desire to talk over the trip to New York with Father however he seems in good spirits— Ever yr devoted Lizzie

1. On July 22, James B. McPherson was killed during Hood's unsuccessful assault on Sherman's lines before Atlanta.

2. There had been decided opposition to the draft, as witnessed by the riots in New York during the previous summer, but the terrible cost in lives of Grant's campaign necessitated another. Lincoln called for a draft of 500,000 men to begin on September 5.

Washington   July 26, 1864

Dear Phil   We reached here No 4 comfortably about 6 olk yesterday & there I was soon handed your letter & the correspondance Naval Laws— After I put Blair to bed— supped next door with my Parents who had to sleep there as they had ordered their entire bedding to be taken out to Silver Spring where Mother said she must go last night— but she met the servants in here & only got them to go out last night & we are to go this morning as soon as I go buy something to eat—

Yesterday just as I was stepping into the carriage to go to the Depot I got an envelope from Horace from his business place containing a letter from you & the $50 check— I have refunded him the 150— I advanced $50 to Betty— Father was quite sufficient escort to the Cars & Aunts waiter relieved him from trouble about the baggage indeed Jacob is an excellent servant & makes far better arrangements than Horace— & so I dispense with taking him out his business & routine whenever I can do so— &

Last night I met Fatty it cost me a struggle to be civil but I was— & I would have written to you after coming in here but felt I might say out too much of the bitterness of my resentments—[1] He insisted that there never was but 3 or 4 thousand Rebels in Md— I gave him a Coast Survey report of the number of camps between Batchelors & Silver Spring— which it made over ten thousand there & I said nothing save to remark— Batchelors was an exact Englishman & self made man of business habits & wealth

After a sober night of thought & without any chance of consulting with Father my own conclusion is— to drop the discussion— Your whole conduct was right— & my faith is so implicit in right doing that no amount of malice can eventually rob you of the approval & reward of good men tis evident— Mr W was not disposed to censure by his talk— & that the letter was the result of subsequent influences This is a plain as anything can be— I shall be just as quiet as I advise you to be— Father read the correspondence but we had Mrs. Sands in the room & he made no comments whatever— but I thought I saw even resentment in his manner to F. & who he almost asked to leave the room— & in divers ways was marked— so when he slurred him about Franks letters— I made the amende by reading them aloud to him & Mother— & shall tell Father what I say to you— possess your soul with patience— Resentment may hurt him— but ourselves too & tis our duty to forbear even in self justification— Mother & I are both of that opinion in Franks case also— Father is full of letter to set the public straight about you & his own son— I have as yet urged anything but a simple short vindication of you— but he replied I dont see why you would deprive me of the pride of identifying myself with my two fighting men—" I have much to do today So will say now good morning Yr devoted wife Lizzie

I had repaid H[orace] the 50 he sent me so— In money I stand $100 in pocket, when I can get my advance to Betty from Father— Your check is not yet drawn— I had enough besides to pay my way home & buy some things for Blair In Phil— & still have some change in pocket—

Mr D. still waits— looks very badly. Capt Smedburg has gone home— I find my premises want cleaning up sadly. so I'll have plenty to do for some days to come— but shall go home with my Parents today—

1. On July 13, when SPL thought Washington was endangered by Jubal Early's attack, he had steamed up the Potomac from Hampton Roads. Severely chastised by the Navy Department for disobeying his orders, Lee returned to his post. Both Lee and his wife were certain that Montgomery Blair's brother-in-law G. V. Fox, who maintained that the capital was not seriously threatened, had been responsible for the reprimand.

Silver Spring   July 27, 1864

Dear Phil   Yesterday started with me by an early letter to you— then picked out my clothing for the Country bought marketting & precious little before starting   Becky came up with a hard look & inquired if I had made arrangements for her to leave on the 1st of the Month To which I replied promptly but quietly— I had— which is true for I wrote to get Catherine— but I missed seeing her— but I shall have no difficulty about servants— Ned takes good care of Blair when there are no other children here to attract him away from him   to soften the parting with Becky I told him he was now seven years old & he must not have a nurse any longer— & tried to get his boyish pride to help his affectionate sorrow— Still he takes— without saying anything— & is troubled about it—

His meeting with his old dog was sweet— you never saw great joy— & I have seen Blair stretched full length on his back— the dog hid & did not return here for over a week— Genl Breckinridge recovered Blairs donkey & put it Jimmy Byrnes care from whom it was stolen   Ned Byrnes went into the Fort & fought— came out in the battle & his display of courage is the talk of the soldiers Mr. Smith says 15 or 16 of them spoke to him— of his courage & skill as a sharpshooter with my Fathers rifle— After such scenes it strike with wonder to see him whistling along joyously— with Blair in whose eyes he is now a great hero as he is in the eyes of some older men— Andrew says that the soldiers say that he killed some five or six Rebel sharpshooters   I do not like to think of anybody so young taking the lives of so many men of course I say this to you only— But this young gardener of mine is no common boy & has shown marked character from infancy—

As to the House tis in marvellous good condition— The books the pictures mirrors parlor furniture— is unharmed— the bureaus closets— house linen eatables & wearables are all gone— This desk was much cut & pulled but they could not force the lock & is the only place looked which was not forced open   it had all my stationery which I had out here— (not much)   I lost nothing but a piece of cotton which had forgotten— & some little trashy things— I left in my drawers— the bureau can be repaired & is not at all defaced—

They took my photographs Blair's blanket & Becky's, & left every other Blanket in the house— took belonging to the Servants & all of their clothing— Fathers & Andrew Blairs— Tore Betty letters dresses— & bureau &

everything is badly used— her bed & mothers were used & badly— whereas mine, Blairs— & all others in the house were found perfectly clean & precisely as we left them hanging over the foot of the bed   I cannot tell what papers are gone until I see [1]

I am very busy putting things away— & looking up things sent by Genl Breckinridge to the Wilsons & those taken away by Mrs Beale— the trees & lawn are untouched   the servants are the greatest sufferers— Yr affecate Lizzie

All the kitchen utensils have gone to Dixie

1. Martha, wife of John T. Barnes, lived near Silver Spring. On September 21, EBL reported that "Mrs. Barnes says a man who was called Col ordered it to be burned & said at the time— 'if he had his way he would not leave a Blair a shed to live under as the whole "*set*" root & branch had done the South more harm than any other "set of people." ' "

Silver Spring   July 30, [1864]

Dear Phil   All of yesterday was spent in gathering up & re-arranging the letters & business papers which massed in confusion dire— up in the garret   Genl Jacksons letter Mr. Van Burens & other prominent men are all safe as far as I can remember the packages look untouched & But the business papers— deeds & etc are torn & gone some are just as you endorsed & fixed them

Uncle Dick covered with a pile of brush one of Blairs setting turkies just in the middle of the lawn— & strange to say she was not much disturbed & has hatched 6 turkies & as many chickens over which he was in a great glee— With Grandma & as to the chickens "they are *gamer* for being hatched by a turkey" so with his dog Ned & these new pets he is quite consoled for his other losses—

We had a letter from Frank— "3 miles from Atlanta—" in fine spirits & he sends his telegraph sent after the battle of Friday saying they were well & safe—" he describes their march to Atlanta as the most trying of all the marches he has yet had—[1] But writes in great satisfaction over the change of purpose & of commanders on the part of the Rebs—

I think if this weather continues many days hot & dry Mother ought to the sea— One cannot get her to be careful   for two days she has resisted even to admit she needed remedies— but today she gave up— & is very feeble tonight from prostration— I bought her a saddle as the Rebs took both of our ladies saddles, cut off the pommels & left them—

Father has convinced himself and *some others* that there was an Army of Rebs here of over 20 thousand their lines extend over 8 miles & their camping fires if made for five or 6 men would count up 15 thousand— so tis a plain case of luck on *our side* but that hurts *our side* & tis governmental *parol* to say there was only a raiding party of 3 to five thousand— so be it   Your devoted Lizzie

1. Frank led the Seventeenth Corps of Sherman's army in the first battles of Atlanta on July 22. Although casualties were extremely high, neither side could dislodge the other, and the siege of Atlanta began.

Silver Spring   July 31, 1864

My dear Phil   Yesterday finished my labors among the papers & piles of rubish in the garret   you have no idea of what a melee filled those rooms All Bettys fineries all torn into ribbons   poor Marion's & Mary Riggs added to some of Apos Mothers— & my rag bag Blairs old toys— forming the compound with some Maps you had sent some of which they carefully took off— Others torn into atoms & the letters of everybody were mixed However they are now all separated & put in bundles— the useful taken out of the trash & Saturday night found this house in the same good order we left it in Saturday night three weeks ago but alas!! minus some thousands in the way of valuables—[1]

Bernie was here today— She sent Jim down here for Ned when she heard the Rebs were at Rockville when he got to Graves' store (Talbots now)[2] he was taken prisoner about 10 olk Monday as they stopped at the spring a shell fell among the trees east of the Spring killed one man & wounded another— they then brought him to the house where there was a perfect saturnalia in progress— One man dressed up in Betty riding habit, pants & all— another in Fathers red (Jessies) velvet wrapper & took a dance others came out of the house in Andrews uniform & clothing— Fathers old coats of all sorts & with one of the Demijohns of Naval whisky bought last fall by Father & they had a great frolic. others went on rummaging & robbing until five olk when up rode Genl Early & Genl Breckinridge— Jim says they were in a great rage with some officer commanding here for stopping here   Genl Early said "You have ruined our whole campaign—" if you had pushed in the Forts this morning at 8 olk we could have taken them— Now they have reinforcements from Grant & we can't take them without immense loss perhaps tis impossible—

Genl Breckinridge began to curse some soldiers with things taken out of the house—[3] the piano cover for a horse blanket— Made him give it & put him in irons & sent for another Regiment to guard the House   Genl Early said tis no use to fret about one house when we have lost so much by this proceeding—" Then Genl B replied— this place is the only one I felt was a home to me on this side of the Mts—" So Jim took this turn of the talk to let him know this was his home too— & step forward to these Generals said he lived here until & that he would like now to go to his Mother who was alone   John Breckinridge then asked him about all of us where we were— & when we left— when Jim told them— John remarked "that accounts for their leaving everything exposed in this way" He sent Jim home with Blairs donkey (Jim asked for it & went to the lane & got it & he started Jim off on it— but he had scarce been home an hour about midnight when five soldiers stopped

& demanded the Grey horse & followed Jim where it was hid & there was poor Jack too— he was seized & again carried off— Jim took Old Ned home too— but he slipped his collar & was not to be seen for a week— Jim was kept here as a prisoner from 10 olk in the morning until 9 in the evening

Andrew started home yesterday evening— the most reluctant boy to go— he was so intensely happy here— He found it what the Rebs say Maryland is compared to Va— "paradise—" Mother is better & the rest all well   Yr affecate Lizzie

1. On August 19, EBL commented: "Strange how zealous we are repairing damages— with so little security for the future—."

2. Graves's store was at Sligo.

3. A cousin, John Breckinridge had been a frequent guest at Silver Spring in the 1850s.

18

"Justice will be meted in time to those who fill soft places & malign men who perform heroic duties—"

August 6, 1864

LINCOLN, PESSIMISTIC OVER HIS CHANCES of winning a second term, bowed to the demands of the Radicals and sacrificed the Blairs: Montgomery resigned from the cabinet and Lee was removed from command of the North Atlantic Blockading Squadron. With the Blairs out, Frémont abandoned his bid for the presidency, and hope rose that Lincoln could be reelected. For the Lees it was a bitter blow. From his first days in command on the Atlantic, Phillips had persistently urged an attack on Wilmington; he was replaced just as serious planning got underway. Distant from the political scene, Frank fought gallantly in the battles around Atlanta.

Silver Spring   August 1, 1864
Dear Phil   Yesterday by the merest ill luck I failed to get my letters— Brother came to breakfast ere the mail was opened & when Charles called at his house for it Daniel had locked up the house, & altho he waited sometime for it— still obeying general orders never to be away from meals & have Mother doing his work— he came to attend to the tea table— he is an excellent servant and is invaluable to us now that we are so short of servants— for as yet I have no one in Beckys place— or Olivia & I think I shall get one person to fill the gap made by the two. Charles wife does all the washing & dairy work— I am house maid pro tem— & I hope to get Catherine. She decided first to come then wanted time to think over it & I am looking for another in case she refuses How I would like a french woman— As I have to render an acct to Mary Riggs of the plundering done to her goods stored away here I think I'll ask her if she cannot find me a woman who talks good french & can do the sewing— or chamber work— in either vocation I could make her look to Blair & talk to him— Mother says now she prefers a white person as an inmate so that when I leave here for a night I can feel she has some one to attend to her or to save her waiting on others   I find Becky has been very rude to Mother refusing to wait on her

Brother told us of an affair which may illustrate *some people* the day after his House was burned Mary Blair & Mr. Ricd Cutts[1] met him at the foot of his steps & condoled with him when he replied "I am not conscious of a sensation about the house— my every feeling is swallowed up by indignation at the imbecility & treason of these men to whom this Capitol has been a peculiar charge & by whom it has been exposed to insult—" Next day— Halleck reports the remark to the President complaining of the insult to him in the presence of one of his aids & said he hoped the P— would dismiss Mr. Blair from the Cabinet— To which the P. replied "Mr. Blair is a man of very decided opinions & I suppose has as much right to express them as any body else—" & then intimated that he was not the person to call him to account for *such* opinions of individuals & therefore did not say anything to Brother about it— Another person reported the affair to Brother who says he did not mention Hallecks name— but thinks he knew his own cap— so put it on— Cutts put the name in perhaps & thereby like all tatlers gets his share of condemnation— So the thing stands for 10 days

I have been busy cutting and fixing house linen & working over the details of this house— & yet with a terror at my heart of another visit from the Rebs which I do not think improbable— I would not be surprised if Lee evacuated Richmond & came en masse here to die out with effect if the rumors are true of the destruction & capture of Petersburg

Brother went off at daylight so Ive no chance today for this letter— the loss of five mules reduces our movements to the carriage horses— even mother's riding horse is helping to get out the Rye which is all the feed left— as the Rebs cleaned out the corn crib— One of the cows came back— she was hard to drive broke a rope— & got home at last— She is the *muley* cow so we have two cows— now— & all the hogs got back too—

Tuesday Aug— Got your letter— the "Steerage Sneers dont hurt me when fired from an ambuscades of grey beard[2] but the other points I confess have made me more angry than I have been for some years Indeed I had hoped that the sobering vicisitudes of the last four years had made a calmer woman— But I hope a lonesome quiet Sunday has got my head clear— I shall go to my routine at the Asylum & try to work hard & cheerfully

I had a long letter from Fanny her boys are injured by the retrospective tax on tobacco & she suggests the hope that the tax may be remitted in their case as they are minors I will inquire about it & do or get done all that it is possible— but their known bad politics about which they are not prudent makes it a bad case— they save themselves— but lose their year's profit—

I told Father your message about the thousand dollars & I said you mentioned it to John—[3] He says he never needed money as he does now the immediate necessity to buy & pay for every thing except tables & bed steads has made him very hard up— I have brought our household things to their use as far as I can— but they will not consent to much of it— besides the family in the house makes the utensils needed there   I think much of robbing was done by others after the Rebs left— flat irons— tubs— are not things they are likely to take   I will write to John today about the money— as Father has a note to pay on the 7 inst of which he never spoke until this moment— Yr affectionate Lizzie

1. Richard Dominicus Cutts, born 1817, was the son of Richard and Anna Payne Cutts. He was aide de camp to Halleck.
2. The "grey beard," Gideon Welles, had written a severe letter, chastizing SPL for his dash up the Potomac to protect Washington, an action Welles thought unnecessary and unwarranted.
3. SPL had purchased a city lot from FPB in June, but no money had changed hands. On August 9, EBL reported: "Father got a note from John enclosing him a thousand dollars— this Raid has now him aground literally & he remembered your offer to pay him the thousand dollars— (which he remarked he would never need)— but you thought differently & wrote to John about it so I told Father who called upon him & his note came with Riggs among his dues there— which makes it peculiarly opportune—."

Silver Spring   August 6, 1864
My dear Phil   Yesterday I felt sure of a letter— but not getting one thought I could comfort myself with my old one so just as I was starting for home I went after it in the desk— where I put it the day I got it— On taking this reading I saw at the date Hampton Roads for the last time   I scrawled a note chat with a woful pen & came with the feeling of having a new letter—
    I was so over careful I feared to bring yr letter out here as there was so much panic about the Rebels in the upper part of the County I wanted to come to the City but the information was so vague that no one but me was frightened here & the weather so hot I scarce dared take my child to the City   I left him here & went in to the Asylum business— passing quantities of refugees & consequently I left my letter & would liked to have had my people behind the Forts too but as they were not I felt I must come after them
    I had not been as well as usual & what is strange the excitement of that day— made a favorable change in my condition— & tho heat & fatigue was the last thing to recommend for my condition still it took me out of a mental rut braced & excited my nerves & Ive been getting better ever since tonight even after a "*town* day" to use Blairs phrase— I am nearly well after a seige of trouble   I have never had the like since our summer in the Mountains— which seemed to give me a new lease on life—
    I left poor Marion in travail—[1] her condition touched me very much— She said I hoped this pain of the body would obliterate that of the mind at least for the day— but it does not & her sorrow was more than ever accute—

I hope her child will be spared to her— the occupation will be of great help to her altho the very charms joys of its infancy will make her sigh for its fathers sympathy in that pleasure above all others— I know well that heart ache— for we [you] have been more than half of Blairs life away from us— & now the infancy of it is past at 7 years old— & he has been so lovely that I have grieved that you have seen so little of him but tis his delight to be Papas big boy— & I fondly pray you may guide & enjoy his boyhood for you love *boys* more than Babies & that has often cheered me

Franks letter to Apo after the battle of the 21st & 22nd—[2] dated 24th came today— twas the "bloodiest" he ever witnessed— & says "I ordered on the 21st a charge for the purpose of carrying a high hill which commanded the whole position commanded by my corps— the hill was carried & held altho' the enemy assaulted us 3 times or 4 times to recover it On the 22nd made a flank movement & attempted to cut off my comand which occupied the extreme left of the whole Army— Fortunately the 16th Army Corps had received orders to take up a position on my left & was moving in my rear at the moment that the enemy opened his attack I had no cavalry on my flank & no means of discovering his movement on my flank & rear until the enemy came upon me in force with the whole of Hardees Corps consisting of four Divisions— Cleburnes, Maurys (formerly Cheathams Walkers & Bates'—[3] The 16th Corps received the attack of the two last named Divisions, which would otherwise have fallen directly upon me in rear— & Cleburne & (Cheathams old Division Commanded by Maury) came upon my two Divisions on the flank & rear passing through the wide interval between my left & the right of the 16th Corps. while a direct attack was made on me in front & the 15 Army Corps upon my right from the direction of Atlanta, by a part of Hoods[4] Old Corps now commanded by Genl Cheatham— My troops were entrenched but being attacked from the rear they were compelled to get on the other side of their breastworks & when attacked from front they had to jump over again & fight from the rear of our works; this continued from about eleven until four oclk— in the afternoon— the enemy assaulting six or seven times in front & rear with the greatest courage & tenacity—

A little after four oclk I changed my line so as to connect it with Genl Dodge[5] of the 16th Corps— giving for this purpose a part of the ground I held in the morning— Dodge repulsed the Divisions that attacked him & held his ground After my line was changed so as to fill up a part of the interval between the 16th Corps & my command— the enemy again attacked me with great fury & pushed up to the breast works on the top of the Hill we had Captured on the 21st & held the ground in front hardly ten paces distant until dark— the fighting was kept up in this position all night long, in a languid & feeble way but in the morning before dailight they fell back to the position held by my extreme left in the morning—

I lost about one fourth of my whole command in the two days fighting in killed, wounded & prisoners— but the enemy must have lost 3 to my one their loss in front of the 16th & 15th Corps was also very heavy— we buried & gave up to the enemy in front of my line which we held 1000 dead bodies before they retreated they carried off their wounded & their officers who were killed & there are still many of their dead lying inside of my picket lines which I had no time to deliver up during the flag of truce for that purpose— I never saw such severe fighting in my life & if it had not happened that the 16th Corps was marching in my rear at the moment of the attack my whole command would have been overwhelmed by the superior numbers & cut off entirely from the rest of the Army. Genl McPherson was killed about three hundred yards from me— & I had two general officers Gresham & Force[6] belonging to my corps severely

I sent you a dispatch yesterday saying that we were all well & hope you will get it in time to feel no disquietude about Andrew & myself!! Now that is the man that Secesh of the Tribune stripe are attacking here— Surely tis by faith we are upheld thro such trials— justice will be meted in time to those who fill soft places & malign men who perform heroic duties— There is a large force above us— & movements which we trust will result in our protection— so I slept with both eyes shut last night Ever your devoted   Lizzie

1. Marian Sands Dutton was in labor and delivered a son, Arthur, hours later.

2. William T. Sherman's Union army faced Hood's Army of Tennessee outside Atlanta on July 21 and 22.

3. Confederate Gen. William Hardee's corps included divisions led by Maj. Gen. P. R. Cleburne, Brig. Gen. George Maney (formerly B. F. Cheatham's division), Maj. Gen. W. H. T. Walker, and Maj. Gen. William B. Bates.

4. On July 18, John Bell Hood replaced Joseph E. Johnston in command of the Army of Tennessee.

5. Maj. Gen. Grenville M. Dodge led the Sixteenth Corps of Sherman's army.

6. Maj. Gen. Walter Q. Gresham led the fourth division of Frank's Seventeenth Corps and was wounded on July 20. Maj. Gen. Manning F. Force of the first brigade of Mortimer D. Leggett's division was wounded on July 22.

Silver Spring   August 8, 1864

Dear Phil   Yesterday was spent at Church & Asylum— & looking at the new baby at No 4[1]   Blair thinks if we had been in town that night it might have been given to us— he then asked me if Marion would love it— I said Oh very much— Well she wants comforting— for she was so sorry when she was here so Mama it may be just sent for her—" This talk Marion thought was wisdom from a Baby— She looks prettier than ever before— & has a tranquil subdued look that was beautiful   I never felt more for her than yesterday with her fatherless babe by her & No husband to rejoice over it with her

On my return from church I met Genl Grant who recognized me more promptly than I did him we chatted 15 minutes Said he had been above us— I told him I knew that, last night & had slept soundly from a new sense of security— he said he has just received a telegram from Genl Butler telling of the retaliatory burning of Seddons house—[2] I said yes— My Brother mentioned that out home & with regret "In which I agree with him said the General— & I fear I have misled Genl Butler by making some comments about the care with which we had guarded Seddons house—" I said it seemed to me to degenerate war when made on the homes of women children & things nonessential— "You are right Madam & I will issue a general order on the subject" was his rejoinder—

When I got home I found Gus here— he referred to my talk & terror about the invasion it seems— that Genl Howe[3] came & made the report that there was only three thousand— when Siegel had retreated & report the *true* state of things— for which he was removed & Genl H— put in his place for his false report— He based his opinions on those of the War Dept— I intimated the Navy Dept ought be self relying— & that my report was true— I did not follow out the similarity between the Depts— Mr Wells was here too with Mr. Faxon they went off in the grounds to look at the Rebel "*traces*—"[4] & I had not much chance to talk with them as I was tired out from the long day in the City— but I asked them to stay to tea & gave them a good supper which they ate heartily & felt I had acted out fully the law of doing good to those who act dispitefully & etc—

All these things are settling down into to but one big feeling with me which Blair's birthday of tomorrow commemorating his seventh year & the fourth since we broke up for *this cause* I want you home— & every thing else is small to that— As the old darkey said we have lost a great deal of good time fun Old Billy is remembered by that one speech only— All by me Father & Mother send love Yr affecate Lizzie

1. Marion Sands Dutton gave birth to her son Arthur at EBL's Washington home.

2. On August 7, EBL commented: "One thing I know Genl. B[utler] would not have been so zealous if he had owned a house in Maryland—."

3. Gen. Albion P. Howe commanded the Artillery Depot and the Offices of the Inspector of Artillery at Washington from 1863 to 1866.

4. Others came to view the damage, as EBL reported on August 21: "There are sometimes 15 & 16 hacks full of people at the Spring— & wandering all over the place to see what the Rebs wrote— & did here & to see the Rebel graves We do not notice now the coming of carriages any more than we do at No 4— We are civil but we do not receive these visitors— Our nearness to the city makes it something like the Mr. Vernon visitors After a while the novelty will wear off & abate what is now a nuisance—." William Faxon was chief clerk of the Navy Department.

Silver Spring   August 11, 1864
Dear Phil   The excessive heat is the universal complaint I feel it by sympathy only thro Blair, Mother, & Father   the latter is very prostrated from it— I rejoice to think of you in a cool healthy atmosphere & would willingly give you Blair until this heated term was past— I never saw anybody as much affected by sea air as he was— & feel now that he would have been sick if I had not taken him to the Seaside   he is well & sprightly & eats peaches— corn everything with a fine appetite

I read yesterday Dalghrens letter about his son Ulrich[1] it will not add to the reputation of the Admiral as a man of taste— tis poorly written & with such a fine subject you feel vexed almost, that he should belittle it with such reiterated twaddle—

There is not a day passes that a new cases of suffering does not come to light— I do not know a single poor man in this neighborhood whose house & garden horse cow & pigs have not all be taken even Bill Gittings[2] was "cleaned out." who has been always so hot Secesh Whilst Riggs— Wilson Birch[3] Beale— & etc have had only their hay forage eaten & the eatables grown by the families— Riggs lost one ox— all his fine blooded cattle was untouched— Our hay was taken to Wilsons to feed Secesh Headquarters horses— but no poor man escaped   Mrs. Jones[4] had nothing left in her house but her bedstead & cupboard— Mrs. Cook—[5] & everybody of that class fared alike   no matter what their politics   this added to the drought makes me look forward to the winter with real anxiety for these poor people—[6]

Many of the men volunteered to fight in the forts but were not allowed to do so— except a few who went in with the Pickets— Colclazers— Ned Byrnes & others— but Ned did [not] stay in the fort— but went after the sharp shooters— & has made a great name here among the soldiers— & people— by his heroic bearing— he is really a great comfort here now— he takes care of the grapery— goes to market makes such sales as never were made before & really is worth any two men on the place— Blair is devoted to him & takes him as a solace for Becky— follows him all day long— until 12 olk when I require Ned to bring him to the house   I am afraid of this hot sun— & he then plays in the shade about the house until five— & gives me no trouble & I think will soon learn to dress & undress himself— he wants to do this by the time you see him again so that he will be a real "*big boy*—" Ever yr affecate Lizzie

1. Col. Ulric Dahlgren was killed on March 2 during a cavalry raid on Richmond. John Dahlgren had never been one of EBL's favorites. On October 6, 1863, she described a letter from him to the Navy Department: "he takes no responsibility & asks— 'the Department' for instruction about every possible movement— it is so timidly inquisitive that it is almost funny."

2. William Gittings lived not far from Silver Spring.
3. Raymond W. Burche was a farmer near Sligo.
4. Nannie Jones was a domestic who lived near the Blairs.
5. Mrs. Joseph Cook (Martha) worked for the Lees and Blairs and lived nearby.
6. On August 18, EBL wrote: "Our old Shoemaker told Blair & Ned that he told them (Secesh) they would never get in Washington— & they had best leave Mr. Blairs house as some people out here would need him for bread to eat— This old man's boldness saved him— Genl Early is said to have told him that the women & old men of Maryland were the bravest Union people he had ever yet met— Maryland women as a general thing gave the Secesh Army a cold welcome—."

Silver Spring   August 15, 1864

Dear Phil   Father in his talk scorns the idea of Fox making any head way against you— I think now— for the first time tis thro his hair that he is *not* friendly which heretofore he has expressed so profusely to Father & Dennison— but now I think the scales have dropt— & so plain that it was rather amusing to me to see for the first since he has been here in office he was extra civil to me— At first it surprised me but when I saw Fathers hard cold look I understood it—

Father's present program is to get an official recommendation in the Annual report for a vote of thanks— when reviewing your squadron & services it can come in well— & I think it can & will be done— & Mr F not consulted or relied on as heretofore— it will be done—[1] The idea of F. being the man of influence which I suggested as thought by some has rather nettled Fathers sensibilities— He has taken considerable pains to let Mr L Mr W— & Fox too see for themselves the extent of the rebel encampments & the result is the Conviction— that Our city was saved by stupidity & slowness of the Rebs— they could have taken the Capitol— Mr. W— think on Monday without the loss of a hundred men— "God was on our side— "& dealt in mercy—" Just here & in close vicinity there must have been 12 to 15 thousand Rebels encamped—

Father tells me over & over that Mr Welles entirely & warmly your friend & tis a positive relief & a good out of evil— to see that he does not remain blind to Mr F amiable professions He says that he will make any request you may desire about a leave in Oct but at the same time he thinks your position one that you claim without any other intervention— any indulgence that suits you but still if it suits your feeling for it come this way— I am to eager for it— to trust to anybody— for you get absorbed in business & may put it off but I want to see you—

Last spring Father I thought saw things in their true light but since then I am convinced that he failed because he relied on F. who promised so profusely— & I was at fault— because I thought the Secy did not need any pushing— but Franks attitude oppressed my father & I shied from any thing that would add to his troubles & I confess that the temper of the Senate also dismayed me not a little— & when the Campaign opened I then hoped from day to day that something would turn up for our benefit— & so it went along unprofitably enough for us   I have begged father to deal with you in the utmost frankness & he suggested that twas best for him to write himself but I see that— he has left out what he meant by points with the Dept— he means replies— & *protests* to their course— If Mr. W— is made to defend it he will more than ever feel father of the folly—" these are my words but his ideas—

Your letter by the Grand Gulf has not yet reached me— this letter I am answering by the Newbern is my first line from you since you left the Roads— I took comfort in having out on the sea— during this hot weather until Mrs Sands said Saty that her husband wrote that you all were suffering intensely on the Blockade from the same thing— All the world cries out with suffering & fright over our intense drought & heat— it makes me dread winter for the poor especially those who are made destitute by the Rebels

Mother is well— Father feeble— but yr Cape wine has revived him in the last 2 days wonderfully   Blair is well— merry & sends love to you from "Your" 7 year old boy— Ever your affectionate Lizzie

1. On August 13, EBL had reported: "Father takes very cheerful views of our affairs— & so as he sugested— he will write them   I read the two last pages— he intimated if somebody warred on yr promotion— there were two males of my maiden name who would war on him—."

Silver Spring   August 16, 1864

My dear Phil   Your's commenced on Blair's birthday— & finished on the 12th inst reached me last night— evening— rather at 5 olk— All you say about Fatty is carefully kept to myself & you may see except in the letter via New York I have been as careful in what I write save in some nom de guerre With Father even I say what I fear is the case & he is silent— but of late sees things in their true light— We had a long talk about things yesterday again— & I *cannot* explain by letter the cause for our keeping at this time quiet about everything[1] There has been the meanest attacks on Frank only equalled & surpassed by those on you in the New York papers— but sorely as Father is tempted to refute by official data— in the case of the battle of the 20, 21 & 22st— Yet it is thought best to sit in silence— Why you will not imagine— until I see you—

The weather has been such that I have been but rarely to the city & then I went to get bread pans— & such like necessities as knives & etc & I thought at first of taking some of ours— but such now cost 15 & 20 dollars— & I knew those for 12 & 10— would pass muster here— & care such as I like is never taken here of anything— & you must also remember that I may be sometimes

1st Leut— but am never Captain— however I have bought a few towels no sheets yet— or blankets & just get along with as few things as tis possible to live comfortably with Henrys Dicks— & Nannys wardrobes had to be all refitted & that with just enough to keep clean I have but little here & every time I go I pick up something of value to carry with me— belonging here— All of Genl Jacksons letters & etc are now at No 4— & I will keep on at it—

You talk of a leave in Novr— I feared you would put it off— Still tis a real comfort to me to have something definite to look forward to— I want a holiday more than I ever sighed for one in my school days & when I feel good for nothing with these head aches which have followed me sorely of late— I grow nervous & low spirited— but with something ahead to cheer I do better— four years is a long cruise for old couples to endure I dare not murmur— but I feel my deprivations

Brother had a long letter from Frank who says he has sent a copy of official report to Apo desiring her to forward it to us—[2] I have already sent you his report of the battles of 21 & 22 to *her*— but Ill copy the report for you— also I am glad to write via Hampton Roads again that is within your command & you can be there when you think best— I suppose Ask for fast ships— have reports made by the Captains of your slow ships about them—[3] You are blamed when tis not yr fault— Now this pirate off New York[4] is also reported as an escape from Wilmington When she was built in England this year— I believe she is direct from there & all these pirates are English to hurt our shipping interest

Blair wishes Papa had some of our peaches to eat I shall put up very few sugar is too high to make it a profitable desert I have some brandy peaches I put up for you last year at No 4 but you would not accept the jars I took to you so I put these away as they are all the better for being old Father is getting hearty on the wine— & tis wonderful to see the improvement in 3 days— in him— Mother keeps well— she & Blair are devoted friends— Your affecate Lizzie

1. On August 19, EBL wrote: "I feel worried about the *seals* of my letters— it seems almost impossible to repress the fullness of my heart & tongue when I write & talk to you & generally say just what I think be it right or wrong—."

2. On September 8, EBL wrote that it had arrived: "we had a reading of Franks Report— to Sherman (which he had copied by permission for his & our fireside)— of the battles of the 20— 21— & 22— it is very fine— & blends his Corp touchingly with the death of McPherson— & entirely free of egotism— indeed tis remarkable in that respect."

3. On September 6, EBL expressed her desire to aid her husband: "I wish I could get you swift ships by croaking & I think I will do some of it if I get any encouragement but so far I have kept to myself— putting a groan into fathers ears when I could venture to utter it aloud— but his deafness increases so much that I often smile to think of yr

horror over my loud as well as long tongue— but between Neddy & Father my lungs are very much exercised— Blair can make both hear him without an effort— but I have sometimes almost screech to get a hearing—."

4. CSS *Tallahassee*, commanded by J. T. Wood, ran the Wilmington blockade on August 6 and in the next nineteen days captured or destroyed over thirty ships before returning to Wilmington.

Silver Spring   August 23, [1864]

Dear Phil   I did not write yesterday— Sunday afternoon I was taken with one my bad sick head aches & kept my bed nearly all of yesterday but I am again well & feel as if I never had been sick— I sometimes think these headaches are revenges for overtaxing my strength & then 24 hours of entire rest brings up arrears & I am well again—

Whilst lying in the dark yesterday my thoughts & dreams were with you & the more my mind dwells on it the more important I think it, that your Captains should report from each ship their fruitless chasing after the block-ade runners at least every noon— & you pile & file them in the Dept as a part of your official record— I have reason to believe that Mr. W. does *not* understand this matter— I think you might write him a *private* synopsis of the State of things based upon these reports— You remember the appeal you made in person a year ago & its effect— Make this in a kindest respectful tone— *in a private letter* to Mr. W. Now this is my own suggestion— & after much cogitation over the matter— I was grieved to have to say anything about Mrs Sands application— but one of Sand's *officers* have given her a terrible fright about her husbands life— but I told her I was sure it is an exaggeration— as his present duty is disagreeable to his officers as tis arduous to him—

Our great event is the rain— a beautiful one which gives the people some hope for their fall crops which are sadly behindhand—

Brother goes north this week when Fatty is expected here— but that you need *not* know— & his absence gives a good reason rather opportunity for the letter which I suggest Let it *not* have any approach— to the reproachful. Now this may be after you have done all this as Father said a thousand times better than I can even think of Still I have thought of little else for some weeks past Still— I want you to get the facts into a certain head proved *beyond cavil*— I hear of quotations from Capt Cushing— differing somewhat from those I heard Now this was about the depth of water on bars & obstructions—[1] over which it was asserted our monitors could go in high tide— & etc   I said nothing— but I am sure it did not accord with what I heard sometime ago—

I am not sure this is a prudent letter for it may go out of a weak head— but from the full heart of yr own   Lizzie

1. One of the problems at Wilmington was determining if the water was deep enough for the Union vessels. After taking soundings, William B. Cushing reported a

depth of fourteen feet; others claimed only eleven or twelve feet at the mouth of the Cape Fear River.

Silver Spring   September 7, 1864

Dear Phil   In spite of the easterly storm of yesterday— I went to see about the Asylum found we had run aground for money— have no debts & no money & children of the poor from the South rapping at our doors in troops— 5 were taken in from Virginia refugees— Whose fathers & Mothers died of unaccustomed work— having to forsake all to escape the Army of Jeff Davis— I come home every first tuesday of the Month heavy hearted with the tales of woe I cannot even give comfort to from the lack of house room and means

Last winter a boy was sent us from the Army— As the child of a persecuted Union man who was then in duresse vile in the South— he got to our Army this summer & has enlisted— & is now promoted to engineering as he is an educated gentleman of that turn— traced his child up & now claims him of us & the little fellow begged to stay with us as he was too little to go with his father & he did not want go to strangers— The Ladies were so worked on by the child that they kept him— but I think I must soon fill his place by one who has no father. The Ladies are full of adding to our house   Mrs Merrick is wild about it but I think the times unpropitious— & I am in hopes the Trustees will sober Mrs Merrick enthusiasm— She thinks our duty is to work hard as to comfort the litle ones as others work for the comfort of the sick & wounded soldier— She is so southern that these calls from the south excite her vastly— thats her hobby— the orphans of our Soldiers Sailors union of these we have 20—

Neddy drove me to the City— Blair went of course & handles the reins knowingly   I said you would be very proud of his care of me— then talked of how you enjoyed well behaved boys   he looked at me quizzingly— & said— Well if he had two chaps like me— he could do without you? I was of course modest & said I would ask you but he seemed ashamed of the idea & begged me not tell you that he was only teazing me— I intimated that "another chap would take my place with him— better than with you   this seemed to hurt him— I tell you all this to let you see him as he is—

Genl Quitman's pretty daughter[1] got a pass from the President to see her husband. Evy Martin is to be married in November & wishes you & I to go to her wedding— I hope to be happy that month myself at home   All well here   Ever yr own Lizzie

1. Antonia Quitman, daughter of Gen. John A. Quitman, married William Storrow Lovell, USN, in 1858. Lovell had resigned from the navy in 1859 and, when war began, joined the Confederate army.

Silver Spring   September 9, 1864
Dear Phil   Your letter about taking Wilmington is a morsel not of easy disgestion in my weakness— consequently on first reading it I did not trust myself to talk it but after a night's thinking & I did it long— for between fort Fisher & Blairs little inflamed limbs— I was duly awake— So yesterday at breakfast I said in the quietest tones— "Phil thinks Father this is a good time to carry out a plan in which he was disappointed two years ago— & I do not know how many times since— Father replied— I am glad to hear it—

After breakfast I heard him call Brother to take a letter for him & have it sent to the Navy Dept   I found he had been writing earnestly & rapidly— Afterwards— remarked to me I have seconded Phil's motion— not that I can impress it as well as he— but to let them know that *his motions* are of moment to me—

After that I went to the City to do some routine business belonging to the first of the month— When I was regaled by a letter from Capt S[ands] to Mrs. S. telling of a confab with you in which he had mentioned certain rumors to you— the first I had ever heard of them— I evinced some feeling about it & remarked that it might be the wish of some— but not of enough to effect it I mentioned it to Father & asked if he would frankly tell me what were the complaints if any had been made— he assured me to the contrary— zeal, system— & unusual executive ability & if such a thing was done they would make a friend *they needed* now an enemy— for they would deserve the condemnation of honest men for such gross injustice—"[1] But Father is intensely anxious that we should keep to ourselves the cause rather source of these matters & have no talks with anybody about it— & lectures me soundly about manner— & even the expression of my face— which he says alters with the mention of even the names of those I think unfriendly to me Of this much I am sure tho' they strike at my vitals & keep it up— Yet in all my life I am unconscious of ever doing any of the concern even one unkindness— & often when stung with these blows have choked down in my heart every utterance even of suffering— So I can leave it all in the Hands of Him who seeth all hearts—[2]

Blair is gradually getting over the irruption   Mother does not think it poison oak— I only sooth the itching— Father sticks to his tar idea— wants two barrel Father repudiates Dame Rumor entirely We are all well— A man (Mr. Thos Parker offered a balance of his shipload of coal at $14.75 it sells now at $17— I think I may take it & if it is not used— I can transfer it to the Asylum Ever affectionate Lizzie

1. On September 14, EBL wrote: "Another thing I have tried to get at— if there has been any sort of *complaint* made   I can get wind of *none of any kind Over zeal* is the worst to be said."

2. EBL reproached herself on September 14: "I ought only to be thankful in these awful times that those so precious are not only spared— but are not maimed & suffering— & we can hope that a good time is coming when we'll be together & too happy in that to care a fig about the ill will of any & that is truly now my one idea to get you home & contented in your feelings to be there."

Silver Spring   September 15, 1864

My dear Phil   Yesterday I went to the City to see after my affairs there & was glad to meet Mr. Sands— who is not near as feeble as his wife feared & seemed very bright and happy amid his family of which they have quite a gathering at No 4   I ascertained that there will be nothing done before winter about the matter which you were desired to report Nobody is ready but the officers.— "tho' they are so eager for the profits of the blockade" that they too can wait— I have heard that given as a reason why DuP— was not willing to close up Charleston— but I shall sleep without dreaming of the Cape Fear fortifications— No more troops can even be spared to Farragut to take Mobile altho it would open a near & better channel to Shermans rear— via Montgomery There is an *aid de Camp* from the front here tonight

I gave some orders about putting the house in good order— & it will be all ready to receive you by the 1st November— carpets & curtains all in place— The Sands leave Saturday & Monday the fall cleaning commences— John called Tuesday— but said they would not come thro this week— & did not say when he & Nelly would come back—

I recd yours by Capt Mitchell[1] Sunday & Capt Sands package yesterday— Blair is charmed with his gift   I gave part to Grandma The rain kept him in & they had played school   Ned teacher— Mother was amazed to hear Blair call his letters— I have so conscientiously avoided teaching him little Freeman girl[2] told Sarah Coleman— "that poor Blair Lee had a good for nothing Mother for he told her he did not know how to read or spell & she had asked him Well what has your Mother taught you then? Nothing at all! was poor Blairs confession—

I hope Gillmore wont be sent to cooperate if that work is done for tho he has some repute for shooting well yet I do not fancy his record   I do not know him— Save by his public career— which however cannot always be judged fairly by what is made public— I was going to put the box in a smaller compass but Mr. S objected. I said I could just as well by closer packing— but he insisted on my sending it just as it was They do not know its contents The wine is for you when need a *little* refreshment tis the best tonic I ever saw for Father & must be good for any body— Ever your affecate   Lizzie

1. Probably William G. Mitchell, aide de camp to Winfield Scott Hancock.
2. Isabel Freeman, daughter of Col. William and Margaret Coleman Freeman, was the same age as Blair.

Silver Spring   September 16, 1864
My dear Phil   Yesterday Blair rode to the city & back on Jenny Lind for the first time— dined with Capt Sands— who can tell you all about the little fellow He got Beckys wedding *card* & I think wanted to go see her And as Betty was going I consented & all three went off. Betty on Woods poney— Ned on little Wille's poney— & Blair between on Jenny— he was very tired & seemed quite willing to be petted & stay on the sofa for a half hour or so— on his return

Becky was married last night after a long engagement they say— but the marriage accounts for her excitability The servants say she would never got married if I had not dissmissed her— as she has put it off from year to year— but I think that tis the nature of many people to become irritable— when anxious & excited to any great degree She is a good woman & I have missed her very much in the comfort of her, every day neat & steady service— I was not conscious of how much I waited on Next week I shall get a good white girl— on whose honesty I can rely— but who will not be half as comfortable— as the double sort of servants black & white go badly together— Still I prefer white people about Blair now that he is getting larger—

We had a visit from Capt Ives who is just out of Dixie[1] he says they are nearly used up— not in eatables but men the women are bitter & gloomy used to bitter & saucy— Everybody confesses to weariness of War— Still are unflinching in their purpose to fight it out to the last— he has been there for thirteen months— is going to see his family & then— to return to the Army— the Rebs are intensely anxious to exchange These officers look well but say our men are enfeebled by the hot climate & confinement whereas theirs come back in the highest condition of vigor— so it is a good exchange for them as they are so scarce of men— & both sides have about 60,000— each— Grant is opposed to exchange—

I heard Mr. Chase had a long confab in his visit to the President yesterday after abusing him every where at the north Tis said he was going to Europe but Sumner persuaded him not to—[2] It is a comfortable fact to us— that gold has gradually gone down— ever since his resignation

I am afraid the Rebs got Franks letter which I enclosed to you I forgot how I sent it— & also fathers fancy for a barrel of tar which I think I best buy here— & give you no trouble about it— All well— Your devoted Lizzie

1. Capt. Ralph O. Ives of the Tenth Massachusetts had been captured in September 1863 and confined to Libby prison. He had been paroled and was finally exchanged on September 19, 1864.

2. On December 6 Lincoln appointed Chase Chief Justice of the Supreme Court.

Silver Spring　September 17, 1864

Dear Phil　I went to the city yesterday with the hope of greeting Nelly & John They had not arrived　I bid the Sands goodbye as they leave today— Mr. S. will give you his impressions about things I listened to all he had to say & have repeated it fully to Father who bids me say to you be of good cheer— & let nothing of this *side sort affect* you—[1] but stick to your duty patiently & weary not in well doing— That the P. told him it was impossible to spare troops to take Wilmington (now)[2] that it would require an Army— & etc— He has talked to the Secy. & has given the matter a full attention & defined your position fully & you take care of your end of this business & he will see to his end of this rope—

Mr. Fox came out here to breakfast yesterday got here just as it was over but got a good one He was full of talk about Dick Wainwrights boy who was rejected— & then Jenny Davenports son[3] was to go in his place— but Dr. Horwitz's[4] testimony on the point of poor Dicks constitution (tho thin always well & active) got him in the academy— & now Jennies boy is in the cold— over which Mr. F. did not grieve as he said "she was hurrahing all over the City for McClellan—" I prophecy she will get him *in* But it was a real pleasure to have the Wainwright boy cared for— his father really died in the service at New Orleans—[5] I know it will gratify you—

Admiral Porter called at No 4. to see Mrs Sands left civil messages for me— Says he has a good time down the Misspi has six horses— & cows & all sorts of luxuries— has given Fox Jeffs fine blooded mare He has made only one hundred thousand dollars & that is *not* enough when *other fellows* are making a half million— & etc　Sands will tell you his view of these matters—

I asked Mr. Sands about Mr Cushing who is so knowing about the waters on the bars & obstructions at Wilmington— & his account chimes just with my notion about him— His reports of his surveys are wonderful feats or Munchausens—[6] This is the only point on which *I* talked & as that was commenced in my presence here— I felt at liberty to make these inquiries of every & anybody—

Porter says it will take the *whole* power of the Navy to take Wilmington— & they must make up their minds to *lose* half they send (*ships*) over the obstuctions— He seemed very full of the matter & I suppose talks so knowing and much that the papers say he is to be sent to do the work—[7] Fox said here he was to go back to his Misspi command— Where P— *hopes* not to stay long as there is no prizes now to be got there— Father laughs at all this & says "wishes father some thoughts—" all well— Ever yr own Lizzie

I told Mr. S. that he like others magnified their prizes— of which they were lucky if they realized one half　enlighten him by yr experience— & he will talk sensibly then You may be sure of one thing— that as far as we can see into the state of things Father can keep things all right— & he has *not* the least uneasy feeling about your position— thinks the Secy heartily your his & your friend— & he gets irritated if I talk anxiously about these things to him— I talk to nobody else & he knows that— says all the time— "let Phil look to his Blockade & I shall look out for him here— & etc— He said your case was for thanks as good as any mans who had received them— & he talks confidently & affectionately about your position— Only be steady at this point in the game & all will go well— Oh how I would enjoy one good long free talk— with you— but as it is— we must abide our time— & I hope it is not too long coming I find the last four years the very longest of my life

1. Lee had received orders that he was to exchange commands with David Farragut, Lee going to the Gulf Squadron and Farragut to the command of the North Atlantic Blockading Squadron. Thus Lee was not to be allowed to fulfill his plan of leading the attack on Wilmington, North Carolina.

2. SPL had added the "(now)."

3. Richard Wainwright did not pass his physical, the doctors thinking they were doing the boy and his widowed mother a favor. When reexamined, although slender and barely tall enough to qualify, he was accepted. Richard Graham Davenport, Henry Davenport's son, entered the naval academy on September 27, one day before Wainwright.

4. Surgeon P. J. Horwitz, assistant to William Whelan at the Bureau of Medicine and Surgery, became chief of that bureau in 1865.

5. The father, Richard Wainwright, had died of malaria on August 10, 1862. He had served under Farragut on the Mississippi River.

6. Karl Friedrich Hieronymus von Münchhausen (1720–97) was a German soldier; his name became synonymous with exaggerated tales.

7. He was: On October 11, SPL learned that Porter, not Farragut, was to replace him in command of the North Atlantic Blockading Squadron.

Silver Spring   September 22, 1864

My dear Phil   Went to the city yesterday— to perserve was much relieved to find my cook more knowing on the subject than I am even— so did some & left the other half for her to do— & shall get her to go on at it—

I received a letter from Nelly yesterday saying that John had been to see them— found them so comfortably situated that he concluded not to bring them home until first She says the boys have gone to Georgetown College again They feel that Emmetsburg is so far from home Even Willie has returned there from the message he left at No. 4— I go over to College soon to see these children & take Blair— Nelly says that Goldie is engaged to Miss Prather[1] but that tis a great secret & must not be spoken of as they have no immediate prospect of marriage—

I received this morning— yours of Sept 15 & Your enclosure was most welcome— tis exactly the thing to send in & shows why & wherefore the *"failure"* if there is any in the blockade The officers have every motive in the world— to make it a success & Yankees believe in a zeal prompted by money. You are right about the fear of our getting rich I have it dished to me on all occasions—[2] when I dined yesterday with my brother when I expected to be alone with him but found a no 3—[3] In the latitude of whose birth wealth is the greatest earthly good & consequently they dont like to see any body obtain any of it they dont fancy but it is funny to see how completely M.B. softens down in manner & tone when left to himself— & how irritable & even bitter when he is in Lowell Portsmouth atmosphere but tis not well to grumble & as long as we have no greater sorrow— I can be thankful— for by simply & patiently doing our duty No harm can come of it save that of some bitterness of heart which I pray truly not to feel—

Blair has a cold & I have to watch him today— tis hard to clothe him right in midday tis hot & at night so cool & I have let him play out too late in the moonlight— When he is so merry tis a self denial on my part to stop his fun The rest are all well & I stand my perserving work stoutly— Your affectionate Lizzie

1. Goldsborough Robinson married Matilda Nicholas Prather, daughter of William and Penelope Pope Prather, in 1867.

2. As commander of the North Atlantic Blockading Squadron for two years, S. P. Lee was entitled to a share of the prize money generated by all captures of his squadron. The increasing effectiveness of the blockade meant that Lee would emerge from the war with the largest amount of prize money in the history of the U.S. navy. On September 25, EBL commented: "I enjoy getting prize money maybe because I fancy there are people who dont want us to have it— but I have always been rich that is I have had every comfort that I wanted & some to spare for the wants of others— that I call riches— Betty asked me if I did not intend to buy some gorgeous silks when I went to Phila I said no— that I had dressed like a lady all my life & if I had all the wealth of the Indies I would not enjoy dressing any better than I have always done."

3. The third person present was Montgomery's wife Minna, who was born in New Hampshire.

Silver Spring   September 24, [1864]
Dear Phil   Brother resigned his place in the Cabinet yesterday[1] & last night when Father was going to bed he handed me the following addressed to Frank who is on leave of 30 days at St Louis now— saying you will please copy that for Phil & send it to him from me— He may want to know my views of *the position* "My Dear Frank

Your brother resigned today and in consequence of a conversation I had with the President when your Brother was at Portsmouth— I called one night on the P. at the Soldiers Home to talk with him about the election— things looking then very gloomy and he had been very much depressed I told him that he might rely on my sons to do all they could for him & suggested that he ought recall you from the army to heal party divisions in Missouri & Stump the States that Montgomery would go the rounds also— and would very willingly be a martyr to the Radical phrenzy or jealousy, that would feed on the Blairs, if that would help He said nobody but enemies wanted Montgy out of the Cabinet with one exception & this man was your friend in the Frémont controversy & was also Montgomerys friend. He told me that he replied to this gentleman that he did not think it good policy to sacrifice a true friend to a false one or an avowed enemy— though he remarked "Montgomery had himself told him that he would cheerfully resign to conciliate the class of men who had made their war on the Blairs because they were his friends— and sought to injure him among the ignorant partizans of those seeking to supplant him

When Montg returned some weeks ago, he broached the conversation I had reported to him again to the President & made the same suggestion, & in some conversations & I believe letters to some of Frémonts associates intimated that he would quit the Cabinet in case Frémont would retire from the Canvass—[2] Some of those who thought this a good suggestion & were glad to get rid of Montgy pressed this matter, I have no doubt on Frémont & got him to resign on this condition & urged the President to avail himself of Montgomerys overture— & he is out—

In my opinion it is all for the best— In the first place if it tends to give a greater certainty of the defeat of McClellan, which I look upon as the salvation of the Republic, it is well The Blairs prefer a restoration of the Union to all their earthly personal interests— Again you know my greatest solicitude for M's advancement is in the line of his profession in which I would have his old age crowned with its highest honor— I know he would wear it with greatest advantage to his Country— This is my ambition for him— Lincoln I know entertains unbounded confidence in his probity, patriotism & judicial capacities— And this act of self sacrifice to him will secure his gratitude & he will be glad to shew it, especially as it will mortify those common enemies of himself & myself who worked this martyrdom—

I hope you will concur with the views I have taken The true interests of the Country require the reelection of Lincoln— McClellan whose depths I sounded lately as I wrote you in my last letter will, if elected by the Copperheads, will close with the enemy on something short of the integrity of the Union— Whatever compromise they may hatch up will end in the dissolution of the great nation of the Western Hemisphere— If Lincoln triumphs the vile Harpies that surround him will be killed off by public opinion If they remain with him to the end it will result in building up a new party of reform & the war which delivers us from Negro slavery, will be followed by a new political era which will establish a popular power in our commonalty— which will preserve our white laboring class from the fangs of a corrupt aristocracy The

Shoddy Aristocracy of the War will perish with the slave aristocracy— All well— Your affectionate father   FPB[3]

There you have the whole as it looks to us— I think I am more hurt than anybody else[4] Betty laughs at my "bruised feelings sticking out" but I confess to a proclivity for Mr. Lincolns first view— of the poor policy of sacrificing his friends to his enemies—" but I can feel— rather— *think*— it is for the best & *feel*— uncomfortable at the same time Brother went to Frederick today to make a speech— he shows a fine manly bearing & I believe it hurts only his wife & me—

Blair still suffers from a severe cold— but it would be a small matter save that it keeps me haunted with fear of croup— I received a letter from Horace & one from Sara— both urging me to go to Aunt Becky who is still feeble— My duties are all here now— Sarah says William Preston & his family are now in Montreal & she sees a great deal of them   Susan Preston a widow the second time was also with them— They are debating about staying there or going to New York to stay   Kentucky is too much in the strife for them to live there comfortably We were robbed of about 300 bushels of perserving peaches this week & this morning there is scarce one left to eat— & one of our neighbors sold his off of 60 trees for $300— so our hundred trees were a great loss— but we are a helpless set of people as you ever saw & yet I see no way of helping to a better condition— Ever your own Lizzie

1. In an effort to appease the Radicals and gain their support for his reelection, Lincoln asked for and accepted Montgomery's resignation as postmaster general on September 23.

2. Frémont withdrew from the presidential contest on September 17. Third-party votes had been significant in both 1844 and 1848, and there was concern that Frémont's candidacy might tip one or more states to McClellan.

3. On October 4, EBL reported that some of Frank's "friends were just on the eve of consumating a plan to denounce Lincoln for the resignation of Brother— when Frank arrived & succeeded in arresting the whole movement These peace men are worse trators than Jeff— '& we must go for the country first last & all the time—.'"

4. On September 26, EBL described Montgomery's reaction: "He is very cheerful not excited— in the least— Mother is however— but shows quite as gallant a spirit as anybody did— in or before Washington—."

[Silver Spring]   [September 27, 1864]

Dear Phil   You are relieved to cheat the public with the idea that Wilmington is to be taken— of which they have not the least idea Mr. W. says tis not his affair so like others we must be patient— I do not know whether you will be permitted to come to see us or not— I do hope that this will soon end our separation   Father is writing you this moment a full account of his interview with Mr. W. You told me not to trouble him but my precious husband I felt it impossible to submit to this without showing that *we* thought at least twas an unmerited thing so far as you were concerned— & consequently I thought it was right in feeling & policy to make this demonstration I think they will find no profit in it However I feel too deeply a thing like a disrespectful course to you more than any earthly thing & am only awake to one other idea— to learn & say all I can to comfort you— I shall come in tomorrow & see if they have permitted you to come home— I do so yearn to see you

We are all well— I sent through the mail a very confidential letter of Fathers Written he said to you & Frank I mailed it on Sunday myself & shall tell Blair Sands to try to get it for you— I would hate of all things old cross eyes to get hold of it— & delayed sending it one day— but concluded to venture it— as you would see Brothers resignation & want to know the undercurrent which is *dead* against us in spite of all the chanting to the contrary— but tis not right for us to resent politically personal injuries or ill will this is rogues reign & it seems a hard alternative to have help to perpetuate it but so it is— & we can only try to do our duty— father has given me his letter & I must stop— & as I really cannot think & only feel more than ever your devoted wife Lizzie

Silver Spring   September 28, 1864
Dear Phil   I scarce know whether to continue to write or not but will send a mere health bulletin under cover as you desired— I am annoyed by having sent my letters— & gave Blair charge to get the 2 mailed on Sunday I had to keep very quiet last night & Father suggested I had best not tell Mother about our affairs until it is necessary & when we can muster a cheerful face— She will take this added to other things dreadfully & since her illness last summer brought on by her feeling at the ill treatment of Frank we have to be very careful of her— Father told Mr. W. he felt this more than *any act* of the Administration— & he thought Mothers resentments will be intense. So I am going to cool down 'ere I tell her & make as light of it as tis possible—

Father thinks from the course indicated by your letter to the Dept— that you are up to the times & its exigencies— but I confess that the closing words of your letter give my heart one big thrill of joy—[1] tis so very very long since I have seen you & to go so far away without having that comfort about you would fill my cup too full— I am afraid with bitterness as well as sorrow— I feel at this moment as if anything were preferable to it any way— but as I said yesterday— I am afraid to advise— your purposes indicated by letter to Dept— & fathers councils are against every feeling *in me* I dont pretend to argue— the matter with either of you but was so from the first moment & a night of sober second thoughts do not abate the feeling— My desire to have you back home "full due—" is the besetting thought & feeling of my heart & mind— Nothing diverts me from you an hour in the entreaty from Ever yr affectionate Lizzie

1. SPL had asked for a short leave before assuming his next command, which he thought was to be the Gulf Squadron.

Silver Spring   September 30, 1864

My dear Phil   Yesterday I went to the City to see the painters & to try to get them to hurry up & get the house in better condition for your use when you come home— but found they had just put on the 3rd Coat & that it would require a week to dry— 'ere the last one could be put on— So it will be unfit for use for two weeks more to come— the Sands kept delaying their departure & deferring all my house cleaning—

Father went to see when we might expect you as he has an invitation to go on a railroad excursion which he wants to turn to electioneering uses— Still will not wish to be away when you are home but they (Mr W. & F—) did not know when to expect you Adl. F—[1] could not be expected immediately— They said if you did not choose to go South you could have the Phila Navy Yard— Father replied that you had accepted the Gulf Squadron & that he would advise you to adhere to that purpose   I prefer anything to more sea service— but tis evident that you can have a good long rest & then we can see what you & I can best do together—

I told Mother of these changes yesterday   She went off by herself & twice told me it was a comfort to her that her children had fortitude— I laughed & said it did not take any fortitude to have you home   that fact obliterated most other feelings save of joy at the prospect of seeing you— I recd a letter from Evy Martin   She is to be married between the 10th & 20 of October— begs us all to come to the wedding—

Frank is at St Louis where the Rebel invasion looks formidable—[2] Brother has returned from New York in great spirits—[3] he had a great oration there & that to the prospect of making money has more than consoled him for the loss of office—[4] Govr D— takes hold of it today—[5] Blair is well & very happy that Papa is coming and that is a vast deal of joy to me & I am a good sailors wife in one respect a bright present puts out of sight for the time a cloudy future which my sanguine nature is prone to illuminate with bright hopes— Your devoted wife   Lizzie

1. Admiral David G. Farragut. Welles first planned for Farragut and Lee to exchange commands. When that arrangement did not suit Farragut, he switched Lee and Porter. On October 1, EBL wrote: "Mr. W. said *it* was thought due to the Adl F[arragut] & that turn about was fair play &c &c— & that the younger men should have the distant posts & some hard work still to be done— I immediately began to think of Galveston with Cape Fear feelings—."

2. On September 19, Sterling Price had begun his last, unsuccessful raid into Missouri. After the Battle of Westport, near Kansas City, on October 23, the rebels began their retreat out of the state.

3. On September 27, EBL had written: "Brother went off last night to New York the Democratic papers are making great use of his resignation— & he was sent for— Sunday night the conclusions come to will be seen in a speech to be made there— I dont know how wisely— but tis all the truth & I think tis always the truest policy to let it be known I hope he will do it gracefully & without egotism— the whole truth I know will *not* be told— & has not been as yet to anybody in my opinion."

4. On September 25, EBL explained: "I think Brother will go hard to work at the Bar— where he made the year before he was Post Genl ten thousand dollars he said Fridy morning that he could not now afford to be idle— that he had spent too much on the hill & now he must work hard to educate his children well—."

5. EBL wrote on September 25: "You will be glad to see that our friend Govr Dennison is Post Master General this appt. was fathers suggestion—."

Silver Spring   October 5, 1864

My dear Phil Yours of Oct 1st came today I heard that Adl. Farragut had come so felt sure of seeing you today— but when I went to No. 6 to say how do you do to Minna met Mr. Fox who told me it was a mistake that Ladner had arrived— that West India Squadron was broken up— I intimated that I would like to know when you would be home— but I got no definite answer He was full of a bout with S[tanton] who with a certain set have commenced operations upon the Navy Dept now—

Frank & Apo write funny accounts of how hard Blow Gratz Brown— & the Mayor had to work to get the Germans to fuss because Rosy put Frank in command of the City of St Louis— Frank was relieved in a few days & was grateful to be relieved of the unsought honor— & seems to have enjoyed the muss among this set of people He writes to beg Father and Mother to come out to see him I think Mother may go— Father dont wish to go gave up his Railroad party— & says he is going to stay home

I received your check and will pay to the painters— I had to get some clothing for Ned & Blair so had not enough to pay them but did not write about it because I knew you would soon be home— they finished today & as soon as dry I'll get things in good order— We have missed the use of it every time we went to the city— Father said his last spell of sickness came from getting a late dinner— I have a dinner at 3 olk— there therefore the dinner never waits here— Blair is entirely over his fit of indigestion We are all well today Ever yr devoted Lizzie

I enclose you a letter from Fanny which I know will gratify you— at first I intended to copy a part— but tis short & it is a real comfort to know that she is again in her own house— Goldy was hurt that Mr. P[ettit] gave up the old home but tis his old plan & I am glad he adheres to it as it gives assurance that he will carry it *all* out—

19

"Shermans march & devastation & Hoods defeat have been telling blows to the Rebs"

December 22, 1864

ALTHOUGH DISAPPOINTED THAT HE would not lead the assault on Wilmington, S. P. Lee accepted his new assignment as commander of the Mississippi Squadron with headquarters at Cairo, Illinois. He set out for his new post in late October, Elizabeth following him as far as Philadelphia.

The closing months of 1864 signaled the beginning of the end of civil war. Sherman's army left a sixty-mile-wide scar across Georgia, taking Savannah as a "Christmas present" for Lincoln. Grant settled down to siege warfare at Petersburg, stubbornly making Richmond less tenable for the rebels. In the West, S. P. Lee cooperated with George H. Thomas to repulse John Bell Hood's attack on Nashville and destroy the Army of Tennessee. The thought of peace became more than a chimerical hope, and Francis Preston Blair made his first trip to Richmond searching for acceptable terms.

Philadelphia   November 4, 1864
Dear Phil   I received a note from Mr. Jacobs[1] saying the carriage was now ready & if I would call today to see if it suited me it would be dispatched tomorrow so I am off in a few moments to inspect the changes— which were the front seat made permanent & wider— & the curtains for the windows which I expect to feel the benefit of as oftentimes this summer I have been worried with the sun in my eyes when my head ached too bad to hold it up—

I received a letter from Nelly last night saying that their servants had announced their purpose to remain with them in all cases save that of two women who would go to their husband on other plantations—[2] She sends me many thanks for you for the childrens winter cloaks   Annie sends me her measure— & the color she would like to have hers— I shall get them to sent to the lassie   I wrote to Fanny yesterday as I see by the announcement of your arrival at Cairo on Monday that you did not go to Louisville— where I thought you might find it convenient to spend Sunday—

Capt Alden[3] called here yesterday & told me the great expedition against Wilmington since this last move of Grant's will have to be postponed or given up   I laughed & told him to be cautious in announcing that yet— next week this time was quite soon enough to come to that conclusion— He professes to be a great Lincoln man— "convert from pro slaveryism—" professed sympathy with you for having credit like himself credit for great prize money wealth— which has all nearly gone to the benefit of land sharks & &— He had given all of his to the Church "Nobody envies your present command that's certain"

Blair is well but getting impatient about going home where I shall go as soon as I can get the things ordered for him & myself Aunt Becky sends her love to you & says she wants me to stay all winter & will take good care of me as long as I will remain— but I must go to those nearer & dearer— Blair sleeps with me & says he will do so until you come home but that is more comfortable than is good for him— I never approved of young children sleeping with old people He now waits to go with me to see Grandma's carriage   Your affecate   Lizzie

1. S. W. Jacobs, carriage and coachmaker in Philadelphia.
2. On April 8, 1864, Nelly had been more pessimistic, as EBL wrote: "Nellys letter which came today says that John has put his slaves upon wages— & yet they are leaving—."
3. Capt. James Alden commanded USS *Brooklyn* in the North Atlantic Blockading Squadron.

Philadelphia   November 9, 1864

My dear Phil   Yours No 2 came this morning— with one from Father wishing me to buy stores of groceries & etc which I think a mistake on his part at this moment but will make inquiries today & the rest of the time I am here— for I have now finished up all my own purchases and if I consulted my own inclinations would keep out the stores & out of temptation for my house is now my besetting temptation— but so far I have resisted & kept my money to my debts at home & have got two or three little things for the house— but have my boy well fitted out for winter. I have everything that I can possibly need for comfort or Luxury

Your letter was a singular confirmation of a remark made here last night by Henry Etting— He said that he inquired of Capt Ammen[1] what cause removed you just at the moment when you were cull fruits of your labors— Ammen replied he was removed because Fox likes Porter the best— that is the whole of it— Etting said that is hardly true because there are family connections & etc— No matter for that replied Ammen   I know the terms between Fox & Porter & much closer than those between him & Lee—" Etting then asked me if this was so   I said it was entirely so—" he then asked how did it come so— I replied "older & earlier associations—" & declined to enter into the family feud—

Fathers letter is very kind & is evidently moved about my sickness but I am well again & not a little helped to it by the quiet of these three rainy days— I got a note from Mr. Riggs in reply to the one I wrote for Aunt Becky asking him to let Boswell visit her— to which he replies that he is now at school in Cont but that he will send him here in his Christmas holidays and to Silver Spring to see Father and Mother   Aunt Becky is by me & sends her love to you & says she thinks Blair "is as good as can be—" She often points out how much he does things in your way— He gave Ned yr message about Jim— then asked me to write to Jim— but I said it was time enough when I went home next week— He immediately asked me for paper & envelope— & went off to Ned— made him write the message to Jim— came & made me copy yr words on a card— & sent them off in half hour after reading your letter to him

Henry Etting who came to vote yesterday says I must salute you with 21 guns of congratulation over our national safety in the reelection of Lincoln—[2] Tis rumored that McClellan resigned last night— under summons to appear before a court martial for insults to the President[3] The sun is out & I will go out too   Yr own affecate   Lizzie

1. Capt. Daniel Ammen was an old friend of SPL and a career naval officer. He had participated in the unsuccessful attack on Charleston in April 1863 and would serve during the coming winter in the capture of Fort Fisher at Wilmington.

2. On November 8, EBL had described election day: "You would never dream that anything important was going on here today— things look as quiet as on any other rainy day— There has been less of parade & noise during the last week than preceeding ordinary elections."

3. After Lincoln's reelection, McClellan resigned from the army, and on November 11, Lincoln accepted his resignation. On November 2, EBL had reported the political comments of David Murray Hoffman, who had been judge of the New York Superior Court (1853–61): "He is for Lincoln— reluctantly— who he says any real earnest patriotic man could have beaten— If McClellan had kicked out the peace plank he would have carried this state almost unanimously. He was lately at a business meeting of 40 men in the interior— every one of whom meant to vote for Lincoln sorrowfully & would gladly have voted for McC. but for his *peace* party alliance—."

Philadelphia   November 15, 1864

Dear Phil   Col Alexander & Evy have not arrived so— I am here still— but shall take up my line of march without them tomorrow— I have much to do at home & nothing here— save to be with Aunt Becky— & I feel as if I had done all that I can in that way—

I got Horace to inquire for some wine for Father yesterday— He says—

the agent who imported for Uncle Joe— asked him how he was off for good wine for Miss Gratz Horace said he had only 3 bottle of the new port wine left— she had lived on it whilst ill in the summer He told him then he had six Demijohns left— & would go halves with him So I have taken one for Father & Horace one for Aunt— & says if you wish the other he will let you have it— Let me know *at home* just as soon as you get this—

I bought Henrys clothing & old Dicks & now will look out for Nannys which will just leave me money to get home with— I am not decided about the Groceries & if I take them— Father will have to send a check for them I paid for the carriage & found the delay about its delivery was owing to the detention of the boat by the Captain so as let his hands all vote for Lincoln which all did, save one— Our coach maker is a Lincoln man too— altho he says— he has known McClellan since infancy & therefore knows— he knows nothing about politics— But thinks him a good soldier

The wound of Genl Canby makes me shiver—[1] I would soon get sick from my fears if I do not get something to do— besides dwelling upon them— Cannot bales of cotton be so fixed as protect the officers it seems so terrible to have them thus assasinated

Aunt Becky has lost her old friend Mrs. Fisher[2] she died Saturday— The President of the Orphan Asylum Board— She was elected in 1810 & Aunt Becky in 1806— Aunt thinks the old set best all go together & has sent in her resignation. She drops her mantle on me & bids me work on. I shall have improve very much to wear it worthily

Blair is well & full of going home tomorrow where all seem more eager to have him than anyone else Ill say good bye tomorrow morning— Your affecate Lizzie

1. Maj. Gen. Edward R. S. Canby, commander of the Military District of West Mississippi, was seriously wounded on November 4 when he was hit by guerrilla fire while on ship's deck traveling up the White River.

2. Sarah W. Fisher, longtime directress of the Orphans' Society of Philadelphia.

Silver Spring [November 22, 1864]
Dear Phil Yours with enclosures came last evening. (Tuesday many thanks for stamps a genuine convenience to me at the moment— father had called on me for sundry helps in that way— I make but one objection to your statement of your money account & that is to the word *spent* as applicable to the furniture & lot— I regard both as capital investments— & that *spent* on Blair— the boys, & me is so well done that I dout it could have been more profitably invested— for we had great, comfort & enjoyment out of it— I think you are entirely right however about making purchases now— I felt reluctance about

the carriage— & had not mentioned it for a year here Still the other with such roads as we have now is no longer safe— besides I knew it would gratify my Parents, as it has done vastly—

My money will hold out to pay the servants & Garrison the 1st of December I pay— Mary 10— Nap 15— my cook Mary Ann 10— & my washerwoman Lucy 12 You may think the first two scarce of my household— Yet it is an acceptable assistance here & you bid me do that when I could make it so— Nap is the gardener here & has won Old Dicks heart by "being willing to work, & to learn" I can get along very comfortably— with $125 a month & most luxuriously with $150— Blair & I have an abundance of clothing of all kinds— & have already gratified almost my every fancy even about the house— & it will look really elegant & pretty when I get it in good order with stair carpet & curtains in place next week— then I shall be sorry because you are not there to enjoy & look amused at me for caring so much about such things— The Roll of Linen came yesterday— but I saw no box with coat in it Shall go see Mr. Tucker about it

I received a letter last evening from your Phila friend asking Father to help him at the Dept which he will do I understood from Mrs Barnes Mother that he was going on the Blockade— but I suppose Capt B. has since

Blair takes Jims disappointment[1] as his own & told Jesup he would like to go to school with but he did not want Ned to lose any more time— Grandma said it would ruin him— & so did Uncle Dick" He is now happy with these children but he is always contented with me— & we always have plenty to do— only my talk & occupations make him think too much— when in the City Gist comes daily to play with him & he is quite as merry with him as with larger children

I hear talk of peace commissioners under certain contingences which give me a glow of joy— for a little while— Ever yr affecate Lizzie

1. On November 21, EBL explained: "I took Jim Byrnes to the city to see if I could not get him started off— found he was too young by three years to fill the position— he was examined at the Navy Yard & was found physically all right— but Mr. Fox of whom father made inquiries said he was too young— but would see about it— I sent him yesterday 'to *see about it*— when he was told by Mr Fox that the law requires him to be 20 yrs old— & Jim is not yet 18— He says he is willing to go as a common sailor under you— I have bid him wait until you answered this—."

Silver Spring   November 27, 1864

My dear Phil   None of us went to Church today— just before dinner Govr Andrew drove up & evidently was in the highest spirits— Amused us by clever stories— good recitations— & imitations— seemed to enjoy his visit so much that he remained to tea— & then begged the girls to go the city with him   Violet seemed to be his inspiration "She is a dream of beauty & father was the richest man he knew in children— more in quality than quantity—"

Mrs. Andrew wished to visit Washington in Jany. & has consequently got a warm invitation to No 4 in that month— "when we will be in town—" so said father   I go there tomorrow to make my preliminary preparations to go to stay on Wednesday— The Hogs are to be killed this week & farm taken out of the hands of Mr Harvey— the hands dismissed & the place put in winter trim— I hardly think they will get it all done before Christmas— & when the Fair is over I may come out here for a week or ten days if the weather is fine because Blair enjoys it & I am lonesome there by myself but I ought to stay in & industriously return my visits— of which I owe a great number— I am taking in everything I own except furniture— & it puts father out of humor to see anything like that going out of the house—

I remarked to Govr Andrew— "Mr Bates has made a change in the Cabinet rather sooner than was expected—"[1] He "has not quite got out yet   I wonder what started up the old gentleman? said the Govr inquiringly— Of course I could not satisfy his curiosity   You would have been amused at some quiet hits at others in the Cabinet— Says there is news of Sherman being in possession of Macon—[2] Says there are provisions in all the southern Ports for Sherman so that he can get supplies just where ever he chooses to take to Salt water— The Georgians & all the South know this are consequently puzzled where to burn up provision— We are all well— I am getting strong again which I have not been since sick in Phila   Your affecate   Lizzie

1. Bates resigned as Lincoln's attorney general on November 24, to be replaced on December 1 by James Speed of Kentucky.

2. There were skirmishes near Macon, Georgia, on November 21, but the town was not occupied by Union troops until April 20, 1865.

Washington   November 30, 1864

My dear Phil   I received your 2 of the 24th— both today & the one for Mr. Dick   I never dreamed how fully P.[1] is master of Gus & of the situation until I read your conclusive & concise history of events & facts— He is adroit in the management of men & nothing now seems in the way of having his ambition fully gratified as his wife said to me 2 years ago. "I am bursting with impatience & so is Porter— to be "*a full Admiral*"   I heard that her quarters were all fixed for her at Cairo & she refused to go there but went to Old Point after P— telegraphed her not to come (Mrs. Thom Patterson[2] told me this) She asked me if I was going to Cairo   I replied I would go gladly— but you felt me to be an encumbrance on board ship— (That is just what Harrison says to me was her reply & when on ship duty he belongs to Uncle Sam— & on Shore he is all mine)— I laughed & replied I had agreed not to grumble over a

half loaf when I married but these last four years had been very weary ones—
& so we parted both busy with the Orphans Fair—

I shall not repeat what you say about the Navy Yark— but will look that
way sometimes only *to see*　Father told me the Secretary had sent Capt Crosby
away for punishment— he had disobeyed his orders deliberately & nothing
but his efficiency as an officer saved him from Court Martial—[3] It seems when
you sent him after the Lilian he asked to go see his wife　The Secretary pre-
emptorily refused the permission & explained why he should return instantly
to you— Regretting to be forced to do so as Capt C. was importunate but the
Secy was as persistent in refusal— In spite of this— he went not only to his
home in Phila but up in the Country after his wife— & disobeyed orders in
the most pointed manner— which has irritated the Secretary very much so
father tells me & he says he will not court martial him as he deserves— but he
will send him on this duty to which he will soon be assigned— & as he is "a
man of high personal & official merit— he spares him the court martial which
would break him or publiclly rebuke him—

John spent last night here with the boys— Nelly will be up (& stays here)
to put her house in order tomorrow & to have her teeth attended to— too
long neglected— I will go with her to Maynard & do all I can to help &
make her comfortable— I spent the first part of this evening with Mrs Dennison— She adds greatly to the charm of our neighborhood Lizzie is not as
pretty as she promised— they are however a lovely family of children & Allen[4]
is a delightful playmate for Blair & a mutual comfort to each other　Ever yr
devoted　Lizzie

1. David Porter.

2. Marie M. Wainwright married Thomas Patterson in 1847. She was the daughter
of Col. Richard Wainwright.

3. Peirce Crosby had taken extra time to visit his wife before reporting for duty at
Beaufort; he had, however, arrived two days before his ship *Keystone State* had come in
from her sea cruise. Welles banished him to duty in the Pacific but in mid-December
rescinded the order.

4. Allen Dennison was the young son of William Dennison and about the same age
as Blair Lee.

　　　　　　　　　　　　　　　　　Washington　　December 4, 1864
My dear Phil　Last night on my return home from the Fair at half past
eleven— where I had been twelve hours I was too tired to write This day has
been one of rest— mind & body & now I am too lazy to go downstairs for some
proper paper— whereon to write— but I was reminded of your disposition
to indulge me so sweetly today that you will forgive me using the privilege of
being so—

This morning when Blair awakened he was full of joy over seeing me after going to bed without me He took my hand in his petting way & found them swollen from fatigue— asked the reason, when I had explained— He said Mama Papa told me to take care of you & I must do it— He does not like you to wait on anybody— I heard him say heaps of times "Lizzie call the servant to do it" or "tell Becky to do it—" & besides when I was walking the Fair yesterday I heard a lady say— "You see that little slim woman— she is head woman here She will do it for you" & the Lady went to you— & you talked to her & she got pleased & went away laughing Now if you are head woman you ought to make the rest of them wait on you & do the work." [1]

He talked on this theme at breakfast to the great amusement of Grandpa— & they said I was so well lectured afterwards that they would spare me this time But the work is done now & the Fair is fairly started & from the sales yesterday it promises to be great success   we have two thousand dollars worth of tickets for Entrance sold already—

I received your letter about the sheeting I took from it all I thought could be sold & made that up— the rest after thinking it over— I will make up immediately— in a form which will be useful to me at least hereafter & you can return me mine!! for Blair which I find he will need. I do not think it is well to have sleeping with me. It is good for neither— & I find tis just as well to have him in one of the single beds as to bring in the crib from Silver Spring

Father & Mother are here today all came in yesterday—Mother returns in the morning but Father remains with me— for the present & I think the whole party will settle down in No 4 before Christmas this winter— The Dennison were here after dinner but after sitting awhile Mrs. D insisted on my going to bed which I did with many thanks to her— & shall do so again now with a good night to you   Ever yr devoted Lizzie

John & Nelly returned home yesterday will return in a few day to keep a Dental appointment— I went to Maynard for Nelly but the Dr declined— he is too rich & sick   Nelly would have remained but John left the children who come with her next time

1. EBL had good intentions of sharing the work load, as she had explained on November 28: "on Wednesday at the meeting of the board I intend to propose a division of labors— by Committees out of 17 persons & make some lazy ones do their part— there yet a few drones on the Board— & I hope to bring their *usefulness* in full light on this occasion At the last Fair Mrs. Cox Mary Merrick Mrs Harris Mrs Hill & myself did all the work." Mrs. Hill was Ellen Corcoran Hill, wife of Stephen Hill and sister of W. W. Corcoran.

Washington   December 6, 1864
My dear Phil   Blair was entirely over his indigestion today & as it was my day for duty at the Fair I went early & have remained late— Mother had Blair in

the carriage to go out home but with streaming eyes he told me he could not go away from me so I would not force him—

I met Mrs Trumbull & she lives so near me that I hope to see much of her. I shall go there in the morning she bade me send a great deal of love to you— She & Miss Hattie are looking remarkably well— Mrs Foster was at the Fair & we had some pleasant chat very few MC patronize us—

Father went to the Opera— the fates are against my ever enjoying that priviledge— in Phila Horace seemed to think it was his only chance this winter whilst I was there for him to have that frolic as he called it— & now the Fair absorbs my whole time & it is really a duty to be there & I suppose when they come again it will be Lent— Our mankind are in full chase after the place—

Minna got a letter from Quandom Purser Allison—[1] begging to know some of the particulars of Judge Taneys death— Maria Taney[2] had heard of it only thro' the papers— does it not seem a dreadful infatuation that would enduce children to war absolutely upon their own old Parent— during the last hours of his life Mrs. Merrick is subdued her tone is much altered in these three weeks— Good night for I am weary & stupid but always Your affecate   Lizzie

Mrs. Merrick says when Mrs Dr Stone & I were very civil in waiting on even shop people they seemed vastly amused at our performance— said it paid well to see "*stuck up Virginians*" waiting on "the people—" She makes a good joke of it

    1. Richard T. Allison, a purser in the U.S. navy, had joined the rebel army.
    2. Supreme Court Chief Justice Roger B. Taney died October 12, 1864. His daughter, Maria Key Taney, was married to Richard Allison.

                                    Washington   December 8, 1864
Dear Phil   Your long & in many ways comforting letter came today   I was "used up" by my Fair work & had to keep in doors all morning— but rallied by evening— & went down with Ned at 8 olk & remained until 12 olk— found them busy— we made a hundred dollars tonight at the managers tables—

John Father Arthur & Johnny dined with me today   John spent the evening with Col Gantt & is still out with him John went to the sale he bought the Carpets at a great bargain— I have persuaded him not to put them down this winter but to pack them away in our garret in tobacco & a linen covering which I have Mrs Coleman has rented the house as it is & I think tis useless to put these elegant carpets there when not required

The things I wanted went off at high rates   the little chairs brought seven hundred dollars— So John did not even make my bid— He said that the appraisers he took there said the whole was worth about $1500— that is, that new furniture could be had for that in New York— LaJambre[1] charges a vast deal more in Phila You ask what parlor I am furnishing   the little one   I have put the library table book press & sofa in the front room next to No 6 for Father & it looks very well indeed I have a sofa & chairs & every thing except a centre table to fit up the small room— & as I am entirely equipped in clothing— & etc for Blair & myself & will have this fair over, In Jany I hope to save enough out that month's allowance to get one— but I saw a beauty at Barrada's[2] & told John to bid for it— but it went too high for my bid—

You made a remark in one of yr letters that touched me— I said I had enjoyed all you had spent for me— but I did *not* say it any part compensated me for the hardships & exposure & trials of all sorts which has been yr lot in the last 4 years— Would they have been any less without these means? If so no one would so gladly forgo all that money can give to have my husband home well & happy as   Your devoted wife   Lizzie

1. A. Lejambre had a furniture store in Philadelphia at 1012 Chestnut Street.
2. Frederico L. Barreda had been Peru's minister to the U.S.

Washington   December 9, 1864
Dear Phil   I have been on my feet from eleven to eleven   this was my day to take charge of the Managers Table— & every day I have to go as 1st Directress so I'll not be sorry when the work is done & I am greatly encouraged about the results we will make seven or eight thousand dollars— & that is a great deal to raise in 40 days for you know I only started this fair the day before you & I went to Phila—[1] At our last fair we had debts to pay— but this will all go to improve our means of getting along with our house full of children and you have no idea what an immense relief it is to me—

John was waiting for me & I think is satisfied with the result of his interviews with Mr Sherman & Mr Stevens about the proposed tax on tobacco— He will return home tomorrow if the snow storm is not too deep— He was recognized by Mr Sherman as your Brother, Col Gantt has been rather depressing in his political talk & is very much of [a] croaker & like all who are "tender *footed*" on the Darkey— thinks Union an impossible thing *now* But he never had any political sagacity or forsight— God night my dear Phil for your wife is a woman but always yr affectionate   Lizzie

1. On December 14, EBL reported that they "had a most successful Fair I hope & with reason that we have made ten thousand dollars."

Washington   December 10, 1864
Dear Phil   I can now realize fully the pleasure with which *hard* working people hail Sunday— I shall keep it well tomorrow   I'll *rest* I hope my poor tired limbs— John left me this morning consequently I did not go to the Fair until two olk as I wanted to see him off

Col Gantt came in just as he was starting & they talked finance & politics— John was blue about the 1st & Tasker the last— it goes hard to resign the negro as a bondsman— & they see none but fearful results consequent—[1] There never was such demand for labor & labor never was better remunerated & yet John forsees all the ills a country can know from the discontents of the masses at the North where the war save in the loss of soldiers— is not felt at all— He holds to views which I hoped the experience of four years would have cured

I think however he grew more cheerful in his tone the last day or so— & I begged him to come often & stay long out of the malaria of Prince Georges it did his spirits good— I think they will spend the week before Christmas with me— to get Nellys teeth fixed & to take the boys home with them— I want them to let Johnny live with me & go as a day scholar   the outside air & living will be better for him— he looks thin & pale— is too ambitious & studious— I have fixed the room above mine with a carpet & two beds & have told the boys it is always at their service & shall be kept for them— Johnny rather likes the place

I had a visit from Mrs. Dennison & Mrs. Trumbull soon after John left They told me no news but we had a most pleasant gossip I dream of the Cumberland[2] now with its heavily wooded Banks nervously— as well as of the Savannas of Geo   Good night   yr own Lizzie

1. On November 21, EBL voiced her own practical opinion: "Father has put all the servants on wages— over which I rejoice as it will I hope save me some weary steps shopping for them—."

2. SPL had steamed up the Cumberland River toward Nashville to cooperate with Gen. George Thomas in the defense of that city.

Washington   December 13, [1864]

Dear Phil   It is late as usual when I got home after the whence Luke escorted me & he waits so patiently every night & renders me so comfortable & independant in my movements that I feel very grateful to the Boy— Your letter of 8th inst with check for $300 came to me today— I rejoiced to hear from more than I can tell you

This Fair is in some respect of great use to me— For such is my wretched anxiety about your situation that it would overwhelm me if I had not resolutely determined to work hard & not give up until weariness made it necessary— then I can sleep[1] Then I am with you on the Cumberland up where I have been when I used to sing what Sara called Phil Lees song   that is the one told where my thoughts wandered—

We hear today that Sherman has communicated with Foster & all is well & safe— Blair was awakened by his Grandma accidently— He says send my love to Papa & come to bed— & as it is to reasonable a request to deny him   Ever your devoted   Lizzie   Gratz Brown spent the evening here— very cordial

1. On December 27, 1862, EBL had commented: "I sometimes think the watchers & waiting among us women during the war have to bear some of its burdens— which some activity would make more endurable."

Washington   December 16, 1864

Dear Phil   Father & Mother spent the day— with me & I did not have the great washing of windows & etc altho a good day for it that I intended Still I did much that I have wished to do for some weeks— All rejoicing over your telegram from the Cumberland— & over Shermans arrival on Sea Water—[1]

Mrs. Porter met Betty & told her that her husband & Butler had at last sailed for Wilmington[2] Birds flock together! Grant is not sorry to have him off— Comstock went to Wilmington ten days ago—

Mr Preston King spent this evening with me   I gave him a cup of tea in-vited to dine here on Sunday to meet Father— he called next door two days ago— but saw Mrs No 6— who did not tell any of us of his being in the City He asked me the cause of your removal   I told him the truth— he said it was plain enough   I said nothing of old sores or scores— but that Porter owned a cunning arsnal & had long done so— & then told of his talk to Mrs. Sands— & other points & coincidences— which affected the result— I did not speak bitterly— he was an eager listener & responded by saying it— "I see it all now— it agrees entirely with my estimate of Porter whose reports had several times contradictory—" I said I did not impugn P.— he wanted the place— had sought & obtained it with considerable tact— I tried to be short & not bitter— I will have a good dinner for this true hearted friend— & will have my Father to meet him—

Blair made Ned read over your telegram over & over & he has kept rather quiet since & just as close by me as he could get We are both well & were tempted to go home today but I'll never get the curtains up if I dont stay in The Chandelier in the small parlor has broken so often & cost me so much in repairs that John advised me to get a new one which I did today for $34 & it is to be put up tomorrow   Your affecate Lizzie

1. On December 10, Sherman's army began the investment of Savannah, Georgia; on December 13, he reached the sea and made contact with the Union fleet after the capture of Fort McAllister.

2. Porter arrived off the Wilmington, North Carolina, coast on December 18.

Washington   December 18, 1864

My dear Phil   I have just directed a letter to Mrs. Cameron[1] inviting her & her daughter to visit us here this winter— You remember the invitation already given to Mrs. A[ndrew] of Boston— so we are to have a house full— I gave our old friend P. King a good dinner of Turkey but the spare ribs were enjoyed with boyish relish— He & I went to see the Dennisons— & the Govr returned here with us & we had an animated chat until Tea was over— The Carriage is here tonight   Father seemed very content "in the town house." as he termed it when Mr. King remarked he felt happier to have him & Mother in the City during the winter— I shall do my part of social civilities but I confess never with less zest for them—

No news today from your part of the world & until things are quieted down & the battles really over— I am unfitted for anything that requires my wits about me— The last week has been one of the most anxious of all this war— & even the tide of victory does not put me at ease.[2] Your movements on the Tennessee intimated in one of yr letters keep me still on the qui vive to hear how & where you are

We had late accounts of Frank today— Minna came from Fox's— saying he had just talked with an officer from Sherman— who had made particular inquiries about Frank & heard he was well & that the Army had had the grandest time in marching across Georgia enjoying the abundance of that rich country— & so far from losing men had recruited & was 5000 men stronger than when they left Atlanta & horses & everything appertaining to war material recruited in the same style— but we will have full accounts in the Herald— for Sherman like Porter & the Knights of old have their Trumpeters

I have very often doubted the wisdom of your pressure upon that Gentry— This is the Peoples war & as such the Press is a channel of communication with the people— tis not in accord with some military ideas but you know my training is more of the Newspaper sort— than of the regular military— Betty is amazed that I never learned to keep step— I insist tis too rigid a movement for either grace or health— but you must forgive me— for these impertinences as they may be too late to be in the least availing— All I know is that you have done hard work & fighting & if any body else had done half as much— the world would have known it & considered him the great man of the war   Ever yr devoted wife   Lizzie

1. Margaretta Brua had married Simon Cameron in 1822.
2. Sherman had reached the sea at Savannah, and on December 16, Thomas had battered Hood's Confederate army before Nashville.

Washington   December 19, 1864
Dear Phil   I am again alone as the rain & mud kept John & Nelly from coming and Father went out home after dinner thinking Mother the most lonesome— Betty is quite sick— Mother rhumatic & they will not hear of my going home— & if John & Nelly come tomorrow Ill not care about staying as all day long I am busy in doors— or out— but I do not go out at night & the weather makes it impracticable—

The little Dennisons were here most of the day & kept the house a merry one for Blair   Mr. Smith called to see me about putting Ned to a school in the evening   I agreed to it so to Blairs great regret he starts at his books— I want to make him an educated Florist— it is a pursuit of profit & needs no capital to start with save some education which we can give this fine lad—[1] & when employed at Silver Spring makes him a good companion for Blair & will teach him gardening by mere association sufficiently to make it a source of *out door* attraction for him all his life I prefer practical gardening for a gentleman greatly to theoretical— it exercises his body & not his imagination—

We enjoy daily Hoods defeat & retreat—[2] but I shall not be satisfied until I hear from you which I have done only thro the papers since the 8th but I took each one of yr telegrams as a letter

Mr Smith told me that there is a rumor in town that Forney is to be made Secy of War— that Brother is to go abroad— which Mrs. M— likes— & some say he is to be senator in the place of Hicks who is to Collector at Balt— as he wants money more than place— & fill up my observations *it looks* as if Mrs. No 6. was going to have another Baby— or has grown hugely stout & may be prematurely old She is nearly 3 yrs my junior She is so out of spirits that I feel sorry for her & more so for him—

I have papered my wood box to make it look *oak like* correspond with the doors & fixed up my manger & endless little housekeeping matters this rainy day & am going to bed at a reasonable hour. Tomorrow I am going to the Asylum to count my Fair Money—[3] & will then visit my acquaintances in & out of Congress most industriously— & fix for Xmas   Blair looks eats & sleeps well— Ever your affecate   Lizzie

1. On July 4, EBL had explained: "I have paid all of Neds charges ever since Blair infancy— that is clothing schooling & doctoring— & now I find my full reward— for as Mr. Smith says he is one of the finest boys he has ever known & that the universal estimation of him—." Ned Byrne became director of the National Botanical Gardens and credited EBL with his success.

2. On December 16, Hood's army began its retreat from the Nashville area.

3. On December 20, EBL counted the profit: "I went to the Asylum today— to count our money   received $8,000 & there is four thousand more to come in— Quite a fine result I think for a few ladies to work out in a few weeks—."

Washington   December 22, [1864]

Dear Phil   Yours from Clarksville on the Iron Clad Cincinnati of the 15th came today— The point in of moment to me is that you are not well   The siege at Nashville was cured & relieved the day you wrote & what strikes me about your letter is that your telegram of that very date announced Thomas'[1] success   You scratch out the pm of your date so I infer the letter was written in the morning   I had another thrill of joy in Thomas' Victory— it was a relief to you— & I now imagine you are a very busy man getting yr boats in the Tennessee River— Everyday only completes the Victory over Hood— & the tone in Richmond gives a hope of peace— never indicated there before— Commissioners to seek peace boldly advocated in Congress. Shermans march & devastation & Hoods defeat have been telling blows to the Rebs

We had two letters from Frank today he writes in a glow of success— they had just taken Fort McCallister[2] Their march thro Georgia was triumphant in the destruction of War Material— Cotton & everything needed by the Rebs to carry on war— Cotton enough destroyed to carry on the war for a year—

Father came in town with Betty Mr Mrs Grey NY. invited by her to dine here tomorrow They tell me Nina Frémont has married an officer of our Army & has chosen a clever fellow—[3] Jessie has now made friends with her again I went to see Lucy Jesup who is with Mary this winter— We have made up a little class of dancing lessons The 3 Dennisons— Jamie Blair Mary Sitgreaves— Ritchie Stone Dick Wainwrights little girl[4] & Blair— & Ill ask Mrs. Lincoln to let her little boy join them— The back parlor is unfurnished & makes a good place for the lessons & the front room is very comfortable with the furniture out of this room— & some red curtains which I have fixed up makes it very pleasant sitting room This room looks pretty—

I have tried another Doctor for our smoking chimnies & shall pay $30 for trying to cure my room— Shall I let him cure the other six fluves if successfull?— every east wind make the great chimney smoke & every west wind makes our room smoke— Last night I had to clear the fire all out after one olk— We are all well Mother comes in for the winter next Tuesday— not a word from John or Nelly Ever yr devoted Lizzie

Old Frank Thomas is our rival for the Senate & is hard to beat & will succeed without *they* come to the city promptly[5] Take good care of my husband— all the good things of this world are nothing to me— when you are sick & suffering— Sarah Coleman has lost her only brother— & yr friend Dr. Fox died at home & from the accounts given me by the Morris'— he had pneumonia & relapsed— I think from going home

1. Gen. George H. Thomas, commander of the Army of the Cumberland, repulsed the rebels in the last major battle in the West. He was a native Virginian. On December 11, EBL had written: "I told Father about your ideas & sympathies for & with Thomas he said— I do hope they will become friends— they have much to unite them—."

2. Fort McAllister, Georgia, fell to Union forces on December 13, allowing Sherman to make contact with the navy and be resupplied.

3. Frances Cornelia Frémont (Nina) was John C. Frémont's niece and ward. She married Henry M. Porter.

4. Ritchie Stone was the son of Dr. Robert K. Stone; Wainwright's eight-year-old daughter was Mariah. Mary Sitgreaves was the daughter of Lorenzo Sitgreaves.

5. With the increase in moderate influence in the Maryland legislature, the Blairs

hoped to make Thomas Hicks collector of customs in Baltimore and move Montgomery into his vacated Senate seat. That plan, however, was foiled by the unexpected death of Hicks in February 1865. The legislature eventually chose Radical congressman John Creswell to fill out Hicks's unexpired term.

Washington   December 26, 1864

Dear Phil   Last night my head would not let me write so I let it sleep all it could— Today it is subject to my wishes again— & I will talk over the hopful aspect there looming up in the South for peace— I hoped & prayed for it— but I never saw a ray of light through this dark war vista until now— Those resolutions which came within one of passing the North Carolina Legislature of dissolving the Confederacy— The resolution for sending commissioners in the Richmond Congress instead of being scornfully tabled were sent to a Committee—[1]

I have seen & felt a great change in the Secesionists here— for instance— Mrs. Stone whose amiability so well tried— has given away to her Secession acerbity but of late it is all Sweetness— & she told me a few days since that her Mother in a late illness wrote that it might comfort her to know that she thought the Government under which she had lived & reared her children was good enough for her & them & was still of that opinion— Three months ago she would not have repeated this— Add Sherman March into Savannah & the victory over Hood— & we are making a good progress to peace—

There is a hope felt here of disposing of the Negro question in a constitutional way   this session—[2] a large number of Democrats are willing to vote for it now— Our people are working hard for it— Brother wrote to the Editor of the World & hopes to move him to advocate it & in doing so spoke of the Democratic party being chastened in their late defeat to a sober view of this matter— John Van Buren in the Editors reply bid him say that the "Blairs had been *Chastened* as much of late & as any set of people he knew— John has just come from the Water cure— & Mother sent him word— his water wit was even better that of wine— We have had a quiet pleasant Christmas— Blair wishes every day was Christmas— he is an exuberantly happy chap   The toys are very welcome to him in the stormy days of winter for the Rebs carried off his store of toys which Becky & Bernie had hoarded from his birth but they may now be gladdening some little ones in Virginia— I have felt disappointed all this Christmas time— for I had put it in to my heart for a year nearly that you would be here[3] & I never felt so let down & anxious & thus it is we nurse up our fancies but our disappointments will come up with more intense realization on some days more than others—[4] I see this in Mother of late years— she avoids much ado about any anniversary   I now look to the end of the War as that is talked of as a thing soon to come— but it must come soon—

All well & been out this rainy day— but me & I stayed home because I felt uneasy & that without reason for it   I received a Christmas pin cushion from

Marion & her Mother they are well— but seem anxious about the Expedition to Wilmington—[5] Ever your devoted   Lizzie

1. During 1863–64, North Carolina was a leader in opposition to the Richmond government and promoted a call for peace efforts in the Confederate Congress.

2. In his annual message on December 6, Lincoln had asked Congress once again to consider passage of the Thirteenth Amendment abolishing slavery. On November 10, EBL had been optimistic at the prospect, writing: "The large majority in Congress will clean out slavery in a regular lawful way— which will settle that question for all time I hope."

3. SPL added a personal note: "Wholly inconsistent with what I saw & felt whilst allowed to be in Washington ten days in October last. SP. Lee A.R.A."

4. On December 24, EBL complained: "This is my fifth lonesome Christmas— & when I add to it, all the "good time" which Old Billy told me I wasted— it counts up a long list of wasted years which I regret more & more bitterly as my sands grow fewer—."

5. Benjamin Butler and David Porter attempted a joint attack against Wilmington on December 25. The attack failed, just as Lee had predicted, from a lack of adequate army support.

Washington   December 28, 1864

My dear Phil   Our party went off to the front[1] and after running to & fro to get Father's clothing fixed up Brother came in to say that there must be eatables put up for the party & that Minna had *not a thing* for them in the house so I had to get to work and help Mother to have *cold victuals* put up for the party consisting of Father, & Brother & late in the day— Mr Fox who upon hearing of the report of Porter's return to Hampton Roads—

Mr. Sumner who has just left here says he had come from the Departments & there they said there was something incomprehensible & contradictory— & the last was that Butler had returned & left Porter shooting away at the Forts[2] in which he may vie with Dalghren til Sherman comes to his aid as theres a hope he will do before very long— if he carries out *our* programme for him   Mother said most confidently that Porter was sure to take the Forts— I said if he failed it would be for lack of troops— & so kept on the prudent & quiet— said very little & that on the amiable—

After Father started on his errand which I pray may bring its blessing Mother & I went to see Mrs. Trumbull & had a very pleasant chat— I gave her your messages in full & she told me to ask you to write to Walter— that he needs encouragement and is very morbid— She says he was very sorry to leave you last summer & said he was never more happy— Miss Hattie is married & happily so in the worldy aspects— & as it is an old affair of 7 or 8 yrs tis enchanting to those who are attached to them— Mrs T. seems wofully sorry to part with her—

Mother takes Fathers trip anxiously & I confess it affects my nerves very much which I think have had enough to endure He took Henry with him to wait on him— Mother suggested Charles— but he is a contraband— & not in style for such errands We heard that Brother & Porter had a muss about the blowing up the ship— & that Grant & Butler dont gee— this is a part of Mr Sumners news I will cultivate him he is a good news monger Ever yr own Lizzie Blair is well— merry & hard to keep clean

1. F. P. Blair had set off for Richmond in hopes of initiating peace talks with his old friend Jefferson Davis. EBL wrote on December 27: "Father leaves here tomorrow & will not return until he sees my Oakland patient for her good & ours I hope— I am worried to have him go from home at this inclement season but he feels that tis *a call* of duty & that no one must now shrink from that in these days of trial & trouble— I cannot be explicit & you may see why—."

2. The first effort to take Fort Fisher at Wilmington had been a fiasco, with Porter and Butler blaming each other. EBL explained in her letter of December 29: "The Army has left Wilmington— & Porter holds on & begs the Government to send Hancock— Army very mortified at this inglorious result— Genl Wietzel it is whispered could not look Porter in the face when he went to announce his Genls determination to withdraw the army from this expedition—."

Washington   December 30, 1864
Dear Phil   John returned home today   Mother & I coaxed him to stay longer— but I think he may return with Nelly next week   I begged for Williams return to College but he said Willy is a Hill— & never were two races as unlike as the Lees and Hills— & then he described their evening family circle   the other children sitting around the lamp reading or chatting   Willy will walk up & down the room— teaze Phil torment every body with his restlessness & then go off to bed by 9 olk— Get up at day light & go over all the Country before breakfast— & taking the closest observations about everything— like Clem Hill or Dick— & like them never studied any but his lessons & found his books always a bore— & now rejoices in his release from School—

He is doubtful what to do with Johnny— he is very delicate & very precocious & he thinks it will not be wise to push his studies just now That country is too sickly to live in long— & I do wish you could persuade & help him to some other place & pursuit— thats the way I would devote some of the prize money He told me to say to you that he had arranged your affairs (which he came to look after) very satisfactorily

I went out visitting with Mrs Dennison— I know almost everybody & she says she enjoys "*her work*" when I go with her— We met Mrs Porter at the Grimes'— declaring with great violence against Genl Butlers "cowardice" She was there with her husbands aid Lt Preston[1] & it was a funny scene, she appealed to me— "You know what an enemy he is to the Navy You know how mean he is" I let her run on which she did— & I asked her how she spent her time & she began to tell of different hospitalities extended to her among them she said even those Butlers "who you know—" I replied— I never saw Mrs. Butler[2] but once— when I called to see her & I know them but very slightly—" Why did not you go down there & stay— I replied my husband did not wish me to come or Father wish me to go—" which double restraint keeps me steady & at home—" Mrs Wise was there & she & Mr. Grimes & Mrs. Dennison listeners Mrs Dennison said to me— when we got in the carriage— Do you like Genl Butler— I never saw you so noncommittal before—" I cannot bear him" I laughed & said I do not envy his reputation— & that is all I know about him—

Porter has a snarl with Banks who is now here before the War Committee—[3] I think you fortunate in have Genl Thomas to cooperate with who is considered by Halleck & Nichols[4] & other Army men here as the *first man* of this war— These saying were repeated to me today by John to whom they were said

Father was detained on the Potomac by a fog We are all well Blair is well & *happy*— Your devoted Lizzie When I read yr telegrams they all seem for me now is not that a happy conceit so I heard from you today

1. Flag Lt. Samuel W. Preston was killed in the successful capture of Fort Fisher in January 1865.

2. Sarah Jones Hildreth, a professional actress, married Benjamin Butler in 1844.

3. The Red River Campaign of Nathaniel Banks, begun in March and ended in late May, had been an abject failure. The army had met disastrous defeats while the navy, under David Porter, was nearly stranded up river by shallow water.

4. Assistant Adj. Gen. William A. Nichols (USMA 1834) had served in the Mexican War. He was promoted to major general in March 1865.

Washington   December 31, 1864

Dear Phil I went out in the snow storm this morning & made all the purchases for Mother's dinner with all of her grandchildren 8 in number— tomorrow— Last year she & Father enjoyed seeing their troop of younglings together & invited this party— for the New Year— Fathers absence was not then anticipated & we all feel it anxiously— in which I have but few grains of hope intermingled Still as Father felt it his duty to go when so bated— by Greely & Co as well as his own friends But this is fearful weather for old men to be out of their houses & home comforts

A long letter came today from Bettys Army correspondant. The one for whom you had a letter last spring—[1] he says to all others he is silent— but he says to her that Porter agreed to be ready on the Seventh & so announced himself Butler set sail on the 13th & waited— 5 days for the Admiral— who lost thus 5 days of the most perfect weather known by the Blockaders for one

year— transports got out of coal water— temper & almost everything else—
On 24 the Admiral made his appearance— with a spell of bad weather— Still
they made a landing & this Genl thinks he could have taken fort Fisher with
his Division altho the Rebs had full benefit of knowing & preparing for their
approach— Butler says Porter lost the chance of a surprise & capture by assault
& he therefore withdrew— not being prepared to besiege the Fort. It has left
a hot fight between two gas bags— who may puncture each other

No News in the papers today about the movements in your part of the
world— & some contradiction as to the News of yesterday— Some of the
papers say Hood is not yet over the Tennessee— the Herald however says he
is— & out of Thomas' & your reach— This paper says Porter is all right &
will yet take Fort Fisher with his sailors & Marines he has taken up the cudgel
for Porter fiercely in the Editorials & there gives room for the fight to go on
between the Army & Navy correspondants— Mother says "Massa Ben had
sent his *Weizel*[2] to get at the state of things— the 5 days delay gives the old
Yankee a great advantage in the business—

Blair is very well & happy & looks with eagerness quite amusing at this talk
about Wilmington This last part of the year has seen me discomfited by the
injury of my only new gown the whole skirt spoilt by a bath of ink— I wish
you could hear Mother talk & laugh over Massa Ben The torpedo ship is the
source of all sorts of jokes—[3] Mother says she must [not] laugh loud enough to
be heard next door but she must say no failure up to this time ever had in it
any consolations before— Grant thinks Sherman will come along quite time
enough for all his plans— Ever yr affecate Lizzie

1. Adelbert Ames (USMA 1861) fought at First Bull Run, Fredericksburg, Chancellorsville, Antietam, and Gettysburg. He would also take part in the successful
capture of Fort Fisher in January 1865.

2. Grant had wanted Butler's subordinate Maj. Gen. Godfrey Weitzel to lead the
Fort Fisher attack, but Butler assumed personal command.

3. Union forces detonated a powder ship 250 yards offshore from Fort Fisher as a
preliminary to attack. The ship exploded but did no damage.

20

"Things look hopeful for our cause"

February 17, 1865

UNDER THE PRETEXT OF RECOVERING personal papers taken during Early's raid at Silver Spring, Francis Preston Blair undertook exploration of peace possibilities with Confederate leaders. With the approval of Lincoln, he made three trips south, twice visiting in Richmond. Although his efforts did not bring peace, they did lead to a meeting at Hampton Roads between Lincoln and Confederate Vice President Alexander Stephens. Southern defeat now seemed inevitable. The occupation of Charleston and the capture of Wilmington closed the last open Southern ports on the Atlantic; Sherman completed his devastating march, moving north through the Carolinas; and Grant continued his unyielding pressure on Petersburg and Richmond. Congress approved the Thirteenth Amendment abolishing slavery, and politicians in the North intensified their fight to control government policy for the reconstruction of the nation.

Washington   January 1, 1865
Dear Phil   A happy New Year to you this cold bright snow clad day— which scarce seemed like Sunday with St John's Bell hushed— We are still without a preacher[1] The Vestry is obstinate So are the people   so is Mr Pyne— & I doubt if we get another clergyman until the election of another Vestry when most probably we will elect one who will induce Mr Pyne to come back again But I doubt if he will do so permanently— he has lately become very rich by an Estate which Mrs. Pyne inherited from a sister— who left her Mr. Pyne & all their children each an independance of three thousand I hear a year— this added to Mrs. Pynes own property make them very rich indeed   I went to the Epiphany[2] & heard an excellent Sermon returned to dine with children   we sat down ten in all— & had a very pleasant good dinner—
    We have been expecting to hear of Father thro' Brother who is expected to return but it is now late & the Boat has not come up   Capt Mitchell is slow & cautious— & there is a great deal of ice in the River & by tomorrow

if it continues this cold it will be closed   Minna said here tonight that Fox told her that Genl Butler is the City— I heard he was intensely indignant at Porters official report—[3] I fear somebodys zeal for his friend will will involve the Secretary in no Small trouble—

Blair has had great joy in the housefull of youngsters   he is very social in his nature & I waited to see if he would wish for you as he always does when he has had "bully time—" Tonight he said Well Ill have go myself to Old Abe & tell him I must have my Papa home— or Ill burn his house down" Of course I disproved this last threat— but agreed to the first— Ever Your devoted Lizzie

1. On November 24, EBL had explained that the Reverend Mr. Pyne had resigned his position at St. John's Episcopal Church because of political differences with some of the members: "the truth is that this whole move against Mr. Pyne is an undercurrent of seceshism— & the loyal men of the congregation ought not to submit to it— I find all who are alienated from him are those who of the *tenderfooted* kind."

2. The Episcopal Church of the Epiphany, located on G Street between Thirteenth and Fourteenth streets. The minister was the Reverend Charles H. Hall.

3. After the failure of the first attack on Fort Fisher, Porter reported his displeasure with General Butler's conduct, claiming that the fort ought to have been taken.

Washington   January 2, 1864 [1865]
Dear Phil   Greek meet Greek— Modern Greeks both in my opinion— Father returned[1] with the news that Butlers report came up with him & was to be published   Grant regretted that this was made necessary by the publication of Porters report to the Navy Dept   Betty has a letter from her Crony at Head Quarters which opens with a bitter complaint against the *leaking* propensities of the Navy Department— (Grant made the same remark to father) This letter is substantially the same I quoted to you but I will copy this one for you tomorrow— I have no doubt this matter will be investigated by a Court of Inquiry

Father sent two letters to our Oakland cronies[2] & waited two days for a reply but receiving none after waiting two days having had a very pleasant trip to Head Quarters seeing & hearing much that was of great interest to him returned home today in the finest spirits possible—[3]

All the world here was out visiting & nearly all the Ladies receiving at their homes— I did not receive because I never intend to do so in your absence but Mother & Betty might have done so— but would not as I would not help   Betty went out with a party of girls & is still out on this New Years frolick— I went to see Mrs Winn & Mrs Smith brought the last home with me gave her a good dinner & sent her home comfortably under Charles convoy—

Father rejoiced tonight that you are out of this muss with Butler I said it was *not at all certain you would have been in any such fix*— but as you were out of it— it was just as well— for the rest of *us* to keep out of it— to which he agreed entirely & I hope will adhere to this purpose Grant I think will make a defence for Butler *like that Mr Rives* once made— & from the very same opinions & feelings Father is quite well which a great relief after such trip & is much cheered with the military vista as seen at Head Quarters where the hope of catching Hood was still felt Ever your affecate Lizzie

1. Blair returned to Washington on January 2.

2. The "Oakland cronies" are the Jefferson Davises, with whom the Lees had vacationed in the summer of 1859.

3. The next day, January 3, EBL wrote: "Father sets out tomorrow to see our Oakland friends— if he had been more patient & less of a hurry to get back home he would have been saved this double trip— God grant the result we pray for—."

Washington January 6, 1865

My dear Phil I hoped for a letter all this day as I read in the Newspapers that Genl Thomas had given orders to his army to return to Nashville— Every body congratulates me upon your good service & I intimated to Govr Dennison that every body seemed *thankful* but Congress—

This has been a pouring rainy day— & yet we women have been up stairs all day as the rooms below were all occupied with Fathers visitors— Among them were Horace Greely who Betty made Nelly quite curious to see— Father's affairs are all arranged and he starts tomorrow[1] Leaves us all well Blair over his croup threatenings & Ned very much better of his nervous attack— Dr Miller says is the result of over work & a lack of strong diet

Miss Japonica[2] has arrived next door & Nelly goes there with me & on my return Ill close my day's gossip Which consisted tonight of the Butler & Porter snarl— the last has sent up here a collection of caractures illustrative Genl B's feats— for private circulation— which are irresistibly funny— Gingy's new equipage & gayeties were the next course— altogether I think Nelly has not had such an instalment of small for many a day She says she has many a good laugh for John in store & I have just been thinking over the laughable points & for the life of me I cant write them— save that she made the discovery that Ellen Woodbury had reached that stage of life when young *ladies* become civil to middle age ladies— I am afraid I getting too old to be appreciative of fun & small talk & *in* that respect Nelly keeps very much my junior— She really enjoys society— twofold in the present— & all that's clever her fine descriptive talent enables her to enjoy over again in the amusement it affords John

It is now 12 olk & still the conclave holds on down stairs Ever your own Lizzie

1. On January 11, Blair arrived in Richmond on his second trip south. On January 4, EBL wrote of the delay in her father's trip: "Father did not get off today & is to go in more *style*— next time and I hope with more results agreeable to us all— He

is well & very full of his proposed plans to work out a happy result— But I can not dilate on them but they *are all in writing*— so there cannot be any mistake about them hereafter—."

In her January 7 letter, she commented: "I am not sanguine— nor is my father— but I never saw him labor mentally so much to complete— which was done & copied— & tied up nicely & etc."

2. Miss Japonica refers to Minna Blair's youngest sister, Ellen Woodbury.

Washington   January 12, 1865

My dear Phil   Whilst Nelly is writing to John for Luke to mail tonight for her I will write to you as my carrier Ned is hors de combat again— he was taken very sick yesterday but is up today— Dr May— who came to attend my bruised hand says he must not go to work again for some days— I hurt my left hand at the Fair— & since then have put arnica & other things for remedies but the place did not improve at all So Mother insisted the Dr must attend to it today— he came & said it must be put in bandage— or the lump would increase on the back of my hand— & I concluded if it got any larger I could not get my gloves on & that would be uncomfortable as well as ugly— It gives me very little pain save when I touch it— & no one observed it until the last two weeks in which time it has increased very much in size The Dr. says it will soon disappear now— he opened what he called the *sac* today— & will put on the bandage tomorrow & in a week it will be all cured—[1]

After he left I walked to Georgetown bridge with Mother— & made six calls among them were Mrs. Sherman[2] of Ohio with whom I am getting well acquainted She asked about you— I spoke of you as Capt Lee— she remarked that you are "Admiral"   I said no you had no real rank but that which you had when the war commenced Mr Sherman exclaimed— why are you are surely mistaken— but of course I was not— & convinced them of it & this was the second time today I had done the same thing & that to our friend Mr. Doolittle

Every body talks Fathers whereabouts to me— & I avoid it & say as little as I can— but luckily most people begin with story about his papers & when I can truly reply— that he said he wished "to recover some deeds & other business papers of import to him—"

Yours from Clifton of 4th inst reached me this morning and I read all that military to Mr. Doolittle— He was very much interested & said he would like to hear all the military reports I got— Mrs Doolittle comes in a few days— when I will ask her & Mrs. Trumbull to dine with us—

Blair is hard at work with his *tools* & Nelly says is the happiest of Boys— She seemed to think him very good— he is the most eager child I ever saw to learn his book He reads one little short lesson a day to me   Ever yr own   Lizzie

1. On January 21, EBL commented: "Someone said to Mother how uncomplaining I was with my hand— I told her it was because I had no one to listen to me— this an honest but a loud thought— for I could not help thinking how much I made of it to

you— even so far away— but you have so often soothed all my aches with yr patient sympathy that even when away I utter more of real feelings to you of all kinds than to any one else—."

2. Margaret Sarah Cecilia Stewart, daughter of Mansfield, Ohio, lawyer Judge James Stewart, married John Sherman in 1848.

Washington   January 14, 1865

Dear Phil   I started out early today to go to market— wound around to the Asylum & then home— The new lines of Railroad along H. Street & F— makes this trip very comfortable one   these new cars are so clean & comfortably full whilst the others are over crowded— Negroes are permitted in the new line & this of course excludes the fastidious who are touchy on these points— I have always thought making them altogether useless— so I use what is convenient & agreeable— & say nothing about it—

At one I went to the White House was received with great kindness— Mr Lincoln said I expect my news from the Admiral is as late as yours— I replied not quite Ive one day later— Then I made some visits among them one to Mrs. Fox— my first this season— They called here on New Years day— Nelly expected John today— but he would not take her home on Sunday— & he gets up too late this short cold days for business— so he will be here tomorrow—

We have no news direct from Father— the Rebel papers announce his arrival in Richmond[1] & he must be there still Mother is very restless & anxious & so is your affectionate Lizzie

I am only so about his health— he is so feeble & old for such a trip

1. Blair met with Jefferson Davis on January 12.

Washington   January 15, 1865

My dear Phil   We have the comfort of knowing that Father is en route homeward bound tonight— Mr. Welles received a telegram from HdQts of the Army of the James saying he had just thro the lines— & was again on board the Don— So we may hope to see him tomorrow or Tuesday the farthest— This is a relief because the delay has been so much greater than we at first expected—

John arrived just before dinner suffering accutely from the cold weather— He said it was too risky to bring the children so Blair another disappointment He will stay up tomorrow and look into the progress of things here on tobacco— & your affairs— & return home next day— I want him to stay and get Fathers report of matters in Richmond— & etc And I think he will— he says Pendleton[1] says there is not a shadow of a shade of hope for peace Sympathisers of his stamp make their wish father to that thought— & whilst they live here in luxury— & not in subdued in their pride which is all they enlist in the war—

Mr. Everett died today of apoplexy—[2] I feel a pang almost personal in parting with any of our great men now— we so need able & patriotic minds to light us over these wretched times— I saw his daughter yesterday— so full of enjoyment and from late letters to father I see the intense pride & affection he had for her— evidently more pride in her & her children who formed "the delight of his old age—" She left her son with him over a year ago when he was only nine years old—

We all went to church & have had a sober home like Sunday— Nelly had her boys to dine with her— & mothers cordiality with them completely won them They are now to dine with us all the days permitted to them I shall resume my visitting work in the morning— & shall give you full reports of all I hear so when I begin you must fill *names* with our old key— if theres a need for it Blair is well & happy as the day is long & says "so sorry that night & bed time comes so soon— Your affecate Lizzie

1. George H. Pendleton was the defeated vice presidential candidate on the peace ticket with McClellan in November 1864.

2. Former congressman and governor of Massachusetts, Edward Everett had served as secretary of state and U.S. senator. He had also been the Constitutional Union party candidate for vice president in 1860. A staunch Union advocate, he had worn himself out from activity in the presidential campaign supporting Lincoln, and he died on January 15.

Washington January 16, 1865

Dear Phil Yours of the 7th came today so did Father who is very tired and silent[1] But says he was most cordially received by our old friends. My Oakland patients were very cordial— & *he* said he would remember me in his prayers even when dying &c&c She met father with "Oh you Rascal, I am overjoyed to see you—" & Never looked as well in her life stout— but fairer well dressed & even a better talker than ever—

Father staid with an old friend of Frank's & fared sumptuously every day— Mrs. Stannard was of course most delightful & delighted she insisted upon father being her guest— but that was too public a place for an incognito— Emily Mason[2] was importunate to know his errand— when he assured her twas to find Genl Jackson long sighted spectacles which were now so much needed to help political vision— She promised to find them if they were in Dixie— which she doubted— It seems Mrs. S. was engaged to Soule[3] & that Robt Lee persuaded her not to marry him She showed father the whole Correspondance— which fact has diverted John not a little— Fathers talk of these people has been of great interest to John & Nelly— but they like Emily want a look out of these spectacles— which has not been fully given to any one as yet— save *one* glympse I caught— I have not sung any since— which is a relief to Blair who like his father does not enjoy my singing— Father has been perfectly well— but seems overwhelmed with the excitement & fatigue of the past 10 days I confess to no small sense of joy to know that he is in his own bed— & sleeping with Mother by his side happier than I have known her to be for sometime past—

I went out visiting with Mrs. Dennison & did relieve my list considerably she does not know people & it seems be a real help & pleasure to have me to go out with her— I never had any rides in Coach No 6 before— To be sure Mrs. No 6 gets some out of Coach No 4 now days— so wags this world— John & Nelly leave us tomorrow and right sorry I am to part with Nelly. I told Blair that Uncle John said Phil did not miss his Mother— Oh yes Mama he must want her but was ashamed to tell— He dont like to be a baby—" but I am one every night for then I want you." He has been just as good as boy can be all this day— Ever yr devoted Lizzie

1. Blair returned to Washington on January 16 with the possibility that a meeting might be arranged to discuss peace.
2. Emily V. Mason of Richmond was a friend of Varina Davis and an acquaintance of the Blairs.
3. Pierre Soule had been a U.S. senator from Louisiana (1849–53) and then minister to Spain for two years. During the war he served on Beauregard's staff.

Washington   January 17, 1865

Dear Phil My hand is painful & the bandages are obliged to be kept tight & I have the prospect of a week more of this endurance vile— I know how give sympathy to our poor fellows who are bandaged for their wounds if this little matter annoys me so much— however I keep busy out doors all day & am sufficiently tired to sleep at night—

John & Nelly left me today & I miss them both. their visit has been a real enjoyment to me— & to us all They grew quite cordial with the Dennisons & I think the blending with society will rub off many Prince George ideas— Nelly laughed & said what would *they all* think to see her so very friendly with Gratz Brown— Dennison & etc— She said considering she never intended to stay more than a day in Washington she had so managed to spend nearly a month here & that too without her children She feared *she* might get fast & etc— She has not looked as well for many years. I miss her cheerful sympathetic company already—

John will be back next week Nelly agrees with me that tis a good thing to get him up here as often as possible for he enjoys society— & he told her— he always meet clever if not congenial people here— He takes a great deal of

notice of our boy & seems to give him a share of love with his own boys—
Of course this touches me in my weakness— for I think there are not many
who quite appreciate him— tho he wins kindness from almost everybody—
but John sees him as I do—

Fort Fisher is capture & Wilmington *can* be shut up— this helps— *the* prospect which I have now most at heart & about which I would enjoy to pour
into yours all the comfort I feel— John exclaimed thank God it stops prize
money— & helps to stop the war— I think P[orter] in using up B[utler]— has
done the country nearly as much service as in capturing the Fort—[1] the City
had an air jubilant— Mrs. Porter called here today— she said to be congratulated I was out but she got what she came for— from Betty & Mother who
were at home I called to see her about ten days ago—

I paid a large number of visits today— among others to Mrs. Doolittle who
I shall ask to dine here with Mrs. Trumbull— Judge spent this evening here I
have worked of late to get thro' my visiting list— that & my hand has kept
me occupied I dropt today my Porte monnaie— & ere I could pick it up a
man caught it up & made off. I pursued but in vain & in mid Lafayette Square
I could call no rescue— so I gave it— After while— he came & delivered it
to me— Father thought I ought to have had him arrested but I was too glad
to get the orphan's money in it— & Mothers— I had just spent nearly all of
my own— but it would have been a loss $50— to me— He said he would give
it to if I could tell him what was in it— luckily as it was asylum & Mothers
money— just given me— I knew to a penny Ever yr affecate Lizzie

1. On January 15, a combined assault by the Union army and navy resulted in the
capture of Fort Fisher guarding Wilmington. Porter and Butler had not worked ami-
cably, and on January 7, Butler had been removed from command of the Department
of Virginia and North Carolina. After hearing of his removal on January 10, EBL
wrote: "Genl G[rant] has been laying in wait for an opportunity for sometime to get
this brought about."

Washington   January 18, 1865
My dear Phil   I went with Bishop Potter's daughter[1] & Mrs. Rochester to
visit the Secretaries— & others today I was introduced by Mrs. Welles to a
niece of her's with Mrs. Emory— as the wife of an Admiral & she as one of
a Majr Genl— I replied "I would be very glad to be an Admiral's wife— but
to my regret the naval list shows my husband's rank to be that of a Capt—"
Mrs. Welles said are you not mistaken? I laughingly replied— "that in all that
touched my husband I am well posted—" Well quoth Mrs Emory— if he is
not an Admiral he has lots of prize money which I prefer to any honors— I
said that was not a naval spirit— country & honor were Jack's first aims— in
which I cordially shared the sailor's ambition Mrs Surgeon Genl Barnes[2] said

persons who were rich might easy feel so— "I rejoined then I have always been rich—" Yes said Mrs. Emory we who had known you longest will all say you have ever been supremely content with your possessions—"

I bowed off under that after thanking her— & made my next bow to Mrs. Stanton where I met Purser Cunningham—[3] who began with a complimentary tirade on the Blairs— I laughed at him in turn— then he began to pump— when I replied I knew nothing of the Davis' since the War— & discanted on Mrs. Davis as I knew her tone her wit & etc— but added she said she could not "take me to her heart as she did her Democrat associates as I was always such a black Republican— &etc &etc— Mrs. Stanton all the while listening— I had not a little fun— but 15 visits has made me weary— when added to an aching hand— which however is better—

I am busy putting matters in order as another visit to my Oakland patients is to be made tomorrow—[4] & I hope it will cure all their maladies— I went out this morning to get flowers with Mrs. Dennison & helped in her entertaining matters— thus you see I am on the go all day sometimes I would like a day or so of Country rest— but as I spend my evenings quietly I get along well— & when my hand gets free of bandages will be comfortable Tomorrow we have seats for the Opera— taken on purpose— but I fear Mother has too much cold to go she & Betty are complaining—

I met Mrs. Porter at Sewards & congratulated her most heartily— The Banks are here— not looking happy— the War Committee are rowing him up Red River—[5] they called here today We are all well but Mother & Betty— Fathers excursions agree with him— he never seemed in better health So we owe some thanks to Capt Parker Blair puts his new french words at me to *stump* me & is as happy & saucy as heart could wish— Ever yr affectionate Lizzie

1. Alonzo Potter, Episcopal bishop of Pennsylvania (1845–65). When his wife Sarah Benedict died in 1864, his daughter Maria was adopted by friends. In 1869 Maria married the sculptor Launt Thompson.

2. Elizabeth M. Collins married Joseph K. Barnes in 1837.

3. John S. Cunningham, purser in the U.S. navy since 1857.

4. On January 18, Lincoln authorized Blair to return to Richmond to pursue peace possibilities. He returned to Washington on January 27.

5. Banks was ultimately mustered out of the army in August 1865 and was then elected to Congress.

Washington January 21, 1865

Dear Phil This has been a day of relentless storm of Sleet & rain I have been to market— & then hearing that I had wounded Mrs Welles by what I said there— & have already repeated— I went to see her— told her what Mother heard from No 6— when she assured me I had said nothing but what most graceful & my little sly tap at Mrs. Emory was perfectly delightful— & upon the whole I was the most agreeable visitor of that day. We parted as she said *nearer* & better friends than ever—

I had scarce been home ten minutes when I got a note from Mrs. Dennison asking me to come help her with her invitation & to council with her what to do— She knows so little about the local people— so I told her in an amiable spirit all about people— & urged her to invite Congress to all her parties— & seek to render the Administration known & popular with the politicians Got home to dinner & to enjoy Blair's frolics with little Henry & Ned both have been away during the week—

No tidings from Father about whom the papers are filled. It seems the powers that be have traced the publication of Fathers movement to the Naval officers of the Don We have read the papers thoroughly & the only event not a week old commented on is the probability of the evacuation of Richmond & Genl. Grant from what I hear is on the qui vive for that event all the time—[1] I need not tell I am very well after this account of myself even the hand is getting better— Your affectionate Lizzie

1. The rebels did not evacuate Richmond until April 2.

Washington   January 22, 1865
Dear Phil   Govr Dennison told me tonight & Brother told Mother yesterday that you had three hundred thousand dollars of prize money[1] & Govr Dennison said that he derived his information from Mr Welles— & it was "not difficult" to discover that the Dept were disposed to make your wealth a motive for not acting about yr promotion *at* present— I told Govr Dennison what you told me as to the amount of your prize money & he said that agreed with what you said to him— & he promised me to follow the matter up & get at the true statement   I am going to write to John about it tonight as I think the truth will benefit you—

I went to church today in [spite] of the weather which is a continued sleet The trees look like spun glass— & then I went to the Trumbulls— & had a pleasant visit— & most kind in their inquiries about you   Your affectionate   Lizzie

1. The estimate of prize money was greatly exaggerated. The final total for payments to SPL was closer to $127,000, and that amount he did not fully receive until the 1880s.

Washington   January 24, 1865
Dear Phil   I recd a pleasant long letter from Nelly saying that John will be up here some day this week— & I bought some lace curtain which Mother said she wanted to make the parlors look nicely furnished— & that added to

the coal— bill repairs on chimneys to prevent smoke— $60— those of the water closet $30— & the fire place in library which I bought from Strung— [?] & paid (who is dead & are selling out) $45 for which I gave last year $50 in Phila, I told John all these arrangements— he thought them sensible— & said he would pay these bills— but I felt reluctant about it when he was here & declined but when two of these Bills came in today for payt— I felt it was more respectable to do as John suggested than to be dunned— so I will get him to pay these Bills if he still can do so conveniently—

Mother wanted to go hear the debate on Genl Butler in the House so I went with her— He was most lucky in his opponent Mr Brooks[1] & was no match at all for Mr. Boutwell[2] or Mr Stevens— it was an excited debate but you will see it better reported elsewhere— Mother is anxious about Father & I really miss Nelly to help me to amuse & cheer her up & who is always so acceptable to Mother— The Radicals are bitter about this matter but they are rabid at heart towards the middle State people as the feel they may used or run over with impunity

I saw the Smithsonian Institute burn down today with real sorrow—[3] it was lost by the most miserable imbecility in the Fire Dept Lucy Jesup is here spending the winter with Mary— She always begs me to tell you how much she misses you I got a letter from Mrs Martin so full of your praises that the next time I have a head ache & I cannot write I enclose it to you as the best substitute & as to Mrs. Trumbull— the Judge & I concluded it was not proper to send you all the love she gives me to forward to you— Your affecate Lizzie

1. James Brooks, Democratic congressman from New York (1863–66).

2. George S. Boutwell, Radical Republican congressman from Massachusetts (1863–69).

3. The *Washington Evening Star* of January 24 reported that response by the fire department was prompt, although there had been a delay because the alarm box had been frozen shut. On the next day, the newspaper commented, "Much damage was done to articles removed in consequence of the crazy manner in which they were thrown from the windows by excited individuals."

Washington   January 26, 1865

My dear Phil   Father has returned home— looking weary & we are exultingly happy to have him safe & sound out of Dixie for the life of me I could not shake off apprehensions for him Your letter of the 17 came also— & Genl Schofield & I am so happy— to hear from you & of you— I have famished for ten days— & began to fear you were sick all those fears are & others so Ill sleep better than for many long day—[1]

We have had a very narrow escape— Rebel Rams all started down the James River— put the Onandagua to flight & all the rest & nothing saved Grants rear but *Mud* the Rebs had delayed their attack one day too long— & the River fell— & when they got to the obstruction— lo they all stuck there which they by sounding knew they could clear the day before— Father told Genl Grant how bitterly you opposed relying on anything but proper ships for the protection of his communicacations— All the talk down yonder is about the mismanagement!! the Capt of the Onondagua[2] is stricken from the— because!! he took to his heels— I have now talked until one olk to Father We expected him from 10 olk to 12 olk when he arrived— & now how gladly I would talk the rest of the night to you but cant—

Blair did his first skating today— in Lafayette Square which is nearly a sheet of ice This has been the coldest day of the winter. I let him go there knowing twas his safest chance to learn— Happy urchin he was—

Judge Doolittle was here this afternoon he is your true friend God bless him— Grant has gone down to Wilmington— with Fox Farragut has gone to City Point in the Ironsides— So your advice is at last followed I went to the Navy Yard and to see all the Ladies there today being the one they fix to receive— Mrs. Zeilan[3] constantly speaks of her husbands friendship for you— She is a first rate woman— Good night— Ever yr devoted Lizzie

1. On January 23, EBL had written: "I sigh now so much to be with you that even letters do not comfort me as they used May tis I get few of them— but in your present overtasked condition I do not expect or ask for any more— There is a hopeful aspect in affairs which does give me comfort & some assurance that tis heavy endless separation from you will have an end—."

2. A Confederate naval assault down the James River to destroy Grant's supply depot at City Point occurred on January 23. All Union ironclads except the *Onondaga* had been removed in anticipation of an attack on Wilmington. The *Onondaga*, commanded by William A. Parker, and the Union gunboats retreated, but the rebel ironclads ran aground at Trent's Reach. The heavy fire from Union shore batteries and from the *Onondaga* caused the rebels to withdraw upstream, and Grant's supply line was safe.

3. Virginia Freeman Zeilin was the wife of the Marine Corps commandant and the sister of Col. William G. Freeman of the adjutant general's office.

Washington   January 31, 1865
My dear Phil This day has been one without note to us save in the Sound of the Big Guns fired over the passage of the act to amend the Constitution prohibiting slavery forever[1] & I hear Mr. Doolittle counting the states over— & they are all fixed to have the act made valid by State action— They passed it by six more than enough— which was four more than they expected— Father did not convert Mr Brown[2] from Minnsota as he hoped but did the others— & some went away—

the rumor that the mission was a failure got abroad thro Mrs. Hetzel who says Mrs Davis wrote her she says that "all of dear Mr Blairs efforts she fears will prove useless." I have no doubt that Sid Hetzel (her hopeful) sold that news to speculators & traders who (dread peace) for a goodly price— It is funny to see how those who have fattened on War dread peace I have a horror of such Cormorants that is too great for expression—

I started out late hoping to see John but he failed to come— Still I had time to go see Mrs Gratz Brown [3] & others— There is a talk here that the Missouri Radicals have split— & that the equality laws [4] are banishing white people out of the state so fast that it has alarmed the Govr & Mr. Blow— [5] who now want to follow moderate counsel— everybody has an axe & this seems a good time for mine— I have no other thought night or day— & seems to me it is now my motive power— I shall be sure to be civil to my guest Camerons & Andrews— for this one short month is all that is left me— if they come Ill entertain them well & I shall spend some money to do it & if I succeed will take all the grumbling in the world without mumuring— I sometimes feel like writing out all my doings— but cannot— I've but one care— I never appear in person— acting on any body Who can vote in the matter except to my cousin & Mother spoke to him— & Mr. Doolittle Father is keen to his part & will do it I think successfully altho my heart has often sickened over this disappointment Ever yr own Lizzie

1. On January 31, 1865, the House of Representatives passed the Thirteenth Amendment to the Constitution. Previously approved by the Senate on April 8, 1864, the amendment was sent to the states for ratification.

2. James S. Brown, Democratic congressman from Wisconsin (1863–65), had been mayor of Milwaukee.

3. Mary Hansome Gunn, daughter of the former mayor of Jefferson City, married Gratz Brown in 1858. She was fifteen years his junior.

4. On January 11, a state convention was called to amend the constitution of Missouri; it voted to abolish slavery and support the passage of the Thirteenth Amendment to the national Constitution. The Radicals then split over the issues of giving the newly freed slaves the vote and the treatment of Southern sympathizers.

5. Thomas C. Fletcher, governor of Missouri (1865–69); Henry T. Blow, Republican congressman from Missouri (1863–67).

Washington   February 1, 1865
Dear Phil   Admiral Farragut & Lady are invited to dine I called today to see them today but they were out & I left a written invitation for them the Doolittles— Secy Welles & etc a dinner of 16.[1] the Farraguts returned our visits promptly & two for one— I have been marked in my attentions as I knew it was to your fancy— I will have it done in a good style The invitations were from Mr Mrs Blair— I cannot start out

You may congratulate me tonight— I have cleared off all my debts in the visiting line— tis late in the season to have accomplish it for I have always done it in the fall— but the Phila visit— the fair then Congressional visits made me postpone my citizen duties & I assure I have often times shied meeting some of them—

I had my coal partly put away today I got from the place that John recommended to me it took more than half of what you sent me to pay for it Wages & Mme Dorman left me so low in funds that I shall ask John to help me out with the dinner party Dr. Mays bill & etc— as he told me he had funds of yours & could meet any reasonable requisition—

I have just come from listening to the Presidents voice— declaring himself on the Constitutional amendment—[2] the point which of late has laid nearest to his & somebody elses heart— Mother came into my room last night about 3 olk & roused me anxiously— saying is the matter— She says I was talking in the loudest & yet distressed tones She heard "Mr. President" even in her room & yet I was sound asleep— I'll do it wide awake in the next 5 days if it is not done & successfully by some one else—[3] I have announced the end of my patience— & now do it to you— Congress is all right & will gladly do its part— I have felt that pulse industriously for 6 weeks & if it was any use it would act instantly— but the thanks have to start from over the way— to be worth more than a compliment. Even Grimes is friendly so I am assured by Judge D.— I have said less than I have thought & done because I have not been happy about it— until the last few days— & I did not wish to harrass you— I am now sanguine that all will go right for us & that quickly—

Blair is well— told me when said "he was a good for nothing chap—" Well I am good for a boy to Papa—" He is out more than the Dennison children— & seems quite as hardy in all but *eating* they are a great resource to him— Ever yr own Lizzie

1. On January 28, EBL had explained her reluctance to give a dinner party: "I would gladly entertain some of these people but the enormous price of things— makes even the daily routine of living swell up to the propotions of old time frolicking & more— $250 dollars wont give now the dinner that $75 used to do— I mean including wines & etc—."

2. On February 1, Lincoln signed the bill for the Thirteenth Amendment to the Constitution.

3. But on February 20, EBL assured her husband that she would not act improperly: "Do not be anxious about my making speeches to any one *now* I have been until lately sorely tempted to do so to the P— but there are reasons not to be written for not doing that— Father had his third talk with Mr. W. today— He says he will immediately recommend you to the P. for promotion—."

Washington   February 2, 1865
Dear Phil   Father took a short drive today— & I hope will cease soon to be considered an invalid   he wants to go out home tomorrow but Mother says that would be a folly—

The world is all agog about the peace commissioners—[1] There is an odd game going on— which would excite you not a little if I dared write it but as I cannot I will only say that Father thinks you would enjoy it— I do not therefore he & I do not agree with him.

Mother & I took a long walk after the french cook— The Vice Admiral and Lady accepted promptly— & we will have a fine dinner for them of 18 persons chiefly Senators— except Mr Rollins[2] who has the credit of carrying the constitutional amendment   Betty is just in from the Morgans— they are to dine with us— & entertain she says magnificently. Rumor says he is to be our Secy of Treasury— as Mr. Fessenden is to be Senator again   Betty is here talking of Ball dresses & beaux until the small hours are upon us— She returned home early as she is to go out to another ball tomorrow night at the Nicholsons'!!

Nothing amazes me so much as people on salaries giving balls with meats at 35 cts a pound— & milk at 25 cts a quart & all else in propotion— Now we have our cow— & strange to say the one next door took ill & died the week ours came— of course we divide as they did before ours came— Betty and Miss Ellen are very formal when they meet— Miss E. does not go out— & Mrs. No 6 "cannot visit—" the reason makes itself more evident daily— The carriage is more frequently borrowed than ever before "The Style is good—" Still I dont see any increase of amiability—

Good night as I am getting so gossiping it is time to stop— I had to scold Blair today— & he had a bitter cry— the first for many a long long day   Yr affecate Lizzie
Of course Mother says I was wrong & Blair right

1. On February 3, Lincoln and Seward met at Hampton Roads with Confederate peace commissioners Vice President Alexander Stephens, Assistant Secretary of War John A. Campbell, and Senator R. M. T. Hunter. The meeting came to naught.

2. James S. Rollins, Missouri congressman (1861–65), was an opponent of the Radicals.

Washington   [February 6, 1865]
Dear Phil   Made some visits this morning with Mrs. Trumbull She has two young ladies with her and has been out to parties & shows the effect of dissipation— both she & Mrs. Dennison are nearly broken down— bad air & late hours are not good things for dames *after* 40 They reproach me for not going out with Betty I have done better things for her so my conscience is easy in putting my boy to bed— & spending the evenings scribbling to his father[1]

I see by the paper that you are in New Orleans & I think of you now coming up the River— I went to see Mrs Gratz Brown today She spoke in very kind terms of you— They dine here on Wednesday— Adl. Farragut called to consult Father upon a point of etiquette made by Mr Seward He remarked to Mr Seward who mentioned that the President intended giving him a dinner on Wednesday— that he could not go as he had an engagement to dine with my Father When Mr. Seward remarked— all engagements must give up to such an invitation from the President who takes precedence of every body— The Admiral called & said he never heard of such a thing & he had no inclination to forgo his engagement & etc at the same time did not wish to offend Mrs. Lincoln who was he heard punctilious— Father told him for once Seward was right & a few hours afterwards Adl & Mrs. Farraguts excuse in full came to hand— He spoke very kindly of the attention which we had extended to him & his wife I have filled their places with Gratz Brown & his pretty wife

Father is evidently depressed by the commission failure as it is announced & is said it went on well enough until they demanded an Armistice[2] which had been declined in Richmond As to the Union & Slavery those points were as explicitly put in writing as the *only* basis the Armistice however was not in writing— I fancy that there was so much applause given to the originator that the thing was postponed— so as to get the credit & applause which the Country seems so eager to bestow on a peace maker— From all I learn we will have war any how— & much fear we will have two enemies to grapple with— Louis Napoleon is very eager to get at the products of Virginia & will not let from what I hear the chance slip for a blow to attain it—[3]

I heard poor Capt Parker[4] is to be tried for his life— he lost from Adl Farraguts account a glorious chance for renown & easily gained they say— it was a moral cowardice for he has behaved well under fire— but it was the great responsibility which unnerved him— It is the Yankee Parker not Foxhall

Gist they say has the mumps & I shall be on the look out for Blair to have it too Altho he has been but little with him of late Father improves slowly— Ever yr affectionate Lizzie Letter from Frank today— well on 30th declines gracelessly the independent command of the Texas Army— while S. is Secy—

1. On February 24, EBL explained: "I must go to bed— nothing so taxes my spirits as company keeping all day I could walk out to Silver Spring with less weariness."

2. R. M. T. Hunter suggested an armistice followed by a convention of all states, an idea rejected by Lincoln.

3. On his peace mission, Francis Preston Blair had proposed to Davis the idea that the North and South could reunite to dislodge the French from Mexico.

4. William A. Parker was senior officer on the upper James River. Grant had requested Parker's removal, and Lincoln sent Farragut to investigate the case. On January 30, Farragut reported to Secretary Welles that Parker ought to be removed.

Washington   February 7, 1865
My dear Phil   This has been an Orphan Asylum day— & election of officers
of the board   they reelelected me unanimously. I alone voted against your wife
for I know better than most people how poor an officer she is— We recieved
from Mr. Corcoran a donation of the North West Corner of his fine lot on 14th
Street of about 2 acres & a half on which we are to build our new Asylum—[1]
Now for a country member— dont you think the Institution has grown somewhat under her direction— We have already 16000 where with to begin our
building for I am anxious to fund all our sales of property so we may have an
income large enough to buy meat & bread— I want an Institution with space
enough to nurture about two hundred children— & with sufficient means to
feed them without begging—

You see I want those who come after me to have an easier time— like most
people who lay up to make their children idlers But I love this work for all
the good it has done others & to me— I took it, to get rid of myself— when
pining unto sickness for my husband [torn page]   gave me work for head, heart
& hands— & a refuge ever ready for me when my life was too lonesome to
be happy— & no matter how much faith one has we must do something for
others to be happy So you see all my charity is after all selfishness—

Sarah Coleman[2] resigned her place at the board— Her sister   Mrs. Freeman is ill— & I fear will long require Sarah's care of her household   Robert
Coleman left his huge estate to his sisters & his brothers children— Andrew
Alexander is a Brigadier Genl— We are anxious about a battle which we
suppose he has taken a part in on the Stono River Tennessee

You [torn page] by the papers my first views about the Meeting in Hampton
Roads has become the general belief— the end of that affair is not yet— Our
Secesh neighbor Birch has lost his house by fire— & his very helpless family
are homeless which reminds me I must go pay our Insurance— Friend Stabler
is here again much to the delight of Blair but I think Grandpa is rather bored
& Ill not mention what Grandma thinks of the matter This has been a day of
storm & snow & a grievance to Blair who has not been allowed his priviledge
of shovelling snow for I feared that if he had any of the mumps infection from
next door it would aggravate it— & so I shall be careful of any exposure in
falling weather— He gets good tickets all the time from Mme Dorman   Ever
yr affectionate   Lizzie

1. The new orphan asylum was built at the corner of Fourteenth and S streets.
2. Margaret Coleman married Col. William G. Freeman.

Washington   February 11, 1865
Dear Phil   With me this day has been spent quietly consequently I am very
much better than for many past Of course this has given me but little chance

to see & hear— but there has been a buz of people in the house all day in which I take less & less interest as I fail to achieve— & to have postponed that which lies so near my heart— until it has grown sick— forever Still— I have a thousand fair promises both from Senators— Reps & Secretaries— which so far come to nothing but promises All admitting that the you have long since earned all we ask for you— the Secy. says of that there is no doubt— but the time is not now propitious— ie the Radicals wont go for him

I have a plan to prove that they like you— & then it may prove auspicious but I hope not as bouyantly as I did two weeks ago not yet do I give up—[1] I wish I was well— with my old time sanguine feeling— but these headaches make me low spirited— Then I am a dead weight upon everybody— but I am better today & hope to go out tomorrow & get fresh air & hopes—

Father went over with Betty to spend an hour or so at the Dennisons to meet Adl Farragut— who is now according to Secy W— consulted *"on all promotions"* Father is wonderfully improved since last Tuesday— Mr. Sherman & Capt Foxhall Parker are to dine here on Monday had a letter from John enclosing one to Majr Mordicai which Ill dispatch today All well with them at the Lodge—

Blair has a little cold— the weather is still cold tho' I do not feel it in this house where the tenderest flowers have grown at the windows all this cold winter We have been well housed— for such a season Nelly says she felt the change on returning home— Ever yr affectionate Lizzie

I see by the papers from N.O. that you are there & yet I get no letters from there

1. On February 24, EBL wrote: "John laughs at my eagerness to be Mrs. Admiral— it seems to me Ill never be allowed to have my husband home until that title crowns his labors & consequently I am more than reasonably eager to get it— but if I had him home & happy I do not think any thing could keep me being 'over all the ills of life victorious—.'"

Washington   February 13, 1865
Dear Phil No letter from you this your natal day— to cheer & comfort your wife I would not say this if it were possible to hear from you regularly— but as I cannot expect it I can at least say what would an acceptable gift to me on this birthday—

Capt Parker & Capt Eastman[1] dined here— they sneer without provocation or encouragement about Porter I think tis best to be entirely silent on that subject I was busy fixing this dinner which Father invited verbally yesterday & today— These naval Captains were civil to him on "The Don—" He invited the Shermans & Mr Odell & Townsend[2] of New York to meet them— the dinner was gay & pleasant & a good one— I however was divided in my thoughts as this is the first day since we last parted that Blair has been confined to his room— but he has cold & I am so afraid of croup that the doctor said it was best to keep him upstairs as it was intensely cold— Nobody ever *heard tell* of such weather in these parts before—

Cabinet movements are all the talk now[3] I am sorry Mr. Morgan declined the Treasury at the same time I think he is right to enter the Cabinet— I like a Senators place best, in that I agree entirely with Mrs Jeff Gold went down with the peace message— & I believe in spite of Ultra effort to prevent it will come with the other lovely & bright things of the year

Govr Hicks died this morning— the Doctors say from the poison of Malaria— taken in his system at his eastern shore home— he leaves two daughters—[4] neither with him when he died— Mr Sherman says Genl Frémont has settled the House in New York & one at Nahant on Jessie & her children & that he once gave her some US Bonds— but that his speculations absorbed them & his luck put $300,000 in his pocket lately & he hopes Jessie will get her bonds again & put them in real estate— He says Jessie has lately become *entirely* gray— more so than my mother There is no end to the rumors & gossip here now about political matters of which the Herald writers give me generally my first tidings Ever your own affectionate Lizzie

1. Thomas H. Eastman joined the navy in 1853. He was promoted to lieutenant commander in September 1862.

2. Moses Fowler Odell was a Democratic congressman from New York (1861–65). He was then navy agent in New York until his death in 1866. Dwight Townsend, Democratic congressman from New York from December 1864 to March 1865, filled out the term of Henry Stebbins, who resigned.

3. Bates had resigned as attorney general and was replaced by James Speed of Kentucky. Fessenden resigned from Treasury to take a Senate seat and was replaced by Hugh McCulloch after Lincoln's inauguration.

4. Gov. Thomas Hicks of Maryland died on February 13, 1865. He had two daughters, Sallie A. and Henrietta Maria Hicks.

Washington February 17, 1865

My dear Phil I went out tonight to see some tableaux vivant given by the girls of Violets class at Mary Blair's— They were very beautiful & Violet is a real beauty— A litle too languid & disposed to be a blue stocking— Still all that will wear off with knowledge of the world— but egotism in any shape is as hard to cure as consumption & both are hereditary— on all sides of her house—

I met Mrs. Wad Cutts[1] there She looks about 25 but She takes all of life with great equanimity & that has much to do with wearing well— I also met Capt Alden there talking about promotions— Says you & he are worse off than at the beginning of the War— had then only Old Captains & Commodores over you— & now have young ones, got some prize money about which you care little & he less for you have those dear to you to indulge & enjoy with

it— & his lot "is utterly desolate" I felt sorry & touched— for Mary Blair
tells me that the Dr now think his wife hopelessly insane— her mania— his
absence— & now she ceases to know him— Capt Glynn[2] told me years ago—
that the Ex Exption[3] cruise had destroyed her— & I believe it   four years is
beyond human endurance

Things look hopeful for our cause & I heard from *over the way*— that there
was another door opening for peace I think the next program will be agreed
upon between G. & L— this fact may facilitate your leave— & yet— egress
will be down your way— & a less vigorous vigilance may be required of you—
You see I catch at all straws when I want anything & more than half believe
always Ill get it— until tis beyond my grasp— Goodnight Blair is well— so
is your affectionate Lizzie

1. Probably Ellen Cutts, wife of J. W. Cutts, second comptroller of the Treasury.
2. Capt. James Glynn, a career naval officer, had joined the navy in 1815.
3. Charles Wilkes's exploring expedition, 1838–42.

Washington   February 21, 1865
My dear Phil   After finding that I could not get the Dept. to be grateful—
Mother said that Congress ought to instruct & protect the Naval officers who
had devoted themselves to protect their Govt— so she made me write a note
to Gratz asking him to come see her— & they had a long talk   I mentioned
their purpose to Govr Dennison who seconded the movement heartily— he
suggested however that he would consult the *brig* [?] confidentially & was *urged*
not to attempt it but the Govr. did not agree with the brig [?] & enclosed is
the result & it will pass the house as it did the Senate unanimously— so that
protests from retirement endorses your recent services— & Father is delighted
& Mother very happy— & I am more hopeful—

The Camerons came to dinner— Mr. & Mrs. C— & their daughter Mrs
Burnside—[1] they are pleasant & seem very comfortable   John came this morning he took off your box of papers— with him to look up for your taxes—
omitted by Mr Simmons— He was well but say Nelly is sick— The rest very
well I urged him to stay but he would not be persuaded I had a spare room—
but he said he had too much to do— Seems very happy in William who is a
very handsome fellow & would like nothing better than to stay up a week or
ten days John is very nervous about his taste for the fooleries of young people
but tis nonsense to try to suppress what all people call nonsense in the young—
Nobody ever takes except in very small doses the experience of others— &
nonsense is delightful to youth— from "Mother Goose up" I got to be so
sympathetic with Blair that I actually enjoyed Mother Goose & Mr. Bigelow
agrees with me in *feeling* it to be delicious poetry—

Genl Ames sent a deer from the Island of Fort Fisher— it is like the elephant to Betty but to Blair tis a good gift He has waited on & petted it all day & Betty says she has grown six feet in his esteem during this day— We have had a great display of flags & feu de joie over the possession Charleston today[2] It is very brutal in the Rebs to fire the city especially that part inhabited by the poor to prevent the Capture of Cotton We are all well— & Mrs Cameron says she never saw a child grow better than ours— Ever yr devoted   Lizzie

1. Rachel Cameron Burnside, widow of James Burnside, Pennsylvania district judge who had died in 1859.
2. On February 17, Confederate forces began to withdraw from Charleston.

21

"Oh horror upon us again—"
April 14, 1865

On April 9 Robert E. Lee surrendered his Army of Northern Virginia at Appomatox Court House, effectively bringing the Civil War to an end. The Blairs hoped that Lincoln could carry out his moderate reconstruction policies and quickly reunite the nation. That hope was dashed within days when John Wilkes Booth assassinated the president. The shocking crime staggered the country; both North and South realized they had lost a wise and able leader. For consolation Mary Lincoln looked across the Avenue to Elizabeth Lee, who devoted herself to comforting the distraught widow. With the fighting over, Phillips Lee faced the complicated task of dismantling his squadron. It would be another four months until Elizabeth was at last reunited with her husband.

Washington   March 4, [1865]
Dear Phil   Last evening Mrs Lincoln sent for Mrs Lee & Miss Blair to go to the Capitol "to bring the ladies (Camerons) with them— so we went— I had been nearly a week in Blairs room & felt that ought to excuse me but as a simi‑lar excuse had induced me to decline the Theatre— Mother insisted I must go— So put my boy to sleep & went— & had a stupid time— however Mrs L was kind & confidential

Today Blair was very bright & up in the window (*closed*) to see the parade— & as Mother would not— I had to go with Mrs Burnside (né Cameron) to see the inauguration— the third I have witnessed in my life   Mr. V. B.s being my last— Whilst Mr. L. was speaking I got a chance to ask Mr Cameron the fate of the thanks & was I bitterly disappointed to that Gratz had read yr letter to the House Committee— & withdrawn yr name He found Schenk was op‑posing it— & said boldly to the Committee that he liked you— but you were linked in with the xxx Blairs— who wanted everything—" This filled my cup for tis a hard trial for me to your Jonah—[1]

Blair is recovering slowly— & would gain strength better but for his close confinement made necessary by the irruption which covers him— & disfigures his dear little face— but I rejoice to see it *out* for all that inflammation inside would have been fatal— & they tell me the attack of gastric fever will *be slight* in consequence— he played marbles— for a while & listened to Grandmas stories but when I got back he got close to me & lay still & was tired for the the rest of the day— I wanted to be still too so we were as we often times are— a mutual comfort to one another & I needed it much this day— Your affectionate Lizzie

Mr. P. King was here— I was surprised at his bitter tone towards even repentant Rebels— He dines here Monday We were very cordial tho' I confess he shocked me

1. The Blairs' moderate attitude toward reconstruction made them anathema to the Radicals in the Republican party. They had forced Frank out of Congress in June and Montgomery from the postmaster general's office in September. SPL was Blair's "other son," and the Radicals were not going to take any action that would advance him.

Washington   March 6, 1865
Dear Phil   We are greatly relieved tonight by hearing that Genl Grant had Telegraphed to the President that he *knew* that Sherman was in communication with Schofield—[1] Since Beauregard has been superceded by Joe Johnston I had grown uneasy Add these tidings to those from Sheridan[2] & it looks as if the Anaconda[3] (Spoken of so vauntingly three years ago)— was really near getting its prey within its coil— & we will soon have peace— for which I do pray so earnestly— & there is such a bitterness growing in the hearts of good men like P. King that I really dread to have it grow by a prolongation of the War— or by the process of frittering— & helplessness It strikes me as such stupidity on the Rebs part— not to see— that they can get better terms whilst they have one powerful Army— *unwhipped* than after it is routed & demoralized—

Blair is better & Ned made him very happy all day even when kept in this room— dear little prisoner— I see his little face at the window I fear without that thankfulness I ought to have— that he can leave his bed— but this irruption on the skin still confines him & his patience surprizes me

Mr. Doolittle was here tonight & wants us to take care of the V.P. & if the speech he made in the Senate is published as he made it will show you that he is certainly not over his late illness—[4] The Camerons are to leave tomorrow   they are kind hearted people— & Mrs. Burnside is to me a very congenial person— They send you many kind messages & invitations to visit them— I told them that— "if you passed through Harrisburg in your journies to come you would call to see them— Mr. Cameron is one who serves his friends— zealously— & he saved J—[5] from being carried off by force almost— for when I heard him say the *day he first resigned* that no honorable man could remain neutral— I went straight to the War Office that hour & he sent for J— *that day* & he says if he had been kept in the Dept Jn should have had H's[6] place for he is "an *abler* & "*an* "*honest man*—" But Ive vowed this Sacrament Sunday not to repine— So I must say good night & your affectionate Lizzie

1. Sherman's army was moving up from South Carolina toward Fayetteville, North Carolina, while Schofield's moved out from New Bern toward Kinston.

2. Philip Sheridan, commander of the cavalry of the Army of the Potomac, was active in the Shenandoah Valley. His force had begun to move from Winchester toward Petersburg.

3. Winfield Scott's plan for victory, Anaconda, called for the blockade of Southern ports, capture of the Mississippi River, and army incursions into enemy territory to squeeze the South to military death just as the anaconda snake kills its enemy.

4. Andrew Johnson, Lincoln's new vice president, had spoken incoherently at the inauguration, causing great embarrassment and prompting allegations of drunkenness.

5. John Lee.

6. Joseph Holt had been appointed judge advocate general on September 3, 1864.

Washington   March 7, 1865
Dear Phil   Your's of the 26th ult & the 2nd inst & the copy of your's to the Secy. all came today. I read the last to Father it pleased him & disappointed me— for that was not my plan for our summer—[1] of which I have spoken only to Blair who strange to say will never speak of anything I ask him not to but I only spoke of my plan as something he & I would enjoy

He went out doors today for the first time since he was taken sick— I did not write last night as I could not hold up my achy head by night & all of today I have been languid & good for nothing & in truth— it is a reaction after my tension about Blair about whom I was much more scared than hurt— but one cannot avoid nervousness about a child with a high fever— for so many days But he sleeps now just as sweetly & quietly as ever in his life & begins to have appetite & *eats & talks* of Beckys bread with great relish & she is certainly a great improvement as a cook upon any body we have ever had[2]

Mr. P. King & the Vice President are both our guests— the first talked a great deal about you & with a kindness that does me good— Govr. Johnson is confined to his room— & is under Dr May's care— who orders absolute quiet— even about the house— & a low diet & he says he will be able to go out in few days— but ought to avoid work & excitement & etc— He has a good servant & occupies the back parlor— as a bed room— The City & papers are full of gossip— but he is a sick man—[3] & Mr. K. says deeply touched by Fathers kindness— Mr K. & he are old friends—

I took Mrs Gratz Brown out yesterday & returned all her visits— We are very much won by her & think Gratz a lucky fellow in winning such a charming wife— Your affectionate Lizzie

1. SPL had withdrawn his application for leave and asserted his desire to continue to serve until the end of the war.

2. On February 24, EBL commented on their former cook: "Mother dismissed Mary Ann whose manners are not civil or cooking good enough for her— & has engaged Becky in her place at which Blair who immediately said now he would have just as good a time in the kitchen as any where else—." Becky had been Blair's nurse but had left EBL's service after becoming exceptionally quarrelsome. She now returned, much to the delight of all the family.

3. On March 30, EBL wrote: "Mr. J. talks of leaving us soon I observe that every day he gets more cheerful— he was at first the most mortified sick *hurt* man I ever saw."

Washington   March 9, 1865

My dear Phil   I have not been out today altho feeling better than for some time past— The Doctor advised me to keep quiet & take some little remedies as I have been suffering so much with my head of late so I took his advice— & feel better for it— & have enjoyed a quiet day & an idle one

Mr. King spent the evening at the Welles with Ad. Farragut— they had hard stories about our other Guest for instance that he took his elegant body servant who he calls "Burnside & introduced him to everybody at the Inauguration Ball— &c— Our friend will get out all this if— these late things are the result of illness— but if it is followed up— why he is lost— & of this he has been made fully aware by his old friend P.K. who says he can resist temptation if he will— for he knows by experience— I have never seen our Stout friend so jolly & agreeable[1]

Brother was offered the Spanish mission today & he declined it— then the Austrian which he also declined saying he did not intend going abroad upon any mission public or private[2]   I suppose that was to soothe for the defeat at Annapolis which could have been otherwise if the P. had so wished My Brother has resumed his professional labors & I hope will adhere to them— as a lawyer he is successful & tis a good rule to stick to that in which one does well—

Blair took a long walk with Grandma & brought me a bunch of violets— & has recoved his strength very rapidly— eats too much— Asks me often if you will answer any of his letters— Your affectionate   Lizzie

1. On March 8, EBL had described Preston King: "Mr. K— rolls about the house like a huge body of feathers— there is no in the house who moves so noiselessly—."

2. On February 12, EBL had discussed her brother's future: "Silver Spring is good enough for mine I think with you theres no watering place like it— especially since Mrs. Hale told me that Mrs. No 6 says she hates it & rejoices that 'the castle is burnt down— it may not be on air built after all if Mr. No. 6 succeeds Mr Hicks who is said to be dying today He is very much like Macawber— waiting for something to 'turn up.' "

Washington   March 10, 1865
My dear Phil   I had a very pleasant letter from Fanny today— giving me the
latest news of you— the Misspi water has agreed with you from her account
as you are so much stouter handsomer & younger than four years ago   I must
take more care of myself or I'll have no countenance for my wrinkles & grey
hair   Marion said the other day that Blair grew more like you & handsomer
every day so I'll have to make him do the looks for me—

I have been visiting today intend paying all my dues in that line so when
I go out to Silver Spring Ill have nothing of that sort to do— Mrs Foster Mrs
Doolittle & Mrs Trumbull spent the evening here & as they came by accident
seemed well pleased & gay— & all agreed that they were more at home in
our house than any other in the City— Mr Hale goes to Spain—[1] well paid
for mauling the Navy Dept— but as Mr. L said when asked why he appointed
Mr. Chase[2] "I needed one more pumpkin in the bag on that side" So this
pumpkin may keep Mr. Welles in place at least that is my cyphering—

I will write to Fanny tonight You may thereby learn that we are all well
Goodnight as it is late & Ive another letter to write   Yr affectionate   Lizzie

1. John P. Hale of New Hampshire was U.S. minister to Spain from March 1865 to
July 1869. He had been a Democratic congressman (1843–45) and antislavery senator
(1847–53), and the Free-Soil presidential nominee (1852) and senator (1855–65).

2. Lincoln had appointed Chase to be chief justice of the Supreme Court, a position that Montgomery Blair had coveted. For political reasons Lincoln had chosen a
political opponent instead of the loyal Blair.

Washington   March 18, 1865
Dear Phil   We spent the day out in the Country greatly to Blair's enjoyment— We weeded & top dressed the daisy bed & hearts ease— which have
already commence to blossom— Every thing gives promise of an early Spring
& my parents talk of moving out early in April.

Father is out at the Opera tonight So Mother & I had Genl Banks all to
ourselves & he has remained very late   he said he wished he could impart to
you tonight all the apprehensions he has about New Orleans— for then you
would soon dispatch a good force there— he fears Taylor[1] from the west side
of the City He looks happier than I've seen him this winter he has had a great
deal of trouble— & I have regretted it because of all that set from Boston
people I like him & his wife best—

Govr Johnson declined seeing him he had received a host of people & was
worn out He improved very much in his appetite— & now enjoys his food
hugely— his breakfast particularly— & now that there are but few of us at
table he talks well & a great deal & is getting happier in his feelings You will

see in todays papers the much talked of speech— is exactly as I remember it— save he reiterated two or three time the point about Tennessee being *a state*— & all the time "She was not dead— she but sleepeth was one of his utterances— but he *ordered* (*wrote*) the Reporter to write it out as exactly according to his notes as it was possible— & he has done it— & it seems to me it reads well— It never occurred to me that he had any thing the matter with him whilst I was listening to him— & I quite shared all the excitement of feeling he evinced as I thought upon his return to that scene when the 1st acts of this war were enacted— & when I heard him say to the departing Senators that if they acted upon the opinions & purposes they had just proclaim— that they earn the infamy & deserve the punishment due to Traitors

We are all well— Since I got Fanny good accounts of you I have not had any aches or pains & am remarkably well— John went off at 7 olk this morning but he had a good warm breakfast 'ere he went

The Dennisons are going west next Monday they want John's house— too many children & Allen is a destructive— So violent in his temper that I no longer interfere to induce Blair to play with him— They fight furiously— but Blair is a great favorite with the two girls— who constantly wish Allen was like Blair Lee Blair says Allen has no sense— gets mad about every thing especially if he gets beat playing marbles—" Mrs D & I have not interfered & have had more hearty laughing at both of them— Yr affecate   Lizzie

1. Confederate Gen. Richard Taylor, son of former president Zachary Taylor, had defeated Banks at Sabine Crossroads in April 1864. Taylor assumed command of the Departments of Alabama, Mississippi, and East Louisiana on September 6, 1864, then became commander of the Army of Tennessee in January 1865.

Washington   March 21, 1865

My dear Phil   I recd your's of the 16th and was very happy by its coming. I needed some little cheering too for Mother has been insisting all day that I shall have the Doctor to examine a lump in my right bosom nearly under the arm— in Jany. I had a whale bone in the body of my dress— which hurt me a little but I soon cut it out & thought no more of it until a week or so afterwards, I discovered this small knot & it has been for a few days on the increase— & I have been trying to get up courage to consult the Doctor— but so far have not done so, Mother says a woman after forty five ought be careful of all her ailments & take good care of herself & in all else my health is excellent for I have been more careful to go to bed & sleep more than I did during the winter—[1]

I received Fannys letter & read it to Blair who was very well pleased but thought she could not understand him as well you did as you knew & loved him better— He has been very happy today out at Silver Spring. Mr. King is still away with the Senatorial party on the Southern tour to Charleston & Savannah—[2] They will be back the last of this week— Mr. Johnson is still with us & improves daily in health & cheerfulness. The Camerons live in Harrisburg— but they are now with Betty &c&c

Father is pleased that you have adopted his letter— Things look squally with the Frenchmen the appointment of Montholon[3] is almost an act of hostility— they are devoted to Maximillian— & are intensely Secesh— I confess if there is a war— with France that I shall rejoice in yr present command at least until that is past & I think we only need a little time to get thro' all of our difficulties— I received a letter from Sarah Moses— she says Mag Preston[4] is flourishing at Montreal with Lordlings & Generals in her train— but she talks prudently

I have a letter to write to Lysink Campbell[5] who is in confinement to Col Gantt's house in St Louis so I must say Good night   Ever yr affectionate   Lizzie

1. On April 2, EBL wrote: "I got a scolding from Mother yesterday for writing you about what I call *my lump* of lead— she seemed to think it was very wrong— & I could *not* plead one of promptings to do it which was the bitter mortification I had felt when I found you had been sick in Phila & never let me know it   I made up my then that it was true affection to share each others burdens— & I never could have lived thro those of my younger days but for you   but for your help— & altho this may annoy you (for it can give no one anxiety) still it is a relief to my feelings to share even this little lump of annoyance & mortification— for it has never given me the least pain except in the day that the whale bone hurt me & that was so little I bore it nearly all day instead of coming home & relieving myself from it—."

2. On March 25, EBL passed along the reports of Betty and Preston King, who, she wrote: "give sad accounts of the deadness of Charleston but the beauty of Savannah seemed to refresh them   The citizens have entirely deserted the first place & keep aloof & quiet at the last."

3. Marquis de Montholon had been France's minister to Mexico and had recently been promoted to minister to the United States.

4. Margaret Preston Wickliffe married her cousin William Preston in 1840. William Preston served in the Confederate army while his family lived in Canada. In 1864, he was appointed Confederate minister to Mexico.

5. Leczinska Campbell Brown, daughter of Judge Campbell of Tennessee, married Richard Stoddert Ewell, her cousin and a general in the rebel army. She took the loyalty oath, and with the assistance of FPB, was granted amnesty, returning to Tennessee. On March 23, EBL explained: "The President granted Lysinka Campbell permission to remain & resume her rights to property & etc— if she takes the requisite oaths of Amnesty & allegiance— I wrote to her some days since— be civil to her if you see her— I have always grieved over her unhappy life— & her future does not [look] any more promising or happier than her past has been—."

Washington   March 22, 1865

My dear Phil   This has been a real March day— Still I took a long walk & paid some visits, went to Church twice— and then to dancing school where I would have doubly enjoyed it if I had you there to see how well our little urchin glided thro the Lancers & the Waltz— he has his Mother's love of dancing & learns it rapidly it was late in twilight when we came together home— when he was as patronizing of his protection of me as possible in between the dances when "the big girls were learning their steps Blair & Ned Freeman[1] were playing marbles in the hall much to Sarah's & my amusement but some others thought of knees of the pants

When I got home Mother had Dr. May here for whom she went herself today and made an appointment   so I had to submit   he says it is a small turmor & he hopes to scatter it by external applications if not the knife is a perfectly safe remedy and that too without pain   I am not in the least troubled about it

I should not mention it to you but my past experience teaches me that when I have tried to save you pain about me— you were hurt by it so I gained nothing for you by depriving myself of yr sympathy— which is the best joy of my life— This thing does not give me the slightest pain & tis my nature to yield easily to remedies— & this may prolong my life for it is my opinion the ailments which in my youth preyed on my vitals has now come to the surface— Dont mention this to anybody— Ive done so to you Mother & the Dr. and even if I have to have it taken out— it will not confine me a day to the house so tis as I tell you a small matter— & it will take sometime to decide whether this will be necessary—

Little Jimmy has the measles— We expect Apo here— next month No news from Betty— Ever yr devoted wife   Lizzie

Capt. Lamson is here— is be executive officer of the Flag Ship Colorado—[2] He has dined here & we will invite him again

1. Nine-year-old Edward Freeman was the son of Col. William and Margaret Coleman Freeman.

2. On January 27, EBL described Roswell Lamson, who had served in the North Atlantic Blockading Squadron under Lee: "he came soon after breakfast— I made him at home & asked him to dine— & he seemed very happy— talks of you with a real affection which is delightful to me & says he has written to you after each affair of Fort Fisher for he knew you would wish to see how it looked to him   his wound is getting well but he looks very thin & colorless."

Washington   March 24, 1865

Dear Phil   I remarked at dinner that you were waiting at Cairo to see Genl Thomas who had now an independant command—[1] the V.P.s eyes brightened

& remarked I rejoice that has been achieved at last— he then went on to show how Genl. T— had been treated—[2] & wound up by saying if we would observe closely— no matter what a southern *man* did was a *small* matter— always— & that throughout this war—the Union of the South had hard knocks from friends & foes— I added he might include the Navy— & he said Admirals especially Father said it was the result of a loss of political power— & even among ourselves the divisions were weakening— & the results from it gave him apprehensions for the future— He dilated on that text— in which he & the VP. accord indeed they seem to pull together like two well broken teams long used to the same burden.

There is much talk about the object of the Presidents visit to the Army & its peace purpose—[3] I know it has been urged upon— to offer over again his old Amnesty proclamation The difficulty is to get it promulgated among the people— the Leaders alone are for keeping up the war— & there was a regiment of deserters passing here yesterday father saw them— for some reason & I can see good ones these *arrivals* are no longer announced in the papers—[4] I hear they have two regiments in the Forts around Norfolk & Old Point— & others are sent to the Indian Country

I copied most of your letter last night & dispatched it this morning as you directed I copied but the courtesy part when I was too tired to proceed with civilities The rest of the family have gone to Silver Spring— but it is very cold & raw— & I shrink from— Blair of course went but with less glee as I did not go I have bought a new bed stead for him with which he is delighted—a miniature of mine & also another exactly like it, for your dressing room or as Blair says for Phil— when he comes— The single iron bedsteads are used by the servants— having a spare which comes into play often as at present for the V.Ps servant—

Mrs. Dennison started to the West Monday left Lizzie & Miss Neil with the son Neil in charge of the house Mother was there to see them yesterday & says they have all the capets up & matting down & in full summer trim— The snow which is now falling must be unexpected to them They have greatly enjoyed their winter campaign— both have La tete monte— badly— which I am happy to say they did not catch from Govr. or Mrs D— I like them both more than ever

Capt Sands is ordered to the Gulf Squadron— his wife is anxious about his health if you enclose a letter to me Ill have it forwarded to him— All well Yr affecate Lizzie

1. On February 10, Thomas's command had been expanded to include the Departments of Kentucky and the Cumberland, save those posts on the Mississippi River.

2. A Virginian and career army officer, George Thomas had been passed over for promotion three times in the past.

3. On March 23, Lincoln began his trip to City Point, Virginia, to confer with Grant.

4. On April 1, EBL commented: "when I have seen such troops of Secesh deserters about the streets without guards— tis more than human that some of [them] should not be revengeful & yet I have scanned hundreds as they passed me— & they are generally people of good countenances indicating generally depression— but never saw an angry or a rude expression in any face yet— But they are greeted & treated with respect & kindness—."

Washington   March 27, 1865

Dear Phil   It is believed here that there is a huge fight going on between Genl Grant & Genl. Lee's armies[1] This idea may have been induced by the fact that the President was expected here early today but his non arrival has started dame Rumor is fresh business—[2]

I went out this morning and as our *new* (but old English gardener) says, I did *choars*— for Mother— Blair went with me & he has since I have been house bound kept with me all I would let him

Mr King and Father off to the Opera being the gay members of the family— I hear the ex Senator has a fancy for a European trip but Bigelows appointment[3] put that plan out of joint— for which we are sorry altho' we like Bigelow & must entre nous admit he is best fitted for the place altho our friend best deserves it from his political friends, indeed few men have labored more truly & ably for the weal of the party & Country. He is very cheerful & I never saw him happier than he is here now Yesterday I had to give him some brandy— as he was not well after his sea voyage but when he came to tea to "resume his rations" the V. P. was diverted with the heartiness of his appetite in which good gift he & Betty are just now well gifted. The V.P. (who is a small eater) & Father have endless fun at their expense—[4] Refugees & prisoners hardly give the Mr Johnson time to eat— The Rebel prisoners from Tennessee judging by their applications to be permitted to take the oath are all deserting the Confederacy en masse—

Miss Hamlin has married a Capt Batchelder & is here on a wedding trip— he is a quandom crony of Bettys— has just got a paymaster's place in the Army— he is ugly enough red hair bald head & etc

We are relieved by having Shermans report of his battles of 16 & 19— in N Carolina[5] for altho I give but little credence Rebel rumors still they have the power of making me uncomfortable. Read the letter in the Tribune on Rebeldom it comes thro our State Dept & has been obtained from a Rebel Congressman whose name is "Kept *Sacredly*" & I *suppose* has got for it secret service money enough to take him abroad—

You will be glad to know that I hope from present symtoms that the present remedies I use will succeed & I hope to escape the certain one because tis severe— which is so mitigated by chloroform however that it is not be much dreaded— as in old times   I learn from the Dr. that this a common trouble among womankind— as it usually comes from bruises or weed & this of mine is just in the spot for which he healed me for the weed & he reminded me of it when Blair was nearly three months old— This is produced however by the bruise or irritation of a crooked whale bone which hurt me all day— & I was wrong to endure it a whole day— The strap which holds my skirts up— pressed it on me— but I hope to escape the penalty of my folly & inertness— All well— Yr affectionate Lizzie

1. On March 25, activity picked up on the stalemated Virginia front when rebels were repulsed in their attack on Fort Stedman just east of Petersburg. On March 28, Grant began to move his army west in preparation for the final Appomattox campaign which began on March 29.

2. On March 28, EBL wrote: "The President had not returned late in the day today and the peace talk is on every lip as the wish is in all our hearts— I fear there is a huge battle going for these two days there is an anxious look about some people's faces which makes me think this may be true— & there is a peculiar smoky look in the atmosphere—indeed this seems now to be a *crisis*— & every body watches the signs as events are now so portentous—."

3. John Bigelow was appointed minister to France in April 1865.

4. On April 1, EBL commented: "Govr Johnson was depressed— & lost all his gayety when introduced & left the table early. alone with us— he is happy but the Moment strangers come along he seems lose all cheerfulness—."

5. The Battle of Averysborough, North Carolina, on March 16 and the Battle of Bentonville, North Carolina, on March 19 were both Union victories.

Washington   April 4, 1865
My dear Phil   Yesterday Mother Betty & Blair went out to Silver Spring (& me of course) On our return we found this city in a tumult of Joy over the fall of Richmond[1] I confess to great disappointment when I found the Rebels had escaped— & did so the Secesh say a week ago—[2] I did hope even to the last that Robt Lee would refuse to be an implement of torture any longer to countrymen but he cannot be truly great and sacrifice himself & the such like few— for the weal of many

I met Mr. John Sherman who returned from Goldsboro[3] last night— he dined with Frank & to use his own phrase— "I was with him all the time—" he says he never saw him look better in his life or in better spirits Father got a letter from him by Mr. Sherman & it hath some bitterness— but tis not profit-able to dwell on— as Mr. Johnson says we middle state "folks have seen bitter hard times—" but we must bear it— for a better one is near at hand— He has made 4 speeches in the last 36 hours & is convincing people hereabouts that they have believed lies—

A funny thing happened at our door yesterday   a fashionably dressed woman came up a step or so towards Maria Smith yesterday when Mr. J— closed his speech— & asked her if that was the man who was drunk on the fourth of March   Maria replied— Get off these steps Madam— nobody can stay here who talks that way— he was no more drunk than you are this minute   The poor soul was utterly abashed & did make *tracks*—

This noise & fatigue used me up & I had to go to bed with head ache— Today however I am entirely well— went to the Asylum— did a great deal of business— was amused with Mrs. M— plucky *sause* did not respond by word or look— but when she got thro' a quiet little body asked with a child like ignorance— Well but do you think they would have left Richmond if they could have helped it?— Mary collapsed & gassed no more— She is trying to bully the board to get her a free ticket for the year over the Railroad— I am as quiet about it as you are— & thus with this year she will leave it— & in many respects she will be a great loss in others a relief—

Adl Farragut & Board have dispersed over ten days ago   Alden & other have been on a court in the Parker case at City Point— & Adl F. has been in Norfolk for a week— It was say promotions would be made certainly before the adjournment & then again in March but so far— there has been none of any prominence indeed Richmd Aulick is the only man of late promoted— Govr J see a great similitude in your treatment & that of Thomas about whom he feels intensely— but says always we must bide our time— it is coming

Mrs. L. wanted the P. to stay with Porter & let her have the Martin[4] to come here in— but refused saying Porter talked too much he could not think where he was— tis thought he will issue a proclamation from Richmond   Blair has enjoyed this jubilee very much tomorrow we will begin to hear of groans of the wounded Your affecate   Lizzie
Yrs of March 28th came today

1. The Confederates left Richmond on April 2, and federal forces occupied the city on April 3.

2. On April 7, EBL explained: "The news of today looks more like peace than even the capture of Richmond— Grant has overtaken Lee's army & the idea here is that it is whipped & surrounded but that I think is a mistake   I think it is whipped & still much of Lee's Army will escape to Lynchburg—."

3. William Sherman's army had reached Goldsborough, North Carolina, on March 23.

4. The Lincoln family was lodged on the *River Queen*, while the Grants were staying on the *Mary Martin*.

Washington   April 5, 1865
My dear Phil   The noise & confusion of joy is past so we are as quiet as if nothing had happened indeed rather more quiet than we have been for a long

time— our guests left us today for Richmond— there were good reasons which were urged on both for going so they went at 3 olk   Mrs. Lincoln & her party at ten olk— They will be back in two or three days— Mr J took all of his luggage— & Mr. King left his trunk here— so we are very quiet Altho Mr. Ben Farrar was at tea & some young ladies at dinner— Blair was ready for bed early have been up later than ever before in his life to see the illumination

I recd a letter from Nelly All well— John busy— but rather disgusted with the *small* style of farming   he has got entirely well   I shall go there in May to see them as Nelly begs me to do so She declines coming to pass Holy week with me which I urged on her   I may be here alone then for I do not intend leaving the City until Lent is over Altho deprived of our old pastor & the substitute we have a poor one still to have the privilege of Church is a very great one to me

Mr Seward was seriously injured[1] I called by on my way from the dancing school to inquire   his arm is broken— & shoulder dislocated head bruised   the Coachman was off the box & the reins were left dangling at the horses feet   Mr. Seward jumped out of the carriage— the ladies sat still & are uninjured— I do not think him in danger but he is very suffering—

I received 3 "service" magazines directed to you shall I forward or keep them?[2]

Mr. Dick spoke of John as "a *good lawyer*—" I intimated I thought *business mind* was a family trait of the Lees— to which he promply assented   he was perfectly kind & easy here— I apologized by saying a house full prevented me urging to stay with us— he replied Farrar could do without him & he could not do without Farrar in the same town He was very bright & is very much improved in his health & appearance— Mrs Warrington sent me word that she met you lately at Memphis & you never looked as well & as handsome in your life You see how my friends know my weakness— Eliza Chubb gave me the message with many kind expressions about you We are all well   Your affectionate   Lizzie

1. On April 5, Seward was injured when he tried to stop his runaway carriage and fell to the ground. In addition to a broken arm and dislocated shoulder, he also suffered a jaw broken on both sides.

2. SPL added this note: "Keep them carefully— SPL."

Washington   April 6, 1865

My dear Phil   We live on tiptoe for events— I cannot help hoping that these stupid secessionists will give up kicking against the pricks—[1] I rejoice to see the mild tones now coming from Beecher[2] & such men— & I really see much in the bitterness of the Secesh army towards the cities & people which shows that the leaders in this rebellion feel that they are deserted by the Southern people—[3] I am hopeful of a speedy peace— & hope that Mr. Lincoln will lean to mercys side—

I spent the morning in walking and visiting— Blair went with Ned & Henry to see the wild beasts and Circus & had "a bully day" I received your letter saying you would go on the morrow to St Louis so tonight Blair & I imagined you with Jim on one side Preston on the other & George on your knee—

The little Woodbury next door is to be called the Mother says Montgomery— the Father still insists on calling it Cary— but of course he will give up about it[4] All the old Ladies & Gentlemen are doing marvels in the baby line— The Wilkes over the square expect daily[5] Stammie Bache Abert—[6] will add another soon to her house full and I might fill a page with such cases which to use Dr. Millers phrase "amaze the faculty" One lady on his list he knows to be *"fifty five—"* He attended my next neighbor & it is from her I learn all this news One little point is funny— *"Tish"* insists that Mrs W. is about "our age— (ie Tish & I were born in the same year & month)— just forty one!!— dont you wish that was *"our* age—" alas I have to own to six more & four of them war years— We are all well   Your affectionate Lizzie

1. On April 7, EBL wrote: "I cannot help hoping that those poor sinful men will give up their bad & now hopeless cause & cease to torture their country All eyes are turned now to our Army— & the news is the only thought anybody seems to have."

2. Henry Ward Beecher, clergyman and a leading abolitionist, supported free soil and the nonextension of slavery.

3. On March 20, EBL explained: "Father got a letter from Frank— he is well & writes in admirable spirits— says the people of the south he '*knows*' are anxious for peace on 'any terms—' the leaders are now doing all the fighting & solely for themselves."

4. On March 14, EBL had announced the arrival of the baby: "Mrs. Montgomery presented her husband a son at seven olk this morning— she took chloroform & got off easy." The baby was finally named Montgomery, Jr.

5. Mary H. Lynch Bolton married Charles Wilkes in 1854. They lived in the Dolley Madison house, at the corner of Madison Place & H Street. Their daughter was named Mary.

6. Henrietta C. Bache married Charles Abert in 1845.

Washington   April 14, 1865[1]

Dear Phil   Yours of the 8th inst today— what a world of good news we have had since then, & it still comes for it is *certain* that Lee has been sent to Joe Johnston & all the other confederate leaders by Grant with the same terms and he has promised to use all his influence at this late hour to bring back our "Erring sisters" back to their duties[2] *Dont repeat*— but he told *Seth Williams*[3] that he had not a dollars in the world— & Longstreet said in Genl. Meigs presence (who told me) that he would go to Mexico— if he had the means but he had "not *even a cent* with which to buy my next meal—"

Lee did not know it— but he was completely enveloped with troops when he surrendered when I read the account to Mother to night from the N.Y. World of today— Blair came in the room about the time I commenced reading it & when I finished I found him sitting behind me— highly excited he exclaimed— no dont stop go on— there is more about it— I of course stopped— but it took me some time to get him in trim for sleep & it was only by promising that I would read some more in the morning.

He has been out in the Country all day with Father & Mother & we all go out to stay on Tuesday next & never did any chap feel better pleased than ours does at this move— I am quite ready to go— all my visits paid & shopping done— I shall want nothing now, from the city but your letters to me & as they are now only weekly bulletins I can get them Sundays when I come to Church!

I recd $225 from John & am very thankful to transfer my accounts to you— I did not object to going to John for fear you might feel that I had some personal reason for it— but I go to you with my wants without a feeling I would not gladly express to you but I cannot say that about going to any other person in the world— I told you what I wished to do— & I did it in part— & would have spent more in that way— but for my normal want of clothing— in which I have not been extravagant at all— My new silk gown is exactly like the one I bought just five yrs ago— when we first came to this house— it is now on my bed as a comfort I mention this little accident in my dress to show you my taste in that line has not changed with the times— *I have to help* along— & I do it in a way to gratify— not to mortify & in all repairs & furniture for which there is a constant call— for a large family in a newly equipped house I have used our means & for servants Gas— coal & etc—

I still hope to escape the knife & by a singular circumstance— I wrote you hopefully but the next day— it began to pain me & Mother saw I suffered— summoned the Dr. & he examined the tumor & & said there was no change— & said the sooner it was taken out the better— I begged delay— until your return he said nothing would induce him to consent to a delay so indefinite— but he agreed to await Govr J. & Mr. Ks departure— so day after they went to Richmond last week— I stopped in my room a little while after breakfast & was surprised to find Mother had chloroform— & everything ready for the Dr. I was shocked but said nothing & for an hour tried to be calm started to write a letter to you but I found that would upset me completely— so tried to think of any thing & anybody but you— The Dr. came & declined to do it that day saying he had been employed that morning on two cases of irecipulas & that disease was now an epidemic & he would not now attempt this case— After he left— I was taken violently sick— which you know excitement will always do for me— but I said nothing about it continued the remedies he had given— & the result is— that the tumor has now entirely disappeared from sight— & I can feel that its whole shape & character is changed— this attack of sickness produced by fright following immediately *on another*— seems to have been a good remedy— & I am full of hope it will entirely relieve me

I am weak— & nervous but keep a quiet exterior— even amid all this excitement— & glow of joy over our glorious victories— but none offer up more heartfelt thanksgivings than your wife This experience has made come to this conclusion that I will await your return home if the Dr. says I can safely do so if it returns— I could not shake off the feeling that morning— that I would die under that knife & chloroform— & to leave the world without seeing you again seemed worse than death— There was nothing reasonable or right in this feeling— & I controlled it— Still I *suffered* more than I will do again willingly—

11 olk *Friday night* Oh horror upon us again— I was surprised just now by the ringing of the door bell— everyone was sleeping but me— I went to the door— Majr Rochester said— it was he— so I opened it— & he announced the assassination of our President & the attempt upon Mr. Seward—[4] My brother was out— Charles had gone to the Country— At the moment Luke took his stand at our front door— I told him to come in— & he is here now all night— I am full of terror for you— for Father Frank & all my dear ones— Mr. Seward lives the jugular was not cut— Another ring Luke went to the door— an officer called to say the provost marshall ordered a guard of 6 men to protect this house— & that it must be examined— I went up stairs & Luke below My Parents & darling boy sleep sweetly— but Ill watch & pray for my precious husband— & Country— Your devoted wife— Lizzie

Mr Johnson is at the Hotel— he went there on his return from Richmond when here yesterday said he was so run down by people— that as he was well he would not[5]

1. EBL had injured her thumb and had been unable to write for several days.

2. On April 9, Robert E. Lee surrendered his army to Ulysses S. Grant at Appomattox Court House, Virginia. On April 12, EBL wrote: "The whole Rebellion this side of Texas will be over before July— The Secesh here take Lee's surrender terribly to heart— some of my acquaintances weep in church & along the streets even— & seem altogether inconsolable They say that they were entirely confident of success even after the evacuation of Richmond— Indeed that was spoken of to me a 'masterly achievement—' 'prearranged of course months since.'"

3. Maj. Gen. Seth Williams, a career army officer, had been adjutant general of the Army of the Potomac and then Grant's inspector general. He had participated in the final campaign leading to Lee's surrender.

4. On April 14, in Ford's Theater, Abraham Lincoln was shot. On the same night, William Seward was stabbed while still in his bed recovering from his carriage accident.

5. The end of the letter not found.

Washington   April 15, 1865

Dear Phil   This dark & dreary day for us all has a silver lining to the clouds which overshadow all— for you & for me The Doctor came this morning to make arrangements with Mother for cutting out the tumor   I was at Church She told him of the changed appearance— he waited to see— & I will never forget the expression of relief & pleasure in his face when he said— I have good news for you—I feared this was cancerous— & therefore I could not conscientiously delay it longer but this change *proves* it to be only a bruise— & I am sure you will get rid of it without the knife This has been the fear which haunted me, And if it had turned out to be so— I intended begging you to come to me. You can never know how bitterly I have felt these last months of our long separation but I must not murmur, but be a thankful & I do pray a better woman

Yours of the 11th reached me today— its joyousness even cheered up this gloomy day— the grief of the people here is sincere & intense— Those of southern sympathies know now they have lost a friend willing— & more powerful to protect & serve them than they can now ever hope to find again— Their grief is as honest as that of any one of our side. Many of whom are not as fortunate in knowing how true & able a man succeeds Mr. Lincoln

Mr. Chase came to Father at the quiet inauguration of today[1] & took his hand & with tearful eyes said "Mr. Blair I hope that from this day there will cease all anger & bitterness between us—" My Father responded promptly & kindly. This whole city is draped in Black— I had our house fixed early in the day— The flag taken in by seven olk— I did not sleep much last night but managed to have the house kept so quiet that my Parents slept all night without any disturbance— The Assasin[2] is a drinking foolish fanatic— whose father has been often a frantic madman from drunkenness— all of English origin & feelings— I hope it proves be a theatrical conspiracy— with which no leading southern man had anything to [do]—

Father & I went over to inquire about Mrs. Lincoln— leaving a note of great kindness for her— I called this evening to enquire about the Sewards— they were better & Dr May thinks young Seward[3] can recover— he is young & without he is of feeble constitution will soon rally— Mr Seward is in no danger— I hear much talk about the future but think it prudent not to write it— I feel no distrust in the future of our Country   Grant is here tonight & that will keep some obstreperous military in order— & the smooth working of our Government only proves its great excellence & will bring to it more love & reverence— & faith than ever yet felt— by even its truest votaries   Blair is well— Ever yr devoted wife   Lizzie

Adl Goldsboroughs only child & daughter is thought hopelessly ill— of hemmorage   write to him   they are heart broken & I hear he is utterly hopeless about her— a sweet gentle good girl—

1. Chief Justice Salmon Chase gave the oath of office to Andrew Johnson at the Kirkwood Hotel, with the cabinet and a small gathering in attendance.

2. Actor John Wilkes Booth.

3. William Seward's son Fred was injured while he struggled with his father's assailant.

Washington   April 17, 1865

My dear Phil   Yesterday was a bright Easter Sunday but all in this city seemed oppressed with gloom— much of the feeling is attributable to the false impressions heretofore— encouraged by those *most* in power about Mr J— the endless queries put at me is proof of this— I feel quite sure if he is spared to the country he will make an able *honest* President & one of which we will be truly proud— &c he commences auspiciously for the news comes that Joe Johnston will lay down his arms without being surrounded—[1] Sherman has referred the matter here & Genl Grant told Father that he had sent the same terms he offered to Lee— Mobile taken & Forrest[2] whipped looks like a winding up of this dreadful war and a return home of our sailors & soldiers—

I saw Mr. King today walking up the Avenue— I hear he is all the time with Mr. Johnson— with whom Mother saw him in a carriage escorted by soldiers— they both looked at her & were evidently tempted to laugh   Mr. J dont fancy the guards at all—

Mrs. Lincolns condition is very pitiable— she has hysteria & has sometimes been very delerious— I have offered my services to watch & wait upon her—[3] they have published that Mrs. No 6 had offered the hospitalities of her house &etc &c— but it was father & I— who did it— but tis not our first act accredited to No 6— They already talk & fret as Mr J— had been their guest— altho but once in the house & *never* asked there   he felt the lack of courtesy among these officials— but dont repeat this for he really cares nothing about so matters— save as a matter of good feeling—

I am not very strong— but in all else well— the lump grows delightfully less daily & it lifts a load off of my spirits[4] Our return is delayed to the country as no one is allowed to go in & out of this city on any of the roads but the railroad— The city today was full of rumors & excitement about the captured Assassins— but nothing certain is ascertained— I think both the Sewards will live— the man nurse[5] is dead— We expect Apo soon— may receive her here— which she will like— tho' the children will prefer the country where Blair & I sigh to go— Your affectionate Lizzie

1. On April 17, William Sherman and Joseph Johnston met near Durham Station, North Carolina, to discuss terms of an armistice.

2. On April 12, Mobile, Alabama, surrendered to the federal troops of E. R. S.

Canby. Nathan Bedford Forrest, commander of the Confederate District of Mississippi, east Louisiana, and west Tennessee, lost Selma, Alabama, on April 2 and continued skirmishing over the next few days led to further rebel retreats.

3. On April 28, EBL described a visit to Mary Lincoln: "I went to see Mrs. Lincoln had a painful time she entreated me to come stay with her the rest of the time she remains here— nobody is as kind and agreeable as I am &etc I plead off—."

4. The lump did not go away, and on May 30 EBL submitted to surgery. Dr. Frederick May performed the operation, assisted by Orphan Asylum manager Mary Wannell, Evy Martin Alexander, and EBL's servant Becky. Her recovery was surprisingly rapid; on June 6, she returned to Silver Spring.

5. Sgt. George T. Robinson had been serving as Seward's nurse. He was injured in the fight to save Seward's life but recovered from his wounds.

[Washington] [April 19, 1865] [1]
My dear Phil Dr. Stone has just been over to ask me to take Mrs Welles [2] place— at four olk by Mrs Lincoln's side— I agreed to do so most promptly & am now all ready to go but must say a word to you— for I may be detained longer than I now expect to be & will be weary after a night of sad watching & need sleep & rest— tomorrow— The Dr. says she spoke of wishing to have me there as one she who had attracted her sympathies & confidence more than almost any one in the City She has always been marked in her kindness of manner to me

Certain it is I feel great pity for her now— it is a terrible thing to fall from such a height to one of loneliness & poverty— And no woman ever had a more indulgent kind husband Some have thought she had not his affections but tis evident to me she had no doubt about it and that is a point about which women are not often decieved after a long married life like theirs— She told me when I last saw her after twitting for not going out more with Betty & enjoying society— I told her I had all the enjoyment it could give me— A little while afterwards she was talking about going to the country— saying she meant to stay with her husband for he needed her care and she meant to a good wife too. looking at me archly She then dilated on the havoc which the labors of the last 4 years had made upon Mr Lincolns constitution—

Mother took Blair out to the country with her this morning— & I meant to have packed up my trunk for a move on Thursday— but after Dr. Stones call I concluded to do nothing fatiguing Mr King was here— I said that he had not come *home*— as he ought to have done— he said he & Mr J. had spoken of that & wished themselves back here most heartily— but to come now would look timid & therefore they had remained where these events found them—

Mrs. Welles now waits for me She begs me not to smile Mrs. L. said Oh I dread to see *Mrs. Lee's smile*—" She laughs— but I have little to make me smile My only fear is Ill weep so good day Yr affecate Lizzie

1. SPL added this note: "probably written April 19/65 *postmarked 20th."*

2. On April 25, EBL commented on Mary Jane Welles: "Today she [Mrs. Lincoln] declined to see Mrs Welles— who is so good & gentle— I am very much won by her since *we* have 'served together' on this sad occasion."

Washington   April 20, 1865

My dear Phil   I did not leave Mrs. Lincoln until after six when her two children had returned from the obsequies of their father— I was so weary from 24 hours of unflagging watching that I undressed & went to bed— & slept until late this morning   I am quite refreshed & the Secy of the Navy has just left me— saying Mrs. Welles wishes me to relieve her— so I am off in a few moments but could not go until I thanked you for your three letter   they cheered & I am ready at any moment to go to you— in all respects save I have not money enough— having spent that I had on my summer outfit which I have much of it still to make up—

I will read your letter to Father about Spencer rifles   have not had time or chance yet   All well   I must hasten away   I never thought of you more in my life in the same time as in this last week nor realized that I am blessed indeed to have you spared to me amid so many perils   May God still so bless us— is unceasing prayer of your devoted Lizzie

Washington   April 22, 1865

My dear Phil   Your reproach that your long absence had made me forget what was due to you— haunted & hurt me— & as I knew no matter how illjudged the outlay had been I never doubted that all I did was within what I thought was the spirit of your wishes— So on my return last night from the White House I spent some hours for I am wofully slow over arithmetic counting up & conning over my account book since Jany 1st— & following are the results of my cogitation & counting for furniture (which I thought the comfort of the house required) and repairs— Insurance & water tax $550.00 Servants wages every month— cook 12— washerwoman 12— chambermaid 10— Man 15— 196 Gas & coal— 200— Blairs french & dancing 52 In groceries— meat bills and confectionary $300 I may have been very ill judged about getting curtains— new fire place for the little parlor & etc— but as we had no elegance in our parlors I felt it was right to make the rooms we occupied as perfectly comfortable as it was possible— & then when I found there was no money elsewhere to pay the above bills— I paid them & felt fully sanctioned in doing by a recent letter from you bearing on this point— And as Father has but fifty thousand dollars that I know of in the world besides his home & its surroundings— I thought it was right without saying anything even Mother— thus to use the means in my power— Hereafter I shall not do so save the amounts specified by you for that purpose— The rest I have spent in some clothing &

indulgences for Blair & myself— the bills making the clothes are to be paid as they are still in the hands of the semptress— Now I feel there is nothing oblivious of you in all this however ill judged it may be— You have always shown so much affection for my Parents that if I have indulged my own towards them I never doubted your sympathy and do not now—

I recd from Baltre yesterday wedding cards from Mr Eugene Van Rensselear— Manor House— and Miss Pendleton— and invitation to Adl. & Mrs Lee from Mr. & Mrs. Kennedy—[1] No 90 Madison Street Baltimore I know some of this party— but infer from the invitation they are among yr acquaintances The enclosed letter I opened without looking at the address as it was handed to me as a letter for me—

Mrs. Lincoln is better physically & her nervous system begins to rally from the terrible shock— I thought her mind had recovered in part its tone— but her grief is terrible & altogether for her husband as her all in life— this makes her sorrow doubly touching I am surprised to find so far that she has not uttered a word of resignation— or religious submission She had her hand on his arm when he was shot he never quivered— the flash of the pistol made her hold him tighter & when she first saw him after it— the "*head had drooped upon his chest—*" *&* "*eyes closed &*" it looked calm *&* "*Thy will be done*" "*his spirit fled then for he was never once moved by my anguish*" She addresses him in sleep & in her delirium from raging fever in terms & tones of the tenderest affection— She constantly refers to his religious faith— but never to her own— I shall return there again this evening & shall continue to go as long as I find I can stand it— or be of any use—

So far I keep well— but am conscious of being continually excited even sleep does relieve me from the idea & memory of scenes of the day— Mother is packing to go home Monday Says I shall go with her or next day— There is a regiment now stationed where the Masstts 10th was encamped— Father has ordered two Spencer rifles & agrees entirely with you about the state of affairs

Blair is well— smells of onions like an old Spaniard— The Dr. advises it as antidote to his tendency to worms— his health has been excellent— better this winter than ever before— Ive had but one really anxious time abt him— & that was much lighter sickness than he had a yr ago— All well Yr affectionate Lizzie

1. John Pendleton Kennedy, Maryland congressman (1840–44), had been secretary of the navy in Millard Fillmore's cabinet.

Washington   April 25, 1865

My dear Phil   I have been hurrying all day to get things off into the country but after all Father and Mother concluded not to go until tomorrow— when they say I must go too Father has accepted your offer & bought the two guns

& he has paid for them today but I told him you would refund them— he believed they were fifty dollars but I have not asked him since his return from the Dept as Mr. Doolittle dined with us so I did not discuss such details—

I think my Parents want to get me into the Country & tho I am not sick yet, feel the quiet & rest of my Country home will be a good thing for me[1] the Mass 10th is in its old camp & I think pickets at both gates so were are as well off there as we are here indeed I feel no anxiety— on that score altho Father adopts your views most cordially but I think we are too near the Forts & pickets which are always at our gate—

Mr. Doolittle listened to Fathers reading of your general order[2] & it was thought excellent— I am off to the White House as soon as Blair gets dressed she wishes us to take charge of her goats which were the pets of her husband— Blair wishes to go see them & get Tad[3] to tell him their names— I feel anxious about your obstinate cold Blair is quite over his which went off on his bowels and stomach— which are his weakest organs— He is wild with joy of going home soon—

I do hope Sherman has not prolonged the war by his mistakes which I think are most unnecesarily enlarged upon[4] If they traitors all get into Texas— & are soon driven out of that state by our immense [?] it cannot last long— But I think Joe has treated for time to let "*the Confederates*" have a chance of escape & he will accept when they are safe— Lees fate— I think the confederates abroad will be proved the active originators & payers for the assassination I have always thought it a foreign plot—

Blair is ready to see the goats so I must close this note I expect write to you from Silver Spring on our wedding day— I do not wish to waste any more of my life This is the 5th consecutive wedding day I have passed away from you— at first I thought you were away the Sixth but you hurried home from Chicago & got on the 27th which I appreciated then & *now* Your devoted Lizzie

1. On April 30, EBL wrote: "I shall come in occasionally to see her but will not stay if I can help it so late at night again but she says night is her terrible time & it is hard to see one suffer & refuse to do what they think will relieve them I found her yesterday in a wild state of excitement— but she became calm in an hour & remain so all the time I was there I left her with her son talking of business which she had not been quiet enough to do before She reminds me constantly of Mary Boswell of whose warmth of heart I alway thought better than most person because I knew her history better." EBL continued to assist Mrs. Lincoln, and wrote on May 4: "I am going to the city tomorrow to see Mrs. Lincoln she begged me so hard yesterday not to leave her that I feel as if it was a duty to go— yet I do dread it— more & more She says no one gives her half the relief or does in the least feel for her as I do I suppose this is flattering Still— she makes me feel of use & therefore I ought to go— Mrs. Welles— Mrs. Kenny (a sister of Mrs. Senator Dixon) are the only persons she receives at all."

2. Lee's order to his command on the death of Lincoln.

3. Thomas Todd Lincoln (Tad), the president's twelve-year-old son.

4. On April 18, Sherman and Joe Johnston had signed a memorandum of armistice which went well beyond any authority granted Sherman and infringed upon reconstruction policies. The cabinet rejected the memorandum, and Sherman was ordered simply to conclude a military end to hostilities and not to negotiate peace terms.

Bibliography

The literature on the American Civil War is so vast that no bibliography of reasonable length can encompass all the significant works. This bibliography, therefore, lists only those materials which have been most helpful in the editing of these letters. For more comprehensive surveys, see Allan Nevins, James I. Robertson, Jr., and Bell I. Wiley, *Civil War Books: A Critical Bibliography*, 2 vols. (Baton Rouge: Louisiana State University Press, 1967–69) and James McPherson, *Ordeal by Fire: The Civil War and Reconstruction* (New York: Alfred A. Knopf, 1982) and his more recent bibliographic note in *Battle Cry of Freedom* (New York: Oxford University Press, 1988).

Manuscript Sources

Alexander Bible Records from Bible of William Alexander. Brought to Woodford County, Kentucky, from Virginia, copied February 6, 1928, by Mrs. Jouett Taylor Cannon, State Chairman of Genealogical Research for Kentucky. Kentucky Historical Society.
Blair Family Papers. Library of Congress.
Blair Family Papers. Western Historical Collection, State Historical Society of Missouri. Columbia, Missouri.
Blair Papers. Missouri Historical Society. St. Louis.
Blair-Lee Papers. Princeton University. Princeton, New Jersey.
Hillcrest Children's Center Collection. Library of Congress.
Lee Papers. Missouri Historical Society. St. Louis.
National Archives. Record Group 24. Records of the Bureau of Naval Personnel.
———. Record Group 45. Naval Records Collection of the Office of Naval Records and Library.
———. Record Group 94. Records of the Adjutant General's Office.
———. Record Group 156. Records of the Office of the Chief of Ordnance.
St. John's Episcopal Church Parish Records. Washington, D.C.

Newspapers

Army and Navy Journal, 1860–97.
Baltimore American Commercial Advertizer, 1860–65.
New York Evening Post, 1860–90.

New York Herald, 1860–65.
New York Times, 1860–98.
New York Tribune, 1860–90.
Philadelphia Inquirer, 1860–65.
Philadelphia Public Ledger, 1860–65.
Washington Daily Intelligencer, 1860–65.
Washington Evening Star, 1860–65.

City Directories

Boyd's Washington Directory, 1860, 1862, 1863, 1864.
Hutchinson's Washington and Georgetown Directory . . . 1863.
McElroy's Philadelphia Directory, 1861, 1862, 1864.
Thomas' Buffalow City Directory for 1862.
Wood's Baltimore City Directory, 1864.

Printed Primary Materials

Ames, Mary Clemmer. *Ten Years in Washington: Life and Scenes in the National Capital as a Woman Sees Them*. Hartford, Conn.: A. D. Worthington and Company, 1873.

Basler, Roy P., ed. *The Collected Works of Abraham Lincoln*. 9 vols. New Brunswick, N.J.: Rutgers University Press, 1953–55.

Bates, Edward. *The Diary of Edward Bates, 1859–1866*. Edited by Howard K. Beale. Washington, D.C.: Government Printing Office, 1933.

Bay, William Van Ness. *Reminiscences of the Bench and Bar of Missouri*. St. Louis: F. H. Thomas and Company, 1878.

Census of the United States, 1850, 1860, 1870. Washington, D.C.: Government Printing Office, 18

Chesnut, Mary Boykin. *Mary Chesnut's Civil War*. Edited by C. Vann Woodward. New Haven: Yale University Press, 1981.

Clarke, Dwight L., ed. *The Original Journals of Henry Smith Turner with Stephen Watts Kearny to New Mexico and California, 1846–1847*. Norman: University of Oklahoma Press, 1966.

Congressional Globe. 46 vols. Washington, D.C., 1834–73.

Fisher, Sidney G. *A Philadelphia Perspective: The Diary of Sidney George Fisher Covering the Years 1834–1871*. Edited by Nicholas B. Wainwright. Philadelphia: Historical Society of Pennsylvania, 1967.

Fox, Gustavus Vasa. *Confidential Correspondence of Gustavus Vasa Fox, Assistant Secretary of the Navy 1861–1865*. 2 vols. Edited by Robert M. Thompson and Richard Wainwright. New York: DeVinne Press, 1918.

French, Benjamin Brown. *Witness to the Young Republic: A Yankee's Journal, 1828–1870*. Edited by Donald B. Cole and John J. McDonough. Hanover, N.H.: University Press of New England, 1989.

Grant, Ulysses. *Personal Memoirs of U. S. Grant*. Edited by E. B. Long. Cleveland: World Publishing Co., 1952.

Johnson, Robert U., and Clarence C. Buel, eds. *Battles and Leaders of the Civil War*. 2d ed. 4 vols. New York: Thomas Yoseloff, 1956.

Meade, George. *The Life and Letters of George Gordon Meade.* New York: Charles Scribner's Sons, 1913.

Moore, Frank, ed. *The Rebellion Record. A Diary of American Events, with Documents, Narratives, Illustrative Incidents, Poetry, etc.* 12 vols. 1861–68. Reprint. New York: Arno Press, 1977.

Official Records of the Union and Confederate Navies in the War of the Rebellion. 30 vols. Washington, D.C.: Government Printing Office, 1894–1922.

Official Register of Officers and Agents of the United States Government for the Year 1861. Washington, D.C.: Goverment Printing Office, 1862.

Official Register of Officers and Agents of the United States Government for the Year 1863. Washington, D.C.: Goverment Printing Office, 1864.

Official Register of the Volunteer Force of the U.S. Army for the Years 1861, 62, 63, 64, 65. 8 vols. Washington, D.C.: Government Printing Office, 1865–67.

Poore, Ben Perley. *Perley's Reminiscences of Sixty Years in the National Metropolis.* Philadelphia: Hubbard Bros., 1886.

Pryor, Mrs. Roger A. *Reminiscences of Peace and War.* New York: Macmillan Company, 1904.

Register of the Commissioned, Warrant, and Volunteer Officers of the Navy of the United States, including Officers of the Marine Corps and Others, to January 1, 1865. Washington, D.C.: Government Printing Office, 1865.

Sands, Benjamin Franklin. *From Reefer to Rear Admiral: Reminiscences and Journal Jottings of Nearly Half a Century of Naval Life.* New York: Frederick A. Stokes Company, 1899.

Smith, Margaret Bayard. *The First Forty Years of Washington Society.* Edited by Gaillard Hunt. New York: Charles Scribner's Sons, 1906.

Spence, Mary Lee, ed. *The Expedition of John Charles Frémont.* 3 vols. Urbana: University of Illinois Press, 1970–84.

Steedman, Charles. *Memoir and Correspondence of Charles Steedman, Rear Admiral, United States Navy with his Autobiography and Private Journals, 1811–1890.* Edited by Amos Lawrence Mason. Cambridge, Mass.: Riverside Press, 1912.

The War of the Rebellion: A Compilation of the Official Records of the Union and Confederate Armies. 70 vols. in 128. Washington. D.C.: Government Printing Office, 1881–1901

Welles, Gideon. *Diary of Gideon Welles, Secretary of the Navy under Lincoln and Johnson.* Edited by Howard K. Beale. 3 vols. New York: W. W. Norton, 1960.

Secondary Materials

Adams, Ephraim D. *Great Britain and the American Civil War.* 2 vols. 1925. Reprint. Gloucester, Mass.: Peter Smith, 1957.

The Army Lawyer: A History of the Judge Advocate General's Corps, 1775–1975. Washington, D.C.: Government Printing Office, 1975.

Ashe, Samuel A'Court, ed. *Biographical History of North Carolina from Colonial Times to the Present.* 4 vols. Greensboro, N.C.: Charles L. Van Noppen, 1906.

Baker, Jean. *The Politics of Continuity: Maryland Political Parties from 1858 to 1870.* Baltimore: The Johns Hopkins University Press, 1973.

Barrett, John G. *The Civil War in North Carolina.* Chapel Hill: University of North Carolina Press, 1963.

Bates, Samuel P. *History of Pennsylvania Volunteers, 1861–1865.* Harrisburg: B. Singerly, 1869.

Bauer, K. Jack. *The Mexican War: 1846–1848.* New York: Macmillan, 1974.

———. *Ships of the Navy 1775–1969.* Vol. 1: *Combat Vessels.* Troy, N.Y.: Renssaelaer Polytechnic Institute, 1969.

Bennett, Frank. *The Steam Navy of the United States: A History of the Growth of the Steam Vessel of War in the U.S. Navy and of the Naval Engineer Corps.* 1896. Reprint. Westport, Conn.: Greenwood Press, 1974.

Biographical Cyclopedia of Representative Men of Maryland and the District of Columbia. Baltimore: National Biographical Publishing Company, 1879.

Biographical Directory of the American Congress, 1774–1971. Washington, D.C.: Government Printing Office, 1971.

Biographical Encyclopedia of New Jersey of the Nineteenth Century. Philadelphia: Galaxy Publishing Company, 1877.

"Biographical Notice of James Melville Gillis." *Annual of the National Academy of Sciences for 1866,* 53–107. Cambridge, Mass.: Welch, Bigelow and Company, 1867.

Blair, Gist. "Annals of Silver Spring." *Records of the Columbia Historical Society* 21 (1918): 155–85.

Blue, Frederick J. *Salmon P. Chase: A Life in Politics.* Kent, Ohio: Kent State University Press, 1987.

Bogue, Allen G. *The Earnest Men: Republicans of the Civil War Senate.* Ithaca: Cornell University Press, 1981.

Bowie, Effie Gwynn. *Across the Years in Prince George's County: A Genealogical and Biographical History of Some Prince George's County, Maryland and Allied Familes.* Baltimore: Genealogical Publishing Company, 1975.

Boyd, T. H. S. *The History of Montgomery County, Maryland, from its Earliest Settlement in 1650 to 1879. . . .* 1879. Reprint. Baltimore: Regional Publishing Company, 1968.

Brand, William F. *The Life of William Rollinson Whittingham, Fourth Bishop of Maryland.* 2 vols. New York: E. and J. B. Young and Company, 1883.

Brown, Orlando. *Memoranda of the Preston Family.* Frankfort, Ky.: Hodges, Todd & Pruett, 1842.

Bryan, Wilhelmus B. *A History of the National Capital from its Foundation through the Period of the Adoption of the Organic Act.* 2 vols. New York: Macmillan Company, 1916.

Bullock, Joseph G. B. *A History and Genealogy of the Families of Bayard, Houstoun of Georgia. . . .* Washington, D.C.: James H. Dony, 1919.

Cain, Marvin R. *Lincoln's Attorney General: Edward Bates of Missouri.* Columbia: University of Missouri Press, 1965.

Cajori, Florian. *The Chequered Career of F. R. Hassler.* Boston: Christopher Publishing House, 1929.

Callahan, Edward W., ed. *List of Officers of the Navy of the United States and of the Marine Corps from 1775 to 1900. . . .* New York: Haskell House, 1969.

Case, Lynn M., and Warren F. Spencer. *The United States and France: Civil War Diplomacy.* Philadelphia: University of Pennsylvania Press, 1970.

Catton, Bruce. *The Centennial History of the Civil War.* 3 vols. Garden City, N.Y.: Doubleday and Co., 1961–65.

Channing, Stephen A. *Crisis of Fear: Secession in South Carolina.* New York: Simon and Schuster, 1970.

Childs, James Rives. *Reliques of the Rives (Ryves), Being Historical and Genealogical Notes of the Ancient Family of Ryves of County Dorset and of the Rives of Virginia.* Lynchburg, Va.: J. P. Bell Company, 1929.

Civil War Naval Chronology. Compiled by the Naval History Division of the Navy Department. Washington, D.C.: Government Printing Office, 1971.

Cleaves, Freeman. *Meade of Gettysburg.* Norman: University of Oklahoma Press, 1960.

———. *Rock of Chickamauga: The Life of General George H. Thomas.* Norman: University of Oklahoma Press, 1949.

Clift, G. Glenn, comp. *Kentucky Marriages, 1797–1865.* Baltimore: Genealogical Publishing Company, 1978.

Coddington, Edwin B. *The Gettysburg Campaign: A Study in Command.* New York: Charles Scribner's Sons, 1968.

Cole, Donald B. *Jacksonian Democracy in New Hampshire, 1800–1851.* Cambridge: Harvard University Press, 1970.

Coleman, Mrs. Chapman. *The Life of John J. Crittenden, with selections from his Correspondence and Speeches, by his daughter.* 2 vols. Philadelphia: J. B. Lippincott and Company, 1871.

Collins, Lewis. *History of Kentucky.* 2 vols. Covington, Ky.: Collins and Company, 1878.

Cooling, Benjamin Franklin. *Symbol, Sword, and Shield: Defending Washington during the Civil War.* Hamden, Conn.: Shoe String Press, 1975.

Cornish, Dudley T., and Virginia J. Laas. *Lincoln's Lee: The Life of Samuel Phillips Lee, United States Navy, 1812–1897.* Lawrence: University Press of Kansas, 1986.

Crippen, Lee F. *Simon Cameron: Ante-Bellum Years.* 1942. Reprint. New York: DaCapo Press, 1972.

Crozier, William Armstrong, ed. *The Buckners of Virginia and the Allied Families of Strother and Ashby.* New York: Genealogical Association, 1907.

Cummings, Damon E. *Admiral Richard Wainwright and the United States Fleet.* Washington, D.C.: Government Printing Office, 1962.

Davis, Charles. *Life of Rear Admiral Charles Henry Davis, Rear Admiral, 1807–1877.* Boston: Houghton Mifflin and Company, 1899.

Dell, Christopher. *Lincoln and the War Democrats.* Madison, N.J.: Fairleigh Dickinson University Press, 1975.

Dorman, John Frederick. *The Prestons of Smithfield and Greenfield in Virginia: Descendants of John and Elizabeth (Patton) Preston through Five Generations.* Philadelphia: The Filson Club, 1982.

Dudley, William S. *Going South: U.S. Navy Officer Resignations and Dismissals on the Eve of the Civil War.* Washington, D.C.: Naval Historical Foundation, 1981.

Dyer, Frederick H. *A Compendium of the War of the Rebellion.* 3 vols. New York: Thomas Yoseloff, 1959.

Farquhar, Roger Brooke. *Historic Montgomery County Maryland: Old Homes and History.* Baltimore: Monumental Printing Company, 1952.

French, David M. "The Brent Family." Alexandria, Va., 1981. Typescript, New England Historical and Genealogical Society, Boston, Mass.

Gamble, Robert S. *Sully: The Biography of a House.* Chantilly, Va.: Sully Foundation, 1973.

"George Madison." *Kentucky Historical Register,* 1903.

Getty, Mildred Newbold. "Montgomery Blair." *Montgomery County Story* 8 (Nov. 1964): 1–10.

——— . *To Light the Way: A History of Grace Episcopal Church, Silver Spring Maryland.* N.p., 1965.

Gibbs, George. *The Gibbs Family of Rhode Island and Some Related Families.* New York: privately printed, 1933.

Gienapp, William E. *The Origins of the Republican Party, 1852–1856.* New York: Oxford University Press, 1987.

Giffen, Jerena East. *First Ladies of Missouri: Their Homes and Their Families.* N.p.: Von Hoffmann Press, 1970.

Goode, Paul R. *The United States Soldiers' Home: A History of Its First Hundred Years.* Richmond: William Byrd Press, 1957.

Govan, Gilbert E., and James W. Livingood. *A Different Valor: The Story of General Joseph E. Johnston.* New York: Bobbs-Merrill, 1956.

Green, Constance M. *The Church on Lafayette Square: A History of St. John's Church, Washington D.C., 1815–1970.* Washington, D.C.: Potomac Books, 1970.

Gunderson, Robert Gray. *Old Gentlemen's Convention: The Washington Peace Conference of 1861.* Madison: University of Wisconsin Press, 1961.

Hall, Henry. *The History of Auburn.* Auburn, N.Y.: Dennis Brothers and Company, 1869.

Hamersly, Lewis R. *The Records of Living Officers of the U.S. Navy and Marine Corps. . . .* Philadelphia: J. B. Lippincott and Company, 1870.

Hamlin, Charles Eugene. *The Life and Times of Hannibal Hamlin.* Cambridge, Mass.: Riverside Press, 1899.

Hattaway, Herman, and Archer Jones. *How the North Won: A Military History of the Civil War.* Urbana: University of Illinois Press, 1983.

Havighurst, Walter. *Ohio: A Bicentennial History.* New York: W. W. Norton, 1976.

Heitman, Francis B. *Historical Register and Dictionary of the United States Army from its Organization, September 29, 1789, to March 2, 1903.* 2 vols. Washington, D.C.: Government Printing Office, 1903.

Henderson, Daniel. *The Hidden Coasts: A Biography of Admiral Charles Wilkes.* New York: William Sloane Associates, 1953.

Hibben, Henry B. *Navy Yard, Washington. History from Organization, 1799 to Present Date.* Washington, D.C.: Government Printing Office, 1890.

Historical Court Records of Washington, District of Columbia Marriages, 1811–1853. Compiled by Homer A. Walker. 14 vols. Privately published (mimeographed), n.d.

Hoffman, Eugene A. *Genealogy of the Hoffman Family*. New York: Dodd, Mead and Company, 1899.

"Honorable Levi Woodbury of Portsmouth, New Hampshire." *The New England Historical and Genealogical Register*, vol. 1, pp. 84–86. Edited by William Cogswell. Boston: Samuel G. Drake, 1847.

Howard, Cecil Hampden Cutts, comp. *Genealogy of the Cutts Family in America*. Albany: Joel Munsell's Sons, 1892.

Howe, M. A. DeWolfe. *Memoirs of the Life and Services of the Rt. Rev. Alonzo Potter*. Philadelphia: J. B. Lippincott and Company, 1871.

Hyde, William, and Howard L. Conard. *Encyclopedia of the History of St. Louis*. 4 vols. New York: Southern History Company, 1899.

Johnson, Robert E. *Rear Admiral John Rodgers 1812–1882*. Annapolis: U.S. Naval Institute Press, 1967.

Jones, Elias. *Revised History of Dorchester County, Maryland*. Baltimore: Read-Taylor Press, 1925.

Keidel, George C. "Jeb Stuart in Maryland, June, 1863." *Maryland Historical Magazine* June 1939: 161–64.

Kieffer, Chester L. *Maligned General: The Biography of Thomas Sidney Jesup*. San Rafael, Calif.: Presidio Press, 1979.

Klein, Philip S. *President James Buchanan: A Biography*. University Park: Pennsylvania State University Press, 1962.

Korngold, Ralph. *Thaddeus Stevens: A Being Darkly Wise and Rudely Great*. New York: Harcourt, Brace & Co., 1955.

Krug, Mark M. *Lyman Trumbull: Conservative Radical*. New York: A. S. Barnes & Co., 1965.

Lee, Edmund Jennings. *Lee of Virginia 1642–1892*. Philadelphia: Edmund Jennings Lee, 1895.

Leech, Margaret. *Reveille in Washington, 1860–1865*. Garden City, N.Y.: Garden City Publishing Co., 1945.

Long, David F. *Ready to Hazard: A Biography of Commodore William Bainbridge, 1774–1833*. Hanover, N.H.: University Press of New England, 1981.

Long, E. B. *The Civil War Day by Day: An Almanac, 1861–1865*. Garden City, N.Y.: Doubleday & Co., 1971.

Malone, Dumas, and Allen Johnson, eds. *Dictionary of American Biography*. 22 vols. New York: Charles Scribner's Sons, 1933–36.

Martin, E. S. *Some Account of Family Stock Involved in Life at Willowbrook and of Neighbors Residents and Visitors Especially in the Latter Part of the Nineteenth Century*. Willowbrook, N.Y.: printed by E. S. Martin, 1933.

May, Robert E. *John A. Quitman: Old South Crusader*. Baton Rouge: Louisiana State University Press, 1985.

McPherson, James M. *Battle Cry of Freedom: The Civil War Era*. New York: Oxford University Press, 1988.

———. *The Negro's Civil War: How American Negroes Felt and Acted during the War for the Union*. New York: Pantheon Books, 1965.

———. *Ordeal by Fire: The Civil War and Reconstruction*. New York: Alfred A. Knopf, 1982.

Meigs, Henry B. *Records of the Descendants of Vincent Meigs who came from Dorsetshire, England, to America about 1835*. Baltimore: John S. Bridges and Company, 1901.

Meirs, Earl S., ed. *Lincoln Day by Day: A Chronology 1809–1865*. 3 vols. Vol. 1: 1809–1848, compiled by William E. Baringer. Vol. 2: 1849–1860, compiled by William E. Baringer. Vol. 3: 1861–1865, compiled by C. Percy Powell. Washington, D.C.: Lincoln Sesquicentennial Commission, 1960.

Mowry, Duane. "An Appreciation of J. R. Doolittle." *Proceedings of the Wisconsin Historical Society* 1909: 281–96.

Munford, Robert B., Jr., *Richmond Homes and Memories*. Richmond: Garrett and Massie, 1936.

Nelson, William, ed. *Nelson's Biographical Cyclopedia of New Jersey*. 2 vols. New York: Eastern Historical Publishing Society, 1913.

Nevins, Allan. *Ordeal of the Union*. 8 vols. New York: Charles Scribner's Sons, 1947–71.

Newell, Captain Joseph Keith, ed. *"Ours." Annals of 10th Regiment, Massachusetts Volunteers in the Rebellion*. Springfield, Mass.: C. A. Nichols & Co., 1875.

Nichols, Roy F. *The Disruption of American Democracy*. New York: Macmillan Co., 1948.

Niven, John. *Gideon Welles: Lincoln's Secretary of the Navy*. New York: Oxford University Press, 1973.

Parrish, William E. *Turbulent Partnership: Missouri and the Union, 1861–1865*. Columbia: University of Missouri Press, 1963.

Patrick, Rembert. *Jefferson Davis and His Cabinet*. Baton Rouge: Louisiana State University Press, 1944.

Paullin, Charles O. *Paullin's History of Naval Administration, 1775–1911*. Annapolis: Naval Institute Press, 1968.

Pearson, Henry Greenleaf. *The Life of John A. Andrew, Governor of Massachusetts 1861–1865*. 2 vols. Boston: Houghton Mifflin and Company, 1904.

Pec, Taylor. *Round Shot to Rockets: A History of the Washington Navy Yard and U.S. Naval Gun Factory*. Annapolis: U.S. Naval Institute Press, 1949.

Peterson, Norma Lois. *Freedom and Franchise: The Political Career of B. Gratz Brown*. Columbia: University of Missouri Press, 1965.

Phelps, Mary M. *Kate Chase Dominant Daughter: The Life Story of a Brilliant Woman and Her Famous Father*. New York: Thomas Y. Crowell Company, 1935.

Poole, Martha Sprigg. "Daniel Carroll of Rock Creek." *Montgomery County Story* 7 (May 1964): 1–12.

Portrait and Biographical Record of the Sixth Congressional District of Maryland. New York: Chapman Publishing Company, 1898.

Potter, David M. *The Impending Crisis, 1848–1861*. New York: Harper and Row, 1976.

————. *Lincoln and His Party in the Secession Crisis*. New Haven: Yale University Press, 1942.

Proctor, John Clagett, ed. *Washington Past and Present: A History*. New York: Lewis Historical Publishing Company, 1930.

Quarles, Benjamin. *Lincoln and the Negro*. New York: Oxford University Press, 1962.

Radcliffe, George. *Governor Thomas H. Hicks of Maryland and the Civil War*. 1901. Reprint. New York: Johnson Reprint, 1973.

Reed, Rowena. *Combined Operations in the Civil War.* Annapolis: U.S. Naval Institute Press, 1978.

Richardson, Hester D. *Sidelights on Maryland History with Sketches of Early Maryland Families.* Baltimore: Williams and Wilkens Company, 1913.

Riggs, John B. *The Riggs Family of Maryland: A Genealogical and Historical Record Including a Study of the Several Families in England.* Baltimore: Lord Baltimore Press, 1939.

Rochester, Nathaniel, comp. *Early History of the Rochester Family in America.* Buffalo, N.Y.: Matthews, Northrup and Company, 1882.

Ross, Ishbel. *The First Lady of the South: The Life of Mrs. Jefferson Davis.* New York: Harper and Bros., 1958.

Scharf, J. Thomas. *History of Saint Louis City and County, from the Earliest Periods to the Present Day: Including Biographical Sketches of Representative Men.* 2 vols. Philadelphia: Louis A. Everts & Co., 1883.

———. *History of Western Maryland.* 2 vols. 1882. Reprint. Baltimore: Regional Publishing Company, 1969.

Scharf, Thomas, and Thompson Westcott. *History of Philadelphia 1609–1884.* 3 vols. Philadelphia: L. H. Everts, 1884.

Sears, Stephen W. *George McClellan: The Young Napoleon.* New York: Ticknor and Fields, 1988.

Semmes, Katherine Ainsworth, comp. *A Historical Heritage: The Washington Navy Yard.* Washington, D.C.: Naval Officers' Wives' Club of Washington, D.C., [195?].

Smith, Edward Conrad. *The Borderland in the Civil War.* 1927. Reprint. Freeport, N.Y.: Books for Libraries Press, 1969.

Smith, Elbert B. *Francis Preston Blair.* New York: Free Press, 1980.

———. *The Presidency of James Buchanan.* Lawrence: University Press of Kansas, 1975.

Smith, William E. *The Francis Preston Blair Family in Politics.* 2 vols. New York: Macmillan Company, 1933.

Spofford, Ainsworth R. *Eminent and Representative Men of Virginia and the District of Columbia in the Nineteenth Century.* Madison, Wis.: Brant and Fuller, 1893.

Stafford, George Mason Graham, comp. *General George Mason Graham of Tyrone Plantation and His People.* New Orleans: Pelican Publishing Company, 1947.

Stern, Malcolm H., comp. *First American Jewish Families: Six Hundred Genealogies, 1654–1977.* Cincinnati: American Jewish Archives, and Waltham, Mass.: American Jewish Historical Society, 1978.

Stockton, Thomas Coates. *The Stockton Family of New Jersey and Other Stocktons.* Washington, D.C.: Carnahan Press, 1911.

Sween, Jane C. *Montgomery County: Two Centuries of Change.* Woodland Hills, Calif.: Windsor Publications, 1984.

Swisher, Carl B. *Roger B. Taney.* Hamden, Conn.: Archon Books, 1961.

Templeman, Eleanor Lee. *The Blair-Lee House: Guest House of the President.* McLean, Va.: EMP Publications, 1980.

Thomas, Benjamin, and Harold M. Hyman. *Stanton: The Life and Times of Lincoln's Secretary of War.* New York: Alfred A. Knopf, 1962.

Thomas, Emory. *The Confederate Nation 1861–1865.* New York: Harper and Row, 1971.

Toomey, David Carroll. *The Civil War in Maryland.* Baltimore: Toomey Press, 1983.

Trefousse, Hans L. *Benjamin Franklin Wade: Radical Republican from Ohio.* New York: Twayne Publishers, 1963.

————. *The Radical Republicans: Lincoln's Vanguard for Racial Justice.* New York: Alfred A. Knopf, 1969.

Turner, Justin G., and Linda Levitt Turner. *Mary Todd Lincoln: Her Life and Letters.* New York: Alfred A. Knopf, 1972.

Upshur, John Andrews. *Upshur Family in Virginia.* Richmond: Dietz Press, 1955.

Van Deusen, Glyndon. *William Henry Seward.* New York: Oxford University Press, 1967.

Wagandt, Charles L. *The Mighty Revolution: Negro Emancipation in Maryland, 1862–1864.* Baltimore: The Johns Hopkins University Press, 1964.

Warner, Ezra J. *Generals in Blue: Lives of the Union Commanders.* Baton Rouge: Louisiana State University Press, 1964.

————. *Generals in Gray.* Baton Rouge: Louisiana State University Press, 1959.

Weigley, Russell F. *Quartermaster General of the Union Army: A Biography of M. C. Meigs.* New York: Columbia University Press, 1959.

West, Richard S., Jr. *Lincoln's Scapegoat General: A Life of Benjamin F. Butler, 1818–1893.* Boston: Houghton Mifflin Co., 1965.

————. *The Second Admiral: The Life of David Dixon Porter, 1813–1891.* New York: Coward-McCann, 1937.

Wharton, Anne Hollingsworth. *Social Life in the Early Republic.* Philadelphia: J. B. Lippincott, 1902.

William, Roger. *The World of Napoleon III, 1851–1870.* New York: Free Press, 1965.

Williams, Frances Leigh. *Matthew Fontaine Maury: Scientist of the Sea.* New Brunswick, N.J.: Rutgers University Press, 1963.

Wilmer, L. Allison, J. H. Jarrett, and George W. F. Vernon. *History of Rosters of Maryland Volunteers, War of 1861–5.* 2 vols. Baltimore: Guggenheimer, Weil and Company, 1898.

Wilson, James Grant, and John Fiske, eds. *Appleton's Cyclopedia of American Biography.* New York: D. Appleton and Company, 1888.

Wise, Jennings Cropper. *Col. John Wise of England and Virginia (1617–1695) His Ancestors and Descendants.* Richmond: Virginia Historical Society, 1918.

Wolfe, Edwin, and Maxwell Whiteman. *The History of the Jews of Philadelphia from Colonial Times to the Age of Jackson.* Philadelphia: Jewish Publication Society of America, 1956.

Woodbury, Charles L. "Levi Woodbury." New England Historic Genealogical Society, *Memorial Biographies* 1 (1845–1852): 295–327.

Wooster, Ralph A. *The Secession Conventions of the South.* Princeton, N.J.: Princeton University Press, 1962.

Index

Page numbers in boldface refer to identifications of individuals.

A Note on the Editor

VIRGINIA JEANS LAAS teaches history in the Social Sciences Department of Missouri Southern State College. She is the co-author (with Dudley T. Cornish) of *Lincoln's Lee: The Life of Samuel Phillips Lee* and has written several articles on EBL.